Constitutional Process

Constitutional Process

A Social Choice Analysis of Supreme Court Decision Making

Maxwell L. Stearns

with a Foreword by Lee Epstein

Ann Arbor
THE UNIVERSITY OF MICHIGAN PRESS

Copyright © by the University of Michigan 2000
All rights reserved
Published in the United States of America by
The University of Michigan Press
Manufactured in the United States of America
⊛ Printed on acid-free paper

2003   2002   2001   2000   4   3   2   1

A CIP catalog record for this book is available from the British Library.

Library of Congress Cataloging-in-Publication Data

Stearns, Maxwell L.
    Constitutional process : a social choice analysis of Supreme Court decision
  making / Maxwell L. Stearns with a foreword by Lee Epstein.
        p.   cm.
    Includes bibliographical references and index.
    ISBN 0-472-11130-2 (alk. paper)
    1. United States. Supreme Court.   2. Judicial process—Social aspects—
  United States.   3. Social choice—United States.   I. Title.

KF8742 .S745   2000
347.73'26—dc21   00-031716

For Harrison L. Winter

This book is dedicated to the memory of Harrison L. Winter, United States Court of Appeals for the Fourth Circuit, for whom I had the privilege of clerking from 1987 to 1988. Although then–Chief Judge Winter would not have fancied himself a law and economics scholar, and although I never discussed social choice theory with him, he greatly influenced my thinking about constitutional process.

In an early chamber conference, a coclerk had raised the specter of a newly arrived Supreme Court plurality decision. She stated that the various opinions were sufficiently contorted that it was difficult to determine the holding, or even to know which opinion expressed it. Judge Winter responded to the effect: "Of course, under the *Marks* doctrine, the holding is stated in that opinion which resolves the case on the narrowest grounds." I will not be so presumptuous as to speak for my coclerks, but my best recollection is that following a collective "of course," I, at least, scurried back to my office to look up this rule that had somehow eluded me throughout the immediately preceding three years of law school. Readers will discover in chapter 3 that this doctrine proves critical in understanding both the dynamics and rationality of Supreme Court decision making and in thinking about that institution from a social choice perspective.

More generally, Judge Winter influenced my thinking about constitutional process through the deep respect and understanding that he exhibited—indeed exuded—for the federal judiciary and for the processes through which that institution created law, even when he disagreed with the results. In an age marked by deep cynicism of governmental institutions, Judge Winter's appreciation for the proper role of the federal judiciary in our scheme of governance remains for me among his great legacies. It is also one that I hope my own students and readers of this book might come to appreciate and share.

Summary of Contents

Foreword

Constitutional Process: A Social Choice Analysis of Supreme Court Decision Making

Most readers of this foreword are, in all likelihood, "legal scholars." This is a term the popular press occasionally uses to refer to those of us who study law and courts. And it is a term we ourselves often invoke, even though we are such a heterogeneous group that a label implying anything else is something of a misnomer. We are lawyers, political scientists, sociologists, anthropologists, psychologists, criminologists, historians, and even mathematicians. And we focus our inquiries on a wide range of problems, from the correlates of judicial behavior to the doctrine judges produce to the impact of their decision on society, to name just a few.

In fact, the list of our concerns is seemingly endless. But the general point should not be missed: To speak of "legal scholars" is to speak of large, diverse group, who do not necessarily see eye to eye on the types of questions to ask, the kinds of theories to invoke to answer those questions, or the sorts of data necessary to assess propositions emerging from those theories.

It is in this spirit that I commend to you *Constitutional Process: A Social Choice Analysis of Supreme Court Decision Making.* For Maxwell Stearns has done the extraordinary: Amid all the division, he has managed to find common ground, to craft a book that "legal scholars" of all stripes will find attractive.

How has he accomplished this seemingly impossible task? One answer centers on his primary research question—a question that is as old as the study of law and courts but is, nonetheless, of enduring value: How do courts make constitutional law? At least in my discipline (political science), I cannot imagine too many of my colleagues for whom this is not a question of central concern—regardless of whether they focus on the approaches justices take to produce doctrine or the doctrine itself. Much the same, I am sure, can be said of scholars toiling in other fields.

But Professor Stearns does more than simply ask a good question. Which takes me to a second point: He invokes a provocative and, to my mind, appropriate methodology to answer it, the theory of social choice. Also known as "public choice," this theory provides a potent set of tools for examining group decision making.

In the political world, social choice approaches are, perhaps, most commonly associated with the study of legislative behavior, but Professor Stearns is not the first to exploit their power to illuminate decision making on collegial courts. Nearly two decades ago, Frank Easterbrook, in his now-seminal "Ways of Criticizing the Court,"[1] relied on the "developing theory of public choice" to explore the Supreme Court's performance in various legal areas. Professor Stearns himself produced an outstanding reader, just three years ago, that brings together some of the best exemplars of the application of social choice to legal problems.[2]

And, yet, even among these classic writings, I can identify nary a one that comes close to harnessing the power of social choice theory to the extent that Professor Stearns does in *Constitutional Process*. Perhaps this is a reflection of the care he takes, in chapter 2, in explaining the basic tools of social choice (including the Condorcet paradox and Arrow's Theorem)—an explanation that, astonishingly, well-versed readers will find insightful and newcomers will find accessible. Indeed, his "Introduction to Social Choice" (chap. 2) is just about the best I have ever read, and will go some distance to encouraging the broader use of these tools by legal scholars, including those who had never encountered them before reading this volume. Or perhaps it is because of a claim Professor Stearns makes throughout: social choice theory enables us to analyze features of the rules courts adopt in ways that traditional approaches cannot readily (or do not attempt to) do. This is a bold claim, to be sure, but one that goes some distance toward explaining the power of *Constitutional Process*. It brings to the fore a point that many other scholars have skirted: If we want to develop a full understanding of constitutional process, we avoid social choice at our own peril.

In theory, this is an argument that anyone who has puzzled through recent Supreme Court decisions must acknowledge as facially valid. To see this point, I need only invoke but one of Professor Stearns's many examples: Why in *Planned Parenthood of Southeastern Pennsylvania v. Casey*,[3] did a majority of the justices empower a minority of their colleagues "to define the critical case issue and thus the direction of constitutional doctrine?" Surely, this question dawned on many of us after reading the case. But, in practice, we tend to put it to the side in favor of those stressing the doctrine itself or the approaches invoked by individual justices in articulating doctrine. What *Constitutional Process* highlights with force is the problem with so doing; namely, we cannot understand the doctrine unless we understand the collective nature of the decision-making process that undergirds it.

This point, this bold claim that Professor Stearns makes, is related to a third explanation for the volume's expansive reach: the evidence the author brings to bear to support it. As a matter of general principle, when it comes to validating hypotheses, those of us in the social sciences are supposed to be committed to the view that there is no one right way to get the job done. Nonetheless, at least some scholars working in my field seem to reject this position in favor of a far more orthodox one: We should only accept hypotheses that researchers have assessed against large-scale, large-n data sets.

Advocates of this stance have, naturally, taken aim at scholars immersed in the study of doctrine, accusing them of relying on "scattershot" and "selective" evidence to validate their hypotheses. More recently, however, they have pointed their cannons at those who ground their work in theories based on assumptions of rationality. Donald P. Green and Ian Shapiro's *Pathologies of Rational Choice Theory*[4] is, perhaps, the most-cited example, but it is hardly the only work to argue that "to date few theoretical insights derived from rational choice theory have been subjected to serious empirical scrutiny and survived."[5]

Constitutional Process provides forceful evidence of why this particular argument, as well those that take the more general form about the need to employ large-scale data sets, often rings so hollow. Professor Stearns does not rely on "numbers" to do the heavy lifting; he presents detailed analyses of court cases. But, in his hands, the cases are not simply sets of stylized facts designed to prove a point; they are, in every sense of the word, "data" and, more to the point, data that are more compelling than much of that culled from large-*n* databases. That is because they enable him to assess systematically his hypotheses *and* to provide keen insights into the development of law. Sheer "numbers," yes, can perform the former, but rarely do they accomplish the latter.

I realize these words seem to contradict my earlier statements about the "something for everyone" nature of this book. After all, what could the "large-scale" crowd gain from reading *Constitutional Process*? Such a response, though, would miss the point: It may be scholars of doctrine who will most appreciate his form of evidence, but it is their data-oriented counterparts who will most benefit from Professor Stearns's rich analyses. They provide, more than any others I have read in the law and courts field, the best evidence of why a commitment to a diversity in evidence is a commitment we all should share.

There is one final feature of Professor Stearns's work that explains its near-universal appeal, and this may be its most important one: the agenda it sets for future research. In the conclusion of his work, Professor Stearns admonishes us to ask a question about outcomes produced by the U.S. Supreme Court—"how are these outcomes shaped by the collective nature of the Supreme Court's decision-making processes"—and reminds us of the lesson he has taught throughout: social choice provides a powerful set of tools for answering it. For some scholars, the next venture will involve following the path Professor Stearns has blazed, investigating the Supreme Court's work in evolving areas of the law or, perhaps, Courts of bygone eras. For others, the task will be to use the tools of social choice to study different American collegial courts, be they appellate panels or state tribunals. For members of yet a third set (and the one into which I fit), *Constitutional Process* will challenge them to think beyond the American legal system to constitutional courts elsewhere, especially in emerging democracies. For years, even decades, judicial specialists have complained about out community's persistent bias toward U.S. courts and away from judiciaries in other countries.

Why this bias exists is a question on which many scholars have speculated, but Herbert Jacob provides a common response when he writes about the lack of a "widely accepted paradigm [with] which to model the relationship between law, courts, and politics in a cross-national context."[6] Social choice theory provides such a paradigm or, at the very least, a set of theoretical tools that our comparative counterparts contend is revolutionizing their field.[7] With the publication of *Constitutional Process,* we legal scholars can now make much the same claim about ours.

Lee Epstein
Washington University in St. Louis

NOTES

1. Frank Easterbrook, "Ways of Criticizing the Court," *Harvard Law Review* 95 (1982): 802.
2. Maxwell L. Stearns, *Public Choice and Public Law: Readings and Commentary* (Cincinnati: Anderson Publishing Co., 1997).
3. 505 U.S. 833 (1992).
4. Yale University Press, 1994.
5. Donald P. Green and Ian Shapiro, *Pathologies of Rational Choice Theory,* 9.
6. Herbert Jacob, Erhard Blankenburg, Herbert M. Kritzer, Doris Marie Provine, and Joseph Sanders, introduction to *Courts, Law, & Politics in Comparative Perspective* (New Haven: Yale University Press, 1996) 2.
7. *See,* e.g., Robert H. Bates, "Comparative Politics and Rational Choice: A Review Essay." *American Political Science Review* 91 (1997): 699.

Preface and Acknowledgments

Constitutional Process: A Social Choice Analysis of Supreme Court Decision Making represents the culmination of an eight-year research project. This research has produced several articles and a course book. While those publications have contributed in varying degrees to this manuscript, I am confident that even readers familiar with my prior work will appreciate the originality of *Constitutional Process*.

Writing a book that builds upon prior scholarship has afforded me a rare luxury. While authors of law review articles sometimes catch and correct discrete errors, they rarely have the opportunity to completely refine or rethink past presentations. In addition to providing me with an opportunity to extend my research into new areas, this book has allowed me to retrace old ground with the benefit of hindsight and, hopefully, with greater wisdom and insight. Of course, doing so has not been entirely costless. More than once I have come to fear that unless readers keep fully current with my writing, they might reasonably assume that I never uncovered some of the very weaknesses in past presentations that I hope to have improved upon here. In addition, I have come to realize that I might have dismissed some past criticism a bit too hastily, especially when the cause was my own failure to convey critical concepts with greater precision. While such criticism has not caused me to abandon my essential thesis, it has forced me to clarify, and thus improve upon, underlying concepts and the manner in which I have presented them.

Any costs along these lines are certainly outweighed by the benefits. The single greatest benefit of writing this book—aside from hopefully advancing the academy's collective understanding of the Supreme Court, a singularly important American institution—is that it has given me the opportunity to solidify past professional relationships and friendships and to develop new ones. I am always impressed when a scholar at another institution who has no personal or professional stake in my reputation willingly invests his or her time to read my work and to provide me with valuable criticism and commentary. This is all the more remarkable when one considers that law review articles routinely approach or exceed one hundred pages. But with this substantially longer and far more comprehensive manuscript, I have experienced such generosity on an unparalleled scale. Because this book performs an intermarriage between a legal subject matter, constitutional law, and an economic discipline, social choice, my commentators were required to come up xiv · *Preface and Acknowledgments*

to speed on at least one foreign discipline (and in some cases two). Commenting on the manuscript was therefore no small task. I was truly astounded by the depth of insight that my commentators provided and by the enthusiasm (which is not to suggest wholehearted agreement) that they expressed for the project. I have no doubt that these numerous, detailed, and often extensive comments have greatly improved the final product. I am also confident that virtually all commentators on earlier versions of this manuscript, and many commentators on related articles, will find their fingerprints somewhere on the pages of this book. While it has become something of a cliché to say so, any resulting errors are entirely my own. The following scholars provided extremely valuable comments on earlier drafts of the entire manuscript: Evan Caminker, Lee Epstein, Tracey George, Michael O'Neil, Bob Pushaw, Mark Ramsayer, David Skeel, Nicolaus Tideman, Todd Zywicki, and two anonymous reviewers.

In addition to comments by individual readers, I have benefited substantially from comments and questions raised in numerous faculty presentations in law, economics, and political science. I have received valuable commentary on chapter 3 from workshops at the following institutions: American Law and Economics Association, the Center for Market Processes, the University of Chicago Law and Economics Workshop, George Mason University School of Law, Hebrew University School of Law, Midwest Political Science Association, the Public Choice Center at George Mason University, Tel Aviv University School of Law, and Temple University Beasley School of Law.

I have also benefited from comments upon earlier published works. While it is not possible to acknowledge every single contributor, I hope that anyone whom I might have omitted will blame simple forgetfulness on my part. The following scholars' comments on earlier works have remained prominent as I developed this book: Robert Anthony, Peter Aranson, Kenneth Arrow, Bruce Chapman, Jim Chen, Lloyd Cohen, John Jeffries, D. Bruce Johnson, Bruce Kobayashi, Saul Levmore, Henry Manne, Richard Murphy, Geoffrey Miller, Erin O'Hara, Jeffrey Parker, Larry Ribstein, Glen Robinson, John Rogers, David Schum, Warren Schwartz, Linda Schwartzstein, Gordon Tullock, and Tom Ulen. In addition, I have benefited from helpful comments from workshops on related articles at the following institutions: American Political Science Association, Emory University School of Law, the University of Florida Fredric G. Levin College of Law, the University of Florida Departments of Economics and Political Science, Florida State University School of Law, George Mason University School of Law, Georgetown University School of Law, and the Institute for Humane Studies. I would also like to acknowledge the generous funding in support of this research from the Law and Economics Center at the George Mason University School of Law and from the Law School administration, which provided me a semester of paid research leave to complete the initial draft of this manuscript. Jennifer Dacey provided outstanding research assistance. Finally, I would like to thank my constitutional law students at George Mason Law School and my public choice students at George Mason Law School, the University of Florida, and

Tel Aviv University, who have patiently endured, and occasionally claimed to find persuasive, my novel theories and who have always edified me with insightful and provocative questions and comments.

While all of the people listed above have left an undeniable imprimatur on this book, two deserve special mention. Over the past two years, I have developed a deep admiration for Professor Lee Epstein. Her in-depth understanding of the judicial process, of the scientific method, and of how those two bodies of knowledge can meaningfully be combined is impressive. More impressive to me, however, is her never ending willingness to share her time (which I am quite confident is limited) and energy (which somehow appears not to be) to support and promote the research of others. I would also like to specifically mention Nic Tideman. From our initial lengthy telephone discussions of the opening chapters through the many discussions of the remainder of the manuscript, Nic provided a critical line-by-line edit of the entire manuscript. During this process, I was given what can best be described as a tutorial in social choice and the economic method, at the reduced rate of about ten cents a minute. Even by state tuition standards, this was an undeniable bargain. Nic not only forced me to refine countless prior arguments and presentations but also enabled me to develop a more integrated approach to the social choice analysis of Supreme Court decision making in the main theoretical presentations set out in chapters 2, 3, and 4.

Although the arguments and presentations from the following articles have been substantially refined, they have all played an important role in the development of this book:

The Misguided Renaissance of Social Choice, 103 YALE L.J. 1219 (1994): Several of the arguments and presentations in chapters 1, 2, and 3 find their genesis in this work. Any portions of text or notes from this article that appear in this book are reproduced with the express written permission of the Yale Law Journal Company and Fred B. Rothman & Company.

Standing Back from the Forest: Justiciability and Social Choice, 83 CAL. L. REV. 1309 (1995): Several of the arguments and presentations in chapter 4 are based upon this work. Any portions of text or notes from this article that appear in this book are reproduced with the express written permission of the California Law Review.

Standing and Social Choice: Historical Evidence, 144 U. PA. L. REV. 309 (1995): Several of the presentations in chapters 5 and 6 are based upon this work. Any portions of text or notes from this article that appear in this book are reproduced with the express written permission of the University of Pennsylvania Law Review.

How Outcome Voting Promotes Principled Issue Identification: A Reply to Professor John Rogers and Others, 49 VAND. L. REV. 1045 (1996): Chapter 3, section 3, finds its genesis in this article. Any portions of text or notes from this article that appear in this book are reproduced with the express written permission of the Vanderbilt Law Review.

Mistretta Versus Marbury: The Foundations of Judicial Review, 74 Tex. L. Rev. 1281 (1996). This small essay contributed to part of the presentation in chapter 4. Any portions of text or notes from this article that appear in this book are reproduced with the express written permission of the Texas Law Review Association.

Should Justices Ever Switch Votes? Miller v. Albright *in Social Choice Perspective,* 7 Sup. Ct. Econ. Rev. 87 (1999): This recent article contributed to portions of the presentation in chapters 1 and 3. Any portions of text or notes from this article that appear in this book are reproduced with the express written permission of the Law and Economics Center of the George Mason University School of Law and the University of Chicago Press.

In addition, several notes and commentaries from Public Choice and Public Law: Readings and Commentary (Anderson Publishing Co. 1997) have contributed to the analyses and presentations throughout this book.

Finally, more than anyone else, I want to thank my family. My wife, Vered, has put up with endless hours of writing, editing, and occasional moments of panic. She has also endured dry runs of many academic presentations in a discipline quite distant from her own (medical oncology, and specifically breast cancer). She has done so in an always supportive manner and sometimes (read on) under less-than-ideal circumstances. My older daughter, Shira (six years old), has put up with the same, minus the presentations, often at the expense of trips to the playground or companionship during a video. And our latest addition, Keren (one year at the time of this writing), like her proud big sister, is simply beautiful.

Maxwell Stearns
George Mason University School of Law
Arlington, Virginia

Contents

Part I

Framing the Inquiry

CHAPTER 1 **Decisional and Doctrinal Anomalies in Constitutional Law**

I. Introduction

This book is about how constitutional law is made. Almost all constitutional scholarship has tended to focus upon two inquiries: first, the various, often conflicting, jurisprudential approaches of federal judges, with a particular focus on Supreme Court justices, and second, the black letter legal doctrine that emerges from constitutional case law. Both of these areas of inquiry are important. Indeed, they comprise the bulk of most introductory courses on constitutional law, including the one that I teach. But these traditional approaches to constitutional law leave many features of that important body of doctrine unexplained. In this book, I will introduce both a novel methodology for analyzing constitutional decision making, the theory of social choice, and a third branch of constitutional inquiry, namely constitutional process.[1] By constitutional process, I mean the study of those formal and informal decision-making rules, beginning at the Supreme Court and filtering down into federal judicial practice generally, that, individually and in combination, transform judicial preferences into constitutional doctrine. This book will demonstrate that the economic theory of social choice is uniquely suited to analyzing the Supreme Court's process-based decisional rules and will show how those rules affect the substantive development of constitutional law.

This book, which has seven chapters, is divided into four parts. Part I, "Framing the Inquiry," contains two chapters. Chapter 1 will set out the legal, doctrinal, and historical anomalies of Supreme Court decision making, which this book is designed to explain. Chapter 2 will describe the methodology of social choice, without which, I will argue, it is not possible fully to understand the Supreme Court's process-based decisional rules. Part II, "Social Choice Models of Supreme Court Decision Making," consists of chapters 3 and 4. Chapter 3 will set out a static model of constitutional decision making that explains how the Supreme Court decides individual cases; and chapter 4 will set out a dynamic model of constitutional decision making that explains how the Supreme Court decides groups of cases over time. Part III, "Historical and Case Evidence," will provide empirical support for the book's most far-reaching theory of constitutional process, namely that of justiciability, and specifically, of standing. Chapter 5 will provide a historical review of the relevant Supreme Court periods, beginning with the New Deal Court and continuing through the present Court, and chapter 6 will provide a detailed examination of the Supreme Court's modern standing case law. Finally, part IV, chapter 7, will provide a brief summary of the main points.

After providing a nontechnical introduction to social choice in chapter 2, this book will focus on three groups of anomalies of Supreme Court decision making, that have remained unexplained under traditional constitutional law scholarship. In this chapter, I will describe these anomalies. The first section of this chapter, which corresponds to chapter 3, will consider why the Supreme Court on occasion appears to thwart the will of a majority of its own members in individual cases in both identifying and resolving underlying case issues. The second section, which corresponds to chapter 4, will extend the problem of suppressed majorities to multiple cases. First, we will consider why the Court employs stare decisis, which has the effect of grounding the substantive evolution of constitutional law in the order in which groups of cases are decided over time. We will then consider why the Court employs a set of doctrines, under the label of standing, that appear sufficiently malleable that by flipping the Court's own analyses in two major cases, the Court could have achieved precisely opposite results. In the third and final section, which corresponds to chapter 5, we will consider an important historical anomaly involving the early development of standing in the New Deal and its later transformation in the Burger and Rehnquist Courts. In chapter 6, we will see that this transformation has had a profound impact on the recent development of constitutional process and on substantive constitutional law.

Before describing each of the puzzles that follow, a few general methodological comments will be helpful. First, this book will demonstrate that the Supreme Court's process-based decision-making rules reflect a pervasive tension between the desire to produce results that make sense, meaning that they can be viewed as the product of rational thought, reflection, and deliberation, and the competing desire to do so based upon a set of rules that are sufficiently balanced and inclusive, as to be accepted as fair. As the next chapter will demonstrate, the tension between rules that promote collective rationality and rules that provide a sense of overall fairness—a tension that afflicts virtually all collective decision-making bodies—lies at the heart of the body of economic literature referred to as social choice. As the name suggests, social choice is about the differences between the social impact of individual and collective decision making. The Supreme Court is a collective decision-making body that presently has nine members.[2] Because it is a multimember decision-making body, and one with the awesome power to define constitutional law for the nation as a whole, it is critical to consider the manner in which the Supreme Court's decisional rules respond to the problems associated with aggregating the expressed views of its members. And yet, with few exceptions,[3] traditional constitutional scholarship has scarcely considered the implications of collective decision making upon the substantive development of constitutional law. This book is the first full-scale analysis of the Supreme Court based upon social choice.

Second, in contrast with much existing literature on the Supreme Court, this book takes the justices' own statements of doctrine, as expressed in their opinions, quite seriously. Many of the anomalies that I will identify in this chapter and the ones that follow depend upon believing—or at least temporarily suspending our disbelief regarding—what the justices say. Virtually all postrealist legal theorists would rightly reject the assertion that published Supreme Court opinions reflect a purely neutral application of previously articulated doctrine to new legal questions. Instead, a more nuanced understanding of the behavior of justices assumes that, having identified their objectives, which are largely influenced by judicial ideology, Supreme Court justices often manipulate doctrine to achieve desired results. And yet, I will argue, an appreciation of articulated doctrine remains critically important. The question, of course, is why. In this book I take doctrine seriously not because I believe that doctrine neutrally drives case results, but rather because I believe doctrine serves as one of several important constraints that influence the manner in which justices achieve desired case outcomes. That said, it will be helpful to articulate a premise that underlies much of the analysis in this book: Justices are strongly motivated to present a set of internally consistent resolutions of identified dispositive case issues—meaning those issues that the justices claim are necessary to the resolution of the case before them—in achieving their preferred disposition of each case. I do not mean to imply that the reasoning in every Supreme Court opinion is beyond reproach. If that were true, different justices could never credibly reach opposite conclusions in the same case. Instead, I am suggesting that if a justice explicitly or implicitly concludes that two preconditions must be met before a statute can be sustained (or struck down), that justice will not reach that result after having determined that only one of those two conditions is met. When operating against a considerable backdrop of existing precedent, achieving even this very modest requirement of internal consistency will require justices to manipulate doctrine in sometimes quite unexpected ways. Such manipulation has the potential to influence considerably the substantive development of constitutional law. I am not suggesting, therefore, that we take stated rationales within Supreme Court opinions strictly at face value. Indeed, I will often explain why a Supreme Court justice has set out a seemingly disingenuous rationale in his or her opinion. But without at least occasionally and temporarily suspending our disbelief regarding the asserted justifications for Supreme Court opinions, it is often difficult to comprehend the manner in which constitutional law has historically evolved, or to appreciate the implications of the Court's various process-based decision-making rules for constitutional doctrine.

Third, throughout this book, I will offer justifications grounded in social choice for several seemingly anomalous Supreme Court decision-making rules and resulting doctrinal developments. It is important to understand, however, that I am not trying to expose the actual motivations, psychological or otherwise, of the justices themselves. Instead, I will assert throughout the book that various rules and doctrines have evolved in a manner that solves, or at least avoids, problems that can best be identified using the framework of social choice. It is neither necessary nor likely, however, that the justices would have understood the difficulties that faced them at various points in the Court's history in terms of the analytical framework of social choice. As explained in chapter 2, social choice analysis, like economic analysis generally, does not provide contemporaneous *explanations* of the decision makers' actual thinking in developing specific rules or doctrines. Instead, social choice is most helpful in providing positive and independent *justifications* as to why certain rules, which the decision makers adopted, have remained in place, in spite of the sometimes enigmatic doctrinal results that those rules produce, and why other suggested rules, which might appear better suited to the task at hand, have either not been adopted or have not survived, given the additional complexities that social choice reveals those rules would produce.

Finally, it is important to consider the practical and theoretical significance of our collective undertaking. As the examples that follow in this chapter and in the remainder of the book will show, the Supreme Court's process-based decisional rules have affected the substantive development of the most prominent and divisive bodies of constitutional law. These include abortion, affirmative action, the commerce clause, criminal procedure, public school desegregation and busing, free speech and press, race-based gerrymandering, and justiciability, just to name a few. This book will discuss many bodies of constitutional law that have rarely, if ever, been considered through an economic lens, and certainly not through the lens of social choice. While no single methodological approach can explain all of the anomalous features of constitutional case law, I hope to demonstrate that social choice substantially complements other, more traditional, approaches by helping to explain how the Supreme Court's process-based decisional rules have influenced several of the most notorious doctrinal developments of that body of law. This book will also consider several increasingly popular proposals for changing the way that the Supreme Court goes about its business. While I will often appear critical of these proposals, my purpose is not to suggest that the Supreme Court is a perfect institution. As I will demonstrate in chapter 2, there is no such thing. Instead, I will suggest that several proposals for reforming the processes of constitutional lawmaking, including facilitating a switch from outcome to issue voting, relaxing stare decisis in constitutional cases, and abandoning or severely curtailing the modern standing doctrine or other barriers to justiciability, would likely produce problems greater than those that they are intended to cure. With that introduction, we are now ready to consider the problem of collective decision-making in the Supreme Court.

II. Individual Case Decision Making: The Problem of Thwarted Majorities over Outcomes and Issues

This chapter will begin by introducing two case studies in individual case decision making. In the first case study, which is based upon the recent decision *Miller v. Albright*,[4] the Court appears to have thwarted the expressed judgment of separate majorities in resolving underlying dispositive issues. In the second case study, which is based upon *Planned Parenthood of Southeastern Pennsylvania v. Casey*,[5] the Court appears to have allowed a minority of its members to define the underlying dispositive issues in a manner that a majority implicitly or explicitly rejected.

A. *Miller v. Albright:* The Divergence of Issues and Outcomes under the Immigration and Naturalization Act

In *Miller v. Albright*,[6] the Supreme Court considered a Fifth Amendment due process challenge to a provision of the Immigration and Nationality Act (INA) that imposed different requirements upon citizen fathers and citizen mothers of children born out of wedlock outside the United States as a precondition to conferring citizenship status on the child, when the other parent is not a U.S. citizen. Petitioner, Lorelyn Penero Miller, was born out of wedlock on June 20, 1970, in the Philippines to a U.S. citizen father and a Filipino mother. Under the challenged INA provision, her father was required to undertake certain affirmative steps before she reached the age of twenty-one, as a precondition to her receiving U.S. citizenship. Had her mother, instead, been the U.S. citizen, petitioner would automatically have received citizenship status from the time of her birth.

The *Miller* Court produced five separate opinions, three opinions of two justices each, which together denied petitioner's claim to citizenship, and two opinions each joined by the three dissenting justices, who would have struck down the challenged INA provision and thus have conferred citizenship upon petitioner. While a majority of six of the nine justices voted to deny petitioner relief, tallying the justices' votes on each of the underlying dispositive issues produces a logical progression leading to the dissenting result.

Under the challenged INA provision, a foreign-born child born out of wedlock to a U.S. citizen father and a non–U.S. citizen mother can acquire citizenship only if the father formalizes his relationship with the child before the child reaches the age of twenty-one. While Congress amended the challenged statutory provision in 1986, lowering the age for formalizing the relationship between the father and the foreign-born illegitimate child to eighteen,[7] and imposing several additional preconditions to receiving citizenship,[8] in his opinion issuing the Court's judgment (joined by Chief Justice Rehnquist), Justice Stevens explained that petitioner's status was to be determined according to the preamendment version of the statute. Under the relevant preamendment provision, petitioner only needed to obtain "formal proof of paternity by age [twenty-one], either through legitimation, written acknowledgment by the father under oath, or adjudication by a competent court."[9]

Petitioner's father, Charlie Miller ("Miller"), served in the U.S. Air Force, where he was stationed in the Philippines at the time his daughter was conceived. After his tour of duty, Miller returned to the United States, where he resided in Texas. Miller apparently had little if any contact with his daughter until she reached adulthood. In November 1991, shortly after she turned twenty-one, petitioner filed an application for registration as a U.S. citizen with the State Department, which was denied in March 1992. Miller then filed a petition in a Texas state court in 1992 to formalize his relationship with his daughter, which was granted in July 1992. After her father obtained the paternity decree, petitioner reapplied with the State Department, but her second application was denied on the ground that her father had failed to formalize his relationship with her before she had reached the age of eighteen, as required by the amended statute. In his opinion announcing the judgment for the Court, Justice Stevens noted that, while petitioner fell within the narrow window that would have allowed the formalization to occur prior to her twenty-first birthday, she still failed to meet the statutory requirement in a timely fashion.

In 1993, petitioner and her father filed a suit in United States District Court for the Eastern District of Texas against the secretary of state, alleging that the INA's differing treatment of citizen fathers and citizen mothers violated Mr. Miller's rights under the equal protection component of the Fifth Amendment due process clause.[10] The district court dismissed Miller from the case on the ground that he lacked standing to raise the due process claim, meaning that the court determined that the daughter, rather than the father, was the real party of interest in the suit. With Miller, the only Texas citizen who was a party to the suit, excluded, the suit could no longer proceed in Texas.[11] The Texas court transferred the case to the United States District Court for the District of Columbia. That court then dismissed the suit on the ground that, even if the challenged provision of the INA violated due process, the Constitution expressly confers the authority over naturalization to Congress and thus federal courts lack the authority to confer citizenship except as specified in a federal statute. In a split panel decision, the United States Court of Appeals for the District of Columbia Circuit affirmed the dismissal, but did so on different grounds. The appeals court began by rejecting the government's challenge to petitioner's standing, reasoning that if petitioner succeeded on the merits of her claim, the court would then hold that she was already a citizen pursuant to other provisions of the INA. On the merits, however, the court reasoned that because citizen mothers and citizen fathers were not similarly situated in this context, it would apply the lowest level of judicial scrutiny, the rational basis test. Under that standard, the court concluded that the scheme rationally furthered the government's legitimate interest in fostering the child's ties with the United States.[12] The Supreme Court granted certiorari to resolve whether the challenged INA provision violates the Fifth Amendment due process clause. In resolving this question, the Supreme Court badly splintered, producing a total of five separate opinions.

In his opinion announcing the Court's judgment, joined only by Chief Justice Rehnquist, Justice Stevens identified three underlying issues, which he deemed critical to the outcome of the case: (1) Does petitioner have standing to raise her father's Fifth Amendment due process clause challenge to section 1409(a) of the INA? (2) does the Court's general standard of review governing sex-based classifications, namely heightened scrutiny (also referred to as intermediate scrutiny), apply, or does a more relaxed standard apply, given that the statute is premised upon real differences between citizen mothers and citizen fathers as it relates to raising foreign-born illegitimate children?[13] and (3) is the chosen standard satisfied in this case? With the exception of Justice Scalia (joined only by Justice Thomas), who concurred in the judgment without addressing the merits of the underlying challenge, and thus declined to reach the second and third issues, each of the remaining justices agreed to Justice Stevens's formulation of the case issues, although they disagreed as to how those issues should be resolved.

Justice Stevens quickly dispensed with the challenge to petitioner's standing. To analyze that issue, Stevens distinguished two due process claims that petitioner raised in her challenge to the INA. With respect to her own claim, as opposed to that of her father, Stevens concluded that petitioner had standing, given that she was seeking a judgment that would affirm "her pre-existing citizenship rather than grant her rights that she does not now possess."[14] With respect to her father's claim, Stevens also concluded that petitioner had standing, given that "her claim relies heavily on the proposition that her citizen father should have the same right to transmit citizenship as would a citizen mother." For Justice Stevens, the same substantive test applied, regardless of whether petitioner was pursuing her own claim or that of her father. As a general matter, Stevens observed, the Court applies heightened scrutiny in cases presenting challenges to statutes that are based upon "overbroad stereotypes about the relative abilities of men and women." In this case, however, Stevens reasoned that the challenged provision of the INA was not based upon overbroad generalizations about men and woman, but rather, was based upon real differences between them. Given that mothers, but not fathers, are inevitably aware of the birth of an illegitimate child, and further given that mothers, but not fathers, will almost invariably be involved in the child's upbringing, Stevens inquired only whether Congress had devised a relevant distinction between citizen mothers and citizen fathers for purposes of the INA's naturalization requirements. With respect to petitioner's own claim, Stevens concluded that her challenge failed even under heightened scrutiny. Stevens identified the following three objectives as "strong governmental interests" that the challenged provision was "well tailored to serve": (1) deterring fraud in citizenship claims; (2) encouraging a healthy relationship between the child and the U.S. citizen parent; and (3) fostering ties between the foreign-born child and the United States. Thus, Justice Stevens voted to sustain the challenged INA provision against both of petitioner's challenges.

In an opinion concurring in the judgment, Justice O'Connor, joined by Justice Kennedy, began by articulating a basic principle of standing, namely the presumption against allowing one person to litigate the claim of another. Justice O'Connor stated: "This Court has long applied a presumption against allowing third-party standing as a prudential limitation on the exercise of federal jurisdiction."[15] By "prudential," Justice O'Connor meant that Congress has the constitutional authority to overcome the presumption against third-party standing by statute, thus creating the power in specified individuals to enforce the rights of others,[16] although Congress had not done so in the INA. Justice O'Connor reasoned that, while petitioner was also presenting a due process challenge to the INA provision on her own behalf, the more serious challenge was based upon the statute's distinction between U.S. citizen fathers and U.S. citizen mothers, and their respective obligations in naturalizing illegitimate children born outside the United States. Because the more serious challenge involved the part of the statute that created an express sex-based distinction, that challenge rested with petitioner's father, rather than with petitioner. O'Connor further recognized one of the several exceptions to the presumption against third-party standing, which she concluded petitioner had failed to meet. The Court has generally allowed an exception to its presumptive rule against third-party standing when the person raising the legal challenge has a sufficiently concrete interest, demonstrates a close connection with the person whose rights have been violated, and further demonstrates that the latter person has been substantially hindered in his efforts to raise his own claim.[17] O'Connor declined to apply that exception in *Miller*, however, because petitioner's father had simply declined to appeal his dismissal from the suit originally filed in the United States District Court for the Eastern District of Texas. Because she concluded that petitioner did not have standing to raise her father's due process claim, O'Connor limited herself to considering petitioner's own constitutional challenge, which did not involve a statutory sex-based distinction. O'Connor stated:

> Although petitioner cannot raise her father's equal protection rights, she may raise her own. . . . Her challenge, however, triggers only rational basis scrutiny. . . . Given that petitioner cannot raise a claim of discrimination triggering heightened scrutiny, she can argue only that § 1409 irrationally discriminates between illegitimate children of citizen fathers and citizen mothers. Although I do not share JUSTICE STEVENS' assessment that the [challenged INA] provision withstands heightened scrutiny, . . . I believe it passes rational scrutiny for the reasons he gives for sustaining it under the higher standard. It is unlikely, in my opinion, that any gender classifications based on stereotypes can survive heightened scrutiny, but under rational scrutiny, a statute may be defended based on generalized classifications unsupported by empirical evidence. . . . This is particularly true when the classification is adopted with reference to immigration, an area where Congress frequently must base its decisions on generalizations about groups of people.[18]

As both dissenting opinions observed, O'Connor's analysis strongly implied that had she reached the opposite conclusion on standing, thus addressing the merits of the father's underlying due process claim, O'Connor would then have applied heightened scrutiny and voted to strike that provision down, with the effect of conferring citizenship status upon petitioner.

In his opinion concurring in the judgment, joined only by Justice Thomas, Justice Scalia also addressed the issue of standing. But rather than addressing what the relevant standard of review was and whether the chosen standard was met, Scalia disposed of the case by resolving an altogether different issue: Even assuming that the challenged INA provision is unconstitutional, do the federal courts have the authority to strike down an allegedly unconstitutional provision of a naturalization statute and then apply the now-revised statute to confer citizenship, when the congressionally mandated provisions for naturalization have not been met? On the preliminary issue of standing, Justice Scalia noted that if he were addressing the question absent binding precedent, he would have agreed with Justice O'Connor and voted to deny standing. He went on to note, however, that in prior cases, the Court had conferred standing upon claimants who had a close relationship with the person whose claim they were raising, even when the third party had suffered far less of a hindrance than Mr. Miller had in this case. Scalia further noted that because petitioner was ultimately pursuing her own claim to citizenship, she was entitled to standing as "the least awkward challenger."[19] Scalia then resolved the question whether federal courts have the power to confer citizenship other than pursuant to a congressionally enacted statute by taking a strict textualist view of the Constitution. Scalia began by noting that under Article I, which states, "The Congress shall have Power . . . To establish an uniform Rule of Naturalization," persons can acquire citizenship only through birth or naturalization.[20] Because petitioner was not U.S. born, Scalia reasoned that for her to gain citizenship status, petitioner needed to establish full compliance with a congressionally enacted statute setting out the requirements for naturalization. Had the State Department made a factual error respecting compliance with the INA, Scalia suggested that the Court might then have had the power to remedy the error because in doing so, it would not have been called upon to confer citizenship other than in a manner consistent with a federal statute. But Scalia reasoned that a federal court lacks the authority to correct even an apparent constitutional defect in a naturalization statute and then confer citizenship based upon the judicially amended version. Having concluded that the Court lacks the power to confer citizenship, Justice Scalia declined to address the merits of petitioner's due process claim.

Of the remaining justices, Justices Ginsburg and Breyer wrote dissenting opinions, which all three dissenters, including Justice Souter, joined. Because the two dissents took substantially similar views of the critical underlying issues, I will treat them together here. Justice Breyer began by concluding that petitioner had standing to assert her father's claim because she had suffered an injury in fact, she had a close relationship with her father, and her father had suffered some hindrance in the pursuit of his own claim.[21] In addition, both Ginsburg and Breyer determined that the relevant test was heightened scrutiny, under which the challenged provision, which each concluded was based upon antiquated sex-based stereotypes, could not survive.[22] Justice Ginsburg noted that under Supreme Court case law, it is not sufficient that those assumptions underlying a sex-based statute are generally true. Instead, she observed, "the Court has rejected official actions that classify unnecessarily and overbroadly by gender when more accurate and impartial functional lines can be drawn."[23] Justice Breyer expressed a similar intuition in suggesting that a scheme distinguishing the caretaker from the noncaretaker parent could achieve the same statutory objectives, without resting upon sex-based stereotype, even if that stereotype applies in most cases.[24]

In addition, both Justices Ginsburg and Breyer noted the anomaly that a majority of the Court appeared to agree that, on the merits, the challenged provision of the INA likely should have been struck down. Thus, Justice Ginsburg stated:

> As JUSTICE O'CONNOR's opinion makes plain, distinctions based upon gender trigger heightened scrutiny and "[i]t is unlikely . . . that any gender classifications based on stereotypes can survive heightened scrutiny."[25]

And after noting that he would have applied heightened scrutiny to both petitioner's own claim and to that of her father, Justice Breyer went on to observe:

> Regardless, like JUSTICE O'CONNOR, I "do not share," and thus I believe a Court majority does not share, "JUSTICE STEVENS' assessment that the provision withstands heightened scrutiny." . . . I also agree with JUSTICE O'CONNOR that "[i]t is unlikely" that "gender classifications based on stereotypes can survive heightened scrutiny," . . . a view shared by at least five members of the Court.[26]

Table 1.1 breaks down the five opinions in *Miller*, based upon each of the identified dispositive issues. In table 1.1, I have employed the following conventions. I have included all four issues that are identified as dispositive in one or more of the five opinions. I have also indicated when a justice failed to reach a given issue or issues. For consistency, I have stated each of the four issues such that a yes response favors petitioner and a no response favors the government. The following implicit assumption is fully consistent with all five of the opinions: To confer relief upon petitioner, each justice must either answer yes to questions A, B, and C, without reaching D, or answer yes to all questions including D. The collective response to these questions means that (A) petitioner has standing; (B) the relevant test is heightened scrutiny; (C) the chosen standard is not satisfied; and (D) separation of powers does not bar relief.[27] The table shows that while separate majorities on the Court resolve issues A through D, all in petitioner's favor (or in the case of issue D, at least not against petitioner), another majority of the Court, composed of Justices' Stevens, O'Connor, and Scalia, and those who join their opinions, succeed in denying petitioner relief.

Table 1.1. *Miller v. Albright:* Analysis of the Five Opinions by Issue

Author of Opinion (and those who join)	(A) Does the petitioner have standing?	(B) Should Court apply heightened scrutiny rather than a more relaxed standard?	(C) Does the statute fail under the chosen standard?	(D) Can Court grant citizenship without violating separation of powers?	Decision on Outcome
(1) Stevens (Rehnquist)	Yes	No	No	Does not reach	Deny relief
(2) O'Connor (Kennedy)	No	Yes	Yes	Does not reach	Deny relief
(3) Scalia (Thomas)	Yes	Does not reach	Does not reach	No	Deny relief
(4, 5) Ginsburg, Breyer (Souter)	Yes	Yes	Yes	Yes	Grant relief
Issue vote (hypothetical)	Yes (seven to two)	Yes (five to four)	Yes (five to four)	Yes (seven to two)	Grant relief (five to four)
Outcome vote (actual)					Deny relief (six to three)

Based upon an analysis of similar cases, in which the Court's combined issue resolutions produce a logical progression leading to the dissenting result, one pair of scholars has advocated that the Supreme Court switch completely from its present practice of outcome voting to issue voting,[28] meaning that the logical progression that follows from the separate majority resolutions of identified dispositive issues would control the case outcome, and another pair of scholars has advocated that the Supreme Court choose between issue and outcome voting by majority vote on a case-by-case basis.[29] In chapter 3, which develops a social choice model of individual case decision making in the Supreme Court, I will demonstrate, first, the limited conditions under which a *Miller*-type voting anomaly is capable of arising, and, second, how these proposals for institutional reform would undermine, rather than further, the objectives of improving the rationality and fairness of Supreme Court decision making.

B.   A Comment on Tiers of Scrutiny

While I have described the requirements of rational basis and heightened scrutiny in the above discussion of *Miller*, for the case study that follows, it will be helpful to provide a more formal introduction to tiers of scrutiny in constitutional judicial review. I will first describe the initial two-tier framework, which did not include heightened—or intermediate—scrutiny. I will then introduce the Supreme Court's 1992 revision in *Planned Parenthood of Southeastern Pennsylvania v. Casey*[30] of the 1973 framework for evaluating the constitutionality of state abortion regulations established in *Roe v. Wade*.[31] Setting aside for now heightened scrutiny, which was at issue in *Miller*, and which is a fairly recent innovation, when a court is presented with a constitutional challenge based upon the Fifth Amendment due process clause (which applies to federal laws) or the Fourteenth Amendment due process or equal protection clauses (which apply to state laws), the court will engage in a two-step process to determine the appropriate tier of scrutiny. First, the court will inquire whether the law infringes upon a fundamental right or draws a suspect classification. Second, if it does, the court will apply strict scrutiny, and if not, it will apply rational basis scrutiny.

In the absence of a fundamental right or suspect classification, the court will employ low-level rational basis scrutiny. Under that test, the court will inquire whether the state has a legitimate interest and whether the means chosen are reasonably drawn in furtherance of that interest. In essence, this test demands only that the state proffer some credible justification for the law under review, even if the proffered rationale was not the real motive,[32] and even if there exists a superior method of furthering the law's actual or proffered objective. On the other hand, if the court determines that the law impinges upon a fundamental right or draws a suspect classification, it will inquire whether the state has a sufficiently strong interest, which in Supreme Court jargon must be "compelling," to overcome that fundamental right or to justify such a classification, and, if so, whether the law under review is "narrowly tailored" to further that interest. In contrast with rational basis scrutiny, under strict scrutiny, the presence of a superior alternative, meaning one that will further the law's stated objective without infringing a fundamental right or drawing a suspect classification, is fatal because it demonstrates that the law in dispute is not narrowly tailored.

Because the Court has on occasion sustained laws applying strict scrutiny and struck down laws applying rational basis scrutiny,[33] the two-tier framework has been criticized by, among others, former justice Thurgood Marshall and Justice John Paul Stevens. Analyzing the root criticism, which Marshall and Stevens shared, to the two-tier approach will help to explain the important process-based function that the framework serves, even though the tiers are not always consistently applied. Marshall and Stevens have both observed that because the choice of scrutiny does not always predict the case outcome, the two-tier framework fails to capture the nuances of the Court's substantially more complex decision-making processes in cases involving suspect classifications and fundamental rights. In the context of fundamental rights analysis, Justice Marshall advocated employing multiple tiers of scrutiny, based upon the importance of the claimed right and the extent of the legal intrusion upon that right.[34] In nearly opposite fashion, although perhaps ultimately with the same effect, Justice Stevens has advocated employing a single, but meaningful, rational basis test, under which the deciding court, and most notably the Supreme Court, would provide the genuine rationale for its decision, rather than rely upon the two-tier framework, which, for him, has a tendency to mask articulable—and important—justifications for sustaining or striking down laws subject to constitutional challenge.[35]

For purposes of constitutional process, it is best to think of the two-tier framework as furthering two critical functions, each associated with judicial administrability in a hierarchical, and pyramidically structured, judiciary. First, each operates as a presumption, the former, in favor of sustaining the law in question, and the latter, in favor of striking it down. The difficulty with the Marshall and Stevens suggestions is that ultimately, whether couched in terms of multiple tiers or a single, but meaningful, tier, the Supreme Court benefits from having an administrative vehicle with which to guide lower courts in sorting constitutional challenges to state and federal laws. Under a multiple-tier approach, it appears likely that, over time, some group of the more finely nuanced tiers would develop that would have the effect of presumptively (albeit not irrebuttably) sustaining certain laws, while other tiers would develop, that would have precisely the opposite effect. Similarly, under a single meaningful tier approach, it appears likely that other characterizations would emerge over time to guide lower courts in determining which critical factors counsel presuming in favor of, or against, the constitutionality of a challenged law.

Second, the framework provides instructions concerning how to rebut these administrative presumptions. In the case of rational basis scrutiny, the absence of either a credible justification or means that rationally further that justification is sufficient to strike down a law that neither infringes upon a fundamental right, nor draws a suspect classification. In the case of strict scrutiny, proof of a compelling state interest and means that are narrowly tailored in furtherance of that interest will rebut the presumption against sustaining the law. The critical difference between these two formulations is who has the burden to prove that the law is or is not constitutional. Under rational basis scrutiny, in which the presumption is in favor of the law's constitutionality, the challenger bears the burden to prove that the test is not met. Under strict scrutiny, in which the presumption is against the law's constitutionality, the state or federal government has the burden to prove that the test is met.[36]

The foregoing analysis of the two-tier framework is important not only to the next case study on abortion, but also because it previews an important insight about the evolution of process-based rules. As this book will demonstrate, many process-based rules are the complex product of a series of evolutionary steps, each of which resolves a problem existing along a relatively large margin, but which, in turn, creates a problem to be solved by a future rule or practice existing along a relatively smaller margin. The two-tier framework solves the large administrative problem of guiding lower federal courts and state courts in ascribing presumptive outcomes in cases involving constitutional challenges to federal and state laws. As with almost all rules, presumptive or otherwise, the tiers of scrutiny are overbroad and underbroad, meaning that they produce displeasing results in at least some cases. The instructions accompanying the two tiers solve problems along a smaller margin of cases by providing a vehicle for overcoming the occasional displeasing presumptive outcomes. To establish that the two-tier framework is deficient, therefore, one would need to establish a superior framework, which would help lower federal courts and state courts to sort constitutional challenges in an effective manner and which would allow for necessary exceptions. The use of either a single meaningful tier, per Stevens, or multiple tiers, per Marshall, I would suggest, would simply replicate the same regime with new language or unnecessary complexity. The Marshall and Stevens criticisms focus on the relatively narrow margin of cases in which presumptive outcomes are rebutted, without appreciating how the framework operates to solve a significant problem of judicial administration along a far larger margin of cases. Later in this book, we will see that arguments in favor of switching from outcome to issue voting, relaxing stare decisis, or abandoning the standing doctrine are subject to a similar criticism. That said, as the next case study demonstrates, the choice of level of scrutiny has proved a major issue in constitutional litigation, precisely because of the power that the underlying presumptions hold.

C. *Planned Parenthood of Southeastern Pennsylvania v. Casey:* Stare Decisis and Issue Definition in Individual Cases

The second case study on individual case decision making will demonstrate how a doctrine essential to constitutional process, stare decisis, can operate to effectively suppress majority agreements and to vest seemingly disproportionate authority over defining case issues and outcomes with judicial minorities. The analysis will also expose how stare decisis (short for *stare decisis et non quieta movere,* meaning "stand by past decisions, and do not disturb settled things")[37] sometimes limits inquiries into the merits of the underlying issues in a case, and thus will raise some of the conceptual difficulties surrounding the doctrine, which I will elaborate upon in the next section.

The 1992 case *Planned Parenthood of Southeastern Pennsylvania v. Casey*[38] presented one in a long series of efforts by Republican administrations to have the Supreme Court overrule the famous (some might say infamous) 1973 decision *Roe v. Wade.*[39] In *Roe,* a majority of the Supreme Court, in a decision written by Justice Harry Blackmun, struck down a Texas statute prohibiting abortions. After determining that abortion was a fundamental right protected by the Fourteenth Amendment due process clause, the *Roe* Court set out the well-known trimester framework for determining the constitutionality of state abortion regulations.

Because the *Roe* Court determined that the right to abort was fundamental, to restrict access to abortion procedures, the state had to advance a compelling state interest, and further demonstrate that the challenged restriction was narrowly tailored to further its compelling interest. The *Roe* Court identified two state interests, which while legitimate (meaning that in the absence of a fundamental right, they would have been sufficient to restrict access to the abortion procedure), did not become compelling until precise points during the pregnancy. Under the strict scrutiny framework, only when these interests became compelling were they sufficient to justify infringing the woman's right to abort. The state's first legitimate interest, in the mother's health, did not become compelling until the end of the first trimester, the point at which mortality rates for live birth were higher than for abortion. The state's second legitimate interest, in the potential life represented by the fetus, did not become compelling until the moment of viability, the point at which the fetus can exist independently of the mother's womb.[40] Based upon these state interests, which had to be weighed against the mother's right to abort, the *Roe* Court determined that the state could not regulate abortion at all during the first trimester. During the second trimester, given the state's compelling interest in the health and safety of the mother, the state could regulate the abortion procedure to promote that objective. Finally, in the third trimester, given its compelling interest in the potential life represented by the fetus, the state could proscribe abortion altogether, except to the extent that abortion is necessary to protect the mother's health or life.

While the *Roe* framework had been challenged on numerous prior occasions, *Casey* represented the most serious challenge since the 1989 decision *Webster v. Reproductive Health Services,*[41] in which a plurality of four advocated abandoning the trimester framework and characterized abortion as a mere liberty interest rather than as a fundamental right. *Casey* presented a challenge to an elaborate set of abortion regulations under Pennsylvania law.*

---

*The Pennsylvania law contained five specific provisions: (1) an informed consent provision, requiring detailed disclosures to the mother—which would rather obviously have had the effect of discouraging the abortion procedure—within twenty-four hours prior

The United States viewed *Casey* as an ideal opportunity to again invite the increasingly conservative Supreme Court to overturn *Roe v. Wade*. Since 1989, when *Webster* was decided, the Court had witnessed the replacement of two of the Court's most liberal justices, William Brennan and Thurgood Marshall, with David Souter, a Bush appointee, whose views on abortion were not well known, and Clarence Thomas, who, upon ascending to the Supreme Court, quickly aligned himself with Justice Antonin Scalia, the Court's most prominent conservative. If the Court were ever ripe for a challenge to *Roe*, *Casey* seemed to present the perfect opportunity. In fact, the *Casey* Court had four Reagan appointees, William H. Rehnquist (elevated to chief justice by President Ronald Reagan from his appointment to associate justice by President Richard Nixon), Sandra Day O'Connor, Anthony M. Kennedy, and Antonin Scalia; and two Bush appointees, David H. Souter and Clarence Thomas. Of the remaining three members of the Court, Byron White was one of only two dissenters (along with Rehnquist) in the original *Roe* decision. It appeared that only two sitting justices would clearly continue to endorse *Roe:* John Paul Stevens, an enigmatic Ford appointee who, with some notable exceptions,[42] generally sided with the Court's liberal wing, and Harry Blackmun, a 1971 Nixon appointee, who quickly moved to the liberal wing and authored *Roe* just two years after his ascendency to the Supreme Court. While *Roe* was the product of a seven-to-two decision, in favor of a right to abort, it appeared that the tables had precisely turned, with six recent Republican appointees plus one Democratic appointee who dissented in *Roe,* totaling seven, against only two obvious continued adherents to *Roe*. For pro-life conservatives, it must have seemed difficult to imagine a friendlier Court.

The *Casey* Court produced a total of five separate opinions, each taking sharply different views on whether stare decisis dictated adhering to *Roe* and on the merits of *Roe* as an original decision. For ease of presentation, it will be helpful to divide the *Casey* Court into three camps: Justices Blackmun and Stevens, concurring in part and dissenting in part, wrote two separate opinions in which they made clear that they preferred the original *Roe* framework to the revised *Casey* framework established in the jointly authored, and controlling, plurality opinion.[43] Both justices voted to strike down the four restrictive provisions of the Pennsylvania abortion statute, but voted to sustain a provision exempting a woman seeking an abortion from those restrictions in the event of a medical emergency.[44] In addition, Justice Stevens voted

---

to the scheduled abortion; (2) a parental consent provision for minors, subject to a judicial bypass mechanism, in the event that the court finds the minor sufficiently informed and mature to make her own decision or finds that it is in her best interest to have an abortion; (3) a spousal notification provision requiring married women to provide, except in cases involving previously reported spousal abuse, signed statements demonstrating that they had notified their husbands of the intended abortion (whether or not the husband approves); (4) exemptions to the above provisions in cases of medical emergencies; and (5) reporting requirements for facilities performing abortions. *Casey,* 505 U.S. 833, 844 (1992) (joint opinion).

to sustain the statute's reporting requirements.[45] In two separate partial dissents and partial concurrences in the judgment, Chief Justice Rehnquist and Associate Justice Scalia (joined by Justices Thomas and White), concluded that because the Constitution nowhere establishes a right to abort, *Roe* was erroneous as an original decision and should be overturned.[46] These four justices voted to uphold all provisions of the Pennsylvania abortion statute. Finally, in a joint opinion, which stated the Court's judgment, Justices Kennedy, O'Connor, and Souter eschewed any inquiry into the original merits of *Roe*. Instead, the joint authors maintained that stare decisis obligated them to adhere to what they characterized as *Roe*'s "basic holding."[47] While Blackmun and Stevens joined part III of the joint authors' opinion, setting out the critical stare decisis analysis, they did not join part IV, which applied that analysis to revise the *Roe* abortion framework.

For ease of reference, I will refer to Justices Blackmun and Stevens as liberal, Chief Justice Rehnquist and Associate Justices Scalia, Thomas, and White as conservative, and the joint opinion authors as moderate.* Both the liberals, who preferred the original *Roe* formulation, and the conservatives, who rejected *Roe* on the merits, observed that what the joint authors labeled *Roe*'s essential holding bore little resemblance to the original 1973 abortion decision. In the name of stare decisis, the joint authors had redefined *Roe* in three important respects. First, they reclassified abortion from a fundamental right, requiring a compelling state interest before the state can infringe it, to a liberty interest subject to substantially greater state regulation. Under the *Casey* formulation, regulations that do not impose an undue burden on the right to abort, defined as not placing a "substantial obstacle" in the path of the woman seeking an abortion, are permissible. Second, the joint authors rejected the trimester framework, which they concluded was not part of *Roe*'s essential holding. Finally, the joint authors determined that *Roe,* and the Supreme Court decisions that followed it, had consistently undervalued the state's interest in the potentiality of human life represented by the fetus.

Among the several noteworthy features of the joint opinion is that, while purporting to be based upon adherence to precedent, it expressly overruled two fairly recent Supreme Court abortion cases, which it determined undervalued the state's interest in the potentiality of human life.[48] In addition, the joint authors' stare decisis analysis, described below, was both controversial and ironic, given the joint authors' extensive reliance upon the Supreme Court's two most famous overrulings in the twentieth century to support their decision to adhere to *Roe*.

The joint authors began by observing that while mere displeasure with existing precedent is not a basis for overruling, when a precedent is fundamentally deficient, overruling is "virtually foreordained."[49] In between these two easy categories are more difficult cases, like *Roe*. In such cases, the joint

*I will provide a more detailed breakdown of the Supreme Court in chapter 5, which does not always neatly match the implicit ideological spectrum suggested here. *See infra* chapter 5, § IV.

authors posited that the Court must weigh four pragmatic considerations. The joint authors quickly dispensed with two of the four factors, concluding that *Roe* "has [not] proved to be intolerable in terms of defying practical workability," and that "related principles of law have [not] left [*Roe*] no more than remnant of abandoned doctrine."[50] The more difficult issues were whether *Roe* had engendered "a kind of reliance interest that would lend special hardship to the consequences of overruling," and whether relevant "facts have so changed or come to be seen so differently, as to have robbed the old rule of significant application or justification."

While Chief Justice Rehnquist quickly dispensed with any claim of reliance as a basis for adhering to *Roe,* observing that if the Court abandoned *Roe,* which he advocated, " 'reproductive planning could take virtually immediate account' of this action,"[51] the joint opinion authors defined reliance more broadly. Thus, they stated:

> To eliminate the issue of reliance that easily, however, one would need to limit cognizable reliance to specific instances of sexual activity. But to do this would be simply to refuse to face the fact that for two decades of economic and social developments, people have organized intimate relationships and made choices that define their views of themselves and their places in society, in reliance on the availability of abortion in the event that contraception should fail. The ability of women to participate equally in the economic and social life of the Nation has been facilitated by their ability to control their reproductive lives.[52]

More interesting than identifying the operative level for defining reliance, however, was the debate surrounding the final prudential concern, namely whether the factual predicate of *Roe* had so changed, or come to be seen so differently, "as to have robbed the old rule of significant application or justification." For the joint authors, this became a vehicle for distinguishing their decision to adhere to *Roe* from the Court's earlier decisions to abandon two of its prior landmark rulings, *Lochner v. New York,*[53] culminating in *West Coast Hotel v. Parrish,*[54] and *Plessy v. Ferguson,*[55] culminating in *Brown v. Board of Education (Brown I).*[56] The critical difference between the analysis of these historical overrulings for the joint authors, on the one hand, and the conservatives, on the other, was that the joint authors claimed that the erosion and ultimate abandonment of *Lochner* and *Plessy,* in 1937 and 1954 respectively, resulted from a change—or at least the perception of change—with respect to the factual underpinnings of the initial decisions.[57]

The *Lochner* doctrine, which protected certain private market transactions from prospective governmental interference in the form of minimum wage and maximum hour laws, came on the heels of the industrial revolution. *Lochner* was the product of a conservative Supreme Court, which tried to limit liberal intervention into a free market economy. As set out more fully in chapter 5,[58] by the early to middle 1930s, Lochnerian jurisprudence had already proved a major obstacle to both Franklin Delano Roosevelt's New Deal initiatives for federal regulatory intervention during the Great Depression and to parallel progressive state laws.[59] In response to perceived Supreme Court obstruction of New Deal programs, FDR proposed his Court-packing plan, under which he would appoint an additional justice for every justice over the age of seventy who did not retire. If implemented, the result would likely have transformed a five-to-four conservative majority into a ten-to-five liberal majority. In large part to avert this plan, Justice Owen Roberts, the often critical fifth vote in striking down a number of key New Deal initiatives, voted with the Court's liberals in *West Coast Hotel v. Parrish,*[60] which sustained a state minimum wage law for women. In effect, Roberts signaled his intent to side with FDR in future challenges to New Deal regulatory programs. Roberts's vote in *West Coast Hotel* later became known as "the switch in time that saved nine."[61]

In part III of their *Casey* opinion, which Blackmun and Stevens joined, the joint authors offered the following alternative account of the Court's decision to abandon *Lochner:*

> In the meantime, the Depression had come and, with it, the lesson that seemed unmistakable to most people by 1937, that the interpretation of contractual freedom protected [by the *Lochner* doctrine] rested on fundamentally false factual assumptions about the capacity of a relatively unregulated market to satisfy minimum levels of human welfare.[62]

In this analysis, the Court rejected *Lochner* as a result of a changed perception of the virtues of a laissez-faire economy, rather than as a result of a shift in the Court's jurisprudential vision concerning what the Constitution protects under the guise of due process.

The joint authors' explanation of the Court's eventual abandonment of *Plessy,* culminating in *Brown I,* is parallel. The *Plessy* Court sustained a Louisiana law, typical of those operating throughout the South, that segregated railway cars based upon race. In his famous dissenting opinion in *Plessy,* Justice Harlan determined that whatever the historical practices in the South may have been with respect to treating the minority race when the Fourteenth Amendment was adopted, the fact remained that both races were here to stay and that their fates were necessarily intertwined. Thus, he stated:

> The destinies of the two races, in this country, are indissolubly linked together, and the interests of both require that the common government of all shall not permit the seeds of race hate to be planted under sanction of law. What can more certainly arouse race hate, what more certainly create and perpetuate a feeling of distrust between these races, than state enactments which, in fact, proceed on the ground that colored citizens are so inferior and degraded that they cannot be allowed to sit in public coaches occupied by white citizens?[63]

While the joint authors in *Casey* acknowledged that "we think Plessy was wrong the day it was decided,"[64] they further posited that *Brown I,* which held that state-mandated segregation of public schools violated equal protection, and which effectively ended the *Plessy* regime, was based upon an historical change in actual or perceived facts:

> The Court in Brown addressed these facts of life by observing that whatever may have been the understanding in Plessy's time of the power of segregation to stigmatize those who were segregated with a "badge of inferiority," it was clear by 1954 that legally sanctioned segregation had just such an effect, to the point that racially separate public educational facilities were deemed inherently unequal. Society's understanding of the facts upon which a constitutional ruling was sought in 1954 was thus fundamentally different from the basis claimed for the decision in 1896.

By, again, grounding the justification for the Court's ultimate decisions to overturn a landmark precedent, this time *Plessy,* in a change in perceived facts, the joint authors were able to present *Roe* as a case that they were compelled to follow, since *Roe*'s factual predicate, however controversial that decision may have been, had not changed. As a result, the joint authors' gloss on history provided a framework, based upon stare decisis, for concluding that the factors that led to the demise of economic substantive due process and of the separate-but-equal doctrine did not counsel abandoning the right to abort.

The chief justice and Justice Scalia criticized the joint authors' historical account as disingenuous. Rehnquist readily acknowledged that the factual predicate of *Roe* had not changed, stating, "Of course, what might be called the basic facts which gave rise to Roe have remained the same—women become pregnant, there is a point somewhere, depending on medical technology, where a fetus becomes viable, and women give birth to children."[65] But for Rehnquist, changed factual underpinnings did not form the basis for abandoning either *Lochner* or *Plessy.* Instead, Rehnquist observed, the real problem underlying *Lochner* was that the Constitution nowhere speaks of "freedom of contract," and that the *Lochner* doctrine vindicated the conservative preferences of a majority of the then-sitting justices on the Supreme Court, rather than the language or design of the Constitution. Rehnquist similarly dispensed with the changed factual underpinnings rationale for abandoning *Plessy,* noting that Justice Harlan had made many of the same arguments, which the *Brown* Court ultimately accepted, in his *Plessy* dissent. Unlike the conservatives who flatly rejected stare decisis as a basis for adhering to *Roe,* the liberals, Justices Stevens and Blackmun, joined the joint authors' stare decisis analysis, but rejected the revision of *Roe* that followed. In their separate opinions, the liberals made clear that they preferred the *Roe* formulation based upon the merits of the original decision.

Although the four conservative justices expressly rejected the joint opinion's stare decisis analysis and the two liberal justices rejected the joint authors' revision of *Roe,* which followed from that stare decisis analysis, in favor of the original *Roe* framework, the joint authors relied upon stare decisis to redefine *Roe's* central holding, to reject the trimester framework, to reclassify abortion as less than a fundamental right, and to expressly overrule two recent Supreme Court abortion decisions. In chapter 3, which provides a social choice analysis of outcome voting and the narrowest grounds rule, established in the important, but relatively obscure, 1977 decision *Marks v. United States,*[66] we will see why minorities on the Court, as in *Casey,* are occasionally empowered to define the critical case issues and thus the direction of constitutional doctrine.[67] And in chapter 4, I will explain the institutional forces that have made the Court resistant to proposals to relax stare decisis in constitutional cases, based upon the high cost of overruling problematic constitutional decisions, advanced by, among others, Chief Justice Rehnquist and Justice Scalia.

We have now seen two examples of problematic individual case decisions, *Miller,* in which separate majority resolutions of underlying dispositive issues produced a logical progression leading to the dissenting result, and *Casey,* in which a minority of the Court defined the dispositive issues with the effect of revising the abortion framework set out in *Roe v. Wade,* and of overturning two recent abortion decisions, based upon a stare decisis analysis that a majority of six justices explicitly or implicitly rejected. We are now ready to consider two examples of anomalous Supreme Court decision making involving multiple cases. The next two case studies involve busing as a means of achieving racial integration in the public schools and the modern standing doctrine. The first will illustrate another dimension of stare decisis, namely how adherence to precedent grounds the substantive evolution of constitutional doctrine in the order in which cases are presented and decided. The second will illustrate how the Court has responded to this problem in recent years by imposing a set of timing-based justiciability barriers, including, most notably, standing, even though that doctrine appears prone to inconsistent applications across cases.

III. The Problem of Case Decision Making over Time: Stare Decisis, Path Dependency, and Standing

The next two case studies present another manifestation of the effective suppression of majority preferences in Supreme Court decision making, this time involving the creation of constitutional doctrine over multiple cases. The first case study illustrates that, as a consequence of stare decisis, the same two cases presented in reverse order can produce precisely opposite legal doctrine. In the language of social choice, stare decisis renders the evolution of legal doctrine "path dependent."[68] One necessary consequence of path dependency is the potential thwarting of majority preferences with respect to the underlying merits in those cases that are subject to controlling precedent. The second case study, which will contrast two standing cases, illustrates a related phenomenon. By switching the frameworks used to grant and to deny standing in two prominent cases, I will demonstrate that the Supreme Court's own analysis would, again, compel achieving opposite results in both cases. In both case studies, we will see that two of the Supreme Court's most important process-based decisional rules, stare decisis and standing, have the effect of grounding substantive constitutional holdings in seemingly fortuitous factors, namely, the order in which case decisions are presented, or the Supreme Court's choice between two seemingly malleable doctrinal frameworks.

A. *Crawford, Seattle,* and the Importance of Case Order

Consider the following tandem of cases: *Crawford v. Board of Education*[69] and *Washington v. Seattle School District. No. 1.*[70] In *Crawford,* the Court was presented with an equal protection challenge to an amendment to the California Constitution, which prevented state courts from ordering busing as a means of promoting racial integration of the public schools unless the court first determined that the order was required to remedy a violation of the Fourteenth Amendment equal protection clause.[71] In *Seattle,* the Court was presented with an equal protection challenge to a Washington statewide referendum that prevented local school boards from ordering busing as a means of promoting racial integration, absent a finding that busing was required to remedy a violation of either the United States or Washington Constitutions.[72] For a two year period, after which the legislature could authorize nonremedial integrative busing by statute, the state's voters would have to pass another initiative to achieve that objective. In contrast with the cases discussed in the prior part, in which at least part of the opinion announcing the Court's judgment was rejected by a majority of the Court, both *Crawford* and *Seattle* were decided by clear majorities. And yet, these two cases had the curious effect of thwarting the preferences of a majority of the very justices on the Supreme Court who decided them.

A brief explanation of the issues underlying *Crawford* and *Seattle* will be helpful for the analysis to follow. These cases involved the intersection of two competing concerns with respect to the integration of public schools. First, unlike southern states, neither California nor Washington had ever legally mandated the segregation of public schools based upon race. Nevertheless, in the aftermath of the prominent northern desegregation case, *Keyes v. School District No. 1, Denver, Colorado,*[73] the Supreme Court began to scrutinize northern states that engaged in practices with the effect of producing de facto segregation of their public schools. The most common of such practices was gerrymandering attendance zones to place African American schoolchildren in one set of schools and white schoolchildren in another. These northern desegregation cases presented the Court with a major conceptual difficulty. The persistence of single-race schools can be attributable to any number of factors, including, but not limited to, genuine racial demographics, which involve no illicit gerrymandering, or awkwardly and deliberately drawn school attendance zones, placing students of the same race in the same schools. The problem for courts presented with school-districting challenges based upon gerrymandering is that, almost invariably, the racial composition of a school is a combination of both demographics and districting. In those cases in which there is any indication that race may have played some role in drawing school district lines, therefore, the party who bears the burden to prove either the presence or the absence of illicit racial gerrymandering will likely lose. As a result, the presumptive force of assigning either rational basis scrutiny or strict scrutiny is most often dispositive. Not surprisingly, the northern school desegregation cases focused, by and large, on developing rules governing who carried the burden of proof to establish the legality or illegality of single-race schools.

Following *Brown I,* the pace of southern desegregation was painstakingly slow, in large part due to the Court's effective abdication to southern resistance under the "with all deliberate speed" formula articulated in *Brown v. Board of Education of Topeka (Brown II).*[74] After the landmark 1971 case *Swann v. Charlotte-Mecklenburg Board of Education,*[75] however, the Court provided lower federal courts with the mandate and broad equitable tools needed to force the meaningful desegregation of southern schools. In the aftermath of *Swann*'s success, the Court was faced with the anomaly that the southern public schools had become the most integrated in the United States.[76] The Court then confronted challenges to the effective segregation of northern school systems, which, although never formally mandating segregation, had engaged in a number of facially race-neutral strategies that had the effect of promoting single-race schools. Between the time of *Swann* and the 1980s, when *Crawford* and *Seattle* were decided, the Court had developed three competing approaches to this problem. In *Keyes,* a liberal group of justices, Brennan, Marshall, and Blackmun, joined by Justice Stewart, a moderate, held that in states that had never segregated their school systems by law, but in which plaintiffs could establish intentional practices within parts of particular school districts that tended to produce single-race schools, the burden shifted to the state to disprove that intentional gerrymandering in one part of a school district also produced single-race schools in other parts of the same district.[77] In contrast, then–Associate Justice Rehnquist stated that it was never permissible to shift the burden to states that had never segregated public schools by law to disprove an equal protection violation based solely upon the racial composition of a school. Instead, the burden remained on the challenger to prove that the existence of particular single-race schools was the product of intentional state action for the entire district.[78] Finally, Justice Powell, in an approach later adopted by Justice Stevens in the context of equal protection challenges to racial gerrymandering of voting districts,[79] would have allowed burden shifting, but not based upon proof of actual intent. Instead, these justices would have shifted the burden to the state when presented with objective factors that tended to evince a subjective intent to gerrymander based upon race.[80] Most typically, such objective indicia include awkward district lines not attributable to natural geographic boundaries, for example, rivers or highways.

While the Court alternated throughout this period among these competing approaches to burden shifting,[81] a single prophylactic measure remained that would allow states to successfully defend against an equal protection challenge based upon either de facto or de jure segregation, regardless of which framework happened to dominate. If schools within a particular district had a ratio of African American to white students roughly equal to the ratio in the population at large, then under any of the three methods, the state would almost invariably succeed in defending against an equal protection challenge. One way to achieve this objective was through a benign form of racial gerrymandering, which deliberately integrated the races. Another was through busing. The major difficulty with busing, however, is that it ran into conflict with the second, competing, concern of parents, especially of younger children, namely providing their children with the benefits of an education in their neighborhood of choice.

The California and Washington laws can be understood as successful efforts by parents to defeat preventative measures aimed at curbing equal protection challenges to de facto segregation, to further neighborhood education. One of the most curious features of these two laws, both of which limited busing as a means of achieving integration in public schools, is that each appeared to have had a built-in safeguard against a federal equal protection challenge. While limiting the power of state judges in *Crawford,* and of school boards in *Seattle,* to order integrative busing, the challenged laws also provided that violations of the federal Constitution's equal protection clause would provide the basis for an exception. The Washington initiative provided an even broader exception, allowing busing to remedy violations of both the federal and state constitutions. In essence, through these two laws, California and Washington voters had attempted to equate their state's equal protection law with federal constitutional requirements for purposes of integrative busing. It appeared that the only way to strike either law would be to hold that a law guaranteeing Fourteenth Amendment equal protection violated Fourteenth Amendment equal protection. And yet, the Court sustained only the California amendment.

To see why, we must consider one more precedent, which intersected with *Seattle* and *Crawford.* In *Hunter v. Erickson,*[82] the Supreme Court was faced with a challenge to an amendment to the city charter of Akron, Ohio. Through the amendment, the voters had effectively repealed a previously enacted fair housing ordinance aimed at remedying unfair housing practices based upon race. As the *Seattle* Court explained, the charter amendment provided that

> ordinances regulating real estate transactions "on the basis of race, color, religion, national origin or ancestry must first be approved by a majority of the electors voting on the question at regular or general election before said ordinance shall be effective."[83]

In effect, the amendment required persons seeking fair housing ordinances aimed at a particular problem, racial discrimination in real estate transactions, to secure the support of a majority of both the city's voters and the city council. All other groups seeking any other type of city ordinance, including fair housing statutes not aimed at curbing racial discrimination, needed to secure only the support of a majority of *either* the city's voters *or* the city council. The *Hunter* Court concluded that this facially neutral ordinance violated the Fourteenth Amendment equal protection clause by requiring persons seeking to secure a particular type of legislation aimed at curbing racially discriminatory housing practices to clear two hurdles rather than one.

We are now ready to consider the manner in which the *Crawford* and *Seattle* Courts effectively thwarted the preferences of their own members in at least one of the two cases. First, we must consider the voting lineup in both cases. In *Crawford,* a majority of six justices, in an opinion by Justice Powell, upheld the California constitutional amendment. Two justices concurred in the judgment and one justice dissented. In *Seattle,* a majority of five justices struck down the Washington statewide referendum, with the remaining four justices dissenting.

The *Seattle* majority was persuaded that the governing authority was *Hunter* and that the state had imposed unique obstacles in the path of those participants in the state's political process who sought to secure the benefits of an integrated education through busing.[84] It did so by raising the governmental level at which this group must secure passage of favorable legislation to the highest in the state for at least a two-year period. Following the statewide referendum, three options remained to secure busing for integrative purposes: first, to prove an equal protection violation, under either the state or federal constitutions; second, to secure another statewide initiative, repealing the one under review; and, third, to secure a two-thirds majority vote of the legislature. Because the referendum achieved this objective only for this limited category of proposed legislation, a majority of the Court, in an opinion written by Justice Blackmun, and including Justices Marshall, Brennan, White, and Stevens, voted to strike down the Washington initiative. Justices Powell, Burger, Rehnquist, and O'Connor dissented.

In contrast, while those challenging the *Crawford* amendment also presented a *Hunter* challenge, the *Crawford* majority was persuaded that the effect of the California constitutional amendment was to equate the state's law governing integrative busing with that compelled by the Fourteenth Amendment equal protection clause.[85] In an opinion by Justice Powell, the *Crawford* majority reasoned that a state constitutional amendment that equates the state's law on integrative busing with federal constitutional requirements *but no more,* cannot violate those very federal constitutional requirements. Thus, Justice Powell, joined by Chief Justice Burger, and Justices Burger, Rehnquist, O'Connor, White, and Stevens, voted to sustain the California constitutional amendment. Justices Brennan and Blackmun concurred separately and Justice Marshall dissented.

Based upon the foregoing discussion, consider the vote lineup across these two cases shown in table 1.2. I have placed asterisks next to the names of five justices, Chief Justice Burger and Justices Powell, Rehnquist, and O'Connor, who joined the majority in *Crawford* and dissented in *Seattle*, and Justice Marshall, who joined the majority in *Seattle* and alone dissented in *Crawford*.[86] For present purposes, I will assume that the views expressed in these opinions are sincere.[87] The opinions reveal that while this group split on how the two cases should be decided (with Marshall reaching the opposite conclusions from those of the remaining four), all five did agree that the two cases were constitutionally indistinguishable, such that whatever the ultimate resolution of either case happens to be, the other case should have been decided the same way.

In Marshall's dissenting opinion in *Crawford,* he expressly stated that the two cases were constitutionally indistinguishable,[88] and in his *Seattle* dissent, joined by Chief Justice Burger and Justices Rehnquist and O'Connor, Justice Powell rejected, what, for him, was the only conceivable distinction between the two state laws under review. Specifically, Powell observed that, unlike the California amendment, which simply curtailed the power of state courts in construing the state's constitution, the Washington initiative removed power with respect to a particular issue affecting race from what had once been the local level to the highest level of decision making in the state.[89]

While *Hunter* provided the basis for a minority of the Court, Justices Brennan and Blackmun, who concurred in *Crawford,* to distinguish the two cases and to vote only to strike down the Washington initiative, Justice Powell and the three justices who joined his *Seattle* dissent concluded that *Hunter*

Table 1.2. Voting Lineups in *Seattle* and *Crawford*

Seattle		
Majority		Dissent
Blackmun		Powell*
Marshall*		Burger*
Brennan		Rehnquist*
White		O'Connor*
Stevens		

Crawford		
Majority	Concurrence	Dissent
Powell*	Brennan	Marshall*
Burger*	Blackmun	
Rehnquist*		
O'Connor*		
Stevens		
White		

was not controlling in either case. For this group of four justices, *Hunter* did not control *Seattle* because the Washington statewide initiative did not raise the hurdles for those interested in securing the benefits of integrative busing. Instead, the initiative simply restored to the state the authority to decide a matter that, at an earlier time, it had conferred upon local school boards. But since the authority originally emanated from the state, Powell concluded that restoring it to the state could not violate equal protection. Allowing *Hunter* to control *Seattle,* Powell reasoned, would create the odd effect that whenever the state provides for local decision making and a local governmental unit does more than the federal or state constitutions require, the state becomes forever barred from rescinding that authority and limiting the protections over the given issue only to those that the state or federal constitutions require.

The merits of these various positions aside, the asterisks demonstrate that for a five-justice majority of the deciding Courts, *Crawford* and *Seattle* presented issues that are constitutionally indistinguishable. Assume for present purposes that the deciding justices adhere to stare decisis in the second of these two cases. Now consider what the effect of stare decisis would have been had these two cases been decided one year apart, rather than the same day. Assuming that the *Crawford* case arose first, such that the California amendment was upheld, the majority that determined that the two cases were indistinguishable would later have confronted the question in *Seattle,* whether *Crawford* was controlling as a matter of stare decisis. Assuming, as the opinions make plain, that a majority of the *Seattle* Court determined the two cases to be indistinguishable, and that this majority adhered to the rule of stare decisis, then the result would have been to uphold the *Seattle* initiative. If so, both the California constitutional amendment and the Washington initiative would have been upheld. Alternatively, if the cases were presented in the opposite order, such that the *Seattle* initiative were struck down first, applying the same logic in the second case, the result would be to strike down the *Crawford* amendment as well. Given the preferences of the justices in these two cases, and assuming that the justices voted consistently with the views expressed in the opinions that they wrote or joined, the order in which the cases were presented would have fully determined the substantive body of constitutional law that they developed. Because the cases were issued at the same time, neither *Crawford* nor *Seattle* controlled the other as a matter of precedent. As a result, the Court was able to issue each of the two decisions without considering the impact of the holding in the other case, even though, taken together, the effect was to constitutionalize a distinction between the two cases, based upon *Hunter,* which a majority of the *Seattle* and *Crawford* Courts rejected.

Together, *Crawford* and *Seattle* present the very same anomaly that we saw in *Miller,* namely that the Supreme Court's decision-making rules sometimes have the curious effect of subordinating majority preferences on the Court. The only difference is that in *Miller,* this problem arose in a single case in which no opinion commanded a majority of the Court, while in *Craw-*

ford and *Seattle,* the problem arose across two cases, each decided by clear majorities.

Based upon the phenomenon illustrated by the above discussion of *Crawford* and *Seattle,* Frank Easterbrook, a prominent legal scholar and federal court of appeals judge, has advocated abandoning, or at least relaxing, stare decisis in constitutional cases. In contrast with Chief Justice Rehnquist, who in *Casey* advocated relaxing stare decisis in constitutional cases due to the difficulty of overruling,[90] Judge Easterbrook has advocated relaxing stare decisis in constitutional cases because of that doctrine's effect in rendering the substantive evolution of legal doctrine dependent upon the fortuitous order in which cases are presented and decided.[91] In chapter 4, which provides a social choice model of stare decisis and of justiciability, I will respond to these arguments and explain, using the theory of social choice, the critical importance of stare decisis in promoting the stability of constitutional doctrine.

B.   Standing *Board of Regents v. Bakke* and *Allen v. Wright* on Their Heads

The next case study also contrasts two cases, *Board of Regents of the University of California v. Bakke,*[92] which presented the question whether a twice rejected nonminority applicant had standing to challenge the University of California at Davis School of Medicine's affirmative action program, and *Allen v. Wright,*[93] which presented the question whether the parents of African American school children had standing to challenge an IRS tax policy, which, they alleged, had the effect of undermining the integration of the public schools that their children attended. In doing so, this case study will present a dimension of standing that is conceptually more problematic than the question of third-party standing at issue in *Miller.* In *Bakke,* the Court granted standing, thus allowing Mr. Bakke to present his equal protection challenge. In *Allen,* the Court denied standing, preventing the federal judiciary from reaching the merits of the plaintiffs' underlying claim. After reviewing the two standing determinations, I will demonstrate that the articulated rationales are sufficiently malleable that employing the *Bakke* framework in *Allen* would have produced the opposite result, as would employing the *Allen* framework in *Bakke.* The next and final section of this chapter will then consider the broader historical anomaly of standing of which *Miller, Bakke,* and *Allen* are a part.

In *Bakke,* the Supreme Court considered a challenge to the University of California at Davis School of Medicine's affirmative action program. The school had an entering class with one hundred seats, of which it set aside sixteen for minorities. Bakke, who had been rejected twice in his application to the medical school, sued, claiming that, as a nonminority, his inability to compete for all one hundred seats, rather than for just eighty-four seats, violated his rights under the Fourteenth Amendment equal protection clause. In addition to defending the merits of its affirmative action program, the medical school claimed that Bakke lacked standing to challenge that program.[94] The school argued that Bakke had failed to articulate a justiciable injury because even if the Court struck down the affirmative action program, Bakke could not prove that he would have been given one of the sixteen seats reserved for minorities. In addition to its prudential doctrine against third-party standing introduced in discussing *Miller,* the Supreme Court has identified three constitutional prerequisites to standing, each taken from the common law of tort: injury in fact, causation, and redressability.[95] In essence, the medical school claimed that Bakke had not alleged the requisite facts with which to prove a constitutional injury in fact because even without the affirmative action program in place, he might not have been admitted. Applying the same reasoning, Bakke also had not established that if the Court struck down the Davis affirmative action program, it would redress his injury.

To understand the Supreme Court's analysis, it will be helpful first to consider the approach to burden shifting set out by the California Supreme Court, from which the United States Supreme Court took certiorari. The California Supreme Court had resolved the problem of proof by analogizing Bakke's equal protection claim to a claim arising under Title VII of the Civil Rights Act of 1964,[96] alleging racial discrimination.[97] Under Title VII, when a plaintiff presents a credible allegation that he has either been fired or passed over for a promotion based upon race, the burden then shifts to the employer to articulate a race-neutral justification for the employment decision. If the employer fails to offer a credible race-neutral rationale, plaintiff prevails as a matter of law. If, on the other hand, the employer does offer a credible race-neutral rationale, the question is then presented to the trier of fact. By analogy, the California Supreme Court, having determined that Bakke had articulated a prima facie case of an equal protection violation, given that his denial of admission was at least partially race based, placed the burden on the medical school to prove that but for the affirmative action program, Bakke would not have been admitted. On petition for rehearing before the California Supreme Court, the medical school, not surprisingly, conceded that it could not carry the shifted evidentiary burden. The California Supreme Court then amended its opinion to order Bakke's admission into the medical school, which was stayed pending review in the Supreme Court.[98]

In addressing the merits of the standing defense, the Supreme Court, per Justice Powell, determined that Bakke had articulated a constitutional injury in fact and that the claimed injury was redressable. Powell reasoned that whether or not Bakke would have been admitted had the affirmative action program not been in place, it was clear that by virtue of the operation of that program, Mr. Bakke was unable to compete for all one hundred seats, rather than just the eighty-four seats reserved for general admission. The Court concluded that Mr. Bakke's inability to compete for the sixteen seats reserved for minorities constituted a cognizable injury in fact. In essence, Powell vindicated Bakke's claim of standing by characterizing his claimed injury as the denial of an opportunity to compete, which, thus defined, would be remedied if the affirmative action program were struck down, whether or not Bakke was ultimately admitted.

Now compare *Bakke* with the 1984 case of *Allen v. Wright*.[99] In *Allen*, parents of African American schoolchildren located throughout the United States challenged a policy through which the IRS determined the tax-exempt status of private schools. Under this policy, the IRS based the tax-exempt status of such schools not upon an evaluation of the merits of the school, but, rather, upon the tax-exempt status of the umbrella organization of which the school was a part. Plaintiffs claimed that while the IRS generally denied tax-exempt status to private schools that discriminated on the basis of race, some schools, through the operation of this tax policy, were afforded tax-exempt status notwithstanding their racially discriminatory practices. Plaintiffs further alleged that if the Supreme Court struck down the IRS policy based upon the Fifth Amendment due process clause, which the Supreme Court had previously interpreted to apply equal protection standards to the federal government,[100] the result might inure to the benefit of their children who attended public schools by effectively removing a taxpayer subsidy for white flight. The Court held that plaintiffs had failed to allege a constitutional injury in fact, and that they therefore lacked standing. Justice O'Connor, writing for the *Allen* Court, reasoned that even if the Court struck down the IRS policy, no fewer than four intervening causal links, involving persons not before the Court, remained between the Court's action and the effective integration of the public schools. Thus, O'Connor explained:

> It is, first, uncertain how many racially discriminatory private schools are in fact receiving tax exemptions. Moreover, it is entirely speculative [whether] withdrawal of a tax exemption from any particular school would lead the school to change its policies. [It] is just as speculative whether any given parent of a child attending such a private school would decide to transfer the child to public school as a result of any changes in educational or financial policy made by the private school once it was threatened with loss of tax-exempt status. It is also pure speculation whether, in a particular community, a large enough number of the numerous relevant school officials and parents would reach decisions that collectively would have a significant impact on the racial composition of the public schools.[101]

In short, O'Connor denied standing to the *Allen* plaintiffs by focusing on the attenuated linkage between the claimed injury, an allegedly unconstitutional IRS tax policy, and the relief ultimately desired, namely the further integration of public schools.

Both *Bakke* and *Allen* present difficult standing analyses in large part because neither involves the most obvious barriers to standing. Unlike *Miller*, for example, neither *Bakke* nor *Allen* involved an effort to raise the claim of a third party.[102] In addition, neither case involved claims that are legally diffuse, as the Supreme Court has employed that term.[103] The Supreme Court employs the concept of diffuse status to prevent adjudication of claims based upon injuries that the claimants share in common with the population or citizens generally, and which are therefore better addressed to the legislature. While the *Allen* plaintiffs were a large class, nominal class size alone is not the basis for denying standing because of diffuse claim status. Provided the court can distinguish the affected class from the population generally, the claim, even if it affects large numbers of people, is legally specific to the affected class.[104] Instead, both cases involved challenges to regulations the absence of which might have produced more favorable market conditions (for entering medical school in *Bakke*, and for providing the benefits of an integrated public school education in *Allen*) and which might ultimately have inured to the benefit of the plaintiff, or, in *Allen*, of the plaintiffs' children.

In *Bakke*, the Supreme Court rejected the argument that standing should be denied even though Mr. Bakke might not actually have benefited in terms of his ultimate admission had the affirmative action program been struck down. Instead, the Court reasoned that the mere denial of an opportunity to compete in a marketplace unimpeded by an unconstitutional admissions regime—and specifically, the opportunity to compete for sixteen additional seats, even if ultimately Bakke would not be given one of them—constituted a judicially cognizable injury in fact.[105] In contrast, the *Allen* Court focused on the multiple links in the chain of causation that rendered the African American parents' claimed injury attenuated.[106] But with little effort, we can easily "flip" *Bakke*, using the *Allen* framework, such that his claimed injury would have appeared deficient for standing purposes, and just as easily flip *Allen*, using the *Bakke* framework, such that the causal link problem would disappear. Indeed, based upon the ease with which one can successfully complete this exercise, numerous legal academics have questioned the legitimacy of this line of standing cases.[107]

First, we will flip *Bakke*. Had the Court in *Bakke*, using the *Allen* framework, focused on the number of causal links between the claimed relief, striking down the affirmative action program, and the ultimate objective, admission to the medical school, it could have devised at least as many as did the *Allen* Court in determining that the claimed injury in that case was unduly attenuated. At a minimum, Bakke's ultimate admission into the Davis medical school turned on (1) whether having struck down the Davis affirmative action program, the medical school would substitute some other, constitutionally permissible, affirmative action program;[108] (2) whether the absence of an affirmative action program or the presence of a newly devised plan would reduce the applications or admissions of minority candidates, relative to nonminority candidates, as compared with the struck Davis program; (3) whether the absence of an affirmative action program or the presence of a newly devised plan would encourage applications by additional and more qualified nonminority students who might have been deterred from applying based upon the impact upon their admissions prospects of the struck affirmative action program; and (4) whether the altered pool of both minority and nonminority applicants that would result from striking the Davis plan would have had a significant enough impact on Bakke's relative qualifications to the others in both pools to change the outcome of his application. One can, of course, go further: (5) whether or not having struck down the Davis program, other medical schools would follow suit, in turn, affecting the composition of their own applicant pools with spillover effects upon that at Davis; and (6) whether the changed admissions regimes at other medical schools would make those schools more attractive for Bakke to apply to and to matriculate, if offered a seat. As in *Allen,* the ultimate question whether striking down the Davis program would have resulted in either Bakke's admission or his attendance at Davis turned upon the impact of the Court's ruling on parties not before it and about whose conduct the Court could only speculate.

My point is not to demonstrate that Mr. Bakke presented a claim that should have been held nonjusticiable; in fact, my own position is that his claim, whatever the merits, was justiciable. Instead, I am simply demonstrating that to the extent that intervening causal links can be said to render the claimed injury in *Allen* attenuated, one can make precisely the same claim in *Bakke.* In fact, as the discussion to follow will demonstrate, the causal chain analysis is equally suspect in both cases.

Now reconsider *Allen* using the *Bakke* framework. The *Allen* plaintiffs alleged that an IRS tax policy used to determine the tax-exempt status of private schools had the effect of creating a loophole through which some discriminatory private schools were afforded tax-exempt status. The policy therefore had the effect of subsidizing white flight.[109] We will now recast the alleged injury in *Allen* employing the framework set out in *Bakke.* The *Allen* plaintiffs did not allege that any particular degree of integration would necessarily follow from striking down the IRS policy affording tax-exempt status to schools that discriminated on the basis of race. Instead, they simply claimed that their children should have been afforded the *opportunity* to receive an education within a market for public and private schools that is undistorted by an unconstitutional IRS tax policy. As with Mr. Bakke, the *Allen* plaintiffs' ultimate position was that once the illegal IRS tax policy (substitute: illegal Davis affirmative action program) is struck down, let the chips fall where they may, whatever the ultimate effect upon the integration of the public schools that their children attend (substitute: upon Mr. Bakke's admission or rejection). Stated differently, the *Allen* Court, in contrast with the *Bakke* Court, focused on the question of what the effect on the margin of a change in the IRS tax policy would be. That, of course, is an empirical question, and one, it turns out, that it was entirely unnecessary for the Supreme Court to have even attempted to resolve. When the *Allen* claim of injury is viewed through a *Bakke* lens, we see the plaintiffs' real claim: *However* many people are on the margin with respect to each of the Court's identified causal links, plaintiffs only seek to change the conduct of those people and of no one else. And certainly a change in the IRS tax policy will change the conduct of *all persons* whose conduct is on the margin with respect to that policy; that, after all, is the definition of being on the margin.[110] Mr. Bakke's claim of injury, which the Supreme Court accepted, can of course be phrased in precisely the same way. Whether or not eliminating Davis's affirmative action program ultimately would have resulted in his admission, which Bakke had no way of knowing, has no logical bearing on whether he should have been allowed to compete in the absence of an allegedly illegal market distortion, the removal of which, if his candidacy *was* on the margin, would have resulted in his admission. Thus viewed, the *Allen* plaintiffs' claimed injury was precisely parallel to that articulated in *Bakke* and for which Bakke, unlike the *Allen* plaintiffs, was given standing.

As we will see in chapter 4, this "flip," which works equally well in both directions, is not unique to the *Bakke* and *Allen* cases; indeed, it is characteristic of all standing cases in the category "no right to an undistorted market." The question then arises: Why have a standing barrier that appears to devolve to a question of how one elects to characterize an injury? As I will demonstrate in chapter 4, while this standing doctrine is prone to such manipulation, social choice provides a strong positive explanation for these case results and for the role of standing in furthering fair constitutional process.

IV. The Historical Anomaly of Justiciability: The Conservative Burger and Rehnquist Courts' Embrace of Liberal Standing Doctrine

This final section will briefly set out an historical anomaly of constitutional law, rather than one based upon the seemingly anomalous resolution of particular cases. I will present a paradox to which legal scholars have paid relatively little attention, but which calls into question traditional explanations of the emergence of the modern standing doctrine and which raises associated anomalies surrounding the doctrines of ripeness and mootness.

The modern standing doctrine finds its inception in the efforts of Justice Louis Brandeis and then-professor (and later justice) Felix Frankfurter to protect progressive regulatory agencies from judicial attack in conservative lower federal courts. And yet, the emerging conservative Burger and Rehnquist Courts, which were far less trusting of governmental regulation and which had a correspondingly greater faith in private orderings, significantly increased their reliance upon, rather than cutting back on, the New Deal standing doctrine. While this section will focus principally on standing, chapters 5 and 6, which will explain the historical anomaly that follows, will further consider two related paradoxes of justiciability, first the Burger and Rehnquist Courts' constitutionalization of all three timing-based justiciability doctrines, ripeness, mootness, and standing, and second, the creation by the same Courts of exceptions, which, individually and collectively, appear to defy the characterization of justiciability as other than a prudential doctrine.

Before explaining the historical anomaly of standing, it is worth considering the doctrine's prominence in modern constitutional adjudication. It is no exaggeration to assert that for the better part of sixty years, standing has greatly affected the development of each of the substantive bodies of constitutional law already discussed, and many others. A brief introduction will help to place the anomaly in context.[111] The history of standing can roughly be divided into three historical periods. Several legal scholars have persuasively demonstrated that early United States practice, both state and federal, and indeed the English practice upon which it was based, allowed public enforcement actions by private citizens against allegedly unlawful government conduct, with no requirement of a direct personal stake.[112] While a number of early federal equity decisions employed language, including the term *standing,* to determine the conditions under which individuals may invoke the federal courts' equitable powers,[113] commentators have observed that such cases invariably involved prudential concerns rather than equitable or jurisdictional powers.[114] In addition, there is a near universal consensus that early federal court cases had not linked the notion of standing to the Article III case or controversy requirement. And while private enforcement actions tapered off in the mid–nineteenth century, that was attributable principally to the increased professionalization of prosecutorial functions, not to any change in the perceived justiciability of such actions.[115]

In an extensive review of early federal equity practice, Professor Steven Winter persuasively established the now widely accepted proposition that the modern standing doctrine was a New Deal invention.[116] To be more specific, Justice Louis Brandeis and his disciple, Felix Frankfurter, developed standing from an earlier set of cases that involved the jurisdictional limits on the equitable powers of the federal courts. To understand why Brandeis and Frankfurter created a doctrine limiting the power of private persons to bring enforcement actions in federal court unless they had a personal stake in the matter, a brief background on the New Deal Court will be helpful. As explained above, to fend off FDR's Court-packing plan, Justice Owen Roberts made his famous "switch in time that saved nine" in *West Coast Hotel.* By voting to sustain the state minimum wage law for women under review, Roberts, the critical fifth vote in striking down a number of prior New Deal initiatives, signaled his willingness to ratify future New Deal initiatives. Following this shift, while his formal Court-packing plan failed, FDR ultimately succeeded in replacing the entire Supreme Court during his long administration. FDR did not, however, have the same success with respect to the lower federal courts, which had been packed in three previous Republican administrations.[117] While the New Deal Court was increasingly willing to ratify FDR's New Deal initiatives, lower federal courts were thus content to continue distinguishing landmark Supreme Court precedents in an effort to strike other such programs down. Even if the Supreme Court had ultimately reversed these lower court decisions, doing so would have been costly as a political matter. The Court would have repeatedly had to distinguish or overrule its own precedents from a recent, but more conservative, era, thus undermining the Court's claim to judicial detachment and legitimacy.

The New Deal Court employed language from early federal equity practice to devise a series of justiciability doctrines intended to prevent lower federal courts, which shared a common conservative vision at odds with the now liberal Court, from reaching the merits of underlying challenges to regulatory programs. The effect of imposing barriers to justiciability, whether in the form of ripeness, mootness, or standing, was to prevent lower federal courts from reaching the merits of underlying challenges, without the need to dictate results. The Court could signal that the doctrines used to dispense with such challenges were new because the regulatory era was new,[118] without having repeatedly to confront underlying doctrinal inconsistencies transparently based upon the Court's changed political composition.

Of these doctrines, standing was the most novel and ultimately the most far reaching. The Court developed the standing doctrine because ripeness and mootness alone proved inadequate to limit legal challenges that threatened to undermine the Supreme Court's appearance of credibility and political detachment in the face of cases that would have repeatedly forced the Court to confront its doctrinal about-face. The relevant cases were mature, or ripe, in that they involved statutory regimes that were fully in force and that affected genuine private interests. In addition, they involved issues that had continuing significance, and thus were not moot.

But, by devising rules governing the conditions under which entities or persons could challenge New Deal regulatory initiatives, the Supreme Court was able severely to restrict lower federal courts in their efforts to address the merits of challenges to New Deal regulatory initiatives.[119] If lower federal courts could not litigate such claims because the challengers lacked "standing," the Supreme Court would no longer have to address lower federal court decisions that distinguished recent Supreme Court precedents and that struck down such programs. For the New Deal Court, this newly minted justiciability barrier, which remained prudential, proved an essential administrative tool in reigning in lower federal courts, which generally possessed a very different vision regarding the scope of the commerce clause and of the Fifth and Fourteenth Amendment due process clauses.

In the later Burger and Rehnquist Court periods, justiciability in general, and standing in particular, underwent a radical transformation, which took two forms. First, while in the New Deal and Warren Court eras, all three timing-based justiciability doctrines—ripeness, mootness, and standing—had remained essentially prudential tools for judicial administration, thus paving the way for federal statutes allowing private enforcement actions, the Burger Court infused each with a constitutional component, grounded in Article III.[120] Second, the Burger and Rehnquist Courts altered the language of standing, infusing no fewer than three requirements, namely injury in fact, causation, and redressability, each drawn from the common law of tort. The Burger and Rehnquist Courts not only changed the contours of standing doctrine, but also, and more importantly, made standing the centerpiece of their justiciability jurisprudence in constitutional cases. In fact, standing has become an essential litmus test in virtually all civil constitutional litigation, and it is often raised *sua sponte,* meaning at the court's own initiative. Beginning in 1992, the Supreme Court has employed the constitutional prong of standing to prevent private litigants alleging injuries with no clear common law antecedents from enforcing the Endangered Species Act,[121] notwithstanding the statute's broad-based standing provision, and to delay consideration of a challenge to the constitutionality of the Line-Item Veto Act,[122] presented in a challenge by, among others, members of Congress, even though the act conferred standing upon members of Congress and called for expedited review in the Supreme Court.[123] Most recently, the Court has suggested a retreat from these substantial restrictions upon Congress's power to circumvent the Court's imposed standing barriers.[124]

This history raises two questions. First, why did the emerging conservative Burger and Rehnquist Courts embrace, rather than set aside, the various barriers to justiciability invented by the liberal New Deal Court to protect federal regulatory intervention from interference in lower federal courts, given the increased faith that those later Supreme Courts exhibited in private orderings? Second, why did the same Courts ground the once prudential justiciability tools in significant part in Article III? In chapter 5, which employs social choice to explain the nature of the modern Supreme Court's political composition, I will explain this historical anomaly.

V. Final Comments

This introductory chapter has introduced three sets of notorious anomalies of constitutional law, each of which remains unexplained under traditional constitutional scholarship. After outlining the theory of social choice in the next chapter, I will use the theory to solve each of the puzzles described above, along with several associated puzzles of constitutional law, and to reveal the basis for the underlying process-based decisional rules that produced them. Part II will provide economic models, grounded in social choice theory, of static and dynamic constitutional process. Chapter 3 will explain why the Supreme Court employs outcome voting even though that rule sometimes appears to thwart the expressed views of a majority of the deciding Court on agreed-upon issues, as in *Miller,* or to allow a minority to define and resolve the dispositive case issues, as in *Casey.* Chapter 4 will extend the analysis to consider why the Court employs stare decisis in constitutional cases, even though the doctrine has the effect of allowing the order of case decisions to substantially affect the substantive evolution of constitutional doctrine. In addition, the analysis will demonstrate that the apparent difficulties notwithstanding, by operating together with stare decisis, standing improves the overall fairness of constitutional decision making. Part III will test this book's most far-reaching theory of constitutional process, namely that of standing, against the historical and case evidence. Chapter 5 will explain why the conservative Burger and Rehnquist Courts transformed standing, a liberal doctrinal creation, into a constitutional requirement and gave it central prominence in its constitutional decision making. Chapter 6 will provide a detailed overview and analysis of the modern justiciability case law with a particular emphasis on standing. Finally, chapter 7 will summarize the main arguments presented throughout the book.

With that introduction, we are ready to begin our journey of analyzing constitutional process, which provides a critical but rarely exposed link between jurisprudence and constitutional law based upon insights gleaned from the multifaceted discipline of social choice.

CHAPTER 2 **An Introduction to Social Choice**

I. Introduction

This chapter will introduce the underlying social choice concepts without which, I will argue, it is not possible to piece together the intricate puzzle of constitutional process. In contrast with the remaining chapters, which are structured around specific doctrinal or historical anomalies in constitutional law, this chapter introduces the methodology of social choice. Interdisciplinary scholarship, and especially interdisciplinary legal scholarship, tends to present the nonprimary discipline in either of two ways. Most commonly, legal scholars introduce the alternative discipline incrementally, through a series of discrete applications. For two reasons, however, in this book, I will follow the alternative approach of introducing social choice systematically, with the applications to follow. First, incremental introductions to a complementary discipline work best when the principles involved are susceptible of early and simple applications, followed by increasingly complex applications. By selecting increasingly difficult applications over time, the incremental approach allows the author to present the alternative discipline by example. In part II of the book, however, I will be presenting economic models of Supreme Court decision making of similar complexity. The models presented in part II explain the processes through which the Supreme Court transforms judicial preferences into constitutional doctrine, both in individual cases and over time and across cases. The difference between the static and the dynamic models of constitutional decision making, presented in chapters 3 and 4, respectively, is not the difficulty of the underlying economic analysis, but rather the nature and scope of the underlying legal issues.

Second, incremental approaches to introducing complementary disciplines often suffer from a lack of rigor. While the purpose of interdisciplinary legal scholarship is to apply the alternative discipline to actual legal problems, there is a tendency in legal scholarship to radically simplify the complementary discipline to the point where its integrity is undermined. As Albert Einstein once stated: "Everything should be made as simple as possible, but not simpler."[1] This is especially true with respect to a discipline like social choice, which contains terminology that appears deceptively accessible. In some instances, the same phrases have nearly opposite meanings when used as terms of art in social choice, on the one hand, and in ordinary discourse, on the other. A systematic introduction to social choice helps to avoid such mis-understandings. In addition, because social choice is less widely known, for example, than price theory, a systematic introduction will help to place social choice within a broader economic perspective. A systematic introduction to social choice will help to expand the range of economic criteria used to eval-uate governmental—as opposed to private market—decision making. Only by expanding the normative range of economic criteria in this manner is it pos-sible fully to understand many of the most profound anomalies of constitu-tional law described in chapter 1. Before formally introducing social choice, a brief comment on the relationship between social choice and economic methodologies more commonly associated with law and economics will be helpful.

A.   Defining Economics and Dimensions of Rationality

One of the principal purposes of this book is to demonstrate the power of eco-nomic analysis to edify our understanding of the manner in which constitu-tional law is made. Economic analysis might initially appear ill suited to explaining those rules that produce seemingly arbitrary legal outcomes, based upon such fortuitous factors as whether issues or outcomes are dispositive in individual cases, the order in which multiple cases are presented for review, or the deciding court's choice among malleable justiciability frameworks. Indeed, the phenomena that I have described in chapter 1 might appear not to have much to do with economic analysis at all. In this chapter, I will demon-strate that economics, properly defined to include social choice, is critical to understanding each of the anomalies of constitutional decision making out-lined in the prior chapter, as well as numerous additional features to be explained in the chapters that follow. To introduce social choice, it will be helpful to consider, first, the relationship between social choice and more tra-ditional, and widely understood, economic analysis.

While the relationship is conceptually backward, social choice is often understood as a subset or offshoot of traditional microeconomics or price the-ory. Instead, to employ a metaphor from biology, within the overall discipline of economic analysis, social choice is better viewed as the genus, and price theory, or microeconomics generally, as a species. Of course, my alternative description of the relationship between social choice and price theory, like that of academics who might be inclined to state it in opposite terms, depends upon a conception of the meaning of economics. There are two competing definitions of economics, one which is commonplace, but potentially mis-leading, and the other of which is not commonplace, but which is more edi-fying. We will start with the first. Consistent with the commonplace under-standing, *Webster's New World Dictionary* defines economics as follows:

> 1. The science that deals with the production, distribution, and con-sumption of wealth, and with the various related problems of labor, finance, taxation, etc. 2. Economic factors.[2]

In this conception, economics is defined with reference to the subject matters of interest to those who study it. Not surprisingly, the above definition accurately captures many of the relevant subject matters of interest to scholars within the field of economics.

A better definition, I would argue, focuses not on the subject matters of interest to scholars in the field, but rather, upon the tools that economists employ, whatever subject matter happens to interest them. So viewed, economics is the social science that analyzes individual and collective human behavior using models derived from the single simplifying assumption of individual rationality. In this conception, economics is defined not with reference to particular substantive subject matters, but rather with reference to its unique disciplinary, or methodological, perspective.[3] Economics is a unique discipline due to the nature of the models economists construct to offer insights into individual and collective human behavior, whatever the context of that behavior happens to be.

The latter definition of economics depends, of course, upon an understanding of the term *rationality*. There are two complementary definitions of rationality, both of which are critical to economic analysis generally and to social choice in particular. The first definition, best articulated by Nobel laureate James M. Buchanan and Professor Gordon Tullock, focuses on the cost effectiveness of engaging in particular activities. This understanding of rationality captures the important intuition that rationality in economics is not commensurate with personal greed:

> [E]conomic theory does not depend for its validity or its applicability on the presence of the purely economic man. This man of fiction, who is motivated by individual self-interest in all aspects of his behavior, has always represented a caricature designed by those who have sought to criticize rather than to appreciate the genuine contribution that economic analysis can make, and has made, toward a better understanding of organized human activity. The man who enters the market relationship as consumer, laborer, seller of products, or buyer of services may do so for any number of reasons. The theory of markets postulates only that the relationship be *economic,* that the interest of his opposite number in the exchange be excluded from consideration.[4]

So understood, individuals are presumed rational whatever their activity of choice, be it charitable giving, building a financial empire, trading votes in a legislative body, or voting in a congressional or presidential election,[5] provided that the marginal benefit to the individual engaging in that activity equals or exceeds the marginal cost. Indeed, it is for this very reason that the growing literature on the economics of charity is not premised upon an internal contradiction.[6]

Within economics, there exists a second component to the assumption of individual rationality. When an individual is able to rank his preferences over a group of three or more options, it is assumed that his ranking of those options will be transitive. For example, if I prefer (and I do) coffee ice cream to chocolate ice cream to vanilla ice cream, most people would assume that I must also prefer coffee ice cream to vanilla ice cream. If I possessed the opposite preference, vanilla ice cream to coffee ice cream, people would rightly infer that there is something wrong with me. The implications of this basic element of individual rationality lie at the core of the problem of social choice. While the first dimension of individual rationality, the cost-effective pursuit of desired objectives, is more commonly associated with price theory, and the second dimension of individual rationality, the condition of transitivity, is more commonly associated with social choice, as I will demonstrate throughout this book, these two complementary dimensions of rationality are both essential to these interlocking economic disciplines. With that understanding of the scope of economics and the meaning of rationality, we are now ready to consider the problem, and discipline, of social choice.

The remainder of this chapter is divided into four sections. The first section introduces the basic tools of social choice, including the Condorcet paradox, the Condorcet criterion, Condorcet-producing and Condorcet-consistent rules, and a brief description of Arrow's Theorem. The second section identifies two fallacies, the fallacy of composition and the isolation fallacy, which legal scholars and economists often commit in relying upon social choice to advance proposals for institutional reform, and provides the methodological tools, based upon social choice, to avoid them. The third section employs social choice analysis to derive an expanded set of normative baselines, beyond economic efficiency, with which to evaluate a wide range of collective decision-making bodies, including markets, legislatures, courts, and agencies. The fourth and final section provides a more systematic introduction to Arrow's Theorem. Arrow's Theorem provides a set of positive tools for evaluating the evolution of the Supreme Court's process-based decisional rules, which often have the effect of allocating ultimate decisional authority among various governmental institutions. The theorem further provides the basis for avoiding an important third fallacy, the nirvana fallacy, in comparative institutional analysis.

II. The Problem (and Discipline) of Social Choice

The intellectual discipline of social choice grows out of a deceptively simple problem that a French philosopher and mathematician, the Marquis de Condorcet, described in a famous essay in 1785.[7] Imagine three persons, each choosing among three options, A, B, and C. These options can represent literally anything, including, for example, the differing amounts of money to spend repairing a road, alternative locations for building a prison, or various restaurants to consider for lunch. Further imagine that the three persons are either the only ones involved in the decision, or that they represent three equal-size groups, for example, in a legislature.[8] Further imagine that these three persons candidly discuss their views of the merits of each option and that, in the course of their discussion, they realize that none of the three options has majority support. One of the group members suggests trying to determine the group's preferred outcome by having each person rank his preferences from most to least preferred, and then taking a series of pairwise contests to select a winner. Person 1 ranks the options A, B, C; person 2 ranks the options B, C, A; and person 3 ranks the options C, A, B. Now the group takes a series of pairwise contests. In the choice of A against B, A wins, with persons 1 and 3 prevailing against person 2, and in the choice of A against C, C wins, with persons 2 and 3 prevailing against person 1. It might appear that because C is preferred to A and A is preferred to B, the group must also prefer C to B. That, after all, is the condition of transitivity, which is a basic tenet of individual rationality. In fact, however, if the group took a final contest between B, the option defeated in round one, and C, the victor in round 2, B would win, with persons 1 and 2 prevailing over person 3.

The above example illustrates what is referred to in the literature as the Condorcet paradox, or simply, the voting paradox. The paradox reveals that the transitivity condition, which operates as a basic rationality assumption for individuals, cannot be assumed for groups. Indeed, in the example just given, each person's individual preferences are fully transitive, and yet the ranking of pairs by majority rule reveals an intransitivity. This deceptively simple insight lies at the core of what has proved to be among the largest and most influential bodies of social science literature, namely the modern theory of social choice.[9] Before discussing modern social choice theory, it will be helpful to consider Condorcet's proposed partial solution to aggregating collective group preferences in the absence of a first-choice majority candidate. Condorcet proposed that in groups of three or more persons choosing among three or more options, in the absence of a first-choice majority winner, the outcome chosen should be that which defeats all other available options in direct pairwise contests.[10] To illustrate, consider a group of three persons choosing from among options A, B, and C, with the following slightly modified ordinal rankings: person 1: A, B, C; person 2: B, C, A; and person 3: C, B, A. While the relative preferences between options B and A are reversed for person 3, all other preferences are the same as in the first example.

Now imagine that these three persons try to select an outcome employing Condorcet's proposed method. In the choice between A and B, B wins, with persons 2 and 3 prevailing against person 1, and in the choice between B and C, B again wins, with persons 1 and 2 prevailing against person 3. The choice between A and C is irrelevant (C wins, with person 1 losing) because option B would defeat whichever option prevails. Option B, the stable outcome in this example, is referred to as the Condorcet winner. Rules that ensure that available Condorcet winners prevail, including the rule just employed, are described as satisfying the Condorcet criterion.

While the Condorcet criterion has two notable defects, described below, social choice theorists often evaluate the competence of collective decision-making bodies in terms of their ability to ensure that available Condorcet winners prevail. William Riker best captured the intuition underlying the confidence that scholars place in the Condorcet criterion:

> This notion [that an available Condorcet winner should prevail] is closely related to the notion of equality and "one man, one vote," in the sense that, when an alternative opposed by a majority wins, quite clearly the votes of some people are not being counted the same as other people's votes.[11]

Despite the confidence that social choice theorists place in the Condorcet criterion, at least two critically important sets of institutional rules, outcome voting in appellate courts and plurality voting in popular elections, have evolved in a manner that thwarts the Condorcet criterion.

As stated above, despite the intuitive appeal of the Condorcet criterion, rules that satisfy the criterion suffer from two well-known defects.[12] First, in groups of three or more that lack a first-choice majority candidate over three or more options, a Condorcet winner will not always exist. Second, the Condorcet criterion does not take into account intensities of preference. As we will see later in this chapter and in chapter 3, the first defect goes a long way toward explaining why appellate court decisional rules have evolved away from the Condorcet criterion. In chapter 4, I will demonstrate that the second defect goes a long way toward explaining why the Supreme Court sometimes imposes justiciability barriers upon potential federal court litigants, thus forcing them to seek redress in the legislature with respect to the issues concerning them. I will further demonstrate in this chapter that legislatures, including Congress, are generally far better suited to producing results that satisfy the Condorcet criterion.

A. Distinguishing Condorcet-Producing Rules and Condorcet-Consistent Rules

To analyze the first defect, we must now distinguish two types of rules that satisfy the Condorcet criterion, which I will refer to as *Condorcet-producing rules* and *Condorcet-consistent rules*. Both sets of rules will select the Condorcet winner as the outcome if one is available, but the outcomes of the two sets of rules differ when there is no Condorcet winner. Condorcet-producing rules effect a phenomenon known as "cycling" when no Condorcet winner is available. Cycling arises when, for any given outcome, another has majority support in a direct binary comparison.[13] Because this is true for all potential outcomes, when a Condorcet-producing rule is employed, no outcome is stable. For this reason, we can conceive of Condorcet-producing rules as possessing the characteristic feature of unlimited majority veto, meaning that pairwise comparisons continue until no majority is thwarted. The first set of preferences set out above, in which there is no Condorcet winner, is illustrative.

Recall that our three persons had the following preferences: person 1: A, B, C; person 2, B, C, A; and person 3: C, A, B. In this example, unlimited pairwise voting, a Condorcet-producing rule, revealed that, while each person's individual preferences are transitive, when those preferences are aggregated, an intransitivity results, such that the group as a whole selects A over B (with person 2 losing) and B over C (with person 3 losing), but also C over A (with person 1 losing). In the language of social choice, these persons lack a Condorcet-winning option, and, thus, employing a Condorcet-producing rule produces instability in the form of cycling.

Let us now consider a universal feature of Condorcet-producing rules. All such rules permit at least the same number of pairwise contests as options.[14] In contrast, when the decisional rule restricts the number of pairwise contests relative to the number of options, then, depending upon the participants' preference structures, the substantive outcomes will sometimes depend upon the order in which options are considered.[15] In the language of social choice, limiting the number of votes relative to the number of options invites "path dependence."[16] Thus, in the preceding example, with only the following two votes, A versus B (A wins) then C versus A (C wins), over the three options, A, B, and C, the outcome was C. Only by resurrecting option B, which was defeated in round 1, and pitting it against option C, the victor in round 2, was the cycle revealed. In fact, if we assume that people vote sincerely based upon their actual preferences, then given the preference structures in that example, a rule permitting only two votes for these three options would allow the person setting the order of votes to achieve any desired outcome. In the language of social choice, the person given this authority is referred to as an *agenda setter,* and the authority she is given is referred to as *agenda-setting authority*. Simply by ensuring that the one option that would defeat her first choice in a direct pairwise comparison is eliminated in the first round, she will produce a voting path leading to her first choice.[17]

While both types of rules satisfy the Condorcet criterion, unlike Condorcet-producing rules that cycle in the absence of a Condorcet winner, Condorcet-consistent rules effect a stable resolution with or without a Condorcet winner. Thus, Condorcet-consistent rules select available Condorcet winners as the outcome, but select an alternative option when no Condorcet winner is available. Several sets of rules are Condorcet consistent. We need only consider one here, however, referred to as the minimax rule, to appreciate the difficulty that such rules would pose if employed by lawmaking institutions.

The minimax rule, as originally devised by social choice theorist Duncan Black, has been defined as follows: "in the event that there is no dominant option [meaning no Condorcet winner], the winner would be the option for which the worst loss to another option in paired comparisons was least bad."[18] Assume that ten participants are choosing among four options, A, B, C, and D. In this regime, each participant votes on each of the potential six binary comparisons. The resulting scores, which are presented in parentheses after each binary comparison, represent the number of votes for the first listed

**Table 2.1.   Matrix of Paired Comparisons
            Illustrating Minimax Rule**

	A	B	C	D
A		–4	–2	6
B	4		–2	–4
C	2	2		0
D	–6	4	0	
Worst binary score	–6	–4	–2	–4

Note: Scores are column letter minus row letter.

option minus the number of votes for the second listed option: A versus B (seven to three); A versus C (six to four); A versus D (two to eight); B versus C (six to four); B versus D (seven to three); C versus D (five to five). The matrix of paired comparisons in table 2.1 summarizes the results for each binary pair.

Each entry in table 2.1 represents the difference between the number of votes for the letter along the left side vertical axis minus the number of votes for the letter along the top horizontal axis, for each binary pair. (The zeros result when two different options receive the same number of votes in a binary comparison, for example C against D; when the same letter appears in both row and column, no comparison is made.) Under the minimax rule, we select as the winner that option whose score for its most negative binary comparison is highest or least bad. If a Condorcet winner were present, the score that option would receive would be a positive number, given that, by definition, no option defeats a Condorcet winner in a direct comparison. This reveals a characteristic feature of Condorcet-consistent rules. Although each is expressed as a single formulation, each can be recast in terms of the following two-part algorithm: (1) Employ a Condorcet-producing rule to select a Condorcet winner if one is available, and (2) in the absence of a Condorcet winner (or upon discovering cyclical preferences by unlimited majority rule), employ an alternative non-Condorcet-producing rule to select a default option.

Because there is no Condorcet winner in this example, the worst binary score for each option, which is listed in the final row, is negative. In this example, although it is not a Condorcet winner, option C wins because its worst binary comparison, –2 against A or B, is better than the worst binary comparison for all three alternatives. Moreover, C is the winner even though in unlimited binary comparisons we would discover a cycle. Although C and D are tied in a direct binary comparison, if we employed a Condorcet-producing rule of unlimited binary comparisons, we would discover that A defeats B, which defeats C, which ties with D, which defeats A, and so on. If p means "preferred to," and r means "at least as good as," the cycle can be summarized as follows: ApBpCrDpA.

The above illustration reveals that not all rules that satisfy the Condorcet-criterion cycle in the absence of a Condorcet winner, but that is because Condorcet-consistent rules include an alternative non-Condorcet-producing default rule in the event that there is no Condorcet winner. In any event, Condorcet-consistent rules are relatively inconsequential for the analysis in this book. First, such rules are too cumbersome in practical application to be functional in either a judicial or legislative setting.[19] Second, as will become more clear when we compare outcome and issue voting in the Supreme Court,[20] even setting aside the problem of administrative complexity, Condorcet-consistent rules have the potential to invite strategic identification of underlying issues, in a manner that would undermine the stability of outcomes. And finally, while cycling is most often presented as the product of an institutional defect, later in this book I will argue that in some institutions, the ability to cycle in the absence of a Condorcet winner has the significant affirmative value of allowing the institution to decline effecting a change from the status quo, when none of the available alternatives is a stable outcome under simple majority rule over all binary comparisons.[21]

B. A Brief Comment on Arrow's Theorem

While I will provide a more formal introduction to Arrow's Theorem in the final section of this chapter, for the analysis to follow, a brief comment on the theorem, and specifically, on its relationship to the Condorcet paradox, will be helpful. Arrow's Theorem is best understood as a generalization of the Condorcet paradox. The theorem posits a group of four conditions, which are closely associated with fair collective decision making, and proves that all four conditions cannot coexist in a decision-making body that ensures collectively rational, or transitive, outcomes.[22] The four conditions are (1) *range:* the collective decision-making rule must select its outcome in a manner that is consistent with the members' selection from among all conceivable ordinal rankings over three available alternatives; (2) *independence of irrelevant alternatives:* in choosing among paired alternatives, participants are assumed to decide solely based upon the merits of those options and without regard to how they would rank options that might be introduced later; (3) *unanimity:* if a change from the status quo to an alternate state will improve the position of at least a single participant without harming anyone else, the decision-making body must so move; and (4) *nondictatorship:* the group cannot consistently vindicate the preferences of a group member against the contrary will of the group as a whole.

Later in this chapter, I will provide a more detailed description of each of these fairness conditions and provide illustrations. For now, it is sufficient to note that Arrow's Theorem generalizes the Condorcet paradox by proving that any rule intended to ensure that collective outcomes meet the transitivity criterion will necessarily produce a feature of collective decision making that is in some significant sense problematic or unfair. One of the critical implications of Arrow's Theorem, explored more fully below, is the trade-off it exposes between collectively rational, or transitive, results and procedural rules that vest seemingly disproportionate power in a minority. If unlimited majority rule has the potential to produce collective instability in the form of cycling, the sole means of ensuring stable outcomes might be to limit majority rule, in at least some contexts, by vesting ultimate decisional power in a minority of the group as a whole. Based upon that insight, we can attribute the difficulties of collective decision making not simply to the problem of collective intransitivity, revealed by the Condorcet paradox, but more generally to the trade-offs in collective decision making revealed by Arrow's Theorem.

C.   Social Choice Implications for Institutional Reform, Negative Legislative Checkpoints, and Riker's Theory of Minimum Winning Coalitions

Based upon the brief introduction thus far, it is important to consider some prescriptions for institutional reform advanced by legal scholars based upon social choice theory. My purpose is not to provide a comprehensive review of the legal literature relying upon social choice theory. It is instead to recognize that a study of constitutional process necessarily requires a comparative analysis of institutions. The varied social-choice-based proposals for institutional reform that follow, for example, are implicitly or explicitly based upon the authors' assessments of the comparative institutional competence of appellate courts and legislatures. By analyzing these proposals, therefore, we can lay the foundation for the social choice analysis of courts and legislatures to follow.

One group of legal scholars, discussed below, has questioned the soundness of legislative outcomes based upon the seeming arbitrariness of those outcomes in institutions prone to cycling. Whether or not legislatures "cycle" in the formal sense, which I will discuss below, several well-known roadblocks within Congress, which I have referred to as "negative legislative checkpoints,"[23] serve to raise the cost of securing proposed legislation. These roadblocks find their historical pedigree in the theory of factions espoused by David Hume and were given constitutional prominence by James Madison.[24] Consistent with the Madisonian vision that the rapid formation of majoritarian factions is to be feared,[25] such devices as bicameralism, presentment, elaborate committee structures, and the Senate filibuster serve to raise the cost of forming successful legislative coalitions. These practices, which increase the size of successful coalitions, have an important theoretical foundation reflected in the writings of the social choice theorist William H. Riker.

Professor Riker posited that, with some noncontroversial assumptions about legislative bargaining,[26] stable coalitions will approach minimum winning size, meaning a simple majority. Riker's theory of minimum winning coalitions is best understood as the public choice analogue to Madison's theory of factions. Riker posited that large, overweighted coalitions tend to break down in favor of smaller, stable coalitions, which can distribute larger per capita payoffs to their members. Both Riker and Madison shared the basic intuition that, in the absence of barriers that raise the cost of forming simple majority coalitions, the consequences of this form of inherent institutional stability within legislatures would be to promote illicit redistributive legislation.[27]

While the various negative legislative checkpoints within Congress provide valuable defenses to factional legislation, they also produce something of a paradox. By vesting minority groups with power to block rapidly forming majoritarian legislation, negative legislative checkpoints afford such minorities with the power to exact rents in exchange for support and to control the often-critical path affecting the substance of legislation that is ultimately adopted. Based upon such insights, some legal scholars, including Lynn Stout,[28] William N. Eskridge,[29] and Jonathan Macey,[30] have called into question the prevailing assumption within our judicial system that, absent a constitutional violation, courts should afford substantial deference (as exemplified, for example, in low-level rational basis scrutiny) to legislatures as rational aggregators of collective constituent preferences.[31] These scholars have counseled judges to liberalize their construction of statutes and to broaden constitutional judicial review in a manner consistent with each of their (widely divergent) normative conceptions of the public good.

In contrast, Professors Daniel A. Farber and Philip B. Frickey have argued affirmatively against relying upon social choice to shift decisional authority from legislatures to courts, and have instead used the theory to proffer proposals for institutional reform within Congress itself.[32] Farber and Frickey have argued that the theory of social choice implies that legislatures cannot function rationally based upon purely pluralist conceptions of government. Unbridled pluralism, they argue, which is conducive to zero-sum politicking and factional violence, is prone to the antinomy of cycling. In turn, these scholars assert that social choice theory supports a limited reversion to small *r* republican principles (as distinguished from large *R* Republican politics), which will tend to increase the base of electoral participation. While presented in a deliberately modest and tentative manner, Farber and Frickey have posited that social choice provides preliminary support for certain campaign finance reform proposals and for what they refer to as "structural due process," meaning a limited judicial check aimed primarily at ensuring legislative deliberation.

Whether focused upon reforming judicial doctrine or legislative practices, the proposals discussed above are largely consistent with what can perhaps best be labeled a growing neorepublican scholarly tradition within the legal academy. In contrast with the proposals for institutional reform discussed in chapter 1, which were based upon perceived defects in the decisional processes of appellate courts, with a particular focus on the Supreme Court, the above proposals for institutional reform are based upon perceived defects in legislative processes, with a particular focus on Congress. Evaluating such proposals for institutional reform, whether targeted to courts or legislatures, requires a comprehensive comparative analysis of the affected institutions. As I will demonstrate below, the theory of social choice, and specifically Arrow's Theorem, provides an exceedingly valuable framework for undertaking such an analysis without falling victim to the pervasive "nirvana fallacy."[33] Through the nirvana fallacy, scholars identify a defect in a given institution and then, based upon the perceived defect, propose fixing the problem by shifting decisional responsibility somewhere else, without fully considering whether the alternative institution for which decisional authority is proposed would be better or worse than the originating institution at performing the assigned task.

Before setting out a more detailed description of Arrow's Theorem, it will be helpful to expose two further analytical fallacies, which will shape our assessment of proposals for institutional reform based upon social choice. Some commentators have observed that because appellate courts generally, and the Supreme Court in particular, are collective decision-making bodies, to the extent that social choice reveals potential defects in the legislative process, so too it reveals defects in the judicial process.[34] Responding to such arguments, Professors Farber and Frickey have suggested that if social choice applies to both legislatures and the judiciary, as a tool of analysis, the model explodes. The authors explain:

> In a sense, the . . . thesis [that cycling plagues both courts and legislatures] proves too much. If chaos and incoherence are the inevitable outcomes of majority voting, then appellate courts (which invariably have multiple members and majority voting rules) and even the 1787 Constitutional Convention are equally bankrupt. As a result the . . . thesis is bereft of any implications for public law, since it tells us to be equally suspicious of *all* sources of law. If we accept the thesis as to legislatures, we are left with nowhere to turn.[35]

My purpose is not to fully analyze each of the above arguments concerning the implications of social choice for institutional reform, although the analysis to follow will have significant implications for each of them. Instead, I wish to show that most, if not all, legal scholars relying upon social choice as a basis for proposing such reform fall subject to one or more of three analytical fallacies: the fallacy of composition; the isolation fallacy; and the nirvana fallacy. When these fallacies are properly understood, social choice can then be used to provide a strong normative foundation for many seemingly enigmatic features of constitutional lawmaking. Holding aside the nirvana fallacy, which we will revisit when I reintroduce Arrow's Theorem at the end of this chapter, in the next part I will expose the other two fallacies, which are closely related to each other and to a conceptual problem of timing that lies at the heart of many social-choice-based proposals for institutional reform.

III. The Composition Fallacy, the Isolation Fallacy, and the Problem of Timing

When Kenneth Arrow published his famous proof, now referred to as Arrow's Theorem, in 1951, economists attempted to find its limits and to refute its seeming universality.[36] Ironically, as suggested above, Professors Farber and

Frickey and others have maintained that the universality of social choice—meaning its seeming application to virtually any collective decision-making body—is as much the theory's weakness as it is its strength. If the theorem truly is universal, meaning that it applies to all institutions in all circumstances, then the theorem suggests that judicial and legislative outcomes may, at best, be random, and at worst, be the product of strategic manipulation by minority groups vested with a form of agenda-setting power. While the theory might then leave us with a deep sense of cynicism, it might be difficult, if not impossible, to derive policy prescriptions based upon social choice to ameliorate that cynicism and to restore some sense of legitimacy to our lawmaking institutions. Among my central aims in writing this book is to dispel this understanding of social choice. My own view is that social choice, perhaps uniquely as a discipline, provides a profound normative basis for restoring our faith in the very institutions the legitimacy of which it is most often relied upon to attack.

I will begin by defining and illustrating the fallacy of composition. I will then give two hypothetical illustrations that, together, help to dispel some of the misconceptions about the implications of social choice for our lawmaking bodies. The first is loosely based upon William Shakespeare, *The Tragedy of King Lear,* and the second is based upon a 1992 Supreme Court case, *New York v. United States.*[37] By demonstrating how the rationality of multiple collective decision-making bodies is improved when they operate together, these hypotheticals will further expose the related isolation fallacy.

A. Understanding the Fallacies and Their Implications for Collective Decision Making

The fallacy of composition is the assumption that if phenomenon X produces result Y, more of phenomenon X will necessarily produce more of result Y. Imagine, for example, a proposed housing development in which the basic model house is brick. A single purchaser (or a small group of relatively dispersed purchasers) could make her home more distinctive by instead opting for a stone facade. But imagine that every purchaser shared the same intuition and that in an effort to render each of their homes more distinctive every buyer opted for stone rather than brick. Purchasing the stone facade would no longer render a home distinctive. Indeed, if all homes were built of stone, a purchaser could then render her home more distinctive by reverting to the original brick. Of course, the same problem would again arise if everyone followed suit.

Similarly, a single homeowner could make her house safer from burglary by installing an alarm. Even if we assume that sophisticated burglars could get past the alarm with relatively little effort, holding all else constant,[38] the alarm would encourage would-be crooks to burgle unalarmed homes, which, at the very least, will take relatively less effort. But if everyone in the housing complex installs an alarm, the relative benefit of having one is greatly reduced. While each home might be slightly more difficult to burgle, the overriding benefit of encouraging would-be burglars to go to a neighboring home would then be lost. In both examples, phenomenon X (a stone facade or a house alarm) produced result Y (distinction or a reduced risk of burglary relative to neighboring homes) *only if* relatively few purchasers within the complex as a whole engaged in the distinguishing strategy. If most or all homeowners followed the same strategy, the payoffs from distinction disappear.[39]

In the context of collective decision making, the fallacy of composition is that if each collective decision-making body is prone to cycling, two collective decision-making bodies will somehow cycle more than one collective decision-making body.[40] The related isolation fallacy is the failure to recognize that individual institutions that are prone to anomalies resulting from difficulties in aggregating collective preferences can avoid those anomalies when operating in conjunction with other institutions. Those other institutions can also be collective decision-making bodies, or they can be pyramidically structured with a single ultimate decision maker.

Even when two collective decision-making bodies are individually prone to cycling, they can collectively reduce cycling by operating in conjunction. This seemingly counterintuitive result applies if the two institutions do not cycle in response to the same factual phenomena. The United States Constitution, I will argue, which establishes two lawmaking bodies, Congress and the Supreme Court,[41] is implicitly premised upon this understanding. In addition, as developed in chapter 4, several Supreme Court doctrines further this intuition by allocating decisional responsibility between these two branches in a manner that promotes the collective rationality of both branches.

The critical difference in the phenomena that lead institutions to cycle, I will demonstrate, is a function of timing. Specifically, institutions are prone to cycling when faced with the prospect of allocating the benefits of an unanticipated windfall or the burden of an unanticipated loss. In contrast, institutions are least likely to cycle when developing facilitating rules or practices that apply generally and prospectively, before the factual circumstances generating such a windfall or loss, capable of generating a cycle, arise. In the first example presented below, a state legislature will prevent cycling among private market actors, and, in the second example, a state legislature will itself be plagued by cycling. I have chosen these two examples because, together, they illustrate the strengths and weaknesses of legislative decision making when confronted with factual circumstances that have the potential to produce cycling. The difference in the factors leading to the state legislature's differing responses in these two hypotheticals provides the key to understanding the importance of cycling in evaluating social-choice-based proposals for institutional reform, whether directed to appellate courts or to legislatures.

B.   The Problem of the Empty Core among Private Actors

The first hypothetical will take as its inspiration William Shakespeare's famous play *The Tragedy of King Lear*.[42] In the original story, an aging Lear vainly disinherits his youngest and most beloved daughter, Cordelia, because unlike her sisters, Goneril and Regan, Cordelia is unwilling to express her love for him in unconditional terms as a precondition to taking her share of the kingdom. As the story unfolds, we learn the devastating consequences of both the disinheritance and the premature conveyance to the remaining sisters for Lear and Cordelia. In our adaptation, Professor Lear, an eccentric mathematics professor, who has recently won thirty million dollars in the lottery, has long been estranged from all three daughters, who are also estranged from each other. Because the three daughters have not had any contact with Lear since their mother died over ten years earlier, they are unaware that he won the lottery five years earlier. To simplify the presentation, assume that the full lottery proceeds were distributed as a single lump sum with no discounting.

Upon winning the lottery, Lear, a very private man, did not change his modest lifestyle. Instead, he placed the full proceeds of the lottery into a trust fund, with the objective of passing the money to his daughters if certain conditions were met. Five years after winning the lottery, Lear was diagnosed with a fatal disease and was told that he had only six months to live. After he was informed of his diagnosis, Lear realized that if he structured the terms of the trust properly, he could witness, for the first time in his life, a controlled high-stakes game-theoretical experiment with real players.

Lear immediately contacted the administrator of the trust and had the terms governing the distribution of the corpus modified such that if those terms were satisfied by the time of his death, the full proceeds would then be distributed accordingly. In the event that the terms were not satisfied by the time of Lear's death, however, the corpus of the trust would, instead, pass into the residuum of Lear's will. The relevant provisions of the trust are set out below:

> The corpus of the trust shall be distributed based upon the consent of any two of Lear's three daughters, provided that the following two conditions are met. First, the amount of the allocations must be communicated in writing by any two or three daughters by five o'clock in the afternoon no later than ten (10) days prior to Lear's death, and must not be superseded within ten (10) days by any alternative division, submitted in writing by two or three daughters prior to Lear's death. The last plan submitted no fewer than ten (10) days prior to Lear's death, without being superseded pursuant to the terms of the trust by any alternative division for a period of ten (10) days, shall become the basis for the final distribution (the "final distribution"). Second, after a submitted plan becomes the basis for the final distribution, any daughter, whether or not a signer to that plan, who tries to alter the terms of the final distribution, either in a court of law or equity, or by agreeing to give up part of her share other than by submitting a revised plan in a timely fashion pursuant to the terms of this trust, shall forfeit her entire share, with the proceeds distributed in equal shares to the remaining daughters. In trying to achieve a resolution to the outcome of the distribution of the trust corpus, the daughters are permitted to employ any governing rules that they choose, except that under no

conditions can any of the daughters rely upon a court of law or equity in an attempt to enforce or to challenge any agreement made between or among them concerning the distribution of the trust corpus. Upon being in receipt of the basis for final distribution for ten (10) consecutive days prior to Lear's death, the trust administrator shall immediately notify Lear of the terms of the final distribution. In the event that no plan forming the basis for a final distribution meets the requirements of the trust, the full corpus of the trust shall pass to the residuum of Lear's will.

Under the terms of Professor Lear's will, the residuum will be donated to a charity. After modifying the trust, Lear notifies his three estranged daughters of his illness and of the terms of his trust.

Before considering how the daughters might respond, a few general comments about the hypothetical will be helpful. Under the terms of the trust, any two of the three daughters are called upon to agree to an outcome governing the distribution of what will be an extremely valuable windfall. In addition, while the daughters are permitted to employ any background rules they wish, they will suffer severe sanctions, in the form of a complete forfeiture, if they try to have those rules legally enforced. Finally, under the terms of the trust, a minimum of two out of the three daughters must agree on the terms of the final distribution for a period of ten consecutive days.

Now consider the options confronting the daughters. One obvious solution exists: Each daughter could take $10 million and the three, now wealthier, sisters could go on with their lives.[43] Based upon this intuition, Professors Farber and Frickey have posited that in hypotheticals of this sort, simple and obvious fairness (or value) solutions, like equal division, provide practical, and potentially stable, solutions.[44] Before evaluating the merits of whether value solutions provide a stable outcome, we need to consider the pathology that underlies our hypothetical. In the language of game theory, this hypothetical has an "empty core." The empty core is identical to the Condorcet paradox. The difficulty that the sisters face is that for any existing coalition, there exists an alternative "superior" coalition that can improve the payoffs for both the excluded party and a defector. Because this holds true for any potential coalition, no coalition is stable. In contrast, a game has a core, thus producing a stable solution, when, for a coalition or set of coalitions, there is no alternative superior coalition that will improve the plight of an excluded party and a defector. Because the game in the text has an empty core, for any proposed solution there exists an alternative favored by a newly formed coalition, thus generating a cycle.

To simplify, I will use a total pool of $30, where each dollar represents one million. Assume that Goneril and Regan begin by submitting a plan for each to take $15 each. Cordelia can now break up that coalition within the allotted ten-day period by offering Regan $20 and agreeing to take only $10. Goneril, the excluded party, can now break up that coalition within the ten-day period by offering Cordelia $20, and herself taking $10. And now Regan can break up that coalition within ten days by offering Goneril $20 and herself taking $10. Of course, now Cordelia can start the ball rolling again, offering Regan $20 and agreeing to take only $10. The coalitions have now come full circle, with Goneril and Regan (15/15), replaced by Regan and Cordelia (20/10), replaced by Cordelia and Goneril (20/10), replaced by Goneril and Regan (20/10), but the last-listed coalition is no more stable than it was in the initial round. It might appear that the whole problem would be solved if the three sisters simply agreed to submit a written plan calling for an equal division. But this too is unstable. After the 10/10/10 plan is submitted, Goneril can approach Regan, offering to cut Cordelia from the coalition and to split her share between them. Goneril and Regan could then submit a revised plan calling for equal division (15/15) between them. That, of course, was the starting point in the prior example, but was not a stable solution.

We can only speculate, of course, what the final outcome would be and whether the daughters would come to a satisfactory resolution before their father's death or whether, as a result of efforts by the excluded sister to improve her payoff by forming a new coalition, the daughters would force the trust corpus into the residuum of their father's will from which they would take nothing. The point, however, is not to predict the actual outcome. Instead, it is to explain that under some circumstances, lawmaking institutions have a comparative advantage over private decision makers in avoiding certain pitfalls that plague collective decision making. And yet, under alternative conditions, lawmaking bodies themselves are particularly prone to the very cycling problem that in other contexts they are able to solve among private actors. As the following variation will show, that comparative advantage is a function of timing. Empty-core problems arise when parties negotiate after the facts arise that produce an unanticipated windfall or loss.

To illustrate, let us now modify the hypothetical such that the sisters can attempt to enforce any interim agreements that they reach without sacrificing any gains that legal enforcement brings. Assume, contrary to the original hypothetical, that Lear's trust does not prevent the sisters from invoking a standard expectancy damages rule for breach of contract enforceable in a court of law. This rule imposes liability upon the breaching party and restores the victim of the breach to the position she would have been in had the breaching party fully performed.[45] While it is not possible to predict which coalitions might initially form for purposes of a breach of contract action, we can predict that if any coalition does form, this basic facilitating rule (meaning a rule governing negotiations, rather than establishing liability in the form of a property right in a particular party) will induce stability. To illustrate, assume that Goneril and Regan form a binding agreement for each to receive $15. If Cordelia offers Regan to form a superior coalition, in which Regan receives $20 and Cordelia receives $10, Regan is likely to decline. If she enters into the superior coalition with Cordelia, Regan will gain $5 but will owe Goneril for $15 in compensatory damages. The principle is fully generalizable. Once any of the coalitions described above has formed, an expectancy damages rule will ensure that any gains to the defector from entering into a superior coalition with the initially excluded daughter will be entirely consumed by an award of compensatory damages. Of course, while any coalition that actually formed would be stable with such a rule in place, the payoffs are such that even at the preliminary negotiating stage, the empty-core problem has the potential to rear its ugly head, thus preventing the creation of any contractually enforceable agreement, and thus the submission of any plan for final distribution.

Alternatively, a legislature can induce stability among private actors facing an unanticipated windfall or loss through a property rule. If Lear had simply died intestate, consistent with the laws of virtually all jurisdictions, the sisters would have taken equal shares. To see why a legislature, unlike the sisters, is able to devise a simple and obvious fairness solution in this situation, imagine a state legislature trying to devise a rule governing the distribution of the assets of a deceased widower or widow among his or her children in the absence of a will. In contrast with Goneril, Regan, and Cordelia, who are confronted with an ex post windfall, and thus confronted with an empty-core problem, the legislators are devising a prospective rule of general application. Because the legislators have no reason a priori to favor any particular category of sibling over any other, for example, based upon birth order or sex, the likely stable outcome, indeed the one in force in virtually every state, is to divide the corpus equally among siblings.[46] In the event that this off-the-rack, or one-size-fits-all, rule turns out not to fit for particular parents, those parents, again in virtually every state, are free to supersede it by the express terms of their will.[47] Not only is the legislature able to devise the intestacy rule, but also it is able to devise the facilitating rule of expectancy damages, which, in the absence of the intestacy rule, operates to break down incentives to defect once any two- or three-party coalition actually forms.

The question then arises why state legislatures are universally able to devise simple fairness solutions as stable, off-the-rack rules governing the allocation of a corpus to three or more siblings in the absence of a will, when, left to their own devices, and with no legislative involvement, the siblings themselves, faced with the same factual phenomena, fall victim to the problem of cycling. To answer this question, which is essential to understanding the different comparative advantages of lawmakers versus private market actors, it will help to consider a second hypothetical in which members of the legislature themselves fall victim to the problem of the empty core and thus cycle.

C. Location of Toxic-Waste Disposal Facility

This hypothetical, which is based upon an adaptation of the facts of the 1992 Supreme Court decision *New York v. United States,*[48] demonstrates the conditions under which a state legislature, the very institution that was able to restore stability among private parties prone to cycling in the prior example, is itself prone to cycling. In *New York,* the Supreme Court struck down the take-title provisions of the Low-Level Radioactive Waste Policy Amendments of 1985. Under the terms of the amendments, states that failed either to join a regional waste-disposal pact with other states or to create their own in-state waste disposal facility within a predetermined time frame were required to take title to low-level radioactive waste or to compensate producers of that waste for liability incurred as a result of the state's failure to do so. The amendments, which followed a series of unsuccessful attempts to solve the national shortage of low-level radioactive waste disposal facilities, were the product of a compromise reached by the states, negotiated through the National Governors' Association. Under the terms of the amendments, Congress created a series of three compliance incentives, intended to encourage self-sufficiency on the part of states by the end of 1992.[49] Of the three incentive provisions, the *New York* Court concluded that only the take-title provisions were constitutionally defective.

The *New York* case illustrates two important points about constitutional process. First, the case facts help to illuminate the conditions under which state legislatures are prone to cycling, and, thus, to explain the nature of the comparative advantage between lawmakers and private actors in ameliorating cycling. Second, Justice O'Connor's analysis of why the take-title provisions violate the Constitution edifies our understanding of the critical process-based differences between legislatures, including Congress, and appellate courts, including the Supreme Court.

By December 31, 1992, the compliance deadline under the 1985 amendments, all but one state, New York, had either joined a regional pact or had created an in-state disposal facility for low-level radioactive waste. As a result, New York alone was subject to the potential operation of the take-title provisions, which it challenged on constitutional grounds. The record revealed that New York had initially opted to join a pact, but then decided to place a disposal facility in-state.[50] The legislature ultimately rejected each of five proposed sites. As a result, New York became the only state not in compliance with the 1985 amendments. To recast the problem that the New York legislature faced in social choice terms, it will help to simplify the facts slightly. Assume that instead of narrowing down the choice of location to five sites, the legislature narrowed it down to only three. Further imagine that the three sites are each located within one hundred miles of a major city, cities A, B, and C. City A is located to the north; city B is located to the southeast; and city C is located to the southwest. Figure 2.1 illustrates this hypothetical.

To simplify the presentation, assume that the state consists only of these three regions and that the legislature has only three members, one from each region, where each member represents a coalition such that any two coalitions contain the requisite votes for a majority. Further assume that each representative's first choice for the location of a waste facility is in the region clockwise to his region; that his second choice is in the region that is counterclockwise to his region; and that his last choice is in his region. Based upon these assumptions, the preferences of the legislators are as follows:

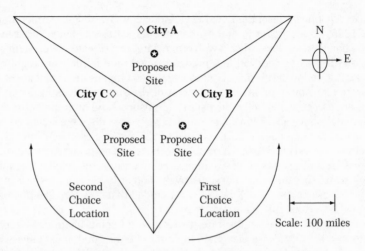

Fig. 2.1.   Proposed locations of toxic waste dump

Region A: B, C, A
Region B: C, A, B
Region C: A, B, C

These are paradigmatic non-Condorcet-winning preferences. Using unlimited pairwise voting, a Condorcet-producing rule, the result would thus be to cycle.

Why in this hypothetical is the state legislature prone to cycling, when in the Lear hypothetical the same institution was able to devise either a facilitating rule or an off-the-rack fairness solution, either of which operates to inhibit cycling? The answer to this question provides the basis for three important insights about comparative institutional analysis. First, institutional comparative advantage is often a question of timing. Second, in evaluating proposals to shift decisional authority from one institution to another, we need to avoid the isolation fallacy and the fallacy of composition. And third, the power of institutional inertia is critical in promoting legislative rationality.

In the Professor Lear hypothetical, the sisters, in contrast with the state legislature trying to devise an off-the-rack intestacy rule, were faced with the issue of how to allocate the proceeds of an unanticipated windfall. In trying to allocate those proceeds, the sisters were not concerned with devising the best (or most equitable) public policy for dividing assets among siblings in the absence of a will. Instead, each was concerned with maneuvering to maximize individual gain, which, in the absence of a core, produced a cycle. In contrast, legislators, in crafting a rule governing intestacy in the absence of a will, are less likely to be interested in trying to maximize personal advantage. In fact, the resolution of the issue in any particular manner would not produce any likely benefit to any one of them. That is because the off-the-rack facilitating rule ultimately adopted would apply generally and prospectively.[51] As a result, the legislators, unlike the sisters, were able to consider the question of how to divide a decedent's estate among siblings in the absence of a will from the perspective of decision makers personally unaffected by the selected rule. Stated differently, for the sisters, the relevant time frame for assessing the outcome of dividing the corpus is ex post, thus leading to strategic behavior and cycling; for the legislature, the relevant time frame is ex ante, which is therefore more conducive to rational reflection and deliberation and thus to the creation of a stable and fair rule. Thus, in the hypothetical in which Lear simply dies intestate, the possibility of cycling among the sisters is a matter of only slight theoretical interest because the off-the-rack rule, calling for equal division among the three siblings, prevents that possibility from occurring in the real world. In other words, the emergence of an off-the-rack rule, produced by an institution that is able to behave as if the relevant facts that had given rise to a potential cycling problem have not yet occurred, can prevent cycling within another institution, or among another group of individuals, that is directly affected by the relevant facts in a manner that produces cycling. This holds true even though *both* institutions, under identifiable conditions, are prone to cycling.

Now reconsider the hypothetical based upon *New York,* in which the state legislature did cycle. In the case upon which the hypothetical was based, the 1985 amendments had the effect of imposing upon the legislature the equivalent of an ex post loss. The legislators knew that their constituents—and specifically the property values of their constituents' homes—would be directly affected by the location of the waste disposal facility. As a result, like the Lear sisters, the state legislators in this example are likely to behave as if the relevant frame of reference is ex post, thus producing a cycle.

While Justice O'Connor offered an historical justification for striking down the 1985 amendments that has been subject to criticism,[52] social choice provides an independent economic foundation for her ruling. O'Connor reasoned that the critical defect in the take-title provisions was that, through them, Congress was not regulating private persons, or even the states, directly. Instead, Congress was forcing the states to implement its own regulatory scheme. Thus, in response to the United States' argument that the amendments gave the states a broad range of compliance options, Justice O'Connor stated:

> This line of reasoning, however, only underscores the critical alternative a State lacks: A State may not decline to administer the federal program. No matter which path the State chooses, it must follow the direction of Congress.[53]

To avoid the operation of then-recent precedents, which suggested that only the political process itself limited Congress's power to regulate the states under the Tenth Amendment, O'Connor pieced together a first-principles argument dating back to the displacement of the Articles of Confederation with the Constitution.[54] Justice O'Connor maintained that, together, the Tenth Amendment and the commerce clause prohibit Congress from "commandeering" the states. O'Connor contrasted the Articles plan with the Constitution. Under the former, Congress lacked the power of direct taxation, was fully dependent upon the states for all forms of revenue, and had no direct regulatory power over individuals. Under the latter, in contrast, Congress possesses taxation authority, is not dependent upon the states to raise revenue, and can regulate individuals directly. For Justice O'Connor, the rejection of the Articles in favor of the Constitution reveals an intent to prevent Congress from regulating through the states. As Justice Stevens observed in dissent, however, O'Connor's historical rendition reveals nothing about whether Congress, if it so chooses, especially with the states' consent, has the power to regulate through the states, rather than regulating the states directly.[55] Instead, the framers of the Constitution rejected the Articles plan because Congress's dependency upon the goodwill of the states to effectuate its intent and to raise necessary revenue did not work. As a result, Stevens observed, the rejection of the Articles was intended to strengthen, not weaken, Congress's power relative to that of the states. At best, O'Connor's historical analysis is indeterminate, but a strong case can be made that, on its own terms, it actually supports a contrary holding.

Despite O'Connor's curious assertion that the Constitution was intended to prevent Congress from commandeering state legislatures, social choice theory might provide a sound economic justification for the Court's holding. The hypothetical (corroborated by the actual case facts) demonstrates that legislative preferences, in at least some cases, are prone to cycling. If Congress were authorized to compel state legislation, the effect would be to require state legislatures to adopt rules that ensure collective outcomes, even when faced with intransitive preferences.* Setting aside Condorcet-consistent rules on grounds of impracticality, state legislatures would then need to adopt non-Condorcet-producing rules to ensure collective outcomes in the event that legislative preferences cycled. The result might well be to undermine state legislative rationality by preventing institutional inaction when confronted with cycling majorities. And notice that if the state legislatures did adopt non-Condorcet-producing rules, presumably those rules would apply generally, meaning that they would not be limited to those rare occasions in which Congress commandeers the states. A contrary holding in *New York*

---

*The same analysis helps to explain the outcome in the famous decision *Youngstown Sheet & Tube Co. v. Sawyer,* 347 U.S. 579 (1952), in which the Supreme Court held that President Harry Truman lacked the authority to seize the steel mills during the Korean conflict to avert a strike. Writing in dissent, Justice Vinson stated, "The President himself closed the door to any [unlimited executive power] when he sent his Message to Congress stating his express purpose to abide any action of Congress, whether approving or disapproving his seizure action." *Id.* at 701. As in *New York,* the *Youngstown* majority's rejection of Vinson's argument establishes the inherent power of Congress as a legislature to make or not make law as it sees fit. The *Youngstown* Court thus prevented President Truman from attempting to shift the burden of congressional inertia by declaring that the legal status quo *will change* unless Congress enacts legislation that reveals its will to ensure that the status quo remains.

would therefore have threatened to move toward merging the functions of legislatures, which have generally evolved toward the Condoret criterion, and courts, which have generally evolved away from the Condorcet criterion. In fact, as I will demonstrate below, the power of legislatures to avoid formal institutional action, which is essential to the *New York* holding, lies at the core of the distinction between these two institutions.

D. Justification versus Legitimacy: A Methodological Comment

Before presenting the next part, which discusses a case study by Professor Saul Levmore on the evolution of parliamentary rules, a comment on methodology will be helpful. While the above hypotheticals demonstrate the possibility of cycling among private actors, within real-world legislatures and appellate courts, it is difficult, if not impossible, to actually observe a verifiable instance of cycling. The divergence between the theoretical plausibility of cycling within each of these settings and the apparent stability of outcomes that the relevant institutions generate has provoked sharp debate about the practical significance of the cycling phenomenon.

In one of the most famous titles in the public and social choice literature, Professor Gordon Tullock sparked an ongoing debate on the significance of cycling simply by asking the question: "Why so much stability?"[56] Tullock noted that while the literature on legislative cycling is pervasive, observed cycling within legislatures is virtually nonexistent. Tullock posited that logrolling, or vote trading, a prevalent legislative practice, promotes stability by allowing participants to commodify preferences, rather than merely to rank them ordinally.

In a prominent series of articles,[57] Professors Kenneth Shepsle and Barry Weingast challenged Tullock's argument, demonstrating that under specified conditions,[58] logrolling itself can lead to cycling. Instead, these authors posited that a variety of institutional structures in Congress, some of which I have already described, including committees, Calendar Wednesday, the filibuster, and bicameralism, induce stability by raising the cost of identifying and codifying cyclical preferences. The Schepsle and Weingast thesis provides an important conceptual link between public choice, or interest group theory, which focuses on the processes through which interest groups influence (mostly in the negative) legislative processes, and the theory of social choice, which helps to provide a positive justification for the emergence of some of those very processes.[59] While social choice might explain the emergence of institutional structures that operate to avoid cycling, the question remains what the normative implications of such structures are for legislative outcomes.

In response to an argument by Professors Farber and Frickey concerning the relevance of cycling for legislatures, Professor Shepsle addressed this question. Farber and Frickey, in considering the apparent paradox of legislative stability in light of the theoretical plausibility of cycling, state, "Arrow's Paradox is both fascinating and illuminating, but it may have little direct relevance to legislative practice."[60] In response, Professor Scheplse observed,

The authors are confused by the fact that even in voting processes victimized by the Arrow result, we are sometimes able to identify equilibria. These equilibria, however, are strongly affected by the underlying incoherence of majority preferences and, because of this, lack a compelling normative justification. Arrow's theorem does not necessarily entail constant flux and indeterminacy; rather, it implies that the manner in which majority cycling is resolved is arbitrary or otherwise morally indefensible.[61]

Shepsle's response consists of two parts, both of which are important to constitutional process. First, relying upon his earlier articles with Weingast, Shepsle argues that institutional structures have emerged within legislatures that reduce the appearance, and quite possibly the actuality, of cycling. Second, he argues that the effect of these institutional structures is to undermine the normative soundness of the resulting legislative outcomes. In a similar vein, Professor Riker has observed that

> [the] consequences [of social choice] are either that power is concentrated in society or that any system of voting can be manipulated to produce outcomes advantageous to the manipulators or at least different from outcomes in the absence of manipulation.[62]

To evaluate the merits of these assertions, we must distinguish what Shepsle refers to as the normative *justification* for legislative outcomes from what I will refer to in this book as the normative *legitimacy* of such outcomes. By legitimate, I mean that societal acceptance of the outcomes follows from the processes through which those outcomes were obtained.[63] As demonstrated below, the same distinction between normative justification and normative legitimacy extends to judicial and market outcomes. By normative justification, Professor Shepsle suggests a comparison, based upon the legislators' preferences, between the merits of the legislature's chosen outcome and the merits of forgone alternatives. Professor Riker suggests the same comparison when he discusses potential outcomes based upon the presence, or absence, of agenda manipulation. In fact, the Schepsle and Riker discussions are parallel to Judge Easterbrook's critique of path dependent judicial outcomes that result from stare decisis.[64] Just as transaction-costs-raising devices induce stable but seemingly arbitrary legislative outcomes by making it more difficult for legislators to identify cyclical preferences, so too stare decisis induces stable but path dependent judicial doctrine by breaking down doctrinal cycles. For each of these scholars, social choice calls into question the normative soundness of resulting outcomes based upon structure-induced equilibrating devices. Based upon these insights, Professors Farber and Frickey claim that social choice theory "proves too much" and that its potential application to both appellate courts and to legislatures leaves us with "nowhere to turn."[65]

Among the central aims of this book is to demonstrate that, properly understood, the theory of social choice greatly strengthens the normative legitimacy, as distinguished from the normative justification, of both structure-induced legislative outcomes and path dependent judicial outcomes. With respect to legislative outcomes, my argument follows from two complementary intuitions. First, when stakes are sufficiently high, legislators will determine through informal means either that preferences cycle or that a dominant, Condorcet-winning, option exists. And they will do so even with non-Condorcet-producing equilibrating mechanisms in place. Through informal iterations, the legislature, unlike an appellate court, will therefore discern the relevant information favoring collective inactivity. Indeed, as the foregoing discussion of *New York* and *Youngstown* reveals, state legislatures have the constitutional authority to remain inert, even against a contrary directive of the United States Congress, and Congress has the constitutional authority to remain inert even against a contrary directive of the President. In contrast, appellate courts, when faced with cyclical preferences in a case properly before them, are institutionally obligated to issue a collective decision.* If the judges', or justices', preferences in a given case are collectively prone to cycling, the effect of this institutional obligation will inevitably be to thwart the will of a majority of the court's own members. This holds true

---

*For some readers, the proposition in the text might appear controversial. As most constitutional scholars would recognize, the Supreme Court has ample means with which to avoid deciding cases and to avoid addressing particular issues within cases. Most obviously the Court's docket is almost entirely discretionary. The certiorari process is governed by the Rule of Four. Once a case is taken, the Court has at its disposal any number of mechanisms for avoiding a merits determination, including dismissing on the ground that the writ of certiorari was improvidently granted (referred to as a "DIG"), dismissing for want of ripeness or standing, or dismissing because the case is moot. And even if the litigant gets past all of these barriers, the Court can decide the case on a very narrow ground, which might even include failing to address the issues that the litigants have raised. While all of these seeming qualifications might appear to undermine the assertion in the text, none of them do. At each stage of its decision-making processes, the Court must provide a formal albeit de minimis institutional disposition of the case. At the certiorari stage, the Rule of Four translates into a formal institutional decision requiring a supermajority of six as a precondition to declining to hear a case. A DIG requires five votes, meaning that a contrary majority of five has the formal institutional authority to insist that a case be heard despite a claimed jurisdictional defect. And each justiciability barrier—ripeness, standing, and mootness—requires majority agreement as a basis for declining to address the merits of the case, as does a determination to resolve the case on a narrow technical ground. *See infra* chapter 3, § IV (explaining that, based upon an application of the narrowest grounds rule, majority agreement can often be implicit, depending upon the coalition structure of the deciding Court). As I will demonstrate in chapter 4, it is precisely *because of* the Court's institutional obligation to decide cases that it has developed each of these institutional mechanisms, which individually and in combination allow the Court to limit the impact of its obligation formally to resolve those cases properly before it. The more important point, however, is that every one of these so-called avoidance mechanisms—from certiorari to standing dismissals—requires a formal institutional decision and thus can be translated into a non-Condorcet-producing rule.

both in single cases, as in *Miller,* and across cases, as in *Crawford* and *Seattle.*[66] Second, faced with cyclical preferences, legislatures, again, unlike appellate courts, have a further means with which to promote institutional rationality. In contrast with appellate courts, which generally eschew vote trading across issues within cases and across cases,[67] legislatures regularly promote, or at least condone, vote trading across issues both within and across bills. Within legislatures, vote trading tends to enlarge policy space, thus allowing legislators to commodify their preferences over a larger set of issues. While the outcome for a given issue over which legislative preferences are cyclical might appear arbitrary, for example, when that outcome is directly compared with forgone alternatives, societal acceptance of the overall legislative package legitimates components that appear irrational when viewed in isolation.

In contrast with appellate courts, in which commodification of preferences is generally regarded as improper, within legislatures, vote trading across issues within or across bills has the potential to thwart the significance of at least some—and quite possible a great many—forgone cycles. While the legislators' preferences for three potential solutions to a given issue might generate cycle if those legislators were asked to rank their preferences ordinally, for some legislators, the presence of some sets of cyclical preferences might be virtually inconsequential. This follows from the limitation that the Condorcet criterion does not consider the intensity of the decision makers' preferences. Imagine, for example, three legislators with the following non-Condorcet-winning preferences: 1: ABC; 2: BCA; 3: CAB. Legislator 3 might be close to indifferent between all three options. If so, he might be perfectly content to allow legislators 1 and 2 to settle upon his ordinal last choice, B, in exchange for the support of those legislators on an altogether different issue of far greater importance to him.

In comparing the legitimacy versus the justification of legislative outcomes, it is important to make one further distinction. When Professors Riker and Shepsle and Judge Easterbrook question the normative justification of a given institution's output, whether it be a piece of legislation or a series of cases producing path dependent doctrine, they suggest a merit-based comparison between the actual outcome and forgone alternatives within the institution under review. In contrast, evaluating the normative legitimacy of a given institution's output requires two different comparisons. First, within the institution under review, we must compare the potential output in all instances, not just the one that provoked immediate dissatisfaction, with and without the equilibrating rule under review in place. This comparison reveals the general value of the equilibrating rule without an excessive focus on our immediate dissatisfaction with a recently generated outcome. Second, after determining the general value of the relevant equilibrating rule, we must compare the merits of leaving decisional authority over the given subject matter under review in a particular institution with the merits of shifting that decisional authority to an alternative institution, after making the same evaluation of the latter institution's equilibrating mechanisms. Thus viewed, our purpose in analyzing the implications of cycling with reference to a zero transaction cost world is to provide a meaningful comparative institutional analysis focused upon the evolution of equilibrating practices and rules within and across institutions.[68] The above analysis has significant implications for those rules and practices that govern the manner in which constitutional law is (and is not) made.

Assuming that equilibrating devices in legislatures encourage legislators sometimes to codify preferences that lack a compelling normative justification when directly compared to forgone alternatives, the question then arises, how might we expect rational legislators to respond? In an article that studies the evolution of parliamentary rules from the perspective of social choice, Professor Saul Levmore addressed this question. Levmore's analysis has significant implications for a comparative assessment of legislatures and courts and, more generally, for constitutional process. The analysis also provides the basis for expanding the breadth of normative criteria, grounded in economics but extending beyond efficiency, with which to evaluate a range of collective decision-making bodies, including markets, legislatures, courts, and agencies. Because the Supreme Court's process-based decisional rules often have the purpose and effect of allocating decisional authority from one institution to another, and thus of sometimes vindicating outcomes that defy the efficiency norm, the analysis has significant implications both for constitutional process and for related proposals for institutional reform.

IV. Expanding the Breadth of Normative Economic Criteria: A Social Choice Analysis of Parliamentary Rules

In a comparative study of a large number of sets of parliamentary rules written in the mid–nineteenth century, including Robert's Rules of Order, Professor Saul Levmore determined that when Condorcet-winning options are likely to be available, the rules are generally Condorcet producing.[69] In contrast, parliamentary rules vary greatly when legislative options are least likely to include a Condorcet winner. Based upon this observation, Levmore posited that, even with no knowledge of the Condorcet paradox, participants in various assemblies seeking to prevent what he refers to as "avoidable dissatisfaction" likely exerted pressure upon those controlling the order of proceedings to abandon rules that defy the Condorcet criterion when a Condorcet winner was likely to be available. Levmore's intuition is straightforward. Imagine a five-person assembly choosing among five options, with the following preferences, which contain a Condorcet winner:[70]

    1:   A, B, C, D, E
    2:   A, B, C, E, D
    3:   C, B, D, E, A
    4:   C, B, E, A, D
    5:   E, D, B, C, A

If the voting procedure is plurality with a runoff, in which everyone votes for her first choice, and, in the absence of a majority winner, the two plurality candidates are directly pitted against each other, the outcome will be to suppress the Condorcet winner. In this example, there is no first-choice majority candidate. The two plurality winners are A and C, with two votes each. As between A and C, C wins, with persons 1 and 2 losing.

Now imagine that on a matter of great significance, option C prevails and that persons 1, 2, and 5 discuss the outcome following the meeting. With little effort, they might discover that each of them preferred option B to option C. With admittedly greater effort, involving persons 3 and 4 as well, they might also have discovered that option B, the Condorcet winner, would have defeated any of the remaining options in a direct pairwise comparison. Whether or not these participants go to the trouble of figuring out the universal appeal of option B, with less effort they could figure out that as a majority of the assembly, they should have been able to prevent an outcome that they all viewed as inferior to an available alternative. Persons 1, 2, and 5 might then voice their dissatisfaction at the next meeting and propose replacing the seemingly deficient plurality-and-runoff procedure with some other voting regime that does not undermine the preferences of a majority of the participants.

It is, of course, impossible to determine whether the assembly, with the support of a majority composed of persons 1, 2, and 5, will immediately supersede the plurality-and-runoff regime with a voting rule that is Condorcet producing. Nor is that necessary to Levmore's thesis. If the assembly adopts another non-Condorcet-producing procedure, then a different majority might at some time in the future find its will frustrated, forcing further tinkering with the rules. Only upon trying a Condorcet-producing rule, for example, unlimited motion-and-amendment voting, will the participants no longer face the prospect of continuing to thwart the will of a majority (although, as the analysis to follow will show, they might face other problems). Thus, with the same preferences and the new regime in place, if person 3 moves to adopt option C, person 1 can then move, instead, to adopt option B. The motion to amend will garner majority support (persons 1, 2, and 5) and, because option B is a Condorcet winner, no other motion to amend will succeed. At that point, the choice of governing rule will be stable.

This simple story is noteworthy in two critical respects. First, it demonstrates the importance of a non-efficiency-based criterion, grounded in economics, for evaluating the evolution of parliamentary rules. While the Condorcet criterion is not necessarily at odds with traditional efficiency principles, it is not difficult to imagine circumstances in which these two economic baselines might conflict. Thus, while option B is the Condorcet winner, that option might be a rather inefficient public policy choice, for example, setting a minimum wage sufficiently high that an industrious class of unskilled workers will be unemployed, or setting a ceiling on rents so low that landlords are no longer willing to engage in otherwise cost-effective repairs and seek to convert affected rental properties into condominiums. Second, the example does not depend upon any actual knowledge of the Condorcet paradox or of the problem of social choice. Instead, the analysis suggests an evolutionary process. Rules that continue to serve our purposes survive; those that do not are abandoned and replaced. Just as species evolve without ever pondering such abstract questions as "would mutating wings help my descendants to survive beyond the Mesozoic era?,"[71] so too rules evolve without the need for theoretical justification on the part of those who push them to change.

I do not intend to suggest that the choice of replacement rules in the evolution of parliamentary process is necessarily random. I am instead suggesting that economic analysis is useful in explaining the evolution of institutions and rules even if the choice among rules is effectively random. In contrast with animal species, which evolve through mutations entirely beyond their conscious control, people, as economic actors, can and do think about the problems confronting them and decide upon possible strategies designed to avoid those problems in the future. Sometimes decision makers get it right; other times they do not. To the extent that individuals do consciously adopt beneficial strategies affecting the evolution of institutions and rules, they quicken the pace of evolution. But whether or not this occurs frequently is not critical to whether economic analysis has the power to explain the evolutionary process.[72]

Levmore's larger thesis concerning the evolution of parliamentary rules is more complex. Levmore posits that while rules that evolve toward the Condorcet criterion prevent avoidable dissatisfaction, not all dissatisfaction is avoidable. In some instances, the likelihood of an available Condorcet-winning option is remote. This is likely to occur, for example, when a legislative assembly is choosing to allocate its annual budget among numerous potential programs or is trying to choose a date for an event or election. In these situations, given the large number of options, and specifically of potentially similar ones,[73] the possibility of cyclical preferences is relatively high. As a result, while dissatisfied coalition members who would prefer an available option to the one chosen might try to force tinkering with the rules, such tinkering is less likely to produce a stable alternative. Levmore posits that we should therefore expect greater variation within the rules when Condorcet-winning options are likely to be elusive. Levmore's review of the various parliamentary rules he studied corroborates this thesis.

Within an important subset of these varied, non-Condorcet-producing rules, Professor Levmore has identified a further common evolutionary thread. As we have already seen, rules that fail to satisfy the Condorcet criterion render outcomes dependent upon the order in which options, or issues, are formally considered. The person vested with the authority to determine the order in which votes are taken will therefore have disproportionate power. In contrast, when a decision-making body employs a Condorcet-producing rule, and when a Condorcet winner is available, the outcome is independent of the order in which votes are taken.[74] While there are many alternative Condorcet-producing rules, when a Condorcet winner is available, these rules all produce the same result. In contrast, rules that defy the Condorcet criterion produce outcomes that vary considerably, whether or not there is a Condorcet winner. Non-Condorcet-producing rules also vary in their susceptibility to agenda manipulation, for example, by a committee chair.[75]

In the absence of a likely Condorcet winner, the legislature might elect to employ a variation on the motion-and-amendment procedure, this time with a prohibition on reconsideration of defeated alternatives.[76] The benefit of this regime is that, in contrast with the unlimited motion-and-amendment procedure, the institution will not cycle, even if there is no Condorcet-winning option. That is because without at least the same number of pairwise contests as options, it is not possible to determine whether the winner satisfies the Condorcet criterion or is the arbitrary product of a voting path. By prohibiting reconsideration of defeated alternatives, the modified regime ensures an outcome, but does so by preventing the institution from taking the requisite number of votes to determine whether or not that outcome meets the Condorcet criterion. Based upon this intuition, Professor Riker criticized a rule employed in both houses of Congress "permitting only four amending motions to a bill or resolution,"[77] which he concluded had the potential to mask voting cycles.

Riker's argument, however, presents two difficulties, which are significant to constitutional process, one that he acknowledged and another that he did not. First, as Riker acknowledged, if the legislature possesses cyclical preferences, expanding the number of permissible amendments will reveal the cycle, but will not help to resolve it.[78] Second, as I will demonstrate more fully below, a formal limit on the number of permissible votes within legislatures relative to the number of options does not necessarily prevent legislators subject to the rule from discovering intransitivities through informal means, especially when the stakes are high. Indeed, as frequently occurs in business settings, important matters are often resolved well in advance of formal meetings. We could expect this to be no less true, and possibly more true, in Congress. If so, there is no effective limit on the number of informal iterations that might occur to identify potential cycles, whatever the limit on formal amendments happens to be. Provided that the legislative culture permits strategic voting and logrolling, such practices will operate as a quasi-market solution that effectively supplants non-Condorcet-producing rules with de facto Condorcet-producing rules, at least when the stakes are sufficiently high.

By limiting the identification of potential Condorcet winners or cyclical preferences, motion-and-amendment voting with a prohibition on reconsideration of defeated alternatives affords the relevant committee chair with substantial power to set the critical voting path. She can do so by controlling who gets the floor and in what order. A motion-and-amendment regime favors early motions because, after the original motion is proposed, members can propose amendments to that motion and, in turn, amendments to that amendment (termed an amendment in the second degree) and to that amendment (amendments in the third degree) and so on.[79] Voting then occurs at the outer edge, pitting the highest ordinal amendments against each other, the victor against the next highest ordinal amendment, and so on, until the victor is directly pitted against the original motion. In contrast with all other motions, the original motion need only survive one round, against the final surviving amendment, before it is voted up or down. Because motion-and-amendment voting favors early motions, Levmore posits that it tends to afford committee chairs with substantial agenda-setting power.[80] It does so by allowing the chair to favor early proponents and to order amendments such that disfavored amendments that could potentially defeat favored initial motions are themselves defeated before a direct comparison.

While motion-and-amendment voting works well when there are few options to consider (because it promises to locate Condorcet winners without producing avoidable dissatisfaction), it is likely to produce dissatisfaction when several options are available because it encourages strategic agenda setting. On the other hand, Levmore suggests that when there are several potential options available, we would expect assemblies to switch to succession voting to avoid agenda setting. In contrast with motion-and-amendment voting, which favors early motions, succession voting favors relatively late motions.[81] Under this regime, motions are voted upon when raised, until a pending motion receives majority support. Again, defeated options cannot be reconsidered. Because it is more difficult for the chair to control the order in which motions will be advanced, it is more difficult to manipulate this process.

Like motion-and-amendment voting with no reconsideration of defeated alternatives, succession voting is a non-Condorcet-producing rule. As a result, succession voting has the potential to produce avoidable dissatisfaction. Levmore thus posits one final evolutionary step, involving the selection among either dates or budgetary allocations. When options have a natural ordering, such as from high to low, one way to increase the likelihood that if a Condorcet winner is available it will prevail is to impose an incremental voting rule, either beginning at the top and working down, or beginning at the bottom and working up. To understand this important final step in the evolutionary process, it is important to introduce three pairs of additional social choice concepts: unipeakedness and multipeakedness; unidimensionality and multidimensionality; and symmetry and asymmetry.[82]

A.   Unipeakedness and Multipeakedness; Unidimensionality and Multidimensionality; Symmetry and Asymmetry

Imagine an assembly with three members that is trying to determine the amount of money to spend repairing a bridge. Further imagine that the proposed amounts, in increments of $10,000, are 1, 2, and 3, each sum representing the first choice of one of the three assembly members. As demonstrated in figure 2.2, we can chart the collective preferences, such that the vertical axis represents the legislators, A, B, and C, and the horizontal axis represents the allocations, 1, 2, and 3.

The legislators' preferences can be represented by a single peaked curve, sloping downward. If we assume that each legislator at the extreme would

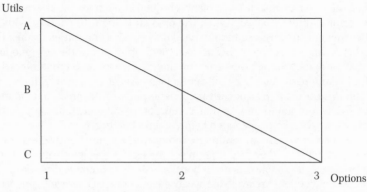

Fig. 2.2. Unipeaked preferences

prefer an allocation in the middle to an allocation at the opposite extreme, then either bottom-up or top-down incremental voting will produce a majority at 2. Each additional increment gains one vote, until a majority is formed at 2, regardless of which procedure is used. Stated more generally, incremental voting in a unidimensional continuum produces a stable outcome at the median option.

Without employing one of these incremental voting rules, however, a two-vote limit would enable a strategic agenda setter favoring one of the extreme allocations, for example, 3, to increase the likelihood of her favored outcome. She could do so by first presenting the middle position, 2, and then, after its defeat, presenting 1, which will also be defeated. The other decision makers would then be forced to select either 3, the agenda setter's preferred option, or to forfeit the bridge repair altogether. By adopting an incremental voting rule, in contrast, the assembly prevents this form of agenda manipulation. At the same time, however, incremental voting might prevent the assembly from discovering preferences that cycle.

To illustrate, imagine that, for one of the assembly members, the low position is the first choice and that the middle position is the last choice. This is less counterintuitive than it first appears. Assume, for example, that the assembly is selecting a date for recess and the options are Thanksgiving (T), Christmas (C), or December 31 (N). As with the prior example, and as illustrated in figure 2.3, the three dates can be plotted along a unidimensional continuum.* Assuming that each person most prefers one of the three dates,

---

*In an effort to simplify the presentations in figures 2.3 and 2.4, I have taken one liberty that is worth noting. Unlike the allocations for repairing a bridge, presented in figure 2.2, which are continuous, the adjournment dates, T, C, or N, and the utilities associated with them, are discrete. While the utility curves shown in figures 2.3 and 2.4 appear continuous, therefore, they are best understood as denoting the relationships between and among three discrete options with three discrete levels of utility, rather than as expressing a continuous series of utilities between each of the relevant options.

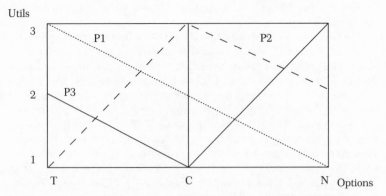

Fig. 2.3. Cycling in a Unidimensional issue continuum

it might appear that incremental voting would produce a stable result at C. It is not difficult, however, to imagine a situation in which this result would not hold. To reflect the unidimensional continuum, each curve will connect the utilities based upon the temporal order of the potential adjournment dates, thus starting with T, and continuing to C, and then to N. As shown in figure 2.4, below, it is precisely because the underlying issue spectrum can be recast to reveal an additional issue dimension that connecting utilities based upon ordinal date of adjournment, per figure 2.3, appears arbitrary. Assume that the ordinal rankings of person 1 (P1), which are single peaked, are TCN. Further assume that the ordinal rankings of person 2 (P2), which are single peaked, but with two slopes rather than one, are CNT. Finally, assume that person 3 (P3) does not celebrate Christmas and most prefers to go through the end of the calendar year, December 31, to provide for a longer summer recess, and least prefers adjourning on Christmas, which provides him no benefit. If so, P3's preferences, NTC, cannot be plotted on a single-peaked curve. The preferences are depicted in figure 2.3.

As this example illustrates, when one of the decision maker's preferences possesses more than a single peak within a unidimensional issue continuum, a cycle may result. Thus, if we consider direct pairwise contests, we see that as between T and C, T wins; as between T and N, N wins; but as between N and C, C wins, thus creating a cycle, in which CpNpTpC. Of course, as

With that understanding, the analysis remains the same. In figure 2.3, cycling arises because the preferences of P3 are multipeaked within a unidimensional continuum. In addition, in figure 2.4, I will demonstrate that cycling can arise even when the preferences of all participants are unipeaked, provided the preferences are properly cast along a multidimensional continuum. As demonstrated, those two characterizations of cycling preferences express the same underlying intuition. As explained in chapter 3, in the context of Supreme Court decision making, justices are most often called upon to choose among discrete, rather than continuous, options, often within a multidimensional issue spectrum.

Professor Riker correctly observed, identifying the cycle does not help to resolve it.

In fact, we can illustrate the same set of cyclical preferences in either of two ways, both of which are helpful in analyzing constitutional process. By plotting all preferences along a unidimensional continuum, as in figure 2.3, we can depict a cycle when the preferences of one of the individuals has more than one peak. In addition, we can depict the same cyclical preferences by expanding the underlying issue spectrum to two dimensions and by presenting each member's preferences as unipeaked.[83] To appreciate the issue expansion, we must recognize that for the three decision makers, the choice of adjournment date raises two implicit issues, first, whether to break to celebrate Christmas, and, second, whether to break to lengthen the summer recess. In figure 2.3, the sorting principle, namely the order of dates, for connecting utilities appears arbitrary; indeed that is the point. Only by expanding the underlying issue spectrum, as in figure 2.4, can we recognize that for P3, an alternative issue dimension generates a more logical ordering that reflects the relationships between and among all three choices. Table 2.2 depicts the relationship between each option—TCN—and the resolution of both underlying issues.

The same assumptions that generated a cycle with multipeaked preferences in a unidimensional continuum can now be expressed as generating a cycle with unipeaked preferences in a multidimensional continuum. Because P1 celebrates Christmas and does not care about lengthening his summer recess, his preferences are TCN. P2 also celebrates Christmas, but unlike P1, would prefer to lengthen the summer recess and celebrate Christmas locally if the choice is to adjourn either on Thanksgiving or on New Year's Eve Day. P2's preferences therefore are CNT. Finally, because P3 wishes to lengthen his summer recess and least prefers adjourning on Christmas, his preferences are NTC. As figure 2.4 illustrates, these paradigmatic non-Condorcet-producing preferences can be plotted in a multidimensional issue spectrum in which each legislator's preferences are unipeaked.

In figure 2.4, the left and right walls represent the same vertical axis, namely adjourning on December 31. To complete the visualization, imagine cutting figure 2.4 from the page, curling it into a tube, and taping the left and right walls together. At that point, P2's curve, which appears to break at the right wall and then resume at the left wall, would be continuous. The result is three unipeaked preference curves that are properly aggregated in a two-

Table 2.2. Choice of Adjournment Dates in Two Dimensions

	Break to Celebrate Christmas	Do Not Break to Celebrate Christmas
Break to lengthen summer recess	C	N
Do not break to lengthen summer recess	T	

Utils

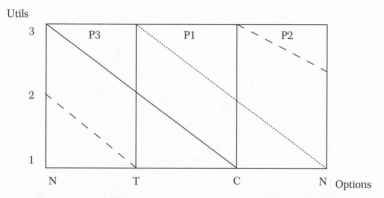

**Fig. 2.4. Cycling in a multidimensional issue spectrum
with asymmetrical preferences**

dimensional issue continuum, represented by the now-curved horizontal axis, thus producing the cycle. Unlike in figure 2.3, which connects utilities for each member arbitrarily based upon the order of dates, in figure 2.4, the utilities for each member are connected across two dimensions and thus appear in a logical descending order from the first to the third choice, based upon utility.

The two graphic depictions, figures 2.3 and 2.4, illustrate precisely the same underlying phenomenon. As shown below, the latter method of illustrating cycling is particularly helpful in explaining the evolution of appellate court voting rules away from the Condorcet criterion. Almost invariably, it is more intuitive to explain the potential for cycling in the Supreme Court based upon an issue spectrum that has more than a single dimension, rather than based upon an issue spectrum with a single dimension, like the order of dates, in which the preferences of a minority of justices are multipeaked. In contrast, depending upon the context of legislative bargaining, legislative cycling can be meaningfully characterized as resulting from either multipeakedness in a unidimensional continuum or from unipeakedness in a multidimensional continuum.

Before leaving this discussion, it will be helpful to introduce one additional paradigm, which will enable us to identify the conditions that are necessary and sufficient to generating cyclical preferences. As figure 2.4 reveals, collective intransitivities can arise when the preferences of the participants exist along more than a single dimension. Even when preferences reveal a multidimensional issue spectrum, however, cycling is not inevitable. Instead, a particular combination of preferences in two dimensions, those that possess the characteristic feature of asymmetry, generates cycles, while the more general case of preferences in two dimensions, those that possess the characteristic feature of symmetry, does not.

To illustrate, let us now change our assumptions about P3. Assume that while P3 continues not to celebrate Christmas, he is consistently more con-

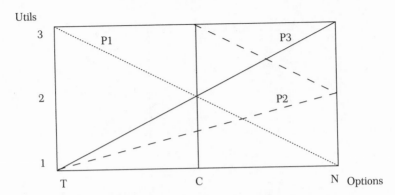

Fig. 2.5. Stable resolution with multidimensional and symmetrical preferences

cerned with lengthening summer recess, thus preferring to adjourn on Christmas over Thanksgiving. If so, his preferences are NCT. As before, the preferences of P1 and P2 are TCN and CNT, respectively. The changed assumptions do not restore the example to a single-issue dimension. For P1 and P2, the critical issue remains whether the adjournment will allow them to celebrate Christmas at home, while for P3, it is whether the summer recess will be long or short. In contrast with the preferences used to generate figure 2.4, in which one of the members who selected N or T first selected C last, even though C was closer along a single-issue dimension of time, in this example both members who select N and T select C second precisely because it is closer than the other option along at least one issue dimension. P1 selects C second because it allows him to celebrate Christmas, and P3 selects C second because doing so lengthens his summer recess. As figure 2.5 illustrates, while our revised assumptions ensure that the preferences exist in two dimensions, they also reveal the symmetrical nature of the underlying preferences.

In this example, if we exclude the preferences of P2, the remaining preferences form an "X" with C as the dominant middle position. The symmetry is further reinforced if we recognize that the preferences of P2, which descend from C to N to T, would result in the selection of C even if they were the mirror image, descending instead from C to T to N.* The symmetrical nature of the preferences for P1 and P3 ensure that regardless of P2's second- and third-order preferences, option C will dominate. Like in figure 2.5, the pref-

---

*Notice also that while the second and third order preferences of P2, NT or TN, appear to cross C, that is because the image is presented in two-dimensional form. Imagine cutting the image from the page and rolling it into two thirds of a tube, this time with the walls for T and N approaching, but not meeting, at the back of the tube. The lower portion of P2's preferences would then form an arc that does not meet C, but rather, that descends directly from N to T along another dimension.

erences in figure 2.4 appear in two dimensions. But unlike in figure 2.5, the preferences in figure 2.4 are not symmetrical around any of the three options, and thus no option dominates.

As I will demonstrate in chapters 3 and 4, the conditions under which Supreme Court decisions are susceptible to the anomaly of suppressed majorities, either within or across cases, can readily be cast in terms of dimensionality and symmetry. When the Court issues decisions with a single dimension, or with two dimensions but with symmetrical preferences, it is easy to locate a dominant, Condorcet-winning, holding. Such cases correspond to figures 2.2 and 2.5, respectively. In contrast, when the Court's preferences exist in two dimensions, but are asymmetrical, then there is no dominant, Condorcet winner, and a voting anomaly, like that present in *Miller v. Albright*,[84] or in *Crawford v. Board of Education*,[85] and *Washington v. Seattle School Dist. No. 1*,[86] can arise. These cases thus correspond to figure 2.4.

B. Return to Evolution of Parliamentary Rules

With that background on various preference structures and their implications for the possibility of cycling in both legislative and judicial contexts, we are now ready to return to Professor Levmore's analysis of parliamentary rules, and specifically to his thesis summary:

> The codes can be regarded as evolving along the lines of, or having adopted, the following reasoning: (1) employ the motion-and-amendment process when there are few alternatives because it promises to find any Condorcet choice without encouraging unavoidable dissatisfaction; (2) when there are numerous alternatives likely to be proposed, facilitate a switch to succession voting because a Condorcet winner is quite unlikely and the switch will make it difficult for the chair to manipulate the order of recognition to unfairly influence the outcome; and (3) when succession voting exposes unavoidable dissatisfaction, tinker with the order in which proposals are considered.[87]

Before evaluating the implications of this complex thesis for constitutional process, we must consider one final step in the evolution of parliamentary rules, which, in Levmore's analysis, appears somewhat paradoxical.

1. The Problem of Electing Committee Chairs

Levmore observes that while the presumptive rule within legislative assemblies is motion and amendment, in the limited context of electing committee chairs, assemblies nearly universally employ plurality voting. Levmore views this as paradoxical given that within legislative assemblies, the cost of repeated votes is relatively low. Levmore offers two tentative explanations for this seeming anomaly. First, some rules that employ paired comparisons, for example, round-robin voting, would undermine perceptions of fairness by allowing one candidate to wait out all other votes, and run only in the final election. Second, a single plurality election, or a plurality with a runoff, reduces transaction costs relative to the more costly round-robin regime. Finally, Levmore observes, "It is interesting, but not terribly helpful, to note that plurality voting often concerns a choice among individuals while motion-and-amendment voting often involves decision making with regard to issues."[88]

The anomaly disappears, however, if we divide the analysis into two parts, first, ruling out the use of a Condorcet-producing rule, and second, comparing the available non-Condorcet-producing rules. As demonstrated in chapters 3 and 4, this two-step process proves critical in explaining the evolution of Supreme Court decision-making rules used to decide individual cases and groups of cases over time.

The first step brings us back to one of the critical defects associated with Condorcet-producing rules.[89] In the absence of a Condorcet-winning option, Condorcet-producing rules, including motion-and-amendment voting, lead to cycling. When choosing whether and how to resolve *issues,* legislatures can and do avoid issuing formal institutional decisions, whether as a result of cycling or following a conscious collective decision to prefer the status quo to any proposed change. In contrast, when choosing among *people* to fill positions, inertia is generally not an option, even when preferences cycle. As a result, the legislature, when choosing among people, gravitates away from employing a Condorcet-producing rule. Having ruled out Condorcet-producing rules, we can then compare the two available non-Condorcet-producing rules, which Levmore describes. Thus viewed, Levmore's assertion that plurality voting appears more fair than round-robin voting is well taken. It is worth noting that this analysis suggests that it is not only interesting, but critical, that plurality voting is employed when choosing chairs, because it is in that context that the legislature is most likely unable to default to the status quo if a cycle is revealed.

C. A Comment on Baselines

The analysis thus far has exposed a number of important baselines for evaluating collective decision-making bodies, including Congress and the Supreme Court, that will prove critical to evaluating the Supreme Court's process-based rules. In the next, and final, section of this chapter, which provides a more detailed presentation of Arrow's Theorem, I will offer a preliminary social choice analysis of these institutions based upon both these baselines and a larger social choice framework. Bear in mind that each of the four baselines in table 2.3, which will inform our analysis of constitutional process, is fully grounded in economic analysis. By that, I mean each is the product of a model built upon the simple rationality postulate.

As table 2.3 demonstrates, we have thus far identified no fewer than four baselines, each growing out of economic analysis properly understood, that,

Table 2.3. Comparison of Baselines for Evaluating Lawmaking Institutions

Baseline	Explanation	Limitations	Preferred Institution or Rule
Efficiency	This is the traditional focus of microeconomic analysis and often operates in competition with rules that promote vote trading among legislators.	Persistent features of our lawmaking institutions fare poorly when evaluated against this baseline, thus inviting additional baselines with which to assess these features.	Free markets, by allowing full cardinalization of preferences, are best suited to meet criterion, subject to accepting present wealth endowments and avoiding externalities.
The Condorcet criterion (or appropriate deference to majority rule)	The Condorcet criterion is often considered an essential condition of fair collective decision making. Because they thwart majority preferences, rules that fail to produce available Condorcet winners generate avoidable dissatisfaction, thus promoting evolution toward Condorcet criterion.	Condorcet-consistent and Condorcet-producing rules fail to account for intensities of preference. Condorcet-consistent rules, while they avoid cycling when no Condorcet winner is present, are unduly cumbersome. Condorcet-producing rules generate cycling when no Condorcet winner is available.	Within legislatures, motion-and-amendment procedures coupled with informal vote trading, which provides quasi-market solution to limits on number of amendments to pending motions, generally meet criterion. By expanding issue space, vote trading sometimes produces rational results that thwart criterion.
Ensuring collective outcomes	Because of administrability problems associated with rules satisfying the Condorcet criterion, institutions that demand collective outcomes generally evolve toward non-Condorcet-producing and non-Condorcet-consistent rules.	Non-Condorcet producing and non-Condorcet-consistent rules are prone to path manipulation by those vested with agenda setting authority.	Limits on permitted number of amendments in legislatures and outcome voting in appellate courts are examples of rules that are neither Condorcet-producing nor Condorcet-consistent.
Avoiding agenda manipulation	Non-Condorcet-producing and non-Condorcet-consistent rules are invariably subject to path dependency, but not all are equally subject to path manipulation.	Path-manipulated results appear arbitrary when compared with forgone alternatives; depending upon how voting path is determined, path dependent results might rightly be regarded as legitimate.	Agenda manipulation is minimized with succession voting and incremental voting within legislatures; justiciability limits in appellate courts; and plurality voting in elections.

when combined, provide a far richer basis for evaluating our lawmaking institutions than any of these baselines operating alone. At this point we can reconsider the relationship between social choice and price theory, with which I opened this chapter. Table 2.3 reveals that microeconomic efficiency is potentially in tension with other economically derived criteria used to evaluate collective decision-making bodies. As the following discussion of Arrow's Theorem will demonstrate, social choice emerges as an umbrella discipline within economics, which is of vital importance in determining the comparative advantage of various collective decision-making institutions and rules in furthering each of the above baselines. In saying that social choice is a genus under which we find the species of price theory and interest group theory, I do not intend to suggest that social choice is necessarily more important than these other economic disciplines.[90] The range of positive price theoretical applications is enormous and thus far has been far more richly tapped than the potential range of positive applications of social choice in explaining how all of our collective decision-making bodies operate, both individually and in combination. But it is important, both conceptually and practically, to place price theory and interest group theory in an appropriate disciplinary perspective, especially since traditional law-and-economics scholarship has tended to focus on the manner in which microeconomic efficiency is so often thwarted by nonmarket collective decision-making bodies, including, most notably, legislatures and courts. Social choice allows us to step back, not by attacking the assumptions that underlie economics or by claiming that the outcomes of positive economic analysis are systematically unfair, but rather, by developing expanded economic models, premised upon the rationality postulate, that expose the tensions between microeconomic efficiency and other economic criteria. Social choice thus helps to explain both the evolution and persistence of the very institutions that fare poorly under the more generally recognized economic baseline of efficiency.

While the foregoing discussion has exposed several non-efficiency-based economic criteria, we are still missing a framework with which to do three things: first, to assess the normative merit of each of these potentially competing baselines; second, to determine which of these baselines are likely to be met or not met in a given collective decision-making body; and third, to determine how to resolve potential conflicts that might arise among institutions in furthering one or more of these baselines. The next and final subsection of this chapter, which introduces Arrow's Theorem, will provide this critical framework. Just as the microeconomic concept of efficiency provides an exceedingly valuable lens through which to assess the evolution of institutions within private markets, Arrow's Theorem provides a multifaceted gem with which we can assess the evolution and persistence of virtually all collective decision-making institutions, including markets, legislatures, courts, and agencies, and many of the formal and informal rules and practices within each of those institutions.

V. Arrow's Theorem

A. An Introduction

Generally speaking, within academics, as in life, failure is just that. Among the most wonderful twists in the modern history of social choice is that one of its most fundamental insights, namely Arrow's Theorem, is the product of an initial failure. Arrow's Theorem resulted from Professor Kenneth Arrow's profound discovery that he could not successfully complete the research project that he set out for himself. For most academics, such a discovery would, at best, result in a waste of time, or, at worst, a tenure denial. For Arrow, it, instead, ultimately resulted in his being awarded the Nobel Prize in economics and his rightful place, along with Duncan Black, as one of the founding fathers of the modern theory of social choice.

Arrow set out to create a set of governing rules to be used by a planning authority that would simultaneously satisfy a fundamental tenet of rationality, namely the ability to ensure that the authority's collective decisions were transitive, and several seemingly noncontroversial assumptions about fair collective decision making.[91] Although then unaware of the work of the Marquis de Condorcet,[92] what Arrow ultimately demonstrated was that any effort to fix the problem of collective indeterminacy or irrationality that results from the problem of cycling will necessarily violate at least one important condition that most people commonly associate with fair collective decision making. Arrow's Theorem has therefore aptly been characterized as a generalization of the Condorcet paradox.[93] Arrow proved that no collective decision-making body can simultaneously satisfy four seemingly noncontroversial assumptions about fair collective decision making and guarantee the ability to produce collective results that are rational, meaning that they satisfy the basic condition of transitivity. Thus, while Condorcet demonstrated that the general assumption of individual rationality cannot be extended to groups, Arrow demonstrated that devices designed to cure collective irrationality will undermine collective fairness in some fundamental way.

Before explaining the four conditions that Arrow presumed to be essential to fair collective decision making, a few comments on methodology will be helpful. Many scholars associated with the law-and-economics movement are distrustful of abstract claims to fairness. That is not because this group of legal academics is systematically less fair than their counterparts, but rather because proposed efficiency solutions to legal problems, including, for example, allowing markets, rather than regulators, to determine the minimum wage,[94] to work toward eliminating discrimination on the basis of race or sex,[95] and to allocate the scarce resource of radio and television bandwidth,[96] are often met with the response, "that's unfair." Unless the term *fair* is specifically defined, such claims operate as a conversation stopper, but one that fails to identify, let alone resolve, underlying philosophical or methodological disagreements. In the axiomatic proof, referred to as Arrow's Theorem, fairness is not an abstract claim. Indeed, Arrow derived each condition using an economic methodology, defined each condition with mathematical precision, and defended each condition on credible normative grounds. That is not to say that every fairness condition is equally important or that all fairness conditions have been universally accepted for their normative validity. Instead, I am suggesting that Arrow used an economic methodology to provide a strong normative foundation for each condition—conditions that individually and collectively are sometimes at odds with traditional economic understandings of both efficiency and rationality.

More importantly, in a profound sense, the whole of Arrow's Theorem is greater than the sum of its parts. By that I mean, even if I were to flatly reject either the normative validity of Arrow's understanding of collective rationality or one or more of his claimed fairness conditions,[97] having done so would in no sense undermine the positive validity of employing the theorem's benchmarks for a meaningful comparative analysis of institutions and rules. That seemingly counterintuitive assertion is closely linked to the "nirvana fallacy."[98] The nirvana fallacy arises when a scholar identifies a defect in a given institution or rule and then proposes either shifting decisional authority elsewhere, or devising a different governing rule, without having first undertaken a careful assessment of whether the proposed alternative would improve or exacerbate the problem that it is offered to cure. The intuition is reflected in the common adage, "Don't let the perfect be the enemy of the good." Although it might seem counterintuitive, the great difficulty in comparative institutional analysis is in identifying what is good enough, not in identifying what is perfect. In essence, Arrow proved the impossibility of achieving what is perfect,[99] without, necessarily, saying what is good enough. To understand this counterintuition, we must first derive from Arrow's Theorem what I will now refer to as Arrow's Corollary.

Arrow's Theorem proves that no single collective decision-making body can simultaneously satisfy four simple conditions of fairness, *range* (the outcome must be consistent with the members' selection among any conceivable ordering over three options), *unanimity* (the *Pareto* criterion, but with a twist), *independence of irrelevant alternatives* (in choosing among options presented, the decision makers are to decide based solely upon the merits and without regard to how they would rank options that might later be introduced), and *nondictatorship* (the decision-making rule cannot systematically honor the preferences of an individual against the contrary preferences of the group as a whole), while ensuring the ability to produce collective results that are rational (transitive).[100] I will provide more detailed definitions of each of these terms below and connect the definitions with several of the examples that we have already seen. The underlying mathematics of Arrow's proof are unimportant for our purposes. It is worth noting, however, that setting aside an initial problem with the first version of Arrow's proof, which he corrected in the second edition of *Social Choice and Individual Values,*[101] virtually every effort to prove Arrow wrong has only confirmed his result.[102] It is also worth noting that Arrow's proof establishes a genuine theorem, meaning that one can generate corollaries from that theorem.

My assertion that Arrow has defined the "perfect," or at least the unattainable, but not necessarily the "good," follows from Arrow's Corollary:[103] Because *no* collective decision-making body can ensure compliance with all five stated criteria (the four fairness conditions plus collective rationality), any collective decision-making body that does function, meaning only that the body actually issues collective decisions, has necessarily sacrificed at least one (and possibly more than one) of these five criteria. Arrow's Corollary, that at least one of five criteria is relaxed in any functional collective decision-making body, implies that not all of the five criteria are essential to the functioning of all institutions. Moreover, as I will demonstrate in the remainder of this book, conditions that are essential in some institutions are easily sacrificed, and are perhaps even detrimental, in others. This argument rests upon the following admittedly normative assertion, which I will defend throughout the remainder of this book: As a society, we do not reject, and in my view quite properly, all of our collective decision-making bodies—including markets, state and federal appellate courts, state legislatures and Congress, and agencies—as being either inherently irrational or unfair. In saying that, I also recognize that, individually and collectively, we are sometimes (perhaps often) dissatisfied with particular results that each of these institutions reaches. If I am correct, my assertion implies that there is some standard for evaluating these various collective decision-making institutions that, although rendering them less than perfect, meaning that they do not meet *all of* the defined conditions of Arrow's Theorem, nonetheless renders them generally acceptable, or good enough.

Arrow's Theorem prescribes the perfect or at least the unattainable, meaning only that Arrow's five criteria provide an objective standard or benchmark for evaluating institutions, knowing that all will come up short in some respect. But Arrow's proof says nothing, necessarily, about which of the particular criteria are most (or least) important in any given institution in terms of furthering (or undermining) their basic claims to fairness and rationality. If we use Arrow's Theorem as the benchmark in making such comparative institutional assessments, however, we can determine the nature of their *different* deficiencies and then determine whether, in light of those deficiencies, the existing allocation of decisional authority is less bad than the likely results of proposed change. In addition, by applying the same analysis to rules within institutions, we can, again, determine whether proposed changes to those rules are likely to ameliorate or to exacerbate the problems that the proponents of change are seeking to cure.

Finally, a full comparative institutional analysis also requires that we avoid the other two fallacies discussed above, the fallacy of composition and the isolation fallacy. One of the critical evolutionary methods for improving the fairness and rationality of our collective decision-making bodies, including, most notably, the Supreme Court and Congress, is through decisional rules that affect the manner in which those institutions operate together to ameliorate each other's institutional deficiencies. One of the most notable examples, which lies at the heart of constitutional process, involves the Supreme Court's evolution away from, and Congress's evolution toward, Condorcet-producing rules and practices. As explained in chapter 4, for example, in response to the efforts of frustrated non-Condorcet-winning minorities to manipulate the order of case decisions in the federal judiciary, with an eye toward ultimately affecting the substantive evolution of constitutional doctrine in the Supreme Court, we might expect the Supreme Court to develop a set of rules, in the form of justiciability doctrines, intended to help encourage decision making in Congress or state legislatures, instead of in the federal courts. Because legislatures are generally better able to identify and select Condorcet winners, and to identify, and remain inert when confronted with, cyclical preferences, the federal courts improve the overall fairness and rationality of lawmaking by erecting justiciability barriers, which encourage ideological litigants to seek redress in legislatures instead of in the federal courts.

B. A More Detailed Application

With that introduction, we are now ready to unveil the gem known as Arrow's Theorem. As stated above, Arrow proved that no single institution can simultaneously satisfy four conditions of fairness and ensure collectively rationality. I will now provide a more detailed definition of each of the fairness criteria and link these definitions to the foregoing discussion. I will introduce several of the concepts to follow in pairs because doing so helps to underscore important relationships between these criteria and to reveal the importance of each criterion to constitutional process.

1. Range (*and the* Condorcet Criterion)

Range requires that given a set of three options, the outcome be the universal product of a decision-making rule that permits all members to rank those options in any order that they choose.[104] For example, when choosing among three options, x, y, and z, there are six sets of potential ordinal rankings (xyz; xzy; zyx; zxy; yxz, yzx). This follows because for the first ordinally ranked preference, the decision maker has three options, leaving two options for the second, and one for the third. The product ($3 \times 2 \times 1$) equals six. Range has two components. First, it requires that each decision maker be permitted to select from any of those potential six combinations of ordinal rankings or, stated differently, that the governing rule not hold any of those six options off limits for the group members. Second, range requires that the outcome be consistent with the members' selections of the various sets of ordinal rankings.[105]

The intuition underlying range is fairly straightforward. If the ultimate choice among the decision makers is the product of a rule that *prevents* some members from selecting any specific ordinal rankings over the available alternatives, then the person who has held certain ordinal rankings off limits has been vested with disproportionate power relative to the remaining group members. We have already seen some examples. Recall that in a group with non-Condorcet-winning preferences (person 1: ABC, person 2: BCA, person 3: CAB), unlimited pairwise voting produces a cycle. But if, out of the six potential options (ABC, ACB, BAC, BCA, CAB, CBA), option CAB is off limits, then person 3 might select CBA, the only remaining option that ranks C first. If so, and if the other preferences remain unchanged, B would emerge the winner, beating both A and C, even though under the original ordinal rankings, A would have defeated B. Assuming that person 2 is the agenda setter, he might choose to hold ordinal ranking CAB off limits, knowing that if people vote sincerely, the result will be to produce a voting path leading to his favored outcome B. Person 2 was able to produce an outcome that achieves the false appearance of transitivity by limiting the effective choice of person 3. In this example, holding option CAB off limits effectively foreclosed option A, the only option that would defeat B in a direct pairwise contest, from emerging the winner.

As stated above, any collective decision-making institution that functions, meaning only that it issues collective decisions, will necessarily relax at least one of the stated Arrovian criteria. In addition, any collective decision-making institution that seeks to translate collective preferences into transitive, and thus stable, orderings—or even the appearance of such orderings—will necessarily violate one of the four Arrovian fairness conditions. In this analysis, range proves critical in distinguishing appellate courts and legislatures, including the Supreme Court and Congress. My basic thesis is that within appellate courts, the condition that is relaxed to generate at least the appearance of transitive orderings—a requirement that is inextricably linked to the rule of law—is range. The collective obligation to produce a judgment and holding in a case that is properly before the Supreme Court, for example, prevents that Court, like virtually all appellate courts, from employing Condorcet-producing rules, given that a regime of unlimited pairwise comparisons by majority rule has the potential to produce a collective impasse. To be clear, I do not assert that the Court *always* must produce a judgment, as, for example, when it determines that certiorari has been granted improvidently or when a case is remanded in light of a recently issued governing case. As stated previously, I also do not assert that the Court has an obligation to issue a holding on the issue or issues of the litigants' choosing.[106] In fact, in chapter 4, I will present a comprehensive social choice model designed to explain the Supreme Court's justiciability doctrines, with a special emphasis on standing, which together often prevent the federal courts from issuing final determinations on the issues presented by litigants. And, of course, the Supreme Court, uniquely within the federal judicial system, has nearly complete docket control, and thus might appear to have the authority never to issue any collective judgments. But each of these junctures in the Supreme Court's decision-making processes—from deciding whether to decide a case, to deciding whether a case is justiciable, to deciding the merits of a case—requires a formal, albeit de minimis, collective institutional decision. Because each of these decision-making junctures demands a formal institutional decision, in the event that the justices possess preferences that, when aggregated, reveal an intransitivity, a rule-satisfying range would potentially violate that institutional obligation. Range is therefore relaxed to the extent that those ordinal rankings that would produce a cycle, and thus, that have the potential not to produce a collective result, are off limits to the justices. As explained more fully in chapter 3,[107] the Court's internal rules have evolved in a manner that effectively excludes consideration of those rank orderings that would produce collective inertia resulting from cyclical preferences.

The collective inability to do nothing, and thus the relaxation of range, has profound implications both for social choice and for constitutional process. An institution can achieve collective indeterminacy in either of two ways. First, it can decide, through an open and deliberative process, that doing nothing is preferred to all potential options for change. In fact, one might argue that the Court's justiciability barriers have this effect. Rather than deciding the underlying issues that the parties have presented, the Court opts to prevent those parties from litigating the claim. But notice that in doing so, the Court *does* issue a judgment and a holding, albeit not on the parties' issue of choice. As a result, denials of standing, or dismissals because cases are either not ripe or are moot, do not involve inertia in the sense discussed here. There is a second method of achieving collective indeterminacy. In an institution that employs a Condorcet-producing rule, but that lacks a Condorcet winner, intransitive preferences can arise. While cycles are largely nonobservable and thus intransitive preferences are difficult to verify, the possibility of cycling proves critical in explaining the evolution of institutions and rules. Absent some barrier to cycling, institutions employing a non-Condorcet-producing rule when faced with intransitive preferences could produce collective indeterminacy. In chapters 3 and 4, which develop social choice models of static and dynamic constitutional process, I will demonstrate that two decisional rules employed by the Supreme Court, namely outcome voting and stare decisis, are non-Condorcet-producing, and are best understood as the product of that Court's collective obligation to produce a judgment and holding in cases properly before it. By excluding from consideration those ordinal rankings that would produce collective indeterminacy in the form of cycling, these two non-Condorcet-producing rules promote results that sometimes appear to thwart the will of the preferences of a majority of the Court's members and further produce legal doctrine that is path dependent. At the same time, however, these rules promote the appearance of transitivity, which undergirds the rule of law.

The Court's use of a non-Condorcet-producing rule tells only half the story. As discussed earlier in the chapter, it is critically important to avoid the isolation fallacy when exploring the implications of social choice for constitutional process. The Court employs the non-Condorcet-producing rule of outcome voting when deciding individual cases and stare decisis when deciding cases over time. I will further demonstrate that in the historical period when the Supreme Court was most likely prone to difficult collective preference aggregation problems, it developed a series of companion justiciability doctrines, which ameliorated the most damaging effects of each of these non-Condorcet-producing rules. Specifically, I will demonstrate the manner in which outcome voting, a non-Condorcet-producing rule that ensures collective outcomes in individual cases, by operating in conjunction with the narrowest grounds rule, increases the probability that if there is a Condorcet-winning opinion, that opinion will state the Court's holding. Similarly, I will demonstrate that by operating in conjunction with stare decisis, a non-Condorcet-producing rule that ensures stable legal doctrine over time, standing grounds the critically important path of case decisions in fortuitous historical events presumptively beyond the control of the litigants themselves. In short, I will argue, both the narrowest grounds doctrine and standing promote fair constitutional process, as fairness is understood in social choice.[108]

I have stated that the application of range marks a critical distinction between appellate courts and legislatures generally and between the Supreme Court and Congress in particular. I have also provided a number of examples of congressional rules that, to use the apt phrasing of Professors Shepsle and Weingast, promote structure-induced equilibria.[109] These devices include elaborate committee structures, bicameralism, filibusters, and limits on the number of permissible amendments for pending legislation.[110] Most obviously, limiting the number of permissible amendments for pending legislation is a non-Condorcet-producing rule if there exist more potential amendments than the rules permit. This rule therefore appears to violate the range criterion. The other rules, while not formally limiting the number of options that the body can consider, have the effect of raising the transactions costs of identifying potentially cyclical preferences, and thus of encouraging seemingly arbitrary outcomes. In fact, however, even with these rules and institutional arrangements in place, I will argue, the general evolutionary path of congressional rules, in contrast with that of Supreme Court rules, is *toward* the Condorcet criterion, at least when the stakes are sufficiently high.

This follows from two complementary intuitions. First, in contrast with the Supreme Court, which has a collective obligation to issue judgments and holdings in cases properly before it, Congress has no collective obligation to produce either a bill or a collective institutional determination that no bill is warranted in response to every legislative proposal. Unlike the Supreme Court, Congress has the power not to formally act at all. This means that, in theory, Congress has the power to adopt Condorcet-producing rules, even if those rules occasionally, or even regularly, produce collective indeterminacy. While this may be defensible in theory, however, the equilibrating devices mentioned above have the potential, and perhaps even the effect, of inducing equilibria even when Congress possesses cyclical preferences. But recall that rules that satisfy the Condorcet criterion do not take intensities of preference over a given set of ordinal rankings—or even of interest in the subject matter of those rankings—into account. Thus, in a group with the following ordinal preferences, P1: ABC, P2: BCA, and P3: CBA, while B is the Condorcet winner, it might also be an inferior social alternative to option C. If, for example, P1 is close to indifferent among all three options, he might happily forgo voting for B in a contest with C, thus allowing C to prevail overall, in exchange for the support of P2, who least prefers option A, in some other matter. Through the commodification of preferences, which I will discuss below under the heading of "Unanimity and Independence of Irrelevant Alternatives," legislators sometimes produce results that are mutually beneficial, while deliberately thwarting the Condorcet criterion.

The second intuition that helps to explain the evolution of congressional rules toward the Condorcet criterion is that while some rules formally limit the number of votes relative to the number of options, in legislatures, unlike in courts, the members are allowed, even encouraged, to determine both their ordinal and cardinal rankings over available options through informal means. Thus, while the number of amendments relative to the number of options might be limited formally, there is no effective limit on the number of iterations that can occur informally. If enough legislators—or at least a sufficiently powerful group—anticipate a path taking them where only the agenda setter wants to go, we might expect that this group will exert appropriate pressure to change that path, or will threaten to vote in a manner that would derail the voting path.[111] We might further expect the probability of such efforts to be positively correlated with the importance of the underlying issue to the affected group. And while the number of congressmen might appear to render the task of exchanging information more difficult, the various negative legislative checkpoints, including most notably elaborate committee structures, facilitate this process. Legislators strongly committed to avoiding those outcomes that might be structure-induced could employ the same mechanisms to achieve their objectives as well. In short, social choice theory suggests a quasi-market solution, which helps to identify potentially cyclical preferences and, thus, which helps to promote inertia within Congress, even when formal congressional voting rules are non-Condorcet-producing.

2. Unanimity and Independence of Irrelevant Alternatives

Unanimity is defined as follows: "If an individual preference is unopposed by any contrary preference of any other individual, this preference is preserved in the social ordering."[112] While commentators often equate this with the condition of *Pareto superiority,* this equation of terms can be deceiving. A move from the status quo to an alternative state is Pareto superior if it benefits at least one participant without harming others. A move is Pareto optimal if no further Pareto superior moves remain (meaning that any changes will have distributional consequences). The Pareto criterion is almost universally applied within private markets. Indeed, the Pareto criterion is often advanced as the normative justification for free-market decision making. If we set aside such problems as initial wealth endowments and externalities, and assume away such illegal circumstances as duress and fraud, market transactions are almost invariably unanimous. From an ex ante perspective, private market exchanges are therefore presumed to improve the utility of at least one, and probably both, of the parties to the exchange; otherwise the parties would not have bothered. Exchange is one of the two vehicles through which private markets create wealth. The other, of course, is production.

The difficulty with applying the Pareto criterion in a public law context is that within legislatures, trades that satisfy the unanimity criterion often have the effect of inhibiting wealth creation in private markets. The intuition that Pareto superior legislative exchanges can produce Pareto inferior results in terms of limiting economic growth is best understood by considering the two competing markets in which the Pareto criterion can be applied. To illustrate, consider two cases, both of which are discussed in chapter 1, *Lochner v. New York*,[113] decided in 1905, and *West Coast Hotel v. Parrish*,[114] decided in 1937. In *Lochner*, the Court held that a state minimum wage law violated the Fourteenth Amendment due process clause.[115] In *West Coast Hotel*, the Court upheld a state minimum wage law for women against a constitutional challenge.[116] By preventing state legislatures from enacting minimum wage statutes, the *Lochner* Court prevented some seemingly Pareto superior or unanimous exchanges supported by affected legislators or their constituents. In doing so, however, the *Lochner* Court *guaranteed* the rights of employers and workers, if they so chose, to enter into employment contracts for less than the statutory minimum wage. In contrast, in *Parrish*, the Supreme Court, by allowing legislatures to enact minimum wage laws, protected Pareto superior legislative exchanges. At the same time, however, the *Parrish* Court allowed the same legislatures to *prevent* seemingly Pareto superior transactions within private markets by employers and prospective employees willing to enter into contracts at below the statutory minimum wage. In short, there are two potential markets in which Pareto criterion can be applied. The Supreme Court can guarantee that Pareto superior transactions are protected over given subject matters in one market or the other, but not both.[117]

A large public choice literature has demonstrated that legislative processes, in Congress and in state legislatures, have a systematic bias in favor of regulatory intervention that undermines private market efficiency.[118] Assuming that legislatures do have such a proregulatory bias, protecting the unanimity criterion within legislatures might conflict with, rather than promote, private wealth creation. To understand the full dynamic of unanimity, and to consider whether it applies within the Supreme Court, it is necessary to introduce what turns out to be a companion fairness criterion, namely independence of irrelevant alternatives.

The independence criterion is defined as follows: "The social choice between any two alternatives must depend only on the orderings of individuals over these two alternatives, and not on their ordering over other alternatives."[119] Stated differently, independence requires that each decision maker base her choice between each pair of presented alternatives solely upon the relative merits of those alternatives, without strategic considerations. Prohibited strategies can include trying to anticipate, and thus derail, the voting path, for example, by voting other than for one's first choice to produce a more favorable result, or by trying to improve one's utility through vote trading. This might be the most counterintuitive and, indeed, most controversial, of Arrow's fairness assumptions. And yet, both Condorcet and Arrow embraced the assumption, albeit based upon somewhat different intuitions. Although both intuitions are related, Condorcet's intuition has greater relevance in applying the criterion to the Supreme Court and Arrow's has more relevance in applying it to Congress. My basic thesis here is the obverse of that with respect to range. While range is relaxed in the Supreme Court to ensure collective results, and adhered to in Congress, given its power to remain inert, the opposite is largely true with respect to Arrovian independence. Subject to an important caveat, described below, I will argue that Supreme Court justices are presumed to adhere to independence, while members of Congress are presumed to violate independence.

Influenced by the republican writings of Jean-Jacques Rousseau, Condorcet proposed that in choosing among options, legislators should focus solely upon the merits of presented alternatives so that in each successive contest, better options are selected, until the best option emerges.[120] In Condorcet's understanding, individuals, upon entering the public sphere, either as legislators or as voters, are expected to subordinate their own objectives in furtherance of their perception of the interest of society.[121] In contrast, Arrow's intuition about the importance of the independence criterion was not driven by republican notions. Instead, for Arrow, independence was necessary to comply with the basic economic principle that systems of governance are presumed unable meaningfully to compare interpersonal utilities.[122] To be clear, there is no difficulty in allowing persons to place weights upon their own utilities, for example, through market exchanges, which allow individuals both to commodify and to reveal their preferences.[123] Indeed, as suggested in the above discussion of unanimity, that is among the primary justifications for private-market decision making. Thus viewed, price theory, or the study of market mechanisms under certain conditions to convey critical information concerning value instantly and spontaneously, with no central coordinating authority, is ultimately an application of this important insight, which finds its conceptual origin in the theory of social choice. Social choice theory thus provides a basis for understanding the comparative advantage of markets in the creation of wealth relative to virtually all other real-world institutions.[124] The economic difficulty arises in trying to devise some objective and verifiable measure of utility when cardinalization cannot be achieved through private market exchange or some other means. It is nearly impossible to conceive of a device that can be employed to measure objectively interpersonal utilities that would not provide substantial opportunities for posturing or strategic behavior among participants, for example, claiming that favored measures would generate greater utility for supporters than disutility for opponents.

Unanimity and independence are largely at odds because one of the principal means of producing Pareto superior exchanges is through agreeing not to pursue objectives that one agrees to in principle, in exchange for having others pursue objectives that we care about more strongly. Within legislatures, this is referred to as logrolling, a process that requires careful attention to the voting agenda and considerable foresight about the relationships between present decisions and future options. Within Congress, for example, vote trading and strategic considerations are a way of life, at least for any congressperson who wants to keep the job. While unanimity is generally adhered to within legislatures, independence is generally relaxed. Alternatively, subject to the following caveat and some exceptions set out in chapter 3,[125] independence is generally adhered to within appellate courts, including the Supreme Court, while unanimity is generally relaxed.

Commentators on the Supreme Court sometimes suggest that justices behave improperly when their decisions are based other than on the merits of available alternatives. Professors Lewis Kornhauser and Lawrence Sager, for example, expressed this intuition in stating that "We strongly lean toward the view of adjudication as an exercise in judgment aggregation; indeed, we understand most plausible schools of jurisprudence to embrace this view."[126] In this conception, I would suggest, justices are presumed to decide cases, and presumably issues within those cases, in a principled fashion, not because of the difficulty in engaging in interpersonal utility comparisons, although that may be a component, but rather to ensure that in choosing among available options, the justices will select the one that is likely to be the most sound. Supreme Court justices are therefore expected not to trade votes or to base their decisions on strategic considerations, as opposed to merits determinations.[127] And yet, recent studies of the Supreme Court, based upon the private papers of individual justices, reveal that justices quite often change their initial assessments of the merits of cases, as indicated in their preliminary postargument conference votes, by the time the written opinions are issued.[128] Most often, justices engage in a form of compromise to secure a majority opinion, without which the case would produce a holding, but would not establish a precedent, even if to do so the holding is cast in substantially narrower terms than originally desired. One might conclude from such studies that justices, no less than members of Congress, are prone to strategic behavior in a manner that contravenes Arrovian independence. In fact, however, a subtle, but significant, distinction remains in applying the independence criterion to these two institutions. As set out more fully in chapter 3,[129] strategic interaction between and among the justices almost without exception appears to involve moves toward the median position on the Court, with the objective of elevating a potential narrowest grounds opinion to majority status. Most critically, such compromise, again almost without exception, arises within single issues and within single cases. This serves as a considerable limitation on the power of justices to commodify their preferences through a systematic practice of strategic voting and vote trading. In contrast, legislators routinely commodify preferences across issues within bills, across bills of the same subject matter, and even across bills of widely differing subject matters. It is based upon this narrower understanding that I assert that justices, unlike legislators, adhere to Arrovian independence.

Moreover, while Professors Kornhauser and Sager have advanced an eminently reasonable normative thesis about Supreme Court decision making, subject to the above caveat, I will argue that as a positive theory about the behavior of justices, it is to a limited extent falsifiable. Specifically, I will argue that the common practice of opinion writing and publication has two important effects. First, published opinions can be understood as a stylized and piecemeal form of ordinal rankings, providing valuable information to other judges and to the bar about the justices' preferences. Second, by encouraging justices to state their preferences, even if in stylized and piecemeal form, published opinions substantially raise the transactions costs of departing from expressed views for strategic gain. In contrast with judges who are commonly expected to explain their reasoning in published opinions, congressmen are not generally expected to explain the bases for their votes (and indeed, when asked, are generally quite good at failing to provide straightforward responses). Indeed, it is well understood that legislators might vote for or against proposed legislation for reasons *other than* a principled commitment to the cause.

3. *Nondictatorship*

Nondictatorship is defined as follows: "No individual enjoys a position such that whenever he expresses a preference between two alternatives and all other individuals express an opposite preference, his preference is always preserved in the social ordering."[130] Nondictatorship appears the most obvious fairness condition in any collective decision-making institution, but, in fact, Arrow's Theorem proves that to preserve transitive orderings in a system that meets the other fairness conditions set out above, it is inevitable that someone be vested with substantially disproportionate decisional authority. While not all justices and members of Congress are truly equal in all contexts, nondictatorship is satisfied in both institutions. That said, it is worth considering the extent and nature of the sometimes unequal distribution of power within these institutions. In the Supreme Court, as in most appellate courts, the chief justice (or in the case of the federal circuits, the chief judge) truly is the first among equals in terms of the weight of his or her vote. But even there, he possesses some limited form of disproportionate power. When the chief justice votes with the majority, he assigns the opinion; when the chief justice votes in dissent, the senior justice voting with the majority assigns the opinion. This, of course, is a far cry from actual dictatorial power, as defined above, but the power of opinion assignments should not be taken lightly.[131] More obviously, a minority of four is given disproportionate power to control the Court's docket through the writ of certiorari. But even this does not defy Arrovian nondictatorship because the rules governing certiorari do not vest the same four justices with power over all certiorari petitions against the contrary will of the Court. Those in a successful minority of four in one round might well find themselves in the unsuccessful majority of five in the next. In any event, setting aside these minor examples of occasional dispro-

Table 2.4. The Supreme Court and Congress through an Arrovian Lens

Arrovian Criterion	Supreme Court	Congress
Range	Collective obligation to produce results prevents the Supreme Court from employing Condorcet-producing rules; impracticality prevents Condorcet-consistent rules.	Collective ability to remain inert has allowed Congressional rules coupled with informal practices to evolve toward Condorcet criterion. In addition, cardinalization of preferences enables members of Congress to achieve collectively rational results while occasionally thwarting the Condorcet criterion.
Unanimity	Vote trading is inhibited in the Supreme Court by publication of written opinions and judgment-based decision making.	Vote trading is encouraged, thus producing Pareto superior legislative exchanges, which often undermine private market efficiency.
Independence of irrelevant alternatives	Judgment-based decision making and publication of written opinions raise the costs of strategic voting among justices; strategic interactions that remain are generally toward median position on the Court and operate within issues and cases.	Congressmen regularly vote strategically, thus cardinalizing their preferences over issues and bills.
Nondictatorship	Generally adhered to, but opinion assignment power and power of certiorari provide occasional disproportionate power to minorities on the Court.	Compromised by practices that afford disproportionate power to committee chairs and to individual congressmen; limited by informal quasi-market checks when the stakes are high.
Condorcet Criterion	Evolution of important rules, including outcome voting and stare decisis are attributable to the Court's inability to employ Condorcet-producing rules. These rules must be evaluated in conjunction with companion rules, e.g., the narrowest grounds rule and standing, which help to improve the Court's overall rationality and fairness.	Important congressional voting rules have evolved toward Condorcet criterion, except when Congress lacks the power to remain inert, including, in selecting legislative leaders. Some limiting rules appear to defy Condorcet criterion, but common voting practices provide quasi-market solution, thus restoring Condorcet-criterion when stakes are high.

portionate power among justices, each of the justices generally has roughly equal voting power in the Supreme Court.

In contrast, within Congress, the various negative legislative checkpoints vest disproportionate power in a limited number of congressmen. While each member of Congress has an equal vote, Congress is an institution in which some members have significantly greater market power and can effectively exercise the votes of others. But here too, the power is not unlimited. As seen in the above discussion of the Condorcet criterion, in the event that a powerful committee chair abuses his or her power, members of Congress can engage in a variety of retaliatory measures intended to limit such abuses in the future. Again, however, the powers of committee chairs are not to be underestimated.

VI.   Concluding Comments and Summary

As stated above, the whole of Arrow's Theorem is greater than the sum of its parts. Even if one or more individual criteria are normatively suspect, the theorem provides a framework for analyzing and comparing institutions in a manner that avoids the nirvana fallacy precisely by demonstrating the ability of a given institution to relax criteria that are inessential to—or that might actually harm—its functioning. Table 2.4 summarizes the preceding discussion. In part II, we will use this social choice framework to analyze how individual cases are decided and how groups of cases are decided over time.

Part II

Social Choice Models of Supreme Court Decision Making

CHAPTER 3

Static Constitutional Process: How Individual Cases Are Decided

I. Introduction

This chapter will begin to develop a social choice model of constitutional lawmaking by focusing on the manner in which the Supreme Court decides individual cases. The social choice model of individual case decision making developed below explains no fewer than three important anomalies, which remain unexplained under traditional constitutional analysis. First, it explains why the Supreme Court, as seen in *Miller v. Albright,*[1] occasionally issues decisions that appear to thwart the will of a majority of the deciding justices with respect to the underlying issues, and it identifies the limited conditions that give rise to this kind of voting anomaly. Second, it explains why the Supreme Court has not adopted, as has been proposed,[2] a voting rule that honors the collective resolution of the deciding justices on the underlying issues, rather than honoring the collective resolution on the most often binary outcome choice, affirm or reverse, even though one could design a non-Condorcet-producing rule that would satisfy either of those two objectives. Finally, it explains why the Supreme Court employs the narrowest grounds doctrine to govern the identification of its holding in fractured panel decisions, even though the doctrine sometimes, as in *Planned Parenthood of Southeastern Pennsylvania v. Casey,*[3] appears to be premised upon an attenuated notion of consensus, and other times, as in *Miller,* proves entirely dysfunctional as a means of identifying the Court's holding.

In addition to explaining each of these enigmatic phenomena, this chapter and the next will provide an economic foundation for an important, and commonly shared, normative understanding that justices on the Supreme Court are presumed to decide cases in a principled fashion.[4] While my own position is that this is an entirely defensible normative assertion, from an economic perspective, it is somewhat counterintuitive, at least if we accept the premise that, holding all else constant, judges would prefer the legal system to embrace their view of the world.[5] Moreover, whatever the normative appeal of this characterization, it certainly fails to capture all interactions of Supreme Court justices. In at least some respects, Supreme Court justices can and often do behave strategically. And yet, I will argue that Supreme Court justices do not uniformly defect from the norm of principled decision making.[6] Identifying the nature and limits of strategic interactions among the justices,

which include tactical decisions on whether to grant or to deny writs of certiorari,[7] and changes by individual justices from their ideal points, as
expressed in conference voting, to those positions embraced in the written
opinions they either join or write,[8] will prove critical in employing social choice
to model Supreme Court decision making. Using social choice theory, I will
develop a model that explains the emergence of several institutional practices that, individually and in combination, operate to constrain justices, thus
promoting judgment-based decision making both in individual cases and
across a larger number of cases. Strategy-limiting practices in individual case
decision making, which I will elaborate on below, include the publication of
written opinions, outcome voting, and the *Marks* narrowest grounds doctrine.

Finally, this chapter will explain the increasingly prevalent, and much
criticized,[9] practice of fractured Supreme Court opinions. In this chapter, I
will employ social choice theory to expose the inevitable trade-off between
the desire for judgment-based decision making, and for the appearance—
albeit arguably a false one—of clear guidance that more unified Supreme
Court opinions would provide.

While explaining each of these phenomena is important, the model
developed in this chapter is significant at a more general level as well. As the
public choice economist Mancur Olson observed: "The persuasiveness of a
theory depends not only on how many facts are explained, but also on how
diverse are the kinds of facts explained."[10] Consistent with Olson's intuition,
it is also important to consider the striking parallels between the analysis of
how the Supreme Court decides individual cases, and both Saul Levmore's
thesis concerning the evolution of parliamentary rules, described in chapter
2, and the social choice theory of how the Supreme Court decides groups of
cases over time, which I will present in chapter 4. Specifically, the Court's
combined use of outcome voting and the *Marks* narrowest grounds doctrine
corresponds with at least two other pairs of companion rules or practices.
These include the relationship between the switch to succession voting when
Condorcet winners are not likely to emerge, and the use of incremental voting in a one-dimensional continuum to limit agenda setting by committee
chairs; and the relationship between stare decisis, which limits doctrinal
cycling but which also promotes path dependent evolution of law, and standing, which presumptively grounds the order of cases in fortuitous historical
events beyond the litigants' control. In all three contexts,[11] a non-Condorcet-
producing rule has emerged that increases the likelihood that the collective
decision-making body will generate outcomes, even if preferences occasionally cycle, and a complementary rule has emerged that increases the probability, but that does not (and cannot) guarantee, that if a Condorcet winner
is available, it will prevail.

If the social choice model of static constitutional process matches up to
actual Supreme Court practice, therefore, the theory very likely has much to
commend it. By that I mean it is less difficult to devise an economic story targeted to explaining a single enigmatic phenomenon observed in the real world
than it is to devise a methodological approach that, in parallel fashion,

explains a broad range of enigmatic phenomena, especially when, as in the case of succession and incremental parliamentary voting, outcome voting and the *Marks* narrowest grounds doctrine, and stare decisis and standing, observers have generally treated them as unrelated.

This chapter will be subdivided into four sections. The first section will explain the evolution of Supreme Court voting rules away from the Condorcet criterion. The second section will explain why, as between the two available non-Condorcet-producing rules,[12] outcome and issue voting, the Court has selected outcome voting, even though that rule on occasion thwarts majority preferences on underlying issues. That section will also provide an economic analysis of how issues are defined in Supreme Court cases. The third section will explain why the Supreme Court has adopted the *Marks* narrowest grounds doctrine even though applying it sometimes depends upon a rather attenuated notion of consensus. That section will also explain how the narrowest grounds doctrine ameliorates the irrationality that outcome voting, a non-Condorcet-producing rule, potentially creates. The fourth, and final section, will demonstrate that the lingering problems associated with the outcome voting/*Marks* regime, which have generated proposals to switch to issue voting, require solutions that can, instead, be accommodated within the framework of existing rules. In the course of developing each of these analytical points, I will also introduce a taxonomy of Supreme Court plurality decisions: plurality decisions with a unidimensional issue continuum, plurality decisions with a multidimensional issue continuum and symmetrical preferences, and plurality decisions with a multidimensional issue continuum and asymmetrical preferences. Except in the case of plurality decisions with a multidimensional issue continuum and asymmetrical preferences, in which no rule is capable of avoiding the underlying voting anomaly, I will demonstrate that the narrowest grounds doctrine works well at identifying a dominant Condorcet-winning holding.

II.   Outcome Voting: The Evolution toward a Non-Condorcet-Producing Decisional Rule

A.   *Kassel v. Consolidated Freightways*

To illustrate why the Supreme Court, like virtually all appellate courts, employs a non-Condorcet-producing rule when deciding individual cases, even though that rule sometimes thwarts the preferences of a majority of the justices on underlying issues, it will be helpful to consider *Kassel v. Consolidated Freightways*,[13] a case that presents the same conceptual anomaly as *Miller v. Albright*,[14] introduced in chapter 1. *Kassel* presented the question whether an Iowa statute that prohibited the use of sixty-five-foot twin trailers in state, with exceptions benefiting in-state trucking interests, violated the dormant commerce clause. The statute's legislative history demonstrated that the law was intended to make, and had the effect of making, it more costly for out-of-state truckers to operate by forcing them to alter their rigs before entering Iowa or to travel around the state. As a result, the statute saved the wear and tear on state highways.[15]

The Supreme Court produced three opinions, a plurality of four by Justice Powell, a concurrence for two by Justice Brennan, and a dissent for three by then–associate justice Rehnquist. The three writing justices distilled the case to two issues: (1) Is the appropriate substantive test the lenient rational basis test, described in chapter 1,[16] or the somewhat more stringent balancing test, under which the court independently weighs the law's alleged safety benefits against the burden it imposes on interstate commerce? and (2) Whatever the substantive test, can evidence in support of justifications for the statute not considered by the Iowa legislature be introduced at trial? Justice Powell, joined by Justices White, Blackmun, and Stevens, voted to strike down the statute, concluding that the relevant test was the balancing test and that the state's attorneys could introduce evidence at trial to support novel justifications for the statute not considered by the Iowa legislature.[17] Justice Brennan, joined by Justice Marshall, also voted to strike down the statute, concluding that the relevant test was the rational basis test, but that the trial court could consider only evidence actually used to support justifications that the Iowa legislature considered.[18] Brennan concluded that the legislative history evinced a protectionist motive, and that the statute was therefore per se unconstitutional, even applying the rational basis test. Finally, Justice Rehnquist, joined by Chief Justice Burger and Justice Stewart, voted in dissent to uphold the statute, concluding that the relevant test was the rational basis test and that the state's lawyers could introduce evidence supporting novel justifications.[19] Table 3.1, which presents the two issue dimensions in *Kassel* along the horizontal and vertical axes, summarizes the positions of the justices.

The opinions reveal that two conditions were both necessary, but neither alone sufficient, to sustain the Iowa statute. Based upon all three opinions, the justices implicitly agreed that if the relevant test were rational basis, the lowest level of scrutiny, and if trial lawyers were free to introduce more, rather than less, evidence with which to find a rational basis, the result would be to uphold the statute. The bolded upper left box thus indicates that to sustain the statute, a majority of justices must fall within that box, thus agreeing to the laxer substantive test and to the laxer evidentiary rule. Alternatively, if *either* the relevant test were the more stringent balancing test *or* the state were not permitted to introduce arguments other than those considered by the Iowa legislature (given that all of the actual supporting justifications evinced a protectionist motive), then the result would be to strike down the Iowa statute. Table 3.1 reveals the anomaly that on an issue-by-issue basis, one majority, composed of those in the upper left and upper right boxes, the Rehnquist and Powell camps, concluded that the trial court should be permitted to consider novel trial evidence, and another majority, composed of those in the upper left and lower left boxes, the Rehnquist and Brennan camps, concluded that the trial court should apply the rational basis test. Thus, on an issue-by-issue basis, the result should be to uphold the statute.

Table 3.1.   Positions of the Justices on the Two Issue Dimensions in *Kassel*

	Rational Basis	Balancing Test
Admit novel evidence	(B) Rehnquist, Burger, Stewart	(A) Powell, White, Blackmun, Stevens
Exclude novel evidence	(C) Brennan, Marshall	

Instead, a separate majority composed of the Powell and Brennan camps, in the upper right and lower left boxes respectively, voted to strike down the statute on the ground that only one of the two necessary conditions for sustaining it was met.

In chapter 2, I posited that the Supreme Court's institutional obligation to resolve those cases properly before it prevents the Court from employing a Condorcet-producing case decision rule.[20] Using language drawn from Arrow's Theorem,[21] in the Supreme Court, range is relaxed,[22] meaning that the Court's decisional rule will not generate an outcome for all conceivable ordinal rankings of the justices over combined issue and outcome resolutions. Stated more simply, Supreme Court justices are precluded from selecting those ordinal rankings over packaged issue and outcome combinations[23] that, in the aggregate, would produce collective indeterminacy in the form of cycling. Using table 3.1, I will now illustrate these propositions with *Kassel*. Recall from chapter 2 that to do so, I need only employ a single Condorcet-producing rule, given that all such rules would produce the same anomaly absent a Condorcet winner.

To demonstrate the difficulty that the Court would have faced had it employed a Condorcet-producing rule to decide *Kassel*, it is necessary to make some assumptions about the justices' positions on the underlying issues. Because the Court employs outcome voting, which is a non-Condorcet-producing case decision rule, the deciding justices are not called upon to choose from a complete list of all possible rankings of available options over combined issue and outcome resolutions. Instead, through their judicial opinions, the justices provide us with what can best be understood as fragmented statements of judgment concerning the resolution of issues necessary to deciding the case.[24] Over a sufficiently large number of cases, these fragments can be pieced together to derive a more general sense of each justice's jurisprudential view of a larger set of issues, although the information invariably remains incomplete.

To illustrate the difficulty that a Condorcet-producing rule would create, I will present a choice among three options, each represented by the package of issue determinations in one of the actual three written opinions. The three positions, represented by the upper right, upper left, and lower left boxes in table 3.1, respectively, are as follows:

A (Powell):   balancing test; admit evidence
B (Rehnquist): rational basis test; admit evidence
C (Brennan):   rational basis test; exclude evidence

After an important methodological comment, I will generate a set of ordinal rankings for all three camps. In doing so, I will assume that each justice ranks his own opinion first and then, based upon a further set of assumptions, I will set out his ordinal ranking over the remaining two options. Before proceeding with this example, it is important to provide a more comprehensive explanation of what each of the options, A, B, and C, represents, and to contrast the hypothetical voting regime that I have set up with both the actual outcome voting regime and the alternative hypothetical issue voting regime.

B.   Methodological Comment: Outcome Voting versus Issue Voting and Ordinal Rankings over Packaged-Issue Resolutions

As the literature on Supreme Court voting rules has developed,[25] the Court's actual case decision-making rule, in which the Court's judgment is based upon the majority resolution of the most often binary choice whether to affirm or reverse, has been described as outcome voting. In contrast, the hypothetical decision-making rule, in which the Court's judgment, instead, would be based upon the logical sequence that follows from separate majority resolutions on each underlying dispositive issue, has been described as issue voting (or sometimes as issue-by-issue voting). Because this terminology is potentially confusing, a clarification of both the terminology and its implications is essential for the analysis to follow.

Outcome voting actually is a form of issue voting in which each justice, in deciding whether to affirm or reverse, selects from a combination of resolved issues that she deems critical to disposing of the case, either as presented by another opinion writer, or as presented in her own separate opinion.* The term *issue voting* could therefore be understood to embrace either of two very different meanings. In actual practice, in deciding how to dispose of a case, each justice selects a combined package that resolves the underlying dispositive issues in a manner that leads logically to her chosen judgment. We could describe this as *endogenous issue voting*, meaning that each justice resolves issues in a manner that is internally consistent with her decision regarding how to vote on the outcome. Instead, the term *issue voting* has been employed to describe a hypothetical regime in which the Court tallies the justices' determinations on the underlying dispositive issues and then bases its judgment on the logic of the aggregated issue-by-issue determinations.[26]

---

*I am setting aside for purposes of this analysis three-judgment cases, in which the Court must decide whether to affirm, reverse, or remand. For a discussion of such cases, *see infra* § V.D.

In a total of three cases, discussed at the end of this chapter, one or more justices have employed a variation on the latter form of issue voting, allowing themselves to be bound by a majority's contrary resolution of a dispositive issue. Having done so, the justices reached one or more issues, that were not necessary to reach based upon the internal logic of their opinions. In each of these cases, the effect was to decide the case in a manner inconsistent with the internal logic of the opinion of the vote-switching justice and to change the Court's judgment.* We could characterize this form of voting as *exogenous issue voting,* meaning that the vote-switching justices allowed themselves to be bound not by the internal logic of their own analyses, but rather by the external resolution of an underlying issue by a contrary majority of the Court. With that clarification, to keep the terminology simple and consistent with the literature, I will continue to use outcome voting, where *endogenous issue voting* is also appropriate, and issue voting, where *exogenous issue voting* is also appropriate.

In addition to clarifying the terminology, it is important to clarify the nature of the options, A, B, and C, each representing a pair of combined issue resolutions in the above discussion of *Kassel,* and to explain the significance of positing ordinal rankings for each group of justices over those options. Commentators have expressed skepticism about applying an Arrow's Theorem framework in analyzing Supreme Court decision making, given that justices appear simply to vote on the most often binary choice of outcome, without ordinally ranking preferences over combined issue resolutions.[27] With respect, the criticism fails to appreciate how an Arrovian framework edifies our understanding of Supreme Court decision making. In most fractured panel cases, the justices are called upon to make two choices simultaneously. To simplify, assume a constitutional case that presents two potential holdings—to strike down or to sustain the challenged law—and two underlying dispositive issues. In the voting anomaly cases, which include *Miller* and *Kassel,* the written opinions, when aggregated, presented two pairs of combined issue resolutions producing one result (in table 3.1, packages A and C produce a decision to strike down the Iowa statute), and one pair of combined issue resolutions leading to the opposite result (in table 3.1, package B produces a decision to uphold the statute).[28] The justices must select simultaneously the binary choice of outcome and a set of issue resolutions, from A, B, or C, that is internally consistent with that binary choice of outcome.[29]

---

*To illustrate, this could have occurred in Miller v. Albright, 118 S. Ct. 1428 (1998), had Justices O'Connor and Kennedy allowed themselves to be bound by the contrary majority resolution on the question of standing. Had they done so and had they further based their outcome vote upon their resolution of the underlying merits as expressed in Justice O'Connor's concurrence, which Kennedy joined, they would most likely have voted to strike down the challenged provision of the Immigration and Nationality Act, rather than to sustain it, with the result of changing the Court's judgment.

In theory, a justice could opt to select a package of issue resolutions that is inconsistent with her chosen outcome vote, although I know of no instance in which this has ever occurred.[30] One might view the disinclination to do this as a form of range restriction, but, properly understood, that characterization does not apply. A range restriction applies when an institution's decision-making rules explicitly or implicitly prevent members from selecting any conceivable ordinal ranking over available options, in this case the available packages of underlying issue resolutions represented by A, B, and C. Viewed from the perspective of the individual justices who themselves are creating available packages of issue and outcome resolutions and also implicitly ranking those packages ordinally, range restrictions can thus be understood as forming an exogenous constraint on individual behavior. The apparently universal disinclination of justices to select a set of governing rationales that is inconsistent with their outcome votes is better explained by individual reputational concerns, and thus as forming an endogenous constraint.

We can now recast the above presentation of issue resolutions in *Kassel* as containing three available and complete packages of issue resolutions coupled with their internally consistent outcomes:

A (Powell):   balancing test + admit evidence = strike down statute
B (Brennan):   rational basis test + exclude evidence =
               strike down statute
C (Rehnquist): rational basis test + admit evidence = sustain statute.

This presentation is fully generalizable, meaning that all *Miller-* and *Kassel-* like voting anomaly cases present at least three such complete packages. And as I will demonstrate below, even in its majority decisions and its fractured panel cases with a unidimensional issue spectrum, the Supreme Court is potentially susceptible to producing three or more complete packages, depending upon the nature of the Court's case decision-making rule.[31] Given the three (or more) available options presented in virtually all Supreme Court cases, therefore, the Arrovian framework proves critical not only in the more obvious context of a case presenting three potential remedies—affirm, reverse, or remand—but also in the more typical case presenting only a binary outcome choice.

As explained below, each justice selects as her first choice the actual package of issue resolutions that she wrote or signed onto and that is consistent with her outcome vote. Her reputational concern for generating results based upon an internally consistent rationale, however, does not preclude her from explicitly or implicitly ranking as a second choice a package of issue resolutions, that would produce an opposite outcome vote. This is especially true in a case, like *Kassel,* that possesses the characteristic features of multidimensionality and asymmetry.[32] Notice that while Justice Powell and Brennan resolve both underlying issues in precisely opposite fashion, represented by A and C in table 3.1, their opposite issue resolutions lead them to the same result, namely to strike down the Iowa statute. As a result of the combination of multidimensionality and asymmetry, there would be nothing internally inconsistent with Justice Powell's taking the position that his first choice is to strike down the Iowa statute because it fails the balancing test, even with novel evidence admitted, but to prefer Rehnquist's position, which would uphold the statute using a rational basis test and also admitting novel evidence, as a second choice, to Brennan's alternative rationale for striking down the statute, which takes an opposite view on both dispositive issues from Powell's first choice.[33] In essence, if Powell were called upon to rank the alternative rationales ordinally, he would be forced to select as a second choice between a closer rationale leading to an opposite judgment, or a more distant rationale leading to the same judgment. As a result, there is no logical basis with which to predict how Powell (or Brennan, who faces the same anomaly) would choose. As explained below, while there is no logical reason to assume that Powell would prefer positions B or C as a second choice, and thus no reputational stake in avoiding ranking Rehnquist's closer rationale leading to an opposite outcome as a second choice, social choice analysis reveals an institutional constraint, operating as a range restriction, that effectively prevents this form of contingent expression of underlying issue resolutions.

The Court's judgment is based solely upon the majority resolution on the binary choice of outcome. Both the Court as a whole and the individual justices, however, are concerned not only with disposing of the immediate case, but also with providing a governing rationale. In fractured panel cases, there simply is no majority selection of packaged issue resolutions consistent with the outcome, and thus, there is no majority support for a governing rationale. In addition, the justices are not formally called upon to rank ordinally the remaining two pairs of combined issue resolutions. In lieu of that, the Court has developed the narrowest grounds doctrine, which operates upon certain premises concerning how the justices would likely have ranked their second and third choices over the remaining paired issue resolutions had they been required to do so. As explained more fully below,[34] the underlying premises about implicit ordinal rankings work well in the vast majority of fractured panel cases, which do not possess the characteristic features of multidimensionality and asymmetry. In all other fractured panel decisions, the narrowest grounds doctrine identifies as the opinion stating the holding that opinion which represents a dominant, and thus stable, second choice. In cases like *Kassel* and *Miller*, however, which possess these characteristic features for a voting anomaly, the doctrine's assumptions break down. In the analyses of *Kassel* and *Miller* that follow, I will demonstrate that if the justices were free to rank their choices over combined issue resolutions in any conceivable order, the potential for generating uncertainty over the outcome, and resulting doctrine, would arise. The analysis demonstrates that through outcome voting, the Court avoids this problem by effectively holding certain ordinal rankings over available packaged-issue resolutions off limits.

Before proceeding, one more clarification will be helpful. It is important to recognize the difference between a lurking collective intransitivity and an actual cycle. Collective intransitivity is a necessary, but insufficient, condition to cycling. While cycling might suggest, at least to some, endless indecision and indeterminacy, even when a collective intransitivity arises, indeterminacy can quite easily be avoided, for example, by a rule that limits the number of binary comparisons relative to the number of options. As a result, collective intransitivity might not manifest itself in the form of a cycle. Generally, it is more intuitive therefore to characterize the voting anomaly in cases like *Kassel* and *Miller* as the product of collective intransitivity, rather than of cycling, given that the Supreme Court does not engage in unlimited binary comparisons in deciding cases.

C. Multidimensionality and Asymmetry Revisited

1. *Lurking Intransitivity in* Kassel

We will now continue our analysis of *Kassel*. I will generate a set of ordinal rankings over all three packages of issue resolutions for the three camps of justices in *Kassel*. Based upon the combined packages of underlying issue and outcome resolutions set out above, whichever ordinal ranking Justice Powell chooses, his second ordinal preference will apply low-level rational basis scrutiny. Assume that Justice Powell believes that even if the test is rational basis, the state should be able to introduce new evidence to support novel justifications that might be rational. If so, his ordinal rankings are ABC. In contrast, whichever package Justice Rehnquist ranks second will apply a more stringent standard on one of the two requisite issues for upholding the state law. Assume that Justice Rehnquist cares more about the substantive test, which implies a strong presumption of validity for state highway regulations, than he does about the evidentiary rule. If so, his ordinal rankings are BCA. Finally, assume that Justice Brennan cares more about the outcome than about which rationale predominates. If so, his ordinal rankings are CAB. These are the paradigmatic non-Condorcet-winning preferences.

Alternatively, one can posit a reverse cycle. This time, assume that Justice Powell cares more about the outcome than about which rationale predominates. If so, his preferences are ACB. Assume that Justice Rehnquist cares more about the substantive test than about the evidentiary rule. If so, his preferences are BAC. Finally, assume that Justice Brennan cares more about creating a precedent on the application of rational basis scrutiny than about the actual outcome in *Kassel*. If so, his preferences are CBA. Again, these are paradigmatic non-Condorcet-winning preferences.[35]

In each case, the hypothetical cycle arises because of the characteristic features of multidimensionality and asymmetry, as shown in table 3.1. Because there is nothing internally inconsistent with Justices Brennan and Powell selecting the packaged-issue resolution leading to the opposite judgment as a second choice, it is possible to generate both the forward and backward cycles. After illustrating how the same phenomenon arises in *Miller*, we will then consider how outcome voting effectively avoids these lurking intransitivities.

2. Miller *Revisited: Narrowing the Issues to*
Reveal a Lurking Intransitivity

We are now ready to revisit *Miller,* this time by narrowing the issues to reveal
the lurking intransivity. Recall that in table 1.1,[36] I summarized the five *Miller*
opinions based upon each of the four issues that one or more of the writing
justices deemed dispositive in their analyses. We can now simplify *Miller* to
reveal the characteristic features of multidimensionality and asymmetry. In
Miller, five camps of justices raised four potentially dispositive issues, each
listed in table 1.1: standing, the choice of substantive test, whether that test
is satisfied, and separation of powers. Having now identified the characteristic features that generate a voting anomaly, we can simplify the presentation
by reducing the number of voting camps to three and the number of dispositive issues to two.

Recall that in *Miller,* the justices who reached the merits of the underlying constitutional challenge were required to choose whether to apply
heightened scrutiny or a laxer test in assessing the merits of the father's equal
protection challenge to the Immigration and Nationality Act, which the
daughter raised on his behalf. All of the justices who concluded that the relevant test was laxer than heightened scrutiny concluded that the test was met,
and all of the justices who instead concluded that the relevant test was heightened scrutiny concluded that the test was not met. For those justices who
addressed these issues, therefore, the choice of test was dispositive of the
merits of the underlying claim. Thus, the decision to apply the laxer test was
equivalent to holding that the test was met, while the decision to apply heightened scrutiny was equivalent to holding that the test was not met. As a result,
issues B and C from table 1.1 (representing the choice of test and the issue
whether the chosen test is met) can now be combined into the single issue
of which test applies.

Recall also that only Justice Scalia (joined by Justice Thomas) addressed
the issue whether separation of powers prevented a federal court from conferring citizenship upon petitioner even if the challenged INA provision were
held to violate the Fifth Amendment due process clause. We can further simplify the presentation by collapsing this issue into the choice of substantive
test. While Justice Scalia concluded that petitioner had standing to raise her
own claim and that of her father, he provided no indication that a contrary
resolution on the separation of powers issue would have changed his outcome
vote. As a result, we can reasonably assume that had Justice Scalia addressed
the issue of which substantive test applies, he would have selected the laxer
test and voted to uphold the statute on the grounds that the test was met.*

---

*Alternatively, one can defend the assumption in the text on the ground that it is more
conservative than the alternative. I do not mean this in an ideological sense. Instead
by conservative I mean that I am assuming a set of conditions that render the possibility of a cycle *less likely* to occur. The opposite assumption, namely that had Scalia
addressed the merits, he would have applied heightened scrutiny and voted to strike

Table 3.2. *Miller v. Albright* **Revisited**

	Petitioner Lacks Standing	Petitioner Has Standing
Laxer test		(A) Stevens, Rehnquist, *Scalia, Thomas*
Heightened scrutiny	(C) O'Connor, Kennedy	(B) Ginsburg, Breyer, Souter

Based upon these assumptions, table 3.2 presents the two critical issue dimensions in *Miller* and further reveals the asymmetrical nature of the underlying judicial preferences.

Two groups of justices take position A, represented in the upper right box, which results in the denial of relief. Justice Stevens (joined by Rehnquist) concluded that petitioner had standing and that the laxer substantive test applied (which implies that the test was met). Justice Scalia (joined by Thomas) also concluded that petitioner had standing, but resolved the case on separation of powers grounds. The italics indicate that while he took a different approach, his analysis was the functional equivalent to selecting the laxer substantive test (again implying that the test was met). Justices Ginsburg, Breyer, and Souter took position B, concluding that petitioner had standing and that the relevant test was heightened scrutiny (which implies that the test was not met). Finally, Justice O'Connor (joined by Kennedy) took position C, concluding that petitioner lacked standing to raise her father's due process challenge, but that if she had standing the relevant test would have been heightened scrutiny (which implies that the test would not have been met). We can now expose the conditions that give rise to the lurking intransitivity in the case. With the exception of Justices Scalia and Thomas, all justices implicitly assumed that if petitioner had standing to raise her father's challenge, and if the relevant test was heightened scrutiny, the challenged INA provision should have been struck down. The bolded lower right box represents those justices who agreed to both conditions that were necessary to ruling in petitioner's favor. While separate majorities agreed to each of those preconditions to striking down the statute, with the Stevens, Scalia, and Ginsburg camps (A and B, totaling seven justices) agreeing that petitioner had standing to raise her father's claim, and the Ginsburg and O'Connor

---

the challenged INA provision down, would have provided two independent bases for intuiting cyclical preferences in *Miller,* the first involving Justice O'Connor (joined by Kennedy), and the second involving Justice Scalia (joined by Thomas). Both would have achieved the opposite outcome vote had they reached the underlying merits, which they avoided based upon their standing and separation of powers analyses, respectively. To illustrate the voting anomaly, I do not need to make this assumption with respect to Scalia, who, in contrast with Justice O'Connor, gave no indication that he would have switched his vote under these conditions. As a result, I have set out assumptions that operate against the possibility of a cycle based upon Scalia's vote.

camps (B and C, totaling five justices) agreeing that the appropriate test was heightened scrutiny, which was not met, a separate majority, composed of the Stevens, Scalia, and O'Connor camps (A and C, totaling six justices) voted to deny petitioner her requested relief. Because only a minority of justices, those in the lower right box, agreed to both necessary and sufficient conditions to striking the provision down, the Court ruled against the petitioner.

As before, the underlying asymmetry, in which those in the upper right and lower left boxes resolved the issues along both dimensions in opposite fashion, but voted for the same judgment, allows us to generate reasonable assumptions to reveal a possible forward or backward voting cycle. Assume that Justice O'Connor (joined by Kennedy) reasons that if forced to choose among the remaining two options as a second choice, she would prefer the Ginsburg/Breyer position, which would send a clear signal that sex-based distinctions based upon overbroad characterizations about men and women will not survive constitutional scrutiny. If so, her preferences are CBA. Further assume that Justices Ginsburg and Breyer reason that while they strongly disagree with both the O'Connor and Stevens analyses and outcomes, they are more concerned about denying standing than they are about the substantive legal test. If so, their preferences are BAC. Finally, assume that Justice Stevens is more concerned about denying petitioner relief than he is with the dispositive rationale. If so, his ordinal rankings are ACB. These, of course, are paradigmatic cyclical preferences. As in *Kassel,* one can posit a cycle in the reverse direction as well. Assume that Justice O'Connor is more concerned about denying petitioner relief than with the choice of dispositive rationale. If so, her preferences are CAB. Further assume that Justice Stevens is more concerned with ensuring that qualified persons receive standing than whether this particular litigant is denied relief and even with whether the test applied in this unusual case is intermediate scrutiny. If so, his preferences are ABC. Finally, assume that Justices Ginsburg and Breyer are more concerned with the choice of substantive test than with the question of standing. If so, their preferences are BCA. Again, these are paradigmatic cyclical preferences.

D.   Outcome Voting as a Cycle-Breaking Rule

Because the justices are not called upon to rank preferences over remaining rationales ordinally, cases like *Kassel* and *Miller* do not allow us to actually prove that cyclical preferences exist. As the above analysis reveals, however, the characteristic features of multidimensionality and asymmetry do allow us to generate two sets of plausible ordinal rankings over the three alternatives, which if selected, would generate an actual cycle. The question then arises how Supreme Court voting rules, and specifically outcome voting, limit the justices in their choice among these sets of conceivable ordinal rankings over the combined issue resolutions. The answer is that outcome voting holds off limits those rank orderings that express contingent outcome preferences. In the preceding analysis of *Kassel,* in which I generated a forward cycle, for example, outcome voting holds Justice Powell's ordinal ranking, ABC, off limits because, in effect, Powell, whose ideal point is to strike down the statute based upon a more stringent substantive test, ranks second Justice Rehnquist's preferred rationale producing the opposite judgment (to sustain the statute), to Justice Brennan's contrary rationale producing the same judgment (to strike down the statute). Similarly, in the preceding analysis of *Miller*, in which I also generated a forward cycle, Justice O'Connor's rankings would suffer the same deficiency of rendering her outcome vote contingent upon which rationale predominates. While there is nothing illogical about either of these hypothetical ordinal rankings, or those underlying the hypothetical backward cycles in each case, the outcome voting rule fails to credit any such expressions of contingency, thereby preventing a justice from conditioning his outcome vote upon whether his preferred rationale either gains majority support, thus establishing a precedent, or states the holding on the narrowest grounds.[37]

As a general rule, outcome voting effectively forces each justice to state his first-choice outcome based upon a rationale—defined as a packaged set of resolutions of the underlying dispositive issues—that he is either willing to sign onto or to write separately.[38] In so voting, however, a justice who agrees to the majority resolution of the case judgment cannot be assured that his rationale will state the holding for the Court. In contrast with issue voting, which would allow justices to state their preferred resolution of underlying case issues without binding themselves on the judgment, outcome voting forces a binding, and noncontingent, vote on the judgment, and produces as the Court's holding that package of issue resolutions, consistent with the case judgment, which predominates either as a majority winner or as a dominant second choice. And it requires justices to so bind themselves even if the opinion that ultimately states the holding does so based upon a rationale that they would rank lower than another opinion producing a contrary judgment.

The analysis thus far reveals that outcome voting has the characteristic feature of preventing justices from implicitly selecting among all conceivable ordinal rankings over available rationales in a given case. In the technical language of social choice theory, outcome voting is a rule that relaxes the range criterion. By preventing the justices from issuing their preferred resolutions of underlying dispositive issues in contingent form, outcome voting prevents the Court from revealing actual voting cycles in which no single rationale is necessarily preferred by a majority to any other rationale, or even to the status quo. While legislative rules and practices generally allow inaction when such preferences arise, in the Supreme Court, outcome voting forges an outcome by demanding only a de minimis consensus, focused solely on the judgment, even if there is no consensus on a dominant rationale.

The analysis can be recast from an Arrovian framework in which we consider the restriction upon hypothetical ordinal rankings over combined issue resolutions, thus relaxing range, to a Condorcet analysis in which we focus on the limits upon conceivable binary comparisons. By failing to allow the justices to rank all available options in any order, outcome voting effectively disallows unlimited binary comparisons over issues and outcomes. As a result, outcome voting fails to satisfy the Condorcet criterion. Specifically, outcome voting effectively prevents a voting path in which the justices first consider separate majority resolutions on each identified dispositive issue, namely rational basis and the laxer evidentiary rule, which would lead to the result of upholding the statute; followed by a separate majority resolution on the binary choice of outcome, leading to the result of striking down the statute; followed by renewed separate majority resolutions on each identified dispositive issue, leading again to the result of upholding the statute; and so on. Instead, the rule vindicates the majority resolution on the most often binary choice to affirm or reverse, even if a hypothetical decision path focusing on the separate collective resolutions of identified dispositive issues would lead to the opposite judgment.

The foregoing analysis also explains why the Supreme Court, given its obligation to dispose collectively of those cases properly before it,[39] again in a de minimis manner, employs a non-Condorcet-producing decisional rule. What it does not explain, however, is why the Court employs the particular non-Condorcet-producing rule of outcome voting, given that both issue voting (in which there is no final outcome vote) and outcome voting (in which there are no binding votes on underlying dispositive issues) could, in theory, ensure a judgment even in cases like *Kassel* and *Miller.* As the next section will show, social choice provides the critical framework with which to explain not only the Supreme Court's evolution away from the Condorcet criterion, but also the Court's choice of the particular non-Condorcet-producing rule of outcome voting.

III. A Social Choice Analysis of Issue Identification: The Selection of Outcome over Issue Voting

A. *National Mutual Insurance Co. v. Tidewater Transfer Co.*

To explain the Supreme Court's evolution toward outcome, rather than issue, voting, it will be helpful to introduce another case that produced a *Miller-* and *Kassel*-like voting anomaly. In *National Mutual Insurance Co. v. Tidewater Transfer Co.,*[40] the Supreme Court addressed the constitutionality of a federal statute granting diversity jurisdiction to federal district courts in cases between a citizen of a state and a citizen of the District of Columbia. Several commentators have observed that while the Court upheld the diversity-granting statute in a five-to-four vote, the opinions reveal that separate majorities supported resolutions of the two underlying issues in a manner that together produced a logical voting path leading to the dissenting result.[41] The case presented four separate opinions, a plurality of three, written by Justice Jackson; a concurrence for two, written by Justice Rutledge; and two separate dissents for two each, written by Justices Vinson and Frankfurter. As in *Kassel,* the *Tidewater* justices distilled the case to two major issues: (A) Under Article III, is a citizen of the District of Columbia a citizen of a state? and

(B) does Article I provide Congress with the power to confer jurisdiction upon federal courts beyond the limits of Article III?[42] The opinions reveal that all of the writing justices agreed that the federal statute is constitutional if the answer to *either* issue A *or* issue B is yes. The statute is unconstitutional only if the answers to both questions are no. Thus, a negative response to each question is a necessary, but insufficient, condition, to striking down the jurisdiction-conferring statute.

For a plurality, Justice Jackson, joined by Black and Burton, concluded that Chief Justice John Marshall's holding in *Hepburn & Dundas v. Ellzay,*[43] that citizens of the District of Columbia are not citizens of a state under Article III, is binding, but that Congress is not limited by Article III in conferring jurisdictional authority upon the federal courts. Instead, Congress, pursuant to Article I, can confer additional responsibilities upon federal courts generally, as it has with those sitting in the District of Columbia, even if doing so extends beyond Article III's diversity requirement.[44] Thus, Justice Jackson determined that the answer to issue A was no, but that the answer to issue B was yes. In concurrence, Justice Rutledge, joined by Murphy, determined that while *Hepburn* held that citizens of the District of Columbia were not citizens of a state for purposes of Article III diversity jurisdiction,[45] *Hepburn* should be overruled because it produces an unfair result not dictated by an original understanding of the purpose of the Article III diversity requirement. Rutledge further determined that Article I does not provide Congress with general jurisdiction-granting power beyond the limits set out in Article III. Rutledge therefore determined that the answer to issue A was yes, but that the answer to issue B was no. Writing in dissent, Justice Vinson, joined by Douglas, concluded that while Article I provides jurisdiction-granting authority to federal courts in the District of Columbia, for all other federal courts, the jurisdiction-granting limits are set out in Article III.[46] In addition, based upon the need for a strict interpretation in this context, Vinson determined that Article III's express language, which limits federal diversity jurisdiction to cases between citizens of different states, was controlling. Finally, writing a separate dissent, Justice Frankfurter, joined by Reed, agreed that for federal courts outside of the District of Columbia, the jurisdiction-granting limits are set by Article III, not by Article I.[47] In addition, Frankfurter determined that based upon the contemporaneous interpretation by Justice Marshall and others and the need for a consistent application of the word *State* as used throughout the Constitution, federal diversity jurisdiction must be limited to cases between citizens of different states.

Table 3.3 summarizes the positions of the justices and reveals the *Tidewater* voting anomaly. In this case, the bolded upper left box indicates the two necessary and sufficient conditions for striking down the jurisdiction-granting statute, namely that D.C. citizens are not state citizens for diversity purposes and that Congress is limited by Article III in conferring jurisdiction. While separate majorities conclude that D.C. citizens are not state citizens for purposes of diversity jurisdiction (the upper left and lower left boxes) and that Congress is limited to Article III in conferring jurisdiction upon the fed-

Table 3.3. The Voting Anomaly in *Tidewater*

	Issue A: D.C. citizens are not state citizens for diversity purposes	D.C. citizens are state citizens for diversity purposes
Issue B: Congress is limited by Art. III in conferring jurisdiction	Vinson, Douglas; Frankfurter, Reed	Rutledge, Murphy
Congress is not limited by Art. III in conferring jurisdiction	Jackson, Black, Burton	

eral courts (the upper left and upper right boxes), leading to the logical outcome that the statute should be struck down, only a minority of the Court, appearing in the bolded box, accepts both necessary and sufficient propositions leading to that result. As a result, a separate majority composed of the Rutledge (upper right) and Jackson (lower left) camps succeeded in upholding the statute on the ground that one of the two necessary preconditions to striking it down is not met. Moreover, as occurred in *Miller* and *Kassel,* two groups of justices in *Tidewater,* represented by Jackson and Rutledge, reach precisely opposite resolutions along each issue dimension but achieve the same judgment vote. *Tidewater* thus presents another illustration of multi-dimensionality and asymmetry.

In the presentations of *Miller, Kassel,* and *Tidewater,* I have thus far assumed that the statements of underlying issues in the justices' opinions control their individual dispositions of the case, even if the collective resolution of one or more of such issues is thwarted for the Court as a whole. Beyond explaining the demand for internal consistency, driven by reputational concerns,[48] I have not explained what motivates justices to identify the issues that they deem dispositive. One critical deficiency with issue-voting proposals, as the next subpart will show, is that those advancing them tend to assume that governing issues exist independently of the Supreme Court's case decision-making rule. In fact, however, a social choice analysis of individual case decision making reveals the economic forces that would drive alternative issue statements under outcome- and issue-voting regimes. In comparing outcome and issue voting, therefore, it is important to consider not only whether those rules vindicate or thwart collective determinations of underlying case issues, but also, and more importantly, how each rule affects the manner in which those very governing issues are framed.

In an analysis of *Tidewater,* Professor John Rogers, in arguing against issue-voting proposals, asserted that the case presented a minimum of seventeen issues.[49] If so, even when faced with a *Tidewater*-like voting anomaly, Rogers argued, issue voting would infuse potentially greater indeterminacy than it is intended to cure. In reply, Professors David Post and Steven Salop, who advocate issue voting, argued in favor of a "stopping rule," which they claimed would produce the two governing issues identified in table 3.2 in *Tidewater*.[50] For present purposes, it is neither necessary to consider all seventeen issues, which Professor Rogers claims are lurking in *Tidewater*,[51] nor to consider whether the stopping rule, which Post and Salop advance, would succeed in reducing that list to two. Instead, using social choice theory, I will show that current Supreme Court decision-making rules have evolved in a manner that produces a more stable set of governing issues than either Rogers suggests or than would exist under issue voting. In fact, I will argue that under the governing outcome-voting regime, but not under issue voting, Supreme Court justices have a strong incentive to produce as definitive, in such cases as *Miller, Kassel,* and *Tidewater,* the dominant issues described in the above discussions of each case, at the same time that the present regime thwarts the Court's majority resolution of those issues. Rather than solving the apparent paradox that these cases produce, issue voting would invite strategic statements of issues intended to create favorable voting paths, which, in turn, would infuse greater indeterminacy into Supreme Court decision making.

To explain the stabilizing effect of outcome voting in defining the governing issues in actual cases, we must first consider the destabilizing effects of the proposed issue-voting regime. Because the issues in *Tidewater* are disjunctive, meaning that a contrary majority resolution of either issue would produce a result opposite the actual holding, I will use that case to illustrate the unique problems that issue-voting rules are capable of posing. While the various justices in *Tidewater* distilled that case to two principal issues, represented as issues A and B in table 3.3, it is relatively easy to subdivide one or more of those issues into subissues such that the relationship between the resolution of the two subissues and of the larger issue possesses the characteristic features of multidimensionality and asymmetry. If so, the subdivision simply embeds the lurking intransitivity at a deeper level in the case.

The following subdivision of issue A, "Are D.C. citizens state citizens under Article III?" while admittedly hypothetical, is based upon discussions from the various *Tidewater* opinions. Issue A can now be subdivided into subissue A-1, "Absent a clearly expressed intent of the framers, should the judiciary interpret the jurisdictional provision of Article III to avoid unfair results, including preventing diversity jurisdiction in cases between citizens of the District of Columbia and citizens of states?"; and A-2, "If so, did the framers clearly express an intent to deny diversity jurisdiction in this context?" If we assume an issue-voting regime, then the outcome of *Tidewater,* based upon the majority resolutions of issues A and B, would be to strike down the federal statute. While we do not know how each of the justices would have decided these potential subissues, it is not difficult to hypothesize a voting lineup parallel to that governing the larger relationship between the outcome vote and issues A and B, this time with respect to issue A and subissues A-1 and A-2. Because issues A and B are disjunctive, meaning that a favorable ruling on either results in upholding the statute, if the further division of issue A into issues A-1 and A-2, as represented in table 3.4, produces an outcome opposite that for issue A, then the effect of the deeper subdivision would be to restore the original outcome vote to sustain the statute.

Writing for a plurality, Justice Jackson inferred from the language of the Constitution an intent to deny Congress the authority to create diversity jurisdiction between citizens of states and citizens of the District of Columbia because allowing such jurisdiction would produce inconsistent meanings for the word *State*.[52] While this supports a finding that the framers might have intended to prevent diversity jurisdiction in this context, if a majority determined that absent clear evidence of such an intent, Article III should not be construed to prevent this unfair result, the same evidence might well fall short. If so, Justice Jackson, even if he rejects the higher hurdle to honoring the framers' intent, might vote yes on issue A-2, but no on issue A-1. Justice Rutledge, writing a concurrence for two, determined that *Hepburn* was incorrect and should be overruled in part because it produced an unfair result.[53] He further stated that the framers simply failed to consider whether Article III was intended to prevent Congress from conferring jurisdiction in this context. Based upon this opinion, we can infer that Rutledge would vote yes on both A-1 and A-2. Justice Vinson, also writing in dissent for two, stated that fairness considerations should not trump the intent of the framers.[54] We might infer from this analysis that the basis for his decision was an understanding that the framers intended not to allow diversity in this context, but that without evidence of such an intent, fairness could be allowed to dictate a contrary interpretation of Article III. If so, he would vote yes on A-1, but no on A-2. Finally, Justice Frankfurter stated that he did not think that limiting diversity jurisdiction to cases with citizens of different states unfair because "no great public interest or libertarian principle is at stake."[55] He further stated that, had the framers intended a contrary result, they could have expressed it clearly. Because Frankfurter reasoned that denying diversity jurisdiction does not produce an unfair result, and that doing so is consistent with the clearly expressed intent of the framers, given their ability to express themselves, we can infer that the question of fairness is relevant to Frankfurter's analysis and might have been controlling absent what, for him, was a clearly expressed contrary intent. If so, Frankfurter, like Vinson, would vote yes on A-1, but no on A-2.

Table 3.4. Subissue Voting on Issue A in *Tidewater*

	Subissue A-1: Must avoid unfair results absent clear intent	Need not avoid unfair results absent clear intent
Issue A-2: Framers did not clearly intend this unfair result	Rutledge, Murphy	Jackson, Black, Burton
Framers clearly intended this result	Vinson, Douglas, Frankfurter, Reed	

If these votes are tallied on a subissue-by-subissue basis, we see that Jackson (for three) alone votes no on A-1, producing a majority of six voting yes, and that a majority of five, composed of Jackson (for three) and Rutledge (for two), vote yes on A-2, with Vinson (for two) and Frankfurter (for two) voting no. If so, then switching to issue voting creates a deeper potential intransitivity, such that by forcing the justices to go one further level down, below issues A and B, Justices Jackson and Vinson can create an alternative favorable voting path that produces the very same result achieved in *Tidewater* under outcome voting. Table 3.4 summarizes the preceding discussion.

In this illustration, the bolded box indicates that only a minority agrees to both propositions necessary to conclude that D.C. citizens are state citizens for diversity purposes, even though separate majorities would produce that result by subissue voting. Thus, table 3.4 reveals one majority, composed of Rutledge and Murphy (upper left), and Vinson, Douglas, Frankfurter, and Reed (lower left), which concludes that the Court must avoid unfair results absent a clear contrary intent, and another majority, composed of Rutledge and Murphy (upper left) and Jackson, Black, and Burton (upper right), which concludes that the framers lacked a clear intent to reach that result. This leads to the logical conclusion that D.C. citizens are state citizens for diversity purposes. And yet, a third majority, composed of the Jackson, Black, and Burton (upper right) and Vinson, Douglas, Frankfurter, and Reed (lower left), concludes that D.C. citizens are not state citizens because one of the two necessary preconditions to a contrary determination is not met. Combining tables 3.2 and 3.3 reveals a cycle such that (1) under outcome voting, the result is to sustain the statute; (2) under issue voting, the result is to strike down the statute; and (3) under subissue voting, the result is again to sustain the statute, thus restoring the original outcome vote.

Admittedly, to contrive the apparent cycle from uphold (outcome voting) to strike (issue voting) to uphold (subissue voting), based upon three different issue levels in *Tidewater*, I took some interpretive liberties with the various written opinions. The point of the exercise, however, is not to demonstrate what would actually occur in a given case under the various voting rules. It is, instead, to demonstrate that the same potential relationship between outcomes and issues that has given rise to proposals to switch, on either a case-by-case or across-the-board basis, from outcome voting to issue voting, can pervade as well the relationships between issues and subissues, thus re-creating the very anomaly that the proposed rule is intended to cure.[56] Indeed, within constitutional law, and probably many other areas of law as well, most articulated issues are actually composites of two or more subissues that the Supreme Court has previously resolved.[57]

The phenomenon that one or more major issues can be subdivided into subissues to produce a deeper voting cycle raises several questions. First, how are issues defined in a given case under the present outcome-voting regime? Second, how would they be defined under a proposed issue-voting regime? And finally, in the event of an impasse with respect to defining the issues in a given case, how would such disputes be resolved? Answering each of these questions, in the next subsection, will help to explain the Supreme Court's ultimate choice of outcome voting.

B. The Unexpected Intricacies of Issue Voting

Under issue voting, justices seeking to avoid the case result produced by the division of an outcome vote into two or more first-level issue votes would have two alternatives. Assuming agreement on what the first-level issues are, if the Court's collective resolution would produce an unsatisfactory result, justices would have an incentive to divide issues further down to produce a more favorable voting path, one leading to the desired result. Generating a deeper intransivity within a single case is admittedly complicated by the need to hypothesize a subdivision that meets the fairly stringent requirement of asymmetry. As demonstrated in chapter 4, however, generating intransitivities becomes easier when the body of cases is expanded. Thus viewed, outcome voting should be understood not only to limit strategic issue identification within single cases, but also as a vehicle that tempers path manipulation by both litigants and deciding justices over a larger number of cases. Of course, in an issue-voting regime, those who would prefer an opposite outcome to that which results from a clever issue division would have the incentive either to resist such efforts or to divide even further down in an effort to restore a favorable voting path. Some rule would then need to be developed to determine how to resolve such disputes.* I would suggest that there are four potential voting regimes that might emerge in an attempt to resolve the resulting issue indeterminacy, which I will label (1) the issue war of attrition; (2) collective voting on issue levels; (3) issue-setting power in one or more justices; and (4) strategic voting. For the analysis to follow, until we consider the possibility of strategic-voting, assume that at whatever level issues are defined, the justices vote consistently with their sincere assessments of the merits of presented alternatives, rather than trying to vote strategically in an effort to generate a favorable voting path. In the language of social choice, the justices are assumed to adhere to Arrovian independence. As we will see,

---

*The analysis further explains why the Supreme Court does not employ Condorcet-consistent rules, meaning those rules that will select available Condorcet winners, but that do not cycle when no Condorcet winner is available. In contrast with the simpler Condorcet-producing rules, Condorcet-consistent rules require for their implementation a matrix of paired comparisons over all conceivable pairs and, therefore, would require in the context of Supreme Court decision making that all potentially dispositive issues be identified in advance. *See supra* chapter 2 (providing illustration). In addition to the general complexity of administering such rules, *see* T. Nicolaus Tideman, Collective Decisions And Voting, chapter 13 (unpublished manuscript, on file with author) (comparing various sets of decisional rules and demonstrating the administrative complexity of those that are Condorcet consistent), in the context of Supreme Court decision making, such a regime would invite the very strategic identification of issues that outcome voting largely avoids.

principled voting in this context does not necessarily imply that justices will base their assessments of the optimal issue *level* on the merits of presented alternative issue levels. (In discussing the fourth voting regime identified above, I will relax even the limited constraint of Arrovian independence.)

1. The Issue War of Attrition

By continuing to divide down in an effort to prevent the other side's preferred voting path from emerging, the likely result would be to draw issues at *either* too great a level of generality *or* at too narrow a level of specificity. While it might at first appear paradoxical that the same voting regime could produce seemingly opposite results, in fact, these two results are manifestations of the same phenomenon. As justices move past the most persuasive presentation of issues in a given case, they are forced either to look to increasingly fact-specific distinctions that can be relied upon to avoid disfavored results, or to articulate issues at a level of generality that avoids the natural consequence of a merits determination of a more credible presentation of the issues. The former presentation of issues can, for example, take the form of "Should the Constitution be construed to avoid unfair results?" or "Should we employ originalism or textualism in constitutional interpretation?"[58]

Alternatively, justices confronted with the possibility of an unfavorable voting path might try to avoid this result by seizing either fact-specific or seemingly disingenuous distinctions. Indeed, even under existing rules, the seeming pretzel logic of many Supreme Court decisions in recent years has likely emerged for just this reason.* The creation of voting paths in the direction of

---

*For two of my very favorite examples, recall Justice O'Connor's analysis in New York v. United States, 505 U.S. 144 (1992); *see supra* at 61–63 (discussing Justice O'Connor's *New York* analysis), in which she presented the history of the rejection of the Articles of Confederation in favor of the Constitution as motivated by the desire to *prevent* federal coercion of the states, when the historical record demonstrates that the real difficulty under the Articles was Congress's inability *to control* the states in the emerging trade wars among them and to raise revenue from the states to support the fledgling federal government. For a related analysis, see Erik M. Jensen & Jonathan L. Entin, *Commandeering, The Tenth Amendment, and the Federal Requisition Power: New York v. United States Revisited,* 15 CONST. COMMENTARY 355 (1998). Without her creative gloss on this historical transformation from the Articles to the Constitution, however, O'Connor would have faced great difficulty in restoring some Tenth Amendment limits at the margins of commerce clause jurisprudence in light of the Supreme Court's seeming capitulation of such limits, most prominently in Garcia v. San Antonio Transit Authority, 469 U.S. 528 (1985) (upholding application of federal minimum wage law to local transit authority, and overturning National League of Cities v. Usery, 426 U.S. 833 (1976)).

Recall also the joint opinion's effort in Planned Parenthood of Southeastern Pennsylvania v. Casey, 505 U.S. 833 (1992); *see supra* at 16–23 (discussing joint authors' stare decisis analysis), to present the abandonment of Lochner v. New York, 198 U.S. 45 (1905), and Plessy v. Ferguson, 163 U.S. 537 (1896), in West Coast Hotel

excessive generality, excessive fact specificity, or creative rendition (even simple distortion) of governing historical or legal principles, results from the efforts of the justices to avoid disfavored results that would have followed from a more candid and straightforward application of precedent to the cases before them. I do not intend to suggest that considerable strategizing of this sort does not occur under present voting rules. The *New York* and *Casey* opinions obviously demonstrate otherwise. Instead, I am suggesting that the present outcome-voting regime substantially raises the cost of such strategies and thereby inhibits them relative to an issue-voting regime. As shown below, outcome voting does so by promoting adherence to the important Arrovian independence criterion, or principled decision making, among justices on the Supreme Court and federal judges generally.

2. *Collective Voting on Issue Levels*

An alternative method of trying to resolve the difficult question of governing issue levels in a given case is to allow a majority vote on that question, in addition to majority votes on the various issues that the justices agree should be dispositive. While Professors David Post and Steven Salop have posited that issue voting should be a mandatory rule,[59] Professors Lewis Kornhauser and Lawrence G. Sager have instead advocated case-by-case decision making on the governing rule in those cases that present a *Miller-, Kassel-,* or *Tidewater-*like voting anomaly.[60] Perhaps counterintuitively, the Kornhauser and Sager proposal has the potential to create even greater indeterminacy than the Post and Salop proposal, although both produce sufficient indeterminacy to explain why Supreme Court practice has evolved differently. Consider, for example, applying the Kornhauser and Sager proposal to the above presentation of *Tidewater.* Recall that based upon the three levels for potential disposition of *Tidewater,* set out in tables 3.3 and 3.4, an outcome vote produces a decision to uphold the jurisdiction-granting statute, an issue vote produces a decision to strike down the statute, and a subissue vote restores the decision to uphold the statute.

Assume that Justice Jackson, writing for a plurality, is most committed to achieving the outcome of upholding the statute, and that, as between outcome and subissue voting, both of which would achieve that result, he prefers subissue voting on the ground that it might be viewed as a precedent for favor-

---

v. Parrish, 163 U.S. 537 (1896), and Brown v. Board of Education, 163 U.S. 537 (1896), respectively, as grounded in a subsequent change in actual or perceived facts. A straightforward reading of the cases makes plain that these famous overrulings resulted, instead, from a fundamental change in the jurisprudential vision of the Supreme Court. Again, without this creative gloss on legal history, it would have been difficult to maintain that traditional principles of stare decisis, rather than an independent determination on the merits, dictated the joint authors' determination not to overrule Roe v. Wade, 410 U.S. 113 (1973).

able issue division in future cases. Jackson therefore ranks the choice of voting regimes as follows: subissue voting (uphold); outcome voting (uphold); issue voting (strike). Assume that Justice Rutledge most prefers outcome voting, but that if forced to choose between issue and subissue voting, he selects issue voting, even though it produces a contrary result. While this might appear counterintuitive, assume that he reasons that, while issue voting in this case produces a displeasing result, the effect of going down as many levels as one can conceive produces a bad precedent for future cases. If so, his ordinal ranking is outcome voting (uphold); issue voting (strike); subissue voting (uphold). Finally assume that both Vinson and Frankfurter, writing in dissent, most prefer issue voting, which produces their favored result, but that if forced to choose between the two alternative regimes, both of which will produce an undesirable result, they prefer subissue voting to outcome voting. They reason that such a vote will provide a valuable precedent for issue division in general should such a case arise in the future. Their ordinal rankings are issue voting (uphold); subissue voting (strike); outcome voting (strike). A brief review reveals that the three groups of justices, any two of which contain the requisite five votes for a majority, possess cycle-producing preferences. A rule permitting the justices to vote upon issue levels therefore has the potential to replicate the very doctrinal indeterminacy that it is intended to avoid. This is not surprising, given that the proposal expands issue dimensionality, and further introduces the possibility of asymmetry, relative to a straightforward (or even not so straightforward) determination of the merits of a given case. Any proposal that replicates cycling by expanding the dimensionality of underlying case issue space simply invites strategic behavior to avoid disfavored results, without providing a genuine cure to the pathology that the justices' substantive preferences create.

3. Issue Setting Power in One or More Justices

One seemingly obvious way to avoid the problem of strategic issue identification that would afflict the war-of-attrition and majority-voting approaches to issue identification would be to vest authority to determine the governing issue level in one or more justices in a given case. The justices could agree, for example, to let the chief justice determine the binding issue levels. This solution affords the chief justice the power to devise a voting path at odds with majority preferences. While this does not formally violate Arrovian non-dictatorship, since the chief justice cannot proceed to judgment in opposition of unanimous contrary preferences,[61] it does violate at a minimum violate the related anonymity condition from May's Theorem.[62] The anonymity condition, which May demonstrated was a central tenet of simple majority rule, demands that the outcome of the voting procedure be independent of who casts which ballot. In the Supreme Court, the chief justice is understood to be first among equals, at least with respect to voting on the case judgment. Vesting him the authority to determine governing issue levels would instead be the judicial equivalent of the infamous line in *Animal Farm,* "All animals [read: jurists] are equal, but some . . . are more equal than others."[63]

We could design a further modification that would mirror the Supreme Court rule governing the opinion assignments. In this regime, the chief justice, if in the majority, or the senior justice in the majority, if the chief justice is in dissent, would determine the level at which issues would be decided. This regime, however, would have the odd effect of reestablishing the very doctrinal incoherence that cases like *Miller, Kassel,* and *Tidewater* create. If, for example, the most senior justice voting with the majority in each of those cases sought to preserve his favored holding, he could simply define outcome voting as the relevant issue level. At that point, the issue-voting regime has not furthered the cause of providing a closer linkage between the Court's holding and the resolution of the underlying issues. Alternatively, this regime could invite a form of strategic behavior, not unlike that occasionally witnessed when Warren Burger, as chief justice, would state at conference his intent to vote with the majority, assign the opinion, and then switch to dissent.[64] Specifically, the chief justice or a justice who would otherwise be senior could initially agree to vote with the majority simply to determine the issue level. In contrast, however, with Burger's vilified tactic of strategically posturing himself solely to assign an opinion, then switching his vote, this tactic would allow the chief justice to increase the likelihood of his preferred outcome in a manner that would make his strategic manipulation less obvious and thus less prone to criticism.

Of course, this all assumes considerably greater knowledge (and candor) than is likely under such a regime. The voting conferences might well turn into strategy sessions in which all votes would be expressed in contingent form, for example, "I vote to affirm if the dispositive issues are A and B, but to reverse, if instead, the dispositive issues are C and D or if issue A is subdivided into issues A-1 and A-2." Social choice amply reveals the potential indeterminacy under such a regime.

4. *Stability through Strategic Voting*

The final, and perhaps most obvious, potential solution to the problems raised in each of the above attempted fixes to issue voting would simply be to invite strategic voting among the justices. To be clear, some strategic voting already occurs, albeit generally in the form of moves toward the median position on the Court.[65] The form of strategic voting I am discussing here is different in kind. Arrovian independence is relaxed when justices vote inconsistently with their preferred merits resolution to secure a superior voting path or trade votes to secure favored outcomes over a larger number of issues or cases. So understood, moves from ideal points, meaning first-choice resolutions of underlying issues as expressed in conference votes, to accommodationist positions needed to elevate the median position to majority status, do not violate Arrovian independence. More importantly, introducing vote trading itself produces several problems. First, strategic voting does not uniformly prevent cycling; sometimes it simply replicates cycling at a different stage of decision making.[66] Alternatively, however, strategic voting can induce stability, in favor of results that sometimes thwart the Condorcet criterion, but which account for disparate intensities of preference.[67] The more important question, however, is not the probability of inducing stability under strategic voting, but rather, the normative merit of a regime in which important principles of law, especially of constitutional law, are determined through the strategic maneuvering of justices. My own position is that this is an indefensible method of determining the substantive content of constitutional doctrine, and of legal outcomes generally, and that it is antithetical to the core distinction between legislatures and courts.[68]

Not only does strategic voting, as a means of producing stable constitutional doctrine, represent a normative affront to traditional notions about the manner in which judges and justices should go about their business, but also, as I will demonstrate in the remainder of this chapter and in the next, it further undermines numerous practices that have evolved in a manner that renders such behavior more difficult in courts, relative to legislatures. Such process-based rules and practices as opinion writing, outcome voting, the narrowest grounds rule, stare decisis, and standing operate, individually and in combination, to promote principled decision making in the federal courts, and to preserve the kind of strategic decision making discussed here in legislatures, including Congress, where it is presumed legitimate. Moreover, because strategic voting could lead to one set of substantive outcomes in a given period and an altogether different set of substantive outcomes in another period, it would greatly diminish the value of judicial decisions in promoting the rule of law. Before discussing these various features of judicial decision making, we will first consider how the present regime of outcome voting, in contrast with issue voting, promotes principled issue identification.

C.   How Outcome Voting Promotes Principled Issue Identification

In contrast with issue voting, outcome voting greatly reduces, although it does not entirely eliminate, the likelihood of an impasse in resolving actual cases. And it does so while encouraging principled, rather than strategic, statements of issues by the justices. With one minor exception, namely cases in which separate minorities on the Court each support one of three potential judgments—affirm, reverse, or remand—and in which none of the judgments has majority support, outcome voting produces a result in virtually all cases.[69] Specifically, outcome voting forces an odd number (a noncoincidental evolutionary feature, given that an even number would not ensure the same result) to select between two alternatives, affirm or reverse. When faced with only two possibilities, provided an odd number of decision makers vote, and the decision is by simple majority rule, a collective outcome is virtually guaranteed. Indeed, even on the rare occasion when one of the justices does not participate in a given case and the remaining justices are evenly split, ensuring an outcome is fairly easy. In actual practice, the Supreme Court has solved this potential problem by employing a default rule that an evenly split Court results in an affirmance without precedential value.[70]

The fact that outcome voting ensures an outcome, however, does not prove that the outcome that it produces is normatively defensible. The normative soundness of outcome voting most obviously is drawn into question in cases like *Miller, Kassel,* and *Tidewater,* in which there is a divergence between the Court's collective resolution of underlying dispositive issues and its holding. In fact, as the next part, which discusses the narrowest grounds doctrine, set out in *Marks v. United States,*[71] will show, this divergence arises within a small margin of cases along a spectrum with four principal categories.[72] With a rare exception,[73] in cases producing a majority opinion, the same majority of the Court agrees to both the outcome and the rationale consistent with that outcome. Plurality cases can be subdivided into three general categories, of which we have seen one, those involving a multidimensional issue spectrum and asymmetrical preferences. In the remaining two categories, cases with a unidimensional issue spectrum and cases with a multidimensional issue spectrum and symmetrical preferences, the narrowest grounds doctrine produces a stable holding, which is a Condorcet winner. In these two categories of plurality opinions, while a majority does not agree to a single dominant rationale as a first choice, if there is a Condorcet winner among the written opinions, the narrowest grounds opinion is likely to be it. It is only in the very limited category of cases with multidimensionality and asymmetrical preferences that the narrowest grounds doctrine produces an impasse. In this category, there simply is no Condorcet-winning opinion and, as a result, no rule is capable of ensuring a stable solution linking the judgment to a dominant rationale. The final category is three-judgment cases in which none of the three potential judgments—affirm, reverse, or remand—commands the support of a majority. These cases have been resolved in practice by individual vote switches, generally from an alternative judgment toward a remand, thus producing a majority disposition.

While outcome voting produces an occasionally problematic result, it is the least-bad alternative not only because it alone ensures a collective outcome (setting aside three-judgment cases, a category for which no rule could ensure a collective judgment), but also because in all cases, including those in which it has the potential to mask cyclical preferences over packaged-issue resolutions, it produces significant benefits for the legal system as a whole. Specifically, in contrast with issue voting, outcome voting encourages opinion-writing justices to craft their opinions in a manner that presents the most compelling statement of issues, based upon a careful assessment of the merits of the case, as the primary means of assembling majority support, rather than by trying to devise a set of issues and issue levels that will produce a favorable voting path. Outcome voting does so by effectively divorcing the statement of issues and the level at which issues are determined from the case outcome. Provided that a majority agrees on nothing more than the binary choice of outcome, that majority will control the outcome even if each justice writes a seriatim opinion taking a completely different approach to the case, and even if, as in the hypothetical based upon *Kassel*,[74] some of those voting consistently with the chosen outcome would have preferred a packaged-issue resolution producing the opposite outcome over an alternative packaged-issue resolution producing the same outcome. If we assume, therefore, that justices are motivated by a desire to have their jurisprudential approaches reflected in case law, outcome voting produces an incentive to write opinions in a manner that is most likely to persuade a majority to join. Otherwise, if, for example, the opinion writer states the issues in the case too broadly, he risks losing not only a majority, but also the opportunity to state the Court's holding.[75] Under *Marks*, if one or more defecting justices prevents the writing justice from retaining a majority and if the defectors further produce an opinion resolving the case on a narrower ground, the result will be to seize the power to control the rule of law announced in the case.

Outcome voting, coupled with the *Marks* doctrine, therefore produces an incentive among the justices to provide the most persuasive statement of the issues in the case as a precondition to using the case as a vehicle for announcing the rule of law. In this manner, judicial self-interest and the interests of constitutional process coincide in that more persuasive, and more stable, statements of issues, as opposed to statements dominated by strategic concerns, ultimately inure to the benefit of the legal system as a whole. And indeed, sounder statements of legal issues even benefit the legal system in cases like *Miller, Kassel,* and *Tidewater.* They do so by providing critical guidance to judges and litigants about important differences in the jurisprudential approaches of members of the deciding Court.

If one takes the long view, instead of focusing solely on the disparity between outcome and rationale in a particular case, outcome voting furthers at least two important objectives of constitutional process. First, outcome voting ensures outcomes in all but three-remedy cases and provides guidance to courts and litigants based upon careful judgment, rather than clever strategy. Second, while issue voting produces the incentive among justices to divide down until issues are stated too broadly or too narrowly to provide substantial guidance about the meaning of the Court's holding, outcome voting produces the opposite incentive, namely to define up in an effort to present the case in the most persuasive manner in an effort to get colleagues to join. With that background, we are now ready to consider what may well be among the most important, and most neglected,[76] cases about constitutional process, namely *Marks v. United States.*

IV. The Narrowest Grounds Doctrine: A Social Choice Perspective

A. *Marks v. United States*

In *Marks v. United States*,[77] Justice Powell produced a remarkable (and short) opinion, holding that the Fifth Amendment due process rights of petitioners, who had been convicted of distributing obscene materials based upon a jury instruction modeled on *Miller v. California*,[78] had been violated when their underlying criminal activities occurred between the time the Supreme Court issued *Memoirs v. Massachusetts*,[79] a plurality decision, in which the Court articulated more stringent limits than the later *Miller* Court on the power of the states (and presumably the federal government as well) to punish the distribution of materials deemed obscene, and the time it issued *Miller.* Prior to both *Memoirs* and *Miller,* the Court had decided the standard for punishable obscenity in *Roth v. United States.*[80] Justice Powell, writing in *Marks,* explained that "*Roth*'s test for distinguishing obscenity from protected speech was a fairly simple one to articulate: 'whether to the average person, applying contemporary community standards, the dominant theme of the material taken as a whole appeals to the prurient interest.' "[81] In *Memoirs,* a plurality of three, composed of Justices Brennan and Fortas and Chief Justice Warren, announced that "three elements must coalesce" before material can be deemed beyond the protection of the First Amendment on the ground that it is obscene:

> [I]t must be established that (a) the dominant theme of the material taken as a whole appeals to the prurient interest in sex; (b) the material is patently offensive because it affronts contemporary community standards relating to the description or representation of sexual matters; and (c) the material is utterly without redeeming social value.[82]

This opinion raised the *Roth* standard for punishable obscenity by adding prongs (b) and (c). As the *Miller* Court later observed, prong (c) of *Memoirs,* requiring that the material be "utterly without redeeming social value," imposed upon the prosecutor "a burden virtually impossible to discharge under our criminal standards of proof."[83] In two opinions concurring in the judgment, Justices Black and Douglas adhered to their "well-known position that the First Amendment provides an absolute shield against governmental action aimed at suppressing obscenity."[84] In a brief opinion concurring in the judgment, Justice Stewart incorporated by reference his belief that only "hardcore pornography" may be suppressed as obscene consistent with the First Amendment, as previously expressed in his dissenting opinion in *Ginzburg v. United States.*[85] Finally, in three separate dissents, Justices Clark and White adhered to the statement of obscenity articulated in *Roth,*[86] and Justice Harlan expressed the view, which he had articulated in *Roth,* that, while the hardcore pornography standard articulated by Stewart is appropriate when the First Amendment is applied to the federal government, the First Amendment requires only that states "apply criteria rationally related to the accepted notion of obscenity."[87]

Finally, in *Miller,* a majority of the Supreme Court, in an opinion by Chief Justice Burger, redefined the standard for punishable obscenity as follows:

> The basic guidelines for the trier of fact must be: (a) whether the "average person applying contemporary community standards" would

find that the work, taken as a whole, appeals to the prurient interest; (b) whether the work depicts or describes, in a patently offensive way, sexual conduct specifically defined by the applicable state law; and (c) whether the work, taken as a whole, lacks serious literary, artistic, political, or scientific value.[88]

The *Miller* Court added, "We do not adopt as a constitutional standard the '*utterly* without redeeming social value' test of [*Memoirs*]."

To summarize, before *Marks*, the Supreme Court issued three relevant decisions concerning the definition of proscribable obscenity. In *Roth* in 1957, the Supreme Court defined obscenity based upon whether, applying "contemporary community standards, the dominant theme of the material taken as a whole appeals to the prurient interest." In *Memoirs* in 1966, the Supreme Court issued the fractured panel decision at issue in *Marks*. A minority in the *Memoirs* dissent continued to adhere to *Roth* or an even laxer standard, namely rational basis. Two concurrences stated that no materials may be proscribed as obscene under the First Amendment. A concurrence of one stated that only hard-core pornography may be proscribed as obscene consistently with the First Amendment. And a plurality of three added two requirements beyond *Roth*, including most importantly, that the material be *utterly* without redeeming social value to be proscribed as obscene. Finally, in *Miller* in 1973, the Court expressly rejected the *Memoirs* plurality's "utterly without redeeming social value" standard in favor of a refined version of *Roth*.

The *Marks* petitioners, who had engaged in criminal activities between the time of *Memoirs* and the time of *Miller*, were convicted of conspiring to distribute and distributing obscene materials based upon a jury instruction modeled on the *Miller* definition of obscenity.[89] The district court rejected petitioners' argument that the jury instruction modeled on *Miller* violated their Fifth Amendment due process rights not to be convicted based upon an obscenity formula announced after the acts giving rise to their prosecution, and which cast a "wider net than *Memoirs*," by which "petitioners charted their course of conduct." Petitioners' argument was analogous to one arising under the ex post facto clause,[90] which, although only applying to legislation, prohibits the retroactive criminalization of conduct. By analogy, in *Bouie v. City of Columbia*,[91] the Court had extended the same protection under the Fourteenth Amendment due process clause to strike down a conviction based upon an unanticipated judicial enlargement of a statute applied retroactively.

For the *Marks* petitioners to succeed, they had to demonstrate both that the *Memoirs* plurality announced the Court's holding and that, following *Memoirs*, *Miller* stated a new rule of law. Like the district court, the court of appeals in *Marks* rejected the argument that *Miller* "unforeseeably expanded the reach of the federal obscenity statutes beyond what was punishable under *Memoirs*."[92] Because the standards announced by the *Memoirs* plurality never commanded the support of more than a minority of three justices at one time, the sixth circuit, in a split panel decision, determined that "*Memoirs* never became the law."[93] As Powell explained, applying this reasoning, the issue in

Marks would have been whether *Miller* significantly altered the obscenity standard articulated in *Roth,* which he agreed it did not. But Powell went on to state:

> [W]e think that the basic premise for this line of reasoning is faulty. When a fragmented Court decides a case and no single rationale explaining the result enjoys the assent of five Justices, "the holding of the Court may be viewed as that position taken by those Members who concurred in the judgments on the narrowest grounds."[94]

Applying the narrowest grounds rule, it was easy to determine that the plurality opinion announced the holding. Justices Black and Douglas would have prevented criminalizing any conduct on grounds that the material in question was proscribable obscenity, and Justice Stewart would only have permitted hard-core pornography to be proscribed as obscene. The Brennan plurality opinion, in contrast, struck down the conviction but would have permitted a broader range of state and federal statutes proscribing materials as obscene to be upheld. As a result, while the plurality struck down the conviction, it did so on the narrowest grounds. Indeed, Powell observed that, except for the Sixth Circuit, every federal court of appeals that had considered the question had so read *Memoirs.** Powell then went on to conclude that "Memoirs therefore was the law," and that "Miller did not simply clarify Roth; it marked a significant departure from Memoirs," by "expand[ing] criminal liability" relative to the *Memoirs* "utterly without redeeming social value" standard for proscribable obscenity.[95]

Table 3.5, which outlines the various opinions in *Memoirs,* will help us to analyze Justice Powell's *Marks* analysis. In contrast with the tables depicting the two dimensions and asymmetrical preferences in *Kassel, Miller,* and *Tidewater,*[96] table 3.5 reveals a unidimensional issue spectrum in *Memoirs.* Under the *Marks* formulation, Justice Powell employed the following intuition. If we were to plot each of the published opinions in *Memoirs* along a unidimensional continuum, from broadest protection of obscenity to narrowest protection of obscenity, we could derive the Court's implicit consensus position. In table 3.5, I have included a double vertical line to separate those opinions, to the left, that are eligible for holding status under *Marks,* from those opinions, to the right, that are not, because they are not consis-

---

*In stating that *Marks* is both important and neglected, I do not intend to suggest that the case changed then-existing practice respecting the construction of Supreme Court fractured panel cases by lower courts. As Justice Powell observed, prior to the Sixth Circuit departure in *Marks* itself, the federal circuit courts had uniformly applied the narrowest grounds doctrine in the form of a custom or norm. But even rare departures can highlight the critical importance that such customs or norms can play. In *Marks,* Justice Powell recognized this point by converting what had once been a custom or norm into the Court's holding, and thus into a binding rule of case construction.

Table 3.5. *Memoirs v. Massachusetts* **in a Unidimensional Issue Spectrum**

(A) Douglas and Black (concurring)	(B) Stewart (concurring)	(C) Brennan, Fortas, and Warren (plurality)	(D) Clark, Harlan, and White (dissenting)
No proscribable obscenity	Hard-core pornography only as proscribable obscenity	"Utterly without redeeming social value" standard for proscribable obscenity	*Roth* standard (Clark and White) or rational basis test (Harlan) for proscribable obscenity

Broad protection of obscenity ◄————————► Narrow protection of obscenity

tent with the outcome of the case. Dissenting opinions can still be plotted based upon the breadth or narrowness of the proposed holding. Indeed, while I have combined the three dissenting opinions, I could have placed the Harlan opinion farther to the right than the other two, given that he would have afforded states broader powers to regulate obscenity than under the *Roth* test, which Clark and White embraced. The reason that the opinions for Clark, Harlan, and White became dissents is that the potential protections that each would have afforded for obscenity was, contrary to a majority of the Court, too narrow to include relief for Marks on the facts of the case.

Justice Powell's analysis implicitly assumes that the positions of the justices embraced in each opinion can be expressed along a unidimensional continuum, namely the breadth or narrowness of the protection for allegedly obscene materials. Assuming that all the participants agree that the sole issue in the case is the breadth of First Amendment obscenity protection, then, using table 3.5, it is fairly easy to locate the median candidate. We can label each of the opinions in the order in which they appear in table 3.5: A (Douglas), B (Stewart), C (Brennan), and D (White). Implicit in the assertion of a unidimensional continuum is the premise that if forced to choose among each of the remaining opinions, those writing or joining the opinions at the outer edge would most prefer the one closest to them and least prefer the one farthest from them. To simplify the presentation, I have treated all three dissents as one, represented by Justice White. While I have included both the Douglas and Stewart opinions in table 3.5, since both are eligible for holding status under *Marks,* for the analysis to follow, I will simplify by treating the Douglas and Stewart opinions as a single opinion A/B, representing three justices. This eases exposition by creating three camps, any two of which contain the requisite five votes for a majority. Otherwise, Stewart, a one-justice camp, could join the plurality or dissent and still be in a minority. Based upon the above assumption, the ordinal rankings of the A/B camp are as follows: A/B, C, D. The ordinal rankings of the D camp are D, C, A/B. The ordinal rankings of the C camp are irrelevant because whether they are C, A/B, D or C, D, A/B, the result is the same. If the only options available are A/B, C, and D, then option C is the Condorcet winner. The analysis illustrates the important proposition that the narrowest grounds rule is best understood as an application of the Condorcet criterion to fractured panel Supreme Court decisions.

B. *Planned Parenthood of Southeastern Pennsylvania v. Casey* Revisited

The above analysis further explains the seemingly anomalous decision in *Planned Parenthood of Southeastern Pennsylvania v. Casey*,[97] introduced in chapter 1. Recall that in *Casey*, a plurality of the Court revised the abortion framework established in *Roe v. Wade*,[98] based upon stare decisis, in a manner that a majority of six justices implicitly or explicitly rejected.[99] Table 3.6 presents *Casey* in light of the *Marks* doctrine, from the perspective of the justices striking down the spousal notification provision.[100]

Recall that in *Casey*, a pair of generally liberal justices, Blackmun and Stevens, joined the stare decisis analysis set out in part III of the joint authors' opinion, but declined to join the application of that analysis to revise the *Roe* trimester framework in part IV, which set out the newly minted undue burden test. Except for the reporting provisions, which Stevens voted to uphold, Blackmun and Stevens voted, contrary to the joint authors, to strike down all remaining restrictive provisions of the Pennsylvania abortion statute.[101] In contrast, the conservative justices voted to uphold all provisions of the abortion statute based upon an assessment of the merits and without regard to *Roe,* which they favored overruling. Finally, the joint authors, O'Connor, Kennedy, and Souter, eschewed any inquiry into the merits of *Roe* as an original decision in part III of their opinion, and voted to revise *Roe* to increase the power of the states to regulate abortion to express respect for the potential life represented by the fetus in part IV of their opinion. Because the breadth or narrowness of the right to abort, as articulated in the various *Casey* opinions, can be cast along a single dimensional issue spectrum, without

Table 3.6. *Casey* through the Lens of *Marks*

Blackmun and Stevens (concurring)	O'Connor, Kennedy, and Souter (plurality)	Rehnquist, Scalia, White, and Thomas (dissenting)
Strike down all restrictive provisions based upon either stare decisis or analysis of merits of original *Roe* decision.	Strike down only spousal notification provision, based upon stare decisis revision of *Roe.*	Uphold all provisions based upon critical analysis of merits of original *Roe* decision.

Broad abortion right   ◄——————————————►   Narrow abortion right regard to the justifications for vindicating or denying the claimed right, it appears improbable that the wings of the Court would have selected an opposite level of protection for that right over the apparent median position represented by the jointly authored opinion, simply to further an agreement that the underlying stare decisis analysis was suspect. As a result, the *Marks* doctrine works well in identifying the jointly authored plurality opinion as the Condorcet winner in *Casey.*

C.   The Narrowest Grounds Doctrine in Two Dimensions with Symmetrical Preferences: *Board of Regents of the University of California v. Bakke* Revisited

While the logic of the narrowest grounds doctrine appears most compelling in cases like *Memoirs* and *Casey,* in which the opinions can readily be cast along a unidimensional issue continuum, as the next example will show, under certain conditions, the doctrine can also apply when the opinions require that the issue spectrum be expanded to two dimensions. To illustrate, reconsider *Board of Regents of the University of California v. Bakke,*[102] this time, however, based upon analysis of the merits of the underlying equal protection claim, rather than on the issue of standing, which was discussed in chapter 1.[103] Recall that in *Bakke,* the Supreme Court considered a challenge to the University of California at Davis School of Medicine's affirmative action program. The school had an entering class with one hundred seats, of which it set aside sixteen for minorities. Bakke, who had been rejected twice in his application to the medical school, sued, claiming that, as a nonminority, his inability to compete for all one hundred seats, rather than for just eighty-four seats, violated his rights under the Fourteenth Amendment equal protection clause.

While *Bakke* produced several opinions, for the analysis to follow, we need only consider the three principal opinions. Justice Brennan, writing for himself and three others, would have applied intermediate scrutiny,[104] and would further have held that the school's effort to remedy the present effects of past discrimination was sufficient to sustain the school's affirmative action program. Justice Stevens, writing for himself plus three others, would have avoided addressing the equal protection issue altogether. Instead, Stevens concluded that race-conscious measures employed by state universities violate section 601 of Title VI of the Civil Rights Act of 1964.[105] Finally, Justice Powell, writing only for himself, but delivering the judgment of the Court, determined that the case presented two issues: first, whether the Fourteenth Amendment equal protection clause or Title VI of the Civil Rights Act of 1966 prevented a state university from using race as a factor in its admissions decisions, and, second, if not, whether the University of California School of Medicine at Davis nonetheless used race in an impermissible manner.[106]

Powell concluded that the medical school could consider race in admissions, but that it could not do so for the school's stated purpose of remedying the present effects of past discrimination. Instead, the school could use race to promote diversity among the student body. Justice Brennan, plus the three justices who joined Brennan's separate opinion, concurred in the relevant portions of the Powell opinion, in which he concluded that the equal protection clause did not altogether preclude the state medical school from considering race.[107] Justice Stevens, plus the three justices who joined Stevens's separate opinion, concurred in the relevant portions of the Powell opinion, in which he struck down the Davis program's use of race to set aside a prescribed number of seats for minorities.[108] Only Justice Powell accepted what for him proved to be a dispositive distinction between the use of race as a plus factor and the use of race to set aside a given number of seats.[109]

In his split opinion for the Court, Powell determined that while Davis could not use race to set aside a particular number of seats from which non-minorities could be altogether excluded, state universities could use race in the manner employed by Harvard University, as one factor among many in its admissions decisions. Powell considered it critical that, unlike Davis, Harvard did not segregate its admissions files by race; instead, it considered all files, minority and nonminority, as part of the same process.[110] In addition, Justice Powell considered the justifications that would allow a state institution of higher learning to employ a race-conscious measure. While Brennan accepted the argument that Davis's use of race was intended to further societal remediation in countering the present effects of past discrimination,[111] Justice Powell flatly rejected remediation as beyond the competence of the Board of Regents.[112] Powell concluded that because the medical school was not a policymaker, it lacked the institutional competence with which to make the requisite findings either to identify past discriminatory practices or to tailor a remedy aimed at curbing any such practices that it did identify. Instead, Justice Powell posited that, if appropriately tailored, for example, like the Harvard plan, a state university could employ race, as one factor among many, as a compelling interest in promoting a diverse student body.

No justice joined either the relevant part of the Powell opinion in which he concluded that diversity was a compelling state interest, sufficient to allow the state to employ a race-conscious measure without violating equal protection, or that part of his opinion in which Powell concluded that in contrast with the Harvard plan, which had used race as one factor among many, the Davis plan was constitutionally infirm because it was not narrowly tailored. Justice Stevens had no need to reach these issues, since he concluded that the use of race by a state institution violated a federal statute.[113] And in Justice Brennan's separate opinion, he eschewed any distinction between the Harvard and Davis plans.[114]

Table 3.7 depicts the two-dimensional issue spectrum in *Bakke* and the positions of each of the three camps along those two dimensions. In table 3.7, I have identified the two issue dimension in *Bakke*, first whether a state could consider race at all in its admissions decisions, and second, whether the University of California at Davis had employed race in a constitutionally permissible manner. Table 3.7, depicting *Bakke*, differs most obviously from tables 3.5 and 3.6, depicting *Memoirs* and *Casey*, respectively, in that the presence

Table 3.7.   Positions on the Two Issue Dimensions in *Bakke*

	State can consider race	State cannot consider race
State properly considered race	(A) Brennan (plus three)	
State did not properly consider race	(B) Powell	(C) Stevens (plus three)

of a second issue dimension increases the plausibility of intuiting a collective intransitivity. Thus, *Bakke* reveals that eight of the nine justices rejected what for Justice Powell proved a dispositive distinction between the Davis and Harvard plans. But table 3.7 further reveals a critical distinction between *Bakke,* a case in two dimensions, and *Miller, Kassel,* and *Tidewater,* which are also cases in two dimensions. Unlike the latter decisions, even with the expanded issue dimensionality in *Bakke,* the requisite criteria for an underlying collective intransitivity are lacking. To see why, notice that the positions embraced by the A and C camps, representing Brennan and Stevens, respectively, agree to both of the underlying issues, but reach opposite resolutions on both of those issues. Moreover, the opposite resolutions on both issues lead each camp to precisely opposite results. In contrast, the Powell position, represented by B, contains one issue resolution in common with each of the alternatives A and C. In addition, Justice Powell's holding for the Court provides each side with a partial victory: Consistent with the Brennan position, states are permitted to continue the use of race in admissions; consistent with the Stevens position, Davis cannot continue to employ race as it had, in the form of a set-aside. A cycle seems implausible in *Bakke* because for either the Brennan or Stevens camps to rank the other ahead of the Powell position ordinally, they would have to accept opposite resolutions on both underlying issues, and an opposite holding, as a second choice, over a seeming intermediate position that affords a partial but incomplete victory in the form of a favorable resolution on one issue and on one part of the two-part holding.[115]

To further bolster the intuition that the Powell position is dominant in *Bakke,* consider the necessary preconditions to an opposite holding, namely sustaining the struck Davis plan against the equal protection challenge. Consistent with all three opinions, we can derive the following premise: The plan can be sustained only if the state is permitted to employ race and if Davis used race in a constitutionally permissible manner. The upper left box is bolded because it alone satisfies these necessary and sufficient preconditions to sustaining the Davis plan. Notice, however, that the Court has apparent majority support for only one of the necessary propositions. While the Brennan and Powell camps form a majority to support the proposition that Davis can employ race, the Brennan camp stands alone as a minority supporting the proposition that Davis had used race in a constitutionally acceptable manner. Because the underlying preferences are symmetrical, it is possible to locate Justice Powell's opinion as dominant even though the issue spectrum is two dimensional.

It might appear that the Supreme Court has solved its collective decision-making problem, given that outcome voting, a non-Condorcet-producing rule, ensures collective outcomes, and that the *Marks* doctrine restores the Court's rationality by singling out as the holding that opinion which is a Condorcet winner. Not surprisingly, however, given the limits of the Condorcet criterion, the *Marks* doctrine creates problems of its own. And yet, I will demonstrate below that the difficulties that the *Marks* doctrine produces can be accommodated, once again, within the framework of existing rules and without the need for major institutional reform. Before doing so, a brief comparative application of the Condorcet criterion, which highlights some of the strengths and weaknesses of the narrowest grounds doctrine in Supreme Court decision making, will be helpful.

D. The Condorcet Criterion in Differing Institutional Contexts: The Median Voter Theorem and the Narrowest Grounds Doctrine Compared

As applied to direct elections, the median voter theorem—another application of the Condorcet criterion—predicts that candidates will converge upon the median voter, and that, as a result, third parties are likely to be squeezed out.[116] While an extended discussion of the median voter theorem would be inappropriate, it is worth noting two peculiarities that have caused political commentators to question the theorem's significance.[117] First, commentators have observed that the median voter theorem rests upon the erroneous premise that our political system can readily be cast in traditional liberal-to-conservative terms, and thus, along a unidimensional issue continuum.[118] Second, commentators have observed that the median voter theorem is premised upon the additional erroneous assumption that all participants vote, or at least that those who do not are effectively spread evenly along the political spectrum.[119]

Because both the median voter theorem and the narrowest ground doctrine are applications of the Condorcet criterion, and because both applications depend upon assumptions about the underlying institutional context that might be unrealistic, it is worth comparing the apparent deficiencies of the Condorcet criterion in each context. Like the median voter theorem, the *Marks* doctrine has been criticized for failing to recognize that Supreme Court decisions do not always fit traditional liberal-to-conservative predictions, and that, as a result, the opinion that is identified as stating the holding under the theorem might not be robust in predicting future directions of Supreme Court doctrine. In one of two rare academic commentaries on the narrowest grounds doctrine, Professors Kornhauser and Sager observed that the doctrine only functions when the relationships between and among the positions taken in the various opinions in a given case can be nested like Russian dolls.[120] Because Russian dolls can be evaluated along the single dimension of size, the metaphor reveals a similar intuition to that presented here. In addition, in a student note, Mark Alan Thurmon has argued that *Marks* provides poor guidance concerning future directions of Supreme Court doctrine.[121]

Holding these criticisms to one side, the above discussion of the median voter theorem bolsters the intuition underlying the application of the Condorcet criterion, under the guise of the narrowest grounds doctrine, to Supreme Court plurality decisions. In contrast with popular voting, the intuition underlying the *Marks* doctrine is strengthened by the presumption in favor of full participation by all members of the Court. Although not all justices vote in every case, a justice's decision not to vote is virtually never dictated by an objection in principle to all potential case outcomes. Also, in contrast with elections, where voting other than for a major candidate is often viewed as, at best, a form of protest, "voting" by Supreme Court justices permits a written decision choosing from any approach that disposes of a case, which has the potential, over time, to gain influence in the subsequent evolution of law.[122] This can include variations on the dominant positions taken along a given issue spectrum, as, for example, Justice Stewart illustrated in alone staking out the position that obscenity is equal to hard-core pornography.[123] It can also include, however, taking an entirely different approach, one that does not fit neatly along the once dominant issue spectrum. When this occurs, it is possible that the positions taken might generate something like a cycle, in which no opinion can be said to resolve the case on the narrowest grounds, precisely because the justices do not agree on how to define the relevant case issues.

We have already seen three cases in which the *Marks* doctrine does not operate to produce a Condorcet-winning holding, and in which the issue space appears to be two dimensional. In *Kassel,* for example, where the Court determined that the Iowa statute limiting the transportation of sixty-five-foot twin trailers in state violates the dormant commerce clause, the two relevant opinions from which to identify the Court's holding, per *Marks,* are those of Powell and Brennan. On the question of which substantive test to apply, Powell chose the balancing test, while Brennan chose the less stringent rational basis test. But on the question of whether to permit trial evidence supporting novel arguments, not considered in the state legislature, Brennan chose to exclude such evidence, while Powell chose to admit it. In constitutional cases where the Court strikes down a statute, the *Marks* doctrine vindicates that opinion consistent with the outcome that preserves the constitutionality of the most laws. Conversely, in constitutional cases where the Court sustains a statute, the *Marks* doctrine vindicates that opinion consistent with the outcome that preserves the constitutionality of the fewest laws. The problem in *Kassel* is that to achieve a contrary result, upholding the Iowa statute, two conditions needed to be satisfied. The trial court would have had to apply the laxer test, rational basis, and would have had to admit more, rather than less, evidence with which to find a rational basis, thus allowing evidence in support of arguments not considered by the Iowa legislature. With respect to the substantive test, Brennan resolved the case on the narrower ground, but with respect to the admissibility of trial evidence, Powell decided the case on the narrower ground. Because favorable resolutions on both issues are necessary to sustaining the Iowa statute, a narrower construction on one does not trump a broader construction on the other. Because the issue spectrum is two dimensional and because the underlying preferences are asymmetrical, the *Marks* doctrine is indeterminate in *Kassel*.

Similarly, in *Tidewater*, to strike down the statute, the justices agreed that two conditions had to be met. The Court needed to determine, first, that D.C. citizens are not state citizens under Article III, and, second, that the limits on Congress's jurisdiction-granting authority derive solely from Article III. If either of those conditions were not met, then the result would be to uphold the statute. For a plurality, Jackson determined that while D.C. citizens were not state citizens for diversity purposes, Congress could grant jurisdiction beyond Article III. In concurrence, Justice Rutledge determined that while Congress could not confer jurisdiction beyond Article III, D.C. citizens were state citizens for diversity purposes. Because the *Tidewater* Court actually upheld the jurisdiction-granting statute, the narrowest grounds opinion is the opinion consistent with the outcome that would uphold the fewest laws. While Rutledge's opinion was narrower on whether Congress could confer jurisdiction beyond the dictates of Article III, Jackson's opinion was narrower on the question whether D.C. citizens are state citizens for purposes of diversity jurisdiction. Because both conditions were necessary to striking the statute down, neither trumps the other. Just as in *Kassel* and in *Miller*, therefore, the *Marks* doctrine is indeterminate in *Tidewater*.

In contrast with popular elections, in which we can only speculate based upon limited evidence as to whether the political spectrum is single- or multidimensional, in the Supreme Court, we can actually demonstrate the impasse that the *Marks* doctrine creates in such cases as *Miller, Kassel,* and *Tidewater*. That is because in the vast majority of cases, the entire Court has voted and all of the justices have signed onto written opinions, which together reveal either a unidimensional or two-dimensional issue spectrum, and, if the latter, further reveal whether the collective preferences are symmetrical or asymmetrical. Thus, in cases like *Miller, Kassel,* and *Tidewater*, we can clearly identify the impasse of applying the Condorcet criterion to locate a dominant opinion. And these cases are not unique.[124] The question then arises why the Supreme Court has adopted a case decision rule that does not work in an empirically verifiable category of cases.

As the next subpart will show, the Supreme Court has selected the *Marks* narrowest grounds doctrine as its vehicle for identifying the holding in fractured panel cases because it achieves the Court's three overriding objectives: (1) ensuring an identifiable holding in the maximum number of fractured panel decisions; (2) ensuring that the holding in such cases is most likely to be a stable outcome, meaning that it is a Condorcet-winning opinion, if such an opinion exists; and (3) promoting, rather than undermining, principled decision making (or adherence to Arrovian independence). After a brief summary, I will consider each of these complementary justifications for the *Marks* doctrine and then discuss solutions to the two categories of cases in which *Marks* produces either potentially unacceptable outcomes or indeterminate results.

E.   Summary of Argument

While the narrowest grounds doctrine produces an impasse in cases producing a *Miller*-, *Kassel*-, and *Tidewater*-like voting anomaly, *Marks* is premised upon the intuition that within the full set of nonmajority Supreme Court opinions, such cases are relatively uncommon compared to cases in which a consensus opinion (or Condorcet winner) exists. In fact, as suggested above, the voting anomaly cases represent but one out of four principal categories for purposes of assessing the soundness of the *Marks* doctrine. With the minor exception of cases in which one or more justices has switched votes to forge a majority,[125] in cases resulting in a majority opinion, there is no collective preference aggregation problem at all; a majority favors *both* the judgment *and* the rationale producing that outcome. Setting aside three-remedy cases, it is only in fractured panel decisions that the potential for a divergence between outcome and the dominant rationale even arises. Fractured panel decisions can be subdivided into three categories, two of which—unidimensional issue spectrum cases and multidimensional issue spectrum cases with symmetrical preferences—produce a consensus opinion (or Condorcet winner) and one of which—multidimensional issue spectrum cases with asymmetrical preferences—does not. The intuition underlying *Marks* is that the two former categories are likely dominant.[126]

F.   The Narrowest Grounds Doctrine and Plurality Voting Compared: *Memoirs v. Massachusetts* Revisited

To fully appreciate the power of the *Marks* doctrine, consider employing an alternative rule governing fractured panel decisions, one in which the plurality opinion announces the ruling in the case. This rule can take various forms, including a simple rule that the opinion consistent with the outcome that obtains the most votes states the ruling in the case, or, alternatively, that no concurrences are permitted. While these two alternatives do not appear identical, social choice analysis suggests that in most cases, the two rules would likely produce the same result. To illustrate, reconsider *Memoirs v. Massachusetts*.[127] In *Memoirs,* given the actual vote lineup in which the plurality disposed of the case on the narrowest grounds, the results would be the same under either the *Marks* doctrine or under a plurality-voting regime.[128] But this is not an inevitable result. There is no reason why the opinion consistent with the outcome that gets the most votes could not articulate a broader, rather than narrower, rationale than the concurrence. Indeed, in *Bakke,* Justice Powell articulated the holding in an opinion, the critical parts of which no one else joined. Imagine that the Douglas/Black/Stewart opinions in *Memoirs*, which would have disposed of the case on broader grounds, had obtained four votes and that the Brennan opinion, which would have disposed of the case on a narrower ground, had obtained only two votes.

Under *Marks*, we consider the implicit choice that the narrowest grounds doctrine ascribes to those justices who join broader opinions consistent with the outcome or who join narrower opinions in dissent, in an effort to locate the consensus, or Condorcet-winning, opinion. In contrast, in the hypothetical plurality-holding regime, we would consider, instead, the options available to those justices joining the narrower concurrence. Those inclined under *Marks* to join the narrower concurrence, if initially in the minority among those favoring the same outcome, and if instead operating under plurality voting, would face a choice either to continue to join a narrower concurrence, which will not state the holding in any event, or to join one of the potentially dominant alternative opinions. If they chose the latter course, they would either sign onto the broader holding expressed by Douglas/Black/Stewart, under which virtually no state can proscribe materials as obscene, or onto one of the dissenting opinions, which in the cases of Justices Clark and White would have continued to adopt *Roth*'s prurient interest test, or in the case of Justice Harlan, would have adopted the even more lenient rational basis test. In contrast with the choice that those authoring the broader or narrower opinions faced under *Marks*, there is little reason to assume that those signing onto a narrower concurrence, if forced to choose between a broader plurality or a narrower dissent, would necessarily have chosen the former. It would have been perfectly rational for those in a potential narrowest grounds concurrence to take the position that they were willing to throw out this conviction because there was no demonstration that the materials in question were utterly without redeeming social value, but to go no further than that. Thus, they could have concluded that, if forced either to protect all obscenity or to employ the *Roth* community standards test, they would prefer the latter.

The same reasoning applies in such cases as *Casey* and *Bakke*. In *Casey*, for example, if the joint authors had lost one vote to the Brennan/Stevens camp, and were forced to choose between striking or sustaining all of the Pennsylvania abortion restrictions, there is no obvious reason to assume that they would necessarily have sided with the more liberal wing of the Court, which voted to decide the case on a broader ground. Similarly, if Lewis Powell were forced in *Bakke* to choose between upholding the University of California at Davis Medical School's affirmative action program based upon intermediate scrutiny or striking it down based upon an application of Title VI of the Civil Rights Act of 1964, there is again no logical basis upon which to predict how he would have voted. As a result, under a plurality-holding rule, the effect is to introduce uncertainty as to which opinion contains the implicit consensus of the Court and thus constitutes the holding. And, of course, in each of these cases, further jockeying could occur. Thus, in *Bakke*, if Powell opted to join the Stevens opinion rather than the Brennan opinion, Justice Brennan could try to rewrite his opinion to attract Powell. The Stevens camp, upon losing Powell, for example, could try to win him back. At best, the outcome would be indeterminate. At worst, the outcome would introduce a regular practice of strategic voting and strategic opinion writing, thus undermining the value of Supreme Court precedent.

In enhancing the likelihood that the prevailing opinion in a fractured panel decision will have the implicit consensus of the Court, the *Marks* doctrine also promotes the sense of fairness in collective decision making associated with equally weighted voting. As demonstrated above, a plurality-holding regime, or a no-concurrence rule, has the potential to vest disproportionate power in a minority of the Court, while the *Marks* doctrine requires implicit consensus, thus constituting majority support around what in most cases likely represents a Condorcet-winning holding. As illustrated below, the *Marks* doctrine, in contrast with a plurality-holding or no-concurrence rule, further promotes adherence to Arrovian independence, or principled voting.

To illustrate, we will again consider *Memoirs*. Imagine that those signing onto Brennan's narrowest grounds opinion for striking down the conviction had been in a minority relative to the remaining opinions achieving the same result. Further imagine that they favored the dissenting *Roth* standard over the hypothetical plurality's absolute-protection standard (represented by Black and Douglas) and to the Stewart near-absolute-protection standard (equating obscenity with hard-core pornography). Based upon these assumptions, if the Court operated under a plurality-holding or a no-concurrence rule, the narrowest grounds justices would have faced the choice *either* to have the Court strike down the conviction based upon a standard that they believed too broad *or* to sustain the conviction, thus announcing a level of First Amendment protection that they believed too narrow. The choice is either to allow a minority, those who are in the now broader plurality, to hijack the holding, setting it more broadly than an implicit, or even an explicit, consensus of the Court would otherwise permit, or to change the holding altogether in favor of an alternative minority, espousing an even narrower view, to avoid the broader rule.

Similarly, in *Casey,* the joint authors, if they were in the minority and were forced to select between upholding all provisions based upon strict adherence to *Roe* or striking all provisions based upon a reversal of *Roe,* would either have had to select a broader or a narrower range of abortion rights than they believed *Roe* required as a matter of stare decisis. Again, either result would not be supported by an otherwise explicit or implicit consensus of the Court. The same analysis applies in *Bakke.* Under a plurality-holding regime, Justice Powell would have faced the choice either to sustain affirmative action programs that he believed to be unconstitutional or to switch his vote to suggest that even the Harvard plan, which he thought constitutionally sound, would also violate equal protection if employed by a state university.

In contrast with the hypothetical plurality-holding or no-concurrence rule,[129] the *Marks* doctrine promotes both principled voting and principled opinion writing. It does so by delinking the statement of the Court's holding from the expressed opinions of the justices. Regardless of where along the voting spectrum individual justices cast their opinions, the holding will be that decided consistently with the outcome on the narrowest ground. At first blush, that might sound circular, but it is not. If the rule were plurality-holding, it is true that the holding will be stated in the opinion consistent with the outcome that garners the most votes, but in contrast with the narrowest grounds opinion under *Marks,* which opinion obtains dispositive status would be a function of the strategic considerations of those who would prefer to decide the case on narrower grounds. If potential narrowest grounds writers vote one way, they are dissatisfied in one direction; if they vote the other way, they are dissatisfied in the opposite direction. Only by designating the narrowest grounds opinion as stating the holding does the Court substantially reduce such strategic considerations in determining the outcome of the case. While those who would prefer to decide on a broader ground might be disappointed, there is nothing that they can do to promote that objective, other than to write a sufficiently compelling opinion to persuade the requisite number of colleagues to join to create a majority or to move sufficiently toward the median position to gain majority support. Similarly, those who would prefer to decide the case on an even narrower ground, which necessarily means that they are in dissent, cannot promote that objective through strategic voting unless they succeed in moving toward the median position. But notice that whichever side captures the median justice produces an opinion with explicit majority support. And if neither side captures the median justice, then as the narrowest grounds author, the median justice captures the implicit support of the Court as the Condorcet winner. As a result, among the relevant potential holding-identification rules, the *Marks* doctrine best promotes the fairness of Supreme Court decision making and limits strategic voting.[130]

V. The Lingering Problems of *Marks*

While the *Marks* doctrine has the benefit of promoting limited adherence to Arrovian independence and of encouraging opinions that provide critical guidance for the future direction of lawmaking on the Supreme Court, the doctrine is not without its costs. We can place the problems generated by the outcome-voting/*Marks* regime under three general headers: (1) guidance problems for lower federal and state courts; (2) voting anomaly outcomes that are unacceptable to individual Supreme Court justices; and (3) the problem of three-remedy cases. In this section, I will explain why, notwithstanding each of these problems, *Marks* remains the least-bad decisional rule governing fractured panel decisions.

A. The Problem of Guidance to Lower Federal and State Courts

In those cases in which the *Marks* doctrine does not operate to identify an opinion stating the governing rationale for the Court's holding because of a

Miller-, Kassel-, and *Tidewater*-like voting anomaly, the doctrine leaves lower federal courts and state courts with a potential problem of doctrinal uncertainty. Professor John Rogers has recognized an apparent solution to this problem; lower federal courts can apply the Supreme Court's holding when the issues creating the Supreme Court holding arise together, but tally votes on a per-issue basis, including the votes of any dissenting justices, when the issues arise individually.[131] Several lower federal Courts have taken just this approach in construing *Tidewater* and similar cases.[132] While this practice is certainly functional, it is also problematic. Lower federal courts and state courts are perfectly capable of applying the Court's judgment when the issues presented in a Supreme Court precedent arise together and of tallying the issue votes when they arise separately, despite the voting anomaly that underlies the governing Supreme Court precedent. Thus, if presented with a law like the Iowa statute struck down in *Kassel,* which evinced a similar protectionist motive, a lower federal court could apply *Kassel* to strike the law down, even though on an issue-by-issue basis, the Supreme Court would achieve the opposite result. The result is no more incoherent at the lower federal court level than it was in the Supreme Court, except that if issued by a district court, it is the product of a single judge. Even so, the applying judge is not being incoherent; she is simply applying a precedent that is itself the product of a Supreme Court voting anomaly.

Now imagine a case in which only one of the *Kassel* issues arises, for example, a state highway safety law that is challenged under the dormant commerce clause, where there is direct legislative evidence sufficient to establish a rational nonprotectionist motive, thus satisfying the rational basis test, but insufficient to establish that the state's stated safety interest outweighs the national interest in commerce, thus failing to satisfy the balancing test. Assume that there is no other evidence. Because all of the relevant evidence concerns actual legislative history, there is no question as to whether evidence supporting novel justifications presented for the first time at trial should be admitted. Thus, the only issue from *Kassel* that the case raises is which test to apply. The lower federal court could readily apply the rational basis test based upon the majority composed of Brennan (concurrence of two) and Rehnquist (dissent of three). Again, while this practice may require reading several opinions instead of one or two, it does allow the application of an otherwise problematic Supreme Court decision.

The difficulty with this approach is that it has the potential to provide different rules of law on one or more issues based upon happenstance. Thus, for example, assume another dormant commerce clause challenge to a state highway regulation in which the legislative history, as in *Kassel,* is insufficient to establish a rational basis because it evinces a protectionist motive, and in which the state's lawyers proffer evidence that is sufficient to establish a rational basis but not to meet the more stringent balancing test. The second case, because it presents both issues that were raised in *Kassel,* would result in striking down the law, implying that either the relevant test is higher than rational basis or that novel-justification evidence should be excluded. One could imagine an opinion stating the holding in the alternative, but at the very least, the holding will suggest a different governing rule on the issue presented in the first hypothetical simply because that issue was presented with the other issue on which *Kassel* turned.

We should not be surprised by the seeming imperfection of the proposed rule that lower courts should head count on issues when they are presented separately and head count on outcome when the issues arise together. After all, there is no reason to assume that a lower federal court can cure the pathology giving rise to such cases as *Miller, Kassel,* and *Tidewater.* At the very least, the proposed rule improves the utility of such precedents. Should two cases provide parties with different legal rights based upon such fortuitous factors as issue convergence, the lower court could independently consider a due process or equal protection challenge to the application of different substantive rules to different parties on like facts. But speculating about such cases is not helpful in resolving real ones before the courts.

B. Voting Anomaly Outcomes That Are Unacceptable to Individual Justices

In a total of three cases presenting a potential *Miller-, Kassel-,* or *Tidewater-* type voting anomaly, one or more Supreme Court justices were unwilling to accept the case result that followed from a strict application of outcome voting. These justices deferred to their colleagues' collective determination on an underlying issue, and thus voted for a different outcome than that which followed from the internal logic of their own opinions. In each case, the vote switches changed the Court's ultimate holding. Because these cases are factually closest to *Miller,* in that they had the potential to cycle over a preliminary issue like standing, I will contrast them with *Miller* in the analysis to follow. In two of these cases, the vote-switching justices sought to avoid a holding at odds with an important substantive constitutional value, and in the third, they sought to preserve the Court's jurisdiction. Each case represents an exception to the outcome-voting/*Marks* regime in that the outcome is determined by a voting path that followed from a contrary majority determination on an underlying dispositive issue. In *Seminole Tribe of Florida v. Florida,*[133] the Supreme Court overturned the most recent of these three cases, *Pennsylvania v. Union Gas Co.,*[134] in part on the ground that the vote switch in question undermined the decision's utility, and thus, its precedential value. *Seminole Tribe* thus suggests a partial solution to the pathology underlying such cases, namely a relaxed application of stare decisis in those cases subject to the voting paradox. Moreover, *Seminole Tribe* might explain the disinclination in *Miller* of Justices O'Connor and Kennedy to concede standing to the contrary majority in order to afford their views on the merits dispositive status. Had they done so, the result might well have been to strike down, rather than to sustain, the challenged provision of the Immigration and Nationality Act.

Professor Rogers, who has written in opposition to issue-voting proposals, has criticized the vote switches that I am about to describe.[135] In contrast, these ad hoc exceptions to outcome voting go substantially less far than advocates of the various issue-voting proposals would prefer.[136] As I will demonstrate below, however, the social choice analysis of individual-case decision-making reveals that these cases exist on a tiny margin, one that has been made so by the combined operation of outcome voting and the *Marks* narrowest grounds rule. The outcome-voting/*Marks* regime provides determinate and rational holdings in all but the small margin of cases that reflect the *Miller-*, *Kassel-*, and *Tidewater-*like voting paradox. Of the cases on this small margin, only three have arisen in the Supreme Court's entire history in which, based upon an overriding substantive constitutional or jurisdictional value, individual justices felt compelled to switch to a limited form of issue voting. I will argue that these very cases belie the need for either a categorical prohibition against discretionary vote switching by individual justices, or the need for a systematic change in Supreme Court decision making in favor of issue voting. My point is not to criticize the decision in *Seminole Tribe* to overturn *Union Gas* based upon the potential doctrinal uncertainty that Justice White's opinion in *Union Gas* apparently produced. The Supreme Court can condone occasional vote switches in cases in which the Supreme Court justices' preference structures produce a voting paradox, while, at a later time, when the Court coalesces around a single contrary rationale, affording the earlier case only the most limited stare decisis value. This approach provides more complete information about the justices' various positions without tying the Court as an institution to the unsatisfying results of the voting-paradox decision in a later period.

1.   Pennsylvania v. Union Gas Co.

Because the three relevant cases share an identical structure, I will discuss only one here in detail, and then briefly summarize the other two. We will start with *Pennsylvania v. Union Gas Co.*[137] *Union Gas* presented two issues, first, whether the Comprehensive Environmental Response, Compensation and Liability Act ("CERCLA"),[138] as amended by the Superfund Amendments and Reauthorization Act of 1986,[139] permits a federal court damages action against a state, and second, whether the statute is constitutional under the commerce clause or, instead, whether Congress lacks that authority under the Eleventh Amendment. The Court produced five separate opinions. In parts I and II of his opinion (joined by Marshall, Blackmun, Stevens, and Scalia), Justice Brennan concluded that the language of CERCLA permits lawsuits against states for damages in federal court.[140] In part III of his opinion (joined by Marshall, Blackmun, and Stevens), Brennan further concluded that allowing such suits does not exceed Congress's commerce clause powers. While Scalia joined as part of the majority in determining that CERCLA authorized suits against the states, in a separate opinion, joined in part by Rehnquist, O'Connor, and Kennedy, Scalia also concluded that such suits violate the commerce clause.[141] Justice White, in an opinion joined in part by Rehnquist, O'Connor, and Kennedy, stated that he did not agree that the language of CERCLA permits such suits, but, in another part of his opinion, written for only himself, went on to state:

> My view on the statutory issue has not prevailed, however; a majority of the Court has ruled that the statute, as amended, plainly intended to abrogate the immunity of the States from suit in the federal courts. I accept that judgment. This brings me to the question whether Congress has the constitutional power to abrogate the State's immunity. In that respect, I agree with the conclusion reached by Justice BRENNAN in Part III of his opinion, that Congress has the authority under Article I to abrogate Eleventh Amendment immunity of the State, although I do not agree with much of his reasoning.[142]

In addition to these opinions, Justices Stevens and O'Connor wrote separate concurring and dissenting opinions, respectively, which do not alter the essential voting lineup.

To simplify, table 3.8 presents the four major voting blocs in the case. Brennan (plus Marshall, Blackmun, and Stevens) determined that CERCLA authorizes damage suits in federal court and that the statute is constitutional. Scalia determined that CERCLA authorizes damage suits in federal court, but that the statute is unconstitutional. White determined that CERCLA does not authorize damage suits in federal court, but, based upon the contrary majority judgment establishing that it does authorize such suits, further determined that authorizing such suits is constitutional. Finally, Rehnquist, O'Connor, and Kennedy determined that CERCLA does not authorize damage suits in federal court and that, if it did, it would be unconstitutional. All justices agreed that if the statute permitted damage suits and if permitting such suits were constitutional, the result would have been to affirm, thus allowing the damages suit to proceed. They further agreed that if either the statute did not allow such suits or if the statute, construed to allow such suits, were unconstitutional, then the result would be to reverse. Table 3.8 summarizes the preceding discussion.

Table 3.8 reveals the two-dimensional issue spectrum with asymmetrical preferences in *Union Gas*. The bolded box contains the minority of jus-

Table 3.8.   Positions on the Two Issue Dimensions in *Union Gas*

	Statute authorizes suit	Statute does not authorize suit
Allowing suit does not violate commerce clause	Brennan, Marshall, Blackmun, Stevens	*White* (moves left)
Allowing suit violates commerce clause	Scalia	Rehnquist, O'Connor, Kennedy

tices who agree to the necessary conditions to affirming the lower court ruling allowing a damages suit to proceed against a state under CERCLA. To affirm and allow the suit to proceed, a majority had to determine both that the statute authorizes suits against the states and that such authorization does not violate the commerce clause. Absent Justice White's decision to resolve the constitutional issue, even though the reasoning of his own opinion rendered that unnecessary, *Union Gas* would have presented a *Miller-*, *Kassel-*, and *Tidewater*-like voting anomaly, in which separate majorities determined that the statute authorizes suit (the upper left and lower left boxes) and that authorizing suit does not violate the commerce clause (the upper left and upper right boxes), but in which the Court reversed because only a minority (the upper left box) found both prerequisites to affirming. The italics and parenthetical entry indicate that by switching his vote, Justice White effectively placed himself in the upper left box, thus voting to affirm and to allow the suit to proceed, even though the logic of his opinion led to the opposite result. But for Justice White's vote switch, he and Justice Scalia would have resolved the two underlying issues in precisely opposite fashion, but leading to the same judgment. In effect, Justice White was not willing to follow the general (range-restricted) rule of expressing a noncontingent outcome vote. While we cannot know with certainty why he failed to follow this rule, it seems apparent that he was unwilling to take the chance that the precedent would be construed in a manner opposite his preferred rationale on both issues. While his first choice was to reverse on the ground that CERCLA did not authorize the damages action against a state, his last choice was to reverse on the ground that, although CERCLA did authorize such suit, it could not do so constitutionally. As a result, he opted for an opposite result, which demanded that he concede the statutory construction issue, thus concluding that the statute authorized suit, to then hold that allowing the suit was constitutional. This is exactly the type of unacceptable ordinal ranking over combined issue resolutions, that outcome voting, in the ordinary case, holds off limits.[143] Stated in the technical language of social choice, in *Union Gas,* Justice White was unwilling to allow himself to operate within a range-restricted voting regime, and thus expressed a resolution of underlying issues in which his second choice produced an opposite holding, rather than the same holding on the rationale he viewed as least favorable.

In a thorough exposition, in which he reviewed over 150 Supreme Court decisions in which he determined such a vote switch could occur, Professor Rogers concluded that Justice White's vote switch, which he criticized, was nearly unprecedented.[144] Rogers determined that with the exception of one prior case, and one post–*Union Gas* case, each discussed briefly below, the only cases in which individual Supreme Court justices voted against the reasoned conclusion that followed from the internal logic of their own opinions was when the Court lacked a majority for one of three judgments—affirm, reverse, or remand—and thus could not produce a judgment.[145]

In overturning *Union Gas,* Chief Justice Rehnquist observed:

In the five years since it was decided, *Union Gas* has proven to be a solitary departure from established law [on the power of Congress to abrogate state sovereign immunity]. . . . Reconsidering the decision in *Union Gas*, we conclude that none of the policies underlying *stare decisis* require our continuing adherence to its holding. The decision has, since its issuance, been of questionable precedential value, largely because a majority of the Court expressly disagreed with the rationale of the plurality.[146]

There are no fewer than three ways that one can read this excerpt from Chief Justice Rehnquist's opinion. If construed to suggest that in voting anomaly cases, future Supreme Courts will apply a relaxed stare decisis analysis to allow the resolution of underlying issues when the foundation for a collective intransitivity is no longer present, then that conclusion would appear to have much to commend it as a matter of policy. After all, when the Court possesses collective preferences that are intransitive, there is no solution to the problem of how to aggregate such preferences in a rational and fair manner. While outcome voting ensures a collective resolution, even in such cases, relaxing stare decisis allows the Court to extricate itself from an inevitably problematic resolution of the issues that such a case produces.

Alternatively, Rehnquist could be asserting that the difficulty in *Union Gas* has nothing to do with the voting anomaly, but rather, that it arises because Justice White expressed disagreement with the very part of the Brennan opinion that he joined and that led to the decision to sustain CERCLA against constitutional attack. Thus viewed, Rehnquist might be focusing on a single issue dimension represented along the vertical axis in table 3.8, in which Justice Brennan concludes that Congress can abrogate state sovereign immunity, Rehnquist concludes the opposite, and White joins Brennan on the result, with reservations but with no independent rationale.[147] If so, Rehnquist's opinion could be construed to suggest an unwillingness to presume that Justice Brennan's opinion states the holding when it is possible that had Justice White stated the basis for his reservations in joining Justice Brennan on the result, he might have offered an alternative rationale that resolved the case on a narrower ground.

Finally, in stating that the *Union Gas* "majority . . . expressly disagreed with the rationale of the plurality," Chief Justice Rehnquist might be including both Justice White and Justice Scalia, who disagreed with what otherwise would have been a plurality (the bolded upper left box in table 3.8) on two separate and independent bases, over which they were split. If by conceding the question of statutory interpretation, Justice White intended to signal agreement on the essential point that Congress has the power to abrogate state sovereign immunity, then there existed a majority, represented by Justice Brennan's plurality of four plus Justice White's concurrence, on that issue. In this alternative reading, for Rehnquist to claim that a majority disagreed with the Brennan analysis, he would have had to include in his majority Justice Scalia, who disagreed with Brennan on an issue of statutory construction, which had no bearing on the constitutional issue presented in *Seminole Tribe.*

While it is difficult to prove conclusively which of these readings is most persuasive, the voting lineup in *Seminole Tribe* itself might provide some insight. In *Seminole Tribe,* the chief justice was joined by Justices O'Connor, Scalia, Kennedy, and Thomas. In his *Union Gas* dissent, which embraced a rationale opposite Justice Brennan's opinion for the Court on *both* underlying issues, the chief justice was joined by Justices O'Connor and Kennedy (appearing in the lower right box in table 3.8). While Justice Scalia (appearing in the lower left box) concluded in *Union Gas* that Congress intended to abrogate state sovereign immunity, he agreed with the chief justice that Congress lacked the authority to do so. The critical fifth vote for overturning *Union Gas* came from Justice Thomas, who succeeded Justice Marshall. While Justice Marshall joined the Brennan plurality opinion in *Union Gas* (appearing in the upper left box), Justice Thomas instead joined the chief justice in ruling that Congress lacks the constitutional authority to overcome state sovereign immunity. So viewed, the Court's decision to overturn *Union Gas* in *Seminole Tribe* might be explained on straightforward ideological grounds, resulting from a critical change in Court personnel, namely the replacement of Justice Marshall, a dedicated liberal, with Justice Thomas, an equally dedicated conservative. Whatever the motivation, the rule produced by this overruling might well remain a stable solution to an intractable problem of how to treat a precedent that is at least in part the result of aggregating collective preferences in a Court that possessed multidimensional and asymmetrical preferences.

In any event, the issue remains whether we can identify the conditions that gave rise to Justice White's decision to switch his vote in *Union Gas.* To answer that question, it will be helpful to briefly consider two additional vote switch cases, and then to compare the results with those in *Miller, Kassel,* and *Tidewater,* in which no such vote switches occurred.

2. Arizona v. Fulminante

In a later decision, *Arizona v. Fulminante,*[148] Justice Kennedy engaged in a vote switch. In Fulminante's capital murder appeal, the three writing justices, Chief Justice Rehnquist and Justices White and Kennedy, distilled the case to three issues: (1) whether the second of Fulminante's two confessions was coerced; (2) if so, whether harmless error analysis applies; and (3) if so, whether admitting the coerced confession was not harmless. All justices implicitly agreed that the conviction would be reversed only if the confession was coerced and, if *either* harmless error analysis did not apply, or if it did, admitting the confession was not harmless error. The individual justices joined parts of the various opinions, producing a total of five voting blocs over the three issues. To simplify, I will present here only the voting tabulations on each issue, and the holding. In a part of his opinion joined by Marshall,

Brennan, Stevens, and Scalia, Justice White determined that the confession was coerced. Justice Kennedy, having instead determined that the confession was not coerced, should have voted to affirm, but instead, he conceded the factual issue, thus treating the contrary majority resolution on the factual issue as binding. In a part of his opinion joined by O'Connor, Kennedy, Souter, and Scalia, Chief Justice Rehnquist determined that if coerced, harmless error analysis applies. And in another part of his opinion, joined by Marshall, Blackmun, Stevens, and Kennedy, Justice White concluded that the coerced confession was not harmless error. Because Kennedy concluded that the confession was not coerced, it was unnecessary for him to reach the two harmless error issues; whether or not the admission was harmful, a voluntary confession would not provide the basis for a reversal. Had Justice Kennedy voted consistently with the internal logic of his opinion, therefore, the result would have been to affirm the conviction, given that absent his vote, only a minority would have concluded that harmless error analysis applied and that the admission was not harmless error. Instead of voting to affirm the conviction, however, Justice Kennedy stated the following:

> My own view that the confession was not coerced does not command a majority.
>
> In the interests of providing a clear mandate to the Arizona Supreme Court in this capital case, I deem it proper to accept in the case now before us the holding of five Justices that the confession was coerced and inadmissible. I agree with a majority of the Court that admission of the confession could not be harmless error when viewed in light of all the other evidence; and so I concur in the judgment to affirm the ruling of the Arizona Supreme Court.[149]

We will now consider the final vote-switch case.

3. United States v. Vuitch

Finally, consider what Justice Rogers identified as the sole precedent for Justice White's vote switch in *Union Gas*,[150] namely *United States v. Vuitch*.[151] The *Vuitch* Court reversed the dismissal of an indictment of a doctor performing abortions in violation of a federal statute operating only in the District of Columbia. The district court had dismissed the indictment on the ground that the statute was unconstitutionally vague, and the government appealed under a statute that allowed direct appeals to the Supreme Court from cases striking down federal statutes on constitutional grounds. On appeal, the Supreme Court produced five opinions in which the justices distilled the case to two issues: first, did the Supreme Court lack direct appellate jurisdiction under the relevant federal statute, given that the underlying statute applies only in the District of Columbia; and, second, if so, was the statute unconstitutionally vague. If the answer to either issue was yes, then the result should have been to affirm the dismissal. Implicit in all opinions was the assumption that the dismissal should be reversed only if the Court had jurisdiction and if the statute was not unconstitutionally vague or otherwise unconstitutional.

As before, I will present only the issue and outcome voting lineups. In a part of his opinion for a majority, consisting of himself and Chief Justice Burger and Justices Douglas, Stewart, and White, Justice Black concluded that the Supreme Court had appellate jurisdiction. Justices Harlan and Blackmun, having instead determined that the Court lacked appellate jurisdiction, should have voted to dismiss, which would be equivalent to voting to affirm the conviction. Instead, Justices Harlan and Blackmun conceded the jurisdictional issue to the contrary majority, thus treating their resolution of the second issue as dispositive of their outcome vote. Thus, in a part of his opinion joined by a separate majority, which included Chief Justice Burger and Justices Harlan, White, and Blackmun, Justice Black concluded that the statute was not unconstitutionally vague. As a result of the Harlan and Blackmun vote switches, which allowed them to join as part of the second majority, the Court reversed the dismissal of the indictment for vagueness, even though the internal logic of the opinions for these two justices suggested that the Court lacked jurisdiction in the case. Justice Harlan provided almost no direct explanation of his vote switch, and Justice Blackmun essentially maintained that he was duty bound to adhere to the majority's contrary determination that the Court had jurisdiction.[152]

4. The Vote-Switch Cases: An Assessment

Professor Rogers not only observed that these vote switches are unprecedented, but also argued that they "portend[] forfeiture of the Supreme Court's claim—implicit in the fact that the Court issues opinions—to be composed of reasoned, and not arbitrary, decision makers."[153] Of course, to evaluate this argument, one needs a working definition of the word *arbitrary*, that does not rest upon the premise that collective outcome determinations are more worthy of respect than are collective issue determinations.[154] In opposite fashion, Professors Kornhauser, Sager, Post, and Salop would look to the potential result in the absence of the vote switches by Justice White in *Union Gas,* Justice Kennedy in *Fulminante,* and Justices Harlan and Blackmun in *Vuitch,* as proving the need for at least an occasional switch to issue voting to avoid arbitrary and unjust results.[155] Both sides are operating from a normative premise about the nature of the judicial process that is defensible and that is actually honored in the overwhelming majority of cases. I would suggest, however, that both sides have failed properly to consider that the relevant margin for assessing the merits of these vote switches is exceedingly narrow.

Thus, except in this rare category of vote-switch cases, in cases decided by a majority opinion, there is no divergence between outcome and the rationale producing that outcome. Among the Court's plurality decisions, most often the relationships among the various opinions exist along a single dimension over which single-peaked preferences can be presumed. In such cases, any divergence of viewpoint is a matter of only academic concern. While such cases lack the precedential effect of majority opinions, the opinion consistent with the outcome decided on the narrowest grounds represents a stable, Condorcet-winning outcome. Moreover, the same analysis applies in cases like *Bakke,* where the issue spectrum is two dimensional but the underlying preferences are symmetrical. But in a very narrow margin of cases, including *Miller, Kassel, Tidewater, Union Gas, Fulminante,* and *Vuitch,* the problems of collective decision making rear their ugly head, producing a potentially irreconcilable divergence between the outcome and the governing rationale. And in an even smaller margin of cases, represented only by *Union Gas, Fulminante,* and *Vuitch,* one or more justices has been unwilling to accept the outcome-based result given the Court's resolution of dispositive issues.

From a pure social choice perspective, by which I mean an analysis of these cases from the viewpoint of coalitions and voting rules, these cases are not distinguishable either in degree or in kind. But (and I will defend this proposition at greater length in chapters 4 and 6, when discussing standing) our judicial system is not universally driven by academic concerns for consistency, either as a matter of substantive constitutional doctrine or as a matter of constitutional process. Instead, our judicial system is driven by the competing concerns of rationality, fairness, and an overriding desire to further the actuality and appearance of justice, even at the expense of doctrinal purity or consistent voting processes. My own view is that these vote-switch cases do not present either an affront to nonarbitrary judicial decision making, or support for a more systematic switch from outcome to issue voting. Indeed, while the sample size is admittedly small, social choice analysis might help to provide some tentative insights as to why the individual justices switched their votes in some but not all of these cases.

There are at least two possible means of reconciling the decisions of individual justices to switch votes in *Union Gas, Fulminante,* and *Vuitch* with the failure of individual justices to do so in *Miller, Kassel,* and *Tidewater.* One explanation focuses on the importance of the underlying issue resolution or holding, which would be suppressed absent the vote switch. Consider for example the substantive issues in *Kassel* and *Tidewater,* which did not generate vote switches. In *Kassel,* the voting anomaly produced the result that a majority of the Court voted to strike down a state law, infringing on commerce, even though a majority on each of the two underlying issues concluded that relevant evidence supported a finding that there was a rational basis to support the law. In *Tidewater,* the voting anomaly produced the result that a majority permitted diversity jurisdiction in federal court between a D.C. citizen and a citizen of a state, even though a majority of the Court determined that Article III limited diversity to citizens of different states and that Congress's power to confer such jurisdiction derived solely from Article III. I do not want to suggest that these cases, and the issues that they present, are unimportant. *Kassel* presents an important question about the power of states to regulate their own affairs without undue federal judicial interference, and

Tidewater presents an important question about the integrity of constitutional interpretation. But one could argue that *Kassel* and *Tidewater* implicate concerns of a somewhat different magnitude of importance than those underlying *Union Gas, Fulminante,* and *Vuitch.*

In *Union Gas,* had Justice White failed to switch his vote, the enforcement mechanism under a federal environmental statute would have been effectively nullified even though a majority determined that the provision anticipated the mechanism and that the mechanism was constitutional. While the Court later reached an opposite merits determination in overruling *Union Gas* in *Seminole Tribe,* that does not demonstrate that Justice White erred in concluding against striking down the statute, given the expressed viewpoints of the then-deciding Court. In *Fulminante,* a man would have been executed based upon a confession admitted at trial even though a majority of the Court determined that the confession was coerced and that its admission was not harmless error. And in *Vuitch,* Justices Harlan and Blackmun deferred to the collective judgment of a majority on a question of the Court's own jurisdiction in a case in which failing to do so would have left in place a district court ruling with which they disagreed, striking down a congressional statute. The difficulty with this explanation, however, is its apparent circularity. We can only know that the underlying issues are important because the vote-switching justices went out of their way to reach those issues. Moreover, and perhaps more importantly, this analysis renders the vote switches in *Union Gas, Fulminante,* and *Vuitch* potentially difficult to reconcile with the absence of a vote switch in *Miller,* given that that case sustained a sex-based distinction in the context of denying a woman her claimed citizenship status.

A better explanation, I will now argue, is grounded in social choice. This explanation turns on the relationship between and among the underlying case issues. In each of the cases generating a vote switch, the conceded issue can be characterized as a gateway issue, meaning an issue that possesses two characteristic features. First, the ultimate resolution of the gateway issue is essential to deciding whether to address the remaining substantive issue or issues. Second, the analytical framework employed in resolving the gateway issue is not inextricably linked with the analytical framework employed in the resolution of the remaining substantive issue or issues. Thus, in *Union Gas,* Justice White conceded to a contrary majority resolution on an issue of statutory construction to reach a question of constitutionality; in *Fulminante,* Justice Kennedy conceded to a contrary majority resolution on the factual question whether a confession was coerced to reach the issue whether, if coerced, its admission constituted harmless error; and in *Vuitch,* Justices Blackmun and Harlan conceded to a contrary majority resolution on whether the Supreme Court had appellate jurisdiction to address whether a criminal statute was unconstitutionally vague. In contrast, in *Kassel,* both underlying issues, whether the lower court could consider evidence in support of the statute beyond that considered by the enacting legislature, and whether the relevant test in evaluating a commerce clause challenge was the balancing test or the rational basis test, were inextricably linked to resolving whether a state law impinging upon a national market violates the dormant commerce clause. While one might view the evidentiary question as a gateway issue, that characterization does not bear scrutiny in this context. *Kassel* is not a case in which the question of evidence logically precedes a substantive issue of constitutional law. For Justice Brennan, the issue of constitutionality involved, first and foremost, the issue of which justifications in support of the law the enacting legislature considered.[156] And in *Tidewater,* most obviously, both underlying issues, whether the District of Columbia is a state for purposes of Article III and whether Congress has the power to go beyond Article III in conferring jurisdiction upon federal courts also exist at the same level of construing federal court jurisdiction under Article III.

To be clear, under this analysis, the critical distinction is not whether a case involves a gateway issue—jurisdiction, statutory construction, a factual finding, or standing—instead of a substantive question of constitutional law; rather, it is whether the case presents two issues operating at different levels. The intuition that a justice is more likely to concede an issue at one level to reach an issue at another level is bolstered by an additional distinguishing characteristic between those multidimensional and asymmetrical cases that produced a vote switch—*Union Gas, Fulminante,* and *Vuitch*—and those that did not—*Miller, Kassel,* and *Tidewater.* Notice that in each vote-switch case, the gateway issue was decided by a majority in a single opinion.[157] In contrast, in the cases that did not produce vote switches, the separate majorities on each issue that produced a logical voting path leading to the dissent was composed of justices over several opinions, including some in dissent.[158] At one level, the lineup is potentially fortuitous, depending, perhaps, on no more than how the issues in the case were initially conceived, and the how opinions were initially assigned. If, for example, *Miller* had been conceived initially as neatly presenting the issues of standing and the choice and application of substantive test for the underlying due process challenge,[159] then it would have been easy to imagine Justice Stevens writing a two-part opinion, the first holding that petitioner has standing, which would have been joined by seven justices out of nine, excluding only O'Connor and Kennedy, and the second, concluding that the relevant test was rational basis scrutiny, commanding the support of only himself and Chief Justice Rehnquist. One can further imagine Justice Ginsburg, as part of the majority on part I of our hypothetical *Miller* opinion, then drafting a separate opinion, seeking majority support, which would hold that the relevant test is heightened scrutiny, under which the challenged INA provision fails. Had this occurred, then structurally, the case would have been identical to the vote-switch cases, in that a clear contrary majority opinion on standing would have presented an obvious opportunity for Justices O'Connor and Kennedy to concede that issue, thus turning Ginsburg's potential dissenting opinion on the choice and application of substantive test (joined only by Breyer and Souter), into a majority opinion (joined also by O'Connor and Kennedy). Notice also that had this occurred, the resulting opinion would not have been decided by a judgment, but rather, by two separately authored majority opinions. Alternatively, the fact that *Miller* was not so structured might have been a deliberate strategy to prevent such a voting path from emerging.[160] That said, from the perspective of aggregating collective preferences, there is no apparent difference between whether a given issue is resolved by a majority in a single opinion or over multiple opinions.

We can now intuit why those justices who switched their votes in multidimensional asymmetrical cases might have done so. When the issues exist at different levels, as made evident in part by majority coalescence in a single opinion resolving one issue, the voting anomaly might be of relatively minor conceptual significance. But for the fortuitous combination of issues that the case happens to present, a majority agrees on how to frame and resolve an underlying substantive constitutional question. When, in contrast, the two issues arise at the same level, vote switching is unlikely because the justices genuinely disagree how to resolve, or even define, the same substantive issue of law. At a minimum, this theory explains *Union Gas, Fulminante, Vuitch, Kassel,* and *Tidewater.*

Again, however, *Miller* appears somewhat difficult to reconcile with these other cases, given that Justices O'Connor and Kennedy could readily have conceded standing, a gateway issue, to address the constitutional challenge to the Immigration and Naturalization Act, a substantive constitutional issue. While one can speculate as to why these justices declined to defer to a contrary majority on standing,[161] the more important point is to remember that in this book, I have developed an economic model intended to explain institutional behavior generally, rather than to explain the behavior or predilections of individual justices in every case. With that caveat, the social choice model fares quite well even within the narrow class of multidimensional cases with asymmetrical preferences in identifying the conditions that are and are not conducive to vote switching. More importantly, given that such voting anomaly cases are rare as a general matter, social choice places all the multidimensional asymmetrical cases within a broader perspective, which reveals the limited circumstances in which the Supreme Court confronts a substantial problem in preference aggregation.

C. Implications for Institutional Reform

My point is not to defend each of these four vote switches on the merits, or to criticize the decision by Justices O'Connor and Kennedy not to switch votes in *Miller,* although I do find each of these decisions defensible. Instead, I want to suggest that the tradeoff that each of these cases represents does not appear either to threaten the integrity of the judicial system or to require that it be massively overhauled. This is especially true given that there simply *is no* solution to the pathology that produces these occasional voting anomalies. To be clear, by offering a limited justification for a regime that permits occasional vote switches, I am not embracing the Kornhauser and Sager proposal, which would require a majority vote on a case-by-case basis on the governing rule in cases in which such voting anomalies arise. Under that regime, all justices would be bound by a collective determination on the governing rule, which, as I have already demonstrated in the discussion of *Tidewater,* could have the effect of simply replicating cycling at a different level in the case. Instead, I am arguing that we can justify the occasional decisions of individual justices to switch their votes, not only to break a judgment deadlock, as seen below, but also to avoid an otherwise unacceptable result that is the product of employing the non-Condorcet-producing outcome-voting rule on a Court that occasionally has multidimensional and asymmetrical preferences and that decides matters of vital importance for the nation as a whole. Indeed, the proposed change to issue voting, either on a case-by-case or across-the-board basis, is as likely to produce a satisfactory result, one that works in all cases, as are the efforts of economists to devise a universal solution to the Condorcet paradox or to disprove Arrow's Theorem. Rather than recognizing that a minor deviation from standard practice ameliorates a fairly narrow problem, which these cases represent, advocates of issue voting risk instead re-creating many of the problems already solved through a series of incremental evolutionary steps, including outcome voting and the *Marks* doctrine, that, together, generally operate quite well in the Supreme Court.

Once we recognize that certain problems associated with collective decision-making are in fact intractable, narrow solutions to clearly identified problems become more attractive than sweeping solutions, which may have unforeseen consequences, and which might re-create problems that have already been solved by existing process-based rules. We know from social choice that any collective decision-making body is prone to issuing decisions that either defy rationality or that undermine some fundamental tenet of fair collective decision making. We should not be surprised, therefore, to find that, on occasion, the Supreme Court's decision-making rules produce results that appear problematic. At a minimum, social choice ought to provide the legal theorist with some sympathy for Supreme Court justices who, on rare occasion, depart from theoretical consistency when making binding decisions for the nation as a whole on critically important constitutional issues.

D. Three-Judgment Cases

In light of the above analysis, the final category of cases implicated by outcome voting and the *Marks* doctrine becomes easy to explain. In cases that present three potential judgments—affirm, reverse, or remand—it is possible that the expressed judgments of the individual justices will fail to produce a judgment for the Court as a whole. In six cases, at least one justice has switched his vote to produce a judgment for the Court.[162] These cases demonstrate the principal rationale underlying the evolution away from the Condorcet criterion in Supreme Court voting. Condorcet-producing rules do not ensure an outcome. While the Court's selection of the non-Condorcet-producing rule of outcome voting does not ensure an outcome in three-remedy cases, any rule designed to solve that problem would necessarily engraft a minority voting regime on the Court, thus producing greater problems than the rule would be intended to cure. As with the above category, the Court's countervailing concern for determinacy provides a justification for the occasionally aberrational outcomes that these vote switches appear to produce. It is worth noting that in all but one case in this category, the vote switch was toward a remand, which, if the issue spectrum is unidimensional, is likely a Condorcet-winning outcome. It is also noteworthy that four of the six cases in this category predate *Marks*.[163] One could argue that even without the vote switches, in those three-remedy cases in which the issue spectrum is unidimensional, *Marks* compels the remand in any event, given that it is the likely Condorcet-winning judgment. If, on the other hand, the issue spectrum is two dimensional, then there is no dominant judgment.

E. Synopsis

In this chapter, I used social choice to explain why the Supreme Court employs the non-Condorcet-producing rule, outcome voting, in deciding cases, even though that rule has the potential to thwart majority preferences on underlying issues in an identifiable class of cases. First, I demonstrated that outcome, rather than issue, voting, both of which are non-Condorcet-producing, is superior in promoting principled issue identification. I then explained that while outcome voting produces occasionally irrational results, the Court has further developed as a companion rule the *Marks* narrowest grounds doctrine, which ameliorates that regime's potential irrationality by ensuring that if a Condorcet winner is available, it will likely prevail. The *Marks* doctrine further promotes adherence to Arrovian independence by delinking the case holding from the expressed judgment of those who would prefer to decide the case on broader grounds. Under the outcome-voting/*Marks* regime, however, in those cases in which issue space is two dimensional and preferences are asymmetrical, and where, as a result, there is the potential for cycling, the narrowest grounds analysis is potentially indeterminate. In those cases, lower federal courts have developed an issue head-counting approach when issues arise separately and an outcome head-counting approach when issues arise together. In a rare group of cases, one or more Supreme Court justices have feared that the voting anomaly produced in such cases would undermine important values, including the due process rights of a death row inmate, separation of powers, and the objective of preserving the Court's own jurisdiction, and have therefore switched votes based upon the Court's majority resolution on an underlying issue. In a final category of three-judgment cases, the outcome-voting/*Marks* regime also produces occasionally indeterminate results, which individual justices have avoided by switching their votes to ensure a majority judgment. With one exception, these vote switches have all been in favor of a remand, which, if the issue spectrum is unidimensional, is the apparent Condorcet winner. Table 3.9 summarizes this chapter's presentation of the social choice analy-

Table 3.9.   Summary of Individual Case Categories

Case Category	Examples	Impact on Supreme Court Rules	Continuing Problems
Majority opinions	The overwhelming majority of Supreme Court decisions	With minor exception, assuming agreement on issues, both outcome and issue voting would produce the same result because a majority agrees on the rationale producing the Court's judgment.	None
Fractured panel decisions in which one opinion resolves case on narrowest grounds	*Casey, Bakke, Memoirs*	Outcome voting/*Marks* regime, by delinking proposed breadth of holding from the case outcome, best promotes such probable Condorcet-producing outcomes.	Sometimes appears to rest upon a strained notion of implicit consensus.
Fractured panel decisions in which no opinion resolves case on narrowest grounds	*Miller, Kassel, Tidewater* (and, but for the vote switches, all cases in the next category)	Outcome voting/*Marks* regime, by delinking statement of issues from case outcome, promotes such outcomes; lower federal courts can apply issue or outcome headcounting approach, depending upon issue combinations.	Produces apparent doctrinal incoherence and has potential to produce displeasing substantive results in important cases.
Fractured panel decisions producing vote switches by individual justices	*Union Gas* (White), *Fulminante* (Kennedy), *Vuitch* (Harlan and Blackmun)	Constitutes exception to outcome voting, intended to avoid unacceptable results.	While doctrinally impure, such cases demonstrate occasional overriding concerns, thus far in cases involving separation of powers, due process, and preserving jurisdiction.
Three-remedy cases	Cites listed in note 162	Constitutes exception to outcome voting, intended to ensure collective judgment.	Consistent with social choice analysis that range is limited in Supreme Court by collective obligation to decide cases properly before it; judgments are likely Condorcet-producing.

sis of individual case decision making by case category within the Supreme Court.

VI. Concluding Comments

The foregoing analysis, which demonstrates that Supreme Court decision-making rules evolve in piecemeal and complementary fashion to ensure fair and rational outcomes, provides the critical bridge from static to dynamic constitutional process. The very cases that reveal fault lines in a given fractured panel decision provide the information to future litigants who will try, if unimpeded, to manipulate the order of case presentations over time in the Supreme Court. As the next chapter will demonstrate, this problem is exacerbated when we consider another non-Condorcet-producing Supreme Court rule, one that works across large numbers of cases, namely stare decisis. Like outcome voting, stare decisis promotes outcomes that are contingent upon the voting path. And, again, as with outcome voting, the Supreme Court has developed a companion doctrine, in fact a series of companion doctrines, that operate to increase the likelihood that available Condorcet winners will prevail, rather than path-manipulated legal doctrine. But in contrast with the *Marks* doctrine, the Supreme Court's justiciability doctrines promote Condorcet winners not on the Court itself, but rather in a coequal branch, the United States Congress. With that introduction, we are now ready to consider dynamic constitutional process.

CHAPTER 4

Dynamic Constitutional Process: How Groups of Cases Are Decided

I. Introduction

In this chapter, I will develop a social choice model designed to explain a series of rules that affect the transformation of judicial preferences into constitutional doctrine over time and across cases. While this chapter will explain stare decisis and a series of timing-based justiciability doctrines, its principal focus is the much criticized standing doctrine. Since the early 1970s, standing, and to a lesser extent the related doctrines of ripeness and mootness, have played a central role in the development of virtually all substantive bodies of constitutional law. In contrast with outcome voting and the narrowest grounds rule, which govern decision making within individual cases, the rules considered in this chapter affect the transformation of judicial preferences into constitutional doctrine over groups of cases. In the discussion of *Planned Parenthood of Southeastern Pennsylvania v. Casey*,[1] I offered a preliminary assessment of stare decisis based upon social choice. In this chapter, I will further develop a social choice model of that doctrine, without which, I will argue, one cannot fully appreciate the functions that the Supreme Court's various justiciability doctrines serve. I will demonstrate that, among the other functions that the doctrine serves, stare decisis operates as a cycle-breaking rule, which stabilizes legal doctrine, but which renders the substantive evolution of constitutional law path dependent. I will then argue that all three timing-based justiciability doctrines—ripeness, standing, and mootness—improve the fairness of constitutional decision making by presumptively grounding the critical path of case decisions in fortuitous factors beyond the control of the litigants themselves.

This chapter focuses largely on standing, which has operated as the federal judiciary's principal justiciability gatekeeper throughout the Burger and Rehnquist Courts. As a result, standing has evoked unparalleled scrutiny and criticism from both judges and commentators. While the literature on standing is abundant, prior commentators have not analyzed the doctrine through the lens of social choice. And yet, social choice is uniquely suited to explain both standing's enigmatic doctrinal features and its rather unusual historical development. Traditional commentaries on standing have focused, by and large, on either its doctrinal inconsistencies or its seeming historical illegitimacy as a constitutional, or even quasi-constitutional, doctrine. Little effort has been spent considering the process-based functions that standing serves. The analysis to follow will demonstrate, however, that standing is, first and foremost, a set of rules governing constitutional process.

While commentators have rightly treated standing as an independent body of constitutional law governing the conditions under which litigants can raise claims in federal court, I will demonstrate in this chapter that standing is different in kind than most substantive constitutional doctrines. Standing is simultaneously a discrete set of black letter constitutional rules and a set of rules governing the conditions under which constitutional law is made. To appreciate standing, therefore, we need to analyze the relative competence of those institutions affected by the Supreme Court's decision to address, or not to address, the merits of the underlying disputes. When the Supreme Court denies standing to raise a claim in federal court, the Court, in effect, forces the frustrated litigant either to accept the status quo or to seek redress of her grievance in the legislature. A complete analysis of standing therefore requires a comparative theory about the relative institutional competence of the federal judiciary, on the one hand, and of Congress and state legislatures, on the other.

This chapter will show that while outcome voting, a non-Condorcet-producing rule, ensures a collective outcome in all but three-judgment cases, it does not prevent all potential cyclical indeterminacy in Supreme Court decision making. Outcome voting prevents cycling within, but not across, cases. Under certain conditions, Supreme Court justices might possess multiple normative frameworks for deciding groups of cases over time, none of which dominates the Court as a whole. Absent a constraint on how issues are framed in cases subject to precedent, the potential would arise for the Court to codify cyclical preferences over multiple cases. The resulting doctrinal instability would diminish the value of Supreme Court case law. Stare decisis infuses stability into Supreme Court case law by presumptively requiring adherence to indistinguishable precedent. Just as outcome voting prevents justices from expressing contingent preferences in a given case, so too the presumptive obligation to adhere to precedent prevents justices from expressing contingent doctrinal preferences across cases. Based upon stare decisis, a justice who believes that two cases are indistinguishable is presumptively prevented from basing his or her outcome vote in the later case upon whether a majority agrees not to distinguish the precedent, or upon a determination that adhering to precedent might generate an unfavorable voting path. Stare decisis infuses doctrinal stability by preventing reconsideration of arguments that were rejected in cases producing binding precedent and that, if freely entertained, might increase the frequency of exposed doctrinal cycles, and thus undermine the rule of law. Stare decisis thus stabilizes Supreme Court decision making, but it does so at the cost of grounding substantive case outcomes in the order in which cases are decided.

Judge Frank Easterbrook has objected that path dependency itself is a vital defect in constitutional decision making,[2] one which counsels in favor of relaxing stare decisis. I will argue, instead, that path dependency is an inevitable, and thus acceptable, by-product of a legal regime that seeks to produce stable constitutional doctrine. The real problem with stare decisis, which is ameliorated by the various justiciability doctrines, is the incentive it creates among potential ideological litigants to try to influence the substantive evolution of constitutional doctrine by manipulating the critically important path of case decisions. The modern standing doctrine is best understood as a set of ground rules that operates in conjunction with stare decisis and that ameliorates the most damaging effects of adhering to precedent. Standing presumptively prevents ideological litigants from strategically timing cases in federal court solely to manipulate the substantive evolution of constitutional doctrine. The principal standing ground rules require that claimants be injured by fortuitous historical circumstances beyond their control as a precondition to litigating in federal court. While the emerging substantive body of constitutional law remains path dependent even with standing in place, standing renders the process of constitutional decision making more fair by making it more difficult for ideological litigants, who are generally non-Condorcet-winning minorities, to exert a disproportionate influence over the path of case decisions.

As stated above, evaluating standing requires a comparative institutional analysis of courts and legislatures. In raising the cost to potential ideological litigants of trying to vindicate their claims in federal court, standing further encourages them to seek redress in Congress or in state legislatures. In contrast with appellate courts, which have largely evolved away from the Condorcet criterion, legislatures, including Congress, have generally evolved toward the Condorcet criterion, and specifically toward Condorcet-producing rules and practices. When faced with cyclical preferences, legislatures have the institutional power to do nothing and to let the various proposals before them die. Alternatively, legislatures can respond by expanding the relevant issue space, thus achieving the requisite level of consensus through vote trading. While the commodification of preferences might produce legislation that is no one's first choice, the resulting package likely has implicit Condorcet-winning support. In effect, given the legislature's comparative advantage in aggregating collective preferences—even those that are cyclical—in a rational and fair manner, the modern standing doctrine is best understood as calibrating adjudicatory lawmaking according to the relative institutional competence of the federal judiciary, on the one hand, and Congress and state legislatures, on the other.

The remainder of this chapter is divided into three sections. The first section introduces the concept of standing and places the doctrine within a broader framework of justiciability, including ripeness and mootness. The second section explains the doctrine of stare decisis in economic terms, and explains why stare decisis creates incentives for litigants to attempt to control the evolution of substantive legal doctrine by manipulating the order, or path, of legal decisions. That section also explains the conditions under which we would expect the Supreme Court to respond to litigant path manipulation by imposing a justiciability barrier in the form of standing. The final section demonstrates the importance of standing in furthering a critical and often overlooked distinction between legislative and judicial lawmaking functions in our constitutional system of government. The next two chapters will then assess the historical development of standing in light of this chapter's analytical framework.

II. An Introduction to Standing: Justiciability, Separation of Powers, and Enigmatic Doctrine

This section will introduce the concept of standing in three different, but complementary, ways. I will begin by placing standing within a broader framework of justiciability. To do so, I will employ two modes of analysis, one based upon timing, and the other based upon the perceived ease or difficulty of the various case categories in promoting path manipulation. I will then consider standing's function in furthering an important aspect of separation of powers. Finally, I will explain some of the doctrine's most notorious doctrinal inconsistencies and the inability of traditional analytical methods to explain them. In the remainder of this chapter, I will expand upon each of these points in developing the social choice theory of stare decisis and standing.

A. Defining Standing: Timing and Agenda-Manipulation Models

Defining standing is a notoriously difficult task. Standing is perhaps better conceived as a somewhat amorphous concept, having to do with the conditions under which individuals can litigate claims in federal court, than as a discrete legal doctrine. To explain standing, it will be helpful to place the doctrine within a broader spectrum of closely related barriers to justiciability, ripeness and mootness. These more easily defined justiciability doctrines serve much the same function as standing in raising the barriers to strategic timing of cases, but have proved historically inadequate to prevent the most egregious manifestations of litigant path manipulation. We can cast the Supreme Court's justiciability spectrum in terms of the following conceptual time line. Ripeness prevents the adjudication of premature claims, including, for example, a challenge to the constitutionality of a statute yet to be enforced.[3] Mootness prevents the adjudication of claims, which although once fully mature, are no longer alive, such as a right not to be penalized for the exercise of a constitutional liberty in a workplace in which the claimant has already voluntarily terminated her employment.[4] Standing operates between these conceptual boundaries to bar as nonjusticiable certain presently live claims, meaning claims that are ripe and not moot. Table 4.1 presents the above justiciability time line.

In contrast with ripeness and mootness, which are fairly easy to define (albeit sometimes difficult to apply),[5] standing is notoriously difficult both to define and to apply. Thus, Justice William O. Douglas once observed, "Generalizations about standing to sue are largely worthless as such."[6] One com-

Table 4.1.   Standing in Time

Doctrine	Ripeness	Standing	Mootness
Analytical Spectrum	premature claims ◄───────────► dead claims		

mentator, Professor Steven Winter, has attributed the term *standing* to the common courtroom practice requiring that one stand to be heard.[7] In this conception, the doctrine is about the conditions under which potential litigants have or lack the figurative power "to stand," and thus to raise their potential claims in federal court. Because the remaining timing-based justiciability barriers already prevent the adjudication of claims that either are not yet ripe or are moot, standing is about the conditions under which persons have or lack the power to litigate presently live claims.

In chapter 1, I contrasted two prominent cases reaching opposite outcomes on standing, *Board of Regents of the University of California at Davis v. Bakke,*[8] and *Allen v. Wright.*[9] Recall that in *Bakke,* the Supreme Court granted Bakke standing to challenge the affirmative action program employed by the University of California at Davis Medical School, which set aside sixteen of its one hundred seats for minority candidates. The *Bakke* Court allowed standing by focusing on the denial of the opportunity to compete, even though Mr. Bakke might not have been admitted to the medical school had the affirmative action program not been in place. In *Allen,* in contrast, the Court denied standing to a group of African American parents who challenged the constitutionality of an IRS tax policy, which based the tax-exempt status of private schools upon that of the umbrella organizations of which they were a part, rather than upon an individualized assessment, even though the effect, the parents claimed, was to afford such status to some schools engaging in racially discriminatory practices. In contrast with the *Bakke* Court, the *Allen* Court denied standing, concluding that even if it were to strike down the allegedly unconstitutional IRS tax policy, the effect might not be to meaningfully further the integration of public schools, given the number of intervening links in the chain of causation, controlled for the most part by persons not before the Court.

The problem is that the *Bakke* and *Allen* Courts could have produced opposite results by employing the other case's conception of injury. Thus, had the *Bakke* Court focused on the attenuated linkage between striking down the Davis affirmative action plan and Bakke's ultimate goal of attendance, it could easily have denied standing, as it did in *Allen.* And had the *Allen* Court defined the plaintiffs' injury in terms of the lost opportunity to pursue an integrated education in a market place unimpeded by an allegedly unconstitutional IRS tax policy, regardless of the ultimate effect on the integration of the schools that their children attended, it could just as easily have conferred standing, as it did in *Bakke.*

In presenting *Bakke* and *Allen* in chapter 1, I observed that both cases fall into the most difficult category of standing.[10] In this chapter, I will further demonstrate that standing itself falls into the most difficult category of justiciability. Later in this chapter, and in chapter 6, I will demonstrate that most standing cases can be divided into one of three general rules: no right to enforce the rights of others; no right to prevent diffuse harms; and no right to an undistorted market. A preview of these rules will help to further develop the justiciability spectrum presented in table 4.1.

Let us assume, as I will argue in the next part, that the modern standing doctrine was developed to improve the overall fairness of Supreme Court decision making by making it more difficult for litigants to influence the substantive evolution of constitutional doctrine by manipulating the order in which cases are presented. If so, we can then reconceive justiciability from a timing-based spectrum, per table 4.1, to conceptual spectrum based upon the ease or difficulty of engaging in path manipulation. To visualize this reconceived presentation of justiciability, imagine folding the timing-based spectrum in table 4.1 in half, thus bringing the outer edges, ripeness and mootness, together. Those two justiciability barriers proscribe the adjudication of claims that have either not yet fully developed or that were once fully developed, but have since expired. Ripeness and mootness thus represent the easiest rules for preventing persons or interest groups from engaging in the strategic timing of cases. With no timing-based barrier preventing claims that have yet to arise, or that have since expired, litigants would be limited only by lawyerly imagination in their efforts to strategically time cases.

Within standing, we can further divide the doctrines based upon the relative ease or difficulty that they pose for strategic path manipulation. While ripeness and mootness avoid the lowest cost method of strategic timing, as explained below, the first two standing doctrines—no right to enforce the rights of others and no right to prevent diffuse harms—avoid the relatively low-cost manipulation of presently live claims. The final category, which includes *Bakke* and *Allen,* is the most difficult, and the most prone to seemingly inconsistent applications, precisely because it involves presently live claims that do not belong to others, and that are not legally diffuse. And yet, even the seemingly inconsistent case outcomes falling into this difficult standing category can be explained based upon the theory of social choice. Table 4.2 presents the reconceived justiciability spectrum.

Table 4.2. Standing in the Path of Agenda Manipulation

Doctrine or Standing Category	Ripeness and Mootness	No Rights to Enforce the Rights of Others or to Prevent Diffuse Harms	No Right to an Undistorted Market
Analytical Spectrum	Relatively easy path manipulation ◄――――――►		Relatively difficult path manipulation
Nature of Claim	Premature or dead claims	live claims	

In this analysis, ripeness and mootness, although opposite from a timing-based perspective, are presented together, given the relative ease of inventing hypothetical claims or of resurrecting dead claims in an effort to manipulate the order of case decisions. It is obviously more difficult to locate live claims. Notice that the relevant spectrum, depicted by the double arrow, continues after the emergence of live claims. That is because within the general category of live claims, some are more difficult to locate—and thus to path manipulate—than others. Some interest groups, like the NAACP Legal Defense Fund and the American Civil Liberties Union, are well equipped to follow relevant legal developments throughout the United States and to time legal challenges accordingly, and others, like Sierra Club and Amnesty International, are able to do that, and even to monitor legal developments abroad. If these organizations could raise legal challenges on behalf of others who might be affected by them throughout the United States, their ability to shape the substantive evolution of doctrine by manipulating the order of case decisions would be greatly enhanced. Alternatively, even a rule prohibiting such groups from vindicating the legal claims of others would pose no meaningful barrier to justiciability if the groups could claim that their members were harmed, albeit in a general and imperceptible way, simply by the existence of illegal governmental activity somewhere in the world. Thus, whether cast in terms of preventing the vindication of claims belonging to others, or claims that are legally diffuse, these standing categories prevent an intermediate level of difficulty in manipulating the order of case decisions.

The final standing category, no right to an undistorted market, is conceptually the most problematic because it does not appear to involve particularly easy conditions for path manipulation. In *Bakke* and *Allen,* for example, the litigants were directly affected by fortuitous historical circumstances beyond their control. In fact, in both cases, the government, or its agent, was in control of all relevant facts. To fully appreciate the justiciability spectrum, and to place these cases in their proper context, we must now expand the presentation in table 4.2 to include one more category. In criminal procedure cases, persons charged with or convicted of crimes are permitted to raise virtually any constitutional challenge to alleged governmental misconduct affecting their case with no credible challenge to the justiciability (as distinguished from the merits) of their underlying claims. In other words, within our legal system, convicted criminals, in their direct appeals or collateral challenges, are presumptively entitled to a judicial resolution of their underlying legal challenges, however dubious the merits of those challenges might be. As demonstrated more fully below, in cases falling within this final category, the Court has issued the most minutely detailed body of substantive case law, and in fact, has sometimes defied its own traditional justiciability principles in doing so.[11] The Court allows the federal judiciary to make such detailed pronouncements of constitutional law in criminal cases because without doing so, convicted criminals would face the most severe restrictions that a state or the federal government is lawfully empowered to impose, namely imprisonment or even death, possibly in violation of their constitutional rights. As a

Table 4.3. Expanded Justiciability Spectrum

Doctrine or Standing Category	Ripeness/ Mootness	Rights of Others and Diffuse Harms	Undistorted Market	Criminal Procedure
Analytical Spectrum	Strong presumption in favor of path manipulation ◄————————►		Strong presumption against path manipulation	

result, the Court generally presumes in favor of the justiciability of such claims, which are almost invariably not motivated by a desire to manipulate the order of case decisions, but rather are driven by the more immediate desire to secure whatever relief a court of law is able to provide. Table 4.3 presents the expanded justiciability spectrum.

In the expanded justiciability spectrum represented in table 4.3, the final standing category, no right to an undistorted market, lies between the relatively easy standing categories, no right to enforce the rights of others and no right to prevent diffuse harms, in which there is a fairly strong presumption in favor of path manipulation (and thus against justiciability), and the criminal procedure cases, in which there is an equally strong presumption against path manipulation (and thus in favor of justiciability). In chapter 6, which will provide a more detailed breakdown of the standing case law, I will argue that in this final standing category, the Court looks for those characteristic features that pull toward either the end of this broader justiciability spectrum in which litigant path manipulation is easily recognized or the opposite end in which, like criminal defendants, the litigants appear to be trying to extricate themselves from a bipolar legal tangle arising from circumstances largely within the government's control or, at the very least, beyond their own.

B. Standing and Separation of Powers: Another Dimension of Timing

Standing not only limits strategic path manipulation, but also preserves a critical, although increasingly neglected, aspect of separation of powers. This aspect of standing implicates another dimension of timing, namely the extent to which the federal judiciary, on the one hand, and Congress and state legislatures, on the other, control the timing of their own decision making. A fundamental tenet of federal court practice, dating to the famous statement in *Marbury v. Madison*,[12] holds that "[i]t is emphatically the province and duty of the judicial department to say what the law is."[13] *Marbury* requires the federal courts to make law as slowly or as quickly as needed to resolve disputes presented in cases properly before them, without regard to whether, in doing so, they are required to make law, and also without regard to whether in making law, they sometimes produce seemingly irrational results. This is the essence of Chief Justice John Marshall's assertion, not just of judicial "province," but also of judicial "duty."* We have already seen that among the costs imposed by this duty is the need for the Supreme Court to adopt non-Condorcet-producing decisional rules to avoid the potential impasse that would otherwise result when the Court is faced with cases for which the preferences of its members are intransitive. This holds true both for decision-making rules employed in individual cases, explaining the choice of outcome rather than issue voting, and for rules employed to decide groups of cases over time, explaining the emergence of stare decisis. In both contexts, judicial duty imposes an obligation upon the Supreme Court and lower federal courts to resolve cases even when in doing so those courts potentially thwart the majority preferences of their own members.

In contrast with appellate courts, which are obligated to decide cases properly before them, legislatures are free to decide—or not decide—issues presented to them for consideration in the form of bills. Legislatures have the institutional power of inertia, meaning that they can avoid taking formal collective action. Unlike appellate courts, legislatures have two avenues for dismissing proposed changes to the status quo that are unpopular. Legislatures can either make a collective determination to vote down such proposals or they can simply fail to act. As shown in the discussion of *New York v. United States*,[14] in which the State of New York declined to locate an in-state low-level radioactive waste disposal facility, the latter method of disposing of proposed change can result from an empty-core problem, and thus from the phenomenon—or at least the threat—of cycling. In contrast, at each stage of the Supreme Court's decision-making processes—deciding whether to grant or to deny certiorari, deciding whether to dismiss on grounds that certiorari was improvidently granted, deciding whether to dismiss for want of justiciability, and deciding the case on its merits—declining to change the status quo requires at least a de minimis formal institutional collective decision. Of course, the Court need not dispose of cases in the manner that the parties request. Standing denials, for example, often represent a judicial decision to avoid the issues that the parties claim to be suitable, or even necessary, for judicial resolution. But as with each of the above stages of Supreme Court decision making, standing denials require a collective institutional decision.

More importantly, standing reduces the extent to which litigants can force the creation of positive law in federal courts, including the Supreme

---

* The insight in the text is also inextricably linked to meaning of the word *case*. The word derives from the Latin *casus*, meaning chance. *See* Robert Pushaw, Jr., *Article III's Case/Controversy Distinction and the Dual Functions of Federal Courts*, 69 NOTRE DAME L. REV. 447, 472 n. 133 (1994). The implication is clear: Litigation presents courts with the opportunity—and duty—to resolve the underlying issues necessary to deciding those cases, which, by chance, happen to be presented. *See also* David E. Engdahl, *John Marshall's "Jeffersonian" Concept of Judicial Review*, 42 DUKE L. J. 279, 303 (1992) ("What makes the judiciary the appropriate decider of a question, and sometimes makes it the last recourse among federal departments on a constitutional (as on any other legal) question, is not the character of the question, but rather the accident of its occurrence in the form contemplated by Article III").

Court, through strategic timing of cases. By declining to address the merits of an underlying constitutional challenge, standing has the effect of protecting the authority of Congress and state legislatures, which have the power to remain inert, to do so unless and until an appropriate legislative consensus has formed. The standing doctrine thus preserves a fundamental distinction between the appropriate nature of judicial and legislative lawmaking, namely the relative difference in control over the timing of decision making. I will further show that a series of Supreme Court cases involving the application of low-level rational basis scrutiny to a variety of state and federal regulations that are challenged as either over- or under-broad is consistent with the analysis of standing presented here. Like standing, the choice of tiers of scrutiny furthers the presumption that legislatures, unlike courts, are the masters of their own timing.

C. The Doctrinal Puzzle: Standing Elements Drawn from Tort

The principal doctrinal elements of standing, which have been extended as well to ripeness and mootness, are derived from the common law of tort. The Supreme Court has stated that at a minimum standing requires the presence of a constitutional injury in fact, causation, and redressibility.[15] Of these elements, injury has proved the most important, and the one most subject to criticism based upon seemingly inconsistent applications. To understand these doctrinal standing elements, it will be helpful first to consider their parallel role in a prima facie tort action.

A widely accepted tenet of tort law holds that if A witnesses B's negligent conduct that does not cause harm to anyone, A will be prevented from suing B for negligence. Judge Cardozo aptly summarized the point when he wrote: "Proof of negligence in the air . . . will not do."[16] Instead, A must wait until B injures her, or someone she has a legal right to protect, before suing. It is relatively easy to envision an alternative regime in which courts would allow A to sue B before B causes anyone, including A, actual harm. Assuming A is willing to incur the costs of suing, the hypothetical regime, which would presumably impose some liability upon B for his noninjurious negligence, would have the obvious benefit of making B's negligent conduct potentially more costly *before* B causes anyone harm. Indeed, in a world in which all persons possess complete information and can transact—or litigate—costlessly, the hypothetical legal regime might seem superior. While A has not been forced to sue B, her willingness to do so appears to provide an important societal benefit, namely raising the cost to B of engaging in tortious conduct before that conduct causes an actual injury.

In tort, the substantial cost of litigation and the scarcity of judicial resources plays an important role in preventing litigation of hypothetical claims, meaning those for which no concrete injury has yet occurred. Some fortunate persons might continue in their negligent conduct without ever causing an injury. Still others might conform their once-negligent conduct to an appropriate level of care before harming anyone. Requiring as a prerequisite to a tort action that the plaintiff suffer actual harm benefits the legal system as a whole by reducing potentially wasteful litigation costs and by conserving scarce judicial resources. At the same time, if appropriate sanctions for negligence are imposed upon tortfeasors who do cause injury, others who have not yet conformed their conduct to the requirements of the law will have an incentive to do so.

While the doctrinal elements of standing are drawn from tort, it is not obvious that the justification for the borrowed tort elements extends as well to the standing context. Do the benefits of conserving scarce judicial resources through standing denials outweigh the costs of denying standing to ideological litigants who, but for standing, might freely challenge allegedly unlawful governmental regulation? To answer this question, it will be helpful to briefly preview the historical foundation for standing, which I will set out more fully in chapter 5.

The antecedents to modern standing were conceived in the New Deal to fend off attacks on mounting and pervasive governmental regulation. The scope of such regulation, and thus the importance of standing, increased throughout the later Great Society in the 1960s. And some have argued that by today's standards, even the New Deal and Great Society programs imposed relatively minor regulatory intrusions.[17] Today, both federal and state regulations intrude upon areas of our lives that, under the once-dominant jurisprudence of *Lochner v. New York*,[18] were deemed altogether beyond regulatory reach.[19] And federal regulatory powers today intrude upon areas once deemed the exclusive subject of state and local control.[20] The liberal New Deal and Warren Courts gave way to the more conservative counterparts beginning in the early 1970s. In contrast with the New Deal and Warren Courts, which condoned state and federal regulatory intervention, typified, for example, by minimum wage and maximum hour provisions, the Burger and Rehnquist Courts tended to exhibit a greater faith in private orderings and a corresponding distrust of governmental regulation. When the modern standing doctrine is placed in a proper historical perspective, therefore, the tort analogy raises an important anomaly, which traditional standing analysis has failed to consider, let alone to explain. The general economic conservatism of the Burger and Rehnquist Courts make implausible the extension of the underlying logic of the injury regime in tort to the context of standing. Simply put, it seems unlikely that those later conservative Courts incorporated the tort elements of injury, causation, and redressibility because a majority believed that the judicial resources saved through standing denials outweighed the potential costs of allegedly unlawful governmental regulation, which, but for standing, conservative ideological litigants could have challenged. And yet, it was during the generally conservative Burger and Rehnquist periods that the Supreme Court infused standing (along with ripeness and mootness) with doctrinal elements drawn from tort. It was also during this period that the Court solidified the constitutional underpinnings of standing, concluding that it was a prerequisite to filing suit in federal court, growing out of Article III.[21]

Not surprisingly perhaps, at least one prominent market-oriented legal scholar, Professor Richard Epstein, has argued that the pervasiveness of government regulation during the last half-century calls for a general relaxation of standing doctrine.[22] But the attacks on the modern standing doctrine are by no means limited to those who strongly favor economic conservatism. In fact, there is a fairly uniform consensus among legal scholars from across the political spectrum denouncing the legitimacy of standing as formulated in the Burger and Rehnquist Courts.[23] Whatever the political or doctrinal implications of relaxing the modern standing doctrine might be, the doctrine's historical development presents an important puzzle that traditional analyses have failed to explain. Assuming that a once sympathetic New Deal Court created the standing doctrine to stave off unwelcome challenges to experimental government programs designed to reverse the depression, the question arises why the later, and more conservative, Burger and Rehnquist Courts did not abandon, or at least severely restrict, the doctrine's application. As an historical matter, nearly the opposite has occurred.

Commentators have criticized not only the present doctrinal formulation of standing and the Court's repeated assertion that the doctrine has constitutional, and not merely prudential, underpinnings, but also the Court's application of standing as inconsistent, and perhaps even as arbitrary. In considering such challenges, it is again helpful to consider the analogy to tort. While the tort injury requirement operates to prevent the adjudication of claims that may never arise or that may manifest themselves in unforeseeable ways, standing's injury prong is often understood to prevent similarly ill defined ideological claims, often in the form of constitutional challenges to government laws or policies. Whether or not such a policy is wise, standing is often seen as a device used by federal courts to fend off challenges to governmental conduct that are brought primarily on an ideological basis. The difficulty with this conception of standing, however, is its inability to explain the many apparent doctrinal inconsistencies. In addition to *Allen* and *Bakke,* discussed above, consider the following cases.

In *City of Los Angeles v. Lyons,*[24] the Supreme Court denied a former choke hold victim standing to raise his due process challenge to the Los Angeles Police Department's continued choke hold practice on behalf of himself and the class he represented. In *Gilmore v. Utah,*[25] the Court applied standing principles to deny an application for stay of execution by Gary Gilmore's mother, who alleged that her son's conviction and death sentence violated several constitutional guarantees. In *United States v. Richardson,*[26] the Court denied standing to a federal taxpayer who alleged that the CIA's failure to release budget information violated the Constitution's statement and account clause. In *Schlesinger v. Reservists Commission to Stop the War,*[27] the Court denied standing to United States citizens who alleged that certain members of Congress were serving in the armed forces reserve in violation of the Constitution's incompatibility clause. And in *Lujan v. Defenders of Wildlife,*[28] the Court denied standing to environmentalist plaintiffs who challenged a regulation on interagency consultation issued under the Endangered Species Act, even though a section of the act expressly granted plaintiffs standing. In each of these well-noted cases, the Supreme Court based its standing denial, at least in part, on its assessment that plaintiff or plaintiffs had failed to allege a sufficiently concrete injury, or that the litigation was being conducted on an essentially ideological basis.

The merits of the above rulings aside, commentators have found difficult, if not impossible, the task of reconciling them with others in which the Supreme Court has allowed standing. In addition to *Bakke,* consider the following cases granting standing. In *Duke Power Co. v. Carolina Environmental Study Group, Inc.,*[29] the Court granted standing to property owners who challenged the constitutionality of a federal statute limiting the liability of nuclear power plants in an effort to halt the planned construction of two such plants near their homes, even though they did not allege and could not prove that striking the liability limit would abate construction. And in *United States v. Students Challenging Regulatory Agency Procedures (SCRAP),*[30] the Court granted standing to a group of environmentalist law students alleging that a railroad rate increase, if approved, would cause harm to the air in Washington, D.C., notwithstanding the unusually attenuated, and rather dubious, causal chain from the challenged conduct to the alleged harm.[31]

Relying upon these and other seemingly irreconcilable standing outcomes, scholars have debated since the inception of standing, first, whether the doctrine serves any valid function not already served by other, more well established, legal doctrines, for example, other barriers to justiciability or the question whether the claimant has a cause of action;[32] second, whether standing should be treated as a constitutional requirement, as the Supreme Court has repeatedly stated, or instead, as purely prudential; and finally, whether standing is merely a vehicle employed by a politicized Supreme Court either to avoid reaching the merits of divisive cases or, precisely the opposite, to provide a preliminary and low-cost indication of how it might rule on the merits at some future time.

In its efforts to clarify standing, the Supreme Court itself has only added confusion. Resting the standing doctrine on both prudential and constitutional grounds, the Court has generated substantial debate among scholars, and in its own ranks, as to whether Congress has the power to grant standing when the Court has denied it. Thus, while Justice O'Connor argued in *Allen,* for example, that standing is designed to protect Congress's power to monitor the executive branch as it sees fit,[33] Justice Scalia, in *Lujan v. Defenders of Wildlife,*[34] denied Congress the power to vest standing in private attorneys general to monitor executive agency conduct. While both justices agree that standing grows out of separation of powers, their separation of powers analyses have led them to precisely opposite outcomes when Congress confers standing by statute.[35] Justice O'Connor, who believes that standing is intended to protect Congress's power to monitor the executive branch as it sees fit, would freely uphold Congress's power to grant standing even to ideological plaintiffs as part of a congressional enforcement scheme. Justice Scalia, on the other hand, would prevent a congressional enforcement scheme that allows private attorneys general to monitor the executive branch in federal court. Justice Kennedy has attempted to find some middle ground between the O'Connor and Scalia positions, allowing Congress to confer standing upon private attorneys general to monitor the executive branch, but only if, in doing so, the statute articulates a minimally acceptable definition of the plaintiff's claimed injury.[36]

Legal academics have proved equally unsuccessful in achieving consensus on either the purpose or legitimacy of standing doctrine. Indeed, academic commentary on standing reflects a seemingly irreconcilable divergence. Some academics take the position that the Supreme Court employs standing to avoid or delay resolving difficult questions of law, often as a matter of prudence or restraint.[37] Others have argued, in nearly opposite fashion, that standing is an inevitably normative inquiry that merely substitutes one substantive determination, albeit in the guise of a procedural ruling, for another.[38] Professor (now judge) William Fletcher has persuasively argued that because there is no objective measure of the term *injury*, virtually all standing denials are substantive rulings.[39] Unless a prospective litigant is lying about the nature of her underlying claim, it is impossible to apply the concept of injury neutrally to deny standing without making a normative judgment that certain claimed injuries will not provide the foundation for a constitutional challenge in federal court.

I agree with Judge Fletcher that, setting aside the possibility of a lying plaintiff, standing denials based upon the absence of an injury in fact are inevitably substantive determinations. But, I will argue, standing denials represent substantially *different* substantive holdings than do grants of standing followed by determinations of the merits of underlying claims. While granting standing, followed by a determination of the merits of the legal challenge under review, would force a legal judgment on a question that the legislature either chose not to resolve or that it resolved differently, thus demonstrating the absence of Condorcet-winning legislative support, denying standing produces a holding only about the conditions under which a person can or cannot present the underlying claim. Standing denials therefore leave open the possibility that the legislature can address the underlying substantive question in the future, should an appropriate consensus arise, or that the Court will address it should it be compelled to do so in circumstances in which justiciability is not meaningfully subject to dispute. In its most essential form, then, the question of standing is about the appropriate process through which law—and most notably constitutional law—is and is not made. We are now ready to develop more formally the social choice model of stare decisis and standing.

III.   Stare Decisis and Standing: A Social Choice Perspective

A.   *Crawford* and *Seattle* Revisited

The social choice model of stare decisis is best illustrated by reconsidering two cases presented in chapter 1, *Crawford v. Board of Education*,[40] and

Washington v. Seattle School District No. 1,[41] which were decided on the same day, this time based upon the framework set out in chapter 3. In *Crawford,* the Supreme Court upheld against a Fourteenth Amendment equal protection clause challenge a California constitutional amendment preventing state courts from ordering integrative busing unless the court first determined that a federal court would have done so based upon the Fourteenth Amendment equal protection clause. In *Seattle*, the same Court struck down on equal protection grounds a Washington statewide referendum preventing local school boards from ordering integrative busing unless the school board first determined that the federal or state constitutions required it. Justice Marshall, who alone dissented in *Crawford,* stated that he believed the two cases were constitutionally indistinguishable. In his *Seattle* dissent, joined by Chief Justice Burger and Justices Rehnquist and O'Connor, Justice Powell also demonstrated that he believed that the two cases could not be distinguished. Setting aside the substantive question whether the two cases are distinguishable, which does not matter for the analysis to follow, these two cases reveal that outcome voting is not alone sufficient to limit doctrinal cycling in the Supreme Court.

Recall that in striking down the Washington statewide initiative, the *Seattle* majority, per Justice Blackmun, determined that *Hunter v. Erickson*,[42] a case in which the Court struck down an amendment to the Akron City Charter, requiring majority support of both the city's voters and the city counsel to enact a fair housing ordinance aimed at curbing racial desegregation in housing, was controlling.[43] In contrast, writing for a majority in *Crawford* and for four dissenting justices in *Seattle,* Justice Powell determined that *Hunter* did not control either case.[44] In *Crawford* and *Seattle,* the Court possessed three seemingly irreconcilable majorities: (1) a majority to uphold the *Crawford* amendment; (2) a majority to strike the *Seattle* initiative; and (3) a majority composed of Chief Justice Burger and Justices Marshall, Powell, Rehnquist, and O'Connor to decide the cases the same way regardless of whether the state laws were upheld or struck down. Table 4.4 recasts the *Crawford* and *Seattle* voting lineups, originally presented in chapter 1,[45] this time using the analytical framework of dimensionality and symmetry.

In table 4.4, I have employed the following conventions. The lower left box is bolded because it alone contains the minority of justices who agree that the actual case results—uphold the *Crawford* amendment and strike the *Seattle* initiative—can be achieved without violating the principle that indistinguishable cases should be decided in like manner. Within that box, the names of Justices Brennan and Blackmun appear in italics because they alone decline to join Justice Powell's majority opinion in *Crawford*. Because Justices Powell, Burger, Rehnquist, and O'Connor, in the upper left box, and Justice Marshall, in the lower right box, voted for consistent outcomes in the two cases, after having established in their analyses that the two cases could not be meaningfully distinguished, table 4.4 reveals that together, the two cases present the characteristic features of multidimensionality and asymmetry, from which it becomes possible to infer a collective intransitivity. Simply put,

Table 4.4. *Crawford* and *Seattle* in Two Dimensions with Asymmetrical Preferences

| | | *Crawford* Amendment | |
		Uphold	Strike
Seattle Initiative	Uphold	(A) Powell, Burger, Rehnquist, O'Connor	
	Strike	(B) White, Stevens, *Brennan, Blackmun*	(C) Marshall

positions (A), represented by Powell, and (C), represented by Marshall, resolve the merits of both cases in opposite fashion. And yet, both (A) and (C) embrace the position that the two cases are constitutionally indistinguishable, and thus suggest that the cases should be decided in the same manner. As a result, even though position (B) affords the (A) and (C) camps a favorable single case resolution, there is no logical reason why either (A) or (C) could not select the other over (B) as a second choice to further the objective of doctrinal consistency. Thus viewed, these two cases present precisely the same underlying phenomenon as *Miller v. Albright*,[46] *Kassel v. Consolidated Freightways*,[47] and *National Mutual Insurance Co. v. Tidewater Transfer Co.*,[48] each described in chapter 3.

In addition to highlighting the parallel characteristics of individual and aggregate case decision making, *Seattle* and *Crawford* further demonstrate the important process-based function that stare decisis serves in breaking potential doctrinal cycles across cases. To illustrate this function, it will be helpful to consider what the results of employing a Condorcet-producing rule to decide these two cases might have been.[49] To illustrate, assume that the two cases arise together, such that neither operates as a binding constraint on the other. Further assume that the justices distill the two cases to the following three issues: (1) whether to uphold the *Seattle* initiative; (2) whether to uphold the *Crawford* amendment; and (3) whether to treat the two cases as indistinguishable, such that both state laws will either be upheld or struck down. To simplify the presentation, I will present three packages of resolutions of these underlying issues, each of which corresponds to one of the occupied boxes in table 4.4. In each package, the name of a case standing alone means that it will be decided consistently with the actual case outcome, and when the name of a case is preceded by a *not*, that means it will be decided contrary to the actual case outcome. The three issues presented above produce the following three sets of resolutions, as they appear in table 4.4:[50]

A: *Crawford*, not-*Seattle*
B: *Crawford*, *Seattle*
C: not-*Crawford*, *Seattle*

Based upon a set of simplifying assumptions, I will now demonstrate that the presence of three frameworks, one allowing states to equate state equal protection with Fourteenth Amendment standards; one preventing the states, based upon *Hunter,* from making more difficult the process of securing particular political benefits for an identifiable minority group; and one based upon a determination that the two cases are indistinguishable and thus that they should be decided consistently (the functional equivalent of stare decisis), together are conducive to doctrinal cycling. After illustrating how a Condorcet-producing decisional rule would generate cycling, I will then show that by elevating consistency from one of several optional normative frameworks to a presumptive constraint, in the form of stare decisis,[51] the cycle breaks down. In fact, stare decisis operates to break the potential cycle across these two cases in precisely the same manner that outcome voting operates to break potential cycles in individual cases.

Assume that each justice now ranks his preferences over the three sets of alternatives and that the Court bases its outcomes in both cases on a series of unlimited binary comparisons, which honor the justices' ordinal rankings. The decisional rule is Condorcet-producing, thus adhering to Arrovian range.[52] Before setting out the ordinal rankings, it will be helpful to explain each option. A justice choosing option A believes that the cases should be decided consistently and that both state laws should be upheld. A justice choosing option B believes that both cases were correctly decided, such that the California constitutional amendment should be upheld, while the Washington initiative should be struck down. And a justice choosing option C, in contrast, believes that the two cases should be decided in the opposite consistent manner relative to option A, with the result that both state laws are struck down. To simplify the presentation without changing the analysis, assume that there are only three voters, any two of whom can decide for the Court, with Justice Powell representing position A, Justice White representing position B, and Justice Marshall representing position C. Any two camps contain the requisite votes for a majority.

As explained in the presentation of *Kassel* in chapter 3, for each justice, there are six possible ordinal rankings over the three available alternatives.[53] Stare decisis proscribes two sets, each of which expresses a form of contingent preference. We will assume that each justice most prefers the outcome consistent with his actual case votes, and then, based upon a set of assumptions, set out his ordinal rankings over the remaining two alternatives. Assume that while Justice Marshall states that he favors consistency, he would actually prefer a partly favorable inconsistent result to a fully adverse consistent result. If so, his preferences are CBA. Assume that Powell favors consistency even if the result is adverse in both cases. His ordinal rankings are then ACB. Finally, while Justice White believes that the two cases are distinguishable, each of the remaining two options treats them as indistinguishable. Assume that Justice White determines that if forced to choose between striking down or upholding both state laws, he would prefer to uphold both, given that a contrary preference would result in striking down a law that he firmly believes to be constitutional. If so, his ordinal rankings are BAC. As in the examples introduced in chapter 3, the same analysis would apply if we posited a reverse set of assumptions. In this example, assume that Justice Marshall truly favors consistency even if the results are fully adverse, to a partially favorable inconsistency. If so, his preferences are CAB. Further assume that Justice White's second choice is to strike down, rather than to sustain, both laws. If so, his preferences are BCA. Finally, assume that Justice Powell prefers a partially favorable inconsistent result to a fully adverse consistent result. If so, his preferences are ABC. Again, these are paradigmatic cyclical preferences.[54]

In the first hypothetical, the problematic ordinal ranking, which stare decisis effectively proscribes, is that of Justice Marshall, who would vindicate consistency only if it is favorable. If consistency produces unfavorable results in both cases, Marshall prefers partially favorable inconsistency. In the second hypothetical, the problematic ordinal ranking is that of Justice Powell, for the same reason. By elevating consistency from an optional framework to a presumptive constraint, stare decisis precludes this form of contingent preference and thus breaks down either of these sets of intransitive collective preferences. To illustrate, imagine that instead of being decided on the same day, *Crawford* and *Seattle* were decided one year apart. The hypotheticals that follow will demonstrate that stare decisis breaks the cycle by splitting the actual majority coalitions in *Crawford* and *Seattle* such that those who view those cases as indistinguishable are presumptively prevented from registering their preferences contingently, even if the result is fully adverse. In doing so, stare decisis forces judicial preferences that although multidimensional, are symmetrical, and thus not conducive to cycling if aggregated by unlimited majority rule.

Assume that while both state laws have passed, no local school board in either Washington or California has brought suit to challenge the constitutionality of those laws and that no court has ordered a revised desegregation plan consistent with the change in state law.[55] Further assume that no private parties have filed suit to challenge the constitutionality of either state's law. Finally, assume that Washington and California each have local branches of two national public interest organizations, which have taken a strong interest in the two state laws. Members of the first group, Citizens Against Busing ("CAB"), are strongly committed to neighborhood education and thus would like the Supreme Court to uphold both state laws. They also believe that while both laws should withstand an equal protection challenge, the California law presents a more attractive case to litigate because, unlike Washington, California did not attempt to alter local school board conduct directly. As a result, the case is less likely to be governed by the potentially adverse precedent, which they believe *Hunter* represents. Instead, California simply tried to cabin the power of state courts to order busing, with federal constitutional requirements as the outer limit. Members of the second group, Bettering Underprivileged Students ("BUS"), are strongly committed to busing as a means of promoting the integration of public schools and of equalizing the disparate educational resources across wealthy and poor neighborhoods. BUS agrees that the Washington initiative is a more attractive for it to litigate because in challenging that initiative, BUS can appeal to those justices who favor using the equal protection clause to integrate public schools, as well as to those justices who might be disturbed by Washington's apparent intrusion into local policymaking regarding public education. By analogy to *Hunter,* therefore, BUS can argue that the Washington referendum altered the structure of lawmaking over a singe race-based issue in a manner that violates federal equal protection.

Further assume that public interest organizations representing affected parents can freely obtain standing to challenge state laws that restrict integrative busing. If we assume that those justices who view the cases as indistinguishable vote in a principled manner, thus adhering to Arrovian independence,[56] and that they treat later precedents as binding over former ones, then the substantive outcome in *both* cases will depend entirely upon the order in which those cases are presented to the Supreme Court. Whichever of the two citizen groups can get its preferred case to the Supreme Court first will control not only the timing and substantive outcome in that case, but also the substantive outcome in the second case.

Imagine that CAB succeeds first in getting its declaratory judgment action seeking to sustain the California constitutional amendment to the Supreme Court. Because the *Crawford* majority does not believe that *Hunter* is controlling and believes that a state cannot be prevented from equating its own equal protection standards governing integrative busing with those operating under the federal Constitution, the Court will likely sustain the state constitutional amendment as it actually did in *Crawford.* In contrast, based upon the above assumptions, when the *Seattle* case reaches the Supreme Court with *Crawford* already decided, the actual majority coalition that struck down the statewide initiative will break down in favor of an alternative majority coalition producing precisely the opposite result. To see why, consider table 4.5, which provides a revised breakdown of the *Seattle* Court, based upon the assumption that *Crawford* was decided first.

The underlying *Seattle* issues presented in table 4.5 are disjunctive, meaning that to uphold the Washington referendum, an affirmative vote on either issue A (left column) or issue B (top row) is sufficient. In contrast, to

Table 4.5. *Seattle* Decided after *Crawford*

	Issue A: *Crawford* governs *Seattle*	*Crawford* does not govern *Seattle*
Issue B: *Seattle* referendum is constitutional	(A) Powell, Burger, Rehnquist, O'Connor	
Seattle referendum is unconstitutional	(B) *Marshall* (need not reach issue B)	(C) Blackmun, Brennan, White, Stevens

strike down the initiative, the justices must determine, first, that *Crawford* does not govern *Seattle,* and, second, that on its merits, the Washington initiative is unconstitutional, thus appearing in the bolded lower right box. In the lower left box, I have placed Justice Marshall in italics, to indicate that his resolution of issue B, in this case a negative assessment of the Washington referendum's merits, is hypothetical. Table 4.5 reveals that, based upon stare decisis, if *Seattle* follows *Crawford,* the case will then present multidimensional, but symmetrical, preferences. Thus the A and C camps reach opposite resolutions on both underlying issues, but also reach opposite resolutions as to how the case should be decided. Thus, if we assume that Justice Marshall, as in the actual case, would prefer to strike down the *Seattle* initiative on its merits, but upholds it based upon stare decisis, then his position, B, is likely the dominant second choice for those in both the A and C camps. Thus, with stare decisis in place, the resolution of the second case is parallel to both *Board of Regents of the University of California v. Bakke,*[57] in which the critical parts of Justice Powell's decision, which only he embraced, became the dominant second choice, and to *Planned Parenthood of Southeastern Pennsylvania v. Casey,*[58] in which the jointly authored plurality opinion represented the dominant second choice.[59] In all three contexts, given that opposite issue resolutions of the identified dispositive issues lead to an opposite ruling, it appears highly probable that whether resolved in a single dimension, per *Casey,* or multiple dimensions, per *Bakke* and the *Seattle* hypothetical in table 4.5, the seemingly intermediate position is a truly dominant, Condorcet-winning, outcome. Table 4.5 thus demonstrates that when stare decisis is imposed as a presumptive constraint, the doctrine effectively removes one of the issue dimensions for those justices who believe that the latter of two cases is governed by an indistinguishable precedent. Indeed, if Justice Marshall did decide the case presented in table 4.5 based upon stare decisis, any opinion he might express as to how he would have ruled in *Seattle,* but for the *Crawford* precedent, would be dictum. As with outcome voting in individual cases, over groups of cases subject to precedent, stare decisis effectively prevents justices who believe that later cases are indistinguishable from registering contingent preference in which they will only apply the consistency principal if the result is to achieve consistently favorable outcomes.

Precisely the same analysis would apply, albeit with opposite case results, if, instead, BUS succeeded in getting its declaratory judgment action seeking to strike the Washington referendum to the Supreme Court first. This time, the Court would first strike the referendum as it did in *Seattle.* When CAB gets its case to the Supreme Court, the Court would then face the voting situation represented in table 4.6.

As before, the issues in *Crawford* as presented in table 4.6 are disjunctive, this time with the result that an affirmative vote on either issue A or issue B will result in striking down the California constitutional amendment. To instead sustain the amendment, the justices must determine that *Seattle* does not govern *Crawford* and that, on its merits, the California constitutional amendment is constitutional, thus falling into the bolded upper right box.

Table 4.6. *Crawford* **Decided after** *Seattle*

	Issue A: *Seattle* governs *Crawford*	*Seattle* does not govern *Crawford*
Issue B: California amendment is constitutional	(A) *Powell, Burger, Rehnquist, O'Connor* (need not reach issue B)	(B) Blackmun, Brennan, White, Stevens
California amendment is unconstitutional	(C) Marshall	

This time, I placed the names of the four justices in the upper left box in italics to indicate that they need not reach the merits of issue B and that if they do reach the merits, their view will be expressed in the form of dictum. In this variation, the four justices in the upper left box are presumptively prevented from rendering a contingent preference for consistency only if the result is to sustain both laws. As in table 4.5, table 4.6 presents multidimensional and symmetrical preferences, this time with position A as the dominant, Condorcet-winning outcome.

In fact, the two cases reached the Court at the same time. Although a majority favored like treatment in both cases, the Court adopted yet a third option, upholding the *Crawford* initiative and striking down the *Seattle* amendment. In an important sense, all three results, the actual result of the two cases and the two hypothetical results set out in tables 4.5 and 4.6, can be viewed as arbitrary or irrational. By that I mean, in each potential set of case outcomes, an actual majority of the Supreme Court (as indicated by those in the bottom left and bottom right boxes in table 4.5 and in the upper left and upper right boxes in table 4.6) has had its will suppressed. In the actual cases, the majority that thought the cases indistinguishable (the upper left and lower right boxes in table 4.4) had its will suppressed, and in each of the hypotheticals, the majorities favoring opposite outcomes in the later case but for the application of stare decisis, had their wills suppressed. This, of course, is simply another way of saying that because table 4.4 revealed a multidimensional issue spectrum with asymmetrical preferences, avoiding a cycle through stare decisis introduced the phenomenon of path dependency.

B. Path Dependency and Agenda Control

Because stare decisis limits the relevant issues for consideration in cases subject to precedent, litigants have a strong incentive to strategically time the presentation of cases in the federal judiciary generally, and in the Supreme Court in particular. If litigants can get the Supreme Court to decide those more likely to result in a favorable ruling first, they can then build upon that success by presenting cases that, although less attractive initially, have a greater chance of producing a desirable ruling with the favorable precedent in place. Through this strategy, ideological litigants can attempt to manipulate the evolution of substantive constitutional doctrine through the strategic timing of cases.

The ability of litigants to effectively time cases depends upon an important assumption, which was not implicated in the above discussion of *Crawford* and *Seattle,* but which will prove relevant to standing doctrine. The analysis assumes that the Court will continue to adhere to its more recent precedents and that it will construe older precedents in light of any relevant subsequent distinctions. Thus, for example, in evaluating whether the 1896 precedent, *Plessy v. Ferguson,*[60] governed the 1954 case, *Brown v. Board of Education,*[61] the Supreme Court considered not only the *Plessy* Court's decision to uphold segregated railway cars, but also the Court's more recent incursions on the separate-but-equal doctrine, which severely restricted that doctrine's application in the context of higher education.[62] The Court's practice of construing older cases in light of more recent precedents provides litigants with a strong incentive to engage in path manipulation. By presenting relatively modest challenges to a disfavored precedent, without the need to have it immediately overruled, ideological litigants can establish beachhead, with the ultimate goal of having the disfavored precedent entirely displaced. Eventually, successful litigant path manipulation erodes the disfavored precedent to the point where it is but a mere shell, stating a legal principle that no longer is generalizable in any meaningful way beyond its application in the case in which the rule was announced. The Supreme Court occasionally recognizes this phenomenon, when it observes, for example, that based upon subsequent case development, a given precedent has been "limited to its facts."[63] On other occasions, the Court simply recognizes the inevitable and overrules. This is what the joint authors in *Casey* meant when they asserted that in some cases, including *Plessy* and *Lochner,* overruling seems "virtually foreordained."[64] Through strategic path manipulation, litigants are thus able fundamentally to transform—and sometimes even to completely reverse—longstanding tenets of constitutional law.

The above discussion assumes that the litigants have unfettered power to strategically time cases, which, of course, they do not.* Instead, through a series of complex rules, the Supreme Court has established the conditions under which litigants can present challenges in federal court. The first part of this chapter presented a preview of the standing analysis by grading the Supreme Court's justiciability doctrines based upon two sets of criteria: first, the timing of the legal claim relative to the development of the underlying facts, and second, the ease or difficulty of employing the underlying legal claim as a vehicle for strategic path manipulation. Recall that while the

---

*The discussion also assumes that litigants have complete knowledge of all judicial preferences in advance, which they also do not. Instead, as I have argued *supra* chapter 2, § V.B, judicial opinions provide incremental and piecemeal statements of ordinal rankings, which litigants can piece together to derive a larger sense of each justice's overall jurisprudence, but which invariably remains incomplete.

ripeness and mootness doctrines appeared on opposite ends of a timing-based justiciability spectrum, those doctrines converged when that spectrum was folded, and the underlying rules were measured instead based upon the ease or difficulty of the prohibited path manipulation. If litigants could resurrect dead claims, or imagine new ones that might never arise, then the power to strategically time cases would be near limitless. But even limiting justiciability to live claims is insufficient to prevent many fairly low cost attempts at strategic path manipulation. Many nationwide interest groups have the resources with which to monitor the emergence of potentially favorable cases, and, but for justiciability, could time their legal challenges with maximum effect. But for the timing-based barriers to justiciability, the NAACP Legal Defense Fund, for example, might monitor criminal cases with which to test the outermost limits of the Fourth, Fifth, and Sixth Amendments, and the American Civil Liberties Union might monitor cases involving infringing upon free speech and religion to test the outermost limits of the First Amendment. Similarly, Sierra Club could regularly monitor the conditions and uses of any number of natural environments, including, but not limited to, national parks, wetlands, or habitats of endangered species in an effort to strategically time cases arising under federal environmental statutes.

Absent any barriers to justiciability, these and other interest groups could raise claims on behalf of individuals or groups who either lack the resources with which to raise their own legal challenges or who are less committed to ensuring that their constitutional or statutory rights received maximum protection.[65] By presenting claims that more obviously affect others, these groups would be able to substantially improve their ability to influence the substantive evolution of legal doctrine.* Alternatively, if the Court established, as it has, a presumptive prohibition against raising the claims of others, the same

---

*Of course organizations like the NAACP Legal Defense Fund can and do sponsor direct appeals and collateral attacks on behalf of convicted criminals, especially death row inmates, thus circumventing the standing rules to a limited extent. Similarly, the ACLU does sponsor civil rights litigation on behalf of persons whose constitutional rights, including most notably those arising under the First Amendment, have allegedly been violated. Recall, however, that the thesis advanced here is not that standing prevents path manipulation. It is instead that standing makes path manipulation more costly and therefore more difficult than in a regime that lacked standing. In two respects, the requirement that organizations seeking to sponsor such appeals identify available and willing litigants with live claims limits path manipulation. First, the criminal convict, rather than the Legal Defense Fund, is the actual client in such appeals, meaning that under the applicable rules of professional responsibility, attorneys representing such criminals must make critical tactical decisions, including but not limited to choosing which issues to raise and whether to present various discretionary appeals, with the best interests of the criminal convict in mind, rather than based upon an assessment of the impact of such strategic decisions on the developing path of case law. Second, although exceptional, as Gilmore v. Utah, 429 U.S. 1012 (1976), demonstrates, not all convicted criminals, and not even all death row inmates, are willing players in the efforts of others to vindicate their claims.

groups could claim that their members have suffered a generalized harm simply knowing that the government has intruded on the constitutional or statutory rights of third parties, or by knowing that the government has failed to adhere to the law. By presumptively preventing the litigation of claims that belong to others or that are legally diffuse, the Supreme Court has imposed a second-order barrier to fairly low cost path manipulation involving presently live claims. In short, while stare decisis improves the rationality of Supreme Court decision making by breaking down doctrinal cycles, the Court's combined justiciability doctrines—ripeness, mootness, and most notably, standing—improve the overall fairness of Supreme Court decision making by limiting the extent to which nondominant, meaning non-Condorcet-winning, minorities can strategically time cases in an effort to influence the substantive evolution of Supreme Court doctrine.

This basic explanation of the relationship between stare decisis and standing still fails to capture many of the important subtleties of Supreme Court decision making. Most effective path manipulation, for example, does not arise, as in the *Crawford* and *Seattle* hypotheticals, over the course of just two cases. Instead, most path manipulation arises over multiple cases and sometimes over the course of several decades. As a result of the increased number of cases involved and the intervening personnel changes on the Court, such doctrinal cycles are more difficult to formalize. Nevertheless, when this occurs, something approaching a doctrinal cycle can arise, with the result of codifying seemingly inconsistent outcomes over time, even with stare decisis in place. To illustrate, consider three cases involving vote districting. Recall from chapter 1 that the Court has taken three general approaches to allocating the burden of proof in cases challenging the constitutionality of race-based gerrymanders.[66] One group of liberal justices, including Brennan and Marshall, preferred to shift to the state the burden to defend alleged race-conscious gerrymanders based upon disparate racial outcomes. A second group of conservative justices, including Rehnquist and Burger, would have prohibited all burden shifting and required that the challengers prove an actual intent to harm the minority race. Finally, a third group of justices whose ideology was somewhat harder to pin down, including Powell and Stewart, would have shifted the burden to the state to defend an alleged race-based gerrymander only if presented with objective evidence from which to infer an illicit intent. The following cases reveal a doctrinal cycle in race-based gerrymandering cases, growing out of these competing approaches.

It is worth adding a note from personal experience. I once represented a death row inmate in a postconviction proceeding. After losing his state collateral challenges, at both the trial and appeals court levels, and his federal habeas corpus challenge at the district court level, the client insisted upon dropping all arguments on appeal that, if accepted, would have resulted in his receiving a sentence of life imprisonment without eligibility for parole, rather than in an acquittal. This meant dropping his strongest claims. The client has since been executed.

C. Path Dependency over Three Cases:
Race-Based Gerrymandering

In the 1979 case *United Jewish Organizations v. Carey*,[67] the Supreme Court upheld a vote-districting plan intended to create an African American safe seat, also referred to as a minority-majority district. In creating the district, the state legislature had divided up a Hasidic Jewish community, thus preventing that community from electing its own representative of choice. In sustaining the plan, the *Carey* Court reasoned that in creating the minority-majority voting district, the New York legislature evinced no intent to harm the members of the Hasidic community. Instead, it intended to benefit the now-joined African American community. Any resulting harm to the Hasidic Jews was simply a negative consequence of a benign desire to create an African American safe seat.

Fourteen years later, in the 1993 case *Shaw v. Reno*,[68] the Supreme Court faced a novel challenge to an apparent race-based districting scheme in which the challengers to the district in question did not disclose their racial identity. Instead, the claimants simply alleged that the districting scheme was so bizarre on its face that it could only be explained on the basis of race. In turn, they alleged that the scheme violated their equal protection rights. In a six-to-three decision, Justice O'Connor, writing for the *Shaw* Court, held that when claimants allege that "redistricting legislation that is so irregular on its face that its rationale can be viewed only as an effort to segregate the races for purposes of voting, without regard to traditional districting principles and without sufficiently compelling justification," they have alleged a cognizable claim under the Fourteenth Amendment equal protection clause.

Two years later, in 1995, the Supreme Court decided *Miller v. Johnson*,[69] a case that implicated the holdings of both *Carey* and *Shaw*. The *Miller* claimants challenged a redistricting scheme that, while quite oddly shaped, was insufficiently bizarre as to be explainable on no grounds but race. As a result, the claimants could not state a *Shaw* claim. But unlike in *Shaw*, the parties virtually stipulated that the district's odd shape was required to produce an African American safe seat. Relying upon *Shaw*, the state defended its minority-majority safe seat against the equal protection challenge, claiming that absent a showing that the challenged district's shape was so bizarre as to be explainable on no grounds but race, the challengers had failed to state a Fourteenth Amendment equal protection claim. In a five-to-four decision rejecting the defense, Justice Kennedy, writing for the *Miller* Court, stated,

> Shape is relevant not because bizarreness is a necessary element of the constitutional wrong or a threshold requirement of proof, but because it may be persuasive evidence that race, for its own sake, and not other districting principles, was the legislature's dominant and controlling rationale in drawing its district lines. The logical implication, as courts applying *Shaw* have recognized, is that parties may rely on evidence other than bizarreness to establish race-based districting.

Over the course of these three cases, without overruling *Carey*, the Supreme Court effectively gutted that case's underlying rationale. In doing so, the Court produced the equivalent of a doctrinal cycle, even with stare decisis in place. To comprehend the cycle, it will be helpful to again parse these cases, this time focusing on the expanded dimensionality from *Casey* to *Miller*.

The *Carey* Court sustained the challenged race-conscious district, in spite of the alleged harm to a cohesive Hasidic community, by focusing on the benign nature of the racial gerrymander to African Americans. In distinguishing *Carey*, the *Shaw* Court noted that there was no indication that the resulting districts, following the division of the formerly Hasidic district, were bizarrely shaped. Writing for a six-justice majority in *Shaw*, Justice O'Connor stated that

> we believe that reapportionment is one area in which appearances do matter. A reapportionment plan that includes in one district individuals who belong to the same race, but who are otherwise widely separated by geographical and political boundaries, and who may have a little in common but the color of their skin, bears an uncomfortable resemblance to political apartheid.

In effect, the *Shaw* Court distinguished *Carey* by redefining the injury that results from a racially gerrymandered district. The *Carey* Court had defined the injury following race-conscious gerrymandering as the potential harm to African American voters, the original target beneficiaries of the equal protection clause. In this conception, so-called benign race-conscious measures were presumed permissible, in spite of any alleged harm to affected non–African American voters. In contrast, the *Shaw* Court eschewed any inquiry into the race of the parties affected by the apparent race-conscious gerrymander. Instead, the mere fact that a district was so bizarre as to be explainable on no grounds but race undermined the appearance of the integrity of the representational process, and thus stated a cause of action. In effect, as table 4.7 illustrates, *Shaw* expanded the issue space in cases that involve race-based gerrymandering from one to two dimensions.

Finally, writing for a five-justice majority in *Miller*, Justice Kennedy rejected the state's *Shaw*-based defense that absent a sufficiently bizarre shape, a race-conscious gerrymander does not violate equal protection. Instead, Kennedy concluded that one could establish an illicit racial gerrymander in either of two ways:

> The plaintiff's burden is to show, either through direct circumstantial evidence of a district's shape and demographics or more direct evidence going to legislative purpose, that race was the predominant factor motivating the legislature's decision to place a significant number of voters within or without a particular district. To make this showing, a plaintiff must prove that the legislature subordinated traditional

race-neutral districting principles, including but not limited to compactness, contiguity, respect for political subdivisions or communities defined by actual shared interests, to racial considerations.

In effect, *Miller* avoided the anomaly that in a truly bizarrely shaped district, the appearance alone provides the basis for a prima facie case of a race-based gerrymander, but that in a slightly less than bizarrely shaped district, the *actual intent* to create a race-based gerrymander would have been insufficient to state an alternative prima facie case of a race-based gerrymander. Prior to *Shaw,* the Court had considered objective factors in districting, including shape, compactness, and contiguity, only to *infer* an actual intent to gerrymander based upon race. *Shaw* effectively elevated such objective evidence to the basis for an independent prima facie equal protection case. To avoid the anomaly that the objective evidence from which to infer an illicit intent supports a cause of action, but that actual evidence of the same intent does not, Justice Kennedy was compelled in *Miller* to retreat from the Supreme Court's once-dominant intuition that racial gerrymandering violated equal protection only if it harmed African Americans as a suspect class.

While the *Miller* Court distinguished *Carey* by characterizing it as a vote-dilution claim, rather than as a claim about race-based gerrymandering,[70] Justice Ginsburg, writing in dissent, made plain that since *Carey,* the Court's doctrine had come full circle:

> I would follow precedent directly on point. In *United Jewish Organizations of Williamsburgh, Inc. v. Carey,* . . . even though the State "deliberately used race in a purposeful manner" to create majority-minority districts, . . . seven of eight Justices participating voted to uphold the State's plan without subjecting it to strict scrutiny. Five Justices specifically agreed that the intentional creation of majority-minority districts does not give rise to an equal protection claim, absent proof that the districting plan diluted the majority's voting strength. . . .
>
> Though much like the claim in *Shaw,* the *UJO* claim failed because the *UJO* district adhered to traditional districting principles.[71]

The problem in *Miller* was that while the racial gerrymander was virtually stipulated, it was also benign in that it was intended to benefit African Americans. Kennedy was also forced to expand the bases upon which litigants can challenge apparently benign race-based gerrymanders to include not only those that are sufficiently bizarre as to be explainable on no grounds but race, per *Shaw,* but also those that are not so bizarre, but that are certain products of a race-based gerrymander. In doing so, however, he placed *Miller* in tension with *Carey.*

Table 4.7 illustrates how these three cases combined to expand the underlying issue dimensionality twice, first from *Carey* to *Shaw,* and second, from *Shaw* to *Miller.* While it is more difficult to formalize the requisite features of multidimensionality and asymmetry, given the intervention of time

Table 4.7.   Racial Gerrymandering in Two Dimensions with Effective Asymmetry

	Direct Evidence of Gerrymander	No Direct Evidence of Gerrymander
Racial gerrymander presumed from sufficiently bizarre district		Case 2: *Shaw* (allow challenge to district)
Racial gerrymander not presumed from sufficiently bizarre district	Case 1: *Carey* (uphold district), Case 3: *Miller* (allow challenge to district)	

and personnel changes on the Court, it is worth noting that through two sets of distinctions, each principally with reference to the immediately preceding case listed in the table, the Court produced the result of two cases that appear in the same conceptual category, but with seemingly opposite results. In effect, this example illustrates that multiple expansions of dimensionality over time can produce the doctrinal equivalent of multidimensionality and asymmetry.

In effect, the *Miller* resolved both of the critical issues—whether a racial gerrymander could be inferred from sufficiently bizarre district lines that could be explained on no grounds but race and whether there was direct evidence of a racial gerrymander, in the same manner as had the *Carey* Court—but with opposite results. In *Carey*, the challenged district, which the Court upheld, was the absolute product of a race-based gerrymander, but was objectively compact. In *Miller*, the challenged district, which the Court did not uphold, was less compact, but was insufficiently bizarre as to be explainable on no grounds but race. Nevertheless, the Court allowed the challenge to proceed, because otherwise the Court would have signaled per *Shaw* that objective evidence of a gerrymander—even if potentially benign—was sufficient to state a cause of action, while direct evidence of a gerrymander in the form of a virtual stipulation—even if the result was again potentially benign—was not. But for *Shaw*, there would have been no need to allow a cause of action based upon direct evidence of a gerrymander when there was no indication that the result was harmful to African Americans.

Not surprisingly, the doctrinal transition from *Carey* to *Shaw* to *Miller* occurred at a time when the Supreme Court's dominant vision of equal protection was shifting from the more traditional two-tier framework,[72] which applied different standards based upon whether the law in question was intended to benefit or to harm African Americans, to color blindness, which applied strict scrutiny to any race-conscious measure, whether or not benign. To avoid the anomaly that under *Shaw*, objective evidence of an intent to gerrymander provides the basis for a cause of action alleging an illicit racial gerrymander, but that direct proof of intent would not, the *Miller* Court distinguished *Shaw* in a manner that created an obvious doctrinal tension with, but that did not overrule, *Carey*. Even though together *Shaw* and *Miller* suggest that objective evidence of a racial gerrymander is only one relevant consideration in evaluating a race-based gerrymander, *Carey* remains good law. To place the resulting doctrinal cycle in historical perspective, now consider the voting lineup in the three cases.

For ease of reference, in table 4.8 I have coded each of the justice's names according to his or her general ideology.[73] Bold lettering indicates that the justice is generally conservative, which in this context means that he or she strongly favors a color-blind approach to equal protection. Italics indicate that the justice is generally liberal, meaning that he or she will condone benign race-conscious measures. Roman typeface indicates that the justice is moderate, meaning that he or she will condone some race-conscious measures, in the absence of objective criteria indicating an illicit intent.

Even though neither *Shaw* nor *Miller* suggested that *Carey* was, or should be, overruled, the five-to-four ruling in *Miller* rested upon a rationale that was almost precisely opposite that in *Carey*. It is worth noting the one-to-one correlation between those liberal justices voting to reject the constitutional challenge to the race-based districting in *Carey*, and those liberal justices dissenting from the decision to sustain the alleged race-based gerrymander against a constitutional challenge in *Miller*. While Rehnquist, a conservative, joined another part of the White plurality opinion in *Carey*, which upheld the voting district on nonstatutory grounds,[74] the result would have been the same even had he voted differently. Chief Justice Burger's vote to strike down the minority-majority district in *Carey* corresponds with Justice Scalia's vote to strike down the minority-majority districts in *Shaw* and *Miller*. After *Carey*, two judicial replacements moved the center of the Court further to the right.

Table 4.8. Path Manipulation across Three Cases: Racial Gerrymandering

	Majority or Plurality	Concurrence	Dissent
Carey	VRA constitutional: **White** , [*Breyer*] *Brennan* [*Souter*], *Blackmun* [*Ginsburg*], Stevens	Stewart [O'Connor], Powell [**Kennedy**]	**Burger** [**Rehnquist**]
	District constitutional even without VRA: **White** [*Breyer*], **Rehnquist** [**Scalia**], Stevens		
Shaw	O'Connor, *Souter*, **Thomas**, **Scalia**, **Rehnquist**, **Kennedy**		*White, Blackmun* [*Ginsburg*], *Stevens*
Miller	**Kennedy**, **Rehnquist**, **Thomas**, **Scalia**, O'Connor	O'Connor	*Ginsburg, Stevens, Breyer, Souter*

The conservative Justices Kennedy and Thomas replaced the moderate Justice Powell and the liberal Justice Marshall, respectively. Both Kennedy and Thomas voted to strike down the *Shaw* and *Miller* districts. In addition, the moderate Justice O'Connor and the increasingly liberal Justice Souter replaced the moderate Justice Stewart and the consistently liberal Justice Brennan. Both O'Connor and Souter joined the majority striking down the *Shaw* district, with O'Connor writing the majority opinion. In addition, O'Connor joined the *Miller* majority, writing a separate concurrence, with Souter dissenting.

To further illustrate the manner in which Justice O'Connor, writing in *Shaw*, expanded the dimensionality of gerrymandering claims, thus generated a voting path that led to a ruling in *Miller* that was in tension with that in *Carey*, imagine how these cases would have been resolved had the order been different. In her separate concurrence in *Miller*, Justice O'Connor expressed her concern that under the majority ruling, challenges might arise with respect to a large number of districts in the House of Representatives, which in her opinion are clearly constitutional. O'Connor recognized that, based upon *Carey*, states have created numerous race-conscious minority-majority districts. While, of course, one can only speculate as to such matters, it is certainly plausible that had *Miller* been presented before *Shaw*, Justice O'Connor might have voted differently in both cases, and Justice Souter might have voted differently in *Shaw*, thus producing a majority in both cases for the opposite holdings. But for the expanded issue spectrum in *Shaw*, O'Connor might have reasoned that *Carey* governs *Miller*. Otherwise, virtually any district in which race was considered would be subject to a potential constitutional challenge, the very concern that O'Connor raised in her *Miller* concurrence. Only by expanding the range of claims in which a party can raise an equal protection challenge to an allegedly race-based gerrymander to include one based solely on the district's physical appearance was O'Connor able to produce a holding significantly in tension with, but distinguishable from, *Carey*. While O'Connor's *Miller* concurrence indicates some reservation about the manner in which she expanded the issue spectrum in *Shaw* relative to *Carey*, O'Connor also made clear that she was compelled to vote with the *Miller* majority, based in part upon her analysis in *Shaw*. O'Connor's *Miller* vote reflects an unwillingness to allow objective indicia of an intent to gerrymander to trump actual evidence of an intent to gerrymander, even if the effect is ultimately to limit *Carey*'s reach to its facts. In effect, through the creation of a doctrinal cycle, *Carey* has been left a mere shell, which the Court has not yet considered sufficiently significant to overrule.

As suggested above, the changed personnel requires a qualification to any absolute claim to a voting cycle. It is not irrational for one group of justices to prefer one result and a later group of justices to prefer its opposite. Indeed, as explained in chapter 5, this has occurred several times over the course of the twentieth century. But if the Court is disinclined to overrule disfavored precedents, then as these and other cases suggest, even with changed personnel, the Court must manipulate precedent by expanding the dimensionality of underlying case issues, to achieve its desired objectives. In these cases, the Court did so in a manner that affected something close to a doctrinal cycle. Moreover, in this example (in contrast with some of the examples that follow), the relevant personnel changes were insufficiently dramatic to explain the change in outcomes from *Carey* to *Miller* absent the requisite doctrinal manipulation capable of generating a cycle. Thus, the path dependency that these three cases represent is made most clear by considering the near perfect match between the White plurality opinion sustaining the *Carey* district against a constitutional challenge and the group of dissenting justices in *Miller.* While the voting lineup has nearly flipped, based upon the manner in which the issues in the later cases were defined, neither *Shaw* nor *Miller* suggested that *Carey* was, or should be, overruled. Instead, these three cases amount to a doctrinal cycle, resulting from the expansion of the issue spectrum from *Carey* to *Miller,* which was completed with stare decisis in place. In contrast with the *Crawford* and *Seattle* hypotheticals, the additional dimension was not that of doctrinal consistency, in the form of adherence to precedent, but rather the manner in which the Court redefined the substantive equal protection injury over time. And, for that reason, even with stare decisis in place, a tension persists between the underlying logic of *Carey* and *Miller.*

D.   Path Dependency over Larger Trajectories: Desegregation

More typically, doctrinal cycles manifest themselves over larger groups of cases and longer periods of time, rendering doctrinal cycles even more difficult to present formally than that involving *Carey, Shaw,* and *Miller.* Over time, significant personnel changes combine with path manipulation to substantially alter existing doctrine. Even so, precedent operates as a considerable constraint,[75] thus rendering constitutional doctrine path dependent. Thus, when the final cases in a long sequence are contrasted with the earliest relevant precedents, we can see the gradual erosion of precedent through path manipulation. In fact, some of the most famous illustrations of Supreme Court path manipulation took several cases, often over several decades, to complete. The single most famous example of ideological path manipulation involves the NAACP's brilliant, and successful, twenty-five year campaign to have the Supreme Court overturn *Plessy v. Ferguson*[76] and to demolish the separate-but-equal doctrine.

In 1929, the NAACP had received a $100,000 grant, with instructions to finance

> a large-scale, widespread, dramatic campaign to give the Southern Negro his constitutional rights, his political and civil equality, and therewith a self-consciousness and self-respect which would inevitably tend to effect a revolution in the economic life of the country.[77]

The planning committee initially devised a strategy in which the NAACP would file taxpayers' suits in each of the seven states with the worst discrimination records: Alabama, Arkansas, Florida, Georgia, Louisiana, Mississippi, and South Carolina. Dr. Charles Houston, dean of Howard Law School, and Felix Frankfurter, then a member of the NAACP, selected Nathan Ross Margold to lead the campaign, but Margold rejected the chosen strategy as unrealistic.[78] Margold devised an alternative plan, which Houston revised and which the NAACP then administered. Under this plan, the NAACP would not "[try] to deprive Southern states of their acknowledged privilege of providing separate accommodations for the two races."[79] Instead, the NAACP would challenge segregation "as now provided and administered." Stated differently, the Margold plan would focus on the inequalities in the actual implementation of the so-called separate-but-equal public school regime.

Houston's alternative formulation varied in several critical respects from the original plan. Houston proposed to attack those inequalities that were most blatant and for which the whites would feel the least threatened. Critically, this meant attacking public school segregation at the end, rather than at the beginning, of the campaign. As a result, Houston proposed to focus initially on higher education, where state programs not merely segregated, but were often nonexistent for black students. Houston observed that there were no graduate or professional schools for blacks in the South other than Howard University in Washington, D.C., and Meharry Medical College in Nashville, Tennessee. For a black student to earn a degree in law or medicine, for example, he would have had to travel to a different region of the country at great expense and inconvenience. As the well-noted commentator, Richard Kluger, has explained:

> Here was an area where the educational facilities for blacks were neither separate nor equal but non-existent. The Supreme Court, unyielding as it had been on the education question, would have trouble turning its back on so plain a discrimination and denial of equal protection. . . . The point now was to establish a real beachhead. If graduate schools were peaceably desegregated, then the NAACP could turn to undergraduate colleges. And then secondary schools. And grade schools. Each new gain would help the advance to the next stage.[80]

Rather than presenting a frontal assault upon *Plessy*, which almost certainly would have failed, the NAACP presented a series of incremental challenges to the Court's separate-but-equal doctrine by challenging state higher educational programs made available to white students, with no counterpart made available to black students. The NAACP achieved a series of successive victories, each chipping away at the margins of *Plessy*, without suggesting the need to overrule.

In *Missouri ex rel. Gaines v. Canada*,[81] and again in *Sipuel v. Board of Regents*,[82] the Court held that, having created a state law school for whites, the state must also provide a comparable in-state educational opportunity for black students who are qualified but for their race.[83] After rejecting a similar claim in *Fisher v. Hurst*,[84] the Court held in *Sweatt v. Painter*[85] that the State of Texas could not meet its constitutional obligation under *Gaines* and *Sipuel* by creating a separate law school for qualified black students that lacked the resources and prestige associated with the University of Texas Law School. Finally, in *McLaurin v. Oklahoma State Regents*,[86] the Court held that the University of Oklahoma Department of Education, which, following a district court decision, had admitted a black man, had nonetheless violated his equal protection rights by physically separating him within the relevant classroom, library, and cafeteria. With these precedents in place, each arguably distinguishable from *Plessy* but with the effect of chipping away at the margins of *Plessy*, the NAACP had successfully set the stage for a frontal attack on the *Plessy* separate-but-equal doctrine, in *Brown v. Board of Education*.[87] Without having eroded *Plessy* in this manner, a direct frontal assault upon *Plessy* would almost certainly have failed.

In effect, these cases twice expanded the issue space over race-based segregation from one to two dimensions. The Court's initial inquiry, per *Plessy*, was whether state-mandated segregation based upon race was inherently unconstitutional, without regard to the differing quality of conditions made available to the black and white races. While *Plessy* is often said to have established the so-called separate-but-equal doctrine, the *Plessy* Court did not condition its decision to sustain segregated facilities upon true equality. The later cases, *Gaines, Sweatt,* and *McLaurin,* however, expanded upon the original *Plessy* issue spectrum by focusing not only on whether separating the races could somehow be deemed reasonable, but also on whether the underlying *differences* in the quality of the separate programs provided an independent basis for striking down segregated regimes. *Gaines* focused upon inequality in its most obvious form, namely comparing the presence of an in-state law school for whites with the absence of an in-state law school for blacks. *Sweatt* and *McLaurin* further expanded the relevant issue space by focusing upon intangible differences even with comparable facilities in place. Thus, the *McLaurin* Court considered the importance of faculty-student and interstudent interaction in striking down a program that segregated students in the same program based upon race, and the *Sweatt* Court considered differences in prestige, holding that a makeshift law school for blacks is not the constitutional equivalent of the prestigious and well-established University of Texas Law School, which was available only to whites. By the time of *Brown,* with these precedents in place, the Court was open to the argument that not only was a substantial inequality of conditions, whether measured objectively or based upon such matters as interaction or prestige, unconstitutional, but also that separateness itself, especially in the context of education, was inherently unconstitutional. That, of course, was a direct affront to the *Plessy* holding.

E.   Heightened Scrutiny for Sex-Based Classifications Revisited

While the preceding story is perhaps the most well known instance of deliberate litigant path manipulation, it is by no means unique. Women's rights advocates, including now-Justice Ruth Bader Ginsburg, adopted a nearly identical strategy in their ultimately successful efforts to afford women a version of heightened scrutiny under the equal protection clause of the Fourteenth Amendment. They, too, chose to chip away at a series of cases denying Fourteenth Amendment equal protection rights to women, resulting in what is now known as heightened or intermediate scrutiny for gender classifications.[88] This was the standard of review that a majority, in *Miller v. Albright,*[89] composed of Justices O'Connor, Kennedy, Ginsburg, Breyer, and Souter, across three separate opinions, believed applicable to the father's underlying equal protection challenge to the sex-based distinction set out in the INA, but that an overlapping majority declined to apply, in part because Justices O'Connor and Kennedy denied petitioner standing to raise the father's challenge.[90] One of the most interesting features of this example of path manipulation was the use of sex-based classifications operating to the disadvantage of men to erode traditional equal protection doctrine, which allowed states to perpetuate sex-based distinctions ultimately thought to disadvantage women. Thus, for example, in the 1973 case *Frontiero v. Richardson,*[91] the Court struck down a federal statute that automatically entitled male members of the armed services to claim their wives as dependents, but that conditioned the same benefit to female members upon a showing that the husband was dependent for at least half of his support. Three years later, in the 1976 case, *Craig v. Boren,*[92] the Court struck down an Oklahoma statute that prohibited the sale of 3.2 percent beer to males under the age of twenty-one and to females under the age of eighteen. And while the Court rejected some equal protection challenges to state and federal laws that drew sex-based distinctions in this period,[93] in two important decisions in 1977 and 1980, the Court struck down both federal and state statutory provisions, conditioning eligibility for retirement benefits for widowers upon dependency, when widows automatically received such benefits.[94] In these two cases, the Court struggled with the question whether provisions conditioning benefits for widowers disadvantaged men, who did not receive the ultimate benefit, or women, who did not receive the insurance equivalent for their families given to similarly situated male employees. In any event, it is certainly no coincidence that those seeking to afford heightened scrutiny based upon sex began the process by challenging statutes that imposed immediate financial hardships upon men. Finally, it is worth noting that *Miller v. Albright* represents a rare recent failure of the Supreme Court to strike down a federal statute expressly disadvantaging men, although the result might well have differed but for the position on standing that Justices O'Connor and Kennedy embraced in that case.

F. Summary

The above analysis shows that stare decisis can stabilize legal doctrine by forging symmetrical preferences during a particular time frame, but not indefinitely. Over a sufficiently long time horizon, even with stare decisis in place, litigants can manipulate the order of cases in an effort to expand the dimensionality of the underlying issue spectrum. Over a sufficiently long time horizon, multiple expansions can have the effect of introducing functional asymmetry, and thus of generating the doctrinal equivalent of a cycle. But absent stare decisis, such cycles could arise with increased frequency, either in snapshot form, as in *Crawford* and *Seattle,* or over longer time horizons, as in *Carey, Shaw,* and *Miller.* Such cycles would potentially reduce the value of Supreme Court precedent and doctrinal predictability, ultimately undermining the rule of law.

In all three contexts described above, racial gerrymandering, the separate-but-equal doctrine, and heightened scrutiny for sex-based classifications, the Court has fallen subject to a kind of path manipulation, with the ultimate effect of shaping legal doctrine in a manner in tension with earlier precedent, through a deliberate exercise in the strategic timing of cases. While these three sets of case trajectories, each of which had the ultimate effect of reversing a course of precedent, were longer than in the *Crawford* and *Seattle* hypotheticals, the underlying social choice analysis is the same. The difference between path manipulation over the course of but two cases in which the Court has cyclical preferences, or five cases, is one of degree, not kind. That is not to suggest that other factors, like personnel changes on the Court, did not affect each of these doctrinal transformations. Certainly they did. But in each case, the litigants trying to discard a disfavored precedent—and one that might have been produced as a result of a cycle—shared the intuition that only by ordering cases properly, thus allowing the Court to erode, without signaling an immediate intent to abandon, such precedents, would the Court come to realize over time that the overwhelming weight of recent doctrine is in conflict with the ultimately disfavored precedent. That is paradigmatic path manipulation. And, in fact, it is path manipulation with a version of the standing doctrine already in place. It is important to recall, however, that my thesis is not that standing prevents path manipulation. Instead, it is that path manipulation would be substantially easier in the absence of standing.

The above three examples suggest that the litigants themselves have significant power over the critically important path of case law in the Supreme Court. To a large extent that is true, but it only tells part of the story. One barrier to litigant path manipulation is standing. But there are others. The next subsection will consider a group of alternative mechanisms that the Court can, and sometimes does, employ to avoid the seeming problems of path dependence and path manipulation, which stare decisis creates. After describing the strengths and weaknesses of these alternative defenses to stare decisis—induced path dependence, we will come back to standing and explain how it operates in conjunction with them, and with stare decisis, to improve both the fairness and rationality of Supreme Court decision making.

G. Potential Defenses to Stare Decisis–Induced Path Dependence

To simplify my argument that stare decisis renders the substantive evolution of law path dependent, thus potentially thwarting the Court's majoritarian preferences over time and across cases, I have omitted several important institutional details that affect the efforts of litigants to manipulate the path of case decisions. Unlike outcome voting, stare decisis is not a universal rule. At least in theory, civilian jurisdictions do not employ stare decisis at all, although, as a practical matter, the differences between civilian and common law regimes are not nearly so stark.[95] In addition, within the Supreme Court, stare decisis is at best a presumptive constraint, especially in constitutional cases.[96] In addition to developing standing and other justiciability barriers as defense mechanisms to stare decisis–induced path dependence, Supreme Court justices have no fewer than four other potential strategies that they can employ to extricate themselves from the constraint that stare decisis appears to impose. Just as we needed to consider possible alternative individual case decision-making rules before we could attribute outcome voting and the narrowest grounds doctrine to the identified underlying social choice phenomena,[97] so too we must consider alternative defenses to path manipulation besides standing before we can attribute that doctrine to the problem of stare decisis–induced path manipulation. First, justices can devise distinctions to avoid the operation of precedents that they disfavor. Alternatively, justices who are unwilling to codify distinctions to produce more favorable results can express disagreement with underlying precedents in dictum. Second, assuming that justices are unable to identify a viable distinction, which they are willing to codify or state as dictum, they can vote to overrule a disfavored precedent. Third, if the affected justices anticipate that they will not be able to locate a viable distinction or that they will not succeed in encouraging a majority of their colleagues to overrule, they can vote to deny certiorari, with the hope of preventing a potentially unfavorable decisional path from emerging. And finally, justices can to some extent limit cycling by summarily disposing of cases, rather than resolving with full opinions those cases that have the potential to expand the underlying issue dimensionality and possibly to introduce asymmetry. (In the analysis to follow, I will treat certiorari and summary dispositions together.)

Throughout its history, the Supreme Court has employed each of these strategies, often in combination, thus limiting path dependency and path manipulation. As demonstrated below, however, an analysis of each of these alternative strategies ultimately strengthens this chapter's central thesis that stare decisis has evolved as a cycle-breaking rule that operates to promote doctrinal stability in the Supreme Court, and that standing has evolved to ameliorate the resulting problem of path dependence by raising the cost to ideological litigants of path manipulation.

1. Case Distinctions (and Dictum)

Perhaps the most obvious mechanism for trying to avoid the operation of a disfavored precedent is to devise distinctions between the case before the Court and the precedent in question. Clever lawyers, a category that certainly includes sitting Supreme Court justices, have earned that reputation through their ability to see nonobvious differences between the procedural or factual contexts of a precedent and of a more recent case in which one wishes to achieve a contrary result. While Supreme Court justices can and do distinguish cases to avoid the operation of precedent, the Supreme Court as an institution cannot avoid path dependence through distinction. While that might at first appear counterintuitive, consider the effect of distinctions on the future development of case law. Clever distinctions devised in one period become the fodder of path manipulation in the next. That is because those justices who are most troubled by the potential application of a precedent but who are unwilling to vote to overrule are likely to find themselves in the median position in a Court in which one group favors the precedent on the merits and the other groups seeks to overrule. The clever distinction is likely to provide an alternative framework for analyzing the case, potentially expanding the issue spectrum from one to two dimensions, either with the effect of becoming the dominant opinion or of rendering the narrowest grounds doctrine unworkable.[98]

The history of the Supreme Court is replete with examples of seemingly disingenuous distinctions codified into constitutional law to avoid the operation of disfavored precedent. To illustrate, consider two recent cases. Recall from chapter 2 that in *New York v. United States,*[99] the Supreme Court, per Justice O'Connor, sought to restore some limits on the power of Congress to regulate state activity based upon the Tenth Amendment. Then as recently as 1985, the Supreme Court, in *Garcia v. San Antonio Transit Authority,*[100] suggested that whatever limits the Tenth Amendment imposed upon Congress were to be determined solely by the political process, rather than in the federal courts. In striking down the take-title provisions of the Low-level Radioactive Waste Policy Amendments of 1985, Justice O'Connor offered a novel argument, intended to distinguish *Garcia,* namely that the framers and ratifiers of the Constitution sought to prevent Congress from commandeering the state legislatures in implementing federal regulatory schemes. In *Garcia,* the Court had upheld a federal minimum wage statute requiring no state legislative involvement, as that statute applied to local transit authority workers. While O'Connor's clever argument allowed the Court to avoid, without overruling, *Garcia,* the *New York* decision has invited new legal challenges to federal statutes, which commandeered various organs of state government, rather than regulating individuals directly.[101] Thus, in trying to avoid the application of *Garcia,* the *New York* Court established an alternative decisional path.

Even if a disappointed justice is not willing to codify a disingenuous distinction into law, the justice is free to express disagreement with a disfavored precedent. To illustrate, reconsider *Crawford* and *Seattle.* If, for example, *Crawford* had been decided first, Marshall might well have chosen to decide *Seattle* based upon *Crawford* even though the result would have been to sustain two state laws that on first principles Marshall would have preferred to strike down. But voting strictly in accordance with stare decisis would not have prevented Marshall from stating that, unconstrained by precedent, he would have voted for the opposite result in both cases. Thus, he might have stated: "While *Crawford* governs *Seattle,* I believe that *Crawford* was wrongly decided as an original matter. But I also believe that concerns for doctrinal stability outweigh the benefits of overruling in this case."[102] Stare decisis stabilizes doctrine, however, by rendering such assertions dictum, since any statement to this effect would obviously not have been necessary to Marshall's contrary outcome vote. But through dictum, or through separate opinions taking an alternative approach to deciding the case, dissatisfied justices can expose potential fault lines on the Court, which, if exploited over time, have the potential to erode disfavored precedents. Stated differently, dictum provides the fodder for effective litigant path manipulation by revealing potentially successful means of expanding the underlying issue dimensionality and, thus, by signaling distinctions from existing precedent that might garner majority support in the future. By tapping into these distinctions, litigants can begin a gradual erosion process, until a disfavored precedent is ready to be discarded altogether.

2.   *Overruling*

While the Supreme Court has, on occasion, been willing to overrule landmark precedents, including, for example, *Lochner* and *Plessy,* in actual practice, Supreme Court overrulings are quite rare.[103] At a minimum, this suggests a strong preference for avoiding the operation of precedent through distinction. It also might reflect a fear that frequent overrulings increase the appearance that changes in constitutional law are due to changes in the political composition of the Supreme Court, rather than to detached and reasoned analysis, applying neutral principles of law to previously unanticipated facts.[104] One of the benefits of infrequent overrulings is that it encourages litigants to devise arguments that allow for seemingly stable doctrine, but that are capable of accommodating change narrowly and incrementally. Infrequent overrulings thus enhance the value and durability of precedent by disciplining not only the justices, but also litigants who would otherwise view personnel changes as an invitation to challenge disfavored precedents. Most often, as explained above, overruling occurs at the end of a series of cases that have had the effect of undermining the value of the precedent in question. As the joint authors noted in *Casey,* for example, the Court discarded *Lochner* and *Plessy* after a series of cases that left those cases but a remnant of otherwise abandoned doctrine.[105]

3.   *Certiorari and Summary Dispositions*

Because the Court is generally disinclined to overrule and because distinguishing precedents renders the evolution of legal doctrine path dependent, the Supreme Court has a further incentive to avoid taking or deciding cases that might promote disfavored decisional paths. Historically, Congress had established two avenues for presenting cases to the Supreme Court. First, in a defined class of cases, the litigants could directly appeal to the Supreme Court. Second, in a larger class of cases, parties could petition for writ of certiorari to the Supreme Court, and the decision to grant or to deny certiorari was within the control of the Supreme Court itself. After several unsuccessful attempts to have Congress eliminate or severely curtail its nondiscretionary docket, the Supreme Court finally succeeded in assuming nearly complete docket control, by statute, in 1988.[106] In that year, Congress eliminated all but a very narrow class of cases for nondiscretionary appeals to the Supreme Court. By long-standing practice, the Supreme Court employs the Rule of Four to decide in which cases it will grant certiorari. A minority of the Court is therefore itself afforded a form of agenda-setting authority.[107] But even before 1988, the Supreme Court had an additional apparent mechanism for limiting some doctrinal cycling, even in those cases that it was required to hear. Evaluating this mechanism has significant implications not only for the Supreme Court, which continues to use it even though it now possesses nearly complete docket control, but also for the lower federal circuit courts, which do not control their own dockets. Through summary dispositions, in which the Court affirms or reverses without a full written opinion, and sometimes remands in light of another recently issued Supreme Court opinion, the Court can effectively manipulate the timing of its own precedents. The federal circuit courts can also to some extent use this practice to manipulate the timing of decisions. In fact, however, there is an effective limit to using both certiorari and summary dispositions as a counterstrategic mechanism to limit litigant path manipulation. Social choice not only reveals the limitations of certiorari and summary dispositions in limiting path manipulation, but also demonstrates how these devices are strengthened when operating in conjunction with standing.

In a nondiscretionary docket regime, summary dispositions and standing are each necessary but insufficient to avoid the most egregious litigant path manipulation. And in a fully (or nearly so) discretionary docket regime—as in the post-1988 Supreme Court—certiorari and standing are each necessary, but alone insufficient, to avoid the most egregious litigant path manipulation. To illustrate, I will hypothesize a legal regime in which the Court has no discretion over its docket and in which it has erected no standing barrier to prospective ideological litigants. I will first demonstrate the limits of summary dispositions as a counterstrategic device. This part of the analysis applies to both the Supreme Court and to the federal circuit courts. I will then reintroduce docket control, which applies only to the Supreme Court, and show that even combined with summary dispositions it is insufficient to limit the most egregious litigant path manipulation. Finally, I will show how standing, operating in combination with both summary dispositions and docket control, substantially ameliorates litigant path manipulation in the Supreme Court in a manner that certiorari and summary dispositions, in the absence of standing, cannot. I will again use *Seattle* and *Crawford* as illustrations.

Before describing the analysis, I will make a single simplifying assumption. Assume that the prospective litigants correctly anticipate the justices' votes and rationales in advance of litigating their claims. While interest groups obviously lack complete or perfect information concerning the preferences of the various justices, published opinions provide prospective litigants with substantial information with which to make educated guesses in developing arguments and in developing case-presentation strategies. Well-informed interest groups routinely identify those justices who are least likely to be sympathetic to their position, those justices who are most likely to be sympathetic to their position, and those justices who are most likely to be subject to persuasion. Informed lawyers will try to direct their briefs and arguments to the last group of justices after closely analyzing available information, based primarily on written opinions, about that group's members. Thus viewed, written opinions over time provide a stylized and piecemeal form of ordinal rankings.

Assuming perfect information, or even fairly credible predictions based upon prior published opinions, consider the incentives of prospective ideological litigants in a regime in which the Supreme Court docket is nondiscretionary and in which the Court has imposed no meaningful justiciability barriers. In this hypothetical regime, an interest group, like BUS, which is dedicated to empowering local school boards or state courts to order integrative busing, would first present *Seattle,* with the result of striking down the statewide initiative based upon *Hunter,* and then present *Crawford,* with the result of striking down the California constitutional amendment based upon *Seattle.* The result would be to strike down both state laws restricting the use of racially integrative busing. Alternatively, an interest group dedicated to neighborhood education, like CAB, could employ the opposite strategy, first presenting *Crawford,* with the result of upholding the California constitutional amendment on its merits, and then present *Seattle,* with the result of upholding as well the Washington statewide initiative. Absent any barrier to justiciability and with a nondiscretionary Supreme Court docket, we would experience a race to the extremes in which interest groups would try to force cases onto the Supreme Court's docket in the most favorable order to affect the substantive evolution of legal doctrine.

If the Supreme Court tried to respond to the potentially opposite lower court rulings in these two cases by summarily affirming or reversing, the effect would be to provide little or no guidance as to how future cases, with similar facts, should be resolved. Summary dispositions are equally problematic as a counterstrategic defense to path manipulation in the federal circuit courts, which lack the power of docket control and in which most cases are decided in panels of three. In fact, the problem of path dependence is likely exacerbated in these courts, where a given panel might not reflect the court's overall political balance. Absent the relatively rare occurrence of overruling en banc,[108] outlier panels, meaning those that do not reflect the entire court's political balance, likely exacerbate the dual problems of path dependence and codification of distinctions with only minority support. The infrequency of en banc reversals could instead be understood, however, to suggest that such practices as full circulation of opinions before publication, the opportunity for comment by judges not on the deciding panel, and the threat of en banc reconsideration itself combine to discipline potential renegade panels. Of course, within federal practice, panel assignments are random. As a result, it is difficult for litigants to predict which judges will hear any given appeal. Even so, variations in the overall political composition of the circuits themselves would provide considerable opportunities for ambitious interest groups to attempt to manipulate circuit splits,[109] with an eye toward manipulating the order of cases in the Supreme Court.

We will now reintroduce certiorari to see if it alone is sufficient to limit path manipulation in the Supreme Court. In a regime with certiorari, but without standing, the same interest groups could readily force a split, either among the federal circuit courts or among the states' highest courts, on whether a state, having initially created a vehicle for allowing integrative busing, has the power to cut it back. The resulting split on this important question of federal law would substantially raise the cost to the Supreme Court of denying certiorari. With the power of certiorari, but without standing, the Court's nominal power of docket control would therefore be a substantially less powerful barrier to litigant path manipulation. Both certiorari and standing are therefore necessary to prevent the most egregious path manipulation.

H. A Comment on Issue Percolation and Stare Decisis in the Lower Federal Courts

The above analysis reveals that within the federal circuit courts, which lack docket control, rational interest group litigants have a strong incentive to try to manipulate the path of case decisions. Because the evolution of legal doctrine within the circuits will sometimes be the arbitrary product of path dependence, the Supreme Court it has a twofold incentive. First, it will seek to ensure that the doctrine of stare decisis is adhered to *within* but not *among* the circuits. *Intra-* but not *inter*-circuit stare decisis avoids the indeterminacy that would result from cyclical preferences within each circuit. At the same time, the regime ensures that path dependent iterations, which produce arbitrary bodies of law within a given circuit, are not automatically replicated across the circuits. Second, to ensure multiple path dependent iterations from which to choose—which provides an apt economic definition of issue percolation—the Court would want the power to decide when to resolve particular issues, rather than to be forced to decide issues based upon a fixed rule. If, for example, the Supreme Court were obligated to resolve cases whenever there arose a circuit split on a question of federal law, then interest groups could readily create circuit splits to manipulate the path of Supreme Court decision making. In fact, all three of these features, each explained by the social choice framework set out in this book—*intra-* but not *inter*-circuit stare decisis, the Supreme Court's power of docket control, and standing—are reflected in actual practice.[110]

IV. Standing Reconsidered: A Comparison of Legislatures and Courts

The above analysis shows that a regime that seeks to stabilize legal doctrine through adherence to precedent will inevitably produce path dependency and thus invite some path manipulation. In some cases, the issue whether to demand consistency itself can provide the critical additional framework, rendering judicial preferences two-dimensional and thus prone to cycling, as in the *Crawford* and *Seattle* hypotheticals, and in others, multiple frameworks can arise independently of adherence to precedent, as in *Carey, Shaw,* and *Miller.* While the Court can attempt to avoid the problem of path manipulation through overruling, devising novel case distinctions, or employing such counterstrategic devices as certiorari denials or summary dispositions, none of these methods, individually or in combination, is sufficient to avoid the most persistent forms of litigant path manipulation. Even with each of these practices in place, therefore, the Court has a strong incentive to employ a series of doctrines that limit the power of ideological litigants to strategically time cases.

The Court's various timing-based justiciability doctrines—ripeness, mootness, and most notably standing—greatly improve the overall fairness of constitutional decision making by limiting the power of non-Condorcet minorities to affect the substantive development of legal doctrine through strategic timing. The justiciability doctrines therefore encourage frustrated litigants to seek redress in Congress or in state legislatures, which are generally superior at avoiding the codification of components of intransitive collective preferences. As discussed in chapter 2, legislatures, unlike courts, have the institutional power to remain inert when faced with proposed legislation lacking majority or Condorcet-minority support. Alternatively, legislatures can rationally codify seeming non-Condorcet-winning preferences by expanding the relevant issue space through vote trading. A legislature can therefore pass a larger package of legislation, which has explicit majority support, or implicit majority support as the Condorcet winner, but which includes provisions that would not have passed had they been presented alone. The above analysis suggests that various decisional processes in Congress and in the Supreme Court afford each institution a comparative advantage over the other for particular kinds of lawmaking. The analysis further suggests that the relative competence of each institution is enhanced through the combined doctrines of stare decisis and standing.

The difficulty with claiming that stare decisis and standing further the relative competence of the Supreme Court and Congress in performing their assigned tasks is that the analysis rests upon several implicit normative conceptions about what those underlying assigned tasks actually are. If, for example, the Supreme Court and Congress have coterminous lawmaking powers, such that each has full authority to decide any policy issue, except as expressly constrained by the Constitution's limiting provisions, then standing undermines, rather than furthers, the process of Supreme Court decision making. It does so by improperly driving policymaking from one coequal branch of government to another.[111] If the Supreme Court and Congress actually are equal in their lawmaking power, then the justiciability doctrines in general, and standing in particular, which operate to constrain the judiciary's lawmaking function, would have no place.

To demonstrate that the Supreme Court and Congress should not be regarded as coterminous in their lawmaking powers, I cannot rest entirely upon the foregoing social choice analysis. As is generally true of positive economic analysis, social choice reveals certain trade-offs, for example the problems that arise in the judiciary with or without stare decisis and standing. But economic analysis itself cannot tell us which of the identified sets of outcomes is normatively superior. To determine whether these doctrines further important objectives of constitutional process, we must test the trade-offs that a positive social choice analysis reveals against a clearly expressed and normatively defensible assessment of the respective spheres of authority between Congress and the Supreme Court. But doing so requires that we step, at least temporarily, outside of the economic model.[112] As shown below, it may be more difficult to articulate, than to defend, a credible normative distinction between Supreme Court and congressional lawmaking. To assist with this task, I will compare two comments, both of which appeared in dictum in two Supreme Court decisions concerning the Supreme Court's lawmaking role, the first by retired associate justice Harry Blackmun and the second by Chief Justice William Rehnquist.

In *Mistretta v. United States*,[113] the Supreme Court rejected a separation-of-powers challenge to the United States Sentencing Commission, established in the Sentencing Reform Act of 1984.[114] The act created a seven-member independent commission, which is located within the federal judiciary and which includes three Article III judges. Under the act, the commission is vested with the authority to implement uniform federal sentencing guidelines, binding upon all federal courts.[115] Mistretta, who pleaded guilty to conspiracy to distribute cocaine, challenged his sentence imposed under the guidelines. He argued that the act violated separation of powers because it improperly vested legislative power in the judicial branch. As a result, Mistretta argued, the act undermined that branch's "independence and integrity."

To understand the difficulty in distinguishing adjudicatory versus legislative lawmaking, consider the following excerpt from Justice Blackmun's majority opinion, upholding the act against Mistretta's constitutional challenge:

> Prior to the passage of the Act, the Judicial Branch, as an aggregate, decided precisely the questions assigned to the Commission: what sentence is appropriate to what criminal conduct under what circumstances. It was the everyday business of judges, taken collectively, to evaluate and weigh the various aims of sentencing and to apply those aims to the individual cases that came before them. The Sentencing Commission does no more than this, albeit basically through the

methodology of sentencing guidelines, rather than entirely individualized sentencing determinations.

When teaching *Mistretta* in my introductory course in constitutional law, I ask my students whether the commission's responsibilities, as Blackmun has described them, sound judicial or legislative. Most students conclude that description sounds legislative. The more difficult question, however, is how to define the difference between those lawmaking functions.

Most students find it easier to reject, than to devise, defensible distinguishing characterizations. First, students reject as simplistic the assumption that legislatures make law and that courts apply law. That is not surprising; after all, constitutional law is essentially a study in judicially created positive law. Second, they dispense with the notion that legislative rules apply generally and prospectively while judicial rules apply retrospectively to the parties before the court. The prevalence of declaratory judgment actions coupled with the widespread use of injunctive relief aptly illustrates that both courts and legislatures not only make law, but they often do so with prospective effect. Finally, students reject the idea that statutes necessarily affect larger numbers of people than do cases. After all, class actions have greatly increased the size of affected plaintiff populations, and the prevalence of broad-based injunctive relief has had the same effect on defendant populations.

Despite the difficulty in articulating a credible normative distinction between legislative and adjudicatory lawmaking, I believe that Blackmun's description of the sentencing commission's function is legislative. To see why, it will be helpful first to compare Justice Blackmun's dictum with that of Justice Rehnquist in his partial concurrence and partial dissent in *Planned Parenthood of Southeastern Pennsylvania v. Casey*.[116] In criticizing the joint opinion's newly announced undue burden test, which the Court had used to strike several provisions of Pennsylvania's restrictive abortion statute, the chief justice stated: "Under the guise of the Constitution, this Court will still impart its own preferences on the States in the form of a complex abortion code."[117] Although coming at the issue from quite different perspectives, the statements both by Justice Blackmun and by Chief Justice Rehnquist rest upon implicit normative conceptions about the differences between adjudicatory and legislative lawmaking, both of which, I will argue, are problematic. Exposing the difficulties in each analysis will allow us to establish a more beneficial set of normative foundations for these two different lawmaking functions.[118]

In Justice Blackmun's normative conception, adjudicatory lawmaking is the aggregation of individual judicial pronouncements, without regard to the circumstances under which those pronouncements are made. Thus, for Blackmun, the Sentencing Commission guidelines are legitimate because they represent the equivalent of the thousands of individual sentencing determinations that are the daily business of judging. Chief Justice Rehnquist's normative conception is nearly opposite. The aggregation of several, or several dozen, independently legitimate judicial pronouncements becomes normatively suspect if the effect, in terms of depth or complexity, approaches that of an elaborate statutory scheme. Both justices focus on the relationship between individual and aggregated judicial pronouncements, but neither does so based upon a consideration of the *process* through which the former becomes the latter. As suggested by this book's title, my own position is that the normative validity of adjudicatory versus legislative lawmaking is precisely a function of the processes through which law—and especially constitutional law—is and is not made. And because constitutional decision making in the Supreme Court is most critically concerned with which organs of government make which decisions under which conditions, social choice reveals that such decision making is fundamentally concerned with our understanding of the processes through which the various organs of government make their decisions.[119]

Within our constitutional system, both the federal courts and Congress undoubtedly create positive law with prospective application that affects large numbers of people. But unlike Congress, the federal courts are expected to do so on an ad hoc and as-needed basis.[120] Although the Supreme Court, for example, makes law, and plenty of it, it does so in the context of cases presented to it by litigants after a grant of certiorari or, less commonly, following a proper appeal. And while Congress has free rein to legislate on any issue it seeks, provided it has properly delegated authority under Article I and that it does not violate any independent constitutional provision, the Supreme Court—like the federal judiciary generally—is limited by the Article III case or controversy requirement in the exercise of its lawmaking powers. Not only are federal courts limited by actual cases in making law, but also, in deciding individual cases, they are generally expected to limit their lawmaking to that which necessarily flows from the resolution of dispositive issues in the cases before them. This is especially true in the context of constitutional adjudication. In contrast, legislatures, in deciding whether to make law, are not subject either to an ad hoc or as needed constraint. The Supreme Court has repeatedly emphasized that legislatures, including Congress, are the masters of their own timing in enacting legislation. Thus, the Court has rejected challenges to economic regulation premised upon the argument that the legislature improperly chose to deal with the underlying policy issue in only an incremental fashion.[121] The Court has also rejected challenges to regulation premised upon the opposite argument, namely that the regulatory scheme neglected to create a mechanism for case-by-case determinations, rather than creating categorical determinations for the regulated class.[122] In applying rational basis scrutiny to such challenges to legislative lawmaking, the Supreme Court signaled that Congress and the state legislatures, in contrast with the federal courts, are presumed to be the masters of their own timing in lawmaking. And in using standing and other timing-based justiciability barriers to limit its own lawmaking to that needed to resolve actual disputes, the Supreme Court has underscored that the federal courts are *not* the masters of their own timing.[123]

The *Mistretta* Court substantially compromised both of these critical distinctions. Certainly it is true that courts, in the aggregate, sentence large num-

202 · *Constitutional Process*

bers of convicted criminals. It is also true that courts, in the aggregate, interpret, and sometimes invalidate, large numbers of statutes, fill in statutory interstitial gaps, and create constitutional law. Within our constitutional system, the federal courts, no less than Congress and state legislatures, make positive law in performing these functions. None of that, however, places courts on a par with the legislature in their lawmaking functions. The constitutional question in *Mistretta* was not whether, in totaling the individualized sentencing determinations, each of which is a proper judicial function, the federal judiciary affects as many people as does a legislative body. The issue, instead, was whether the Sentencing Commission, which included three Article III judges, unconstitutionally exercised legislative powers by creating positive law in the form of uniform sentencing guidelines *other than* on an ad hoc and as-needed basis. The answer to that question was almost certainly yes.

Now compare Justice Blackmun's conflation of adjudicatory and legislative lawmaking with Chief Justice Rehnquist's attempt to distinguish these two functions. The chief justice suggested that the Supreme Court improperly exercises a quasi-legislative function when, in the name of constitutional adjudication, it devises a sufficiently detailed set of commands that the emerging body of law resembles an elaborate statutory scheme in level of specificity. If that were true, however, we would need to dispense with huge bodies of constitutional case law developed throughout our 210-year history, most of which carry nowhere near the political baggage associated with the abortion case law. The Supreme Court, throughout its history, has devised bodies of positive law, based upon the Constitution, that bear a striking resemblance in level of specificity to complex federal statutes. While detailing any particular substantive area is unnecessary, listing a few well-noted bodies of codelike case law will suffice.

Prior to abandoning all pretense of imposing Tenth Amendment limits on the commerce power, the Supreme Court developed a codelike body of case law attempting to distinguish activities affecting commerce from activities that were deemed inherently local in nature. While abandoning this effort greatly simplified the affirmative side of the commerce clause, it did not remove the complexity from the codelike dormant commerce clause cases. During the New Deal, the Court developed a codelike body of case law concerning which substantive provisions of the Bill of Rights were incorporated against the states under the Fourteenth Amendment due process clause. After incorporating all but four provisions of the Bill of Rights,[124] the Warren and Burger Courts began the continuing process of creating an even more codelike set of interpretations governing the Fourth Amendment prohibition against unreasonable searches and seizures, the Fifth Amendment privilege against self-incrimination, and the Sixth Amendment right to counsel and a fair trial, to name only a few. During the Warren, Burger, and Rehnquist eras, beginning with *Brown v. Board of Education*,[125] the Court developed an exceptionally detailed and codelike body of case law concerning the obligations of previously segregated school systems to desegregate their schools. In the

1970s, the Court went further, rejecting Justice Powell's plea for uniform national standards on desegregating public schools,[126] and began to create yet another complex body of codelike case law on the obligation of the northern states, which had never segregated their public schools by law, to integrate their de facto segregated schools. The Court also has created codelike bodies of case law related to the First Amendment establishment and free exercise clauses and the Fifth Amendment takings clause. While this list is by no means exhaustive, it is sufficient to demonstrate that the level of judicially imposed detail in any particular body of case law, if used to challenge its legitimacy, would undermine numerous vast and important bodies of constitutional law, some dating to the earliest days of the republic.

While criminal procedure cases, as demonstrated above, are by no means unique in their codelike complexity, they are particularly relevant to the evolution and function of the modern standing doctrine. The Supreme Court has not only ruled on which substantive provisions of the Bill of Rights apply against the states, but also has provided detailed instructions in numerous cases to state and local police officers on the timing and method of securing a search warrant, when a search warrant is and is not necessary, what constitutes exigent circumstances, what may and may not be searched in exigent circumstances, how to secure an arrest warrant, what constitutes probable cause to search and to arrest, when suspects may be apprehended short of probable cause, when police officers must inform suspects of their constitutional rights, what specific constitutional rights police officers must identify,[127] what to say and do when a suspect seeks to exercise each of those rights, and when the state is and is not obligated to provide counsel. As before, this list is not exhaustive. Certainly this body of case law is at least as codelike, and is probably more codelike, than the pre- or post-*Casey* abortion case law. Its legitimacy, however, is not determined—or undermined—by its codelike detail. Instead, it is determined by the Court's need to interpret specific constitutional clauses, thus creating positive law, in determining the substantive rights of convicted criminals when those criminals present proper appeals and collateral challenges to the Court. To determine the legitimacy of any area of constitutional case law, one cannot look at the aggregate level of detail. Instead, at the level of each individual case, one must determine whether the judicial creation of positive law was required to resolve the dispositive issues before the Court. If, in deciding several—or several dozen—cases for which the answer to that question is yes, the Court creates a codelike body of case law, one can only conclude that creating that body of detailed positive law was a necessary part of the Court's job.

And yet, we have seen that precisely because the Court needs to resolve cases properly before it, it has developed decisional rules, including the doctrine of stare decisis, that render the substantive evolution of positive law largely subject to the control of those dictating the order of case presentations. Stare decisis, a doctrine adhered to within but not across the circuits, when coupled with the power of docket control, enables the Court to wait until a sufficient selection of path dependent iterations among the circuits has emerged from which to choose. The Court has also increasingly relied upon its standing doctrine to mitigate the most damaging effects of path dependency, not only in the Supreme Court, which can control its docket, but also among the circuits, which cannot control their dockets. Standing performs this function by increasing the role of fortuity—as opposed to advertent litigant path manipulation—in ultimately shaping the substantive development of constitutional law. In criminal procedure cases, the substantive evolution of perhaps the Supreme Court's most codelike body of case law was largely dictated, curiously, by convicted criminals. The question then arises: If we know that the order in which cases are presented for decision affects the substantive evolution of legal doctrine, and not just the timing, does it make any sense at all to provide convicted criminals with complete agenda-setting power over such an important area of case law? Explaining why the answer to this question is yes will help to pierce some of the seemingly enigmatic features of standing doctrine, discussed earlier in this chapter.

A. The Shadow Case Analysis: The Independence of Standing from Cause of Action, Ripeness, and Mootness

The above analysis not only distinguishes legislative and adjudicatory lawmaking, but also suggests the need to employ a novel standing analysis that pierces the Supreme Court's language in describing the barriers to justiciability. Rather than comparing cases directly, for example, based upon the presence or absence of "injury" or the zealousness with which litigants will present their underlying claims, a process-based analysis requires that we compare the relationship between the relevant cases in which standing was either conferred or denied, with their "shadow cases," namely those cases in which the same claims could be presented with no credible standing barrier. The need to employ a shadow case analysis, rather than to compare directly the results of standing cases, is most easily illustrated by considering four actual standing cases. In contrast with the direct comparison approach, which dominates traditional standing analyses and which highlights the doctrine's seeming inconsistencies, the shadow case analysis reveals those critical facts that likely enabled the deciding court to intuit the need to shift *or not shift* the burden of legislative inertia. Specifically, the analysis reveals whether the claimant is seeking to influence the critically important path of case decisions or, instead, has been burdened with the consequences of a fortuitous historical event beyond her control, but which inflicted significant and direct legal harm.

In *City of Los Angeles v. Lyons,*[128] a released choke hold victim had obtained a preliminary injunction on behalf of himself and the class he represented, based upon a holding that the Los Angeles Police Department's practice of restraining suspected criminals with choke holds violated several constitutional guarantees, including the Fourteenth Amendment due process clause and the Eighth Amendment prohibition on cruel and unusual punishment. Lyons argued that as a prior choke hold victim, he had a substantial chance of being so held a second time. The Supreme Court rejected the claim, holding that Lyons had not alleged a sufficient injury to warrant a judicial determination on the constitutionality of the police choke hold practice, except as applied to him in the past in an action for damages.

In *Gilmore v. Utah,*[129] Gary Gilmore's mother sought to challenge the constitutionality of her son's capital murder conviction and pending execution. Mrs. Gilmore alleged that because her son had not filed his own collateral attack on his conviction and sentence, he was certain to be executed, in violation of several claimed constitutional guarantees,[130] if she were not permitted to raise the constitutional challenges on his behalf. The Court again rejected the claim, terminating the stay of execution that it had previously entered. In two separate concurring opinions, four of the six deciding justices expressly concluded that Mrs. Gilmore lacked standing to press her son's claims,[131] reasoning that Mrs. Gilmore had not alleged a sufficient injury to qualify for standing.

In criticizing these case results, scholars have compared cases in which the Court, faced with attenuated, and sometimes dubious, causal chains, held that plaintiffs were sufficiently injured for standing purposes. Thus, for example, in *Duke Power Co. v. Carolina Environmental Study Group, Inc.,*[132] a group of homeowners was granted standing to challenge the constitutionality of the Price-Anderson Act, a federal statute that limited the liability of nuclear power plants, including a proposed plant to be constructed near their homes. Plaintiffs did not allege, however, that if they were afforded standing, and then succeeded on the merits, thus striking the liability limitation, the construction would necessarily be abated. Even though plaintiffs' injury might therefore have occurred independently of the requested judicial relief, the Court rejected the challenge to plaintiffs' standing. Similarly, in *Regents of the University of California v. Bakke,*[133] Mr. Bakke was granted standing to challenge a state medical school's admissions process that created two pools, the first with eighty-four seats for which all students, minorities and nonminorities, could compete, and the second, an affirmative action pool of sixteen seats for which only qualified minority students could compete. Like the *Duke Power* plaintiffs, Bakke did not allege that had he initially been considered for all one hundred seats, he would necessarily have been admitted into the medical school. While the Court granted standing to both the *Duke Power* plaintiffs and to Bakke, who undeniably presented, at best, contingent claims of injury, in *Lyons* and in *Gilmore* it denied standing notwithstanding actual prior or pending injuries that would inevitably arise in the absence of judicial relief. In contrast with *Duke Power* and *Bakke,* if the Court had reached the merits and granted relief in *Gilmore* and *Lyons,* plaintiffs' claimed injuries would necessarily have been prevented. Gary Gilmore would not have been executed or, at the very least, he would have received a new trial or sentencing phase, and the Los Angeles Police Department would have been enjoined from continuing its choke hold practice.

The problem with the above analysis, however, is that in comparing the cases directly, we lose sight of the critical distinction between adjudicatory and legislative lawmaking. In doing so, we also lose sight of the real purpose underlying the standing inquiry, and indeed of justiciability generally. Properly understood, the injury-in-fact prong of the standing inquiry is not really about injury at all. Instead, the term *injury* is a metaphor. The relevant inquiry in comparing these and other standing cases is whether the facts alleged are sufficient to overcome the burden of legislative inertia. While Congress and state legislatures do not issue collective determinations on the constitutionality of legislation, for most if not all cases involving a constitutional challenge to governmental conduct, the legislature has the authority to proscribe that conduct directly by statute. For example, the California legislature could proscribe choke holds, which Lyons challenged, and the Utah legislature could abolish the death penalty, which Gilmore faced. Congress could also amend or rescind the liability limitation that was subject to challenge in *Duke Power,* and California could prohibit its schools from considering race in the manner employed by the University of California at Davis Medical School. In fact, through Proposition 209, California recently did just that.[134] And in some instances, the Court has suggested that Congress has the authority to expand the scope of rights under the Fourteenth Amendment equal protection, even if in doing so, it provides broader protection than the Supreme Court itself.[135] Under this reasoning, using its enforcement authority under section 5 of the Fourteenth Amendment, Congress might have the authority to limit certain state practices as unconstitutional directly. At the time these cases were decided, however, Congress and the relevant state legislatures had remained inert with respect to these issues. In each of these cases, those challenging the underlying laws effectively sought to shift the burden of legislative inertia onto the federal courts, thus reversing the general presumption that when a legislature is silent, the status quo governs. The standing question, then, is not which plaintiff has alleged a more serious or acute injury at some abstract level. Instead, it is which plaintiff has alleged the necessary facts to justify forcing a federal court to consider shifting the burden of legislative inertia on the underlying substantive legal question. Stated differently, the critical standing inquiry is whether plaintiff has sufficiently demonstrated the need for an ad hoc judicial creation of positive law on the underlying legal issue or whether the Court is better served by denying standing, even though in doing so it will issue another, albeit less prominent, substantive legal ruling.[136]

While some commentators have argued that standing is ultimately a heuristic for the presence or absence of a cause of action,[137] the above analysis explains why the standing and cause-of-action inquiries are necessarily independent. One of the many substantive issues that the Supreme Court resolves in its positive lawmaking is whether to infer a cause of action from relevant statutes and constitutional provisions in a given case. As with any other substantive area of Supreme Court decision making, the determination of whether to infer particular causes of action is subject to path dependence. The standing inquiry is not about whether a particular cause of action may be inferred from any particular statutory or constitutional clause. Instead, in cases that involve the issue of whether to infer a cause of action, the standing inquiry is about whether plaintiff has alleged the requisite facts with which to justify shifting the burden of legislative inertia regarding that substantive legal question. In other words, the standing issue in such cases is whether *this case* presents the appropriate opportunity for the Court to resolve the substantive issue whether the statutory or constitutional provision under review implies the proffered cause of action.

As we have seen in the criminal procedure context, the Court is not shy about providing detailed and codelike rules when needed to resolve actual cases. This includes providing detailed information about the nature and scope of implied causes of action when required to resolve concrete cases that are presented to the Court. And yet, notwithstanding the Court's willingness to create detailed positive law when required, the Court effectively denied Mrs. Gilmore standing, even though in doing so it virtually ensured that her son would be executed. If the Supreme Court, in failing to consider a particular case, has virtually ensured that plaintiff's son will be executed, and if the Court is willing, in resolving cases, to create positive law on an as-needed basis, an obvious question arises: What, then, could "as needed" possibly mean?

The judicial creation of positive law is "needed" if a judicial decision is required to prevent the infringement of plaintiff's constitutional or statutory rights. Mrs. Gilmore never alleged that the wrongful execution of her son violated *her* constitutional rights. Instead, she alleged that her son's rights were being violated. In denying her standing, therefore, the Court has held that, as a matter of substantive law, Mrs. Gilmore does not have the right to enforce the rights of others, even those of her son. It is easy to understand why the Court willingly issued this modest substantive holding, best understood as a denial of standing, rather than reaching the merits of Mrs. Gilmore's underlying legal claim. To litigate the underlying constitutional issues, a ready alternative was available: Gary Gilmore was free to file his own collateral attack.

Similarly, Mr. Lyons had not alleged that absent judicial resolution, *his* constitutional rights would have been violated. Instead, he alleged that without a judicial resolution, someone's rights at some unknown time in the future might be violated. But again, there is an obvious solution. If someone is convicted of a crime following an unconstitutional apprehending choke hold, that person, like Lyons, can file a retroactive damages suit and, unlike Lyons, that person can try to challenge the constitutionality of his detention in a direct appeal from his conviction or sentence. In fact, in *Tennessee v. Gardner,*[138] two years after *Lyons,* the Supreme Court did reach the issue whether a police officer must have probable cause to believe a fleeing suspect is dangerous before employing deadly force. In that case, Gardner raised the claim and obtained a favorable holding on the very issue for which Lyons brought suit, but in a context in which there was no credible standing barrier. More generally, in virtually all criminal procedure cases, the claimant who received relief did so either in a direct appeal following a criminal conviction and sentence or in a subsequent collateral attack. And in those criminal procedure cases presenting novel legal questions based upon the application of broad-based textual provisions in the Bill of Rights to a previously unknown set of facts, the Court willingly created positive law. Standing is rarely at issue in such proceedings because a judicial determination is needed to determine whether plaintiff's constitutional rights have been, or are being, violated.[139]

This analysis also explains why the standing inquiry is inevitably separate from such related justiciability inquiries as ripeness and mootness. As with judicially inferred causes of action, the judicial resolution of the substantive rights of convicted criminals based upon broadly worded constitutional provisions is subject to path dependence. There is virtually always the possibility that at some future time, a criminal defendant will be convicted and sentenced based upon an allegedly erroneous interpretation of a constitutional clause, or that a criminal was so convicted in the past. There may also be some convict, who, if he chose to do so, could force a judicial determination of the limits of a particular constitutional clause in an appropriate direct or collateral challenge to his conviction or sentence. For those convicts who could force the further judicial creation of positive law, timing is not in issue. The claim is ripe, given that a conviction or sentence has already been imposed, and is not moot, given that a contrary constitutional interpretation would result in a meaningful remedy, for example, a reversal or remand for a new trial or sentencing phase.

If public interest organizations dedicated to furthering the reach of these substantive constitutional provisions could freely test the limits of such constitutional clauses by identifying a convicted criminal, somewhere, for whom a ripe and nonmoot constitutional claim exists, we would again be subject to the very same sort of litigant-controlled path manipulation that standing operates to prevent.[140] As stated above, however, standing does not prevent path dependence. The preceding analysis suggests that we vest nearly complete agenda-setting power over as important an area as constitutional criminal procedure in convicted criminals because, generally speaking, they present their difficult cases for judicial resolution for only one reason—to get relief from their convictions and sentences. They do not do so out of any desire to manipulate the order of precedent based upon some ideologically driven desire to benefit society at large. Instead, when we allow convicted criminals to force judicial creation of positive law in proper appeals and collateral challenges, we further the likelihood that fortuity, rather than advertent litigant path manipulation, will control the substantive evolution of inevitably path dependent legal doctrine.

The above analysis also helps to explain another anomaly in the standing case law. In some standing cases, the Court has asserted that the doctrine is intended to promote zealous advocacy.[141] And yet, on occasion, the Court appears to deny standing *because of* rather than *in spite of* the zealousness with which the claimant will litigate the case. As with injury-in-fact, the anomaly is removed once we recognize that zealousness is a metaphor. Zealousness is intended to capture the essence of a traditional bipolar legal dispute in which there is no question of standing, namely a case grounded in the rights and obligations of particular parties, rather than one based upon generalized principles. The zealousness metaphor is apt inasmuch as most litigants who can credibly justify shifting the burden of legislative inertia on the ground that without a judicial ruling on the issue they are presenting, their rights will be infringed, tend to present their claims zealously. But the correlation between zealousness and the need to shift the burden of legislative inertia is just that. The difficulty is that most contested standing cases involve ideological litigants who, although they might not allege facts that justify forcing the federal courts to create positive law, will zealously represent their side of the legal dispute. Ironically, at least if we are to credit the Court's language in describing the standing criteria, it is because of the zealousness with which ideological litigants seek to thrust a quasi-legislative function onto the federal courts that the Court denies standing in such cases. The anomaly is removed, however, when we realize that zealousness is not an independent objective of justiciability. It is instead a convenient—albeit imperfect—heuristic that the Court employs to ascertain whether the present case satisfies the traditional criteria justifying it to shift the burden of legislative inertia, thus forcing judicial creation of positive law.

In *Duke Power* it was true that construction would not necessarily be halted if the Court granted the requested relief. But there was no shadow case, as in *Gilmore* and *Lyons,* in which plaintiffs' claims could be presented for resolution with no standing barrier. Once we realize that, the injury-in-fact metaphor is easily translated to secure standing: Absent a judicial determination whether the liability-limiting statute is constitutional, plaintiffs might have been subjected to a severe infringement of their right not to have a nuclear power plant with federally limited liability constructed near their homes based upon the assumption that a federal statute will limit the plant's potential financial exposure. The financial consequences of the construction in *Duke Power* were imminent, and the potential personal consequences were severe. In short, there was no alternative plaintiff or forum in which to protect the plaintiffs' claimed constitutional rights. Plaintiffs therefore alleged facts that more closely resembled those in cases in which the Court has no choice but to create positive law in the face of Congress's unwillingness to change the status quo. Moreover, the *Duke Power* plaintiffs could credibly argue that whatever ultimately happened with the construction of the nuclear power plant, they had already suffered a substantial economic hardship in the present decline in property values resulting from the announced intent to proceed with construction, based largely, if not entirely, on the Price-Anderson Act's liability cap.

Similarly, Mr. Bakke appeared closer to the traditional litigant whose circumstances were governed by fortuity—or at least by circumstances primarily within the government's control—rather than advertent or ideological path manipulation. While it is true that even if he were considered for all one hundred minority seats, Bakke might still have been rejected, it is also true that no alternative plaintiff, or forum, existed in which Mr. Bakke could meaningfully have vindicated his claimed constitutional right. Moreover, it is also possible that if considered for the additional seats, he would have been admitted. The consequence of denying standing, and thus guaranteeing no admission, for this plaintiff was again potentially serious to a specific individual. Both *Duke Power* and *Bakke* lacked compelling shadow cases. As a result, judicial abstinence would have been inappropriate and standing was, therefore, properly granted. That is not because plaintiffs' injuries were more concrete at some theoretic level than in those cases in which standing was denied. It is instead because, having recognized injury for what it is—a metaphor for when plaintiffs have alleged the necessary facts to justify shifting the burden of legislative inertia—these plaintiffs met the injury test. In that respect, *Duke Power* and *Bakke* are hybrids of traditional bipolar litigation in which standing is not in dispute and of those cases in which path manipulation is presumed and thus standing is denied.

This analysis further explains why the final standing category, no right to an undistorted market, is among the most difficult. As stated above, the cases in this category are best understood as hybrids, lying somewhere in the middle of a spectrum, reproduced as table 4.9.

Table 4.9. Expanded Justiciability Spectrum Revisited

Category of Cases	Ripeness/ Mootness	Rights of Others and Diffuse Harms	Undistorted Market	Criminal Procedure
Analytical Spectrum	Strong presumption in favor of path manipulation	←————————→	Strong presumption against path manipulation	

At one extreme, we have those cases that involve facts presumptively beyond the litigants' control and for which judicial relief will unquestionably remedy the alleged harm. In criminal procedure cases, for example, path manipulation is rarely a concern; the litigants are pursuing their claims not out of any sense of ideological altruism, but, instead, out of a narrow desire for personal gain. At the other extreme are moot or nonripe cases, which, because they involve claims that are not live, are likely driven by ideological concerns. In between we have the various categories of standing. The first two ground rules of standing, no right to enforce the rights of others and no right to prevent diffuse harms, involve intermediate categories of cases with relatively low-cost path manipulation. While the underlying claims are specific and live, they are either specific to someone else or are stated broadly to create a first-party claim, which might appear better suited to legislative resolution. Legislative processes are presumptively superior at addressing the merits of such underlying claims because legislatures, unlike courts, have a comparative advantage in identifying and in selecting available Condorcet winners, and in remaining inert or expanding issue space when confronted with collective intransitive preferences. In denying standing, the Court does not forever hold the underlying claim off-limits. Instead, it sends a signal that when a proper shadow case arises as a result of factual developments beyond the litigants' control, it will resolve the case. Until then, the litigants are free to participate in the legislative process. Finally, between the relatively easy standing ground rules and the criminal procedure cases are the most difficult standing cases, those typified by *Duke Power* and *Bakke*. In those cases, the Supreme Court identifies those factors that pull more strongly toward path manipulation, at one end of this expanded justiciability spectrum, or toward compelled judicial lawmaking at the other, and determine justiciability accordingly.

V. Conclusion

This chapter has explained three phenomena. First, based upon the theory of social choice, this chapter has explained the development of stare decisis and standing as complementary doctrines that improve the overall rationality and fairness of Supreme Court decision making. Second, the analysis has placed standing within a broader framework of justiciability doctrines, including ripeness and mootness, based both upon the conceptual timing of case decision making and upon the more important criterion of the ease or difficulty of the underlying cases to path manipulation, which the various justiciability rules operate to limit. Finally, the chapter has provided a normative framework with which to evaluate this book's central thesis, that the Supreme Court's process-based decisional rules further the core distinctions between adjudicatory and legislative decision making. The ultimate paths of constitutional case law are to a significant extent arbitrary when contrasted with potential alternative decisional paths. But with meaningful barriers to justiciability that ground those paths in fortuitous factors beyond the control of the litigants themselves, the resulting doctrine is also the product of a constitutional process that we all can accept as fair. In the next and final part of this book, we will test the social choice model developed in this part against the historical and case evidence.

Part III

Historical and Case Evidence

CHAPTER 5

The Burger and Rehnquist
Courts in Historical Context

I. Introduction: The Nature of Economic Testing

In evaluating the merit of an economic model, it is misleading to use such terms as *correct* or *incorrect*. Economic models are neither true nor false. Instead, the value of a positive economic analysis depends upon the extent to which the model generates meaningful insights about enigmatic phenomena in the real world. Because economic models are intended to be manageable images of reality, a tension necessarily arises between a model's descriptive accuracy and its manageability. Developing an economic model, therefore, differs from developing a theory in one of the natural, or "hard," sciences. While even a single contrary datum can raise questions about the accuracy of a genuinely scientific theory,[1] even the most robust economic models are unable to account for a considerable amount of data. As a result, locating one or more data unaccounted for in an economic model may be of no more value in refuting the model than observing that the model and reality are different.

There are, then, two alternative tests with which to evaluate an economic model. The first, and most ambitious, test is to inquire whether the proffered model accounts for more—and more varied[2]—data than do alternative models or explanations. This test is intuitively appealing for two reasons. First, it avoids the criticism that the proffered model fails if it is unable to explain one or more anomalies in the real world. And second, it demands the more difficult—and more useful—criticism of offering up an alternative model that either explains all the data that the proffered model explains, *plus one,* or that explains an overall greater quantity of data after accounting for the inability of both models to explain some—but perhaps different—data. The second, somewhat less ambitious, test is to inquire whether the proffered model can be combined with existing models to provide a more fully realized understanding of the underlying real-world phenomena than any single model can provide operating alone. At a minimum, this test, which evaluates a model according to whether it provides a basis for a broader understanding of a given subject matter, might rightly be regarded as more collegial in that it accommodates preexisting theories. The two articulated tests might be better viewed as points along a single evaluative spectrum, rather than as independent inquiries. Thus viewed, the social choice analysis of Supreme Court decision making can be evaluated according to the following points along a single dimensional continuum: (1) whether it explains more, and more varied, data than do alternative theories (satisfying the robustness test); (2) whether it provides the basis for important insights not explained under existing theories, in a manner that complements those theories (satisfying the accommodationist test); and (3) whether it simply fails to provide important insights either as a free-standing theory or as the basis for a more complete theory in combination with other theories (failing both tests).

As suggested above, the robustness and accommodationist tests themselves might be viewed as complementary, rather than competing. The social choice theory of Supreme Court decision making developed in this book, like economic theories in general, is not intended to identify actual psychological motivations of the justices in the creation of the various doctrines under review. I do not claim, for example, that the justices continued the practices of outcome voting or stare decisis, carried over from England, because they recognized that those decision-making rules limit cycling. Nor do I claim that the justices devised the narrowest grounds doctrine because they understood the implications of the Condorcet criterion or of the median voter theorem for their decision-making processes. Finally, I do not claim that the Court developed standing as it did when it did because it understood that it was prone to multidimensionality, occasionally coupled with asymmetry. Instead, I recognize that the justices embraced some of these doctrines, and most notably outcome voting, the narrowest grounds doctrine, and stare decisis, because they were familiar, and others, including most notably ripeness, mootness, and standing, because they solved at a particular point in time a problem that was largely the product of unique political conditions facing the Court. The social choice analysis is most helpful in explaining the stability of long-standing rules, in identifying the conditions that have led the Court to change existing doctrines, and in explaining why certain doctrinal changes have remained stable, while others have not. Just as the evolutionary story of parliamentary rules introduced in chapter 2 did not turn on familiarity of the decision makers with social choice theory, nor does the explanation of various Supreme Court decision-making rules. In that sense, social choice theory does not, and indeed cannot, *refute* arguments concerning the actual motivations of the justices in developing any particular doctrine discussed in this book. Thus viewed, the social choice model necessarily complements, rather than replaces, the work of Supreme Court historians who seek to unmask actual motivations underlying judicial behavior. On the other hand, throughout this book, I have argued that more traditional explanations of the doctrines under review have failed to consider why those doctrines have persisted for such a long period of time, despite the apparently anomalous and sometimes problematic outcomes that they produce.

Thus viewed, the social choice analysis of Supreme Court decision making set out in this book should rightly be viewed as a success if it passes, at a minimum, the accommodationist test, meaning that it contributes to our understanding of the Supreme Court decision-making processes and the implications of those processes for the evolution of constitutional doctrine. Nevertheless, my own position is stronger. Without trying to suggest that the model supersedes alternative theories, I would suggest that along the spectrum described above, the social choice analysis set out in this book lies closer to the robustness end, given that it explains some of the most important anomalies of modern constitutional decision making in a more satisfactory manner than do other theories standing alone. As stated above, however, it is not necessary that the reader accept this more ambitious proposition to find value in the social choice model established here.

In this book, I have offered a novel economic model of Supreme Court decision making that explains outcome voting, the narrowest grounds doctrine, stare decisis, and justiciability. While it is not possible here to provide detailed empirical support for the social choice model of each of these doctrines, this chapter and the next will test what may well be the most novel and far-reaching theory developed in part II, namely the social choice theory of standing. The standing analysis provides what may be the most valuable opportunity for empirical testing because the Supreme Court developed its standing doctrine in a fairly recent historical period and in a manner that is strikingly counterintuitive based upon traditional analyses, whether historical or doctrinal. Of course, once a seeming anomaly is properly explained, counterintuition becomes intuition. And so it is here. In this chapter, I will describe the historical and doctrinal evolution of standing. In doing so, I will demonstrate that the social choice theory I offer provides a far more intuitive understanding of why the apparently conservative Burger and Rehnquist Courts elevated and constitutionalized a doctrine conceived in the New Deal to shield emerging federal and state governmental regulation of the economy from attack in the federal courts. In chapter 6, I will then provide a detailed overview of the standing cases themselves.

This chapter will provide a social choice analysis of the following three relevant Supreme Court periods, which are critical in analyzing standing doctrine: the New Deal Court, the Warren Court, and the Burger and Rehnquist Courts. The New Deal Court, relying upon earlier equity cases,[3] developed the standing doctrine to further progressive regulatory objectives associated with the New Deal. The Warren Court then relaxed standing (along with justiciability generally) to invite litigation expanding the reach of the substantive provisions of the Bill of Rights. Finally, the Burger and Rehnquist Courts redeployed and further solidified standing to meet an altogether different set of objectives. Because those Courts were prone to multidimensionality, accompanied by occasional asymmetry, in casting underlying issues within important cases, these later Courts transformed standing to raise barriers to path manipulation by ideological interest groups. In addition to explaining the evolution of standing in these three Supreme Court periods, I will also trace the doctrinal evolution of the injury in fact, causation, and redressability standing elements, which have been extended as well to ripeness and mootness. The analysis will show that these elements, which grew out of a questionable exercise in statutory interpretation, have become constitutional preconditions to justiciability.

Finally, in chapter 6, I will revisit the expanded justiciability spectrum, introduced in chapter 4,[4] which places ripeness and mootness at one end and constitutional criminal procedure at the other. I will demonstrate that the overwhelming majority of standing cases can be graded based upon the ease or difficulty of the susceptibility of underlying claims to path manipulation, which the particular justiciability rules operate to prevent. I will conclude by demonstrating that social choice certainly supplements our understanding of standing doctrine as set out in existing theories, and that in fact the theory advanced here can be credibly embraced as providing a better account for the historical context in which the modern standing doctrine emerged and for the manner in which the doctrine has developed in the actual cases than has been offered in competing theories.

A. Overview: The Three Supreme Court Paradigms

This chapter will show that, while Justice Louis Brandeis and then-professor Felix Frankfurter developed standing to shield progressive regulatory programs, culminating in the New Deal, from attack in the federal courts, the Burger and Rehnquist Courts fundamentally transformed standing from its New Deal roots to serve a substantially different purpose. In contrast with the two major Courts that preceded it, the New Deal Court and the Warren Court, the Burger and Rehnquist Courts were prone to multidimensionality, and occasional asymmetry, with respect to at least an important subset of the most controversial and pressing issues of the day. Each of these three periods on the Supreme Court—the New Deal Court, the Warren Court, and the Burger and Rehnquist Courts—represents a different social choice paradigm, with substantially different implications for constitutional process generally and for justiciability in particular.

The New Deal Court was marked by a judicial retrenchment from a previously identified set of constitutional rights, growing out of the Fifth and Fourteenth Amendment due process clauses. The Hughes Court, which Franklin Delano Roosevelt inherited, employed these constitutional provisions to protect a fundamental right to own property and to contract free of prospective legislative interference. President Franklin Delano Roosevelt succeeded in replacing all of those justices who would employ economic substantive due process, in combination with other constitutional doctrines, to thwart his New Deal initiatives. While this period was marked by a sharp transition from one jurisprudential vision to another, for the most part it was not marked by multidimensionality. Instead, because the emerging liberal majority was readily willing to discard disfavored precedents, the two dominant frameworks that competed in the transitional period from the conservative Hughes Court to increasingly liberal New Deal Court could be evaluated along a unidimensional issue spectrum, with the liberal justices gaining control over time.

In contrast with the New Deal Court, the Warren Court was typified by an expansion, rather than a retrenchment, of constitutional liberties. The Warren Court focused upon vindicating the claimed rights of racial minorities and of the criminally accused, based upon two competing paradigms, the incorporationist approach, championed by Justices Hugo Black and William O. Douglas, and the fundamental rights approach, championed by then-Justice Felix Frankfurter. While the Warren Court was also sharply divided, and perhaps prone to multidimensionality, it was generally not prone to asymmetry. The critical difference between these two liberal Supreme Courts was that in the New Deal, liberalism was generally associated with protecting the regulatory powers of the state, while in the Warren era, liberalism was generally associated with protecting the individual against the regulatory powers of the state. From a social choice perspective, in the Warren era, the relationship between the two critical competing approaches to identifying protected liberties—incorporation and fundamental rights—in any given case was disjunctive, meaning that the theories generally provided alternative bases for the same claim of relief. Thus, even if the justices differed sharply on the underlying rationale, the Court was able meaningfully to predict its outcomes provided that a cross-camp majority of the Court agreed to a given result.

In marked contrast with these two prior judicial periods, the Burger and Rehnquist Courts were typified by no less than three persistent but non-dominant jurisprudential approaches. These Courts were characterized by a partial and incomplete retrenchment from Warren-era liberalism. In contrast with the New Deal Court, which also involved a retrenchment of constitutional rights protected in the immediately preceding era, however, this period gave rise to three frameworks rather than two. In the Burger and Rehnquist Courts, an emerging bloc of centrist justices eschewed the ideologies of the left and right in favor of decisions based upon such neutral principles as stare decisis and justiciability. Therefore, because these Courts possessed one group of justices that favored liberal Warren-era precedents on their merits; a second group that favored an affirmative retrenchment of liberal precedents, even if it required overruling; and a third group that favored decisions based upon neutral principals, the conditions were ripe for both multidimensionality and asymmetry, and thus for path manipulation. In the New Deal rights retrenchment, the growing majority of liberal justices had little concern for precedent, and thus, predictability turned on a straightforward numbers game. In a Court that can generally be graded on a traditional liberal-to-conservative scale, absent defections, the dominant side wins. In the Warren era, in contrast, while the Court was faced with two competing approaches in a period of rights expansion, in any given case, the relationship between the issues was disjunctive. A claimant would succeed provided that a majority agreed that the claimed right was *either* incorporated *or* was fundamental. In contrast, in the Burger and Rehnquist era, retrenching upon a Warren-era ruling required a majority to agree to what was essentially a conjunctive set of legal claims, namely that the claimed right in question was *both* erroneous on its merits *and* that the precedent establishing the right should not be respected as a matter of stare decisis. It is the presence of this third, neutral, stare decisis–based framework, during an era of rights contraction, that set the stage for multidimensionality and asymmetry, and for the transformation of standing from its New Deal roots into its present form.*

In effect, the analysis reveals that certain periods of rights retrenchments may be subject to what we can think of as a judicial ratchet effect.[5] A ratchet effect signifies a tendency of certain phenomena to move more steadily in a single direction and to be subject to fits and starts in the opposite direction. In this context, it is more difficult for a conservative Supreme Court to retrench upon recently vindicated rights than it is for a liberal Supreme Court operating against a neutral backdrop that neither embraced nor rejected the claimed rights in the past, to add new ones. That is because in the absence of an adverse precedent during a period of rights expansions, alternative jurisprudential theories suffice, independently or in combination, to afford relief. In contrast, to retrench upon a judicially recognized right, a majority must agree both that the original decision was wrong and that, whether or not it was wrong, the precedent should not be respected as a matter of stare decisis. Thus, under these conditions, while individual justices need only embrace a single theory to vindicate a claimed right, later judges must simultaneously embrace no fewer than two theories to abandon a right that has already been established. The analysis that follows will show that, in contrast with the liberal New Deal and Warren Courts, the Burger and Rehnquist Courts were subject to this judicial ratchet effect precisely because they were prone to multidimensionality and occasional asymmetry in an important subset of cases.

In the remainder of this chapter, I will provide a more detailed analysis of each of these judicial periods and their relationship to the emergence and transformation of the modern standing doctrine.

II.   The New Deal Court

The first period begins, of course, with President Franklin Delano Roosevelt's initial frustration with the Supreme Court that he inherited from the conservative Hoover administration. This frustration ultimately led to FDR's famous, albeit unsuccessful, Court-packing plan. The plan to add one justice for every justice over the age of seventy who did not retire was intended to

---

*The analysis in the text is not to suggest that the same multidimensionality and asymmetry could not arise in the context of a rights expansion. This could occur if the relevant background rules included a clear precedent denying the existence of the claimed right and if one group of justices favored retaining that result on the merits, a second group favored reversing the precedent to vindicate the claimed right, and a third group favored applying neutral principles like stare decisis or justiciability to resolve the case. The analysis in the text simply recognizes that the creation of multidimensionality and occasional asymmetry in the Burger and Rehnquist Courts was more generally typified by rights contractions than by rights expansions.

limit the influence of the four conservatives, sometimes referred as the "Four Horsemen," who predictably voted to thwart FDR's New Deal efforts: Justices James C. McReynolds, Pierce Butler, Willis Van Devanter, and George Sutherland. In addition, a fifth justice, Owen Roberts, produced significant anxiety in the administration when he sided with the Four Horsemen in several major early cases challenging New Deal initiatives.[6] The most famous single instance of the collective efforts of these justices to thwart the New Deal programs occurred on May 27, 1935, which became known as "Black Monday." On that date, the Court struck down the National Industrial Recovery Act and the mortgage moratoria in the Frazier-Lemke Act in *Louisville Joint Stock Land Bank v. Radford*.[7] The Court also issued *Humphrey's Executor v. United States*,[8] which prevented FDR from removing a commissioner on the independent Federal Trade Commission.

Had FDR succeeded, the Court packing would have allowed him to appoint an additional six justices, thus transforming a generally conservative five-to-four majority to a liberal ten-to-five majority. Justice Roberts's defection in the 1937 case *West Coast Hotel v. Parrish*,[9] referred to as the "switch in time that saved nine," turned the tide for FDR on the Supreme Court and rendered his originally devised Court-packing plan unnecessary to the survival of New Deal initiatives. As many contemporaneous commentators have observed, the Washington minimum wage statute, which the Court sustained in *Parrish,* appeared indistinguishable from the New York minimum wage statute, which the Four Horsemen plus Roberts had stuck down just one year earlier in *Morehead v. New York ex rel. Tipaldo*.[10] More important than marking the effective reversal of *Tipaldo,* however, was that *Parrish* effectively marked the end of the long-dominant era of substantive due process, associated with *Lochner v. New York*.[11] In voting to sustain the Washington statute, Roberts signaled bare majority support, with no need to pack the Court, for future New Deal programs against challenges based upon economic substantive due process. While historians have speculated on the justifications for the famous vote switch, for our purposes the rationale is less important than the fact that it was widely perceived as averting the need for the Court-packing plan.

Even without approval of the formal Court-packing plan, with the sole exception of Justice Roberts himself, FDR ultimately replaced every member of the Court during his long administration.[12] Shortly following the famous vote switch, which provided Roosevelt a bare five-to-four majority in cases involving challenges to his New Deal initiatives, one of the four conservatives, William Van Devanter resigned. Replacing him would allow Roosevelt to increase his comfort margin on the Supreme Court from a bare five-to-four majority to a supermajority of six-to-three. Although the next appointment had initially been promised to the loyal but conservative southern Democratic Senate majority leader, Joseph T. Robinson,[13] Senator Robinson died shortly after the Court vacancy became public. Instead, Roosevelt appointed Hugo Black, a liberal who was personally close to Robinson and who would go on to champion a restrictive interpretation of the Constitution based upon strict textualism.[14] The following year, Roosevelt appointed Stanley Reed to replace George Sutherland, leaving Justices Butler and Reynolds as the sole conservatives, until Roosevelt replaced them with Justices Frank Murphy and Frank F. Burns, in 1940 and 1941, respectively.

From a social choice perspective, the emerging Roosevelt Court was noteworthy in two critical respects. First, while they did not always agree on the underlying rationale, the FDR appointees were uniformly disinclined to continue the once dominant insistence upon a constitutionally imposed laissez-faire regime, under the guise of economic substantive due process. Second, the newly appointed justices generally shared a minimal ideological commitment to respecting precedents that were adverse to FDR's regulatory programs.[15] For that reason, the Court in this period was typified by two general approaches to the most pressing jurisprudential issues of the day, the conservative approach of the Hughes era and the emerging liberal approach, which ultimately came to characterize the New Deal Court. Which of those two approaches prevailed in any given case turned on which camp was larger.

Not only did the New Deal Court abandon *Lochner*-era conservativism, thus allowing New Deal programs to survive economic substantive due process challenges, but also, beginning in the landmark year 1937, the Court marked two other major doctrinal shifts. First, the Court began to clear the way for the creation of what is now commonly referred to as the "fourth branch."[16] While the Supreme Court upheld some fairly simple delegations as early as 1813,[17] in the 1928 decision *J.W. Hampton, Jr. & Co. v. United States*,[18] the Court stated that it would only sustain delegations in which Congress articulated an "intelligible principle," which the federal courts could employ to ensure against the unlawful transfer of lawmaking powers. From 1935 to 1936, the Supreme Court issued three decisions, each striking down a federal statute on nondelegation grounds.[19] In 1939, the Court began to reverse course and by the early to middle 1940s it consistently sustained substantial delegations of lawmaking power.[20] By ultimately abandoning the intelligible principle test, the Court allowed Congress to undertake a major expansion of regulatory agencies. The regulatory agencies created in the New Deal were relatively modest in both scope of authority and size by more modern standards, but their creation and approval during the New Deal Court proved critical for later regulatory expansions, including most notably the Great Society program during the 1960s.[21] During the latter period, with the occasional—and exceptional—use of the now moribund nondelegation doctrine to limit the substantive scope of federal regulatory statutes as a means of avoiding constitutional challenges,[22] Congress's authority to confer substantial regulatory authority upon independent agencies was largely assumed, based upon New Deal precedents. Today, the once limiting nondelegation doctrine poses virtually no barrier to delegating broad-based regulatory authority to agencies.

Second, beginning in 1937, the Court began to reverse the once restrictive application of the Tenth Amendment to limit congressional commerce clause powers. The combined effect of these jurisprudential shifts—restricting substantive due process, abandoning the nondelegation doctrine, and broadening congressional commerce clause powers—was to remove each of the then-perceived doctrinal barriers to the efforts of Congress, through prospective regulation, to pump the economy out of the Great Depression. Tracking the change in commerce clause jurisprudence is particularly helpful in distinguishing the New Deal Court from its successors from a social choice perspective.

A.   Expansion of Commerce Clause Powers

For the first 150 or so years following the Constitution's adoption, the Supreme Court interpreted the commerce clause narrowly and the Tenth Amendment broadly. As explained in chapter 2, in the discussion of *New York v. United States*,[23] the commerce clause is stated in the form of a regulatory grant of power to Congress. The Tenth Amendment states, "The powers not delegated to the United States by the Constitution, nor prohibited by it to the States, are reserved to the States respectively, or to the people."[24] As Congress expanded the use of its commerce powers, the relationship between these two constitutional provisions became increasingly apparent. If the commerce clause were construed as an unlimited grant of power, then the Tenth Amendment is hortatory at best. But if the commerce clause is construed as a genuinely restrictive grant, then its contours might be defined, at least in part, by the powers traditionally understood to be exercised solely by the states. As a result, the Court's commerce clause and Tenth Amendment jurisprudence largely evolved in lockstep fashion over the course of challenges to allegedly excessive congressional commerce clause powers.

Beginning with the landmark 1824 decision *Gibbons v. Ogden*,[25] Chief Justice Marshall established that while Congress's power is "plenary," meaning complete within its sphere of authority, the commerce clause itself represents a specific delegation of power, rather than a universal grant.[26] Following *Gibbons*, the Supreme Court developed a series of formalist distinctions governing whether a given activity was part of commerce, and thus within Congress's regulatory powers, or was outside of commerce, and thus presumed to be within the exclusive regulatory powers of the states. Of these distinctions, the most important involved manufacturing, which was generally understood to precede commerce. Thus, in the 1895 decision *United States v. E. C. Knight Co.*,[27] the Supreme Court invalidated the application of the Sherman Act to the American Sugar Refining Company's acquisition of four sugar refineries. The *E. C. Knight* Court held that because manufacture precedes commerce, Congress lacked the power to prohibit the acquisitions. In the 1918 decision *Hammer v. Dagenhart*,[28] a case that proved to be a major obstacle to New Deal initiatives, the Supreme Court relied upon the *E. C. Knight* distinction between manufacture and commerce to hold that Congress lacked the authority to prohibit the interstate transportation of goods produced by child labor that exceeded certain minimum age and maximum hour requirements. The *E. C. Knight* Court held that, through the Child Labor Act,

Congress had effectively attempted to regulate the processes of production. Finally, in one of the leading 1936 decisions that animated FDR's Court-packing plan, *Carter v. Carter Coal Co.,*[29] the Court struck down the collective bargaining provisions of the Bituminous Coal Conservation Act of 1935. In doing so, the Court rejected a statement in the statutory preamble that was intended to avoid such precedents as *E. C. Knight* and *Hammer.* The preamble stated that "just and rational relations" between labor and management "directly affect[ed] interstate commerce." After observing that the preamble reflected a desperate attempt to regulate activities outside the purview of the commerce clause, the Court went on to state that an indirect effect on interstate commerce "does not become direct by multiplying the tonnage."

From 1936, when the Court decided *Carter,* to 1942, when it decided *Wickard v. Filburn,*[30] the Court produced what might well be characterized as a complete doctrinal cycle. And yet, it would be misleading to attribute this cycle to the factors giving rise to path manipulation in the later Burger and Rehnquist Courts. In contrast with the Burger and Rehnquist, which, because they were prone to multipeakedness and occasional asymmetry in an important subset of cases, could not uniformly predict their own outcomes, the New Deal Court's transition of commerce clause and Tenth Amendment jurisprudence was very much the subject of its own careful control. The wholesale replacement of personnel in the New Deal Court effectively invited litigants to expand the relevant issue space in an effort to avoid immediate overruling. As a result, the Court was a partner to any consequent path manipulation. Two events combine to reveal the resulting doctrinal cycle in the Supreme Court's commerce clause cases. First, in *United States v. Darby,*[31] the Court overruled *Hammer.* Second, in *Wickard,*[32] the Court employed the very multiplier analysis rejected in *Carter Coal Co.,* but this time to achieve the opposite result of sustaining an exercise of congressional commerce clause powers. When a Court employs the very same analysis to reach precisely opposite outcomes within a relatively short time frame, a strong possibility exists that the underlying issue spectrum has been expanded from one to two dimensions, with the effect of producing a doctrinal cycle.

The Court's process of eroding the once restrictive commerce clause jurisprudence began with the seemingly exceptional case of *NLRB v. Jones & Laughlin Steel Corp.*[33] In *Jones & Laughlin,* the Court upheld the collective bargaining provisions of National Labor Relations Act against a Tenth Amendment challenge. In his opinion for the Court, Chief Justice Hughes observed that Jones and Laughlin Steel Corporation, the fourth largest producer of steel in the United States, was so large that its impact upon commerce was virtually unparalleled.[34] But, over time, the Court made clear that such extraordinary facts were not a prerequisite to the exercise of congressional commerce clause power. In *United States v. Darby,*[35] which overruled *Hammer,* the Court sustained a minimum wage and maximum overtime law against a Tenth Amendment challenge, stating that the Tenth Amendment states "but a truism that all is retained which has not been surrendered."

Finally, as stated above, the *Wickard* Court adopted precisely the same argument to sustain a federal statute on commerce clause grounds against a Tenth Amendment challenge, which the *Carter* Court had expressly rejected. In upholding the Agricultural Adjustment Act's wheat production quotas against Filburn, an Ohio diary farmer, who raised small amounts of wheat for his own livestock, for making flour at home, and for seeds, with leftovers for sale, the *Wickard* Court observed:

> That appellee's own contribution to the demand for wheat may be trivial by itself is not enough to remove him from the scope of federal regulation where, as here, his contribution, taken together with that of many others similarly situated, is far from trivial.[36]

In effect, the New Deal Court through a series of three principal cases expanded the relevant issue space from a formalist inquiry concerning whether the regulated activity was within or without commerce, to a more subtle economic inquiry into whether the activity was of sufficiently large scope as to have a substantial impact upon commerce. But once the Court used this expanded issue space to gut the previously dominant formalist distinction between manufacture and commerce, the stage was set for its complete abandonment in *Wickard,* regardless of the scope of the underlying economic activity. Thus, not only did *Wickard* allow the regulation of manufacture, but also it did so in an unprecedented context, this time because the scale was virtually minuscule. As stated above, the transformation from the formalist doctrinal cases, represented by *E. C. Knight* and *Hammer,* to the modernist cases, represented by *Jones & Laughlin, Darby,* and *Wickard,* can be translated into a successful effort on the part of litigants facing a receptive Court to reverse a previously set doctrinal course by expanding the dimensionality of underlying case issues. By expanding the issue spectrum from one to two dimensions, the Court was able to rid itself of one disfavored precedent, *Hammer,* and to distinguish others without the immediate need to overrule. At the same time, the Court substantially broadened congressional commerce clause powers, consistent with the progressive objectives of the New Deal.

B.   The Ideological Divergence between the Supreme Court (and State Courts) and the Lower Federal Courts

Not only did the New Deal Court substantially change the landscape of individual rights by cutting back upon economic substantive due process, and of separation of powers by relaxing the once-restrictive commerce clause jurisprudence and nondelegation doctrine, but also it developed, for the first time, a formal set of barriers to justiciability in the form of standing. To be sure, through a long-standing tradition, the Supreme Court, then as recently as 1923,[37] had imposed limits on the ability of litigants to invoke the equitable powers of the federal courts. But until the New Deal, the Court had not formally developed these jurisdictional limiting principles from equity into a general set of preconditions for litigating all federal court claims.[38] With the help of his protégé, then-professor Felix Frankfurter, Justice Louis Brandeis, an early New Deal proponent, transformed these limited equitable precedents into an emerging standing doctrine, which the Court then used to shield progressive regulatory initiatives from attack in the federal courts.[39] While Brandeis and Frankfurter conceived standing at a time when the Supreme Court itself was generally hostile to a progressive regulatory agenda, the doctrine proved equally valuable after FDR forged a liberal majority on the Supreme Court. In contrast with its modern counterparts, the New Deal Court employed standing to discipline lower federal courts, which did not share its liberal ideological agenda. While President Roosevelt ultimately succeeded in forging a Court that shared his constitutional and political vision, he did not have the same success in the lower federal courts. Those courts, having been packed in the three preceding Republican administrations, were sympathetic to the formalist constitutionalism that typified the earlier Hughes Court, and were therefore generally hostile to FDR's regulatory agenda.[40]

In its earliest incarnation, standing served a very different purpose from that which it later served in the modern Burger and Rehnquist Courts. In the New Deal, standing was a low-cost mechanism that enabled the emerging liberal Supreme Court to stave off unwelcome challenges to progressive regulatory programs. Standing allowed the Court to achieve this objective without having to incur the political costs—or embarrassment—associated with determinations on the merits of underlying claims, which differed widely from the recent era typified by Lochnerian substantive due process and a restrictive understanding of both congressional commerce clause powers and permissible delegation. Absent standing, an ambitious, or contrarian, circuit could have effectively forced the Supreme Court to address the merits of those cases, highlighting the Supreme Courts' several doctrinal turnabouts, by striking down particular New Deal programs based upon dubious case distinctions. The resulting circuit splits would not have afforded the Supreme Court the luxury of using a shorthand vehicle to leave favored programs in place. But, through standing, the Supreme Court could impose a greater degree of doctrinal uniformity throughout the circuits, by preventing recalcitrant lower courts from creating distasteful bait.*

---

*The above analysis not only explains the development of standing, but also explains the development of the closely related *Erie* doctrine. It is no coincidence that the architects of the standing doctrine, Justices Brandeis and Frankfurter, were also the architects of the famous decision Erie R.R. v. Tompkins, 304 U.S. 64 (1938), which Brandeis authored. In *Erie,* the Supreme Court ended the long-standing practice in which federal courts sitting in diversity jurisdiction would promulgate their own common law, often operating in competition with the common law of the states in which those courts sat. Beginning with the Judiciary Act of 1789, federal courts sitting in diversity jurisdiction had been required to apply that jurisdiction's substantive law in resolving cases. In the 1842 decision, Swift v. Tyson, 41 U.S. (16 Pet.) 1 (1842), the Supreme Court

C. The New Deal Standing Doctrine

Before describing the transformation of standing in the Warren Court, it will be helpful to consider the doctrinal framework for standing developed in the New Deal Court. Scholars have divided the earliest standing cases, which began during the New Deal, into three conceptual paradigms:[41] first, some federal statutes expressly denied standing to affected claimants;[42] second, some statutes expressly conferred standing upon affected claimants;[43] and, third, some statutes failed to address the question of standing altogether.[44] In the first two categories, where Congress specifically addressed the question of standing, the Supreme Court almost invariably deferred to Congress's express will. Faced with congressional silence, on the other hand, the Court devised an amalgam of standing presumptions drawn from the common law of property, contract, or tort. In this historical period, standing emerged as a largely prudential doctrine, meaning that even when the Court drew upon

---

held that state judicial decisions did not count as state law under the Judiciary Act. In reversing *Swift,* the *Erie* Court effectively nullified a complete set of parallel federal common laws operating for nearly a century in diversity cases.

Brandeis was motivated to end the parallel track of federal common law because during the New Deal, not only were the lower federal courts more conservative than the Supreme Court, but also they tended to be more conservative than the parallel state courts. This is not surprising given that in many states, judges are popularly elected, while federal judges are appointed for life. Thus, while the lower federal court judges were appointed by three prior conservative Republican administrations in an era of economic growth, the state judges were often elected during the depression itself. By relying upon conservative principles typical of the *Lochner* era, the lower federal courts were able to use such diversity cases to limit the reach of progressive state initiatives, which, like their federal counterparts, were thought to intrude upon the rights to own property and to contract free of prospective governmental interference. As one commentator has explained:

> The federal courts' domination by conservative judges and Justices who opposed much of the progressive legislation that Frankfurter and other liberal intellectuals and politicians supported . . . helps explain Frankfurter's antidiversity position. Through diversity jurisdiction, cases that would otherwise have been in the state courts found their way into the federal courts, where they were heard by the type of judge whom Frankfurter and his progressive colleagues opposed.

William A. Braverman, Note, *Janus Was Not a God of Justice: Realignment of Parties in Diversity Jurisdiction,* 68 N.Y.U. L. Rev. 1072, 1096 (1993) (citations omitted); *see also id.* at 1099 (collecting authorities on joint efforts of Brandeis and Frankfurter to curtail the lower federal courts of authority to produce a parallel track of conservative common law). Like standing, *Erie* proved an essential tool in disciplining the conservative lower federal courts. While standing prevented the lower federal courts from interfering with progressive federal programs, *Erie* prevented the same courts from interfering with progressive state law programs.

common law notions to deny standing, Congress was free to reverse the presumption to favor justiciability by statute. This is not surprising, given that standing was largely intended to shield New Deal programs from attack in the lower federal courts.

For the New Deal Court, the concept of legal injury was central to this early approach to standing. A plaintiff relying upon a federal statute that was silent on the question of standing would be afforded standing if she alleged an injury cognizable at common law. While the legal injury doctrine did not prevent Congress from creating novel claims, it had the practical consequence of allowing the federal judiciary, including most notably the Supreme Court, to protect Congress in its creation of New Deal programs at lower political cost than if those courts reached the merits of every constitutional challenge to a federal regulatory expansion. It also had three significant benefits associated with judicial administrability. First, it had the effect of reducing the number of such actions, thus conserving judicial resources. Second, by creating presumptive rules to govern the determination of injury, grounded in common law principles with which the lower federal courts were intimately familiar, it enabled the Supreme Court to promote a relatively consistent application of standing in lower federal courts. And, finally, it helped to prevent recalcitrant lower federal courts from addressing the merits of challenges to administrative agency regulations, thereby decreasing the potential for circuit splits on important questions of federal law.

The nearly simultaneous retreat from Lochnerian substantive due process and the erection of a judicial-standing barrier in this historical period is no coincidence; indeed, the two doctrinal developments are inextricably linked. The linkage of standing to a cognizable legal injury, grounded in the common law or a relevant statute, would not have protected New Deal programs from attack in a regime that recognized a fundamental right to contract and to own property free of prospective governmental regulation. Curiously, however, the linkage worked in both directions: In a regime that rejected *Lochner* and that allowed substantial governmental intrusion into private orderings, a justiciability doctrine designed to stave off unwelcome challenges to governmental regulation would appear unnecessary, or at best, redundant. After all, without *Lochner*, the very challenges that standing was intended to prevent would have been denied on the merits. Because the New Deal justices shared substantially common preferences, at least in their willingness to condone regulations that the *Lochner* Court held off limits, they could predict with considerable certainty the outcome of challenges to many regulatory programs. The outcome would be to uphold many, or most, of the regulations that the newly created standing doctrine protected from attack.

In that respect, and as demonstrated more fully below, New Deal standing differs from modern standing. Litigant path manipulation arises primarily in courts whose members share multidimensional and asymmetrical preferences. This requires no fewer than three jurisprudential frameworks, none of which has majority support. Because President Roosevelt succeeded, by threat of political force, in forging a Court willing to remove the then-perceived constitutional barriers to his New Deal policies, the New Deal Court's preferences were closely aligned on the most important doctrinal issue of the day, namely whether his regulatory policies would withstand constitutional attack.

The early and flexible approach to standing is noteworthy in two additional respects. First, inherent in the approach is a nearly complete deference to Congress, both in its power to regulate the economy and in its power to confer upon public and private parties the power to litigate in federal court. The degree of partnership, or kinship, between the New Deal Congress and the New Deal Court, while echoed, albeit somewhat more faintly, in the Warren Court era,[45] was largely lacking during much of the Burger and Rehnquist Court eras, when the modern standing doctrine took its present form. Second, by employing common law analogies, the Court merely created a set of legal presumptions. Presumptions, of course, are simply vehicles to be deployed in the face of congressional silence and to be abandoned in the event of congressional redirection. In that sense, the newly erected standing barrier was neither unique nor unusual. In the face of legislative silence or statutory ambiguity, federal courts routinely resolve cases by filling gaps, often based upon common law principles.[46] Those presumptions, however, are generally abandoned when Congress enacts a statute expressing a contrary command. And while common law presumptions, when applied in an era typified by novel legislative intrusions into the marketplace, might prevent many meritorious legal challenges, that is not necessarily an undesirable result. After all, courts, unlike legislatures, generally lack the power of institutional inertia. To the extent that the members of the New Deal Court shared preferences that differed from those of the population at large, lower federal courts, or members of Congress, standing further prevented the Court from becoming drawn into a lawmaking function, with the effect of thwarting contrary majority preferences.

III.   The Warren Court

In creating a Court more favorably disposed to governmental regulation, President Roosevelt himself ultimately created a second rift in the Supreme Court that replaced the former rifts over economic substantive due process, the non-delegation doctrine, and the commerce clause. Having packed the Court sufficiently to ensure that New Deal regulatory programs would withstand a variety of constitutional challenges, which were limited in number by the new standing doctrine, President Roosevelt forged a Court that was sharply divided on the jurisprudential framework for interpreting the Fourteenth Amendment due process clause.[47] The resulting rift was not settled until well into the Warren Court. From the New Deal to the Warren era, the Supreme Court agreed that the due process clause did not protect economic liberties, but was divided on how to identify protected liberties and on the rationale for the jurisprudential change. One camp, led by Justices Hugo Black and William O.

Douglas, employed strict textualism to limit the scope of protected constitutional rights. Through the incorporation doctrine, Black and Douglas sought to provide a textually limited means of ending Lochnerian jurisprudence (given that the rights to contract and to own property free of prospective governmental interference are nowhere expressly mentioned) and of limiting the power of states to continue practices perceived to be unfair to powerless groups. Another camp, led by Justice Felix Frankfurter, employed a fundamental rights framework to achieve a similar objective concerning *Lochner,* given that the rights to contract and to own property free of prospective governmental interference were no longer considered fundamental. While Frankfurter believed that the history of the Bill of Rights did not evince an intent to apply its substantive provisions against the states, he also believed that certain rights—some included in the Bill of Rights, others not—were sufficiently fundamental that the due process clause of the Fourteenth Amendment applied them to the states. Because a majority of the Court agreed that economic liberties were no longer protected, and that prospective economic regulation was therefore permissible, the different bases on that question were initially of little concern. More importantly for our purposes, the resulting doctrinal rift was different in social choice terms than that which emerged in the New Deal. While the New Deal Court consisted of two camps, one favoring a progressive regulatory state and the other opposing it, the later Warren Court consisted of two camps that, although disagreeing on a dominant underlying rationale, often agreed to the results in particular cases.

Historically, the relative size of these two jurisprudential camps on the Warren Court changed, such that the number of justices espousing Justice Frankfurter's fundamental rights view decreased and the number of justices espousing the incorporationist view espoused by Justices Black and Douglas increased. Because either of the two dominant jurisprudential approaches, incorporation or fundamental rights, sufficed to vindicate many claimed constitutional rights against disfavored state practices, the Court was able to produce stable results, even if it was not able to ensure that a majority would embrace a single rationale. But because the Court began systematically to protect rights included in the Bill of Rights against state laws, even if the underlying rationales differed over time, those embracing the incorporationist view were able to develop an independent justification for continuing to do so. Thus, by 1968, in *Duncan v. Louisiana,*[48] Justice White reasoned that the Bill of Rights had increasingly edified the Court's understanding of which rights were fundamental to *our* system, as distinguished from which rights might be fundamental at some abstract level. Thus, Justice White observed that by the time of *Duncan,* the critical question in fundamental rights jurisprudence had become "whether . . . a procedure is necessary to an Anglo-American regime of ordered liberty." And, of course, in answering that question, the Bill of Rights was uniquely informative. As a result, as the Court continued to shift toward the incorporationist camp, the ability to link outcomes to a predictable and dominant rationale substantially increased.

The circumstances leading to the expansion of noneconomic liberties in the Warren Court differed significantly from those that produced the contraction of economic liberties in the New Deal Court. Whereas President Roosevelt had succeeded in creating a strongly liberal Court, following his threatened Court-packing proposal, ultimately replacing all but one justice, Owen Roberts, during his presidency, the circumstances giving rise to the Warren Court era were more fortuitous. President Eisenhower appointed Earl Warren as chief justice as part of a political payback for support that helped to land Eisenhower the Republican nomination and, ultimately, the presidency.[49] In addition, he appointed Associate Justice William Brennan, with the hope that together Warren and Brennan would help restore the liberal Supreme Court to a less prominent role associated with an earlier era. Eisenhower ultimately lamented both choices, labeling the appointment of Earl Warren one of the biggest mistakes of his presidency, and further expressing regret over the appointment of William Brennan.[50]

In contrast with the New Deal Court, the Warren Court tended to invite, rather than to resist, cases testing the outermost limits of federal judicial power. The transition from New Deal liberalism to Warren Court liberalism is striking because the changing liberal political agenda required a nearly opposite set of federal judicial strategies to succeed. The success of New Deal liberalism required a tremendous expansion of both federal and state regulatory powers, and a corresponding retrenchment of conservative federal judicial power. This was achieved in large part through the creation of the standing doctrine. In contrast, the success of Warren-era liberalism, which involved expanding the rights of racial minorities and of the criminally accused, required a tremendous expansion of federal judicial power, most often at the expense of states, and sometimes also at the expense of Congress. Not surprisingly, perhaps, this involved a general relaxation of standing and of justiciability generally.

Much of the Warren Court's success in furthering policy objectives related to the rights of the criminally accused, the desegregation of public schools, and, with the help of Congress, racial equality in places of public accommodation, has been attributed to Chief Justice Earl Warren's charisma and political acumen. Through political acumen, perhaps more than through intellectual force, Earl Warren transformed the role of chief justice, at least for a time, from that of coequal jurist and administrator to that of majority whip.[51] At the same time, Associate Justice William Brennan provided strong intellectual leadership on the left that lasted well into the Rehnquist Court. While the Warren Court was often viewed as political, that perception was due in part to the leadership's ability to bring even those who doubted the propriety of a more activist Supreme Court into the fold in major cases. Defections within the Court generally signaled disagreements in particular cases, rather than on the propriety of a more activist judicial role.

The Warren Court fundamentally redefined—at least for a period—the role of the federal judiciary within our constitutional scheme. It did so by eschewing traditional limiting principles of originalism and textualism in favor of an overriding sense of fundamental fairness. I do not mean fairness in the social choice sense, but rather, in the sense that the Warren Court understood that term. To the Warren Court, fairness required using the federal courts to advance the interests of politically and economically disadvantaged groups. The Warren Court further promoted the notion that the judiciary—and especially the Supreme Court—was the institution of last resort for those whose most ardent claims were resisted in both state and federal political processes.

It is not necessary to detail the history of the Warren Court, which has been amply documented elsewhere.[52] We need only observe that the most controversial decisions issued by the Warren Court were far more controversial outside than inside the Supreme Court chambers. While the landmark opinions *Mapp v. Ohio,*[53] requiring that states exclude illegally seized evidence, and *Miranda v. Arizona,*[54] requiring police to provide a specified set of warnings upon arrest, were decided by narrow majorities, other controversial cases were issued with supermajority or unanimous support. These cases included *Brown v. Board of Education,*[55] which ended the lawful segregation of public schools; *Cooper v. Aaron,*[56] which forced the recalcitrant governor of Arkansas, not party to *Brown,* to abide the Supreme Court's mandate in that case; and *Gideon v. Wainwright,*[57] which established a constitutional right to the assistance of state-provided counsel. While the Warren Court obviously did not share the preferences of the citizenry whose popular will it often thwarted, its members shared a sufficiently common, and perhaps more enlightened, vision that enabled it to predict with considerable certainty both how critical case issues would be defined and resolved.

During Earl Warren's tenure as chief justice from 1953 to 1969, the Court fundamentally altered the nature of constitutional interpretation in several separate but complementary ways. First, the Court greatly expanded constitutional criminal rights by reading broad protections into the Bill of Rights on behalf of state and federal criminal defendants.[58] Second, the Court created, seemingly from whole cloth, other fundamental rights in the individual against the state, including, for example, the right to vote in state elections and the right to have one's vote weighted equally with others.[59] In doing so, the Court intruded upon what had been, for our entire history, an exclusive state legislative function. Third, the Court afforded Congress broad regulatory power to prohibit racial discrimination in places of public accommodation,[60] in a manner that had foreboding implications for the once-restrictive state action doctrine.[61] Finally, and perhaps most notably, the Warren Court handed down *Brown v. Board of Education.*[62] In that one decision, the Court not only reversed nearly a century of postemancipation race-based segregation in the South, but also, in a single stroke of the pen, forever pitted the notion of judicial restraint, founded upon originalism and textualism, against the most fundamental notions of justice and morality.

Moreover, some of the major rights expansions that occurred in the Burger Court owe their foundations to the earlier Warren Court. Thus, for example, while the Burger Court issued *Roe v. Wade,*[63] establishing a right to abort, Justice Douglas's opinion in *Griswold v. Connecticut,*[64] establishing the right of married couples to purchase contraceptives, issued during the Warren Court, provided *Roe* with the necessary (if analytically suspect) foundation. It did so by distinguishing the fundamental right of privacy from the discredited doctrine of substantive due process.

A.   Standing in the Warren Court

While the Warren Court maintained the New Deal Court's general doctrinal approach to standing, that Court relaxed standing at the margins in an effort to invite novel constitutional challenges.[65] This was most apparent in the 1968 decision *Flast v. Cohen,*[66] which limited the reach of a 1923 decision, *Frothingham v. Mellon,*[67] concerning the limits on federal court equity jurisdiction. *Frothingham* was not understood to be a case about standing, and standing was not understood to be rooted in Article III, until later.[68] In *Frothingham,* the Supreme Court prevented a plaintiff from invoking federal equitable jurisdiction to enjoin the enforcement of the Maternity Act of 1921, which he alleged violated the takings clause of the Fifth Amendment by spending his tax dollars contrary to the Constitution. Without reaching the merits of the constitutional challenge, a majority of the Court held that because plaintiff's alleged injury was shared by all taxpayers, it was de minimis and thus insufficient to invoke federal equitable powers. In *Flast,* a majority of the Court narrowly distinguished *Frothingham,* granting standing to a taxpayer who challenged the constitutionality of providing federal tax revenues to a religious organization under the establishment clause. The *Flast* Court thus carved out an exception to *Frothingham,* holding that a challenge to the expenditure of tax revenues under the establishment clause establishes a sufficient nexus between the taxpayer's constitutional claim and the government's spending action to create standing.

Not surprisingly, by 1982, the Burger Court restored standing by limiting the reach of *Flast.* In *Valley Forge Christian College v. Americans United for Separation of Church and State,*[69] a sharply divided Court relied upon *Frothingham* and distinguished *Flast,* denying standing to a taxpayer who alleged that the federal government had unconstitutionally donated surplus land to a sectarian college.[70] Notwithstanding the economic equivalence of the two governmental actions, and over the dissent of four justices, the Court held that the *Flast* nexus exception to the general *Frothingham* prohibition against allowing taxpayers to challenge federal statutes in court did not apply to land grants pursuant to Congress's property clause powers.

In fact, the relaxation of justiciability in the Warren Court was more general. Thus, in the famous 1962 decision *Baker v. Carr,*[71] the Supreme Court relaxed the once-restrictive political question doctrine to allow a challenge to a state's apportionment system under the equal protection clause. Until *Baker,* state apportionment challenges had invariably been presented under Article IV section 4 of the Constitution,[72] which provides: "The United States shall guarantee to every State in this Union a Republican Form of Government." Throughout the twentieth century, the Supreme Court has construed all claims arising under the guarantee clause as presenting nonjusticiable political questions, based upon the 1849 decision *Luther v. Borden*.[73] In fact, as has been recently demonstrated, the holding in *Luther* was actually quite limited and did not prevent the Supreme Court in the latter half of the nineteenth century from adjudicating guarantee clause claims.[74] Nonetheless, *Baker* came on the heels of a long history of cases that construed *Luther* to require the dismissal of such claims.[75] In *Baker*, the Court allowed plaintiffs to recast their challenge to the state's apportionment scheme from one arising under the guarantee clause to one arising, instead, under the equal protection clause. Writing for the *Baker* Court, Justice Brennan went on to reject the state's political question defense, holding that, in contrast with challenges under the guarantee clause, the Court had developed a set of judicially manageable standards with which to resolve equal protection challenges. The *Baker* Court thus converted what had long been a nonjusticiable political question into an equal protection claim, justiciable in federal court. Like *Flast*, *Baker* represented the Warren Court's willingness to broaden justiciability to invite novel challenges to a variety of disfavored state practices, which had been previously thought to involve diffuse harms.

IV.   The Burger and Rehnquist Courts

A.   Three Nondominant Frameworks

While the New Deal and Warren Courts were characterized by a shift from one dominant jurisprudential framework to another, the Burger and Rehnquist Courts were instead typified by the breakdown of liberal dominance, with no single jurisprudential framework to replace it. As explained above, this was due in large part to the differing natures of rights expansions versus rights retrenchments during these periods. In the absence of a precedent rejecting or creating the claimed right, either of two (or more) alternative bases will generally suffice to create a new right, provided a cross-coalition majority agrees to the outcome. The same does not hold true, however, of efforts to cut back upon previously expanded rights. Instead, cases seeking to retrench upon a recent expansion of rights generally present conjunctive, rather than disjunctive, issues. To reverse a case vindicating a claimed constitutional right, a majority must agree to both of two propositions, first, that the precedent in question should not be honored as a matter of stare decisis, and, second, that the precedent was wrong on the merits. The failure of a majority to agree to both of these propositions is sufficient to prevent the retrenchment of a previously identified constitutional right.

Over a significant subset of cases, the Burger and Rehnquist Courts presented a paradigmatic case of multidimensionality, sometimes coupled with asymmetry, in which retrenchment was inevitably partial and incomplete. In contrast with the New Deal Court, which also witnessed a period of rights retrenchment, but which lacked an overriding commitment to precedent, the Burger and Rehnquist Courts had no fewer than three persistent, but non-dominant, camps, any two of which contained the requisite votes to produce a majority. A shrinking minority of liberal justices continued to embrace the once-dominant liberal Warren-era jurisprudential vision. A growing minority of conservative justices, in opposite fashion, called for an affirmative retrenchment of such precedents. And a third group of moderate justices eschewed the ideological approaches of the left and right in favor of case-specific applications of such neutral principals as narrow issue definitions and resolutions, sometimes unpredictable case distinctions, respect for precedent, and avoiding unnecessary constitutional decision making except when the circumstances are truly compelling. Not surprisingly, perhaps, the resulting doctrine has often had the characteristic feature of an uneasy hybrid between a general tendency toward conservativism and judicial restraint, and an equal commitment, among at least some justices, to adherence to precedents, even those that they disfavored as an original matter. Because a majority must agree to reject both stare decisis and the merits to overturn a liberal precedent, the stage was set for an era of fits and starts, rather than an era—like that in the New Deal—of a systematic rights retrenchment.

Not surprisingly, perhaps, given these three nondominant analytical frameworks, the Burger Court was marked by a series of hybrid decisions. Thus, during Warren Burger's tenure as chief justice between 1969 and 1986, the Court located for the first time, and then cut back upon, a fundamental right to abortion;[76] issued a hair-splitting decision upholding a state medical school's use of race as an admissions criterion, while invalidating the school's process of setting aside a specified number of places for candidates admitted through affirmative action;[77] located, for the first time, an executive privilege, but then allowed a special prosecutor to overcome that privilege by issuing a subpoena;[78] and upheld a literacy test for the District of Columbia Police Department, notwithstanding disparate race-based outcomes, because no purposeful discrimination was found,[79] while, in extending the equal protection clause to require northern states to desegregate their de facto segregated public schools, willingly inferred a discriminatory intent to segregate an entire system based upon proof of segregative intent for only a part of that system.[80] Because of the hybrid nature of these rulings, or of the doctrines that they produced, the Burger Court's legacy is largely one of a transitional bridge between two more ideologically driven Supreme Court periods.[81]

And while the several generally conservative Rehnquist Court appointments have moved that Court's center of gravity to the right, especially in recent years, that Court too has largely continued the Burger Court legacy of multidimensionality and occasional asymmetry and thus uneasy rights contractions. Some members of the Rehnquist Court, most notably, the chief justice and Justices Scalia and Thomas, even if sometimes disagreeing at the margins, undoubtedly share a common conservative constitutional ideology. That ideology is largely associated with substantially reducing the extent of the federal judiciary's policymaking role and leaving that function to Congress and state legislatures. One might be inclined to label such an ideology as one of judicial restraint, but that seemingly noncontroversial label itself has profound normative underpinnings. Thus, academics have not hesitated to assert that the process of "restoring" the Court to a less influential policymaking role, in the face of precedents tending in the opposite direction, requires its own form of judicial activism.[82] Not surprisingly, therefore, the present activists on the right, like the liberal activists in the New Deal, have sought to relax stare decisis, especially in constitutional cases.[83] On the opposite side, until the early 1990s in any event, a liberal bloc of comparable size, consisting of Justices Blackmun, Brennan, and Marshall (and sometimes Stevens), demonstrated an equal commitment to preserving, and expanding upon, the victories of the Warren and early Burger Court eras. Again, not sur-

Table 5.1. Multidimensionality in the Burger and Rehnquist Courts in Four Periods

	Liberal	Moderate	**Conservative**
Period One: 1969 to 1972	*Black* [Powell 1972] *Fortas* **[Blackmun 1970]** *Brennan* *Douglas* *Marshall* *Total:* 5, then 4	White Harlan **[Rehnquist 1970]** Stewart Total: 3, then 2	**Burger** Total: 1, then 3
Period Two: 1972 to 1986	*Blackmun* *Brennan* *Stevens* *Marshall* *Total:* 4	White Stewart [O'Connor 1981] Powell Total: 3	**Burger** **[Rehnquist 1986]** **Rehnquist** **[Scalia 1986]** Total: 2
Period Three: 1986 to 1994	*Blackmun* [Breyer 1994] *Brennan* [Souter 1990] *Stevens* *Marshall* **[Thomas 1991]** *Total:* 4, then 1	White [Ginsburg 1994] O'Connor Powell [Kennedy 1988] Total: 3, then 5	**Rehnquist** **Scalia** Total: 2, then 3
Period Four: 1994 to present	*Stevens* *Souter* *Ginsburg* *Breyer* *Total:* 4	Kennedy O'Connor Total: 2	**Rehnquist** **Scalia** **Thomas** Total: 3

prisingly, this bloc, like the shrinking bloc of conservatives in the New Deal Court, insisted upon a strong stare decisis doctrine. The so-called centrist Republican appointees—Stewart (then O'Connor), Powell (then Kennedy), and, early on, Souter (replacing Brennan)—forged a middle path, striking a difficult, and certainly unpredictable, balance between the objectives of restoring the judiciary to a less prominent role and of respecting the high-profile precedents laid down in a more liberal era. Since then, Justice Souter has moved toward the liberal end of the Court.

Most recently, President Clinton has appointed Justices Ruth Bader Ginsburg (replacing White) and Stephen Breyer (replacing Blackmun), both of whom can best be described as liberal to moderate. On the present Court, four justices—John Paul Stevens, David Souter, Ruth Bader Ginsberg, and Stephen Breyer—have often emerged as a uniform liberal-to-moderate bloc, in dissent, with the remaining justices split between furthering a conservative agenda and respecting more liberal precedents as a matter of stare decisis. Despite the structural similarities between the present Court and that in periods two and three, there is a notable difference. In contrast with the earlier periods, the present Court's liberals are generally more cautious and conservative than their liberal predecessors.[84] Thus, while I have placed them under the liberal heading in table 5.1, given their relative status as compared with the remainder of the present Court, we might think of them as liberal-to-moderate when they are contrasted with liberals of an earlier period, for example, on the Warren, Burger, and early Rehnquist Courts. Thus, while the locations of the justices' issue space have remained multidimensional, the Court's center of gravity has generally tilted toward the right.

Because of the number of years that the Burger and Rehnquist Courts have spanned, I have provided a graphic depiction of the shifting coalitions from the beginning of the Burger era to the present Court, which is divided into four periods.

Table 5.1 employs the following conventions: italics indicate liberal justices; boldface indicates conservative justices; and Roman typeface indicates moderate justices.* In brackets after each justice who has been replaced appears the name of the replacing justice, in his or her appropriate typeface, along with the date of replacement. Some of the characterizations are certainly subject to debate. I have characterized Justice Kennedy, for example, as a moderate, while others could credibly argue that his vote in *Casey*

---

*It is important to emphasize that, in using the terms *liberal, moderate,* and *conservative,* I do not intend to suggest a unidimensional issue spectrum. I have used these commonly employed conventions for ease of reference. My general thesis, however, is that the Court's multidimensionality belies a neat liberal-to-conservative continuum. It is also important to bear in mind that the particular classifications are less important to the social choice analysis than the relationships between and among the various camps, and specifically, whether any two of three camps possess the requisite votes to produce a majority.

notwithstanding, he is generally a doctrinal conservative. In addition, the initial use of boldface and the subsequent use of italics for Justice Blackmun indicate that he started as a conservative, but then quickly moved to the liberal block in period two. At the bottom of each group, I have listed the total number of justices that appear in the given category for the relevant period. In periods one and three, I have listed a range, suggesting the loss of one or more core members.

Without trying to suggest that each of the above classifications is airtight (and admitting that some might disagree with particular judgment calls I have made), table 5.1 demonstrates that in period one, coming out of the Warren Court era, the liberals, while still in control of the Court, were losing their reign. With only five justices, the liberal camp could not afford any net defections—meaning defections not compensated for with a crossover vote from a justice in one of the other camps—if it were to issue a predictable ruling in a given case. In periods two, three, and four, which represent the middle to late Burger Court and the early to present Rehnquist Court, no single camp dominated the Court. In theory, any two camps could form a majority coalition, although in intensely divisive cases, ideology can be expected to flatten out potential intransitivities. Even so, as the increased frequency of fractured panel decisions in this period, including in several of the important cases described in chapter 3,[85] also suggests, the potential and sometimes actual breakdown of traditional coalitions rendered the Court most ripe for the formation of the modern standing doctrine in this historical period. Moreover, as shown in chapter 4, the breakdown of coalitions can manifest itself across groups of cases, rather than only in individual decisions.

In the current period, period four, the Court has produced a fairly consistent liberal-to-moderate bloc, often appearing in dissent, consisting of Justices Stevens, Souter, Ginsburg, and Breyer. In this period, Justices O'Connor and Kennedy appear to operate as the fulcrum, sometimes balancing respect for precedent with a generally conservative jurisprudential vision, and sometimes deliberately forging an expansion of issue dimensionality to achieve a desired objective without the immediate need to overrule. The Court is again prone to multidimensionality.[86] Notably in periods two and three, Justice Powell was often the fulcrum, as White, Stewart, and O'Connor, the other moderates, often voted with the conservative blocs. Although Justices O'Connor and Kennedy continue to hold the balance, they have generally moved the center of gravity toward the conservative end of the political spectrum. Finally, it is noteworthy that while one might predict that as the fulcrums of the present Court, Justices O'Connor and Kennedy would invariably seize the opportunity to define the Court's doctrine on underlying questions of federal law, *Miller v. Albright*[87] represents an important recent exception in which these two justices effectively denied themselves that opportunity by deliberately expanding the issue dimensionality in the case to include standing, thus forging a case with multidimensional and asymmetrical preferences.

B.   Social Choice Analysis: Four Case Paradigms

To continue the social choice analysis of the Burger and Rehnquist Courts, we will need to make a few assumptions. In fact, in an effort to increase the number of potential cases captured in the analysis, I will provide four paradigms, based upon four different sets of assumptions. In the end, however, all four paradigms will illustrate the same point: The Burger and Rehnquist Courts have generally been unable to ensure with any reasonable degree of certainty that, in resolving some significant set of cases, quite possibly involving the most divisive issues of the day, they would not thwart the will of a present majority. In turn, those Courts risked producing at least some arbitrary or irrational results. I do not intend to suggest that the outcomes of the Burger and Rehnquist Courts have been systematically irrational. Instead, I am suggesting that in a sufficiently important subset of potential cases, the characteristic features of multidimensionality and occasional asymmetry have had the potential effectively to thwart the preferences of a majority, or more typically, to generate seemingly arbitrary paths of case law, thus producing doctrinal anomalies over time. Either prospect is of sufficient concern that we could predict that the Court might respond by erecting and maintaining barriers to justiciability in the form of standing.

In chapter 3, I presented the first paradigm, in which the Rehnquist Court was not prone to cycling. In both *Planned Parenthood of Southeastern Pennsylvania v. Casey*[88] and *Board of Regents v. Bakke,*[89] the Court produced a fractured panel decision in which the preferences of the justices could be graded on a unidimensional liberal-to-conservative scale, and in a two-dimensional issue spectrum with a clearly dominant, Condorcet-winning, opinion, respectively. In *Casey,* for example, it seems implausible to suppose that the Court's liberal and conservative wings would have preferred the analysis embraced by the opposite extreme to the jointly authored hybrid analysis based upon stare decisis. While the dimensionality in *Bakke* was expanded relative to *Casey,* the same analysis applies. Even though only Justice Powell concluded that Davis could use race, but that it had done so in an impermissible manner, and that it could do so to promote diversity, but not for societal remediation, it again seems probable that each of the Court's wings preferred his opinion to that of the opposite wing, which reached an opposite conclusion on both dispositive issues and on both parts of the two-part holding. In both cases, *Casey* and *Bakke,* the holdings, while embraced by minorities of three and one, respectively, were likely Condorcet winners.

Notice also that *Casey* presents a classic illustration of the disjunctive relationship in cases involving rights contractions. Because a decision either to adhere to the merits of *Roe v. Wade,*[90] or to decline to overrule *Roe* based upon stare decisis, sufficed to continue the right to abort, the *Casey* Court produced that result. And this was so, even though only a minority—albeit a dominant one—agreed to the joint authors' application of stare decisis to rewrite *Roe v. Wade,* with the effect of redefining the trimester framework and of classifying abortion as something less than a fundamental right.

As explained in chapter 3, the narrowest grounds rule, announced in *Marks v. United States*,[91] is premised upon the intuition that within the overall set of fractured panel Supreme Court cases, most decisions possess a Condorcet-winning opinion. The second paradigm, those cases falling into the narrower subset in which the *Marks* doctrine does not apply, result from the combination of multidimensionality and asymmetry. As we have already seen, this can occur in a single case, as in *Miller v. Albright*,[92] *Kassel v. Consolidated Freightways*,[93] and *National Mutual Insurance Co. v. Tidewater Transfer Co.*[94] The same characteristic features can arise, however, over groups of cases, as in *Crawford v. Board of Education*,[95] and *Washington v. Seattle School District No. 1*.[96] In both contexts, even if we assume that each of the justice's preferences was fully transitive, under reasonable assumptions, it is possible to intuit a collective intransitivity. Moreover, even without formal asymmetry, through the repeated expansion of multidimensionality over time, the Court can generate the functional equivalent of a doctrinal cycle, as seen in the evolving equal protection analysis of race-based gerrymandering from *United Jewish Organizations v. Carey*,[97] to *Shaw v. Reno*,[98] to *Miller v. Johnson*.[99] We cannot with certainty identify cycling majorities in any of these three contexts, given that we do not have complete information about the preferences of all justices over all possible issue-and-outcome combinations presented in each case or over the combined frameworks that multiple cases present. But by observing the difficulty in identifying a clear holding in *Kassel*, in devising a supportable distinction between *Crawford* and *Seattle*, and in the nearly complete erosion of *Carey* through redefinition of issues related to racial gerrymandering in *Shaw* and *Miller*, we can make credible assumptions about judicial preferences that are consistent with the notion of an underlying doctrinal cycle. It is not surprising that all of these cases were decided in a period in which, as table 5.1 reveals, the Court was particularly prone to multidimensionality and occasional asymmetry.

While the Supreme Court's process-based decisional rules themselves reduce the manifestation of actual cycling, it is worth considering two further paradigms in which cycling could, in theory, occur. While such cases are difficult, if not impossible, to locate, that is likely attributable to the very process-based rules that this book explains. The possibility of such cycling paradigms thus helps to explain the development and use of doctrines that reduce the incidence of such cases. Assume that the Court is composed only of the three paradigmatic camps described above, which for ease of presentation, we will refer to as the (A) conservative bloc; (B) liberal bloc; and (C) moderate bloc. For the first paradigm, assume that the Court grants certiorari in a case that provides an opportunity to reverse a liberal Warren Court precedent. The conservative bloc would most prefer to issue a strong ruling that signals a retreat from the position established by the Warren Court. If required to uphold the precedent, however, the conservative bloc would prefer to do so on the basis of whatever independent rationale the liberal bloc offers rather than to rely upon the moderate bloc's rationale, which rests upon stare decisis. While this might appear counterintuitive, assume the conservative bloc members reason that a ruling that rests upon stare decisis might limit their ability to reverse Warren-era precedents in future cases more than a ruling that rests upon a set of substantive principles, even ones with which they disagree. In that sense, the liberal bloc's proposed ruling might be viewed as more narrow than the moderate bloc's proposed ruling with respect to the particular facts of the case. Based upon those assumptions, the conservative bloc's preferences are (A, B, C). Assume that the liberal bloc would most prefer to rule in accordance with its own principles. Failing that, it would prefer upholding the precedent based on the moderate bloc's stare decisis analysis to overturning the precedent based upon the conservative bloc's analysis. The liberal bloc's resulting preferences are (B, C, A). Finally, assume that the moderate bloc would most prefer to rest an affirmance on the doctrine of stare decisis. Failing that, it is more inclined to overrule based upon the conservative bloc's principles, which, but for stare decisis, it agrees with, than to uphold based upon the liberal bloc's principles. The moderate bloc's preferences are (C, A, B). The resulting preferences lack a Condorcet winner. Of course, the Court would issue an opinion, but, in doing so, it would inevitably thwart the will of a majority of its members.

In the fourth and final paradigm, cycling results from a reverse form of stare decisis. Consider the case of *Bowers v. Hardwick,*[100] where the Court upheld the conviction of a man charged with violating a Georgia statute prohibiting consensual acts of sodomy. The state had prosecuted on the basis that as applied to heterosexual acts of sodomy, the statute was unconstitutional. As applied to the defendant, a gay man, the state maintained that the act was constitutional. Thus, to reverse the conviction, the Court would have had to expand the reach of the privacy cases to include protection for consensual acts of homosexual sodomy.[101] Ruling in the defendant's favor would have required departing from a long history in which the constitutionality of such statutes was assumed. This time the moderate block initially aligns itself on the result with the conservative bloc, in favor of affirming the conviction. Its rationale is not an ideological commitment to the propriety of the underlying statute, or even, necessarily, to principles of federalism or a more limited judicial role. Instead, the moderate bloc would rule on a much narrower ground, one that might be viewed as a form of *reverse* stare decisis. Members of the moderate bloc determine that the privacy cases, for which they also lack an overriding ideological commitment, have not extended sufficiently far to cover this case and that the history of such state statutes suggests that their constitutionality has long been assumed.

Assume that the liberal bloc would most like to reverse and issue an opinion that expands the reach of the privacy cases. If required to uphold the conviction, however, the liberal bloc members would prefer doing so on the conservative bloc's rationale because the moderate bloc's rationale, if generally employed to assume the constitutionality of statutes that have long been on the books and not challenged, might be more restrictive in future cases involving rights expansions. The liberal bloc's resulting preferences are (B, A, C). Assume that the conservative bloc, which would most like to issue a strong ruling suggesting that the Constitution does not protect a generalized right of privacy, would next prefer upholding the conviction based upon the moderate bloc's more limited rationale than to reverse. The conservative bloc's resulting preferences are (A, C, B). Finally, while the moderate bloc initially aligns itself with the conservatives, assume that if forced to choose between the liberal and conservative combined positions on both result and underlying rationale, the moderate bloc would prefer to reverse, based upon the liberal bloc's rationale, than to uphold the conviction, thereby suggesting a wholesale rejection of recently issued privacy cases. The moderate bloc's resulting preferences are (C, B, A). The direction of this cycle is the opposite of that in the prior example because the moderate bloc's first-choice preference—resting the case analysis on a technical narrow ground—is with the conservative rather than the liberal bloc. Again, the preferences lack a Condorcet winner.

In considering the inability to readily identify cases representing the last two paradigms, recall Professor Shepsle's observation that cycling does not generally manifest itself in either endless stalemate or uncertainty of outcomes.[102] Instead, cycling is reflected in the manner in which decisional rules evolve either to avoid outcomes that are irrational, meaning that they lack majority support when compared with available alternatives, or to facilitate the identification of collective intransitivities, which might conduce to collective inertia. In this book, I have argued that within individual cases, outcome voting operates to break down such cycles, although in doing so, it sometimes produces such doctrinal anomalies as *Miller, Kassel,* and *Tidewater.* In addition, across cases and over time, stare decisis operates to break down doctrinal cycles, but, again, in doing so, it promotes path dependent legal doctrine. Outcome voting therefore purchases stable case outcomes at the cost of occasionally thwarted majority preferences over underlying issues, and stare decisis purchases doctrinal stability over time at the cost of inviting ideological litigant path manipulation. Just as legislative assemblies shift decisional rules away from those most prone to agenda control when faced with cyclical preferences,[103] so too the Supreme Court has established companion doctrines to improve the outcomes of its two non-Condorcet-producing rules, outcome voting and stare decisis. Within individual cases, the *Marks* doctrine increases the probability that holdings will be expressed in a Condorcet-winning opinion. And across cases and over time, the Court's various justiciability doctrines, and especially standing, raise the cost of ideological agenda manipulation and thus of generating non-Condorcet-winning judicial outcomes. The various justiciability barriers, and most notably standing, achieve this objective by presumptively shifting decisional responsibility in the first instance to the legislatures, which are *relatively* better equipped than appellate courts to respond rationally when confronted with cyclical preferences. Not surprisingly, the Supreme Court has developed these barriers to justiciability in the very period that the social choice analysis predicts.

The multidimensionality of the Burger and Rehnquist Courts is noteworthy in two critical respects. First, it ensured that in a significant subset of potentially important cases, the Court's members could not exert any reasonable degree of control over substantive rulings. Instead, the Court's members were only able to predict that if a majority were unable to secure enough votes to resolve the case in a particular manner, the Court's substantive ruling would reflect the preferences of some minority of the Court, as in such individual cases as *Miller v. Albright, Kassel,* and *Tidewater,* and in such groups of cases as *Seattle* and *Crawford,* and *Carey, Shaw,* and *Miller v. Johnson.* The result, namely suppressing the will of a present majority of the Court's members, will hold even if all members possess full knowledge of everyone's preferences in advance. The possibility is increased when, as is more typically the case, such preferences are either not known or can only be guessed at based upon incomplete fragments of judgment assembled over the course of multiple opinions. Given its general obligation to issue rulings in those cases properly before it, a multidimensional Supreme Court has two principal options: It can either decline certiorari in controversial cases to avoid the possibility that it will issue non-Condorcet-winning opinions in some, or it can devise a doctrine, or set of doctrines, that will enable the Court to consider such cases, but to reach a collective outcome on something *other than* the merits, except when absolutely necessary. The latter option would serve to minimize, but not to eliminate, the Court's collective irrationality. This intuition, that the Court employs standing to avoid ruling on the merits, has led many scholars to suggest that standing is no more than a politically expedient means with which to avoid deciding difficult cases. I would argue, however, that for two reasons this explanation is unsatisfying, or at the very least incomplete. First, denying certiorari is the more obvious mechanism for avoiding difficult cases. As explained in chapter 4,[104] however, standing and certiorari are each necessary but insufficient conditions to reduce the most egregious instances of litigant path manipulation. The difficulty is that lower federal courts, which lack the power of docket control, are even more susceptible to litigant path manipulation than is the Supreme Court. Furthermore, absent standing, ideological interest groups could manipulate circuit splits to effectively force upon the Supreme Court the obligation to resolve those splits. And they could do so even with the nominal power of docket control in place.[105] Perhaps for that very reason, the Supreme Court's standing precedents are generally understood to apply to federal courts generally. Second, as the discussion of criminal procedure cases in chapter 4 reveals, the Court routinely resolves cases on the merits in a manner that the political-expedience story does not predict. Indeed, as the discussion of two standing cases in chapter 6 will show,[106] the Court sometimes has contorted its own standing principles to address the merits of highly suspect claims arising under the guise of constitutional criminal procedure.

In fact, if standing were actually intended to enable the Supreme Court to avoid deciding difficult cases, the doctrine would quickly backfire. Ideological litigants would happily take the avoidance signal as an invitation to force judicial creation of positive law at the district and circuit court levels. The resulting precedents, if favorable, would be no less attractive within the affected circuits than if decided by the Supreme Court, which will have signaled an intent to keep them in place. And, if unfavorable, the precedents would only invite further litigation elsewhere designed to create circuit splits that render the Supreme Court's hands-off approach unpalatable. The avoidance strategy, even if successful in the very short term, would promote, rather than inhibit, ideologically based federal court litigation. If so, in short order, the Supreme Court would likely cut back upon, or perhaps even abandon, standing as yet another example of a doctrine that has proved unworkable over time. But the historical record is flatly inconsistent with that thesis. Standing has remained the Supreme Court's most prominent justiciability doctrine in the very period in which traditional analyses—in marked contrast with social choice analysis—would predict its decline.

Judicial multidimensionality is noteworthy in a second critical respect. Multidimensional preferences attract litigants who seek to force the judicial creation of positive law, and specifically of positive law that lacks majority popular legislative support, for the very same reason that multidimensional preferences create angst among the justices who, in the aggregate, possess them. Because its decisional processes render the Supreme Court unable to ensure collective rationality in processing multidimensional preferences for decision in an important subset of cases, interest groups view the Court as a free-for-all in which such fortuitous matters as timing can lead to major victories in individual cases or over time that would have been considerably less likely to occur in a legislative forum.

Unlike the Warren Court, which confronted the fundamental rights/ incorporation debate, the Burger and Rehnquist Courts could not meaningfully predict in a critical subset of cases how the relevant case issues would be defined, or where along any given political spectrum particular Court rulings would lie. Because the Burger and Rehnquist Courts were prone to multidimensionality and occasional asymmetry, the conditions were ripe for the creation of a doctrine designed to prevent the inevitable irrationality that arises when a collective decision-making body is forced to resolve disputes in the face of intransitive collective preferences. Thus, while the New Deal Court imposed standing in a united front against unwelcome challenges to favored New Deal programs and to discipline recalcitrant lower federal courts, the Burger and Rehnquist Courts built on those early roots to transform standing into something else entirely. In the Burger and Rehnquist Courts, standing became a necessary vehicle to prevent the irrationality of the Court's own creation. Even an institution that could not agree either on how to define or resolve divisive issues could agree on one principle: Better not to decide, or to encourage Congress or state legislatures to decide, the most difficult issues presented than to condone outcomes no more predictable than a role of the dice. In the Burger and Rehnquist Courts, the conditions were ripe for the transformation of standing into its present form, set out below, and for the elevation of standing to its present level of doctrinal and practical significance. The next subsection will explain the origin of the metaphors the Burger and Rehnquist Courts employed—injury in fact, causation, and redressability—in devising the modern standing formulation.

C.   Standing Doctrine in the Burger and Rehnquist Courts: A Doctrinal Preview

Before analyzing the development of the standing case law in the Burger and Rehnquist Courts in chapter 6, we will need to consider briefly the doctrine's radical transformation from its New Deal roots. This analysis begins with the Administrative Procedure Act ("APA"),[107] enacted in 1946, which the Supreme Court construed in the 1970 case, *Association of Data Processing Service Organizations v. Camp.*[108] The APA can fairly be characterized as an umbrella statute that was intended to add uniformity to the already burgeoning field of administrative law and procedure. The APA addressed the question of standing in somewhat cryptic terms. Section 10(a) provides standing to "person[s] . . . adversely affected or aggrieved by agency action within the meaning of a relevant statute."[109] Since its adoption, academics have been sharply divided as to what section 10(a) means.[110] To the extent that a consensus has formed as to the section's meaning, the consensus is largely contrary to prevailing Supreme Court interpretation.[111] While social choice theory is not particularly helpful in explaining the Court's initial interpretive error, it is helpful in explaining why the Court has continued to adhere to the framework set out in the much criticized *Data Processing* decision.

In *Data Processing,* the Court infused the APA's standing provision, section 10(a), and ultimately the case or controversy requirement of Article III, with an important and controversial substantive gloss. Despite the near universal condemnation that *Data Processing* has generated among academics, the Court has largely adhered to that decision's basic approach. The *Data Processing* Court determined that plaintiffs relying for standing upon APA section 10(a) and a substantive federal statute must satisfy a two-prong test: The plaintiff must allege, first, that she falls within the zone of interests protected or regulated by the relevant statute; and, second, that she has suffered an injury in fact. The *Data Processing* Court further stated that the injury-in-fact prong of its standing formulation was of constitutional dimension.[112] As a result, based upon *Data Processing,* every federal court plaintiff, whether relying upon the APA, the Constitution, or some independent statute, must satisfactorily demonstrate an injury in fact, or be denied standing. Since *Data Processing,* the Supreme Court has added two further elements, causation and redressability, to its prima facie standing elements.[113] In a 1987 case, *Clarke v. Securities Industry Association,*[114] the Court observed that it has continued to adhere to the essential division established in *Data Processing* by requiring claimants who rely for standing upon the Constitution to satisfy its injury-in-fact test (and the subsequently added causation and redressability tests), and by limiting the zone-of-interest test to APA section 10(a) standing cases.[115] In the course of interpreting section 10(a) of the APA, the Court has effectively metamorphosed three common law tort analogies—injury in fact, causation, and redressability—to the level of quasi-constitutional doctrine.

The principal difficulty with the *Data Processing* approach to standing is that the statutory history of the APA strongly suggests that the standing provision, section 10(a), was not intended to have independent substantive content.[116] Instead, it was intended to continue the New Deal approach to standing by operating as a conduit through which plaintiffs would allege standing in accordance with the underlying substantive statute or constitutional provision.[117] By itself, this erroneous gloss would seem no more problematic than any other questionable exercise in Supreme Court statutory interpretation. As discussed in the section on statutory standing in chapter 6, however, the Supreme Court has, since 1992, begun to superimpose its standing elements not only upon litigants raising constitutional claims, but also federal statutory claims. The Court has also suggested that the various standing elements limit the power of Congress to define and create justiciable injuries by statute. And in the intervening twenty-nine years since *Data Processing*, the Court has used that decision's framework to transform standing from a largely prudential doctrine to a series of nonnegotiable justiciability requirements regardless of the origin of the underlying claim.

In imposing its standing requirements upon Congress, the Supreme Court may have signaled an unwelcome retreat—albeit an inconsistent one[118]—from the long history of public litigation in England and in the United States at the time of the Constitution's framing.[119] Thus, while the Court has allowed standing for housing market testers and community residents under the Fair Housing Act of 1968 to challenge discriminatory residential real estate marketing practices, even though the litigants themselves had no interest in securing housing,[120] in the 1992 decision, *Lujan v. Defenders of Wildlife*,[121] the Court denied standing to environmental litigants in spite of their reliance upon a statute that expressly afforded citizens private attorney general status. In many respects, *Lujan* was unprecedented. More recently, however, the Supreme Court has continued to rely upon *Lujan*, with sometimes unforeseeable results. Most notably, in the unanimous decision *Bennett v. Spear*,[122] Justice Scalia relied upon the very standing provision that he deemed inadequate to support standing in *Lujan*, this time to confer standing, based upon an expansive zone-of-interest analysis, upon claimants seeking to limit the use of the Endangered Species Act to protect the environment in a manner that they claimed harmed their economic interests. While legal scholars are generally in substantial disagreement over the justifications and doctrinal implications of modern standing, an emerging area of agreement is in criticizing the *Lujan* framework for preventing Congress from defining novel justiciable claims.

V. Conclusion

This chapter has shown that standing underwent a radical change in the New Deal, Warren, and Burger and Rehnquist Court periods, for reasons that can be explained based upon principles of social choice. While the New Deal Court developed standing to shield liberal New Deal initiatives from attack in conservative lower federal courts, and while the Warren Court relaxed standing to invite novel constitutional challenges to federal and state laws, the Burger and Rehnquist Courts deployed standing for an altogether different purpose. In contrast with their predecessor Courts, the Burger and Rehnquist Courts have employed standing to prevent high-stakes institutional dice rolls, in which no one, including a majority of the Court's own members, is able to predict, or is likely to be satisfied with, the resulting outcomes in an important subset of politically divisive individual cases or groups of cases over time. With that introduction, we are now ready to consider the modern standing case law.

CHAPTER 6

Standing in the Burger and Rehnquist Courts: The Cases

I. Introduction

This chapter will review the justiciability case law, with a particular emphasis on standing, as it has been developed in the Burger and Rehnquist Courts. For ease of presentation, I will first comment briefly on the easiest justiciability barriers, ripeness and mootness, and then divide the modern constitutional standing case law into the following groupings: (1) no right to enforce the rights of others; (2) no right to prevent diffuse harms; and (3) no right to an undistorted market. In describing the cases within each grouping, I will consider cases in which the claimants have relied for standing upon the Constitution and upon federal statutes, including section 10(a) of the Administrative Procedure Act.[1] I will then revisit statutory standing conferrals in light of the 1992 decision *Lujan v. Defenders of Wildlife*[2] and its progeny. This will help to explore the differences between the standing doctrine's constitutional and prudential foundations. Before describing the three principal groupings of standing cases, it will be helpful to explain my general approach.

As before, I have classified the various justiciability rules according to the susceptibility of the target cases to path manipulation. The framework is based upon table 6.1, reproduced from chapter 4.

Table 6.1.   Expanded Justiciability Spectrum

Category of Cases	Ripeness/ Mootness	Rights of Others and Diffuse Harms	Undistorted Market	Criminal Procedure
Analytical Spectrum	Strong presumption in favor of path manipulation	◄————————►	Strong presumption against path manipulation	

Based upon this framework, I have again placed ripeness and mootness, which are opposite on a timing-based spectrum, together, given that these rules impose the lowest cost barriers to the strategic timing of cases. Within standing, I have employed three principal categories. The first, no right to enforce the rights of others, is most commonly referred to in the literature as "no third-party standing." This standing rule represents the lowest cost mechanism for avoiding the strategic timing of presently live claims. I have described this category, and the others, using a declarative statement of law to emphasize that standing denials invariably mask substantive legal rulings. Thus, in *Gilmore v. Utah*,[3] in terminating the stay of execution that it had previously entered, the Court effectively denied Mrs. Gilmore standing to raise the claims of her son, Gary Gilmore. While the doctrinal standing analysis suggests that the Court avoided reaching the merits of the underlying constitutional claims, the *Gilmore* Court also held as a matter of substantive law that Mrs. Gilmore lacked the legal right to pursue the claims of her son. The Court has generally prevented claimants from raising the legal rights of others, but it has not done so in all cases.[4] In addition, until fairly recently, the Court has generally allowed Congress to alter its presumptive third-party standing rule by creating a statutory right to enforce particular third-party interests.

The second grouping, no right to prevent diffuse harms, represents a slightly more costly method of preventing the strategic manipulation of presently live claims. While the proscription against third-party standing generally leaves open the possibility for a future challenge by someone else, this ground rule sometimes has the effect of preventing anyone from litigating particular claims. That is because certain claims only arise in a diffuse manner. As with the presumptive rule against third-party standing, the Court, until recently, has permitted Congress to define as individual rights, enforceable in federal courts, injuries that traditionally would have been viewed as diffuse.[5] Beginning with the 1992 *Lujan* decision,[6] however, the Court has suggested that Congress itself is limited in its power to transform generalized injuries into an enforceable legal right, especially when preventing such injuries requires that the federal courts monitor the executive branch.[7]

The third grouping, no right to an undistorted market, represents the most costly barrier to the strategic manipulation of presently live claims because it involves legal challenges that belong to the persons raising them and that are not legally diffuse.[8] Denying standing in these cases therefore not only has the potential to prevent anyone from litigating the underlying claim, but also raises a serious question whether the usual disclaimer that injured parties can resort to the political process is meaningful. And yet, this category of standing is analytically the richest in many respects. As with the other groupings, these cases, in which the Court has denied standing because the causal chain between the alleged misconduct and the plaintiffs' claimed harm was attenuated,[9] invariably involve substantive legal determinations. When properly analyzed, these standing cases, and their underlying substantive determinations, reveal both the critical social choice and separation of powers dimensions that underlie the modern standing case law.

While that completes the categories of timing-based justiciability cases, it does not complete the justiciability spectrum. As before, completing the spectrum requires considering a group of cases not generally assumed to involve justiciability. Because I have described several of them already,[10] it is unnecessary in this chapter to present those cases falling into this final category along the spectrum, namely constitutional criminal procedure. But it will be helpful to consider the relationship between that category and the various justiciability rules described above. As explained in chapter 4, in its criminal procedure cases, the Supreme Court has exhibited a willingness to set out the most arcane and detailed body of case law in a context in which justiciability is largely assumed. Indeed, in the discussion of third-party standing, I will demonstrate that the Court's presumption in favor of justiciability in criminal cases is so overwhelming that it sometimes misses most obvious instances in which standing should be held improper.[11]

In any event, none of the three groupings is entirely distinct. And within each grouping, which can perhaps be better thought of as a presumptive doctrine, exceptions can be found. As stated above, scholars writing about standing have relied upon the resulting inconsistencies to challenge both the doctrine's foundations and applications. Much of that literature has been summarized already. In contrast with most legal scholars, I have started from the premise that if we assume that Supreme Court justices, whatever their individual tastes and preferences happen to be, can be expected generally to behave rationally, we should be able to understand why standing developed as it did when it did and what functions that doctrine presently serves. I have also started from the premise that, as with all areas of substantive Supreme Court doctrine, we cannot expect entirely consistent standing case law. I have already demonstrated the function that standing served in the New Deal Court, and I have posited that that function has changed over time. By analyzing the modern standing cases according to the groupings set out above, the remainder of this chapter will explain the modern function, and durability, of this enigmatic doctrine. Before doing so, I will briefly summarize the lowest cost barriers to litigant path manipulation, namely ripeness and standing.

II. Ripeness and Mootness:
The Lowest Cost Barriers to Path Manipulation

A. Ripeness, Chilling, and Overbreadth

Like standing, the ripeness doctrine has been aptly described as a "twentieth-century creation."[12] Early federal equity practice generally condoned the adjudication of public claims in federal court. The development of ripeness is parallel to that of standing in several respects, including, most notably, its origins in the interpretation of a federal statute and its eventual transformation into a quasi-constitutional requirement of justiciability. The modern ripeness doctrine owes its origins to the Supreme Court's narrowing construction of the Declaratory Judgment Act ("DJA").[13] While the DJA, which was modeled on parallel state declaratory judgment acts, had been proposed in several sessions of Congress before its ultimate adoption,[14] the proposals had uniformly been rejected in the aftermath of a series of Supreme Court cases failing to allow suit under the state declaratory judgment acts in federal court. Shortly after the Supreme Court sustained one state's declaratory judgment act, in 1933, Congress enacted the DJA, which the Supreme Court sustained in 1937.[15]

The DJA provides in relevant part:

> In a case of actual controversy . . . any court of the United States, upon the filing of an appropriate pleading, may declare the rights and other legal relations of any interested party seeking such declaration, whether or not further relief is or could be sought. Any such declaration shall have the force and effect of a final judgment or decree and shall be reviewable as such.[16]

The statute was intended, by and large, to permit interested parties to determine their rights and liabilities under federal regulatory law without having to wait until they became defendants in a direct enforcement proceeding. The essential purpose of the DJA was to allow prospective litigants to avoid the Hobson's choice of either complying with a statute that they believed to be unconstitutional (or with a regulation that they believed to contravene a federal statute), or of assuming that the statute actually is unconstitutional and then suffering the consequences if their predictions proved wrong in court.[17] Not surprisingly, perhaps, Justice Felix Frankfurter, who as a professor had helped to develop the New Deal standing doctrine with his mentor, Justice Louis Brandeis, also developed ripeness through a narrowing construction of the DJA. While the DJA was largely intended as a jurisdictional measure, in the 1950 decision *Skelly Oil Co. v. Phillips Petroleum Co.*,[18] Justice Frankfurter narrowly construed the statute to prevent the adjudication of claims that did not meet his fairly stringent understanding of justiciability. In doing so, he helped to develop the ripeness doctrine, which legal scholars have demonstrated has no clear antecedents either in early federal practice or in English practice, upon which early federal practice was based.[19]

In two articles on the DJA, Professors Donald L. Doernberg and Michael B. Mushlin demonstrated that the statute was intended to enlarge the Court's jurisdiction by creating four new categories of claims that could be litigated in federal court. Instead, the *Skelly* Court interpreted the DJA as "procedural only," meaning that federal court litigants could not rely upon the DJA, as Congress had intended, to expand the scope of federal court jurisdiction. In effect, Justice Frankfurter limited the act to those cases in which the court had federal question jurisdiction and in which the plaintiff had a coercive claim presenting a federal question.[20] In so limiting the DJA, the *Skelly Oil* Court imposed a newly minted justiciability barrier in all but one of those four case categories.[21]

As Professors Doernberg and Mushlin observe:

> In at least three other situations, however, a plaintiff might necessarily plead a federal issue in a complaint seeking declaratory relief: (1) a

"mirror-image" case, in which the party seeking the declaratory judgment would have been the defendant in a traditional federal-question coercive action but has not yet been sued; (2) a "federal-defense" case, in which the defendant asserts a federal defense to the plaintiff's nonfederal coercive action; and (3) a "federal-reply" case, in which both the complaint and the answer would include only state claims but where the plaintiff's remedy would raise a federal issue.[22]

As with section 10(a) of the APA in the context of standing, the Court soon transformed its limiting construction of the DJA into a constitutional barrier to the justiciability of nonripe claims. While various commentators have questioned the soundness of the Court's limiting construction, when viewed in its historical context, the motivation is not difficult to understand. The Supreme Court likely construed the DJA narrowly to prevent lower federal courts from employing any of the alternative case categories, described above, as vehicles for challenging increasingly liberal Supreme Court rulings, and possibly circumventing its standing requirements. Frankfurter's narrowing construction of the DJA, enacted in the New Deal, appears somewhat anomalous, given his general approach of judicial deference to congressional initiatives. But in this limited context, *Skelly Oil* might have represented Frankfurter's attempt to cure, what, for him, was a misguided liberalization by Congress of federal court practice itself.

Beginning in the 1970s, the Burger Court not only constitutionalized ripeness, but also it superimposed the constitutional standing elements, injury in fact, causation, and redressibility, onto its ripeness doctrine. The Supreme Court has recently employed ripeness to prevent the adjudication of claims that have a congressional imprimatur.[23] As explained below, however, the Supreme Court has not been altogether consistent in its insistence upon ripe claims. As with standing, the Court has violated its ripeness principles in cases in which it has generally failed to even consider employing a ripeness framework for analysis. The most notable exceptions to modern ripeness arise in two contexts, first, the First Amendment prior restraint and overbreadth doctrines, and, second, the criminal procedure vagueness and overbreadth doctrines.

In First Amendment case law, litigants are sometimes afforded the power to challenge statutes restricting speech on their face, even if the statute is constitutional as applied to them.[24] The Court has allowed such cases to proceed on the theory that even absent an immediate enforcement that would violate the First Amendment, the mere presence of an unconstitutionally overbroad restriction on speech can have an undesirable "chilling" effect.[25] The vagueness and overbreadth doctrines in criminal law are parallel. In some cases, criminal defendants are permitted to challenge the constitutionality of a statute on its face, even if the statute is clearly constitutional as applied to the conduct with which the defendant has been charged.[26] Technically, vagueness and overbreadth have different meanings. A statute is vague if the defendant could not anticipate its application to him based upon unclear wording;

a statute is overbroad if, in addition to prohibiting unlawful conduct, it also prohibits constitutionally protected conduct.[27] As a practical matter, however, the relationship is quite close. Courts will rarely strike down a statute on vagueness grounds unless the statute's vagueness has the potential effect of inhibiting constitutionally protected activity. As with the First Amendment chilling and overbreadth doctrines, the traditional justification for these criminal law doctrines is that allowing facial challenges to allegedly vague or overbroad criminal statutes prevents their potential application to constitutionally protected activities. Both sets of doctrines, chilling and overbreadth in First Amendment, and vagueness and overbreadth in criminal law, defy the presumptive rule prohibiting the adjudication of nonripe claims. These exceptions to ripeness are premised upon the notion of a present injury associated with the existence of a law that has the immediate potential to inhibit constitutionally protected activity.

As with standing, social choice is helpful in explaining both the presumptive, indeed quasi-constitutional, requirement of ripeness and the doctrine's apparent exceptions. While Frankfurter developed ripeness, or at least its statutory equivalent, based upon his construction of the DJA in *Skelly Oil,* to discipline lower federal courts, the Burger and Rehnquist Courts transformed ripeness into a presumptive doctrine that operates in a manner that avoids the lowest cost manipulation of potential legal claims. Absent a ripeness barrier, ideological litigants would have virtually free reign to manipulate the order of cases. Indeed, they would not even need to wait for the enforcement of a statute to bring a constitutional challenge. And yet, as discussed above, the Court occasionally permits such actions to proceed, without considering those actions through the formal lens of ripeness.

The exceptions to ripeness are best understood as ensuring justiciability to challenge an actual present injury, albeit one that has not manifested itself in a manner conducive to a traditional lawsuit. While claims involving vagueness and overbreadth are admittedly subject to a kind of path manipulation, the potential is reduced by the general requirement that the challenge be presented in a traditional criminal proceeding, even if one in which the statute, as applied, appears to be constitutional. The First Amendment chilling and overbreadth doctrines raise more difficult conceptual problems, for example, when no enforcement has yet taken place and when there is no proceeding, criminal or otherwise, beyond the challengers' control. In such cases, it is difficult to reconcile these exceptions with ripeness, other than on the apparent basis that the Court has placed a higher value on free speech than on inhibiting the resulting path manipulation.

B.   Mootness and Its Exceptions

While, together, ripeness and mootness represent the lowest cost barriers to justiciability, in one respect, mootness is the most peculiar justiciability barrier.[28] Unlike both standing and ripeness, which serve to prevent the adjudication of some claims of injury that may simply never come to fruition or that have not directly affected the litigants in a manner beyond their control, in all cases barred as moot, the requisite injury in fact has, by definition, already occurred in a manner harming the claimant.[29] As a result, if we were to accept the Supreme Court's nominal justifications for the various timing-based justiciability doctrines, including ensuring a justiciable injury, concreteness, and adversity, mootness would seem unnecessary and perhaps redundant. Admittedly, the inability to litigate claims that, although once ripe and sufficient to support standing, are now moot, increases slightly opportunities for litigant path manipulation.[30] But since the only cases that claimants have an interest in continuing to litigate are those in which the apparent mooting event has not afforded complete relief, the relevant margin might appear sufficiently small so as not to justify the doctrine's cost. This difference between mootness and its counterpart doctrines of ripeness and standing may help to explain why some commentators have maintained that mootness should always be cast solely in prudential terms.[31] Although earlier cases had cited the Article III case or controversy requirement in connection with mootness along with ripeness, the Burger and Rehnquist Courts established a firm constitutional foundation for mootness doctrine, thus demanding a constitutionally sufficient injury-in-fact, causation, and redressibility.[32]

As with ripeness, the mootness doctrine is perhaps best understood by considering the exceptions. If, in fact, as the Court has repeatedly stated, the requirement that claims not be moot is grounded in Article III,[33] it would appear difficult to reconcile the mootness doctrine with the exceptions for claims "capable of repetition yet evading review,"[34] and for claims in which, despite defendant's voluntary cessation of offensive conduct, plaintiff can credibly allege the potential for a recurring harm.[35] The first exception arose most notably in *Roe v. Wade*,[36] where the Court determined that absent an exception to mootness, given the short duration of pregnancy and the protracted pace of litigation, there might never be a final judicial resolution of the underlying constitutional claim. The second exception arises in cases in which a defendant voluntarily ceases her offensive conduct, leaving open the possibility that, without a final judicial disposition of the claimed injury, she may resume that conduct.[37] One can escape the doctrinal anomaly by asserting the tautological proposition that mootness applies to bar state claims, unless there is an exception, of which two have been recognized. A far more satisfying explanation, however, can be found in social choice.

The difficulty with mootness is that most litigated cases are very close to the margin, meaning that the plaintiffs have some credible claim of continuing injury, often the fear of repeat harm or the desire to further a point of principle that they believe was not remedied by the alleged mooting event. But lifting the mootness barrier altogether would allow for the litigation of claims farther from that margin, even if based entirely on strategic concerns, including, most notably, the desire to manipulate the order of precedents by pressing dead claims solely for the benefit of strategic timing. As a result, the Court has erected a general barrier to the adjudication of moot claims, but in doing so, it has created the anomaly that some claims may never have the potential to be litigated. Prohibited claims could include issues surrounding pregnancy and abortion, and situations in which litigants may live under a perpetual cloud resulting from the fear of recurrence. While doctrinally imperfect, the mootness doctrine and its exceptions operate to prevent the obviously low-cost manipulation of dead claims that could arise in its absence, while also preventing the unfairness of potentially continuing or recurring injuries, which the exceptions allow claimants to litigate in federal court.

Having considered the most obvious timing-based barriers to manipulating the order of precedent, we are now ready to reconsider the most important justiciability barrier, namely standing, which prevents the strategic adjudication of a significant class of presently live claims.

III. Standing Revisited

A. No Right to Enforce the Rights of Others

Because this first standing ground rule, which is most commonly referred to as third-party standing, limits the most obvious attempts to manipulate the order of presently live claims, it lies at the core of the modern standing doctrine. Traditional analyses of third-party standing have failed adequately to consider, first, the doctrine's relationship with cases arising in constitutional criminal procedure, and, second, the illusory nature of the Supreme Court's claim that the doctrine is intended to promote zealous advocacy.[38] In fact, the social choice analysis of this standing rule reveals that quite often the opposite is more nearly correct. Third-party standing denials are designed to promote *appropriate* advocacy rather than *zealous* advocacy. Ironically, one feature of appropriate advocacy is that it not be overly zealous.

In evaluating this standing rule, it is important to recognize that third-party standing denials can invariably be recast as substantive legal rulings. To illustrate, consider the following two cases. In the first, *Gilmore v. Utah,*[39] while not technically resolved by a majority on standing grounds, the Supreme Court declined to reach the merits of the underlying constitutional claims that Mrs. Bessie Gilmore presented on behalf of her son, Gary Gilmore, in challenging his conviction and death sentence. In doing so, the Court also held that Mrs. Gilmore lacked the substantive legal right to enforce the rights of others in federal court, even if the person who was harmed was her son. In the second case, *City of Los Angeles v. Lyons,*[40] the Supreme Court declined to reach the merits of a constitutional challenge presented by Mr. Adolph Lyons, a prior Los Angeles Police Department ("LAPD") choke hold victim, to the LAPD's choke hold practice. In doing so, the Court effectively held that Mr. Lyons, based upon the facts that he alleged, lacked the substantive right to raise the constitutional challenge of potential future choke hold victims in his community.

In each case, in the guise of a technical determination on standing, intended to prevent a substantive ruling on the merits of the underlying legal issue, the Court has issued an alternative substantive ruling limiting the claimant's legal rights. Had it done otherwise, however, it would have significantly reduced the cost to ideological litigants of manipulating the order of presently live claims. To illustrate, consider the alternative options that the Court faced in these cases. In *Gilmore,* the Court had the choice either to grant Mrs. Gilmore standing and to resolve the merits of the constitutional challenges to Gary Gilmore's conviction and death sentence, even though Gary Gilmore had not chosen to press those claims, or to deny Mrs. Gilmore standing and to hold, as a matter of substantive law, that she lacked the power to challenge a conviction and death sentence of someone else, which she alleged, violated the Constitution. There was no third option that would have allowed the Court altogether to avoid making positive law. And in *Lyons,* the Court faced a similar choice. It could either have granted standing and resolved the underlying constitutional challenge, or it could have denied standing and waited until a convicted victim of a choke hold challenged the practice as part of his direct appeal, collateral attack, or retroactive damages action. In each case, the Court had to choose between two alternatives, both of which involved the judicial creation of positive law, and decide which option was least bad. In making these determinations, the Court explicitly or implicitly viewed two values as critically important. First, the Court was explicitly concerned with the extent to which its ruling would encroach upon the legislature's lawmaking function, which includes the power not to resolve a given issue by statute unless and until an appropriate consensus has formed. Second, while the justices would not have framed the inquiry in these terms, we can now translate the holding as expressing an implicit concern with the Court's own ability to aggregate preferences in a rational manner in those cases it does resolve on the merits.

As demonstrated in the case discussions in chapters 3 and 4 and in the historical overview in chapter 5, in an important subset of cases, the Burger and Rehnquist courts were prone to multidimensionality coupled with occasional asymmetry. These characteristics, when joined with decisional rules that prevent the requisite number of iterations to reveal cycles within or across cases, limit the certainty with which the Court can ensure that if it addressed the merits of at least some important and controversial cases, it would not thwart the preferences of a present majority. For the same reason that members of a Supreme Court with such a set of preference structures are likely to be reticent in controversial cases, ideological litigants—especially those who are frustrated in the political process—are likely to be enthusiastic about presenting such cases to that Court. While such minority litigants are by no means ensured success at codifying their desired agenda into law, almost any other preference configuration would ensure failure. The sole exception, of course, is a nondominant preference in the public with majority support on the Supreme Court. This may well have been the situation in the Warren Court for those ideological litigants seeking to further an ambitious liberal agenda. In any event, if one takes enough shots at securing a favorable precedent, given the value of path dependence, the chances of long-run success increase.

One substantive body of case law that particularly tends to attract ideological litigants involves the rights of the criminally accused. Holding aside the merits of *Gilmore* and *Lyons,* we can see why the Court, faced with the choice either to grant or to deny standing, elected the former course. Even assuming that the Court's preferences in these two cases were unidimensional, or multidimensional but with symmetrical preferences, conferring standing and addressing the merits of the underlying claims would have invited interest group manipulation of cases over a long enough trajectory to create the functional equivalent of a doctrinal cycle. Had the Court granted standing in these cases, it would have invited ambitious interest groups to forage for litigants who have chosen not to press their own constitutional claims. Especially in the criminal procedure context, countless claims exist at any given time, even though many or most of the affected parties—the majority of whom are in jail—either are unaware of their possible existence as a test case or elect not to pursue them. As a result, the government's arguably illegal conduct often goes unpunished, and therefore undeterred, at least until a convicted criminal chooses to challenge that conduct in an appropriate proceeding.

As explained in chapter 4, the injury-in-fact requirement in standing is analogous to the personal injury requirement in tort. Of course, both legal regimes rest upon an implicit—and substantive—understanding of injury. In tort, the legal regime could easily expand the definition of injury to include as injured persons who are disturbed when negligence that causes no ultimate physical harm goes unpunished. Similarly, the Supreme Court could expand its definition of injury for standing to include as injured persons who are simply disturbed by the continuous illegality of governmental conduct.[41] Instead, both legal regimes limit judicial action to those cases in which the consequences of governmental conduct are direct and significant to specific claimants, thus increasing the likelihood that the principal motivation to litigate is something other than the desire to make new law. While lobbying cannot guarantee a legislative response, filing a lawsuit can force at least a de minimis judicial response, and very possibly a full judicial opinion on the merits of the underlying claim. Where there is no shadow case—that case in which a different litigant could present the same claim with no credible standing barrier[42]—courts generally cannot avoid creating positive law in resolving those issues necessary to the resolution of the case, regardless of the structure of underlying judicial preferences. Thus, when a convicted criminal challenges the constitutionality of his conviction or sentence in a proper appeal or habeas proceeding in federal court, that court lacks the luxury of delaying the creation of positive law. Courts cannot wait either until an appropriate legislative consensus forms, or until the Supreme Court's preferences coalesce around a dominant jurisprudential framework. In such cases, the federal courts cannot avoid shifting the burden of congressional inertia. Without the presumption against third-party standing, however, ambitious ideological litigants could force the federal judiciary to make law at will, simply by locating an affected party who was not aware of the test case potential her situation represents, or who has chosen not to enforce her own legal rights.[43] Such litigants could affect the path, and thus the substance, of legal doctrine by controlling the order or timing of case presentations.

But in denying standing, the Court has not avoided making positive law. Instead, it has determined, as a matter of substantive law, that the third-party claimant lacks the legal right to pursue another person's underlying claim. This, of course, was the position that Justices O'Connor and Kennedy embraced, albeit for a minority, in *Miller v. Albright*.[44] In a Court prone to multidimensionality, occasionally coupled with asymmetry, however, the substantive legal ruling resulting from a standing denial is often likely to be more attractive than the alternative of granting standing and addressing the underlying claim on the merits. First, the standing denial has a presumptive—rather than absolute—character. Thus, until recently in any event, the Court had permitted Congress to alter, by statute, its presumptive rule against third-party standing. In a series of cases arising under the Fair Housing Act ("FHA"),[45] the Supreme Court has vindicated a variety of claims by ideological litigants who, but for the federal statute, would have been denied standing. For example, the Court granted standing under the FHA to housing market testers who challenged the discriminatory dissemination of residential real estate marketing information even though they themselves were not in the market for housing;[46] to residents not seeking housing but who wished to secure "the social and professional advantages of living in an integrated community";[47] and to a multiracial fair housing organization seeking to ensure nondiscriminatory dissemination of housing information.[48] In the final case, the Court, per Justice William Brennan, quoting Justice Thurgood Marshall, observed that "[t]he actual or threatened injury required by Art. III may exist solely by virtue of 'statutes creating legal rights, the invasion of which creates standing.' "[49] Presumably, had the claimants relied solely upon the equal protection clause rather than a federal statute for their claims, the Court would have dismissed the case based upon third-party standing principles.

Second, and more importantly, creating positive law through a denial of standing might be more attractive to a Supreme Court prone to multidimensionality and asymmetry because the standing denial tends to discourage future litigants from attempting to force upon the Court cases presenting issues over which the justices' judgments, when aggregated by majority rule, are cyclical. In fact, one issue on which sitting justices on a Court operating under these conditions could agree is that it is better to wait for a case in which they have no choice but to rule on a divisive issue than to allow ideological litigants to come in and place their bets but force the Court to roll the dice.

1. Powers, Campbell, *and Displaced Third-Party Standing Analysis*

As explained in chapter 4,[50] the shadow case analysis—in which we compare cases resulting in standing denials with those in which litigants could raise the same underlying legal claims with no credible standing barrier, rather than directly comparing claimed injuries themselves—provides a ready explanation for such cases as *Gilmore* and *Lyons*. And yet, the Supreme Court has not been altogether consistent in applying its third-party standing doctrine. When the justiciability spectrum is properly expanded, as it must be, to include criminal procedure cases, however, we can explain some of the resulting inconsistencies. To illustrate, consider the following line of cases.

In the well-known 1880 decision *Strauder v. West Virginia*,[51] the Supreme Court held that the Fourteenth Amendment equal protection clause prevents a state, in the criminal trial of an African American defendant, from systematically excluding members of defendant's own race from the jury. In so holding, the Court made clear that the claimed right existed in the criminal defendant, rather than in the prospective African American juror subject to exclusion.[52] The *Strauder* case thus contained two critical limitations: It did not hold that the prospective minority juror had a right to serve on the jury and it did not hold that an African American criminal defendant had a right to have members of his own race serve on the jury. Instead, the Court suggested that, regardless of the composition of the ultimate jury, the defendant's equal protection rights are satisfied if African Americans, as members of the defendant's race, are not systematically excluded by law from the jury venire from which the grand and petit juries are drawn.

In the 1970 case *Carter v. Jury Commission*,[53] the Supreme Court cut back upon one of *Strauder*'s apparent limiting principles, namely that the excluded jurors do not have a constitutional right to serve. The *Carter* Court held that a set of jury selection procedures, while "devoid of any mention of race," operated in a manner that systematically excluded African Americans from both grand and petit juries. In holding that an excluded African American juror could sue for a violation of his own equal protection rights,[54] however, the *Carter* Court did not suggest an intent to cut back on *Strauder*'s second limiting principle, namely that the African American criminal defendant has a right to prevent the systematic exclusion of members of *his own race* from the jury.

In 1986, the Supreme Court considered a question closely related to that presented in *Strauder*, namely whether the Fourteenth Amendment equal protection clause prevented state prosecutors, through race-based peremptory challenges, from producing all-white, or predominantly white, juries in criminal cases with African American defendants. In *Batson v. Kentucky*,[55] an African American criminal defendant challenged the prosecutor's systematic exercise of peremptory challenges against prospective African American jurors. The *Batson* Court held that in a trial involving an African American criminal defendant, if the defendant objects to the prosecutor's exercise of a peremptory challenge on the ground that it was race-based, the prosecutor must provide a race-neutral justification for the exclusion. In so doing, the *Batson* Court extended *Strauder* to cover not only systematic legal exclusions of African American jurors, but also peremptory challenges of African American jurors in such trials. Like *Carter*, *Batson* did not alter *Strauder*'s second premise, that an African American criminal defendant has the right not to have members of his own race excluded from jury service.[56]

If we assume that the *Strauder, Carter,* and *Batson* Courts correctly identified the substantive rights in question, then the next case becomes quite difficult to reconcile with the Supreme Court's third-party standing principles. And yet, this book's social choice analysis helps to explain the resulting anomaly. In *Powers v. Ohio,*[57] the Supreme Court addressed the question whether a white criminal defendant can raise a *Batson* challenge when the prosecutor has allegedly employed race-based peremptory challenges to exclude African Americans from the jury. In vindicating Power's claim, the Court conferred standing where it should not have, to pursue a substantively hollow legal challenge. In *Powers,* the Court effectively redefined the injury articulated in *Batson* to include the prospective juror's *Carter* right not to be excluded on the basis of race, and conferred standing upon the defendant, who was white, to litigate the excluded juror's claim.

The difficulty in *Powers* is identifying whose equal protection rights had been violated. If Powers had raised the same injury at issue in *Batson,* namely the right of a minority not to have members of *his own race* systematically excluded from jury service, then the case would not have implicated standing principles at all. Instead, Powers simply would have raised a nonexistent claim. Members of his race had not been systematically excluded from service on the jury that convicted him. Powers argued, instead, that the excluded African American jurors' equal protection rights had been denied and that, as a criminal defendant who was convicted by the jury from which these African Americans had been excluded, he had standing to raise their claim. In accepting this argument, the Court effectively perverted both the underlying legal claims articulated in *Strauder, Carter,* and *Batson,* and its third-party standing analysis.

The *Powers* Court redefined the underlying legal claim, which it had previously suggested rested with the criminal defendant, to rest now with the excluded jurors. But if we assume that the *Powers* Court properly defined the underlying injury as violating the juror's right not to be excluded based upon race, per *Carter,* this time peremptorily, then a proper shadow case rested with the excluded juror himself. As a result, the criminal defendant should have been denied standing to raise that claim. Alternatively, if we assume that standing was proper, then there was no substantive claim to vindicate. Members of the defendant's own race had not been excluded, either systematically, per *Strauder* and *Carter,* or peremptorily, per *Batson.*

Before explaining the *Powers* result, it is worth noting that the Supreme Court in *Campbell v. Louisiana,*[58] recently extended *Powers,* thus allowing a convicted white murderer to challenge the exclusion of an African American from the position of foreman of a grand jury. In doing so, the *Campbell* Court, in an opinion by Justice Kennedy, articulated the following conditions for allowing the vindication a *Powers*-type claim:

Recognizing our general reluctance to permit a litigant to assert the rights of a third party, we found three preconditions had been satisfied: (1) the defendant suffered an "injury in fact"; (2) he had a "close relationship" to the excluded jurors; and (3) there was some hindrance to the excluded jurors asserting their own rights.[59]

The *Campbell* Court then went on to conclude that it was unnecessary to determine whether a white defendant's equal protection rights were violated when black persons were excluded from the grand jury, holding instead that Campbell can raise the well-established right of African Americans not to be excluded from serving on the grand jury because of their race. In his separate opinion, Justice Thomas criticized the Court's reasoning, asserting that he could not "understand how the rights of blacks excluded from jury service can be vindicated by letting a white murderer go free."[60] Addressing the issue of third-party standing, Justice Thomas quite clearly recognized the anomaly that both *Powers* and *Campbell* represent. Thus, Thomas stated:

> Furthermore, there is no reason why a violation of a third party's right to serve on a jury should be grounds for reversal when other violations of third-party rights, such as obtaining evidence against the defendant in violation of another person's Fourth or Fifth Amendment rights, are not.

To understand *Powers* and *Campbell*, we need to recognize that the Court fell victim to its own use of metaphor in analyzing (or in failing to analyze) the question of standing. In essence, the *Powers* Court implicitly placed the case at the wrong end of its expanded justiciability spectrum, as shown in table 6.1.[61] In most third-party standing cases, the Court is implicitly concerned that if it allows ideological litigants to identify and to rely upon the rights of others in forcing the judicial resolution of legal claims, it will afford such litigants with substantial power to manipulate the critical path that influences the substantive evolution of legal doctrine. The third-party standing doctrine does not prevent path dependency, which is an inevitable consequence of decisional rules that prevent the requisite number of votes to reveal cycles. But, by ensuring that fortuity, rather than advertent path manipulation, controls the order of case decisions, the doctrine makes the outcome of its path dependent voting procedures and of its constitutional process more fair. The Supreme Court has infused its standing analysis with traditional notions borrowed from tort law—injury in fact, causation, and redressability—not because those features have abstract significance to justiciability, but instead because those features serve as apt metaphors for when the Court is unable to avoid shifting the burden of congressional inertia. They are apt because they are virtually always present in those cases appearing at the opposite end of its justiciability spectrum in which the Court presumes against path manipulation. Specifically, these features are routinely present when a convicted criminal in a direct appeal or collateral attack alleges that her conviction or sentence was secured in violation of her constitutional rights. In such cases, the courts, including the Supreme Court in a case properly before it, do not have the luxury to abstain from making positive law with respect to the convicted criminal's underlying legal claims. Unless the courts address the claims on the merits, the convicted criminal will incur the most severe consequences that the state or federal government can impose. In such cases, the claimant is least likely to be concerned with path manipulation; instead, she simply wants whatever relief a court is willing to provide. Simply put, because there generally is no shadow case in criminal appeals and habeas proceedings, courts are willing to make law, even at the risk of producing results that defy the Condorcet criterion or that meet the criterion, but nevertheless contribute to long-term path dependency.

Because the *Powers* Court implicitly construed its standing elements literally, rather than metaphorically, it treated Powers's equal protection challenge as if it arose in a traditional criminal context in which justiciability is presumed.[62] The *Powers* Court recognized that if Powers had been convicted and sentenced in violation of the Constitution, the government's illegal conduct could be said to have caused him a concrete injury. But while that is true, it is also circular. The government caused him a concrete injury only if we assume that *his* constitutional rights, rather than *someone else's,* were violated. If the jury exclusion violated the potential juror's rights under *Carter,* rather than those of Powers under *Batson,* then the exclusion caused the potential juror, but not Powers, a concrete injury. The Court further recognized that if it reversed Powers's conviction and sentence, it would redress any injury that he might have suffered. But that too is circular. If we assume that Powers, as opposed to the prospective juror, had no injury, there was nothing for the Court to redress. By implicitly viewing injury in fact, causation, and redressibility as abstract elements of justiciability with independent content, rather than as metaphors designed to limit the Court's lawmaking powers except on an ad hoc and as needed basis, the Court effectively conferred upon Powers third-party standing to raise an excluded juror's substantive legal claim, even though it had repeatedly held that, in general, litigants lack the right to enforce the rights of others. Of course, the same analysis applies to *Campbell.*

2. Third-Party Standing, Statutory Standing, and a Preliminary Inquiry into Zone-of-Interest Analysis

Commentators criticizing the third-party standing doctrine have focused largely on two other cases that lie along the doctrine's periphery, *Sierra Club v. Morton*[63] and *United States v. Students Challenging Regulatory Agency Procedures.*[64] The Sierra Club, an organization that described itself as having "a special interest in the conservation and the sound maintenance of the national parks,"[65] brought suit to challenge the construction of a recreational area in a national park. In denying standing, the Court observed that the plaintiffs had failed to allege that their members had actually used the national park in question. The Court stated that while "aesthetic, conservational, and recreational" harms could satisfy standing's injury requirement, it was unwilling to abandon the requirement that the claimant herself suffer such an injury. One difficulty with *Sierra Club* is that, as shown in the above discussion of *Powers*, the Court has occasionally linked the injury requirement to the promotion of zealous advocacy.[66] At the very least, this case appears to render that justification dubious. Certainly the Sierra Club would have been an effective and zealous advocate on conservation matters.

In fact, zealousness, like the more formalized standing requirements, has been employed largely as a catch phrase, or metaphor, intended to capture a very different concern. Zealousness, like injury in fact, causation, and redressibility, is closely correlated with those cases in which the Court cannot avoid shifting the burden of congressional inertia. But, in fact, the zealous advocacy metaphor appears less apt than the other standing metaphors. The Court actually has denied third-party standing because the advocates in question would litigate too zealously rather than not zealously enough. Certainly, the *Gilmore* and *Sierra Club* claimants would have litigated as ambitiously as the parties whose interests they sought to vindicate.[67] Ironically, the difficulty with the Sierra Club was not the lack of zealousness, but too much zealousness. Because the Sierra Club stated that its goal was to promote "conservation and the sound maintenance of the national parks, game refuges and forests of the country, regularly serving as a responsible representative of persons similarly interested,"[68] it was likely to present its case in a broader manner than would litigants seeking to ensure that their particular uses of the park were not harmed. Similarly, if Mrs. Gilmore were afforded standing, ideological interest groups like the NAACP Legal Defense Fund ("NAACP") might use the precedent as a vehicle to strategically present the rights of numerous criminals who sit on them. The NAACP might, for example, attempt to raise cases in the most favorable order, and it might choose to vary the breadth of particular claims with the ultimate objective of affording maximum reach to the substantive provisions of the Bill of Rights.

To understand why the Court denied standing to Sierra Club, despite the zealousness with which it would have presented its claim, consider the frequently contrasted case, *United States v. Students Challenging Regulatory Agency Procedures (SCRAP)*.[69] In *SCRAP*, a group of law students and an environmental interest group challenged the failure of the Interstate Commerce Commission ("ICC") to suspend a railroad rate increase. SCRAP claimed that the new rate structure would increase the cost of recyclable goods relative to nonrecyclable goods, which in turn would both increase the use of natural resources and the disposal of waste in and around Washington, D.C.[70] Despite this unusually attenuated, and rather dubious, causal chain, the claimants could credibly argue that they had Congress's imprimatur, or at the very least, that the federal judiciary could not avoid making that determination through a standing denial. Thus, the plaintiffs argued that the ICC, in denying the suspension, failed to comply with the National Environmental Policy Act ("NEPA"), which required a "detailed environmental impact statement" before a rate increase could be approved. While NEPA was silent on the question of standing, the statute's substantive provisions provided a credible basis upon which to maintain that Congress intended to confer standing broadly.[71] At the very least, congressional silence on the question of standing implied that to deny standing, the Court would have had to construe the requirement of an environmental impact statement in NEPA as not protecting the claimants' interests. In essence, the Court interpreted NEPA's requirement of an environmental policy statement as protecting individuals' "aesthetic and environmental well-being," no less than their financial well-being.[72]

In contrast, the *Sierra Club* plaintiffs principally relied for standing upon section 10(a) of the APA.[73] The cost of denying standing, therefore, may well have been lower in *Sierra Club* than in *SCRAP* because the plaintiffs in the latter case had relied upon a federal statute that was at least arguably susceptible to a construction affording them protection. In effect, the Supreme Court's zone-of-interest test, which emerged in *Data Processing*, recognizes that statutory standing denials necessarily imply that Congress did not intend the statute under review to protect the plaintiff's claimed interests. Indeed, that is among the critical differences between constitutional and statutory standing denials. When the Court denies standing based upon the Constitution, it says nothing, necessarily, about the merits of the underlying claim. But when the Court denies standing based upon a statute, it implicitly holds that the statute is not intended to protect, or does not by its wording protect, the claimed right on the facts of the case. Thus, while a constitutional standing denial generates an alternative and generally more modest substantive holding, a statutory standing denial is tantamount to a denial *on the merits* of the underlying claim.

In distinguishing *Sierra Club,* the *SCRAP* Court spoke largely in terms of third-party standing, claiming that the difficulty in *Sierra Club,* which was overcome in *SCRAP,* was that the plaintiffs had failed to allege that *they* were adversely affected by the government's conduct.[74] The Court's distinction, if adhered to, would appear to relegate the third-party standing doctrine to the status of an empty pleading requirement. After all, the Sierra Club certainly has sufficient resources with which to secure members who are users of virtually every national park or to send one of its members to every national park that is the subject of its planned litigation. The Court's third-party standing language notwithstanding, applying the shadow case analysis to these cases reveals that something greater may have been at stake.

In *SCRAP,* the litigants alleged that the ICC failed to comply with a particular federal statute, the language of which suggested a right of public enforcement.[75] In *Sierra Club,* the plaintiffs presented statutory and regulatory challenges that, with the possible exception of the regulatory public hearing provisions,[76] they claimed harmed others. Denying standing in *Sierra Club* did not, therefore, require the Court to determine whether Congress intended to confer standing upon individuals who alleged injuries resulting from claimed statutory violations. Instead, by holding that the Sierra Club did not have the right to enforce the rights of persons who may be harmed in the future, the Court allowed itself to wait for a proper shadow case before construing the cited statutes. In a proper shadow case, someone who used the park could force the Court to determine whether the particular statute upon which the Sierra Club relied was intended to confer standing upon him or her.

In contrast, given that the *SCRAP* plaintiffs alleged that they themselves were harmed, there was no obvious shadow case. Denying standing in *SCRAP* would necessarily have meant that, as a matter of substantive statutory interpretation, the requirement of an environmental impact statement under section 102(2)(C) of NEPA was not intended to protect individuals whose use of public recreational areas might be adversely affected by the resulting government activity. Thus, denying standing in *SCRAP* would have meant that, as a matter of substantive law, the plaintiffs did not fall within the relevant zone of interest of NEPA's procedural provisions. But because the *SCRAP* plaintiffs claimed to be using public lands that would be harmed by the rate increase, the obvious question such a ruling would raise is whom those provisions were intended to protect. In contrast, in *Sierra Club,* because the plaintiffs failed to allege that they themselves were harmed, the standing denial did not require the Court to issue a substantive determination on the scope of the underlying statutes.

When the Supreme Court or a lower federal court denies standing to press a constitutional claim, the Court can avoid substantively construing the cited constitutional provision by holding that the claimant lacks standing. The standing denial satisfies the Court's collective obligation to resolve the case, while, at the same time, it leaves open the underlying substantive issue either for Congress to resolve or for itself to resolve in a case in which it cannot avoid making law. Such cases include proper criminal appeals and collateral attacks. But when the basis for a claim is, instead, a federal statute, a determination that the claimant lacks standing necessarily means that, on the facts of the case, the statute does not afford relief, or stated differently, that the claimants do not fall within the statute's zone of interest. A denial of standing in the statutory context, therefore, *is* an assessment of the merits of the underlying claim. At the very least, this means that the cost of denying standing in a case in which the claimant relies upon a federal statute (independent of section 10(a) of the APA, which itself is but a conduit to vindicate a substantive claim arising under another federal statute) is higher than the cost of denying standing in a case in which the claimant relies solely upon the Constitution. Because the Sierra Club did not allege a credible statutory injury, the standing denial in *Sierra Club* was less costly in terms of the judicial creation of positive law than a standing denial in *SCRAP* would have been.

For two more recent cases, which aptly illustrate this point, consider *International Primate Protection League v. Administrators of Tulane Educational Fund,*[77] and *Air Courier Conference of America v. American Postal Workers Union.*[78] In *International Primate Protection League,* the Supreme Court held that the plaintiffs, who had filed a lawsuit in a Louisiana state court challenging experiments on primates, had standing to challenge the removal of their action to federal court by the National Institutes of Health ("NIH"), even though the Court agreed that, had they filed their lawsuit in federal court, the plaintiffs would have lacked standing to pursue their underlying legal claim. To understand the seeming counterintuition that claimants have standing to challenge the removal and dismissal in federal court of a suit for which they presumably lack standing, it is important to consider the purpose of the underlying federal removal statute.[79] The plaintiffs argued that the federal removal statute was intended to allow only federal officials, and not federal agencies, including NIH, to remove suits filed in state court to federal court. Conversely, the statute was intended to protect the choice of forum by litigants against whom removal was improper. Thus, whatever the merit (or lack thereof) of their underlying claim, plaintiffs fell squarely within the protected zone of interest of the federal removal statute and thus had standing to ensure that their claim would be presented (and probably dismissed) in the forum of their choosing.[80]

In contrast, in *Air Courier Conference of America*,[81] the Court denied standing to the plaintiffs, including the postal union, to challenge an exception to the postal monopoly established in a group of statutes referred to as Private Express Statutes ("PES"), involving international remailing. The PES were reenacted as part of the Postal Reorganization Act ("PRA"). In conferring standing upon the postal union, the Court of Appeals determined that the "key impetus and principal purpose of the PRA was to implement various labor reforms that would improve pay, working conditions and labor-management relations for postal workers."[82] The issue in the case was whether the union could claim standing to challenge the exception to the postal monopoly pursuant to the PES, based upon the protections afforded workers under the PRA. In reversing and denying standing, Chief Justice Rehnquist determined that the historical justification for establishing the postal monopoly, which the PES relaxed, was not to benefit postal workers. Instead, it was to ensure that potential competitors with the postal service did not elect to compete in only the most profitable postal routes, thereby driving down the price in those areas, and leaving the postal service to serve the more costly outlying areas without the benefit of cross subsidization. In essence, the postal monopoly was established in recognition of the high fixed costs associated with maintaining a national mailing service. To provide equal cost service throughout the nation, it was essential to provide monopoly power to the postal service, which would allow the profits from the lower cost routes to subsidize the additional costs of service to the less profitable routes. Because this history did not reflect a desire to ensure that the postal employees received the benefits of working in a monopolistic industry, the Court denied the postal union standing.

As in *SCRAP*, each of these statutory standing cases represents a substantive ruling. In *International Primate*, the Court ruled that the federal removal statute protected the right of state court plaintiffs to their choice of forum, regardless of the merits of the underlying claims. In *Air Courier*, the Court held that the postal employees had no right to the employment security and benefits associated with the continued existence of the federal postal monopoly. Both of these holdings appear to be defensible applications of the Court's zone-of-interest test. What renders these holdings legitimate is their apparent fidelity to the intended scope of the underlying statutes on which the claims of standing are based. The removal statute is rather obviously intended to allow the removal of a certain class of state lawsuits by particular defendants to federal court, for which the federal court would have had proper jurisdiction originally. Conversely, the statute is intended to protect the choice of forum by plaintiffs when an improper defendant attempts removal or when the federal court would have lacked original jurisdiction, and thus when removal is improper. A contrary ruling in *International Primate* would have prevented state court plaintiffs from challenging the removal of their lawsuits in the future unless the federal court determined that the state law claim was meritorious. Because the merits of most underlying claims, including justiciability determinations surrounding those claims, are more difficult to evaluate than those in *International Primate,* a contrary holding would have undermined the statute's intended protection of choice of forum by state court plaintiffs in cases in which removal is improper. In contrast, the postal monopoly statute was rather obviously intended to facilitate the delivery of mail in a cost-effective manner at a time when the start-up costs of establishing a national postal service were viewed as potentially prohibitive. Over time, however, Congress recognized that certain related services provided by the United States, including international remailing, no longer need to be safeguarded from competition to promote the original purpose of the postal monopoly. Congress therefore relaxed that part of the monopoly. Allowing the postal employees to challenge the removal of the monopoly would have created the potential for any federal employees to challenge in federal court changes in the structure of the agencies for which they work, if those changes potentially operated to the detriment of their employment. *Air Courier* appears sound as a matter of constitutional process because it presumptively denies standing to federal employees who might raise other, potentially frivolous, lawsuits challenging changes in working conditions that result from amendments to mandating statutes, the primary purpose of which was not to benefit them.

3. Summary of Analysis

This discussion has illustrated two important points underlying the presumptive rule against enforcing the rights of others. First, the rule's purpose is neither to ensure zealous advocacy nor to ensure concreteness of injury at some abstract level. Instead, the rule is intended to prevent the strategic timing of cases and to preserve the autonomy of the legislature to make, or not to make, positive law unless and until an appropriate consensus has formed. This concern is especially acute on a court prone to multidimensionality, and occasionally asymmetry, and thus to issuing path dependent bodies of case law. Second, because third-party standing rests ultimately on separation-of-powers concerns, the doctrine, however it is formally characterized, is logically presumptive, or prudential, in nature, at least with respect to Congress.

This analysis further suggests that the Court should be less inclined to dismiss on standing grounds cases in which plaintiffs rely upon a federal statute the violation of which, they allege, harms them, than cases in which plaintiffs rely for such claims principally upon the Constitution or section 10(a) of the APA. In addition, the Court should be less inclined to dismiss on standing grounds cases in which plaintiffs rely upon federal statutes, the violation of which harms third parties, when the statutes appear to invite such claims. In nonstatutory standing cases, the Court, relying upon such metaphors as zealousness and injury in fact, considers whether it should shift the burden of legislative inertia. At the very least, denying standing when a plaintiff advances a direct claim of injury based upon a federal statutory violation is, therefore, a more costly judicial endeavor, because in such cases, the Court's standing determination is inevitably a substantive ruling on whether plaintiffs fall within the relevant zone of interest of the statute under review. As the discussion of the next two standing ground rules will demonstrate, litigants can strategically time cases through other means than by seeking to enforce the rights of others.

B. No Right to Prevent Diffuse Harms

Because interest groups can manipulate the path of case law in more than one way, a presumptive prohibition against enforcing the rights of others is not alone sufficient to prevent advertent path manipulation by ideological, non-Condorcet-winning interests. If prevented from vindicating the claims of others, ideological interest groups could instead argue that they themselves are harmed by the fact of governmental conduct in violation of the law. Indeed, ideological interest groups could raise such claims even if no person was directly affected by the challenged governmental conduct. In *Valley Forge Christian College v. Americans United for the Separation of Church and State, Inc.*,[83] for example, the Supreme Court denied the claimant standing to challenge a government land grant to a sectarian college. The ruling in *Valley Forge,* as with any denial of standing, can readily be transformed into a substantive ruling: Plaintiffs lack the right to prevent the government from transferring real property, owned by the citizenry at large, to a sectarian college, allegedly in violation of the First Amendment establishment clause, because the resulting harm to any particular citizen is too small. *Flast v. Cohen,*[84] which preceded *Valley Forge,* represents a nearly opposite substantive holding. In allowing the plaintiffs to challenge the grant of tax revenues to a church on establishment clause grounds, the *Flast* Court held that individuals have the right as taxpayers to challenge the expenditure of federal tax dollars to benefit a church. The Court reasoned that while the resulting injury to any particular taxpayer is de minimis, there is a peculiar nexus between the expenditure of tax dollars and the establishment clause. As demonstrated below, when plaintiffs seek standing based upon the Constitution to prevent a generalized harm, *Valley Forge* more closely represents the rule and *Flast,* an exception, probably owing to the Warren Court's general relaxation of standing to invite novel constitutional challenges.[85]

The two most well known diffuse harm cases are *Schlesinger v. Reservists Committee to Stop the War*[86] and *United States v. Richardson*.[87] In *Schlesinger,* the Court denied standing to an organization attempting to unseat members of Congress who were members of the military reserves, based upon the Article I incompatibility clause, which provides that "no Person holding any Office under the United States, shall be a Member of either House during his Continuance in Office."[88] The Court reasoned that because all citizens were injured equally by Congress's allowing these representatives to be seated, plaintiff's injury was not sufficiently concrete for standing purposes. In a similar holding, issued the same term, the *Richardson* Court denied standing to a taxpayer who claimed that the Central Intelligence Agency Act of 1949, by providing that Central Intelligence Agency ("CIA") expenditures not be made public, violated the Article I statement and account clause. That clause provides that "a regular Statement and Account of the Receipts and Expenditures of all public Money shall be published from time to time."[89] The Court specifically rejected as a basis for conferring standing the plaintiff's argument that, if he were denied standing, no one would have the power to challenge the constitutionality of the statute. The Court reasoned that the Framers had not set up an "Athenian democracy or a New England town meeting to oversee the conduct of the National Government by means of lawsuits in federal courts." Instead, the Court noted, our representative form of government, while slow to action, provides alternative means of redress to dissatisfied citizens, namely the political process.

As in the context of third-party standing, Congress's power to rebut the presumptive standing rule, thus converting generalized grievances into individual rights enforceable in federal court, has long been assumed. Perhaps the most well known examples illustrating this proposition are the Freedom of Information Act,[90] which transforms government accountability into the status of individual right; the Fair Housing Act cases,[91] described above, in which the Court has affirmed Congress's power to confer upon individuals the right to have housing information disseminated fairly and without regard to race; and, until recently, cases that have upheld the broad-based standing provisions contained in several federal environmental statutes.[92] In each context, the Court has affirmed Congress's power to transform a generalized interest into an individual right. These cases and statutes strongly suggest that the principal basis for standing has, until quite recently in any event, rested primarily on the Article III case or controversy requirement and the desire of the federal courts to protect Congress's power to make or not to make law as it deems appropriate. Thus, when Congress chooses to convert third-party rights or generalized harms into individual rights enforceable in federal court, the Court has generally not superimposed its standing requirements to limit standing among those relying for justiciability upon such statutes. Perhaps the Court's clearest articulation distinguishing constitutional from statutory standing was Justice Marshall's assertion in *Linda R.S.*

v. Richard D.[93] that "Congress may enact statutes creating legal rights, the invasion of which creates standing, even though no injury would exist without the statute." This distinction has allowed the Supreme Court to employ the diffuse harms standing barrier to limit relatively low-cost path manipulation of constitutional claims, while, at the same time, it has preserved the power of Congress to define novel causes of action. The 1992 Supreme Court decision, *Lujan v. Defenders of Wildlife,*[94] significantly challenged this conception of standing.[95] The *Lujan* court denied standing to environmental plaintiffs who relied upon a broadly worded standing provision in the Endangered Species Act to challenge federal agency funding of projects abroad, which, they alleged, harmed the habitats of endangered species. Writing for the *Lujan* Court, Justice Scalia stated that "[t]here is absolutely no basis for making the Article III [standing] inquiry turn on the source of the asserted right." Before revisiting the question of congressional grants of standing and providing an analysis of *Lujan* and its progeny, however, we must first consider the final constitutional standing case category, no right to an undistorted market.

C. No Right to an Undistorted Market

As demonstrated above, the Supreme Court often employs technical language in its standing cases to give those rulings a procedural rather than substantive gloss. A careful analysis of the standing cases, therefore, requires that we pierce the language to identify the underlying substantive legal rulings that the standing denials represent. The point is perhaps best illustrated by comparing three actual standing cases, in which the Supreme Court ultimately held that the plaintiff has no right to the benefits of a market that is undistorted by an allegedly unconstitutional regulatory practice, even if she credibly alleges that removing that market distortion would ultimately inure to her benefit. In two cases discussed in chapter 1, *Allen v. Wright*[96] and *Board of Regents v. Bakke,*[97] the Court appears to have issued rulings resting upon opposite standing principles. Reconsidering these cases here, along with others falling into this standing category, will help to illustrate the social choice and separation of powers dimensions that underlie the Supreme Court's standing precedents.

Recall that in *Allen,* the parents of African American schoolchildren, who were attending public schools throughout the United States, challenged an Internal Revenue Service ("IRS") tax policy on equal protection grounds. Plaintiffs alleged that the IRS policy based the tax status of private schools on the status of the umbrella organization of which the schools were a part, rather than on the schools' individual merits, and that, but for the policy, plaintiffs' children would have had a greater likelihood of receiving an integrated public school education. The *Allen* plaintiffs alleged that, based upon this tax policy, the IRS had afforded tax-exempt status to numerous private schools engaging in racially discriminatory practices throughout the United States. The plaintiffs did not allege that any of their children had applied to, or had been denied admission into, the private schools that had been given tax-exempt status. In fact, all of the plaintiffs' children attended public schools. Instead, the plaintiffs alleged that if the tax policy were struck down on equal protection clause grounds, their children would have had a greater likelihood of receiving an integrated public school education. The *Allen* Court held that the plaintiffs lacked standing, observing that the number of links in the causal chain between the allegedly unconstitutional tax policy and the students' denial of an integrated education was too attenuated to satisfy the Court's causation test. Extending the analysis used in the above discussion of third-party standing, we can translate the denial of standing in *Allen* into a substantive legal ruling. The *Allen* Court effectively ruled that parents of African American schoolchildren attending public schools have no legal right to a public and private education marketplace that is undistorted by allegedly unconstitutional tax incentives, even where plaintiffs allege that removing the market distortion would ultimately inure to their children's benefit.[98]

The Court had employed a similar causal-chain analysis to deny standing in two earlier standing cases, *Warth v. Seldin*[99] and *Simon v. Eastern Kentucky Welfare Rights Organization*.[100] In *Warth,* the Supreme Court denied standing to a group of residents and organizations in Rochester, New York, who alleged that a zoning ordinance in the neighboring town of Penfield prevented them from securing housing in Penfield, thus discriminating against them in violation of the Fourteenth Amendment equal protection clause on the basis of their income and racial minority status. Plaintiffs alleged that, as a result, their property taxes in neighboring Rochester had increased. As in *Allen,* the plaintiffs did not allege that had the zoning ordinance been struck down, they would necessarily have been successful in their efforts to secure low- to moderate-income housing in Penfield.[101] They did claim, however, that the zoning ordinance caused them to secure less desirable, and more expensive, housing elsewhere. Again, piercing the Court's analysis of the plaintiffs' alleged injury in fact reveals that the Court, in denying standing to the *Warth* claimants, engaged in an important substantive legal determination, rather than a merely technical procedural ruling. In effect, the Court held that the plaintiffs did not have the right to a housing market that was undistorted by an allegedly unconstitutional zoning ordinance.

Finally, in *Simon,* the Court denied standing to a group of indigents challenging an IRS tax policy affording tax-exempt status to hospitals that provided only emergency medical services to the poor, allegedly in violation of the Internal Revenue Code.[102] As in both *Allen* and *Warth,* the plaintiffs did not allege that if the IRS policy were struck down, they would necessarily have secured medical services in the private hospitals that were afforded tax-exempt status. Instead, they alleged that if the tax-exempt status were removed, and if conferring tax-exempt status were conditioned upon providing indigents with medical services, more medical services might become available to them in the future. In denying standing, the Court again focused on third-party links in the chain of causation, including hospitals not party to the lawsuit, and concluded that, even if the tax-exempt status were removed, there was no guarantee that the hospitals in question would provide more medical services to the poor. Stating this as a substantive ruling, rather than as a standing determination, the *Simon* Court held that plaintiffs have no legal right to a market for medical services for the poor that is undistorted by tax incentives created by IRS operating policies allegedly in violation of the Internal Revenue Code.

By transforming each of these standing determinations into a substantive legal rule, I do not intend to suggest that any of them is necessarily incorrect. In fact, from the perspective of constitutional process, each of the rulings appears normatively defensible. In the absence of a judicial ruling striking down the IRS tax provisions and the Penfield zoning ordinance, the question remains where such lawmaking responsibility properly rests. The most obvious place, of course, is in Congress or the state legislature. This is especially true in the *Allen* and *Simon* cases, where the allegedly illegal rule is an IRS tax policy, which Congress has full authority to reverse by statute.[103]

In evaluating these cases, it is helpful to contrast the landmark decision *Marbury v. Madison,*[104] in which the Supreme Court established the power of judicial review. While Chief Justice Marshall, writing in *Marbury,* did not cast the holding in these terms, we can now express the power of judicial review created in that opinion as follows: When Congress acts by statute, and when the statute violates the Constitution, it is both the province and the duty of the Supreme Court to *invalidate* that congressional *action* by striking the statute down. The *Allen* and *Simon* holdings can be recast in parallel fashion: When Congress *fails* to act and when its failure to act allegedly results in a constitutional violation, the Court generally will *not invalidate* congressional *inaction,* thereby creating positive law on Congress's behalf. Instead, the Court, unless forced to create positive law in a case where it cannot decline to do so, will prefer to wait for an appropriate, and presumably Condorcet-winning, consensus to form in Congress. Because the Court is unable to ensure that its rulings will implement a Condorcet winner, its reluctance to overcome congressional inertia, except when absolutely necessary, is understandable.

But the comparison remains incomplete until we consider a critical third group of cases in which the Supreme Court regularly supplants legislative inaction, including that of Congress, with new substantive constitutional rulings. This category is, of course, criminal procedure. Thus, for example, in *Weeks v. United States,*[105] in which the Supreme Court established the exclusionary rule for illegally seized evidence under the Fourth Amendment, and in *Mapp v. Ohio,*[106] in which it applied that rule to the states under the Fourteenth Amendment, the Court overcame the burden of legislative inertia. It did so by choosing from the potential set of remedies then available to legislatures a single remedy for the identified constitutional violation, in the face of legislative silence. The same holds true in *Miranda v. Arizona.*[107] In that case, the Court selected from the potential range of legislative options (and applied that remedy to benefit the litigant before it) the prophylactic requirement of the now-famous *Miranda* warnings when faced with a coerced confession that violated the Fifth Amendment privilege against self-incrimination. In each case, the Supreme Court effectively selected for the legislature one of several potential remedies for the identified constitutional violation in a context in which the failure to select a remedy would have been direct and severe for the defendant. In doing so, the Court implicitly recognized that the conditions for overcoming the burden of legislative inertia had been amply satisfied. As this book is going to press, the Supreme Court is considering whether Congress acted within its constitutional authority in substituting *Miranda* with an alternative set of remedies for allegedly coerced confessions.[108] It is important to remember, however, that the absence of any statutory remedy at the time that the Court issued the decisions establishing the exclusionary rule and the requirement of *Miranda* warnings suggests that political support for their creation was then lacking. In contrast with Congress, which could avoid resolving such issues, the Court, when confronted with an established constitutional violation, was required to establish a meaningful remedy in order to resolve the case. This, of course, brings us back to the early insight that the Supreme Court, given its collective obligation to produce case results, has evolved away from Condorcet-producing rules, which, because they confer unlimited majority veto, risk undermining that collective obligation.[109]

With this three-part division of justiciability in mind, represented by *Marbury, Allen,* and *Weeks,* it is now worth noting an important distinction between this grouping of standing cases, no right to an undistorted market, and the first two groupings discussed above, no right to enforce the rights of others or to prevent diffuse harms. Denials of third-party standing are implicitly premised upon the existence of a shadow case in which some other potential litigant can raise the identical claim without a credible standing barrier. And denials of standing to challenge diffuse harms are implicitly premised upon the intuition that third-party standing claims can easily be recast as diffuse harms claims, thus inviting anew litigant path manipulation. Cases in this final category, in contrast, are premised on the notion that, with slightly altered facts, the same claimants would be better situated to present a judicially cognizable claim. In *Allen,* for example, the plaintiffs would have been able to present a cognizable claim challenging the IRS policy if their children had applied to and been rejected from the discriminatory private schools receiving favorable tax treatment. Similarly, in *Warth,* the plaintiffs would have been able to present a more cognizable claim challenging the Penfield ordinance if they had themselves applied for a variance, which had been denied, based upon race or upon a wealth classification. That is not to suggest that the plaintiffs would necessarily have prevailed had the facts differed. It is only to suggest that they would more likely have been afforded standing. The Court did not deny standing in these cases because the plaintiffs were less well suited than some other person; it denied standing because the underlying legal issue would have been better presented in a case with different facts.

These results, of course, raise the question as to why the Court viewed the facts alleged in these cases as deficient for standing purposes. The social choice analysis suggests that in these standing cases, the Court is seeking facts that appear closer to the traditional bipolar litigation end of the spectrum than to the interest group path manipulation end, which is typified by cases in the third-party standing and diffuse harms categories. Specifically, the Court is looking for facts that more closely correlate with fortuitous conditions, beyond the claimants' control, as the justification for resolving the underlying case issues, as opposed to leaving such issues for potential future resolution in the legislature. But because the Court has employed metaphors that capture only part of the relevant justiciability image, it has rendered decisions that appear inconsistent. As set out below, inconsistencies arise because the cases in this third category in which standing is either granted or denied are distinguishable, not in kind, but in degree. Superimposing ill-fitting metaphors to categorize these cases, therefore, creates the anomaly revealed below that, with little effort, the language in a case in which standing was granted can be used to recharacterize the case such that standing should have been denied. The reverse also holds.

For that very reason, the *Allen, Simon,* and *Warth* cases might appear troublesome to many readers. In these cases, the Court has used standing to deny seemingly powerful legal claims related to the integration of public schools, the provision of medical services, and the availability of housing for minorities and the poor. The cases seem particularly troublesome when they are contrasted with those cases in which the Court, notwithstanding congressional silence, has willingly created very detailed and codelike interpretations of broad-based constitutional clauses, including the equal protection clause. Why, then, did the Court decline to make positive law on the scope of the equal protection clause when faced with congressional inertia on issues as important as those presented in these cases? And why did it decline to address the underlying legal claims when, in the very act of denying standing, the Court inevitably made an alternative substantive legal ruling, namely that plaintiffs have no right to the benefits of a market that is undistorted by allegedly unconstitutional laws? Again, to understand the anomaly, we need to consider the options that the *Allen* and *Simon* Courts faced.

The *Allen* and *Simon* Courts faced two alternatives. First, those Courts could have allowed the litigants to force the federal judiciary to monitor the IRS's internal operating policies, even though that is generally a congressional function and even though the Court could not guarantee that in doing so it would not generate an unfavorable path of case law through the expansion of dimensionality or that it would not issue an immediate ruling that was the product of asymmetry, and thus that would thwart the will of a majority of its own members. Second, those Courts could have issued a more modest substantive ruling, on which a majority of justices could agree, that claimants do not have the right to come into court to have removed an allegedly illegal market distortion. The latter option does not prevent the underlying issues from ever reaching the Court. If, for example, the parents of an applicant to a private school who had been rejected based upon race brought suit seeking admission, and if the Court ruled that as a result of its tax exempt status, the school could not discriminate on racial grounds in its admissions processes, the decision would then force the school to abandon either its tax exempt status or its racially discriminating admissions policies. That, of course, is the very choice that the *Allen* plaintiffs sought to impose upon such schools, but in a factual context in which the Court denied standing. Using the Court's own metaphors, the hypothetical case, like the traditional case in which the Court resolves the legal claims of convicted criminals on appeal, possesses those qualities that resemble the tort elements of injury, causation, and redressibility. The hypothetical case does not resemble—or at least does not resemble as much as the original *Allen* claim—an attempt by an ideological litigant to shift the burden of legislative inertia onto the federal courts. Neither of the options that the Court faced in *Allen* was ideal, but the standing denial more closely accords with limiting judicial lawmaking to an ad hoc and as-needed basis.

While the Court, in effect, chose what it considered to be the least bad of two imperfect options in these cases, the inconsistency with which it applied its standing analysis makes it difficult to predict how the Court will rule in any given case. Consider, for example, the following two standing cases issued within two days of each other, *Duke Power Co. v. Carolina Environmental Study Group, Inc.,*[110] and *Board of Regents v. Bakke,*[111] the second of which I have described already. In *Duke Power,* the plaintiffs, residents of a neighborhood adjacent to a proposed nuclear power plant and an environmental interest group, challenged the constitutionality of the Price-Anderson Act which set a $560 million liability cap for nuclear accidents. The plaintiffs did not allege that if the act's liability limit were struck down, the proposed construction would not proceed.[112] Instead, the plaintiffs alleged a substantial likelihood that the construction might not proceed if the potential cost of nuclear accidents had not been artificially capped by the act, which, they further alleged, violated their due process rights by preventing full recoveries in the event of a nuclear accident. As in the previous cases, the plaintiffs sought to have the Court remove an allegedly unconstitutional market distortion. Unlike the Courts in *Allen, Simon,* and *Warth,* however, the *Duke Power* Court, focusing on both the imminent nature of the potential reduction in the value of the plaintiffs' homes, and the much greater potential damage that would result in the event of a nuclear accident, granted standing.

Similarly, as we have already seen, the *Bakke* Court granted standing to the plaintiff, a white medical school applicant who had twice been rejected from medical school even though he did not allege that had he been allowed to compete for all of the seats (including the sixteen seats that had been set aside for minority applicants), he would have been admitted.[113] To justify the grant of standing, the Court defined Mr. Bakke's injury broadly. Rather than characterizing the injury as the denial of admission into the medical school, the Court determined that Mr. Bakke was injured in his exclusion from competition for all one hundred medical school seats and that this amounted to a violation of the equal protection clause.[114] The difficulty is that the very same reasoning could have been used to achieve a contrary result in both *Allen* and *Simon.*

If the *Allen* Court, for example, had defined the plaintiffs' injury, not as the denial of an integrated education (an assertion that the plaintiffs could not support because of the attenuated causal chain), but rather, as the denial of appropriate market incentives to foster integration, the plaintiffs' injury would have been no less concrete than that in *Bakke*. The same analysis applies in *Simon*, where if the Court had defined the relevant injury, not as the right to receive medical services (an assertion that, again, the plaintiffs could not support because of the attenuated causal chain), but instead as the right to a market for indigent medical services that is undistorted by illegal tax incentives, the causal chain would again have been no less attenuated than that in *Bakke*. Flipping the analysis around and broadening Mr. Bakke's claimed injury reveals the same doctrinal incongruity. Had the *Bakke* Court focused on the requisite links in the causal chain before Mr. Bakke would have been admitted to medical school, it might have found, as it did in *Allen* and *Simon*, that his alleged injury was insufficient to support standing. And *Duke Power* can be "flipped" in the same manner as *Bakke*.

Why, then, did the Court grant standing to the *Duke Power* plaintiffs and to Mr. Bakke when it denied standing to the *Allen* and *Simon* plaintiffs? Again, we need to consider the options that the Court faced. These cases are best viewed as representing points along the Supreme Court's expanded justiciability spectrum, depicted in table 6.1.[115] They are not different in kind, but they are different in degree. Differences in degree, however, can be both important and comprehensible. The *Duke Power* Court could have denied standing, ruling that the homeowners and environmental groups have no right to a marketplace unaffected by an arguably illegal distortion—the Price-Anderson Act's liability cap—even if without that cap the proposed construction might not proceed. Similarly, the *Bakke* Court could have ruled that Mr. Bakke has no right to an education market that is undistorted by a state's arguably unconstitutional selection criterion, even if he might benefit by the removal of that criterion.

To understand these cases, we must pierce the Court's rhetoric on such matters as injury in fact, causation, and redressibility, and focus instead on what these catchphrases are intended to capture. The social choice analysis reveals that these terms are metaphors intended to capture those circumstances in which plaintiffs have adequately alleged the need for the Court to consider shifting the burden of congressional inertia and to make positive law, even given the possibility that the Court's preferences might be multidimensional and perhaps even asymmetrical, and thus that judicial resolution could generate an unfavorable voting path or even produce a seemingly irrational result. Applying this analysis, we can place these cases, in their factual contexts, along the revised spectrum shown in table 6.2, which will help to explain the seemingly disparate results.

As demonstrated earlier, third-party standing operates as a presumptive rule that prevents ideological litigants from forcing favorable precedents through path manipulation by locating someone who is unaware of, or who has been sitting on, her rights. While such cases as *SCRAP* and *Sierra Club*, which lie at the outer edge of standing doctrine, might obfuscate the doctrine's purpose, the purpose is restored when we consider those cases at the core, namely those in which convicted criminals, who are only interested in

Table 6.2. No Right to an Undistorted Market Cases within Broader Justiciability Spectrum

Case Characteristics	Attenuated claim of injury; major pre-cedential impact, beyond immediate parties			Concrete claim of injury; facts arose due to events beyond litigants' control
Doctrines, Standing Categories, and Case Results	Ripeness/ mootness; rights of others; diffuse harms	No Right to an Undistorted Market		Criminal appeals and collateral challenges
		Allen; EKWRO; Warth	*Bakke; Duke Power*	
Analytical Spectrum	Presumption in favor of path manipulation ⟵——————————⟶			Presumption against path manipulation

securing relief on their own behalf with no larger agenda, seek favorable rulings. When convicted criminals raise constitutional challenges, the federal courts cannot avoid addressing the underlying claims on the merits, and thus cannot avoid shifting the burden of legislative inertia.

Thus viewed, *Sierra Club* might be seen as representing the opposite extreme, namely an effort to secure a favorable precedent where the justification for shifting the burden of legislative inertia is weak. Given the absence of concrete injuries and the ideological nature of the claims involved in *Sierra Club,* the political process seemed adequate to the task of resolving the issues presented. Except for the procedural protections in NEPA, the same analysis would likely have applied in *SCRAP.* Moreover, congressional resolution of these issues is less susceptible to path manipulation than is judicial resolution. As shown in table 6.2, the bolded box presents those cases falling into the standing category discussed in this subsection, no right to an undistorted market, which fall along a spectrum between those two extremes.

While it is true that in *Duke Power* relief on the merits, which was ultimately denied, would not have guaranteed that the proposed construction would have ceased, no shadow case existed in which the challenge could have been raised in a sufficiently timely manner to protect the plaintiffs' interests. Moreover, the very fact that a nuclear power plant was being proposed for construction near the plaintiffs' homes created a *present* injury in the form of reduced property values. If the construction ultimately proceeded, the reduction in value was likely to be severe. Thus viewed, *Duke Power* appears closer to those cases in which convicted criminals are attempting to force judicial creation of positive law to secure relief than it does to those in which the plaintiffs are attempting to manipulate the substantive evolution of legal doctrine by controlling the order of precedent.

Similarly, while the conferral of standing in *Bakke* would not have ensured that Mr. Bakke would be admitted to medical school, a contrary ruling on standing would certainly have prevented him from being admitted into the University of California at Davis Medical School. The *Bakke* Court likely ruled as it did because Bakke, having twice applied and having twice been denied admission into medical school, would probably never study medicine if the Court had not addressed the merits of his claim. Again, applying the Court's justiciability metaphors, Bakke's claim contained traditional notions of injury, causation, and redressibility, thus justifying the Court's decision to consider shifting the burden of congressional inertia. Thus viewed, *Duke Power* and *Bakke* are hybrids between the criminal procedure cases, in which a convicted criminal challenges her conviction and sentence on appeal, and the third-party and diffuse claims cases, in which a claimant is presumed to be attempting to manipulate the order of precedent in a Court that possesses potentially cyclical preferences. While these cases contain elements of both extremes along the spectrum, the Court likely viewed them as closer in kind to those involving criminal appeals, or at least traditional bipolar disputes. In contrast, the *Allen, Simon,* and *Warth* decisions appear closer to the other end of the spectrum in which ideological litigants are pressing generalized grievances because the chance of a favorable, non-Condorcet-winning ruling in the federal courts is greater than is the chance of securing non-Condorcet-winning legislation in Congress. This is partly reflected by the fact that the *Allen* and *Simon* plaintiffs, who were not seeking particular educational or medical benefits, were spread throughout the nation.

I do not intend to suggest that Bakke's claim or the *Duke Power* plaintiffs' claim was more important than those of the *Allen, Simon,* or *Warth* plaintiffs. In fact, in characterizing the injuries at stake in these cases, many would conclude that the rights to an integrated public school education, to the provision of medical services, and to the fair marketing of housing are more important, and perhaps more concrete at some level, than the rights not to have property values diminished or to study medicine. That is the point. Concreteness of injury is not an abstract inquiry. Instead, it is a metaphor, intended to capture a single but complex concept, namely the circumstances in which a litigant has provided a sufficiently compelling set of facts to justify forcing a Court prone to possessing cyclical preferences in a two-dimensional issue spectrum to shift the burden of legislative inertia.

D.   The Empirical Test Revisited

At the opening of chapter 5, I set out two alternative tests—or two points along a common analytical spectrum—for evaluating my social choice theory of standing. While a recent line of cases remains to be discussed, it is now appropriate to revisit the more stringent of those tests in light of the preceding historical and case evidence. If that test is met, then the laxer, accommodationist test, is also necessarily met. To justify claiming that my social-choice-based theory of standing is more robust than are existing models of standing, including political explanations, my theory would have to account for more, and more varied, data. These data include the history surrounding the adoption and transformation of standing, and the cases themselves. Most often, political explanations are irrefutable because in response to an apparent inconsistency, one need only say that "it's political."* For the same reason, such theories are also not scientific, meaning that they are not generally capable of being falsified. But in this case, even political explanations of standing are less robust than that which I offer. Political explanations fail to place standing within a broader justiciability spectrum, one that includes other bodies of case law, most notably constitutional criminal procedure. Such explanations are also not terribly nuanced in explaining the details of the standing cases themselves.

I do not deny the existence of inconsistencies within the standing case law. But I have argued that the shadow case analysis reveals the inconsistencies to be less pronounced than most commentators have admitted. Moreover, using this analysis helps to explain away several of the most notorious inconsistencies. If the social choice theory of standing accounts for more data than the next available theory, my model of standing should be regarded as having passed the test of robustness. Based upon the empirical evidence thus far, I would argue that the social choice model of standing better captures three critical sets of data than alternative theories: (1) the historical context in which the New Deal standing doctrine emerged and in which that doctrine was critically transformed during the Burger and Rehnquist Courts; (2) the jurisprudential independence of standing from related justiciability doctrines, including ripeness and mootness, and the question of whether a plaintiff has a cause of action; and (3) most importantly, the standing and nonstanding cases themselves. At a minimum, I would suggest that the theory advanced here can be combined with others to advance our general analysis of standing doctrine, thus satisfying the accommodationist test.

Before revisiting congressional grants of standing in a recent line of cases, it is worth contrasting another plausible political explanation. A more cynical analysis of standing might suggest the following alternative story: The Court, which until quite recently was overwhelmingly composed of upper- or upper-middle-class white males, is more sympathetic to the plights of a medical school applicant denied admission because of so-called reverse discrimination, or of a property owner whose property value is threatened, than to the parents of African American public schoolchildren or of indigents seeking either housing or medical services. At the very least, the former claims would appear to have a greater possibility of affecting the justices or those close to them than the latter claims. In fact, despite any apparent intuitive

---

*Recall that such explanations include positing standing as a judicial avoidance device or as a low cost mechanism for signaling potential future rulings on the merits. *See* *supra* chapter 4 § II. C.

appeal such a theory might hold, the explanation fails the test of accounting for more, and more varied, data than does the social choice model. Consistent with this explanation, we would not expect members of the Court to be particularly sympathetic to convicted criminals or even to criminal defendants. And yet, the Court routinely allows convicted criminals to bring to federal court countless—often frivolous—constitutional claims, which quite often compel the Court to make new law. In fact, as seen in the prior discussion of *Powers v. Ohio,*[116] and *Campbell v. Louisiana,*[117] the Court sometimes goes out of its way to permit the adjudication of claims that appear to defy its own justiciability principles, solely because the claim was presented in a criminal appeal. The analysis in this book accounts not only for more cases than political explanations of this sort, but also accounts for the relationship between the various justiciability doctrines and the voluminous body of case law under the general heading of constitutional criminal procedure. In short, even the generally nonfalsifiable standing-is-politics explanation is substantially less robust than the social choice model of standing.

VI. Congressional Grants of Standing Revisited: *Lujan, Bennett,* and *Raines*

In chapter 4, I explained that the Burger and Rehnquist Courts were prone to possessing cyclical preferences in a multidimensional issue spectrum due to a divergence among conservative justices on whether stare decisis provides its own neutral justification for declining to overrule some of the most controversial precedents from the more liberal Warren Court era. In fact, within standing doctrine itself, another parallel conservative divergence has recently emerged on the question whether Congress has the constitutional authority to define standing more broadly than is acceptable under traditional notions of injury, informed by the common law. Recall that in its earliest incarnation in the New Deal Court, when plaintiffs relied for standing upon a federal statute, the Court employed common law analogues to determine justiciability. In doing so, the New Deal Court allowed Congress to reverse its standing presumptions by statute. In this era, standing was a prudential justiciability barrier in which common law conceptions of injury were intended to facilitate judicial administration in the absence of a clear congressional mandate. As shown in the above discussion of diffuse harms standing, Congress has since expanded standing in a variety of contexts to allow claims of injury that lack clearly identifiable antecedents in the common law.[118]

Beginning in the famous 1992 decision *Lujan v. Defenders of Wildlife,*[119] the Supreme Court's moderates and conservatives have been divided over whether Congress's authority to define novel injuries is unlimited, or instead whether it is subject to an irreducible set of minimum justiciability requirements, each taken from the common law. Together with the more recent, unanimous decision *Bennett v. Spear,*[120] which construed the same standing provision from the Endangered Species Act ("ESA") that was at issue in *Lujan,* the Court has suggested two critical transformations of modern standing doctrine. First, these cases suggest the Court's willingness, using common law standing presumptions and zone-of-interest analysis, to effectively alter the design of a major federal statute. In *Lujan,* the Supreme Court denied standing to two environmentalists relying upon the ESA's broad standing provision, holding that they had failed to articulate a justiciable injury. In doing so, the *Lujan* Court suggested, contrary to long-standing federal court practice, that standing doctrine imposes a set of minimum justiciability criteria to which even Congress is bound. In the 1997 *Bennett* decision, the Court went further, holding that plaintiffs alleging economic injuries resulting from the government's compliance with the ESA fall within the zone of interest of the same ESA standing provision, even though they were seeking to limit, rather than to advance, the protection of endangered species. This counterintuitive result—denying standing under an environmental statute to protect endangered species, but allowing standing under the same statute to limit the protection of endangered species—follows from the Supreme Court's novel applications of the concepts of injury in fact and zone of interest.

These cases are remarkable in a second respect. Recall from the discussion of *Allen v. Wright* that Justice O'Connor rested the denial of standing on the Court's objective of preserving, at least until the Court could not avoid ruling on the underlying issue, the power of Congress to make law. That power included monitoring the executive branch as Congress saw fit. In this analysis, the constitutional underpinnings of standing rested firmly in Article III, and in the desire to prevent, through path manipulation or otherwise, the federal courts from making law in a manner inconsistent with fair constitutional process. Notably, fair constitutional process includes not thwarting congressional inertia except on an ad hoc and as-needed basis. Through the ESA's citizen-standing provision, Congress had established a vehicle for private attorneys general to use the federal courts as forums in which to ensure federal agency compliance with the ESA. In *Lujan,* plaintiffs were seeking to employ the ESA to ensure federal agency compliance in two foreign projects that, they alleged, threatened the habitats of endangered species. In denying standing, the *Lujan* Court noted that standing not only furthered the objective of judicial discretion, but that it also prevented individuals from using the federal courts to monitor executive agencies. The *Lujan* Court thus suggested that the constitutional underpinnings rest, at least in part, in Article II and in the desire to protect the executive branch, in addition to Article III.[121] Because of the importance of these cases, I will discuss each more fully below.

In *Lujan,* the Supreme Court denied standing to environmentalist plaintiffs under the ESA's citizen-suit provision. Under the ESA, which divides the responsibilities for protecting endangered species between the secretary of the interior and the secretary of commerce, federal agencies whose activities might endanger such species are required to consult with the secretary of the interior. Reversing a prior joint regulation, which required interagency consultation for all agency activities that might jeopardize endangered species in the United States, on the high seas, and in foreign nations, the secretary of the interior and the secretary of commerce issued a revised joint rule reinterpreting the ESA. In the revised rule, the two departments limited the geographic scope of the statute for purposes of interagency consultation to those activities within the borders of the United States or on the high seas. The plaintiffs, environmental organizations and two citizens interested in preserving the habitats of particular endangered species abroad, sued the secretary of the interior, claiming that federal agencies were funding projects that jeopardized the habitats of particular endangered species abroad without having first consulted the secretary of the interior. The plaintiffs claimed that the revised joint rule, which did not require such consultation given that the threatened habitats were within foreign nations, violated the ESA's substantive provisions requiring interagency consultation.

Plaintiffs relied for standing upon the following citizen-suit provision contained in the ESA: "[A]ny person may commence a civil suit on his own behalf (a) to enjoin any person, including the United States and any other governmental instrumentality or agency . . . who is alleged to be in violation of any provision of this chapter."[122] In denying the plaintiffs standing, Justice Scalia, writing in part for a majority and in part for a plurality of four, determined that plaintiffs had failed to satisfy both the injury and redressability prongs of the Court's standing formulation. The majority rejected each of three injury theories: first, an actual injury grounded in the plaintiffs' interest in the species whose habitats were endangered by projects that received partial funding from federal agencies; second, a procedural injury resulting from the failure of the relevant agencies to consult with the secretary of the interior, as required by statute; and third, and most importantly, three nexus theories under which individuals with an interest in endangered species, or who use any part of a contiguous ecosystem, are afforded standing when the habitats of those species, or any part of their ecosystems, are endangered.

One petitioner averred by affidavit that she had traveled to Egypt in 1986, where she "observed the traditional habitat of the endangered Nile crocodile," and that, although she did not see the crocodile directly, she hoped to do so when she next traveled to Egypt. She admitted, however, that she had no specific plans to return. Another petitioner averred that she had traveled to Sri Lanka, where she observed the habitat of the Asian elephant and the leopard, which, she alleged, was threatened by a project funded by the federal Agency for International Development ("AID"). In a subsequent deposition, the same petitioner admitted that, although she hoped to return to Sri Lanka, she had no specific plans because that country was engaged in a civil war. Both petitioners alleged that the failure of the agencies funding the programs abroad to consult with the secretary of the interior, as required by statute, had injured them.

Writing for a majority, Justice Scalia stated that, even assuming, which he found questionable, that "these affidavits contain facts showing that certain agency-funded projects threaten listed species," the petitioners lacked the requisite injury to justify granting them standing under the statute. Justice Scalia held for the Court that "'some day' intentions—without any description of concrete plans, or indeed even any specification of *when* the some day will be—do not support a finding of the 'actual or imminent' injury that our cases require." Justice Scalia also rejected the petitioners' claim that the ESA's citizen-suit provision, quoted above, created in all persons a right to challenge the failure of a funding agency to consult with the secretary of the interior. Scalia thus rejected the analysis used by the United States Court of Appeals for the Eighth Circuit, which had denied the government's motion for summary judgment on standing, stating:

> To understand the remarkable nature of [the Eighth Circuit holding] one must be clear about what it does *not* rest upon: This is not a case where plaintiffs are seeking to enforce a procedural requirement the disregard of which could impair a separate concrete interest of theirs (*e.g.*, the procedural requirement for a hearing prior to a denial of their license application, or the procedural requirement for an environmental impact statement before a federal facility is constructed next door to them). Nor is it simply a case where concrete injury has been suffered by many persons, as in mass fraud or mass tort situations. Nor, finally, is it the unusual case in which Congress has created a concrete private interest in the outcome of a suit against a private party for the Government's benefit, by providing a cash bounty for the victorious plaintiff. Rather, the court held that the injury-in-fact requirement had been satisfied by congressional conferral upon *all* persons of an abstract, self-contained, noninstrumental "right" to have the Executive observe the procedures required by law. We reject this view.

As stated above, *Lujan* marks an important rift within the present Supreme Court concerning the constitutional underpinnings of standing. In criticizing Justice Scalia's rejection of the plaintiffs' claim of injury, Justice Blackmun, joined by Justice O'Connor (who authored the *Allen* decision), wrote in dissent:

> The Court expresses concern that allowing judicial enforcement of "agencies' observance of a particular, statutorily prescribed procedure" would "transfer from the President to the courts the Chief Executive's most important constitutional duty, to 'take Care that the Laws be faithfully executed,' Art. II, § 3." . . . In fact, the principal effect of foreclosing judicial enforcement of such procedures is to transfer power into the hands of the Executive at the expense—not of the courts—but of Congress, from which that power originates and emanates.[123]

Finally, Justice Kennedy offered a third position:

In my view, Congress has the power to define injuries and articulate chains of causation that will give rise to a case or controversy where none existed before, and I do not read the Court's opinion to suggest a contrary view. . . . In exercising this power, however, Congress must at the very least identify the injury it seeks to vindicate and relate the injury to the class of persons entitled to bring suit.[124]

While Kennedy tried to strike a middle ground between the Scalia and Blackmun opinions, if adopted, his suggestion would appear to render *Lujan* fairly inconsequential. Congress could then avoid the *Lujan* result by simply defining as injured, persons who intend to travel to locations in which federal agency funding, in violation of the ESA, threatens the habitats of endangered species. Fairly read, Justice Scalia's majority opinion does not appear to countenance this form of subterfuge for its more rigid injury requirement based upon analogues from the common law.

In any event, if, as Justices Blackmun and O'Connor suggest, the constitutional basis of standing lies in the Court's desire to protect Congress's power to monitor the executive branch, it follows that courts should treat a claim of standing based upon a federal statute differently from a claim of standing based upon a constitutional provision. By conferring standing to enforce claimed substantive rights based upon broad constitutional provisions, the Court effectively shifts the burden of congressional inertia. In doing so, the Court might effectively prevent Congress, to the extent that the underlying ruling is grounded in constitutional interpretation, from acting in the future, should a Condorcet-winning legislative preference then arise. In contrast, when faced with a federal statute that confers standing to press an otherwise generalized grievance against the executive branch, that is no longer a concern. Superimposing an abstract injury-in-fact requirement as a precondition to congressional grants of standing has the ironic effect of protecting Congress's power to enact Condorcet-winning statutes by striking down Condorcet-winning statutes. If that sounds nonsensical, that is the point.

Consider, for example, Justice Scalia's assertion in *Lujan* that "there is absolutely no basis for making the Article III inquiry [on injury in fact] turn on the source of the asserted right." While the analysis allowed the Court to prevent a claim that it might have preferred to avoid, either because of its potential for inviting future challenges based upon broadly worded standing provisions within federal statutes, or because of the underlying policy of using federal courts to curtail federal agency conduct allegedly harming endangered species or their habitats abroad, the effect was to limit Congress's power to govern through its method of choice, rather than to protect its ability to govern in the future. Alternatively, if, as Scalia appears to suggest, the constitutional foundation of standing rests upon the Court's desire to protect the executive branch from judicial interference, then whole bodies of constitutional precedent become difficult to comprehend. Consider, for example, Justice Scalia's claimed reliance upon *Marbury v. Madison*,[125] for the proposition that "[t]he province of the court . . . is, solely, to decide on the rights of individuals."[126] In the paragraph of *Marbury* that followed this quote, Chief Justice Marshall went on to state:

> if it be no intermeddling with a subject, over which the executive can be considered as having exercised any control; what is there in the exalted station of the officer, which shall bar a citizen from asserting, in a court of justice, his legal rights, or shall forbid a court to listen to the claim; or to issue a mandamus, directing the performance of a duty, not depending on executive discretion, but on particular acts of congress, and the general principles of law?[127]

Since *Marbury*, the Court's power in a proper case to invalidate executive branch actions that violate the Constitution or federal statutes has largely been assumed. Indeed, a careful analysis of *Marbury* makes plain that the constitutional defect with the Judiciary Act of 1789, which the Court struck down, was not that it invaded the executive prerogative of President Thomas Jefferson, or of his agent, Secretary of State James Madison. While Marshall discussed the political acts doctrine as shielding certain executive conduct from judicial consideration, he also made plain that the obligation to deliver the commission for justice of the peace to Marbury was purely ministerial. Indeed, but for the constitutional defect of attempting to confer original jurisdiction upon the Supreme Court where Article III permitted only appellate jurisdiction, Chief Justice Marshall asserted that the power to issue a writ of mandamus to compel delivering the commission, for which Marbury had a vested right, would have been proper.[128]

While one could argue that the failure to deliver the commission in *Marbury* produced a more concrete injury than did the failure to comply with the ESA's interagency consultation requirements in *Lujan*, that would simply beg the question whether Congress has the power to transform otherwise abstract injuries into cognizable and justiciable individual claims. If Congress has this power, then it can effectively transform abstract injuries into injuries that are concrete, at least as a matter of justiciability doctrine. And that, ultimately, was the question that *Lujan* presented. Whether or not Congress has that power, which I—and others[129]—would suggest it does, should not turn on whether judicial enforcement of an otherwise constitutional statute requires courts to intrude upon executive enforcement of the laws, at least if the required enforcement involves a ministerial task.

As stated above, *Lujan* has not only transformed the prior understanding of what constitutes a justiciable injury, suggesting that Congress has less power than traditional analysis assumed to define novel injuries enforceable in federal court, but also it has suggested a new conception of standing's constitutional underpinnings. As with many other aspects of standing doctrine, I would suggest that the resulting confusion about the meaning of standing results from the Court's tendency to take its standing metaphors literally. The injury-in-fact requirement of the Supreme Court's standing doctrine is intended to protect Congress's power to govern. Critical to that power, as social choice reveals, is the power not to make law unless and until an appropriate consensus forms. Because the federal courts, unlike Congress, generally lack the power of institutional inertia, they invite challenges by litigants who are dissatisfied with the outcomes of this important congressional power. This is especially true when courts, including the Supreme Court, signal that less than majority support on an underlying issue is sometimes adequate to force favorable judicial outcomes. Because the Court cannot guarantee a rational result when there is no Condorcet winner, its decisions, precisely because they thwart the will of a present majority, invite ideologically driven litigation. In fact, the generality of this invitation, coupled with path dependent voting procedures, promotes what could fairly be termed a race to the extremes in which ideological litigants, on all sides of any given issue, seek to prevent opponents—or fortuity—from controlling the critical path, in their efforts to achieve the non-Condorcet-winning results that they favor. Rather than permit this form of litigant free-for-all, the Court, at a time when it mattered most and when it was least able to control the outcomes of an important subset of important case decisions or the trajectories of path dependent case law resulting from the repeated expansion of issue dimensionality, elevated standing to a critical status. This doctrine not only serves to discourage advertent litigant path manipulation, but also, by preventing litigants from forcing cases upon the federal courts that would require them to supplant the status quo with judicially created positive law, preserves the power of Congress to govern. Such phrases as *injury in fact, causation,* and *redressability* played a role in this process, but—contrary to Scalia's *Lujan* analysis—not because they are requirements with independent jurisprudential significance. Instead, they played a role because those cases in which the Court is unable to avoid creating positive law correlate with claims that satisfy these traditional tort principles that have emerged in the context of traditional bipolar litigation.

While this chapter has demonstrated that all standing denials can be translated into substantive rulings, until *Lujan* the Court had used standing, by and large, to protect the power of Congress and state legislatures to control the timing of their own lawmaking powers. By resting the constitutional basis for standing in Article III, the Court reinforced the foundation for judicial review, dating back to the famous assertion in *Marbury* that "it is emphatically the province and duty of the judicial department to say what the law is."[130] Critical to *Marbury*'s conception of judicial lawmaking was the notion that while the federal judiciary had the final say on matters of constitutional interpretation, the contrary expression of coordinate branches notwithstanding, the federal courts were presumed to be passive participants in the lawmaking process, the timing of which was presumptively beyond their control.[131] And while congressional enactments in the *Marbury* conception remained subject to judicial correction based upon constitutional judicial review, the Court would only issue such correctives in a proper case, one meeting the requirements of Article III. Standing furthered these objectives by establishing a readily administrable framework with which the Supreme Court, and lower federal courts, could identify those factors in a given case that counseled for or against reaching the merits of an underlying constitutional challenge. Absent the requisite facts with which to demonstrate an injury, causation, and redressibility, resulting from factors presumptively beyond the control of the litigants themselves, the Court was able to infer a significant possibility that the claimants were not seeking judicial relief from a set of circumstances beyond their control, that caused them significant and direct harm. Instead, plaintiffs were likely seeking to force judicial decision making because of the benefits of strategic timing in a Court prone to possessing intransitive preferences. The various justiciability metaphors helped the Court to infer where to place close cases along the now-expanded justiciability spectrum.

Now consider the Supreme Court's application of the zone-of-interest test to expand the reach of the ESA standing provision in the 1997 decision *Bennett v. Spear*.[132] In *Bennett*, Justice Scalia, the author of *Lujan*, issued a unanimous decision construing the same ESA standing provision at issue in *Lujan*. The *Bennett* Court granted standing to two Oregon irrigation districts and to the operators of two ranches within those districts who sought to use the ESA to restrict the authority of the Fish and Wildlife Service (the "Service"), as delegate to the secretary of the interior, to protect the habitats of endangered species. In doing so, the Supreme Court effectively rewrote the ESA's standing provision to protect economic interests, through the operation of a procedural requirement that the Service consider the environmental impact of its actions, based upon an expansive zone-of-interest analysis, while continuing to limit the provision's application to allow private attorneys general to protect endangered species and their habitats based upon a restrictive injury analysis. At the same time, the combined *Lujan* and *Bennett* decisions reversed the long-standing justiciability practice, dating to the New Deal, of employing common law analogues for the limited purpose of identifying cognizable legal injuries in the absence of a clear and contrary congressional directive. In these two cases, the Supreme Court, instead, employed common law analogues to prevent Congress from defining a novel injury, in which a generalized interest in endangered species and their habitats is transformed into a private right of action enforceable in federal court.

In *Bennett*, the Service had issued a Biological Opinion in accordance with the ESA concerning the operation of the Klamath Irrigation Project by the Bureau of Reclamation (the "Bureau") and the impact of that project on the lost river sucker and the shortnose sucker, two species of fish listed as endangered. The project, which was among the "oldest federal reclamation schemes," consisted of a "series of lakes, rivers, dams and irrigation canals in northern California and southern Oregon." The secretary of the interior undertook the project and the Bureau administered it under the secretary's jurisdiction. In 1992, the Bureau notified the Service that the project might adversely affect the two listed species of fish. After the required consultation with the Bureau, the Service issued its opinion, as required under the

ESA, concluding that the "long-term operation of the Klamath Project was likely to jeopardize the continued existence of the Lost River and shortnose suckers." The opinion further identified "reasonable and prudent alternatives," including, most notably, maintaining minimum water levels in the Clear Lake and the Gerber reservoirs, which the Service concluded would avoid this danger. After receiving the opinion, the Bureau notified the Service that it intended to operate the project in compliance with the recommendations.

The petitioners, two Oregon irrigation districts and the operators of two ranches within those districts, claimed a competing interest in the water, which the Service's opinion declared necessary to the preservation of the endangered fish. Petitioners alleged that the jeopardy determinations, requiring the maintenance of minimum water levels for the Clear Lake and the Gerber reservoirs, from which they received their water, violated section 7 of the ESA. Petitioners further alleged that the Service had implicitly determined the critical habitat of the endangered fish without first giving adequate consideration to the economic impact of that designation, in violation of section 4 of the ESA.[133] Petitioners sued the regional director of the Service and the secretary of the interior, relying for standing upon both the ESA's broadly worded standing provision and section 10(a) of the APA.

The district court dismissed for lack of jurisdiction and the United States Court of Appeals for the Ninth Circuit affirmed, holding that only litigants seeking to preserve endangered species or their habitats fell within the zone of interest of the ESA's citizen-suit provision. The Supreme Court reversed, rejecting the Ninth Circuit's zone-of-interest analysis, and further rejecting three alternative defenses offered by the government to deny standing. The principal difference between the analysis of the Ninth Circuit and the Supreme Court was that the former construed the scope of the citizen-suit provision in light of the overall purpose of the ESA, while the latter strictly construed the terms of the citizen-suit provision, eschewing any inquiry into how that provision fit within the overall scheme of the statute.[134] The citizen-suit provision states in relevant part that

> any person may commence a civil suit on his own behalf—
> (a) to enjoin any person, including the United States and any other governmental instrumentality or agency . . . who is alleged to be in violation of any provision of this chapter or regulation issued under the authority thereof; or . . .
> (c) against the Secretary [of Commerce or the Interior] where there is alleged a failure of the Secretary to perform any act or duty under section 1533 of this title which is not discretionary with the Secretary.

Writing for the *Bennett* Court, Justice Scalia described the citizen-suit provision's "remarkable breadth," as compared with statutory standing provisions generally, and even when compared with the generally broader environmental standing provisions. One of the wonderful ironies of Justice Scalia's *Bennett* analysis is his rejoinder to the Ninth Circuit opinion, which relied upon *Lujan* for the proposition that the broad language of the ESA citizen-suit provision notwithstanding, Congress did not intend to confer standing upon any conceivable litigant. The Ninth Circuit stated:

> As *Lujan* makes clear, Congress may not permit suits by those who fail to satisfy the constitutionally-mandated standing requirements. For that reason, suits under the ESA, no less than suits under any statute, are clearly not available to "any person" in the broadest possible sense of that term.[135]

In contrast, Justice Scalia, writing for the *Bennett* Court, relied upon *Trafficante v. Metropolitan Life Ins. Co.,*[136] a case that vindicated a nontraditional statutory injury of the sort called into question in *Lujan,* this time to confer standing upon plaintiffs whose interests, he admitted, were generally inconsistent with the ESA's overall purpose.[137] Recall that in *Trafficante,* the Supreme Court conferred standing under the Fair Housing Act upon housing testers challenging the dissemination of nontruthful housing information based upon race, even though the testers themselves were not in the market for housing. The *Bennett* Court stated that *Trafficante* established that using appropriate statutory language, Congress can expand standing to the "full extent permitted under Article III."[138]

A further irony might help to explain the decision of the Court's liberal and moderate camps to join Scalia's decision. While the *Lujan* Court denied standing to environmental plaintiffs on the ground that none of their three articulated nexus theories sufficed to establish a meaningful interest in furthering the habitats of endangered species abroad, the *Bennett* Court expressly rejected such limitations on environmental injuries. Thus, writing for the *Bennett* Court, Justice Scalia stated:

> Our readiness to take the term "any person" at face value is greatly augmented by two interrelated considerations: the overall subject matter of the legislation is the environment (a matter in which it is common to think all persons have an interest) and that the obvious purpose of the particular provision in question is to encourage enforcement of so-called "private attorneys general."

The irony is deepened when we recognize that whether or not it is common to think that all persons have an interest in the environment, the *Bennett* Court conferred standing to plaintiffs seeking to limit the application of a federal statute to protect the environment. To the extent that the interest in the environment is collective, that interest is one of preservation against private encroachments. The opposite is also true. To the extent that the claimed environmental interest is one of encroachment, that interest is entirely private, rather than general and shared. Stated differently, few would claim a general interest in having a public resource depleted for private gain, while many would claim an opposite interest in preserving a public resource against private encroachment.

To understand how the *Bennett* Court expanded standing under an environmental statute to plaintiffs seeking to limit the statute's enforcement, it will be helpful to again compare the Supreme Court and Ninth Circuit approaches, and to cast those approaches in terms of the expanded justiciability spectrum developed in this chapter. In allowing standing to limit the enforcement of the ESA, Justice Scalia, writing for the *Bennett* Court, relied upon administrative law principles to assert that one need not allege an ultimate injury to claim the protections of a procedural statutory provision. Thus, Scalia reasoned that petitioners had standing to challenge the failure of the Service, in issuing its opinion, to consider, as required by statute, the economic impact of its decision. Scalia stated: "It is rudimentary administrative law that discretion as to the substance of the ultimate decision does not confer discretion to ignore the required procedures of decision making."

In contrast, the Ninth Circuit reasoned:

> We do not believe that in setting forth factors to be weighed in formulating a plan for protecting species, Congress intended to do more than ensure rational decision making by providing guidance for governmental officials. Certainly, it did not intend impliedly to confer standing on every plaintiff who could conceivably claim that the failure to consider one of those factors adversely affected him. . . . To interpret the statute [otherwise] would be to transform provisions designed to further species protection into the means to frustrate that very right.[139]

The critical difference between the Supreme Court and Ninth Circuit approaches is perhaps best understood by considering where along the expanded justiciability spectrum, represented by table 6.2,[140] those courts implicitly placed petitioner's claim of injury. In *Lujan,* Justice Scalia rejected petitioners' claim of procedural injury, based upon the failure of interagency consultation, stating: "[t]his is not a case where plaintiffs are seeking to enforce a procedural requirement the disregard of which could impair a separate concrete interest of theirs."[141] In *Bennett,* in contrast, Justice Scalia reasoned that for standing purposes, it was not necessary that the claimed procedural injury, requiring that the Service adequately consider the environmental impact of its jeopardy determination, result in petitioners' continued supply of the same amount of water from the two affected reservoirs. As with those cases falling into the "no right to an undistorted market" standing category, petitioners did not allege, and could not prove, that if the Service did go back and consider the economic impact of its classification and opinion, that it would rescind the recommended minimum water levels for reservoirs. Moreover, petitioners did not allege, and could not prove, that if the reservoirs maintained their water levels consistently with the opinion, they would not continue to receive the same supply of water. It was possible that those who received water from those reservoirs might not be equally affected, if, for example, the resulting differences in allocation were not made on a pro rata basis. Thus viewed, the case might appear closer to the *Allen, Warth,* and *EKWRO* than to *Bakke* and *Duke Power,* given the number of links in the chain of causation. This is consistent with the Ninth Circuit analysis. In contrast, under the Supreme Court's analysis, petitioners were principally affected by factors exclusively within the government's control. As a result, as with criminal prosecutions, even if protecting against the procedural harm would not have resulted in the ultimate relief sought, the *Bennett* Court determined that standing was proper. In this analysis, the case is closer to *Bakke* and *Duke Power.*

That said, a critical difference remains between *Bennett* and these other standing cases. In each of these other cases, the plaintiffs relied principally for standing upon the equal protection and due process clauses. In this case, petitioners relied, instead, upon a statutory standing provision, set out in the ESA. While the Supreme Court has, since the inception of standing, considered common law analogues for injury in determining justiciability, it has generally done so in cases in which the litigants rely upon the Constitution for standing. When, instead, plaintiffs rely upon a statute, the Court, as in *Traficante,* the very case Scalia relied upon to confer standing in *Bennett,* has traditionally afforded them more latitude. *Lujan* suggested that even Congress is subject to some limits in conferring standing, grounded in both Articles II and III. But even that case was not terribly problematic if Congress defined the justiciable injury with the requisite specificity, or linked the outcome to some concrete form of relief.[142] In *Bennett,* however, the Supreme Court has suggested using common law analogues for a very different purpose, one that, I would argue, is in tension with the central function of standing in furthering the core distinction between legislatures and courts. If the purpose of standing is to limit lawmaking in the federal judiciary to an ad hoc and as-needed basis, then the use of common law analogues is helpful in construing ambiguous statutes because they permit the Court to draw upon a body of case law, which is widely available and which operates in the background of statutory drafting, to determine justiciability. But judicial passivity requires that the federal judiciary not limit Congress if it chooses to alter the presumption in favor of, or against, standing, by statute. In effect, through broad standing provisions of the sort in the ESA, Congress has signaled a desire to accelerate the pace of judicial lawmaking to meet some perceived problem that Congress, either based upon the absence of dominant substantive alternative to the status quo or based upon a majority decision to assign the judgment elsewhere, has chosen not to handle fully on its own. Even then, we might understand *Lujan* as a signal to Congress that the Court will accept the invitation to advance the pace of judicial lawmaking, but only if given appropriate guidance in the underlying statute. So viewed, *Lujan* might be akin to a limited revival of the now-moribund nondelegation doctrine.[143] *Bennett* is, again, troublesome, however, in that it is not premised upon the desire for stronger judicial guidance; instead, as the district court and the Ninth Circuit recognized, conferring standing appears flatly inconsistent with whatever general guidance Congress gave about the overall purpose of the ESA.

While *Lujan* was a divided opinion, with two concurrences and two dissents, *Bennett* was unanimous. This seeming anomaly can be understood, at least in part, as follows. While the *Bennett* Court used standing to alter the mission of the ESA by protecting economic claimants against environmental regulation, in doing so, it also necessarily cut back upon some of the more troublesome aspects of *Lujan*. Specifically, *Bennett* restored to a limited extent the intuition that Congress is free to expand the zone of interest to include potentially novel injuries, as it had in the Fair Housing Act, at issue in *Trafficante,* and to confer standing broadly upon individuals who would seek to have those injuries remedied in the federal courts. While *Bennett,* operating in conjunction with *Lujan,* effectively rewrote the ESA standing provision to permit lawsuits protecting against, rather than pursuing, aggressive environmental enforcement, nothing in those opinions prevents Congress, in future environmental statutes, from limiting the scope of otherwise expansive standing provisions to those seeking to further the overall objectives of the statute. Had the ESA's standing provision stated that "only those seeking to further the overall objectives of this statute, and specifically, to protect endangered species or their habitats, shall have standing," then the *Bennett* plaintiffs would have been denied standing, even under the *Lujan* and *Bennett* analyses. The liberals and moderates on the Court might still hope, therefore, that with appropriate statutory clarification, future standing determinations will limit the force of *Lujan* based upon the expansive logic of *Bennett*.

Before concluding our review of the standing case law, we must consider one final recent standing opinion, *Raines v. Byrd,*[144] issued the same term as *Bennett,* and the follow-up decision, *Clinton v. City of New York.*[145] In *Raines,* the Supreme Court issued a seven-to-two opinion denying standing to five present members and one former member of Congress, who challenged the constitutionality of the Line-Item Veto Act. In doing so, the Supreme Court reversed a long-standing practice of the United States Court of Appeals for the District of Columbia Circuit, which afforded standing to members of Congress who challenged statutes that compromised their constitutionally established lawmaking powers.[146] At the same time, the *Raines* Court infused uncertainty into the underlying ground rules of legislative bargaining in Congress.[147] And it did so in a manner that appears inconsistent with the chilling, vagueness, and overbreadth exceptions to ripeness doctrine.[148]

On April 4, 1996, President Clinton signed the Line-Item Veto Act,[149] into law. While the act did not use the term *veto,* it provided the president with the authority to "cancel" certain spending and tax benefits after he has signed them into law. The act provided in relevant part:

> The President may, with respect to any bill or joint resolution that has been signed into law pursuant to Article I, section 7, of the Constitution of the United States, cancel in whole—(1) any dollar amount of

discretionary budget authority; (2) any item of new direct spending; or (3) any limited tax benefit; if the President—

(a) determines that such cancellation will—(i) reduce the Federal budget deficit; (ii) not impair any essential Government functions; and (iii) not harm the national interest; and

(b) notifies the Congress of such cancellation by transmitting a special message . . . within five calendar days (excluding Sundays) after the enactment of the law [to which the cancellation applies].[150]

In the case of direct spending allocations, cancel means to rescind, and in the case of limited tax benefits, cancel means to prevent the benefit from having legal effect.[151] The act further defined limited tax benefit to include revenue-losing provisions benefiting one hundred or fewer persons under Title 26 in any fiscal year, or a tax provision providing temporary or permanent transitional relief for ten or fewer persons.[152] Under the act, a cancellation becomes effective when the House and Senate receives the president's "special message" providing notice of the cancellation. The act further establishes that within thirty days of receipt of the special message, Congress could disapprove a cancellation through ordinary legislation, meaning a simple majority vote in both houses. If the president then vetoes the disapproval bill, Congress would then need to override with a two-thirds majority of both houses.[153]

Congress included two provisions to expedite judicial review of the act. First, Congress included the following standing provision:

[A]ny member of Congress or any individual adversely affected by [this act] may bring an action, in the United States District Court for the District of Columbia, for declaratory judgment and injunctive relief on the ground that any provision of this part violates the Constitution.[154]

In addition, Congress included provisions for expedited judicial review in the United States District Court for the District of Columbia and for direct appeal and expedited review of any order concerning the act by the district court to the United States Supreme Court.[155]

The *Raines* plaintiffs alleged that the act injured them in their capacity as members of Congress by altering their constitutional role in the drafting and repeal of legislation. As Justice Stevens explained in dissent, as a technical matter, the act limited the ability of members of Congress to repeal enacted legislation through the constitutionally prescribed procedure of simple majority vote in both houses subject to the presidential veto.[156] Instead, the act allowed the president to sign bills into law, then after they became law, to cancel certain items unilaterally. But, as Justice Stevens further observed, as a practical matter, the act further constituted "a simple denial of their right to vote on the precise text that [would] ultimately become law." Thus, plaintiffs alleged that the act injured them in their official capacities in each of the following ways:

The Act . . . (a) alters the legal and practical effect of all votes they
may cast on bills containing such separately vetoable items, (b) divests
the [appellees] of their constitutional role in the repeal of legislation,
and (c) alters the constitutional balance of powers between the Legislative and Executive Branches, both with respect to measures containing separately vetoable items and with respect to other matters
coming before Congress.

The government moved to dismiss on the grounds that the case was not
ripe and that the plaintiffs lacked standing. The district court denied the
motion, rejecting both justiciability challenges, and held the act unconstitutional. On direct appeal to the Supreme Court, Chief Justice Rehnquist, writing for a majority of six, held that plaintiffs lacked standing to challenge the
constitutionality of the act. While the Court issued four opinions, the majority opinion by Chief Justice Rehnquist, a concurrence by Justice Souter, and
two dissents by Justices Stevens and Breyer, the majority opinion and Justice
Stevens's dissent are most important for our purposes.

From a purely doctrinal perspective, Chief Justice Rehnquist's opinion
appears to be straightforward and perhaps defensible. And yet, if we pierce
the Court's standing rhetoric, as I have argued we must in this book, and consider, instead, the underlying purpose of the Court's various justiciability
ground rules, then Stevens's alternative analysis becomes more persuasive.
The critical difference in their analyses was how the writing justices conceived the claimed injury to the process of legislative bargaining. For Chief
Justice Rehnquist, the claimed injury was the failure to have one's vote properly counted in the legislative process, which had yet to occur. As a result,
Rehnquist concluded, plaintiffs lacked standing. For Justice Stevens, it was
instead, the then-present inability to anticipate the consequences of one's
vote, in light of the president's power to alter the nature of legislative bargains after bills had been passed. In this analysis, plaintiffs suffered a present and continuing injury, which was therefore ripe and for which they had
standing.

Chief Justice Rehnquist began his analysis by observing that because Congress conferred standing, the Court's inquiry was limited to the constitutional
standing requirements, the most important of which is a personal injury or
stake. Rehnquist observed that the personal injury requirement furthers separation of powers by limiting the judiciary to its proper role in resolving concrete disputes. The difficulty in *Raines*, Rehnquist reasoned, was twofold. First,
as members of Congress, plaintiffs did not allege a personal injury; instead,
they alleged an injury in their official capacities. In this part of his analysis,
Chief Justice Rehnquist discredited the long-standing practice in the United
States Court of Appeals for the District of Columbia, which had allowed members of Congress to challenge statutes that allegedly infringed upon their constitutional powers.[157] Second, even assuming that they were personally injured
or that injury in their official capacity sufficed for standing purposes, Chief

Justice Rehnquist concluded that members of Congress suffered no concrete harm in their ability to perform their legislative function.

To support the latter point, Rehnquist distinguished the 1939 standing decision *Coleman v. Miller*.[158] In *Coleman*, twenty of Kansas's forty state senators had voted to ratify the proposed "Child Labor Amendment" to the United States Constitution. Ordinarily, the deadlock would have resulted in the failure to ratify the amendment. Instead, as the presiding officer, the lieutenant governor cast a deciding vote in favor of the amendment. The amendment was then approved in the state house of representatives. The twenty senators who voted against the amendment brought suit, alleging that their votes had effectively been nullified. In a divided opinion, the *Coleman* Court held that the plaintiffs had standing to challenge the ratification, but denied relief on the merits.

Chief Justice Rehnquist construed *Coleman* narrowly for the proposition that a group of legislators whose votes were sufficient to enact or to defeat a proposed bill have standing when the legislative action is opposite, on the ground that their votes have been completely nullified. In contrast, Rehnquist reasoned, the votes of the *Raines* plaintiffs, each of whom opposed the passage of the Line-Item Veto Act, had not been nullified. Instead, the plaintiffs had simply lost. Moreover, Rehnquist observed that in future appropriations or tax bills subject to the act, plaintiffs, or those who hold their seats, will continue (even with the act in place) to have the same power to vote for or against the proposed legislation.

In contrast, Justice Stevens identified a present injury that flowed from the enactment of the Line-Item Veto Act, even though it had not yet been exercised. Simply put, for Stevens the act had the effect of preventing congressmen from knowing with respect to bills subject to the act, whether the bills that they voted for would be the same once those bills became law. Thus, Stevens explained that "the Line-Item Veto Act establishes a mechanism by which bills passed by both Houses of Congress will eventually produce laws that have not passed either House of Congress and that have not been voted on by any Senator." In Stevens's analysis, plaintiffs' injury was thus analogous to those for which the Court has carved exceptions to its ripeness doctrine.[159] In effect, the injury was the inhibition of present legislative trades, which flowed from the uncertainty concerning whether the terms of those trades would subsequently be honored. Stevens further read *Coleman* broadly to support the proposition that legislators whose votes had been denied full effectiveness have standing to challenge the diminution of their legislative power.[160] Stevens reasoned that the very injury that he claimed supported standing, also demonstrated the constitutional defect in the act, namely that it established a procedure for the repeal of statutes in a manner inconsistent with the requirements of Article I, section 7.*

---

*Article I, § 7, cl. 2 states in relevant part:
    Every Bill which shall have passed the House of Representatives and the Senate, shall, before it becomes a Law, be presented to the President of the United States;

The critical difference between the analyses of Rehnquist and Stevens is ultimately one of timing. Rehnquist's viewpoint is after the fact. By that I mean Rehnquist focused on the period of actual legislative voting, with or without the act in place. Either way, the votes of congressmen would be counted in support of, or against, particular proposals, even if those proposals, when passed, were then subject to the president's line item veto power. In contrast, Stevens's viewpoint is before the fact. Specifically, Stevens considered the implications of the act for the process of legislative bargaining. For Stevens, the act improperly introduced a significant element of uncertainty concerning whether present legislative bargains would be honored after the underlying legislative proposals were passed, and after the president signed those bills subject to the line item veto into law. Because the Constitution establishes a clear set of procedures for creating statutes, upon which members of Congress necessarily rely in the process of legislative bargaining, the line item veto introduced a present injury by undermining such reliance.

As *Raines* demonstrates, mechanical applications of standing doctrine, which has taken the form of metaphors intended to capture the conditions under which the federal courts should presume for or against shifting the burden of legislative inertia, sometimes conflict with the underlying purposes of the doctrine itself. And yet, there is a significant administrative benefit to having articulable justiciability elements. The problem here is that the elements admit of sufficient flexibility to render both the Rehnquist and Stevens applications plausible. To determine which should have prevailed, I would argue, it is critical to consider the costs and benefits of each possible ruling. The majority ruling delayed, for a relatively short period, the determination of the underlying question whether the act is constitutional. But, as the next subsection shows, even in this short period, legislative bargaining occurred under a cloud of uncertainty, which itself undermined the objectives of constitutional process.

A.   *Clinton v. City of New York* and the
Fallacy of Substantive Equivalence

The Supreme Court was forced to address the merits of the constitutional challenge to the Line-Item Veto Act soon after denying standing in *Raines*. In *Clinton v. City of New York*,[161] a case that revealed the elusive nature of characterizing the Court in strictly political terms, Justice Stevens (who had dissented from the standing denial in *Raines*), produced a majority opinion for six justices voting to strike down the act. Stevens was joined by Chief Jus-

---

If he approve he shall sign it, but if not he shall return it, with his Objections to the House in which it shall have originated, who shall enter the Objections at large in their Journal, and proceed to reconsider it. If after such Reconsideration two thirds of that House shall agree to pass the Bill, it shall be sent, together with the Objections, to the other House, by which it shall likewise be considered, and if approved by two thirds of that House, it shall become a Law.

tice Rehnquist, and Justices Kennedy, Souter, Thomas, and Ginsburg, with Justices Breyer, O'Connor, and Scalia dissenting.[162] Aside from the unusual lineup on both sides of the case, *City of New York* was noteworthy for what it did not say. Justice Stevens reasoned that after the president's exercise of the line item veto, the version of an affected statute that became law would have differed from when it passed both houses of Congress and was presented to the president. As a result, Stevens concluded that the act violated the presentment requirement of Article I, section 7.[163] The majority did not, however, address the argument pressed vigorously in Justice Stevens's *Raines* dissent, that the act was unconstitutional because it altered the background rules of congressional bargaining. As explained below, however, from the perspective of constitutional process, the act did alter that bargaining process in an unconstitutional manner. To see why, we must first consider the arguments in defense of the act raised in the two dissenting opinions.

In their separate dissents, Justices Stephen Breyer and Antonin Scalia, although generally on opposite ends of the Court's political spectrum, advanced quite similar arguments in support of the act. Comparing the two defenses of the act sheds substantial light on legislative bargaining from the perspective of constitutional process, much in the same manner that comparing the distinctions between legislative and adjudicatory lawmaking advanced in Justice Blackmun's majority opinion in *Mistretta v. United States*,[164] and in Chief Justice Rehnquist's partial concurrence and partial dissent in *Planned Parenthood of Southeastern Pennsylvania v. Casey*,[165] shed light on the proper understanding of constitutional lawmaking.[166] Justice Breyer began with the premise that Congress is effectively prevented from achieving the same results as those under the Line-Item Veto Act through an alternative regime, which although constitutional, would be impractical to implement. Breyer explained:

> Congress cannot divide such a bill into thousands, or tens of thousands, of separate appropriations bills, each one of which the President would have to sign, or to veto, separately. Thus, the question is whether the Constitution permits Congress to choose a particular novel means to achieve the same, constitutionally legitimate, end.[167]

In a similar vein, Justice Scalia defended the act's constitutionality by imagining a regime in which Congress continues to group items into bills as it does now, but further includes within specific bills language that renders the expenditures on particular items completely discretionary with the president. Scalia explained:

> Insofar as the degree of political, "law-making" power conferred upon the Executive is concerned, there is not a dime's worth of difference between Congress's authorizing the President to cancel a spending item, and Congress's authorizing money to be spent on a particular item at the President's discretion.[168]

In both the earlier comparison of adjudicatory and legislative lawmaking based upon a comparison of opinion language by Justice Blackmun and Chief Justice Rehnquist, and here, the justices have committed what we can now label the *fallacy of substantive equivalence*. By that I mean, the justices have defended regimes that they favor by arguing that one could achieve a substantively equivalent outcome through constitutionally acceptable means. The fallacy is in failing to consider that the Constitution is not strictly concerned with the substantive equivalence of political or legal outcomes, but also with the constitutional legitimacy of the means employed to achieve those outcomes. In assessing the Line-Item Veto Act, the proper inquiry is not whether Congress could achieve the same substantive result some other way. It is instead whether the analysis of the processes of lawmaking set out in the Constitution reveals the deficiency—and thus the irrelevance—of the supposedly equivalent alternative.

The problem is that the Line-Item Veto Act alters the incentives of legislative bargaining. Without the act in place, members of Congress who are seeking to have their desired items of direct spending or special tax benefits enacted into law can succeed only by forming part of a larger successful coalition.[169] In doing so, such congressmen will trade their votes for the inclusion of items that otherwise would not be enacted as free-standing measures. In that regime, members of Congress who are seeking to have their desired items of direct spending or special tax benefits enacted into law are quite unlikely to accept an offer by the sponsor of a bill to include their favored item in exchange for their vote if they are also told that the bill will include language that gives the president complete discretion over whether to spend the money or to retain the tax break. Similarly, the same members of Congress are quite unlikely to accept an offer by the sponsor of a bill to include their favored item in exchange for their vote if they are also told that the entire bill will then be disaggregated and presented to the president as a series of separate bills, to preserve the president's authority to veto each item separately. In both hypothetical alternatives, provided that some other bill sponsor is willing to offer a better deal, one in which the congressman seeking his special interest item will have that item included in a bill that effectively ties the president's hands such that if the president chooses not to veto the entire bill, he will be forced to accept the special interest item, the congressman will take the latter offer every time. That said, there is absolutely nothing *unconstitutional* about these alternative regimes. But that provides no basis for sustaining against a constitutional challenge a statute that employs neither constitutional alternative, and instead, seeks to achieve the same result through a form of unconstitutional coercion in which members of Congress lose their power to negotiate better legislative bargains in the manner contemplated by Article I, section 7. While Congress could, in theory, package items in the manner that Breyer and Scalia suggest, Congress has not done so precisely because the Constitution instead establishes a regime that affords members of Congress substantially greater protections for the special interest items that they negotiate into larger bills as the price of forming successful coalitions. And it is that process of lawmaking that the Line-Item Veto Act threatened to undermine.

B. Return to *Raines*

In this book, I have argued that if we pierce the Court's often malleable standing language, we see that the doctrine operates as a set of ground rules that improve the fairness of constitutional process by raising the cost of advertent litigant path manipulation. Recall that fairness in social choice is a term of art, which ultimately is grounded in the majoritarian norm. Standing presumptively prevents potential Condorcet-winning legislative outcomes from being thwarted in the federal courts, except on an ad hoc and as-needed basis, as indicated by the emergence of facts, directly affecting the litigant before the court, that are beyond the litigant's control.

The difficulty in *Raines* was that it elevated form over substance. On the one hand, the Court was correct that the claimed injury, namely not to have one's vote diluted through the possible subsequent exercise of a line item veto, appeared tenuous. It was altogether uncertain that the nominal plaintiffs or those they represented would necessarily have fallen victim to an immediate exercise of the president's line item veto power. On the other hand, standing is about preserving the integrity and inclusiveness of the legislative process, a point that the Court in *City of New York* implicitly recognized, and that Justice Stevens explicitly recognized one year earlier in his *Raines* dissent. Perhaps more than any other statute in recent history, the Line-Item Veto Act undermined fairness in the social choice sense by allowing the president to undo legislative bargains that presumably had majority, or at least Condorcet-winning, legislative support. The act, therefore, could not help but change the nature of legislative bargaining, all of which occurred under the act's shadow for over a year. As Justice Stevens recognized in his *Raines* dissent, this was one area in which a clear mandate was of critical importance. Moreover and more importantly, *Raines* did not present a case in which path manipulation was of particular concern. The underlying issue presented a binary choice; the act either *was* or *was not* constitutional, and it was difficult to imagine that anything between the time of *Raines* and the time of *City of New York* was going to change the Court's analysis. In contrast, the uncertain status of the Line-Item Veto Act likely did alter at least some congressional output during the same period.

VII. Conclusion

In this penultimate chapter, I have traced both the history of the Supreme Court's timing-based justiciability doctrines, with a particular emphasis on standing, and the standing cases themselves. While the Supreme Court has employed a number of heuristics, which roughly correlate with the underlying objectives of justiciability, it has failed to devise a comprehensive theory that ties those heuristics together and that meaningfully explains the seeming inconsistencies in its standing doctrine. In this chapter, I have employed the theory of social choice to place standing doctrine on a firmer theoretical foundation that establishes its critical role in furthering separation of powers and fair constitutional process.

While several inconsistencies remain in the Supreme Court's standing case law, some developed quite recently, I would argue that the social choice theory of standing is substantially more robust than alternative theories in the literature, and that, at a minimum, it adds substantial value to those theories. Once the underlying purposes of the Supreme Court's standing doctrine are properly understood, we can appreciate the doctrine's seemingly counterintuitive historical development and dissipate many of the apparent inconsistencies within the case law.

Part IV

Summary and Conclusion

CHAPTER 7 **Summary of Argument**

I. Introduction

My interest in exploring the relationship between social choice theory and constitutional law began in my very first semester teaching law school at George Mason Law School eight years ago. When teaching the introductory constitutional law course that semester, I stumbled across *Kassel v. Consolidated Freightways*.[1] I immediately recognized that the collective resolution of underlying dispositive issues produced a logical progression leading to the dissenting result. At that point, I had been introduced to Arrow's Theorem, but knew little about it. I recognized that the *Kassel* Court was in some sense having difficulties aggregating its own collective preferences, and I passed that insight onto my students. But I was unable to offer any deeper analysis of that aspect of the case. Later the same semester, I stumbled across *Crawford v. Board of Education*[2] and *Washington v. Seattle School District No. 1*.[3] I recognized that a similar preference aggregation problem was involved, but again lacked a larger analytical framework with which to connect those two cases, each decided by clear majorities, with *Kassel*, which was decided by a judgment of the Court with no majority opinion. Finally, during the same semester, I came across several law review articles in which the authors relied upon Arrow's Theorem to argue that the Supreme Court should be more skeptical of the results achieved in the legislative process, and should therefore increase the scope of constitutional judicial review.[4] I immediately recognized a tension between the argument that the Court should attempt to correct for collective preference aggregation problems in Congress and state legislatures through expanded judicial review and the above cases, in which the Court appeared to have had some difficulty in aggregating its own collective preferences.

For the next several years, I became fascinated with the body of legal and economic literature in which Arrow's Theorem has played a central role. While my interest was initially piqued by the desire to say something meaningful to my students about a few seemingly anomalous Supreme Court decisions, I have come to view social choice as an exciting vehicle for explaining a host of important anomalies within our system of constitutional governance and lawmaking.[5] In a sense, this book has been the culmination of the intellectual journey that I have taken over the past eight years into the rarely linked worlds of social choice and constitutional law. In the remainder of this closing chapter I will provide a brief overview of the book's main points.

II. Summary

A. Part I: Framing the Inquiry

As chapter 1 reveals, the journey began with some of the very problems that prompted my initial inquiry into considering the Supreme Court from the perspective of social choice. In chapter 1, I provided several examples of seemingly anomalous Supreme Court decisions. These anomalous decisions include *Miller v. Albright*,[6] a case like *Kassel,* in which the majority resolutions of identified dispositive issues produces a logical voting path leading to the dissenting result; *Planned Parenthood of Southeastern Pennsylvania v. Casey*,[7] a case in which a minority of three justices who state the holding for the Court as a whole have defined the underlying case issues in a manner that the remaining justices explicitly or implicitly reject; *Crawford* and *Seattle,* two cases that separate majorities resolve in opposite fashion, but in which an overlapping majority makes plain that the cases are indistinguishable; and *Board of Regents of the University of California at Davis v. Bakke*[8] and *Allen v. Wright*[9] two cases reaching opposite outcomes on standing, but in which the outcomes in each case would have been opposite if each deciding Court had instead employed the other case's framework for analysis. I also raised an historical anomaly surrounding the circumstances under which standing was initially conceived in the New Deal Court and then transformed in the Burger and Rehnquist Courts. In essence, chapter 1 defined the major puzzles that I hoped to piece together using the theory of social choice.

In chapter 2, I provided a comprehensive, nonmathematical, overview of the relevant social choice concepts needed to piece together the puzzles introduced in chapter 1, along with several related puzzles introduced later in the book. As a framework for introducing the underlying concepts, I described three common fallacies that legal scholars employing the theory of social choice to analyze issues of public law and policy sometimes commit: the fallacy of composition, the isolation fallacy, and the nirvana fallacy. While some scholars have argued that the universality of social choice—the fact that all collective decision-making bodies are prone to the anomaly of cycling— implies that we can derive no normative implications for public lawmaking, I instead argued that two collective decision-making bodies, each prone to cycling under specified conditions, can avoid cycling by operating together, provided that they respond differently to the underlying factual phenomena that give rise to cycling. The analysis further revealed that the phenomenon of cyclical preferences by majority rule was most likely to occur when the members, whether private individuals or legislators, were presented with an unanticipated windfall or loss.

I then introduced the voting paradox (also known as the Condorcet paradox), which reveals that under certain conditions, aggregating the preferences of three or more persons by unlimited majority rule, even when their individual preferences are fully rational (or transitive), can generate cycling. I also introduced the Condorcet criterion, which is helpful in identifying the limited conditions under which cyclical preferences by majority rule are likely to arise. When preferences can be cast along a unidimensional issue spectrum and when the preferences of each member are unipeaked, or when preferences can be cast along a two-dimensional issue spectrum, but the preferences are symmetrical, a dominant outcome, referred to as the Condorcet winner, exists. In contrast, when preferences are cast along a unidimensional issue spectrum but the preferences of one member are multipeaked, or when preferences are cast along a two-dimensional issue spectrum, but the preferences are asymmetrical, then there is no dominant outcome (or Condorcet winner) and a cycle arises. (In fact, these are two different methods of expressing the same relationships between and among collective preferences). Based in part upon these concepts, I summarized an evolutionary analysis of parliamentary rules, which relied upon social choice theory. The analysis allowed us to expand the relevant group of baselines growing out of economic analysis beyond efficiency, to include, first, the ability to ensure that available Condorcet winners prevail; second, the need to produce a collective outcome; and third, the desire to prevent agenda manipulation. The analysis was also significant in helping to evaluate the incremental evolutionary process in the generation of parliamentary rules. Specifically, the analysis revealed that the evolution of rules does not require that the members have any understanding of social choice theory. Instead, provided that the members face avoidable dissatisfaction, meaning that the rules fail to achieve a desired objective that some superior rule could reach, then the members are likely to force further tinkering until dissatisfaction is no longer avoidable. At that point, rules tend to converge. On the other hand, if the resulting dissatisfaction is not avoidable, any tinkering will produce results that are not stable and that will vary considerably across institutions and rules.

Finally, I introduced Arrow's Theorem. Arrow's Theorem sets up a group of four conditions that Arrow deemed fundamental to fair collective decision making, and proves that those conditions cannot be met simultaneously in an institution that seeks to ensure collectively rational, or transitive, outcomes. For that reason, Arrow's Theorem has been aptly described as a generalization of the paradox of voting. For our purposes, Arrow's Theorem is most important for the corollary proposition that in any institution that actually produces collective decisions, at least one of the underlying fairness conditions, or the requirement of rationality, is necessarily relaxed. To avoid the nirvana fallacy, it then becomes critical to identify for each institution under review, which Arrovian conditions are adhered to, and which are relaxed, before evaluating any proposals to shift decisional responsibility between or among affected institutions.

B. Part II: Social Choice Models of Supreme Court Decision Making

In chapters 3 and 4, I then developed the social choice models of Supreme Court decision making for both individual cases and for groups of cases over time. Together, these models help to explain each of the case anomalies described in chapter 1, based upon the framework for analysis set out in chapter 2. The models developed in chapters 3 and 4 are parallel and complementary. Both depend upon the following series of incremental steps: first, an evolution away from Condorcet-producing or Condorcet-consistent rules; second, an evolution toward a particular type of non-Condorcet-producing rule that has the ability to break down potentially cyclical preferences in a manner that is readily administrable; and finally, an evolution toward a companion rule or set of rules, that limits the harm that the non-Condorcet-producing rules would otherwise create in failing to aggregate collective preferences in a fair manner.

In chapter 3, I introduced the social choice model of individual case decision making. I began by explaining the evolution toward outcome voting, a rule that breaks down cyclical preferences by requiring justices to express their preferred resolution of dispositive case issues in a form that is not contingent upon how the case is ultimately decided. The analysis reveals that the Supreme Court faces a problem of social choice not only in the obvious case, which presents a choice among three or more potential judgments—affirm, reverse, or remand—but also in binary outcome cases. This anomaly arises because even when the choice is to affirm or reverse, there is always the potential for no fewer than three rationales, two leading to one result and one leading to the other. In those cases in which judicial preferences possess the characteristic features of multidimensionality and asymmetry, the potential further arises that a justice might prefer as a second choice a rationale that is conceptually closer to his ideal point, but that would produce the opposite result, to an alternative rationale that is conceptually the farthest, but that would lead to the same result. Because outcome voting can be translated into a rule requiring justices to select among no fewer than three potential rationales (meaning packaged resolution of identified dispositive issues), the issue arises as to how outcome voting breaks down the potential underlying cycles with respect to those rationales.

Outcome voting, a rule that relaxes the Arrovian range criterion, effectively requires the justices to select one set of preferred resolutions of identified dispositive issues in the case that lead to their preferred case outcome. Outcome voting effectively prevents the justices from conditioning their preferred resolution of underlying case issues upon whether the majority resolution of those issues produces a voting path leading to their preferred case outcome. By limiting the strategic identification of issues, outcome voting produces more stable results than would the proposed alternative of issue voting. In chapter 3, I explained that by expanding the dimensionality of the underlying case, issue voting would tend to exacerbate the problem of indeterminacy that arises when the Court is confronted with multidimensional and asymmetrical preferences.

The outcome voting rule is best understood in light of three case paradigms, each of which correlates to one of the categories of collective preference aggregation set out on chapter 2. In a small subset of fractured panel decision cases, those in which the justices possess multidimensional and asymmetrical preferences, outcome voting produces seemingly anomalous results. The voting anomaly arises in those cases, which include *Miller, Kassel,* and *Tidewater,* because the two dominant rationales leading to the Court's judgment are opposite on each dispositive issue, while the rationale leading to the dissent contains one issue resolution in common with each opinion leading to the judgment. As a result, there is no logical reason to assume that the justices voting consistently with the judgment would prefer the opposite, same-judgment rationale to the closer, opposite-judgment rationale. While there is no logical reason to assume away such preferences, however, outcome voting prevents the contingent expression of such issue resolutions, thus leading to these occasional anomalous case outcomes.

In two other, more common, categories of cases, those in which the justices' preferences can be cast along a single dimension, for example, *Memoirs v. Massachusetts,*[10] and those in which they are multidimensional but symmetrical, for example, *Bakke,* the result, instead, is to produce a single dominant holding, which is the likely Condorcet winner, for the Court as a whole. In these cases, the holding will be expressed in an opinion that is the ideal point of only a minority of the Court, but that represents the Court's dominant second choice, or Condorcet winner. The narrowest grounds doctrine, articulated in *Marks v. United States,*[11] ensures that such cases produce these stable outcomes. In *Marks,* the Court recognized that when the preferences of the justices in a fractured panel case can be cast along a single issue continuum, for example the level of obscenity protection under the First Amendment, it is probable that the wings of the Court would prefer the rationale embraced in the narrowest grounds decision to that embraced by the members of the opposite wing. While *Marks* dealt with the narrow context of a unidimensional issue spectrum, in chapter 3 I extended the principle to show that the same analysis applies in the case of multidimensional and symmetrical preferences. The narrowest grounds doctrine can readily be translated into an application of the Condorcet criterion for fractured Supreme Court decisions. The doctrine thus explains cases like *Casey,* with a single dimension, in which the justices defined the issues in a seemingly nonobvious manner, and *Bakke,* with two dimensions, in which a single justice alone embraced each of two distinctions necessary to the Court's holding.

In chapter 4, I extended the social choice analysis of Supreme Court decision making to explain the conditions under which multidimensionality and asymmetry can affect groups of cases. In *Crawford* and *Seattle,* for example, which were decided in opposite fashion by clear majorities, a crossover majority believed that the cases were indistinguishable. These two cases together possessed the characteristic features of a cycle. As a result, if the two cases were presented a year apart, rather than together, and if we assume that those who believed that they were indistinguishable voted sincerely, the result would have depended entirely upon which was presented first. Had this occurred, while stare decisis would have introduced another issue dimension in the second case, it would have avoided the possibility of asymmetry. In effect, like outcome voting, stare decisis is best understood as a range-relaxed cycle-breaking rule. As a result of stare decisis, the order of cases becomes critically important to the substantive evaluation of doctrine, or, in the language of social choice, renders the evolution of doctrine path dependent. In chapter 4, I argued, however, that the real problem with stare decisis is not path dependency, which is inevitable in a regime that seeks to achieve stable doctrine, but rather it is the incentive that the doctrine creates among litigants to try to manipulate the order of case decisions.

The Supreme Court's timing-based justiciability ground rules, including ripeness, mootness, and most notably standing, can best be understood as devices intended to limit the ability of ideological litigants to strategically time cases in the federal judiciary generally, and in the Supreme Court in particular, with an eye toward exerting a disproportionate influence on the substantive evolution of legal doctrine. In chapter 4, I further explained that other defenses to stare decisis–induced path manipulation—case distinctions, overruling, denials of certiorari, and summary dispositions—are individually and collectively inadequate to minimize the most egregious examples of litigant path manipulation. In effect, standing encourages litigants to seek redress in the political process, where legislatures are better suited than are the federal courts to avoid anomalous outcomes when their underlying preferences are prone to cycling by majority rule.

C. Part III: Historical and Case Evidence

In chapters 5 and 6, I provided comprehensive historical and case support for the social choice theory of standing set out in chapter 4. I began by explaining the creation of standing in the New Deal Court, and its later transformations in the Warren Court and in the Burger and Rehnquist Courts. The New Deal Court conceived standing as a tool to discipline lower federal courts, which having been stacked in three prior Republican administrations, shared a far more conservative ideology than the Supreme Court that President Franklin Delano Roosevelt forged. In the New Deal Court, standing was a set of presumptive rules—meaning that Congress could overcome those rules by statute—that prevented the federal judiciary from addressing the merits of underlying claims unless those claims were based upon common law analogues of injury. The newly conceived standing rules prevented lower federal courts from addressing the merits of cases, which would have highlighted the Supreme Court's recent doctrinal about-face in three areas: relaxing the long-standing *Lochner* regime; relaxing the Tenth Amendment limits on federal commerce clause powers; and relaxing the once-restrictive nondelegation doctrine. President Roosevelt's various New Deal initiatives had been struck down in the Supreme Court based variously on each of these three sets of conservative doctrines. By continuing to address the merits of such cases, the lower federal courts, which generally continued to oppose the progressive New Deal initiatives, threatened to embarrass the now liberal Supreme Court by revealing that the recent doctrinal changes were due to the remarkable change in Court personnel over a short period, rather than to a detached and reasoned analysis under new conditions.

In the Warren Court, standing was generally relaxed to invite novel constitutional challenges consistent with that Court's liberal agenda on issues of civil rights and liberties. More importantly, beginning in the Burger Court and continuing into the Rehnquist Court, standing was considerably changed. These later Courts imposed a series of specific justiciability criteria, including injury in fact, causation, and redressability, and insisted that standing was a constitutional prerequisite to litigating in federal court, growing out of the case or controversy requirement of Article III. One irony is that unlike their earlier counterparts on the New Deal and the Warren Courts, the Burger and Rehnquist Courts were increasingly conservative. One might have predicted, therefore, that these later Courts would have relaxed standing to invite, rather than to fend off, challenges to increasingly pervasive governmental regulation. Social choice theory helps to explain why the opposite occurred, and why instead those Courts constitutionalized standing and made it the centerpiece of their justiciability jurisprudence.

In contrast with the New Deal and Warren Courts, the Burger and Rehnquist Courts were faced with three persistent, but nondominant, frameworks for analyzing the most pressing constitutional issues of the day. One group of holdover justices continued to embrace liberal Warren-era precedents on the merits. A second group of conservative appointees sought to retrench upon the liberal Warren era to and to restore the Supreme Court to a more passive judicial role, even if that required overruling landmark cases. A third group of hybrid justices eschewed the ideologies of the liberal and conservative wings in favor of pragmatic, reasoned decision making often based upon neutral principles, including stare decisis and standing. This combination of frameworks, none of which could predictably dominate for the Court as a whole, set the stage for difficulties in aggregating Supreme Court preferences in an important subset of the most divisive cases of the day. As a result, the unique configuration of preferences that confronted these Courts created an incentive among litigants to try to exert a disproportionate influence on the evolution of legal doctrine by manipulating the order of cases, and in turn, created an incentive among the justices to respond by imposing a now-strengthened barrier to justiciability in the form of standing.

Finally, in chapter 6, I provided an extensive review of the justiciability case law, as it has been developed in the Burger and Rehnquist Courts. While the review was too comprehensive to invite summary, I will make a few comments. In chapter 4, I suggested that one could cast the Supreme Court's justiciability barriers in terms of timing: ripeness, then standing, then mootness. I also suggested that a more meaningful spectrum folds the timing-based spectrum in half, such that ripeness and mootness appear together. In this revised analysis, the various rules are evaluated based upon the ease or difficulty of manipulating the order of underlying claims. The ripeness and mootness doctrines prevent the lowest cost methods of manipulating the order of cases. And within the category of live claims, standing can be conceived as setting up three levels of barriers to path manipulation. The inability to raise the claims of others and to raise claims involving diffuse harms prevent fairly low-cost attempts at manipulating live claims. The most difficult category involves the rule preventing claims premised upon illegal market distortions. Cases in this category, which includes *Allen* and *Bakke,* appear inconsistent because they do not involve the claims of others or claims that are diffuse. Instead, in these difficult cases, the Court implicitly looks to both extremes on the justiciability spectrum to determine whether those characteristic features that pull in the direction of presuming for or against path manipulation—size of class, scope of desired relief, concreteness of remedy, zealousness of advocacy—predominate. As explained in chapter 6, the standing dimensions of *Allen* and *Bakke* are indistinguishable in kind, but they are different in degree. To appreciate this final hybrid category, we must recognize that law is anything but an exact science. The decision makers are human beings, and their assessments of differences in degree often prove critical. But once we define properly the underlying spectrum, we can understand what drives the justices to sort these cases as they do.

Before closing this summary, I should note that beginning with *Lujan v. Defenders of Wildlife,*[12] the Supreme Court has infused some unpredictability into its standing case law by suggesting that even Congress is limited in its ability to avoid the operation of the Court's doctrinal standing requirements. *Lujan* has been roundly criticized, and most recently, the Court has suggested a retreat.[13] *Lujan* presents a tension with the underlying social choice model in that the model suggests that standing is intended to preserve, until a proper consensus forms, the power of Congress to govern. In *Lujan,* however, Congress chose to govern by creating a private attorney general to monitor the executive branch in the federal courts and the Supreme Court said no. The recent erosion of *Lujan* notwithstanding, it may well be premature to forecast a complete judicial capitulation to Congress to determine the scope of standing to enforce federal laws.

III. Conclusion

The United States Supreme Court is vested with the awesome power to decide final matters of interpretation of constitutional and federal statutory law. While there are few institutions about which as much ink has been spilled as the Supreme Court, until now efforts to consider that institution from the perspective of social choice have been quite limited. Of course, no single model can provide a fully comprehensive analysis of any institution, and the

Supreme Court is no exception. At a minimum, however, I would suggest that this book has revealed the importance of adding the question, "How are these outcomes shaped by the collective nature of the Supreme Court's decision-making processes?" to any repertoire on the Court or on constitutional law. In the end, I hope to have shown that no theory or model intended to explain the United States Supreme Court is complete that does not also consider the implications of collective decision making on an en banc institution that is obligated, even in the most de minimis way, to resolve cases properly before it. I hope that, in the end, this book provides those who are interested in these fundamental questions with a set of powerful tools with which to begin their own intellectual journeys.

Notes

CHAPTER 1

1. Several important works might rightly be viewed as studying constitutional process. Consider, for example, JAMES BUCHANAN & GORDON TULLOCK, THE CALCULUS OF CONSENT (1965), which applies the theory of public choice to edify our understanding of several important features of constitutional democracy in the United States; JOHN HART ELY, DEMOCRACY AND DISTRUST (1980), which analyzes the role of the Supreme Court in furthering the processes of representative democracy; and BRUCE ACKERMAN, WE THE PEOPLE: FOUNDATIONS (1991), and BRUCE ACKERMAN, WE THE PEOPLE: TRANSFORMATIONS (1999), which consider the important role of the Supreme Court in affecting transformations throughout United States history. While each of these seminal works can properly be described in these terms, each is notably different from the undertaking set out here. This book studies the processes through which the Supreme Court, through case decision making, creates constitutional law.
2. The size of the Court has changed throughout its history. In 1789, the Court began with five members and immediately went to six in 1790. The Court size increased to seven in 1811, where it remained until 1836. Since 1837, the Court has had nine members. See GEOFFREY R. STONE, ET AL., CONSTITUTIONAL LAW xcvi–ciii, 31 (3d ed. 1996) (providing comprehensive time line of Supreme Court membership and description of change in Court size); JETHRO K. LIEBERMAN, THE EVOLVING CONSTITUTION: HOW THE SUPREME COURT HAS RULED ON ISSUES FROM ABORTION TO ZONING 635–44 (1992) (same).
3. See infra chapter 3, §§ I and II, and cites therein.
4. 118 S. Ct. 1428 (1998). For a more detailed description and analysis of Miller, see Maxwell L. Stearns, Should Justices Ever Switch Votes? Miller v. Albright in Social Choice Perspective, 7 SUP. CT. ECON. REV. 87 (1999).
5. 505 U.S. 833 (1992).
6. 523 U.S. 420 (1998).
7. See Miller, 523 U.S. 420, 426 n.23 (1998) (Stevens, J., announcing the judgment of the Court) (noting that while, in 1986, the INA was amended to change the age from twenty-one to eighteen, petitioner, who was born prior to 1986, "[fell] within a narrow age bracket whose members may elect to have the preamendment law apply").
8. The amended statute states that
Citizenship of such persons is established if:

   (1) a blood relationship between the person and the father is established by clear and convincing evidence,

(2) the father had the nationality of the United States at the time of the person's birth,

(3) the father (unless deceased) has agreed in writing to provide financial support for the person until the person reaches the age of 18 years, and

(4) while the person is under the age of 18 years—

    (A) the person is legitimized under the law of the person's residence or domicile,

    (B) the father acknowledges paternity of the person in writing under oath, or

    (C) the paternity of the person is established by adjudication in a competent court.

U.S.C. § 1409 (a) (as amended 1986). *Miller*, 523 U.S. at 431 (Stevens, J., announcing the judgment of the Court).

9. 523 U.S. at 432 (Stevens, J., announcing the judgment of the Court).

10. For historical reasons, the Court has construed the Fifth Amendment due process clause to include an equal protection component. *See* Bolling v. Sharpe, 347 U.S. 497 (1954). Because the Fourteenth Amendment, in which the equal protection clause appears, applies only to the states, following Brown v. Board of Educ. of Topeka, 347 U.S. 483 (1954), the Court employed the Fifth Amendment due process clause to end segregation of public schools in the District of Columbia, which were regulated under federal, rather than state, law. This maneuver avoided the anomaly that congressionally controlled schools could continue race-based segregation, while public schools in the states could not. Inspired by the earlier doctrine of incorporation, through which the Supreme Court construed the Fourteenth Amendment due process clause to apply the substantive provisions of the Bill of Rights to the states, *see infra* chapter 5, § III (describing the incorporation doctrine), the doctrine established in *Bolling* has become known as "reverse incorporation," suggesting the historical counterintuition of interpreting an earlier constitutional amendment in light of a judicial construction of a later one.

11. Technically, with the only Texas citizen removed from the case, venue was no longer proper.

12. 523 U.S. at 427.

13. Although Justice Stevens never articulates the relevant test for asserting the gender-based distinction drawn in the challenged INA provision, he does question whether heightened scrutiny applies in this context. *See id.* at 434–35 n. 11. When discussing petitioner's independent challenge arising from her status as the foreign-born illegitimate daughter of a citizen father in section IV of his opinion, Stevens employs a mixture of characterizations drawn from both rational basis scrutiny and heightened scrutiny, *see, e.g., id.* at 440 ("We are convinced not only that strong government interests justify the additional requirement imposed on children of citizen fathers, but also that the particular means used in § 1409(a)(4) are well tailored to serve those interests."); *id.* at 439 ("It was surely reasonable when the INA was enacted in 1952, and remains equally reasonable today, for Congress to condition the award of citizenship to such children on an act that demonstrates at a minimum, the possibility that those who become citizens will develop ties with this country—a requirement that performs a meaningful purpose for citizen fathers but normally would be superfluous for citizen mothers."). In contrast, in discussing the gender-based challenge, Stevens reasons that the "gender equality principle," at issue in those cases in which dis-

crimination "is merely the accidental by-product of a traditional way of thinking about females," *id.* at 442 (internal quotations omitted), "is only indirectly involved in this case." *Id.* Stevens fails to articulate which standard applies and inquires only whether Congress has devised a relevant gender-based distinction. Thus, Stevens reasons that "[n]one of the premises on which the statutory classification is grounded can be fairly characterized as an accidental by-product of a traditional way of thinking about members of either sex. The biological differences between single men and single women provide a relevant basis for differing rules govering their ability to confer citizenship on children born in foreign lands." *Id.* at 444–45. That part of Stevens's opinion can be read in either of two ways. First, Stevens might be suggesting that real differences satisfy the heightened scrutiny test, albeit one that is more relaxed than the "skeptical scrutiny," recently embraced in United States v. Virginia, 518 U.S. 515, 531 (1996). See *Miller,* 118 S. Ct. at 434–35 n. 11 (declining to apply *Virginia* standard for heightened scrutiny). Second, consistent with the intuition expressed by the United States Court of Appeals for the District of Columbia Circuit, he might be suggesting that when a gender-based statutory distinction is founded upon real differences, the relevant test is rational basis scrutiny, under which the Court will inquire only whether Congress embraced a relevant distinction. The argument that follows in the text applies whichever reading one finds more persuasive. Under either reading, Stevens (joined by Rehnquist), appears as part of a minority applying a more relaxed standard than heightened scrutiny as employed by the *Virginia* Court and as part of a minority concluding that his chosen standard is satisfied in this case.

14. 523 U.S. at 432 (Stevens, J., announcing the judgment of the Court).
15. 523 U.S. at 445 (O'Connor, J., concurring in the judgment).
16. For examples in which the Supreme Court has allowed liberal standing based upon the Fair Housing Act, see Havens Realty v. Coleman, 455 U.S. 363, 373–74 (1982); Gladstone, Realtors v. Village of Bellwood, 441 U.S. 91, 109–15 (1979); Village of Arlington Heights v. Metropolitan Hous. Dev. Corp., 429 U.S. 252, 264 (1977); Trafficante v. Metropolitan Life Ins. Co., 409 U.S. 205, 212 (1972). *See also* Maxwell L. Stearns, *Standing and Social Choice: Historical Evidence,* 144 U. PA. L. REV. 309, 391 (1995) (collecting authorities); David A. Logan, *Standing to Sue: A Proposed Separation of Powers Analysis,* 1984 WIS. L. REV. 37, 64–81 (same).
17. *See Miller,* 423 U.S. at 447 (O'Connor, J., concurring in the judgment). In fact, Justice O'Connor effectively raised the standard for vindicating the claim of another under this exception, as previously articulated in Powers v. Ohio, 499 U.S. 400, 411 (1991), from "some hindrance," *see id.* at 411, to "substantial hindrance." *See Miller,* 423 U.S. at 447 (O'Connor, J., concurring in the judgment). As a result, in his separate concurrence, Justice Scalia stated that while he would have agreed with Justice O'Connor's decision to deny petitioner standing to raise her father's claim as an original matter, the Court's standing precedents, which had afforded third-party standing in similar circumstances with even a lesser hindrance, prevented him from doing so in *Miller. See Miller,* 523 U.S. at 454–55 n. 1 (Scalia, J., concurring in the judgment).
18. 523 U.S. at 451–52 (O'Connor, J., concurring in the judgment).
19. 523 U.S. at 454–55 n.1 (Scalia, J., concurring in the judgment).
20. *See* U.S. CONST. art. I, § 8, cl. 4; *see also Miller,* 523 U.S. at 453 (Scalia, J., concurring in the judgment).

21. 523 U.S. at 473 (Breyer, J., dissenting).
22. 423 U.S. at 460, 469–70 (Ginsburg, J., dissenting); *id.* at 476, 482 (Breyer, J., dissenting).
23. 523 U.S. at 460. (Ginsburg, J., dissenting).
24. 523 U.S. at 482–83 (Breyer, J., dissenting).
25. 523 U.S. at 460 (Ginsburg, J., dissenting).
26. 523 at 476 (Breyer, J., dissenting).
27. In table 3.2, chapter 3, § II.C.2, I will simplify this presentation of *Miller* by reducing the relevant number of issues to two and the relevant number of voting camps to three. This simplification, which does not change the analysis, reveals the requisite features for a voting anomaly, namely multidimensionality and asymmetry.
28. See David Post & Steven C. Salop, *Rowing against the Tidewater: A Theory of Voting by Multijudge Panels,* 80 GEO. L. J. 743 (1992); David Post & Steven C. Salop, *Issues and Outcomes, Guidance and Indeterminacy: A Reply to Professor John Rogers and Others,* 49 VAND. L. REV. 1069 (1996).
29. *See* Lewis A. Kornhauser & Lawrence G. Sager, *The One and the Many: Adjudication in Collegial Courts,* 81 CAL. L. REV. 1 (1993).
30. 505 U.S. 833 (1992).
31. 410 U.S. 113 (1973).
32. In chapter 3, we will see that former justice Brennan, contrary to a majority of the Court, took the position that whatever substantive test the Court applies, even low-level rational basis, the asserted justification in support of the law had to be the actual legislative motive at the time of the law's adoption. *See infra* chapter 3, § II.A (discussing Kassel v. Consolidated Freightways, 450 U.S. 662 (1981)).
33. For a prominent recent example of striking down a state statute under rational basis scrutiny, consider Romer v. Evans, 517 U.S. 620 (1996). In *Romer,* the Supreme Court was faced with the following Colorado state constitutional amendment:

No Protected Status Based on Homosexual, Lesbian, or Bisexual Orientation.
Neither the State of Colorado, through any of its branches or departments, nor any of its agencies, political subdivisions, municipalities or school districts, shall enact, adopt or enforce any statute, regulation, ordinance or policy whereby homosexual, lesbian or bisexual orientation, conduct, practices or relationships shall constitute or otherwise be the basis of or entitle any person or class of persons to have or claim any minority status, quota preference, protected status or claim of discrimination. This Section of the Constitution shall be in all respects self-executing.

Romer, 517 U.S. at 624 (quoting Amendment 2 to the Colorado Constitution). In essence, the amendment was intended to prevent gays and lesbians from claiming any protected status under Colorado law by virtue of their sexual orientation. The *Romer* Court, in an opinion by Justice Anthony Kennedy, eschewed any inquiry into the question whether sexual orientation constitutes a suspect class, holding, instead, that the amendment fails the rational basis test. *Id.* at 632. For Kennedy, the Colorado amendment exhibited an illicit animus toward a politically unpopular group, a justification that Kennedy concluded can never rationally further a legitimate governmental interest. *Id.* at 634.
For an example in which the Supreme Court sustained a state law under strict scrutiny, see Maine v. Taylor, 477 U.S. 131 (1986). The *Taylor* Court sus-

tained Maine's prohibition on importing live baitfish from out of state against a dormant commerce clause challenge. Maine contended that live baitfish, which were not native to Maine, were parasitic on a native fish population. *Id.* at 133. Notwithstanding the application of strict scrutiny, the Court sustained the law, holding that protecting its native fish population against parasites was a compelling state interest and that the method chosen was narrowly tailored, given the absence of available alternatives. *Id.* at 151–52. For another, much vilified, example in which the Court, applying strict scrutiny, nonetheless sustained a federal law excluding Japanese Americans from their homes and ordering them to go to detainment centers, see Korematsu v. United States, 343 U.S. 214 (1944).

34. *See, e.g.,* San Antonio Indep. Sch. Dist. v. Rodriguez, 411 U.S. 1, 98–99 (1973) (Marshall, J., dissenting) ("A principled reading of what this Court has done reveals that it has applied a spectrum of standards in reviewing discrimination allegedly violative of the Equal Protection Clause. This spectrum clearly comprehends variations in the degree of care with which the Court will scrutinize particular classifications, depending, I believe, on the constitutional and societal importance of the interest adversely affected and the recognized invidiousness of the basis upon which the particular classification is drawn").

35. *See, e.g.,* Bush v. Vera, 116 U.S. 1941, 1977–78 (1996) (Stevens, J., dissenting) ("The conclusion that race-conscious districting should not always be subject to strict scrutiny merely recognizes that our equal protection jurisprudence can sometimes mislead us with its rigid characterization of suspect classes and levels of scrutiny. As I have previously noted, all equal protection jurisprudence might be described as a form of rational basis scrutiny; we apply 'strict scrutiny' more to describe the likelihood of success than the character of the test to be applied"). This approach is obviously consistent with the conflated standards of review that Justice Stevens applied in *Miller,* see *supra* note 13.

36. Alternatively, the government can succeed upon proving that the ultimate outcome of the state's challenged conduct would have been the same, even absent an illicit classification or infringement upon a fundamental right. This has arisen, most notably, in the First Amendment context. Thus, for example, in Mt. Healthy City Sch. Dist. Bd. of Educ. v. Doyle, 429 U.S. 274 (1977), the Court initially applied strict scrutiny in a lawsuit alleging that a termination decision was based upon the exercise of First Amendment rights, but allowed the state to prove, as an alternative means of avoiding liability, that even absent the protected conduct, it would have reached the same decision. *See also* Village of Arlington Heights v. Metropolitan Hous. Dev. Corp., 429 U.S. 252 (1977). For a seemingly contrary result, see Pickering v. Board of Educ., 391 U.S. 563 (1968) (holding that where plaintiff had engaged in protected First Amendment activity, the state could not fire her, even though school alleged that teacher's statements harmed the school system).

37. Harry W. Jones, *Dyson Distinguished Lecture: Precedent and Policy in Constitutional Law,* 4 PACE L. REV. 11, 18 (1983)

38. 505 U.S. 833 (1992).

39. 410 U.S. 113 (1973).

40. The explanation for choosing viability was circular:

With respect to [the] interest in potential life, the "compelling" point is at viability. This is so because the fetus then presumably has the capability of meaningful life outside the mother's womb.

Id. at 163. Rather than stating a justification for the choice of viability as the cut-off before which the state's interest is not compelling, Blackmun simply restated the definition of viability.

41. 492 U.S. 490 (1989) (Rehnquist, C.J., for a plurality of four).

42. In addition to *Miller, supra*, in which Justice Stevens joined Justice Rehnquist in denying petitioner relief, see also *infra* chapter 3, § IV.C (explaining that Stevens sided with the conservative wing in a four-one-four split majority opinion in Board of Regents of the Univ. of Cal. v. Bakke, 438 U.S. 265 (1978)).

43. *Casey,* 505 U.S. at 914 (Stevens, J., concurring in part and dissenting in part); *id.* at 930 (Blackmun, J., concurring in part, concurring in the judgment in part, and dissenting in part).

44. *Id.* at 920, 922 (Stevens, J., concurring in part and dissenting in part); *id.* at 922, 938–39 (Blackmun, J., concurring in part, concurring in the judgment in part, and dissenting in part).

45. *Id.* at 922 (Stevens, J., concurring in part and dissenting in part).

46. *Id.* at 979–80 (Scalia, J., concurring in the judgment in part and dissenting in part); *id.* at 944, 952–53 (Rehnquist, C.J., concurring in the judgment in part and dissenting in part).

47. *Id.* at 845, 869 (joint opinion).

48. The *Casey* Court overturned Akron v. Akron Ctr. for Reproductive Health, Inc., 462 U.S. 416 (1983), and Thornburgh v. American College of Obstetricians and Gynecologists, 476 U.S. 747 (1986). *See Casey,* 505 U.S. at 881–82 (joint opinion); *see also id.* at 954 (Rehnquist, C.J., concurring in the judgment in part and dissenting in part).

49. *Casey,* 505 U.S. at 854 (joint opinion).

50. *Id.* at 854–55. The joint authors determined that *Roe* derived from two lines of precedent, first, those privacy cases protecting individuals with respect to matters of sexuality and reproduction, beginning with Griswold v. Connecticut, 381 U.S. 479 (1965) (establishing the right of married couples to use contraceptives based upon penumbral right of privacy), and Eisenstadt v. Baird, 405 U.S. 438 (1972) (extending the right of nonmarried couples to use contraceptives based upon equal protection), and, second, those cases protecting individuals against bodily intrusion at the hands of the state, beginning, most notably, with Skinner v. Oklahoma, 316 U.S. 535 (1942) (invalidating statute allowing forced sterilization of habitual criminals convicted of specified "felonies involving moral turpitude," which include larceny, but not embezzlement, even though they are comparable offenses, based upon equal protection clause). The authors concluded that these lines of precedent had not been undermined through subsequent doctrinal developments, nor proved to be unworkable over time. *Casey,* 505 U.S. at 858–59. Alternatively, given the unique nature of the abortion right, the authors reasoned that *Roe* could be viewed as sui generis. *Casey,* 505 U.S. at 857. If so, the joint opinion authors concluded, *Roe* itself cannot be viewed as either a remnant of abandoned doctrine or as creating a framework for analysis that has proved unworkable over time. *Id.*

51. *Id.* at 955 (Rehnquist, C. J., concurring in the judgment in part and dissenting in part (quoting, in part, the joint opinion at 833)).

52. *Id.* at 856 (joint opinion).

53. 198 U.S. 45 (1905).

54. 300 U.S. 379 (1937).

55. 163 U.S. 537 (1896).

56. 347 U.S. 483 (1954).

57. *Casey,* 505 U.S. at 863–64 (joint opinion).
58. *See infra* chapter 5, § II.
59. The most famous Supreme Court overruling of federal New Deal statutes came on May 27, 1935, which became known as "Black Monday." On that date, the Court struck down the National Industrial Recovery Act and the mortgage moratoria in the Frazier-Lemke Act in Louisville Joint Stock Land Bank v. Radford, 295 U.S. 555 (1935), and issued Humphreys Executor v. United States, 295 U.S. 602 (1935), preventing President Roosevelt from removing a commissioner on the independent Federal Trade Commission. For an excellent discussion of this historical period, see WILLIAM E. LEUCHTENBERG, THE SUPREME COURT REBORN: THE CONSTITUTIONAL REVOLUTION IN THE AGE OF ROOSEVELT (1995); *see also* Stearns, *Historical Evidence, supra* note 16, at 368; *infra* chapter 5, § II.
60. 300 U.S. 379 (1937). For a discussion of two scholars who have recently questioned the accuracy of the switch in time account of *Parrish, see infra* chapter 5, section II n. 11.
61. *See* LEUCHTENBERG, *supra* note 59, at 177.
62. *Casey,* 505 U.S. at 861–62 (joint opinion).
63. *Plessy v. Ferguson,* 163 U.S. 537, 560 (1896) (Harlan, J,. dissenting).
64. *Casey,* 505 U.S. at 863 (joint opinion).
65. *Id.* at 955 (Rehnquist, C.J., concurring in the judgment in part and dissenting in part).
66. 430 U.S. 188 (1977).
67. In chapter 3, I will introduce a seemingly more extreme case illustrating the same proposition, namely Board of Regents of the Univ. of Cal. v. Bakke, 438 U.S. 265 (1978), in which only one justice out of nine, Lewis Powell, agreed to the identification and resolution of the two dispositive issues in the case, and yet his opinion became universally accepted as stating the holding in the case on both issues. *See infra* chapter 3, § IV.C.
68. For a more detailed discussion of path dependency, and its implications for the evolution of legal doctrine, see *infra* chapter 4, § III.
69. 458 U.S. 527 (1982).
70. 458 U.S. 457 (1982).
71. Crawford v. Board of Educ., 458 U.S. 527, 529 (1982). The California Supreme Court had previously interpreted the California Constitution to prohibit de facto segregation and to require reasonable steps to alleviate it. *Id.* at 530 n. 2.
72. *Seattle Sch. Dist.,* 458 U.S. at 462, 464.
73. 413 U.S. 189 (1972).
74. 394 U.S. 294 (1955).
75. 402 U.S. 1 (1971). For an interesting review of the history of *Swann,* including an explanation of how the majority opinion's author, Chief Justice Burger, came to embrace the substantive positions initially advanced in Justice Stewart's draft dissent, see LEE EPSTEIN & JACK KNIGHT, THE CHOICES JUSTICES MAKE 106 (1998).
76. *See* JOHN C. JEFFRIES, JR., JUSTICE LEWIS F. POWELL, JR.: A BIOGRAPHY 298–99 (1994); Keyes v. School Dist. No. 1, Denver, Colo., 413 U.S. 189, 218 n. 3 (1973) (Powell, J., concurring in part and dissenting in part).
77. *Keyes,* 413 U.S. at 208.
78. *Id.* at 262–63, 265 (Rehnquist, J., dissenting).
79. *See Keyes,* 413 U.S. at 224, 227–28 (Powell, J., concurring in part and dissenting in part); *see also* City of Mobile v. Bolden, 446 U.S. 55, 90 (1980) (Stevens, J., concurring in the judgment) ("In my view [a voting scheme should be struck down on equal protection grounds only if]: (1) [it] was manifestly not the prod-

uct of a routine or a traditional political decision; (2) it [has] a significant adverse impact on a minority group; and (3) it [is] unsupported by any neutral justification and thus [is] either totally irrational or entirely motivated by a desire to curtail the political strength of the minority").

80. While Powell and Stevens agreed on the formula for determining the presence or absence of burden shifting, their underlying rationales differed. Justice Powell believed that the standards for northern and southern desegregation should be the same, especially since, post-*Swann,* the South was the most integrated region in the country. Powell hoped that a single standard operating throughout the nation would discourage the Supreme Court from promoting continuous federal judicial intervention into southern school districts, which were actually more integrated than their northern counterparts. For an excellent discussion of Powell's jurisprudence on school desegregation in this historical period, see JEFFRIES, *supra* note 76, at 282–83. The objective-manifestation standard would have provided a ready tool that would have operated both in states in which segregation had been mandated by law, thus avoiding the nearly irrebuttable presumption that statistical disparities in the racial composition of public schools resulted from the continuing effects of past segregative practices, and in the North, given the near impossibility of disproving illicit legislative motivations once a racial gerrymander is established in part of a school system.

For Stevens, in contrast, the objective-manifestation standard helped to solve another dimension of inconsistency, but not necessarily across the North and South. The difficulty for Stevens was that if the Court focused upon the subjective motivations of legislators, assuming that it is even possible to prove such motivations, the very same statutes in two different states, or districting schemes in two different districts in the same state, could produce precisely opposite results on constitutionality, making it difficult for future lawmakers to rely upon Supreme Court decisions.

81. For a discussion demonstrating that the Court has continued to shift among these approaches in the vote districting, see *infra* chapter 4, § III.C.

82. 393 U.S. 385 (1969).

83. *Seattle,* 458 U.S. at 467–68 (quoting *Hunter,* 393 U.S. at 357).

84. *Seattle,* 458 U.S. at 470–71.

85. *Crawford,* 458 U.S. at 535.

86. In chapter 4, I will provide a simplified presentation of these cases, which will reveal that, together, they possess the same characteristic features of multidimensionality and asymmetry that is present in *Miller v. Albright. See infra* chapter 4, § III.A.

87. I will revisit, and defend, this assumption, in chapters 3 and 4.

88. *Crawford,* 458 U.S. at 457–58 (Marshall, J,. dissenting).

89. *Seattle,* 458 U.S. at 495 (Powell, J., dissenting) ("It is a strange notion—alien to our system—that local governmental bodies can forever pre-empt the ability of a State—the sovereign power—to address a matter of compelling concern to the State"). One additional distinction remained between the two cases; while the California amendment allowed busing only for identified violations of the federal constitution, the Washington initiative allowed busing for that and for identified violations of the state constitution. Of course, to the extent that this distinction mattered at all, it would have resulted in the opposite holdings in both cases, namely upholding the law that provided stronger equal protection rights, namely the Washington initiative, which the Court struck down, and striking down the

law providing the narrower protection, namely the California amendment, which the Court upheld.

90. *See supra* § II.C (discussing Rehnquist and Scalia approaches to stare decisis in constitutional cases).

91. *See* Frank H. Easterbrook, *Ways of Criticizing the Court,* 95 HARV. L. REV. 802, 820 (1982) (observing, "The order of decisions has nothing to do with the intent of the framers or of the other things that might inform constitutional interpretation").

92. 438 U.S. 265 (1978).

93. 468 U.S. 737 (1984).

94. Board of Regents of the Univ. of California v. Bakke, 438 U.S. 265 (1978).

95. *See Allen,* 468 at 752–53, 753 n. 19.

96. 42 U.S.C. §§ 2000e—17 (1970 ed. Supp. V).

97. *See Bakke,* 438 U.S. at 280 (Powell, J., announcing the judgment for the Court).

98. *See id.* at 281.

99. 468 U.S. 737 (1984).

100. *See supra* note 10 (explaining reverse incorporation).

101. 468 U.S. at 758.

102. While *Allen* might appear at first to involve third-party standing, since the parents are raising claims on behalf of their children, the courts have created an obvious *parens patriae* exception to this general rule, which applies in that case. There was no suggestion in *Allen* that standing was denied on this basis.

103. *See, e.g.,* United States v. Richardson, 418 U.S. 166 (1974) (preventing taxpayer standing to force CIA to release budget information under the Constitution's statements and account clause); Schlesinger v. Reservists Comm'n to Stop the War, 418 U.S. 208 (1974) (preventing citizen standing to prevent seated members of Congress from serving in the military reserves in violation of the Constitution's incompatibility clause).

104. *See* Federal Elections Comm'n v. Akins, 524 U.S. 11, 23–25 (1998) (distinguishing diffuse claim status based upon abstract nature of injury from justiciable injuries that are concrete but widely shared).

105. *Bakke,* 438 U.S. at 280 n. 14 (Powell, J., announcing the judgment for the Court).

106. *Allen,* 468 U.S. at 759.

107. *See* Maxwell L. Stearns, *Standing Back from the Forest: Justiciability and Social Choice,* 83 CAL. L. REV. 1309, 1326–29 (1995) (collecting authorities); *infra* chapter 4 (discussing standing).

108. In striking down the Davis plan, which employed a quota, Justice Powell, delivering the judgment of the Court, stated that the Harvard plan under which the school considered race as one factor among many in its admissions decisions, and considered all files as part of a single process, rather than treating minority files separately, was constitutionally permissible. *See Bakke,* 438 U.S. at 316–20 (Powell, J., announcing the judgment of the Court).

109. *Allen,* 468 U.S. at 784, 788 (Stevens, J., dissenting).

110. Justice Stevens, in his dissenting opinion in *Allen* expressed a similar intuition:

This causation argument is nothing more than a restatement of elementary economics: when something becomes more expensive, less of it will be purchased. [The] process of desegregation will be advanced [since the] withdrawal of the subsidy for segregated schools means the incentive structure facing white parents who seek such schools for their children will be altered.

468 U.S. at 788. How many parents are on the margin is beside the point, since a change in the rule obviously will not change the conduct of parents who are inframarginal in their decision to send their children to private discriminatory schools. As demonstrated in the text, the same holds true in *Bakke.*

111. I will provide a more detailed history of standing in chapter 5, and a detailed review of the standing case law in chapter 6.

112. Professor Gene Nichols has aptly summarized this literature, stating:

> In separate, major, and compelling efforts, Louis Jaffe in 1965, Raoul Berger in 1969, and Steven Winter in 1988 have demonstrated that injury was not a requisite for judicial authority in either the colonial, framing, or early constitutional periods. The Judiciary Act of 1789, like several contemporaneous state statutes, allowed "informer" actions. English practice included prerogative writs, mandamus, *certiorari,* and prohibition, all designed to "restrain unlawful or abusive action by lower courts or public agencies," and requiring only "neglect of justice," not individual injury. Stranger suits and relator practice countenanced the assertion of judicial power without the existence of a direct personal stake in the controversy.

> Gene R. Nichols, Jr., *Justice Scalia, Standing, and Public Law Litigation,* 42 Duke L.J. 1141, 1151–52 (1993) (citations omitted); *see also* Stearns, *Standing Back from the Forest, supra* note 107, at 1327–28 n. 69 (collecting authorities). For a related discussion in a recent Supreme Court decision, *see infra* chapter 5 n. 119 (discussing Steel Company v. Citizens for a Better Environment, 523 U.S. 83 (1988).

113. Equitable jurisdiction arises when a person seeks a form of relief other than monetary damages. Historically, courts of law and equity were separate, but within the United States they have been merged. In BLACK'S LAW DICTIONARY (6th ed. 1990), the editors explain the nature of equity jurisdiction in United States practice as follows:

> In the federal and most state courts there has been a merger procedurally of law and equity actions (*i.e.,* the same court has jurisdiction over *both* legal and equitable matters) and, hence, a person seeking equitable relief brings the same complaint as in a law action and simply demands equitable relief instead of (or in addition to) monetary damages.

> *See id.* at 541 (italics in original) (defining "Equity jurisdiction").

114. *See* Steven L. Winter, *The Metaphor of Standing and Problem of Self-Governance,* 40 Stan. L. Rev. 1371, 1446–47 (1988) (observing that while early federal court practice condoned private enforcement actions that are presumptively barred under current standing doctrine, the origins of modern standing terminology have their roots in late-eighteenth-century equity practice); Stearns, *Historical Evidence, supra* note 16, at 366 (describing late-eighteenth-century origins of standing terminology); Stearns, *Standing Back from the Forest, supra* note 107, at 1326–27 n. 66 and 1327–28 n. 69 (collecting authorities on historical origins of modern standing doctrine and on tension between present doctrine and early private enforcement suits); *infra* chapter 5 (providing more detailed historical development of modern standing doctrine).

115. *See* Winter, *supra* note 114, at 1414 (positing that "[a]s public agencies such as district and county attorneys were established [in the 1840s and 1850s], the need decreased for private attorneys general").

116. *See generally id.* For a discussion of the relationship between the pre–New Deal cases, Frothingham v. Mellon, 262 U.S. 447 (1923), and Fairchild v. Hughes, 258 U.S. 126 (1922), which are often described as standing cases, and later standing doctrine developed in the New Deal, see *infra* at 233 n. 68, and cites therein.

117. *See* Stearns, *Historical Evidence, supra* note 16, at 398 ("While President Roosevelt succeeded in forging a Court that shared his constitutional (and political) vision, the same was not true for the lower federal courts, which having been packed in three preceding Republican administrations, were sympathetic to *Lochner* and hostile to FDR's regulatory agenda"); PETER IRONS, THE NEW DEAL LAWYERS 13 (1982) (observing that the Hughes Court "shared with their lower-court brethren an equal commitment to the precepts of constitutional fundamentalism and a similar 19th-century perspective"); Joseph L. Rauh, Jr., *Lawyers and the Legislation of the Early New Deal,* 96 HARV. L. REV. 947, 949 (1983) (book review of PETER H. IRONS, THE NEW DEAL LAWYERS, 1982) (observing that prior to the Roosevelt administration, "three successive Republican administrations had stacked the lower federal courts with judges hostile to federal action of almost any kind").

118. *See* Stearns, *Historical Evidence, supra* note 16, at 397–98 n. 282.

119. In fact, as I will demonstrate *infra* at chapter 5, standing served the same purpose in this historical period in disciplining lower federal courts with respect to challenges to federal New Deal initiatives that Erie R.R. v. Tompkins, 304 U.S. 64 (1938), played in preventing the same courts from employing a parallel track of federal common law to limit similarly progressive state deal regulatory initiatives. *See also* Stearns, *Historical Evidence, supra* note 16, at 394, 398–99, and cites therein.

120. *See infra* chapter 5 (describing evolution of standing in these historical periods).

121. *See* Lujan v. Defenders of Wildlife, 504 U.S. 555 (1992).

122. *See* Raines v. Byrd, 521 U.S. 811 (1997).

123. The Court later considered the constitutionality of the Line-Item Veto Act and struck it down in Clinton v. City of New York, 524 U.S. 417 (1998).

124. Since the completion of this book, the Court issued Friends of the Earth v. Laidlaw, 120 S. Ct. 693 (2000), a case that appears to be in rather obvious tension with Lujan.

CHAPTER 2

1. THE NEW INTERNATIONAL BOOK OF QUOTATIONS 281 (Hugh Rawson & Margaret Miner eds., 1986).

2. WEBSTER'S NEW WORLD COLLEGE DICTIONARY, Third Edition 430 (1996).

3. One might quibble that I have defined *economic analysis* rather than *economics.* I would argue, however, that, just as statistics is the study of various subject matters from the perspective of statistical analysis, so too economics, properly understood, is the study of various subject matters from the perspective of economic analysis.

4. JAMES M. BUCHANAN & GORDON TULLOCK, THE CALCULUS OF CONSENT: LOGICAL FOUNDATIONS OF DIRECT DEMOCRACY 17–18 (1962) (internal citations and footnote omitted).

5. For a debate on whether the common practice of voting is at odds with the economist's understanding of individual rationality, compare Daniel A. Farber & Philip B. Frickey, *The Jurisprudence of Public Choice,* 65 TEX. L. REV. 873 (1987) (posit-

ing that voting is at odds with the economic understanding of rationality and is often based upon ideology, rather than the instrumental desire to affect the outcome of elections), with Michael E. DeBow & Dwight R. Lee, *Understanding (and Misunderstanding) Public Choice: A Response to Farber and Frickey*, 66 Tex. L. Rev. 993 (1988) (explaining that the consumption value of voting restores the act's rationality using the economist's understanding of that term), *see also* Maxwell L. Stearns, Public Choice and Public Law: Readings and Commentary 64–69 (1997) (discussing economist's understanding of rationality as it relates to noninstrumental act of voting, and collecting authorities).

6. Consider for example the recent difficulties faced by United Way and the fact that, holding all else constant, rational persons would prefer to give to charitable organizations with a lower ratio of administrative costs to the ultimate distribution of proceeds, than to give to charities with a higher ratio. For a discussion of the economics of charity, see Jack Hirshleifer, Price Theory and Applications 81–83, 157–60, 183, 545–46 (2d ed. 1980).

7. *See* Iain McLean & Arnold B. Urken, *Did Jefferson or Madison Understand Condorcet's Theory of Social Choice?*, 73 Pub. Choice 445, 446 (1992) ("Condorcet's standing as the principal founder of social choice rests largely, but not entirely, on his *Essai sur l'application de l'analyse à la probabilité des décisions rendues à la pluralité des voix* of 1785. . . . This work investigates the logical relationship between voting procedures and collective outcomes").

8. While the equal-size assumption is not necessary, it makes the presentation easier. This and future hypotheticals will work equally well with three groups of unequal size, provided that any two-group combination is sufficiently large to create a majority. We have already seen an example of such groups in the discussion of the three relevant camps within the Supreme Court. *See supra* chapter 1, § II.C (discussing two-three-four lineup in *Casey*).

9. *See* Amartya K. Sen, *Social Choice and Justice: A Review Article*, 23 J. Econ. Lit. 1764, 1765 n. 7 (1985) (observing that the "number of books and papers published in formal social choice theory has now certainly exceeded a thousand, the bulk of it coming in the last decade and a half"); *see also* Maxwell L. Stearns, *The Misguided Renaissance of Social Choice*, 103 Yale L.J. 1213, 1224 (1994) (describing proliferation of social choice literature).

10. *See* H. P. Young, *Condorcet's Theory of Voting*, 82 Am. Pol. Sci. Rev. 1231, 1239 ("Condorcet proposed that whenever a candidate obtains a simple majority over every other candidate, then that candidate is presumptively the 'best.' This decision rule is now known as a 'Condorcet's criterion,' and such a candidate (if it exists) is a 'Condorcet winner' or a 'majority candidate' ") (citations omitted). *See also* Stearns, *The Misguided Renaissance, supra* note 9, at 1253 (describing Condorcet criterion and collecting authorities).

11. William H. Riker, Liberalism Against Populism: A Confrontation Between the Theory of Democracy and the Theory of Social Choice 100 (1982); *see also* Stearns, *The Misguided Renaissance, supra* note 9, at 1255 n. 128 (collecting authorities on universal appeal of Condorcet criterion among social choice theorists).

12. *See* Saul Levmore, *Parliamentary Law, Majority Decisionmaking, and the Voting Paradox*, 74 Va. L. Rev. 971, 995 n. 69 (1989) ("The Condorcet concept has at least two well-known defects: Preferences do not necessarily, or even usually, deliver a Condorcet winner, and the concept does not take into account intensity of preference"); Stearns, *The Misguided Renaissance, supra* note 9, at

1255–56 (describing limitations of Condorcet criterion and providing illustrations).

13. *See* Stearns, *The Misguided Renaissance, supra* note 9, at 1233–47 (providing several illustrations of cycling and collecting authorities). Employing the language of game theory, cycling occurs when the preferences of the decision makers produce an empty core. The game theoretical concept of the empty core is virtually identical to the absence of a Condorcet winner in social choice. *See id.*

14. *See* William H. Riker, *The Paradox of Voting and Congressional Rules for Voting on Amendments,* 52 AM. POL. SCI. REV. 349, 354 (1958) (explaining need for number of pairwise votes equal to the number of options to ensure that Condorcet winner, if available, will prevail, and demonstrating non-Condorcet-producing rules that limit permissible number of amendments in Congress); *see also* Stearns, *The Misguided Renaissance, supra* note 9, at 1264–65 n. 171 (collecting authorities).

15. *See* Riker, *The Paradox of Voting, supra* note 14, at 354; Stearns, *The Misguided Renaissance, supra* note 9, at 1264–65 n. 171.

16. *See* Maxwell L. Stearns, *Standing Back from the Forest: Justiciability and Social Choice,* 83 CAL. L. REV. 1309, 1329–50 (1996) (describing phenomenon of path dependency, providing illustrations and collecting authorities).

17. We have already seen the path leading to C. If, instead, the agenda setter most prefers option A, she would first present B versus C (B wins), then B versus A (A wins). Option C, the sole option that would defeat A in a direct pairwise contest, was defeated in the first round. And if the agenda setter most preferred option B, she would first present C versus A (C wins), and then present C versus B (B wins). In this example, option A, the sole option that would defeat option B in a pairwise contest, was defeated in the first round.

18. T. NICOLAUS TIDEMAN, COLLECTIVE CHOICE AND VOTING, chapter 13, p. 43 (1999) (unpublished manuscript, on file with author); *see also* DUNCAN BLACK, THE THEORY OF COMMITTEES AND ELECTIONS 175 (1958). The example that follows is taken from Professor Tideman.

19. For a thorough presentation that demonstrates that all Condorcet-consistent rules suffer from this defect, see TIDEMAN, *supra* note 18, at 65 (providing detailed comparison of seventeen rules based upon thirteen normative criteria, broken down into the categories of "responsiveness," "pairing consistency," "stability," and "qualitative attractiveness").

20. *See infra* chapter 3, § III (describing endogeneity problem in issue identification under issue-voting regime).

21. *See infra* chapter 4 (explaining role of standing as promoting decision making in Congress, which is better suited to remaining inert than is the Supreme Court, when each institution lacks a Condorcet-winning option).

22. As explained more fully *infra* note 91, with one exception, I am employing William Vickrey's more simplified proof in lieu of either Arrow's original or revised proof. The statement of range in the text, which is taken from Arrow's original proof, is less general than either Vickrey's alternative formulation or the revised version in Arrow's second proof. Because I will demonstrate that Supreme Court voting fails to meet the range requirement in Arrow's first proof, it necessarily follows that such voting also fails to meet the more general statements of range, set out in these two alternative formulations of the theorem.

23. *See* Maxwell L. Stearns, *The Public Choice Case Against the Item Veto,* 49 WASH. & LEE L. REV. 385, 408 (1992).

24. *See* STEARNS, PUBLIC CHOICE AND PUBLIC LAW, *supra* note 5, at *xx–xxi*.

25. *See* THE FEDERALIST No.10 (James Madison).

26. Riker's theory provides that "[i]n n-person, zero sum games, where side-payments are permitted, where players are rational, and where they have perfect information, only minimum winning coalitions will occur." *See* WILLIAM H. RIKER, THE THEORY OF POLITICAL COALITIONS 32 (1962).

27. *See id.; see also* THE FEDERALIST No. 10 (James Madison) (discussing potential redistributive legislation that results from factional violence).

28. *See* Lynn Stout, *Strict Scrutiny and Social Choice: An Economic Inquiry into Fundamental Rights and Suspect Classifications,* 80 GEO. L.J. 1787, 1799 (1989).

29. *See* William N. Eskridge, *Politics Without Romance: Implications of Public Choice Theory for Statutory Interpretation,* 74 VA. L. REV. 275 (1988).

30. *See* Jonathan R. Macey, *Promoting Public Regarding Legislation Through Statutory Interpretation: An Interest Group Model,* 86 COLUM. L. REV. 223 (1986).

31. For my more detailed response to these proposals, see generally Stearns, *The Misguided Renaissance, supra* note 9; *see also* STEARNS, PUBLIC CHOICE AND PUBLIC LAW, *supra* note 5.

32. *See generally* DANIEL A. FARBER & PHILIP B. FRICKEY, LAW AND PUBLIC CHOICE: A CRITICAL INTRODUCTION (1991) Daniel A. Farber & Philip P. Frickey, *Legislative Intent and Public Choice,* 74 VA. L. REV. 423 (1988).

33. Harold Demsetz, *Information and Efficiency: Another Viewpoint,* 12 J.L. & ECON. 1,1 (1969). Demsetz explains the fallacy as follows:

> The view that now pervades much public policy economics implicitly presents the relevant choice as between an ideal norm and an existing "imperfect" institutional arrangement. This *nirvana* approach differs from a *comparative institutional* approach in which the relevant choice is between alternative real institutional arrangements. In practice, those who adopt the nirvana viewpoint seek to discover discrepancies between the ideal and the real and if discrepancies are found, they deduce that the real is inefficient. Users of the comparative institutional approach attempt to assess which alternative real institutional arrangement seems best able to cope with the economic problem; practitioners of this approach may use an ideal norm to provide standards from which divergences are assessed for all practical alternatives of interest and select as efficient that alternative which seems most likely to minimize the divergence.

See id.

34. *See, e.g.,* Frank H. Easterbrook, *Ways of Criticizing the Court,* 95 HARV. L. REV. 802 (1982); *see also* Einer R. Elhauge, *Does Interest Group Theory Justify More Intrusive Judicial Review?,* 101 YALE L.J. 31 (1991).

35. FARBER & FRICKEY, PUBLIC CHOICE, *supra* note 32, at 55. In a similar vein, Professor Herbert Hovenkamp has argued that Arrow's result is not limited to "distributive" legislation as opposed to "efficiency" legislation, but rather that the theorem suggests "that *all* legislative solutions, whether efficiency or otherwise, are inherently unstable and cannot yield determinative social welfare functions." Herbert Hovenkamp, *Arrow's Theorem: Ordinalism and Republican Government,* 75 IOWA L. REV. 949, 972 (1990).

36. As explained *infra* note 101, Arrow's original proof, set out in KENNETH ARROW, SOCIAL CHOICE AND INDIVIDUAL VALUES (1st ed. 1951) [SCIV I], was proven to contain an error, which Arrow then corrected by modifying some of the conditions, *see* KENNETH ARROW, SOCIAL CHOICE AND INDIVIDUAL VALUES (2d ed. 1963) [SCIV II].

37. 505 U.S. 144 (1992).
38. This includes assuming that the presence of an alarm does not signal higher value of contents in the home to steal.
39. One might respond that even if everyone in the complex built stone homes or installed alarms, all homeowners would benefit as the community as a whole becomes more distinctive and safer against crime relative to other communities. This, of course, merely extends the geographic reach to which the fallacy of composition applies. Precisely the same phenomenon described in the text can now arise with respect to the relationship between and among various communities within the relevant geographical area if all communities follow suit.
40. While the fallacy of composition and the isolation fallacy appear to converge at this point, the two fallacies remain distinct as both a conceptual and practical matter. One mechanism for preventing cycling in a given collective decision-making body is to have that institution work in conjunction with another that is not itself a collective decision-making body. This method of avoiding cycling implicates the isolation fallacy but not the composition fallacy because a single decision maker cannot cycle. Most examples in this book implicate both fallacies simultaneously. One exception is delegation. At least one scholar has tentatively suggested that by working in conjunction with a hierarchically structured administrative agency, Congress might be able to improve its rationality. *See* William Ty Mayton, *The Possibilities of Collective Choice: Arrow's Theorem, Article I, and the Delegation of Legislative Power to Administrative Agencies,* 1986 DUKE L.J. 948. If so, Congress's improved rationality is achieved by working in conjunction with another institution that is not itself prone to cycling. In any event, this theory, which, in fairness, Professor Mayton advanced cautiously, is contested. *Compare* Peter H. Aranson, Ernest Gellhorn, & Glen O. Robinson, *A Theory of Legislative Delegation,* 68 CORNELL L. REV. 1 (1982) (arguing in favor of renewing the nondelegation doctrine based upon insights drawn from public choice) *with* Jerry Mashaw, *Prodelegation: Why Administrators Should Make Political Decisions,* 1 J. L., ECON. AND ORG. 81 (1985) (arguing in favor of vesting administrative agencies with authority to resolve matters requiring flexibility and discretion). The item veto operates on a similar intuition, namely affording the president, a single decision maker, with the seeming authority to curb legislative irrationality. For my own critical analysis of the item veto, written before the adoption of Line Item Veto Act, 2 U.S.C.A. § 691–692 (1996) (amending Title X of the Congressional Budget and Impoundment Control Act of 1974, 2 U.S.C. § 681 *et seq.*), see Stearns, *Item Veto, supra* note 23 (arguing, based upon public choice theory, that the item veto is more likely to afford the president with authority to control the direction of overall legislative policy than with the power to excise the most egregious pork barrel legislation). In any event, while virtually all delegations have withstood constitutional challenge since the New Deal, the Supreme Court has recently struck down the Line Item Veto Act. *See infra* chapter 6, § IV.A (discussing Clinton v. City of New York, 524 U.S. 4217 (1998)).
41. Article III of the United States Constitution establishes the Supreme Court and provides Congress with the authority to create lower federal courts. *See* U.S. CONST. art. III.
42. WILLIAM SHAKESPEARE, THE TRAGEDY OF KING LEAR (The Riverside Shakespeare, Houghton Mifflin Co., 1974)
43. This outcome is sometimes referred to as the Schelling Point. *See* THOMAS C. SCHELLING, THE STRATEGY OF CONFLICT (1960). A Schelling Point, which need not be a stable outcome, as the example in the text illustrates, is the one thing that

people can agree to if something unexpected happens and if they cannot communicate. Thus, if two persons are to meet in Manhattan at a set time and date, but for some reason are unable to communicate to set a location, we might expect them to both arrive at the top of the Empire State Building or the World Trade Center. The problem in the example in the text is that the sisters cannot bind themselves to the Schelling Point of equal division.

44. The authors state that

> this solution is a sort of equilibrium. It is true that any player could offer an amendment that would beat th[e] [equal division] outcome—but what would be the point in doing so and thereby setting off a round of endless cycling? In a sense, the existence of massive cycling provides the basis for a new form of equilibrium adopted precisely to avoid the cycles.

> Farber & Frickey, *Legislative Intent, supra* note 32, at 434. As the following discussion in the text makes plain, unless one defines disequilibrium to be synonymous with equilibrium (which renders the whole exercise absurd), whatever normative appeal equal division might carry, it cannot be characterized as representing "a sort of equilibrium."

45. *See* John D. Calamari & Joseph M. Perillo, Contracts § 14–4, at 543–46 (4th ed. 1987).

46. *See* William M. McGovern, Trusts and Estates: Including Taxation and Future Interests § 1.2, at 3–4 (1988).

47. *See id.* § 1.4, at 21.

48. 505 U.S. 144 (1992).

49. In her opinion for the *New York* Court, Justice O'Connor explained that by 1979, two of three existing low-level radioactive waste disposal sites, those located in Washington and Nevada, had been forced to close, leaving only the disposal facility in South Carolina. *See id.* at 150. In 1980, the governor of South Carolina announced that he intended to reduce waste intake by 50 percent. In response to the looming national crisis, Congress enacted the Low-Level Radioactive Waste Policy Act of 1980, based upon a report of the National Governors' Association ("NGA"). *Id.* at 150–51. The act authorized states to enter into regional pacts for the disposal of such waste and to allow the sited and pacted states to reduce waste intake from nonmembers by progressive amounts each year, and to refuse altogether to take the waste of nonmembers by 1986. By 1985, only three pacts had formed, all around the three previously sited states, and leaving thirty-one states with no waste outlets beginning in 1986. *Id.* at 151. Effectively ratifying an agreement reached by the NGA, Congress enacted the Low-Level Radioactive Waste Policy Amendments of 1985, at issue in *New York*, which (1) provided that each state is responsible for its own waste disposal; (2) authorized the creation of interstate compacts for such waste disposal; (3) required the sited states to accept waste from every state, but beginning in 1986, to impose a surcharge, in increasing amounts each year, on waste from nonpacted members; and (4) after January 1, 1993, permitted sited states to exclude waste from nonmember states altogether. *Id.* at 151–52.

The amendments created three sets of incentives, designed to promote compliance with the extended time frame relative to the original 1980 statute. First, the amendments provided that one-quarter of the surcharges collected by the sited states would be transferred into an escrow account administered by the secretary of energy. *Id.* at 151–52. Funds from this account would then be transferred to states that met the amended statute's progressive series of compliance deadlines. *Id.* at 152–53. Writing for the *New York* Court, Justice O'Connor upheld this provision, concluding that Congress had expressly and unambiguously authorized states to burden interstate commerce. O'Connor further held that Congress had properly taxed such commerce and had ordered the expenditure of the proceeds in a constitutionally acceptable manner. *See* South Carolina v. Dole, 483 U.S. 203 (1987) (setting out four-part constitutional test for congressional spending). Second, the amendments provided that states that did not meet the series of compliance deadlines could be charged increasing amounts to dispose of their waste. The *New York* Court upheld this provision on the grounds that it gives states the option to either regulate low-level radioactive waste disposal or be preempted by federal regulations and that, in contrast with the take-title provisions, any sanctions for noncompliance fall onto private parties. *New York,* 505 U.S. at 173–74. The *New York* Court struck down only the remaining provision, which provided that states that did not either join a pact or otherwise become self-sufficient in low-level radioactive waste disposal must either take title to the waste or reimburse producers for their failure to do so. The *New York* Court based its holding alternatively upon the Tenth Amendment and the commerce clause, which O'Connor concluded were "mirror images" of each other. *Id.* at 155, 176–77.

50. *Id.* at 196–97 (White, J., concurring in part and dissenting in part).
51. It is worth comparing the original King Lear. One of the reasons Lear, in his effort to ensure "that future strife / May be prevented now," WILLIAM SHAKESPEARE, THE TRAGEDY OF KING LEAR, act 1, sc. 1, lines 44–45, failed dismally is that the legal regime he sought to create—in which the daughter whose most profuse statement of adoration for him would secure the most favorable portion of the kingdom—was not the product of a detached decision maker trying to create an appropriate off-the-rack rule designed to apply generally and prospectively. Instead, Lear was intimately involved in the distribution, the terms of which affected, most immediately, those closest to him.
52. For an interesting article critical of the majority analysis in *New York,* see Erik M. Jensen & Jonathan L. Entin, *Commandeering, the Tenth Amendment, and the Federal Requisition Power: New York v. United States Revisited,* 15 CONST. COMM. 355 (1998) (concluding that Justice O'Connor's historical evidence goes to the propriety, rather than to the constitutionality, of federal requisition orders that demand state legislative compliance).
53. *New York,* 505 U.S. at 176–77 (O'Connor, J., for the Court).
54. As we will see in chapter 4, O'Connor's decision to place a gloss on the relevant history can be explained based upon insights drawn from social choice. *See infra* chapter 4, § III.G.1.
55. *New York,* 505 U.S. at 210–11 (Stevens, J., concurring in part and dissenting in part). *See also* Jensen & Entin, *supra* note 52.
56. Gordon Tullock, *Why So Much Stability?* 37 PUB. CHOICE 189–205 (1981).
57. Kenneth A. Schepsle & Barry R. Weingast, *Structure-Induced Equilibrium and Legislative Choice,* 37 PUB. CHOICE 503–19 (1981); Kenneth A. Schepsle & Barry R. Weingast, *The Institutional Foundations of Committee Power,* 81 AM. POL. SCI. REV. 85 (1987).
58. Specifically, cycling can arise through logrolling when the participants do not have different intensities of preference. *See* DENNIS MUELLER, PUBLIC CHOICE II 82–83 (1989); STEARNS, PUBLIC CHOICE AND PUBLIC LAW, *supra* note 5, at 370–71.

59. *Accord* Farber & Frickey, *Jurisprudence, supra* note 5, at 906 (stating, "Legislatures are not characterized by chaos, but the threat of disorder posed by Arrows's Theorem may determine much of their structure. Understanding the threat can illuminate the importance of legislative procedures").

60. Farber & Frickey, *Jurisprudence, supra* note 5, at 904.

61. Kenneth A. Schepsle, *Congress Is a "They," Not an "It": Legislative Intent as an Oxymoron*, 12 INT'L REV. LAW AND ECON. 239, 242 n. 6 (1992).

62. RIKER, LIBERALISM AGAINST POPULISM, *supra* note 11, at 137.

63. Thus, the OXFORD ENGLISH DICTIONARY VIII 811 (1989), defines *legitimate* as "to declare to be lawful, to cause to be regarded as lawful offspring," and "Comfortable to law or rule; sanctioned or authorized by law or right; lawful; proper," and further describes the etymology as follows: "[T]he word expresses a status which has been conferred or ratified by some authority."

64. *See supra* chapter 1, § III.A and cites therein.

65. FARBER & FRICKEY, PUBLIC CHOICE, *supra* note 32, at 55.

66. *See supra* chapter 1, § II.A and III.A.

67. This is not to suggest, of course, that the justices never engage in strategic behavior in their efforts to promote desired policy objectives in a given case. *See generally* LEE EPSTEIN & JACK KNIGHT, THE CHOICES JUSTICES MAKE (1998). As explained *infra* chapter 3, § III.B, and cites therein, such behavior is generally limited to compromise along a unidimensional issue continuum within a case, almost invariably toward the median, rather than across issues within a case or across cases. For an interesting recent article exploring such strategic interactions and questioning whether they are invariably characterized by unilateral moves along a single issue continuum, see Evan H. Caminker, *Sincere and Strategic Voting Norms on Multimember Courts*, 97 MICH. L. REV. 2297 (1999).

68. *Cf.* R. H. Coase, *The Coase Theorem and the Empty Core: A Comment*, 24 J.L. & ECON. 183, 187 (1981) (critiquing zero transactions costs model intended to illustrate the limitation of cycling on the Coase Theorem among three or more players, stating that the purpose of the radical zero transactions cost assumption is not to "divin[e] the future by the minute inspection of the entrails of a goose").

69. *See generally* Levmore, *supra* note 12; *see also* STEARNS, PUBLIC CHOICE AND PUBLIC LAW, *supra* note 5, at 356–62 (1997) (discussing Levmore thesis).

70. This example is taken from my earlier discussion of Levmore's article; *see* Stearns, *The Misguided Renaissance, supra* note 9, at 1254.

71. In fact, the prevailing scientific wisdom that birds are modern-day descendants of dinosaurs has recently been called into question. *See* John Schwartz, *New Evolution Research Ruffles Some Feathers: Paper Contradicts Increasingly Popular Theory That Birds Descended from Dinosaurs*, THE WASH. POST, Nov. 15, 1996, §A, at 3 (observing that while "[t]he notion that birds are descendants of dinosaurs—or even that they are modern-day dinosaurs—is increasingly popular in the community of paleontology," newly discovered fossils reveal that ancestors of modern birds instead might have antedated dinosaurs by 76 million years).

72. Thus, for example, whether or not the first person to try vertical integration had in mind solving a potential long-term bilateral negotiating problem, or, instead, was simply a power monger, to the extent that the strategy worked to avoid difficult bilateral negotiating problems among the affected actors, it was destined to survive. Future economic actors facing such problems, again whether or not they understood the economic theory of the firm, might opt to mimic the initial entrepreneur's strategy for no other reason than that he is doing better than they are under otherwise similar conditions. For a seminal discussion of the theory of

the firm, see Ronald Coase, *The Nature of the Firm: Origin*, 4 J.L. Econ. & Org. 3 (1988).

73. Increasing the number of like options has the potential to promote cyclical preferences. *See* Tideman, *supra* note 18, chapter 9, at 15–16 (observing that the increased frequency of elections containing at least one cyclical anomaly is a function of the increased number of candidates).

74. *See* Riker, Liberalism Against Populism, *supra* note 11, at 69 ("There are many rules that utilize paired comparisons of alternatives to discover a Condorcet winner. If a Condorcet winner exists, then all these methods come out the same way. If a Condorcet winner does not exist, however, these rules typically produce different results, no one of which, in my opinion, seems more defensible than another").

75. *See* Levmore, *supra* note 12, at 1024–31 (discussing occasional attraction of succession voting).

76. While not yet labeled as such, we have already seen an example of this in the judicial setting, namely stare decisis. *See supra* chapter 1, § III.A; *infra* chapter 4, § III.

77. Riker, *The Paradox of Voting, supra* note 15, at 354; *see also* Stearns, *The Misguided Renaissance, supra* note 9, at 1273 n.199.

78. Recognizing this problem, Riker observed:

Even if both houses were to provide this method of discover[ing potentially cyclical preferences], they would still need a procedure for resolving the intransitivities discovered. . . . But, as Arrow has shown, an intransitivity, once in existence, cannot be eliminated simply by juggling the techniques of voting.

Riker, *The Paradox of Voting, supra* note 15, at 364.

79. *See* Levmore, *supra* note 12, at 1012–23 (discussing motion and amendment voting and providing examples).

80. *See id.* at 1024 ("[W]ell informed and clever chairpersons can manipulate motion-and-amendment voting by recognizing favored motions first so that their motions need not survive a great many votes") (footnote omitted).

81. *See id.* ("In contrast [with motion-and-amendment voting], succession voting often favors later—but not too late—entries into the fray, but since it is difficult for the chair to judge the quantity of alternatives yet to be proposed, it is difficult to position one's favorite correctly").

82. While Professor Levmore discussed unipeakedness in his article, the other concepts are derived more generally from the social choice literature. The concepts of symmetry and asymmetry are derivative of the social choice literature, but are defined in an original manner, one that helps to edify the discussion to follow and in chapters 3 and 4.

83. The analysis is consistent with Professor Ordeshook's assertion that "the existence of multipeaked preferences implies that the issue space is not unidimensional, but multidimensional." P. Ordeshook, Game Theory and Political Theory: An Introduction 56–65 (1986). As the discussion in the text shows, this means that multipeaked preferences in a unidimensional continuum can also be expressed as unipeaked preferences in a multidimensional continuum.

84. 523 U.S. 420 (1998).

85. 458 U.S. 527 (1982).

86. 458 U.S. 457 (1982).

87. *See* Levmore, *supra* note 12, at 1026–27.

88. *See id.* at 1013 n. 122.
89. The analysis is based upon the discussion in STEARNS, PUBLIC CHOICE AND PUBLIC LAW, *supra* note 5, at 359–60.
90. By way of analogy, scientists recently discovered a new animal living on the mouths of lobsters that has "a life cycle and anatomy so unusual that it belonged in a new phylum, the second broadest classification in biology." *See New Phylum Found on Lobsters' Mouths; Other Developments,* SCIENCE, Dec. 31, 1995, A1, at 1014. While the discovery of a new phylum is extremely interesting as an academic matter, most would surely agree that it is less important than, for example, a new medical breakthrough benefiting the human species.
91. Arrow's initial results were set out in ARROW, SCIV I, *supra* note 36. For an accessible summary, see MUELLER, *supra* note 58, at 384–99. After an error in the initial proof was exposed, *see infra* note 101, Arrow set out a revised and apparently incontrovertible proof in ARROW, SCIV II, *supra* note 36. With one exception, explained *infra* note 105 (discussing range), following MUELLER, *supra,* I am employing the definitions from William Vickrey's more accessible proof, *see* William Vickrey, *Utility, Strategy, and Social Decisional Rules,* 74 Q.J. OF ECON. 507–35 (1960), in lieu of those set out in Arrow's revised proof. This provides two benefits. First, as explained below, Vickrey's presentation is simpler. Second, for one of the fairness conditions, unanimity, the Vickrey formulation provides a more meaningful benchmark for a comparative analysis of the relevant institutions and rules under review. While the terminology that Vickrey and Arrow employ is quite similar, some notable differences remain. For interested readers, I will point out differences between Arrow's corrected proof and the simpler Vickrey presentation. *See also infra* notes 104 and 112. It is not necessary to track these differences, however, to follow the presentation in the text.

   At the outset, in contrast with Vickrey, who set out only one axiom, transitivity, Arrow set out two axioms, connectedness (commonly understood as completeness) and transitivity, which together are at odds with his four identified fairness conditions. Completeness is the requirement that "For all x and y, either x R y or y R x," where R means "at least as good as." ARROW, SCIV II, *supra* note 36, at 13 (As explained *infra* note 104, Vickrey implicitly incorporated Arrow's connectedness axiom into his statement of range.) Despite the seemingly modest nature of this axiom, it is almost never satisfied. Completeness is not satisfied by a single snapshot comparison between x and y, but rather is satisfied only if the identified relationship persists when new information, for example, the introduction of an additional option, is presented, and in spite of efforts to subvert an identified relationship between x and y through a manipulated voting path. Thus, with preferences—P1: ABC; P2: BCA; P3: CAB—we can assert through a simple binary comparison that A is preferred to B. But after we introduce C, we discover that B is preferred to C, which is preferred to A, thus calling the initial stated relationship between A and B into question, and thus violating connectedness. Indeed, one of the fundamental implications of Arrow's proof is in underscoring the manipulability of rules and the importance of order in dictating outcomes. That said, one rule does meet the connectedness axiom. If the rule is "preferred by a majority in a direct comparison with," then even with the above cyclical preferences, a stable outcome can be stated for each conceivable binary comparison. Thus A is preferred by a majority in a direct comparison with B, B is preferred by a majority in a direct comparison with C, and C is preferred by a majority in a direct comparison with A. Each stated binary relationship is persistent and nonmanipulable, thus satisfying completeness. The problem is that when the group of relationships is aggregated, it becomes clear that the stated relationships are largely meaningless as a normative matter, as evidenced by the fact that ApBpCpA, where p means "preferred to." Thus, we can understand Arrow's introduction of his second axiom, transitivity, which holds that "For all x, y, and z, x R y and y R z imply x R z," where R means "at least as good as." Arrow, SCIV II, *supra* note 36, at 13. Because this is a statement about aggregate collective preferences, rather than about individual preferences, the Condorcet paradox itself shows that, as a general matter, the axiom does not hold. In essence, Arrow's Theorem reveals that to meet both of his axioms, a collective decision-making body must relax at least one of four conditions that he deemed essential to fair collective decision-making. *See infra* notes 104, 112, 119, 130, and accompanying text (describing and comparing the fairness conditions as articulated in Arrow's revised proof and in Vickrey's simplified presentation).

92. Before Arrow published his result, Duncan Black had published a famous work on social choice in which he provided one of the best histories of the movement, including contributions by Condorcet, Borda, and LaPlace, in the late eighteenth century, and C. L. Dodgson (Lewis Carroll) in the late nineteenth century. *See* Duncan Black, The Theory of Committees and Elections (5th printing 1987).

93. *See* Riker, Liberalism Against Populism, *supra* note 11, at 116 (positing that Arrow's Theorem is "a generalization of the paradox of voting").

94. *See, e.g.,* Jack Hirshleifer, Price Theory and Applications 436–41 (2d ed. 1980).

95. *See, e.g.,* Richard Epstein, Forbidden Grounds: The Case Against Employment Discrimination Laws (1992); Gary Becker, The Economics of Discrimination (2d ed. 1971).

96. *See, e.g.,* Ian Ayres and Peter Crampton, *Deficit Reduction Through Diversity: How Affirmative Action at the FCC Increased Auction Competition,* 48 Stan. L. Rev. 761, 782 (1996) (discussing impact of bandwidth auction procedures on media diversity).

97. Professor William Riker, for example, strongly questioned the validity of independence of irrelevant alternatives, *see* Riker, Liberalism Against Populism, *supra* note 11, at 130; *see also* Stearns, Public Choice and Public Law, *supra* note 5, at 368–70 (critiquing Riker thesis). In addition, Professors Richard Pildes & Elizabeth Anderson have questioned the validity of collective rationality. *See* Richard H. Pildes & Elizabeth S. Anderson, *Slinging Arrows at Democracy: Social Choice Theory, Value Pluralism, and Democratic Politics,* 90 Colum. L. Rev. 2121, 2146–58, 2192 (1990); *see also* Stearns, *The Misguided Renaissance, supra* note 9, at 1251–52 n. 115 (describing Pildes and Anderson thesis).

98. *See supra* note 33, and accompanying text (quoting Demsetz's statement of nirvana fallacy).

99. Of course Arrow himself did not set out to devise the perfect institution; instead, he set out to devise an institution that satisfied what he considered to be certain minimal criteria of rationality and fairness. The impossibility of achieving the perfect institution, however, follows automatically from the impossibility of achieving one that meets these minimally acceptable criteria.

100. *See supra* note 91 (describing differences between Arrow's revised proof and Vickrey's simplified presentation of Arrow's Theorem).

101. For proof of the error in Arrow's initial theorem, set out in Arrow, SCIV I, *supra* note 36, see Julian Blau, *The Existence of Social Welfare Functions,* 25 Econometrica 302–13 (1957). Arrow's revised proof, which required that he strengthen his condition of universal domain (which William Vickrey later termed "range"),

and include the Pareto criterion, appears in the second edition, published in 1963, *see* ARROW, SCIV II, *supra* note 36.

102. *See* Michael E. Levine & Charles R. Plott, *Agenda Influence and Its Implications,* 63 VA. L. REV. 561, 561 n. 2 (1977) (observing that "[a]n entire literature has grown out of [Arrow's] effort, consisting mostly of attempts to escape the rather depressing implications of this theorem and of attempts to identify the range of circumstances to which it applies," and adding that "attempts to sabotage the theory or to weaken its implications . . . have not been nearly as successful as originally hoped").

103. *See* Maxwell L. Stearns, *Standing and Social Choice: Historical Evidence,* 144 U. PA. L. REV. 309, 330–39 (1996) (describing Arrow's Corollary and its implications for constitutional process).

104. Of the four fairness criteria in Arrow's Theorem, the range criterion, sometimes referred to as universal domain, is perhaps the most difficult to conceptualize. One of the difficulties is that it has been articulated in no fewer than three forms. In Arrow's initial proof, he stated universal domain as Condition 1, which follows:

Among all the alternatives there is a set S of three alternatives such that, for any set of individual orderings $T_1, . . ., T_n$ of the alternatives in S, there is an admissible set of individual orderings $R_1, . . ., R_n$ of all alternatives such that, for each individual i, xR_iy if and only if xT_iy for x and y in S.

ARROW, SCIV II, *supra* note 36, at 24. After the initial error in Arrow's proof was revealed, *see supra* note 101, and cite therein, Arrow then reformulated the range condition to Condition 1', which follows: "All logically possible orderings of the alternative social states are admissible." ARROW, SCIV I, *supra* note 36, at 96. Finally, Vickrey reformulated the range condition to require the following:

There is some "universal" alternative u such that for every pair of other alternatives x and y and for every individual, each of the six possible strict orderings of u, x, and y is contained in some admissible ranking of all alternatives for the individual.

MUELLER, *supra* note 58, at 385.

In Arrow's initial formulation, he required that within the universe of alternatives, there exist some set of three options, such that the members were free to select among all conceivable ordinal rankings over those options. This is the version presented in the text. In his revised proof, Arrow generalized the criterion to require that the members be able to select among any conceivable ordinal ranking over all available alternatives. Finally, Vickrey's formulation requires some universal outcome that is consistent with the selection by all members of the ordinal rankings that follow from a combination of u with any other pair of alternatives. In Vickrey's formulation, range is met provided that when u is combined with options x and y, the members are free to select any of the resulting six ordinal rankings, and when u is combined with options a and b, the members are free to select among any of the resulting six ordinal rankings, even if the members are not free, for example, to select among any of the six ordinal rankings over a, x, and y. Vickrey's formulation of range, which seeks a universal alternative contained in some admissible ranking, effectively combines Arrow's connectedness requirement with a less stringent statement of Arrow's condition of universal domain, and lies somewhere between the statements of universal domain set out in Arrow's first and second proofs. *See supra* note 91 (describing Arrow's connectedness axiom). Because Supreme Court voting rules fail to satisfy even the least general range requirement, Condition 1 from Arrow's original proof, it necessarily follows that such rules also fail to satisfy both Vickrey's somewhat more general statement of range, and Arrow's complete generalization, set out as Condition 1' in his revised proof. Moreover, applying Condition 1 is more intuitive in analyzing Supreme Court voting rules. In virtually all cases, the critical number of options, in the form of rationales leading to a judgment, can be reduced to three, implying that each justice is faced with a potential set of six ordinal rankings over available options from which to choose. *See infra* chapter 3, § III.A and C. As shown in chapters 3 and 4, however, even this less stringent statement of range is relaxed by Supreme Court rules, which prevent a justice from implicitly selecting those ordinal rankings over underlying rationales that would allow them to express their preferred judgment in contingent form. *See id.* Stated differently, in a case in which the justices are deciding to affirm or reverse, Supreme Court voting rules prevent a justice from ranking second that rationale which would produce a judgment opposite her actual case vote, over an alternative (and precisely opposite) rationale leading to the same judgment. If, as demonstrated in chapters 3 and 4, Arrow's Condition 1 is not met in Supreme Court decision-making rules, then a fortiori, Vickrey's reformation and Arrow's complete generalization in the form of Condition 1' are also not met.

105. In prior presentations, I have split range and universal domain into these two separate conditions. *See, e.g.,* Stearns, *The Misguided Renaissance, supra* note 9, at 1247–48; *id.* at 1258–76. Consistent with both the Arrow and Vickrey formulations, I will present them as two components of the same condition throughout this book.

106. *See supra* at 65 n.*.

107. *See infra* chapter 3, § II.

108. Specifically, as explained in chapter 4, by raising the costs to special interest groups of attempting to manipulate the path of case decisions, standing renders constitutional process more fair by protecting legislative issue space for future resolution, given that legislative decision making is by design more inclusive and more prone to producing results that are collectively rational. Standing thus promotes the identification of Condorcet winners in Congress, when such options are available, and congressional inertia, when such options are unavailable.

109. *See supra* note 57 and cites therein.

110. On the role of bicameralism in inducing stable equilibria in a multidimensional issue spectrum, see Geoffrey Brennan & Alan Hamlin, *Bicameralism and Majoritarian Equilibrium,* 74 PUB. CHOICE 169–79 (1992).

111. In a recent article, Saul Levmore advanced the related proposition that interest-group participation in the political process is likely to be positively correlated with collective intransitivities. Levmore reasons that, holding all else constant, such groups have a greater likelihood of manipulating voting procedures or decisional paths than they do of altering underlying preferences as the vehicle for obtaining desired legislative objectives. *See* Saul Levmore, *Voting Paradoxes and Interest Groups,* 28 J. LEG. STUD. 259 (1999).

112. MUELLER, *supra* note 58, at 385. In contrast with range, where by relaxing the requirement of complete universality, Vickrey set out a less stringent requirement than Arrow, in this case Arrow set out the less stringent condition in his revised proof, which Vickrey then strengthened. Arrow set out Condition P, the

Pareto principle, as follows: "If x P_i for all i, then x P y," *see* SCIV II, *supra* note 36, at 96, meaning that if the group unanimously ranks x ahead of y, the institution must also rank x ahead of y. With the tastes of a mathematician, Arrow's stated this criterion in the weakest form to determine its implications for collective decision making. As the prior discussion of range illustrates, if this weak-form criterion could not be satisfied, then a fortiori, the stronger, and more common, Pareto criterion, which Vickrey incorporated into his proof, also could not be satisfied. Vickrey's alternative formulation requires that if a change from the status quo benefits one person without harming others, then the change must be made. This condition is far more useful in a comparative institutional analysis of Congress and the Supreme Court because, as set out in the text, it is generally satisfied in legislatures, which condone and even encourage logrolling (even when, if they were to vote upon them separately from the resulting package, the entire institution would disapprove the resulting trades), but is generally relaxed in appellate courts.

113. 198 U.S. 45 (1905).

114. 300 U.S. 379 (1937).

115. *Lochner,* 198 U.S. at 52–53, 64.

116. *West Coast Hotel,* 300 U.S. at 391, 398–400.

117. I added the caveat "over certain subject matters," because even in the *Lochner* era, legislatures did prospectively proscribe certain forms of contracting, with no apparent constitutional difficulty. Examples include prohibitions on dispensing medical or legal services without a license, prohibitions on purchasing certain drugs in all circumstances and alcohol below a certain age, and virtually all contracts for sexual services. Thus viewed, *Lochner* was not about whether state governments could prospectively interfere with contracting. They already did. Instead, it was about the list of subject matters over which states could prospectively interfere with contracting, with a particular emphasis on minimum wage and maximum hour regulations, and on which rationales, if any, were sufficient to justify such prospective interference.

118. For one of the leading articles, see Peter H. Aranson, Ernest Gellhorn, & Glen O. Robinson, *A Theory of Legislative Delegation,* 68 Cornell L. Rev. 1 (1982).

119. *See* Mueller, *supra* note 58, at 386. In this case, while the substantive terminology is different, the criterion from Arrow's revised proof is essentially identical to Vickrey's. *See* Arrow, SCIV II, *supra* note 36, at 27.

120. *See* Stearns, *The Misguided Renaissance, supra* note 9, at 1250 n.108 (discussing Rousseau's influence on Condorcet and collecting authorities).

121. Keith M. Baker, Condorcet: From Natural Philosophy to Social Mathematics 230 (1975) ("All men, Rousseau and Condorcet agreed, have the right to follow their own opinion. But reason dictates that on entering political society, they consent to submit to the general will—or, in Condorcet's phrase, 'the common reason'—those of their actions that must be governed for all according to the same principles").

122. *See* Mueller, *supra* note 58, at 394 ("It was the desire to establish a welfare function that was not based upon interpersonal utility comparisons that first motivated Arrow"); Riker, Liberalism Against Populism, *supra* note 62, at 101 (explaining that Arrovian independence "prevent[s] the rigging of elections and the unequal treatment of voters"); *see also* Stearns, *The Misguided Renaissance, supra* note 9, at 1250 n. 108 (distinguishing bases for adherence to independence by Condorcet and Arrow).

123. *Accord* Mueller, *supra* note 58, at 394–95.

124. Among the frequently noted deficiencies of markets is that while commodification of preferences allows market actors to internalize many of the costs and benefits of their decisions, there are times when they can, instead, pass some costs and benefits onto others. In the case of positive externalities, for example, when a potential real estate developer considers bringing a marginal neighborhood back to life, the result might be underinvestment if the entrepreneur cannot recoup all of the anticipated benefits of her efforts. In the case of negative externalities, for example, pollution, the difficulty is the opposite, namely an overproduction of those goods or services that result in costs not borne by the producers. While it is relatively easy to locate externalities, both positive and negative, the question remains whether regulators seeking to promote activities with positive externalities or to inhibit activities with negative externalities are better suited than markets to correct such deficiencies, or instead, are likely to exacerbate the inefficiencies by either providing too strong a set of incentives in the case of positive externalities, or the opposite, too strong a set of sanctions, in the case of negative externalities, thus promoting some inefficient activities on the one hand or thwarting some efficient activities on the other.
125. *See infra* chapter 3, § III.C.
126. Lewis Kornhauser & Lawrence G. Sager, *Unpacking the Court,* 96 YALE L.J. 82, 88–89 (1986).
127. This holds at least once the Court has decided to take a case. In the case of petitions for writ of certiorari, one commentator has observed that internally inconsistent, and perhaps strategic, behavior among the justices is commonplace. *See* H. W. PERRY, JR., DECIDING TO DECIDE: AGENDA SETTING IN THE UNITED STATES SUPREME COURT (1991). While I agree with Perry's observation about voting at the stage of deciding whether to take a case, I disagree that strategic behavior in the context of voting on certiorari petitions allows us to infer that the same will be the norm in deciding cases once certiorari has been granted. In the case of petitions for writ of certiorari, justices rarely produce written opinions explaining their votes. We should not be surprised therefore that they do not consider themselves bound by such votes in the future. In contrast, most cases, other than summary dismissals, are decided with written opinions, which raise the cost to the justices of departing from their expressed views in future cases. While we should not expect adherence to Arrovian independence in the case of certiorari petitions, we should expect at least presumptive adherence to Arrovian independence once the Court has committed itself to resolving the case by means of a written opinion.
128. *See generally* EPSTEIN & KNIGHT, *supra* note 67.
129. *See supra* chapter 3, § III.C.
130. MUELLER, *supra* note 58, at 385. As with independence of irrelevant alternatives, the Arrow and Vickrey formulations of nondictatorship are essentially the same. *See* ARROW, SCIV II, *supra* note 36, at 30.
131. While this does not violate formal nondictatorship, it does violate the Anonymity criterion of May's Theorem, which holds that "D is determined only by the values of D_i, and is independent of how they are assigned. Any permutation of these ballots leaves D unchanged." *See* MUELLER, *supra* note 58, at 97 (describing May's Theorem, which holds that only simple majority rule satisfies the conditions of decisiveness, anonymity, neutrality, and positive responsiveness).

CHAPTER 3

1. 523 U.S. 420 (1998).

2. *See, e.g.*, David G. Post & Steven C. Salop, *Rowing Against the Tidewater: A Theory of Voting by Multimember Panels*, 80 GEO. L. J. 743 (1992) (arguing that the Supreme Court should regularly employ issue voting); Lewis A. Kornhauser & Lawrence G. Sager, *The One and the Many: Adjudication in Collegial Courts*, 81 CAL. L. REV. 1 (1993) (arguing that the Supreme Court should choose issue or outcome voting by majority vote on a case-by-case basis); *see also* John M. Rogers, *"Issue Voting" by Multimember Courts: A Response to Some Radical Proposals*, 49 VAND. L. REV. 993 (1996) (arguing against issue-voting proposals on ground that they would increase problem of doctrinal indeterminacy and undermine integrity of rule of law); David G. Post & Steven C. Salop, *Issues and Outcomes, Guidance and Indeterminacy: A Reply to John Rogers and Others*, 49 VAND. L. REV. 1069, 1079 (1996) (defending issue-voting proposal and offering "stopping rule," which, authors claim, would improve doctrinal determinacy under issue-voting regime); Maxwell L. Stearns, *How Outcome Voting Promotes Principled Issue Identification: A Reply to Professor John Rogers and Others*, 49 VAND. L. REV. 1045 (1996) (arguing against issue-voting proposals based upon insights drawn from social choice and demonstrating deficiency of "stopping rule" proposed by Professors Post and Salop).
3. 505 U.S. 833 (1992).
4. *See, e.g.*, Lewis A. Kornhauser & Lawrence G. Sager, *Unpacking the Court*, 96 YALE L. J. 82, 89 (1986) (stating that "we strongly incline toward the view of adjudication as an exercise in judgment aggregation; indeed we understand most plausible schools of jurisprudence to embrace this view").
5. *See, e.g.*, Erin O'Hara, *Social Constraint or Implicit Collusion? Toward a Game Theoretic Analysis of Stare Decisis*, 24 SETON HALL L. REV. 736, 738 (1993) (assuming that judges "will be motivated by a desire to impose [their] normative views on the society in which [they] live[]"); William Landes & Richard Posner, *Legal Precedent: A Theoretical and Empirical Analysis*, 19 J.L. & ECON. 249, 272–73 (1976) (arguing that the desire to impose normative worldviews helps to explain why "judges might want to create precedents rather than just resolve disputes").
6. There are at least two distinct dimensions of principled, or judgment-based, decision making. The first involves the normative merit of the bases that go into a particular judge's decision. For Professors Kornhauser and Sager, judgment, in this sense, requires that the decision be based upon premises founded upon a notion of "truth," such that all right-thinking persons would agree. *See* Kornhauser & Sager, *Unpacking the Court*, *supra* note 4, at 84. In contrast, Professor Amartya K. Sen has defined the same general conception of judgment as grounded in an exogenously imposed or agreed-upon set of norms, including, most commonly, a governing set of legal materials or a defining set of natural law principles. *See* Amartya K. Sen, *Social Choice Theory: A Reexamination*, 45 ECONOMETRICA 53 (1977), *reprinted in* AMARTYA K. SEN, WELFARE AND MEASUREMENT 158 (1982). The second dimension of judgment-based decision making, which is more directly edified by an understanding of social choice, requires that the decision makers, in this context judges, base their decisions upon their own analyses of the relative merits of presented alternatives, whether or not they have previously articulated their assessment in one or more written opinions. *See* Maxwell L. Stearns, *Standing Back from the Forest: Justiciability and Social Choice*, 83 CAL. L. REV. 1309, 1343 n. 113 (1995) (defining judgment-based decision making as grounded in principled assessments of the merits of presented alternatives, whatever normative framework the individual judge employs). The latter

conception of judgment-based decision making is, in essence, a restatement of the Arrovian independence criterion. Later in this chapter and in chapter 4, I will demonstrate that Supreme Court decision-making rules have evolved in a manner that significantly promotes the latter form of judgment-based decision making. While the two identified conceptions of judgment-based decision making remain distinct, I will further demonstrate that adherence to the latter form also limits to a considerable extent the ability of judges to claim reliance upon noncredible sources in their written opinions, thus indirectly furthering, as well, adherence to judgment-based decision making, as Kornhauser, Sager, and Sen conceive that term.

7. *See generally* H.W. PERRY, DECIDING TO DECIDE: AGENDA SETTING IN THE UNITED STATES SUPREME COURT (1991).

8. *See infra* note 65 and cites therein.

9. It is noteworthy that before she joined the Supreme Court, Court of Appeals judge Ruth Bader Ginsburg herself expressed concern over the increasingly prevalent practice of fractured panel decision making in the Supreme Court. *See generally* Ruth Bader Ginsburg, *Remarks on Writing Separately,* 65 WASH. L. REV. 133, 142 (1990) (positing that "[c]oncern for the well-being of the court on which one serves, for the authority and respect its pronouncements command, may be the most powerful deterrent to writing separately"). *See also* Edward P. Schwartz, The Concurrence Dilemma (working paper, Harvard University Dept. of Government, 1999) (characterizing practice of filing separate concurrences as a form of judicial defection).

10. MANCUR OLSON, THE RISE AND DECLINE OF NATIONS: ECONOMIC GROWTH, STAGFLATION, AND SOCIAL RIGIDITIES 36–37 (1982).

11. In fact, there is a fourth parallel. In general elections, the combined effect of plurality voting, a non-Condorcet-producing rule, and the tendency of candidates to converge toward or on the median voter, increases the probability that if a Condorcet winner is available, she will prevail. For a more detailed comparison of the Condorcet criterion in electoral voting and in case decision making, see *infra* § IV.C.

12. As explained *supra* chapter 2, § II.A, I am excluding Condorcet-consistent rules on the grounds of complexity in practical operation. For an excellent discussion of these rules, see T. NICOLAUS TIDEMAN, COLLECTIVE DECISIONS AND VOTING, chapter 13 (1999) (unpublished manuscript, on file with author). I will briefly revisit Condorcet-consistent rules, *infra* at 117 n.*. in the context of discussing the problems of complexity and endogeneity, which plague issue-voting proposals.

13. 450 U.S. 662 (1981).

14. 523 U.S. 420 (1998).

15. Such protectionist legislation is antithetical to the commerce clause, which states: "The Congress shall have Power . . . To regulate Commerce with foreign Nations, and among the several States and with the Indian Tribes" U.S. CONST. art. I, § 8, cl. 3. Although stated in the form of a grant of regulatory power to Congress, the clause has consistently been interpreted to prevent state legislation that impinges upon the national market. *See, e.g.,* City of Philadelphia v. New Jersey, 437 U.S. 617 (1978); Hunt v. Washington State Apple Advertising Comm'n, 432 U.S. 333 (1977); Gibbons v. Ogden, 22 U.S. (9 Wheat.) 1 (1824). The clause, which is best understood as a constitutionally imposed multilateral most-favored-nation treaty among the states, is designed to compel the states to act as a single economic union, rather than as separate economic sovereigns, enacting laws in response to constituent pressures at each others' expense. Indeed, the perceived

need to end the protectionist rivalries that plagued the states under the Articles of Confederation, by providing Congress with uniform regulatory power over commerce, was among the animating forces driving the rejection of the Articles in favor of the Constitution.

16. *See supra* chapter 1, § II.B.

17. *Kassel,* 450 U.S. at 678–79 (Powell, J., for a plurality).

18. *Id.* at 680–81 (Brennan, J., concurring).

19. *Id.* at 689–91, and 702 (Rehnquist, J. dissenting).

20. Recall that Condorcet-producing rules can readily be conceived as possessing the characteristic of unlimited majority veto, meaning that the process of decision making does not end until every potentially thwarted majority on an underlying issue or on the outcome has been satisfied. *See supra* chapter 2, § II.A.

21. Recall from chapter 2 that in setting out Arrow's Theorem, unless otherwise noted, I have employed William Vickrey's simpler conventions in lieu of Arrow's original or revised proofs. *See supra* chapter 2, § V.

22. *See supra* chapter 2, § V.B (defining *range* and providing illustrations).

23. *See infra* § II.B (explaining methodological approach of setting out ordinal rankings over packaged issue and outcome combinations).

24. While I have assumed judgment-based decision making (see supra chapter 2, § V.B.), the analysis is unaffected by the contrary assumption of preference-based decision making.

25. *See, e.g., supra* note 2, and cites therein.

26. I will provide a social choice critique of this form of voting, and explain why the Court does not actually employ it, *infra* § III.

27. *See, e.g.,* Kornhauser & Sager, *Unpacking the Court, supra* note 4, at 109 n. 37 and accompanying text (explaining, in response to Frank Easterbrook's application of Arrow's Theorem to analyze Supreme Court decision making, "[w]hile Easterbrook assumes that judges choose among multiple rationales, most of our discussion assumes that judges make a binary choice between judgment for plaintiff and judgment for defendant"); *see also id.* at 107 n. 35 (positing that "Easterbrook apparently conceives of a court . . . conducting a series of futile pairwise votes [capable of generating a cycle]"); *see also* Frank H. Easterbrook, *Ways of Criticizing the Court,* 95 Harv. L. Rev. 802 (1982) (employing Arrow's Theorem to defend Supreme Court against argument that it behaves improperly when it issues fractured panel decisions or renders occasional incoherent decisions). For a more detailed analysis of these articles, see generally Maxwell L. Stearns, *The Misguided Renaissance of Social Choice,* 103 Yale L.J. 1219 (1994); see also Maxwell L. Stearns, Public Choice and Public Law: Readings and Commentary 465–71 (1997).

28. I will demonstrate below that *Miller* can be simplified to reveal two dispositive issues. *See infra* § II.C.

29. Recall from chapter 2 that when three or more members of a collective decision-making body select among three options, the members' aggregate preferences can produce a cycle either when one member's preferences possess more than a single peak along a unidimensional issue continuum, or when the aggregation of preferences reveals multidimensionality and asymmetry, even if each member's preferences have a single peak. *See supra* chapter 2. In chapter 2, I provided an illustration demonstrating that, in fact, these are simply two ways of expressing the same underlying phenomenon and that one can translate the case of cycling in a unidimensional issue spectrum in which one member's preferences are multipeaked into a case in which the aggregate members' preferences

reveal multidimensionality and in which the group cycles even though all members' preferences are single peaked. The discussion that follows takes the analysis from chapter 2 one step further and illustrates that in the context of Supreme Court decision making, even in selecting between the most often binary choice to affirm or reverse, if the Court employed a Condorcet-producing case decision rule, it would be capable of generating a cycle when two conditions are met. First, the Court must be capable of generating three sets of rationales over the two outcomes, with two of the underlying rationales leading to one outcome and the third rationale leading to the opposite outcome. Second, each justice must be capable of logically ranking any of the three underlying rationales in any order, including selecting as a second choice a rationale that produces an outcome opposite her first choice. When these two conditions are met, as illustrated in the text that follows, the Court is capable of generating cyclical preferences because the underlying issue spectrum can readily be conceived as multidimensional and because the underlying preferences are capable of generating an asymmetry.

30. In three cases discussed at the end of this chapter, one or more justices conceded to a contrary majority resolution on an underlying issue, with the result of changing their votes. In doing so, however, those justices ultimately selected a package of internally consistent issue resolutions consistent with their outcome vote. *See infra* § V.B.

31. *See infra* § III.C (explaining different incentives to divide issues under outcome- and issue-voting regimes).

32. *See supra* chapter 2, § IV.A, figure 2.4 (illustrating and describing multidimensionality and asymmetry).

33. The *Kassel* decision thus presents a precise parallel to table 2.2 and figure 2.4, *supra* chapter 2, § IV.A, which together depict the characteristic features of multidimensionality and asymmetry. In that example, person 3, who ranked New Year's Eve first as an adjournment date, resolved issues along both dimensions in opposite fashion relative to the person who ranked Thanksgiving first as an adjournment date. And yet, because he did not celebrate Christmas, he ranked the Thanksgiving adjournment ahead of the Christmas adjournment, even though the latter was closer along the dimension of lengthening summer recess.

34. *See infra* § IV.

35. While one might object to the assumptions needed to generate the two cycles described in the text, the objection will not bear scrutiny. In the two cycling hypotheticals, I have generated both conceivable ordinal rankings for each voting camp over the two alternatives represented in the other two opinions. It is, of course, possible that two camps might select the same second choice, thus avoiding the cycle, but to generate that stable outcome, one must make assumptions about individual preferences that are no more or less obvious than those needed to generate either of the hypothetical intransitivities in the text.

Recall from chapter 2 that for three options, adhering to range means allowing each justice to choose from among six possible ordinal rankings. *See supra* chapter 2, section V.B. For the six potential sets of ordinal rankings in *Kassel,* outcome voting holds two off-limits, ABC and CBA, both of which share the feature of rendering the outcome vote contingent upon the governing rationale. As shown below, the same analysis applies in *Miller.*

36. *See supra* chapter 1, § II.A.

37. In the *Kassel* hypothetical involving the forward cycle, *see supra* § II.C.1, Justice Brennan's ranking, CAB, places second Justice Powell's alternative rationale leading to the same result, namely striking down the Iowa statute. Justice Rehnquist

has no choice but to place second a rationale leading to an opposite result, given that neither of the two remaining opinions would uphold the statute. His ordinal ranking, BCA, cannot be viewed as contingent, and is therefore not problematic. The problematic ranking, ABC, belongs to Justice Powell, who, based upon the foregoing assumptions, prefers switching his outcome vote, applying Rehnquist's rationale, to achieving the same result, applying Brennan's rationale. The same analysis applies in *Miller,* revealing that in the forward cycle, only O'Connor's ordinal ranking, which is continent on the outcome, is problematic. *See supra* § II.C.2; *see also infra* § IV (analyzing narrowest grounds doctrine).

38. One exception, discussed *infra* note 65 and accompanying text, involves decisions by justices to move from their ideal point toward the median position on the Court, thus elevating a potential plurality or concurring opinion to majority status.

39. *See supra* chapter 2 at 65 n.* (defending assumption that Supreme Court is collectively obligated to decide cases properly before it).

40. 337 U.S. 582 (1949).

41. *See* Post & Salop, *Rowing Against the Tidewater, supra* note 2; Kornhauser & Sager, *Collegial Courts, supra* note 2.

42. *See Tidewater,* 337 U.S. at 586–88, 589–90 (Jackson, J., for the plurality); *see id.* at 606–7 (Rutledge, J., concurring); *see id.* at 627, 645 (Vinson, J., dissenting); *see id.* at 648–49, 652–53 (Frankfurter, J., dissenting).

43. 2 Cranch 445 (1804).

44. *See Tidewater,* 337 U.S. at 591–92, 600 (plurality).

45. *Id.* at 606 (Rutledge, J., concurring) (citing *Hepburn,* 2 Cranch 445 (1804)).

46. *Id.* at 638–40 (Vinson, C.J., dissenting).

47. *Id.* at 648–52 (Frankfurter, J., dissenting).

48. *See supra* § II. B.

49. *See* Rogers, *"Issue Voting," supra* note 2, at 1002–4 (listing issues).

50. The proposed stopping rule is as follows:

> a *primary* issue on which multimember courts should vote is a question of law presented by a case that (a) is logically independent of any other questions presented by the case, in the sense that the question can be resolved as a logical matter without reference to any other accompanying questions, (b) is potentially dispositive of the outcome of the case, in the sense that resolution of the question can uniquely determine the outcome of the case, and (c) cannot be further decomposed into separate subquestions that fulfill criteria (a) and (b).

> Post & Salop, *Issues and Outcomes, supra* note 2, at 1078. In fact, Professors Post and Salop concede that their stopping rule will likely produce indeterminate results in the very category of cases for which it is presumably designed. Thus, the authors go on to state:

> The issue decomposition rule will produce a unique set of primary issues defined vertically. That is, it provides a manageable "stopping rule" for the vertical issue decomposition process. However, cases may present alternative primary issues at any level of decomposition defined horizontally. For example, a judge presented with [a given case] may believe that [it] should be disposed of on grounds entirely unrelated to [those that the authors identified as dispositive].

Id. at 1083. Aside from failing to solve the problem that Post and Salop describe as horizontal issue division, the proposed stopping rule further limits Supreme Court range by preventing majority preferences on subissues from dictating the results of issues even when the Court's own members would prefer to follow the internal logic of such an issue division. In essence, the proposed rule fails when the issue spectrum is multidimensional. It also masks the very problem that it purports to solve, namely that the division of a macro issue into micro issues sometimes produces an opposite result. While in *Tidewater*, the macro issue was the outcome vote itself, as demonstrated in the text to follow and in table 3.4, the same anomaly can arise with respect to the division of an underlying issue into subissues. Moreover, enforcing the proposed rule, or any other rule that is determinative on issue levels, would likely invite either strategic efforts to redefine issues in a manner that produces a favorable voting path, or to vote strategically, rather than in a principled manner, to avoid the outcome that the disfavored voting path would produce. Finally, as demonstrated *infra* § III.C, outcome voting itself solves the problem of vertical issue definition by encouraging justices to avoid drawing unpersuasive issue statements designed solely to generate a favorable voting path. For my more detailed analysis of the proposed stopping rule, see Stearns, *Outcome Voting, supra* note 2.

51. For my more detailed criticism of Rogers's statement of the *Tidewater* issues, some of which are discussed below, see Stearns, *Outcome Voting, supra* note 2.
52. *See Tidewater,* 337 U.S. at 587–88 (Jackson, J., for a plurality).
53. *See id.* at 606 (Rutledge, J., concurring).
54. *See id.* at 644–45 (Vinson, C.J., dissenting).
55. *Id.* at 651 (Frankfurter, J., dissenting).
56. It is also worth considering the impact of an issue-voting regime on decisions to grant or to deny certiorari. Justices might be more inclined to strategize in considering such petitions based upon their ability to anticipate the likely division of issues in the case. Thus, even if it is difficult to create a favorable voting path in a given case by going down multiple levels, when the range of potential cases is expanded, creating the same voting path through creative issue maneuvering across multiple cases becomes much easier. For a discussion of path dependency and manipulation across cases, see *infra* chapter 4.
57. Recall, for example, the discussion, *supra* chapter 1, § II.B, on tiers of scrutiny as composite issues.
58. A review of just two of the issues that Professor Rogers claimed to be lurking in *Tidewater* reveals just this phenomenon. Consider Rogers's issue L: "Should words in the Constitution be construed to have different meanings?" If that issue governed the outcome in *Tidewater,* given the high level of abstraction, that seemingly inconsequential case would have become the tail wagging the dog in the far more significant body of cases presenting the question whether the Fourteenth Amendment due process clause incorporates the substantive provisions of the Bill of Rights. After all, the incorporation doctrine gives very different meanings to identically worded provisions in the Fifth and Fourteenth Amendments. Also consider Rogers's issue G: "Should the Constitution be interpreted to avoid unfair results?" which inspired subissue A-1 in table 3.4. Had that issue governed, *Tidewater* would have had foreboding implications across perhaps an unprecedented range of seemingly unrelated bodies of constitutional law. *See* Rogers, *"Issue Voting," supra* note 2, at 1003.
59. *See* Post & Salop, *Rowing Against the Tidewater, supra* note 2.
60. *See* Kornhauser & Sager, *Collegial Courts, supra* note 2.

61. *See supra* chapter 2, § IV.B (discussing Arrovian nondictatorship criterion).

62. Mueller states the condition as follows: "*D* is determined only by the values of D_i, and is independent of how they are assigned. Any permutation of these ballots leaves *D* unchanged." DENNIS C. MUELLER, PUBLIC CHOICE II 97 (1989). As explained *supra* chapter 2, § V.B, and cites therein, May's Theorem posits that only simple majority rule satisfies the four conditions of decisiveness, anonymity, neutrality, and positive responsiveness.

63. GEORGE ORWELL, ANIMAL FARM 118 (Harcourt Brace Jovanovich ed., 1990).

64. *See* BERNARD SCHWARTZ, THE ASCENT OF PRAGMATISM: THE BURGER COURT IN ACTION 14 (1990) (describing practice and observing, "Voting with the majority in this way certainly appears contrary to the spirit, if not the letter, of the Court's assignment practice"); LEE EPSTEIN & JACK KNIGHT, THE CHOICES JUSTICES MAKE 127–33 (1998) (providing examples of seemingly erroneous opinion assignments by Chief Justice Burger). Professors Jeffrey Segal and Harold Spaeth have questioned the accuracy of such accounts, asserting that

> [belying] the accuracy of [assertions that Burger improperly cast initial conference votes to assign opinions, when his ultimate vote was in the minority] is Burger's record during his term of office, a record unmatched for equal distribution of any of his five immediate predecessors.

JEFFREY A. SEGAL & HAROLD SPAETH, THE SUPREME COURT AND THE ATTITUDINAL MODEL 271 (1993). Formal numerical equality in opinion assignments, however, is not necessarily inconsistent with assertions, later documented by Professors Epstein and Knight, *see supra*, that Burger cast false initial conference votes in particular cases, presumably of importance to him, to control at least some opinion assignments.

65. In their extensively researched study of strategic interactions among the justices, Professors Epstein and Knight provide no examples in which justices actually traded votes over issues within a case or across cases. *See* EPSTEIN & KNIGHT, *supra* note 64, at 56–111. Virtually all examples involve strategies to bring in the necessary fifth justice to create a majority, which usually involved moving the opinion from the author's ideal point, as expressed in his initial conference vote, closer to that of the marginal justice. Professors Forrest Maltzman and Paul J. Wahlbeck recently described such a change from an original conference vote to the final vote in Wardius v. Oregon, 412 U.S. 470 (1973). *See* Forrest Maltzman & Paul J. Wahlbeck, *Strategic Policy Considerations and Voting Fluidity on the Burger Court,* 90 AM. POL. SCI. REV. 581 (1996). In *Wardius,* the Court, per Justice Marshall, recognized a defendant's right to reciprocal discovery. In an initial draft, Marshall took a position on the state's exclusionary rule, which Chief Justice Rehnquist, a potential marginal justice in the case, considered unacceptably broad, thus forcing him into dissent. Before casting his final vote, however, Rehnquist circulated a memorandum, in which he stated:

> I voted to affirm in this case at Conference, but before writing a dissent to Thurgood's proposed opinion I think I will wait to see if anything narrower is written.

Maltzman & Wahlbeck, *supra* at 583 (quoting memorandum from William Rehnquist to Warren Burger (Mar. 14, 1973) (available in William J. Brennan's Papers, Box 303, Library of Congress)); *see also* Tracey E. George, *Developing a Positive*

Theory of Decisionmaking in the U.S. Court of Appeals, 58 Ohio St. L. Rev. 1635, 1660 (1998) (providing *Wardius* as illustration of opinion writing and signing negotiations). Maltzman and Wahlbeck then go on to describe the events that followed:

> On June 4, Justice Marshall circulated a new draft with a cover letter stating that "since the Court appears hopelessly splintered on the disposition of petitioner's contentions concerning the state's exclusionary rule, I have decided that it may be best to leave that question for another day." On June 6, Marshall's decision to limit the breadth of his opinion was rewarded when Rehnquist joined his opinion to reverse.

Maltzman & Wahlbeck, *supra* at 583 (quoting Memorandum from Thurgood Marshall to the Conference (June 4, 1973)). This form of strategic interaction reflects a successful move along a single-issue continuum needed to elevate the median position, represented by Rehnquist, to majority status, through the revised Marshall opinion, which moved from the author's ideal point, taking a broader view, to an accommodationist opinion, taking a narrower view. For another recent study of interactive strategies among Supreme Court justices, see Evan H. Caminker, *Sincere and Strategic Voting Norms on Multimember Courts,* 97 Mich. L. Rev. 2297 (1999).

66. In response to Professor Tullock's analysis in *Why So Much Stability?* 37 Pub. Choice 189 (1981), which suggested that logrolling induced legislative stability, Professors Shepsle and Weingast demonstrated that, under specified conditions, when the underlying preferences of decision makers cycle, logrolling has the potential to simply replicate, rather than abate, cycling. *See generally* Kenneth Shepsle & Barry Weingast, *Structure-Induced Equilibrium and Legislative Choice,* 37 Pub. Choice 503 (1981).

67. *See* Mueller, *supra* note 62, at 82–83 (providing illustration); *see also* Stearns, *The Misguided Renaissance, supra* note 27, at 1278–79 n. 223 (same).

68. For my more detailed discussion distinguishing legislative from adjudicatory lawmaking, *infra* chapter 4; *see also* Stearns, *Standing Back from the Forest, supra* note 6, at 1386–93 (describing the elusive distinction between adjudication and legislation based upon theory of social choice); Maxwell L. Stearns, *Mistretta Versus Marbury: The Foundations of Judicial Review,* 74 Tex. L. Rev. 1281 (1996) (describing same distinction based upon comparison of Marbury v. Madison, 5 U.S. (1 Cranch) 137 (1803), and Mistretta v. United States, 488 U.S. 361 (1989)).

69. Three-judgment cases are discussed *infra* § V.D.

70. *See* United States v. Pink, 315 U.S. 203, 216 (1942); Hertz v. Woodman, 218 U.S. 205, 213–14 (1910); Etting v. Bank of the United States, 11 Wheat 59, 78 (1826).

71. 430 U.S. 188 (1973).

72. *See infra* § VI, table 3.9. The discussion in the text treats the category four from table 3.9, fractured panel decisions producing vote switches by individual justices, as a subset of category three, fractured panel decisions in which no opinion resolves the case on narrowest grounds. Identifying cases within this category is complicated by the fact that after the vote switch, the result is a majority opinion, or a combination of separately authored majority opinions.

73. *See infra* § V.B (describing vote-switch cases).

74. *See supra* § II.

75. Even if we assume that justices are principally motivated by the desire to determine policy, rather than to resolve cases in accordance with legal principles, *see generally* SEGAL & SPAETH, *supra* note 64 (describing attitudinal model of Supreme Court decision making and providing detailed empirical support); EPSTEIN & KNIGHT, *supra* note 64 (asserting that policymaking is the principal objective. of justices), then outcome voting can be understood to further that objective.

76. While *Marks* is well cited, I have found only a single student note specifically devoted to a careful assessment of the narrowest grounds rule that that case established. *See* Mark Alan Thurmon, Note, *When the Court Divides: Reconsidering the Precedential Value of Supreme Court Plurality Decisions,* 42 DUKE L.J. 419 (1992) (criticizing *Marks* doctrine on grounds that it fails to produce meaningful guidance for future Supreme Court decision making and that it often rests upon an attenuated notion of judicial consensus). Others have discussed the narrowest grounds doctrine briefly as part of a larger analysis of Supreme Court voting rules. *See, e.g.,* Kornhauser & Sager, *Collegial Courts, supra* note 2, at 45 (arguing that the *Marks* doctrine only functions properly when issues in a given cases can be nested together like Russian dolls); *see also* Rogers, *"Issue Voting",* *supra* note 2, at 1008 (arguing that lower courts can divine guidance from Supreme Court cases where issues cannot be nested like Russian dolls simply by tallying the votes within all opinions on an issue-by-issue basis, when issues arise separately, and by applying the Court's holding when issues creating voting anomaly arise together, even though in doing so, the result on at least one of the underlying issues will differ under these two approaches). I have located no articles that offer a comprehensive analysis of why the Supreme Court has adopted the narrowest grounds doctrine in spite of the doctrine's apparent faults. I have also checked several major constitutional law textbooks. While some mention *Marks,* they include it for its substantive First Amendment content, rather than for the narrowest grounds doctrine. One of the remarkable features of all this is that a student can make it through law school without ever learning how to construe a fractured Supreme Court decision. In a recent essay, I argued that *Marks* warrants its own treatment in introductory course books in Constitutional Law. See Maxwell L. Stearns, *The Case for Including* Marks v. United States *Within the Canon of Constitutional Law,* 17 CONST. COMM.—(forthcoming 2000).

77. 430 U.S. 188 (1977).

78. 413 U.S. 15 (1973).

79. 383 U.S. 413 (1966).

80. 354 U.S. 476 (1957).

81. *Marks,* 430 U.S. at 192 (quoting *Roth,* 354 U.S. at 476).

82. *Memoirs,* 383 U.S. at 418.

83. *Miller,* 413 U.S. at 22.

84. *Marks,* 430 U.S. at 193 (discussing *Memoirs* concurrences).

85. *Memoirs,* 383 U.S. at 421 (concurring in the reversal for reasons stated in dissent in Ginzburg v. United States, 383 U.S. 463, 499 (1966)).

86. *Id.* at 443 (Clark, J., dissenting); *id.* at 460–61 (White, J., dissenting).

87. *Id.* at 454–46 (Harlan, J., dissenting) ("My premise is that in the area of obscenity the Constitution does not bind the States and the Federal government in precisely the same fashion").

88. *Miller,* 413 U.S. at 24.

89. *See Marks,* 430 U.S. at 191.

90. U.S. CONST. art. I, § 9, cl. 3 ("No Bill of Attainder or ex post facto Law shall be passed").

91. 378 U.S. 347 (1964).

92. *Marks,* 430 U.S. at 192.
93. *Id.*
94. *Id.* at 193 (quoting, in part, Gregg v. Georgia, 428 U.S. 153, 169 n. 15 (1976)).
95. *Marks,* 430 U.S. at 194.
96. *See supra* § II.A, table 3.1 (depicting *Kassel*); § II.C.2, table 3.2 (depicting *Miller*); § III.A, table 3.3 (depicting *Tidewater*).
97. 505 U.S. 833 (1992).
98. 410 U.S. 113 (1973).
99. *See supra* chapter 1, § II.C.
100. Recall that the opposite analysis applies for fractured panel decisions upholding a law against a constitutional challenge. To apply *Marks* to the part of *Casey* that upheld the remaining abortion restrictions, we would need to place a double vertical line between the opinions of Blackmun and Stevens and the joint opinion. In this analysis, only the opinions to the right of the double vertical line would be eligible for holding status, producing, again, the joint opinion as the stable outcome.
101. They did not vote to strike down a nonrestrictive provision, which provided for an exception to each abortion restriction in the event of a medical emergency. *See supra* chapter 1, § II.C. (discussing *Casey*).
102. 438 U.S. 265 (1978).
103. *See supra* chapter 1, § III.B.
104. *Bakke,* 438 U.S. at 361–62 (Brennan, J., concurring in the judgment in part and dissenting in part).
105. *Id.* at 412 (Stevens, J., concurring in the judgment in part and dissenting in part) (citing § 601 of the Civil Rights Act of 1964, 42 U.S.C. § 2000d).
106. *Id.* at 281–82, 287–88, 305–6 (Powell, J., announcing the judgment for the Court).
107. *Id.* at 272 (Powell, J., announcing the judgment for the Court); *id.* at 379 (Brennan, J., concurring in the judgment in part and dissenting in part).
108. *See id.* at 271 (Powell, J., announcing the judgment for the Court); *id.* at 421 (Stevens, J., concurring in the judgment in part and dissenting in part).
109. *Id.* at 316–20 (Powell, J., announcing the judgment for the Court).
110. *Id.* at 317. Indeed, Justice Powell was so enamored of the Harvard affirmative action program that he appended a copy of that plan, in which race was used as a plus factor to be considered along with numerous other variables in the university's admissions decisions, to his opinion. *Id.* at 316, 321–23.
111. *Id.* at 362 (Brennan, J., concurring in the judgment in part and dissenting in part).
112. *Id.* at 306 (Powell, J., announcing the judgment for the Court).
113. *Id.* at 412 (Stevens, J., concurring in the judgment in part and dissenting in part).
114. *Id.* at 379 (Brennan, J., concurring in the judgment in part and dissenting in part).
115. This case, which presents multidimensional but symmetrical preferences, is therefore parallel to that presented in chapter 2, § IV.A, figure 2.5.
116. For a comparative analysis of the implications of the median voter theorem in direct presidential elections and in the selection of the prime minister within parliamentary systems, see STEARNS, PUBLIC CHOICE AND PUBLIC LAW, *supra* note 27, at 126–29 (positing that the median voter theorem would predict stable two-party systems with direct presidential elections, but that in parliamentary systems, we would instead predict multiple parties, including small parties, given that in voting for the prime minister, a market develops for parties hoping to become critical in forming a minimum winning coalition).

117. For commentators critical of the practical significance of the median voter theorem, see, e.g., Charles K. Rowley, *The Relevance of the Median Voter Theorem,* 140 J. INST'L AND THEORETICAL ECON. 104 (1984); Randall G. Halcombe, *An Empirical Test of the Median Voter Model,* 18 ECON. INQUIRY 260 (1980); Thomas Romer & Howard Rosenthal, *The Elusive Median Voter,* 12 J. PUBLIC ECON. 143 (1979).

118. The recent election under plurality voting of Jesse "the Body" Ventura to the governorship of Minnesota is illustrative. *See* Helen Kennedy, *Ex-Wrestler Elected Minn. Governor,* DAILY NEWS (New York), November 4, 1998, at 11. Commentators had observed that Ventura appealed to both economic conservatives and to social liberals, thus defying the conventional spectrum in which Republicans are assumed to be conservative on both economic and social issues and Democrats are assumed to be the opposite. *See,* e.g., *Dane Smith,* Rivals Assail Ventura's Remarks on Prostitution; Consider Legalizing It to Control It, He Says, STAR TRIB. *(Minneapolis, Minn),* Oct. 22, 1998, at 1B.) ("Ventura's sympathies toward legalizing drugs and prostitution aren't new revelations. They are consistent with the libertarian principles he generally espouses—less governmental control in both the economic and social spheres"). In effect, Ventura attracted as part of his constituency members from both of these traditional voting coalitions. While Ventura won the plurality election with 37 percent of the vote, however, he might not have been a Condorcet winner. Minnesota could increase the probability of electing a Condorcet winner in its gubernatorial elections by holding a runoff between the two candidates who receive the highest percentage of votes when no candidate commands a majority in a plurality election. It is worth noting, however, that while this regime would increase the likelihood of ensuring a Condorcet winner, it will not guarantee that result. For an analysis comparing various voting regimes according to the criterion of Condorcet efficiency, meaning the percentage likelihood of yielding available Condorcet winners based upon the number of condidates, see MUELLER, *supra* note 62, at 113–16. It remains possible that a candidate who trails the first and second place plurality winners might still defeat each of those candidates in a direct binary comparison. By way of analogy, the Powell opinion is the Condorcet winner in *Bakke* even though both the Brennan and Stevens opinions secured more votes. Recall from chapter 2, *supra* § IV.B.1, that elections generally eschew the Condorcet criterion precisely because Condorcet-producing rules have the potential to produce inertia when no Condorcet winner is available.

119. Consider, for example, Jesse Jackson's not-so-subtle threats during the 1988 presidential campaign that unless Michael Dukakis embraced certain positions of interest to African American voters, Jackson could not guarantee that Rainbow Coalition members would make it to the polls. For more detailed discussions, see Richard Stengle, *An Indelicate Balance; in Picking Bentsen, Dukakis Looked Right and Needlessly Blindsided Jackson,* TIME, July 25, 1988, at 20 ("What [the Democrats] need to settle on is a solution that will satisfy Jackson. He maintains that he wants precisely what he has wanted all along—a place at the table, a chance to be truly involved in shaping a new Administration, the same right to be consulted that white leaders with far less of a constituency are accorded").

120. *See* Kornhauser & Sager, *Collegial Courts, supra* note 2, at 45.

121. *See* Thurmon, *supra* note 76.

122. Witness, for example, the transformation of Associate Justice William H. Rehnquist from the "lone dissenter" to his present status as a chief justice who often votes with the majority and who has imposed a significant imprimatur on the Court. *See* Bernard Schwartz, *Term Limits, Commerce, and the Rehnquist Court,*

31 Tulsa L.J. 521, 528 (1996); John A. Jenkins, *The Partisan: A Talk with Justice Rehnquist,* N.Y. Times, Mar. 3, 1985, § 6 (Magazine), at 28, 34.

123. *See Memoirs,* 383 U.S. at 421 (Stewart, J., concurring in the reversal for the reasons stated in his dissent in Ginzburg, 383 U.S. at 499).

124. For a group of cases with a two-dimensional issue spectrum in which one or more justices deferred to the Court's majority resolution on an underlying issue, see *infra* § V.B.

125. For a discussion of such cases, see *infra* § V.B.

126. This intuition is consistent with the work of attitudinal scholars who posit that judicial ideology, or attitudes, is uniquely predictive of voting patterns in individual Supreme Court cases. *See generally* Segal & Spaeth, *supra* note 64 (providing comprehensive overview of attitudinal model along with empirical support). To the extent that ideology is predictive, it is because in the vast majority of cases, the issue spectrum is unidimensional or is multidimensional but the preferences are symmetrical, and thus can be generally understood in ideological terms. It is precisely in those cases in which the issue spectrum is multidimensional and preferences are asymmetrical that we would predict that the attitudinal model might lose its predictive force.

127. 383 U.S. 413 (1966).

128. *See supra* § IV.A (analyzing *Memoirs* under *Marks*).

129. For another interesting variation, consider the unanimity norm in the Delaware Supreme Court. *See* David A. Skeel, Jr., *The Unanimity Norm in Delaware Corporate Law,* 83 Va. L. Rev. 127 (1997). Providing several case illustrations, Professor Skeel explains the tendency of the norm to mask doctrinal cycles that would otherwise be exposed if the justices of that court were free to express differing viewpoints on underlying dispositive case issues. One particularly interesting manifestation, which is fully consistent with the social choice analysis of issue identification, *see supra* § III, is the apparently high degree of fact specificity included in potentially divisive opinions. Professor Skeel explains:

In a very real sense, the decisions suggest not a choice among approaches, but "of" all of them. In striking contrast to a nonunanimous regime, the unanimity norm encourages the justices to adopt a combined approach that is acceptable to all [justices], rather than [to] articulat[e] their differing views on the appropriate doctrinal approach.

See id. at 147. In the United States Supreme Court, in contrast, justices are free to set out any supporting rationale for their outcome vote. The contrast between the Delaware Supreme Court and United States Supreme Court therefore reveals the trade-off between a regime that provides the appearance—albeit potentially a false one—of agreement on underlying issues, and a regime that allows, and perhaps even encourages, the airing of genuine doctrinal disagreements.

130. As stated previously, the argument in the text is not intended to suggest that the *Marks* doctrine prevents all forms of voting among the justices that one might characterize as strategic. *See supra* note 65 (explaining nature of strategic interactions of justices). Justices who would prefer to express a broader statement of law can behave strategically in a limited sense, even with *Marks* in place. They can choose to concur in the judgment on broader grounds, and if they are the marginal vote, to relegate the holding to case-disposition, rather than precedential, status. (As *Marks* itself makes clear, however, this distinction is less airtight than it once was.) Alternatively, as suggested in the text, the justice can try to

maneuver the narrowest grounds author closer to his position to capture his vote. For a recent illustration of the trade-off confronting a would-be author of a broader concurrence, consider Adarand Constructors, Inc. v. Pena, 515 U.S. 200 (1995). In *Adarand*, Justice Scalia joined the majority, which, including his vote, totaled five justices, "except insofar as it might be inconsistent with the views expressed" in his separate concurrence. An analysis of the opinions reveals that while Justice O'Connor, writing for a five-justice majority, including Scalia, determined that strict scrutiny should apply to federal minority business set-aside programs, the application should not be "strict in theory, but fatal in fact." *Id.* at 237 (internal quotations omitted). In contrast, Justice Scalia made clear that for him, the application of strict scrutiny should be fatal in fact, because "under our constitution there can be no such thing as a creditor or debtor race." *Id.* at 239 (Scalia, J., concurring). Ordinarily, one might have expected Scalia to state his broader proposed holding in a separate opinion and to concur in the judgment. Of course, since his proposed holding would have been broader, doing so would not have allowed him to state the rule of the case in any event. Moreover, Scalia saw *Adarand* as the first opportunity for the Court to issue a majority opinion holding that both federal and state race-based affirmative action programs are subject to strict scrutiny.

In effect, the analysis reveals the limited issue space available to the narrowest grounds opinion writer. While it has become commonplace to describe the apparent median justice—presently often claimed to be Justice Kennedy—as the most powerful, *see infra* chapter 5, § IV.A, and cites therein (discussing lineup of present Court), or even as the most dangerous, *see* Paul H. Edelman & Jim Chen, *The Most Dangerous Justice: The Supreme Court at the Bar of Mathematics,* 70 S. Cal. L. Rev. 63 (1996), social choice analysis reveals the limited force of such characterizations. In those cases in which the justices' preferences can be cast along a unidimensional issue spectrum, the median justice has some negotiating room (or issue space) in which to forge a majority, but if he is unwilling to negotiate by moving toward the right or left to capture a majority, he or she risks standing alone as the narrowest grounds concurring justice. (The relationship between the median justice and those whose support he needs in order to forge a majority can also be expressed in terms of a bilateral monopoly.) If so, the median justice will express the Court's holding, but will do so with less force than if he accommodated enough justices by moving off his ideal point to create a majority. This analysis also helps to explain the frequent observation that justices tend to issue more candid statements of their own views of law in separate concurrences and dissents than they do as authors of majority opinions. Absent the payoff associated with forging a majority, justices writing separately have no need to move off their ideal points to accommodate the views of others. Simply put, the assertion that any particular justice is most powerful is ultimately no more than a recognition that the justice stands in the median position of a Court that most often expresses unidimensional or multidimensional with symmetrical preferences.

131. *See* Rogers, *"Issue Voting," supra* note 2, at 1008.
132. Professors David Post and Steven Salop and Professor John Rogers have identified several illustrative lower federal court cases. For cases taking this approach with respect to *Tidewater*, see Detres v. Lions Bldg. Corp., 234 F.2d 596 (7th Cir. 1956) (applying the Jackson plurality and Rutledge concurring opinions in *Tidewater* to uphold statute creating diversity jurisdiction with citizens of the Territory of Puerto Rico and of a state); Siegmund v. General Commodities Corp., 175 F.2d 952 (9th Cir. 1949) (applying same analysis to uphold statute creating diver-

sity jurisdiction with citizens of the Territory of Hawaii and of a state); Greene v. Teffeteller, 90 F. Supp. 387 (E.D. Tenn. 1950) (applying *Tidewater* result in challenge to post-*Tidewater* jurisdiction granting statute for citizens of the District of Columbia and of states, in which the word " 'States', as used in [the relevant] section, includes . . . the District of Columbia."). For other cases taking the same general approach, see Service Oil, Inc. v. North Dakota, 479 N.W.2d 815 (N.D. 1992) (applying American Trucking Ass'ns., Inc. v. Smith, 496 U.S. 167 (1990)); Banco Nacional de Cuba v. Chase Manhattan Bank, 658 F.2d 875 (2d Cir. 1981) (applying First Nat'l City Bank v. Banco Nacional de Cuba (Citibank I), 406 U.S. 759 (1972)); *see also* Rogers, *"Issue Voting," supra* note 2, at 1008 (collecting cases); Post & Salop, *Rowing Against the Tidewater, supra* note 2 (same).

133. 116 S. Ct. 1114 (1996).
134. 491 U.S. 1 (1989).
135. See Rogers, *"Issue Voting," supra* note 2; John M. Rogers, *"I Vote This Way Because I'm Wrong": The Supreme Court Justice as Epimenides,* 79 KY L.J. 439 (1991).
136. *See* Post & Salop, *Rowing Against the Tidewater, supra* note 2; Kornhauser & Sager, *Collegial Courts, supra* note 2.
137. 491 U.S. 1.
138. 42 U.S.C. § 9601 *et seq.*
139. Pub. L. No. 99–499, 100 Stat. 1613 (1986).
140. *See Union* Gas, 491 U.S. at 13–15, 19–20.
141. *See id.,* 491 U.S. at 29–30, 39–41 (Scalia, J., concurring in part and dissenting in part).
142. *Id.* at 56 (White, J., concurring in the judgment in part and dissenting in part).
143. *See supra* at 116–19 (providing illustration based upon *Kassel* hypothetical).
144. *See* Rogers, *Epimenides, supra* note 135.
145. This group of cases is discussed in the next subsection.
146. *Seminole Tribe,* 116 S. Ct. at 1128.
147. I am indebted to Evan Caminker for suggesting this reading of Justice Rehnquist's *Seminole Tribe* opinion.
148. 499 U.S. 279 (1991).
149. *Id.* at 313–14.
150. *See* Rogers, *Epimenides, supra* note 135, at 463.
151. 402 U.S. 62 (1971).
152. Justice Harlan stated that he reached the second issue "substantially for the reasons set forth . . . in Justice Blackmun's separate opinion." United States v. Vuitch, 402 U.S. 62, 96 (1971) (Harlan, J., dissenting as to jurisdiction). Justice Blackmun wrote:

Although I join Mr. Justice Harlan in his conclusion that this case is not properly here by direct appeal under 18 U.S.C. § 3731, a majority, and thus the Court, holds otherwise. The case is therefore here and requires decision. The five Justices constituting a majority, however, are divided on the merits. . . .

Because of the inability of the jurisdictional-issue majority to agree upon the disposition of the case, I feel obligated not to remain silent as to the merits. . . . Assuming, as I must in light of the Court's decision, that the Court does have jurisdiction on the appeal, I join Part II of Mr. Justice Black's opinion and the judgment of the Court.

Id. at 97–98 (opinion of Blackmun, J.).

153. *See* Rogers, *"Issue Voting," supra* note 2, at 998 (emphasis in original).
154. It is noteworthy that deferring to contrary majority judgments or resolutions of underlying issues cannot universally be condemned as inconsistent with the assumption that the Court is composed of reasoned, nonarbitrary decision makers. Had the *Union Gas* issues come up in separate cases, such that the Court determined first that CERCLA authorizes damages actions against states, in a case which did not present a constitutional challenge, and had Justice White dissented from the majority holding that CERCLA does authorize such suits, it would be difficult to maintain that in a subsequent case in which the constitutionality of the suit-authorization provision was challenged that Justice White would have abdicated his judicial responsibility by accepting the Court's earlier holding on the construction of CERCLA, and then voting that Congress has the constitutional authority to allow such suits. Indeed, as I will demonstrate *infra* chapter 4, § III, if justices were not presumptively bound by contrary majority resolutions of underlying dispositive issues from prior cases, the result would be to introduce considerable uncertainty into constitutional doctrine, a result which one could also attack on credible normative grounds. The difference between the two forms of deference to contrary majority resolutions of underlying dispositive issues, then, has less to do with normative merit than with the nature of the Court's differing decision-making rules as they operate within single cases and across groups of cases over time.
155. *See* Kornhauser & Sager, *Collegial Courts, supra* note 2, at 38–39; Post & Salop, *Rowing Against the Tidewater, supra* note 2, at 751–53.
156. While Brennan consistently embraced the position that, regardless of substantive test, lower courts could only consider the enacting legislature's actual justifications, with the exception of United States v. Virginia, 116 S. Ct. 2264 (1996) (Ginsburg, J., for a majority) (concluding that in the context of an equal protection to challenge a sex-based classification benefiting men, the state could only defend with an actual legislative purpose), his position generally did not command majority support. For an earlier case in which Brennan embraced this position, see Michael M. v. Sonoma County Superior Court, 450 U.S. 464, 1214 n. 2, 1217 (1981) (Brennan, J. dissenting) (rejecting majority rationale that sex-specific statutory rape law furthers an important governmental interest by "roughly 'equaliz[ing]' the deterrents of the sexes," in part on the ground that "the historical development of [the statute] demonstrates that the law was initially enacted on the premise that young women, in contrast to young men, were to be deemed legally incapable of consenting to an act of sexual intercourse," and because "[female] chastity was considered particularly precious").
157. *See Union Gas,* 491 U.S. at 13–15, 19–20 (Brennan, J., for a majority) (concluding that CERCLA authorizes damages suits against states); *Fulminante,* 499 U.S. at 287–88 (White, J., for a majority) (concluding that the confession was coerced); *Vuitch,* 402 U.S. at 64–65, 72–73 (Black, J., for a majority) (concluding that the Supreme Court had jurisdiction in this case).
158. *See supra* § II.C.2 (explaining that in *Miller,* Justices Stevens, Scalia, Ginsburg, and Breyer, and those who joined their opinions, formed a majority to find that petitioner had standing, and that Justices O'Connor, Ginsburg, and Breyer, and those who joined their opinions, formed a majority to apply heightened scrutiny and to strike down the challenged INA provision on the merits); § II.A (explaining that in *Kassel,* Justices Brennan and Rehnquist, and those who joined their opinions, formed a majority to apply rational basis scrutiny, and Justices Powell

and Rehnquist, and those who joined their opinions, formed a majority to admit novel evidence); § III.A, explaining that in *Tidewater,* Justices Jackson, Vinson, and Frankfurter, and those who joined their opinions, formed a majority concluding that citizens of the District of Columbia are not citizens of the United States for diversity purposes, and Justices Rutledge, Vinson, and Frankfurter formed a majority concluding that Congress is limited by Article III in conferring jurisdiction upon the federal courts).

159. At a minimum, the question for which the Court granted the writ certiorari did not make this division of issues immediately apparent. That question was the following:

Is the distinction in 8 U.S.C. § 1409 between "illegitimate" children of United States citizen mothers and "illegitimate" children of United States citizen fathers a violation of the Fifth Amendment to the United States Constitution?

Miller, 118 S. Ct. at 1434.

160. It is noteworthy that Justice Stevens resolved the issue of standing in part III of his opinion, in which he also stated:

[The] only question presented by the facts of this case is whether the requirement in § 1409(1)(4)—that children born out of wedlock to citizen fathers, but not citizen mothers, obtain formal proof of paternity by age 18 [which he later explained was twenty-one as applied to petitioner], either through legitimation, written acknowledgment by the father under oath, or adjudication by a competent Court—violates the Fifth Amendment.

Miller, 523 U.S. at 432. This statement provided the analytical foundation for parts IV and V of Stevens's opinion in which he concluded that the relevant test was rational basis scrutiny, under which the challenged INA survives. Justice Stevens thus failed to structure his opinion in a manner that naturally would have invited the dissenting justices to join in an effort to forge a clear majority on the issue of standing.

161. For further speculation on why these justices did not switch their votes along with a more detailed exposition of the cases themselves, see Maxwell L. Stearns, *Should Justices Ever Switch Votes? Miller v. Albright in Social Choice Perspective,* 7 SUP. CT. ECON. REV. 87, 128–46 (1999) (suggesting that their disinclination to switch votes might have followed from their own separation of powers analysis of standing, which in the context of *Miller,* closely resembled Justice Scalia's independent basis for declining to address the merits; because they construed *Seminole Tribe* as an opinion that discredited the practice of vote switching; or because the *Miller* opinion did not package the case issues in a manner that produced a single majority opinion on the issue of standing, to which they could comfortably defer).

162. *See* Bragdon v. Abbott, 118 S. Ct. 2196 (1998) (Stevens, J., concurring) (casting vote to remand rather than to affirm to produce majority judgment); Connecticut v. Johnson, 460 U.S. 73, 89–90 (1983) (Stevens, J., concurring) (casting vote to affirm, rather than to dismiss certiorari, to produce majority judgment); Maryland Casualty Co. v. Cushing, 347 U.S. 409, 423 (1954) (plurality opinion) (breaking deadlock by voting to remand, rather than to reverse, consistent with concurring opinion); Klapprott v. United States, 335 U.S. 601, 618 (1949) (Rutledge, J., concurring) (breaking deadlock by voting to remand, rather than to

reverse, consistent with plurality opinion); Von Moltke v. Gillies, 332 U.S. 708, 726–27 (1948) (plurality opinion) (observing that two concurring justices have agreed to break deadlock by voting with plurality to remand, rather than voting to reverse); Screws v. United States, 325 U.S. 91, 134 (1945) (Rutledge, J., concurring) (switching vote to remand to allow disposition and observing "Stalemate should not prevail for any reason, however compelling, in a criminal cause or, if avoidable, in any other").

163. One of the two post-*Marks* cases involved a decision to affirm, rather than to dismiss on the ground that certiorari was improvidently granted. *See* Connecticut v. Johnson, 460 U.S. at 89–90 (Stevens, J., concurring).

CHAPTER 4

1. 505 U.S. 833 (1992); *see supra* chapter 1, § II.C.
2. *See* Frank Easterbrook, *Ways of Criticizing the Court*, 95 HARV. L. REV. 802 (1982).
3. *See, e.g.*, Poe v. Ullman, 367 U.S. 497 (1961) (holding unripe a constitutional challenge to a Connecticut prohibition on the use of contraceptives, which had been on the books since 1879, but had yet to be enforced).
4. *See, e.g.*, Arizonans for Official English v. Arizona, 523 U.S. 43 (1997) (holding moot a bilingual state medical malpractice claims processor's challenge to the constitutionality of a statewide referendum prohibiting the use of languages other than English in government services, when the claimant had voluntarily terminated her employment two months after the district court ruled in her favor).
5. *See infra* chapter 6, § II (discussing ripeness and mootness doctrines and exceptions).
6. Association of Data Processing Serv. Orgs. v. Camp, 397 U.S. 150, 151 (1970).
7. Steven L. Winter, *The Metaphor of Standing and the Problem of Self-Governance*, 40 STAN. L. REV. 1371 (1988).
8. 438 U.S. 265 (1978).
9. 468 U.S. 737 (1984).
10. *See supra* chapter 1, § III.B.
11. For two cases in which the Supreme Court erroneously failed to impose a third-party standing barrier in a criminal procedure case, with the effect of vindicating a nonexistent claim, see *infra* § III.A.1 (discussing Powers v. Ohio, 400 U.S. 400, 412–14 (1991), and Campbell v. Louisiana, 532 U.S. 392 (1998)).
12. 5 U.S. (1 Cranch) 137 (1803).
13. *Id.* at 177.
14. 505 U.S. 144 (1992); *see also supra* chapter 2, § III.D.
15. *See* Allen v. Wright, 468 U.S. 737 (1984).
16. Palsgraf v. Long Island R.R., 162 N.E. 99, 99 (N.Y. 1928) (quoting SIR FREDERICK POLLOCK, THE LAW OF TORTS 455 (11th ed. 1920)).
17. As Professor Theodore Lowi explains:

Depending on who is doing the counting, an argument can be made that Congress enacted more regulatory programs in the five years between 1969 and 1974 than during any other comparable period in our history, including the first five years of the New Deal. It is possible to identify 130 major regulatory laws enacted during the decade of 1969–79. Moreover, an even stronger argument can be made that the regulatory policies adopted during that period were broader in scope and more unconditional in delegated discretion than any other programs in American history.

Theodore J. Lowi, *Two Roads to Serfdom: Liberalism, Conservativism and Administrative Power,* 36 Aм. U. L. Rev. 295, 298 (1987).

18. 198 U.S. 45 (1905).

19. *See, e.g.,* Heart of Atlanta Motel, Inc. v. United States, 379 U.S. 241 (1964) (upholding federal statutes that prohibit private discriminatory conduct once deemed beyond regulatory control); Katzenbach v. McClung, 379 U.S. 294 (1964) (same); West Coast Hotel Co. v. Parrish, 300 U.S. 379 (1937) (upholding state minimum wage statute and restricting substantive due process right to contract, which had previously rendered such regulation unconstitutional).

20. *See, e.g.,* Wickard v. Filburn, 317 U.S. 111 (1942) (upholding federal agriculture statute regulating farmer's wheat crop primarily intended for farm use and home consumption). The Supreme Court recently suggested that some Tenth Amendment limits remain on congressional commerce clause powers. *See, e.g.,* United States v. Lopez, 514 U.S. 549 (1995) (striking federal criminal statute prohibiting the possession of guns within specified distance of public schools); New York v. United States, 505 U.S. 144 (1992) (holding that commerce clause or Tenth Amendment prevents congressional commandeering of state legislatures).

21. To be sure, the Court had previously given hints that standing and mootness, but not ripeness, might have some linkage to Article III, but the earlier cases did not come close to a categorical demand that each doctrinal element of justiciability be met as a constitutional prerequisite to suit in federal court. In Doremus v. Board of Educ. of the Borough of Hawthorne, 342 U.S. 429, 432 (1952), for example, the Court, in an opinion by Justice Jackson, denied standing to challenge a state law that required Bible readings at the opening of each school day. Jackson, writing for a majority of six, reasoned that "federal" jurisdiction is cast in terms of 'case or controversy,' " and thus "taxpayer's action can meet this test . . . only when it is a good-faith pocketbook action" rather than one seeking to resolve a "religious difference." And in Liner v. Jafco, 375 U.S. 301 (1963), a case in which a unanimous Court, per Justice Brennan, reversed a state court determination that a labor dispute was moot, the Court stated in a footnote (and in dictum):

> Our lack of jurisdiction to review moot cases derives from the requirement in Article III of the Constitution under which the exercise of judicial power depends upon the existence of a case or controversy.

Id. at 305 n. 3. It is noteworthy that as support for the proposition that the mootness doctrine derives from Article III, Brennan cited no case law, but rather only a law review article and a student note. *See id.* In contrast with standing and mootness, the Court gave no hints that the ripeness doctrine was linked to Article III until Steffel v. Thompson, 415 U.S. 452, 458 (1974) (holding that petitioner, who sought to enjoin the application of the Georgia criminal trespass statute to prevent the distribution of handbills at a shopping center in protest of the Vietnam War, "presents an 'actual controversy,' a requirement imposed by Art. III of the Constitution and the express terms of the Federal Declaratory Judgment Act").

22. *See, e.g.,* Richard A. Epstein, Bargaining with the State 216–17 (1993) (arguing against standing limitations on citizen and taxpayer challenges to constitutionality of government regulation).

23. For criticisms of the Supreme Court's standing formulation informed by a more liberal perspective, see Cass R. Sunstein, *What's Standing after* Lujan? *Of Citizen Suits, "Injuries," and Article III,* 91 Mich. L. Rev. 163 (1992); Winter, *supra* note 7.
24. 461 U.S. 95 (1983).
25. 429 U.S. 1012 (1976). While this case was not formally disposed of on standing grounds, two separate concurrences, one by Chief Justice Burger (joined by Justice Powell), the other by Justice Stevens (joined by Justice Rehnquist), make clear that it was decided based upon standing principles. *See id.* at 1013, 1017.
26. 418 U.S. 155 (1974).
27. 418 U.S. 208 (1974).
28. 504 U.S. 555 (1992).
29. 438 U.S. 59 (1978).
30. 412 U.S. 669 (1973).
31. Since I wrote this book, the Supreme Court issued what may well be its most liberal recent decision on statutory standing, Friends of the Earth v. Laidlaw, 120 S. Ct. 693 (2000), a case that is in significant tension with *Lujan.* In an opinion by Justice Ruth Bader Ginsburg, the *Laidlaw* Court granted standing to a group of private litigants under the Clean Water Act who challenged the defendant's failure to comply with the requirements of an emissions permit. The attenuated nature of the claimants' injury is manifest by the district court finding, which the Supreme Court did not disturb, that the emissions permit violations had produced no discernible environmental harm. In dissent, Justice Scalia insisted upon a chain from a permit violation to environmental harm to injury to the claimant as a presumptive requirement of constitutional injury in fact. *Id.* at 714 (Scalia, J., dissenting) (positing that "[w]hile it is perhaps possible that a plaintiff could be harmed even though the environment was not, such a plaintiff would have the burden of articulating the nature of the injury"). In contrast, Justice Ginsburg, writing for a majority, stated:

    [t]he relevant showing for Article III standing . . . is not injury to the environment but injury to the plaintiff. To insist upon the former rather than the latter . . . is to raise the standing hurdle higher than the necessary showing for success on the merits in an action alleging noncompliance with [the required] permit.

    Id. at 703–4. With the possible exception of a claimant who alleges a reduction to property value resulting from documented permit violations near her property, even absent environmental harm, it is difficult to imagine a set of facts that would allow Justice Scalia to avoid his rigid insistence upon actual environmental harm in such a case. In contrast, Justice Ginsburg would allow standing to redress other forms of injury, for example to redress the psychological harm of knowing about a violation of federal law, provided that Congress conferred standing by statute. In a recent article, I have extended the model of standing developed in this book to account for the apparent inconsistency in the Court's transformation from *Lujan* to *Laidlaw, See* Maxwell L. Stearns, *From* Lujan *to* Laidlaw: *A Preliminary Model of Environmental Standing,* 11 Duke Envtl. L. & Pol'y F.__(forthcoming 2000).
32. For an article taking the position that standing is a substitute for the question whether plaintiff has a cause of action, see Sunstein, *supra* note 23. The social choice analysis of standing demonstrates, however, that standing and cause of

action are necessarily distinct. Depending upon the order in which cases are presented for review, the same court might reach different outcomes on the question whether to infer a particular statutory or constitutional cause of action. As a result, the legal inquiry into cause of action is subject to the same litigant path manipulation as are other bodies of substantive case law.

33. *See* Allen v. Wright, 468 U.S. 737, 760. Justice Blackmun's dissenting opinion in Lujan v. Defenders of Wildlife, 504 U.S. 555, 601–6 (1992), which Justice O'Connor joined, is consistent on this point with O'Connor's analysis for the *Allen* majority.

34. 504 U.S. at 571–78.

35. The analysis is complicated by Bennett v. Spear, 570 U.S. Ct. 154 (1997), in which the Supreme Court, per Justice Scalia, conferred standing upon petitioners who sought to limit the application of the Endangered Species Act (ESA) to further their economic interests against a contrary environmental claim and who relied upon the very ESA standing provision for which the *Lujan* Court denied environmental plaintiffs standing. The *Bennett* Court distinguished *Lujan* on the ground that the former was based upon the absence of a constitutional injury, while the latter was based upon a broad application of the zone of interest test. For an informative analysis of these cases, see Robert A. Anthony, *Zone-Free Standing for Private Attorneys General,* 7 GEO. MASON L. REV. 237 (1999). For an analysis of *Lujan* and *Bennett,* see *infra* chapter 6, § IV.

36. *See Lujan,* 504 U.S. at 579–81 (Kennedy, J., concurring):

In my view, Congress has the power to define injuries and articulate chains of causation that will give rise to a case or controversy where none existed before, and I do not read the Court's opinion to suggest a contrary view. In exercising this power, however, Congress must at the very least identify the injury it seeks to vindicate and relate the injury to the class of persons entitled to bring suit.*Id.* at 580 (citation omitted).

37. *See, e.g.,* Louise Harmon, *Fragments on the Deathwatch,* 77 MINN. L. REV. 1, 61 n.120 (1992) ("Standing, however, is only one of many judicial inventions designed to avoid constitutional decisionmaking"); Michael Wells, *The Impact of Substantive Interests on the Law of Federal Courts,* 30 WM. & MARY L. REV. 499, 513 (1989).

Sensitive to its status as the antidemocratic branch of government in a nation founded on the principle of majority rule, the Court seeks to avoid unnecessary constitutional decisions and to eschew judicial intervention unless the litigant seeking it makes a compelling case that he is so entitled. In recent years the Court has implemented these policies chiefly through its standing doctrine.

Id. at 518 (footnote omitted) ("The jurisdictional policy against standing to assert generalized grievances is sensitivity to the separation of powers, which in this context refers to a policy of restricting the exercise of judicial power by avoiding unnecessary constitutional decisions."); *see generally* ALEXANDER M. BICKEL, THE LEAST DANGEROUS BRANCH: THE SUPREME COURT AT THE BAR OF POLITICS 115–27 (1962) (asserting that justiciability doctrines including standing promote federal judiciary's "passive virtues" as the least majoritarian branch). In Gladstone Realtors v. Village of Bellwood, 441 U.S. 91 (1979), the Supreme Court lent credence to the prudential avoidance position, stating that, "even when a case falls within [appropriate] constitutional boundaries, a plaintiff may still lack standing under the prudential principles by which the judiciary seeks to avoid deciding questions of broad social import where no individual rights would be vindicated." *Id.* at 99–100.

38. *See, e.g.,* Robert A. Sedler, *Standing, Justiciability, and All That: A Behavioral Analysis,* 25 VAND. L. REV. 479, 480–81, 512 (1972) (positing that courts often employ standing as a disguised merits determination); Mark V. Tushnet, *The New Law of Standing: A Plea for Abandonment,* 62 CORNELL L. REV. 663, 663 (1977) (same); Winter, *supra* note 7, at 1373 (observing that some commentators "have concluded that the doctrine of standing is either a judicial mask for the exercise of prudence to avoid decisionmaking or a sophisticated manipulation for the sub rosa decision of cases on their merits") (footnote omitted).

39. *See* William A. Fletcher, *The Structure of Standing,* 98 YALE L. J. 221 (1988).

40. 458 U.S. 527 (1982).

41. 458 U.S. 457 (1982).

42. 393 U.S. 385 (1969).

43. The *Hunter* Court concluded that the amendment fundamentally altered the political process with respect to an issue affecting a distinct group of voters based upon race and, thus, that the amendment violated the Fourteenth Amendment equal protection clause. *Hunter,* 393 U.S. 385.

44. Powell reasoned that the Washington statewide initiative simply restored to the state level decision-making power, which it had once conferred upon local school boards, and that the *Crawford* amendment simply equated the state's equal protection standard to that under the federal Constitution. *Seattle,* 458 U.S. at 495–99 (Powell, J., dissenting).

45. *See supra* chapter 1, § III.A.

46. 523 U.S. 420 (1998).

47. 450 U.S. 662 (1981).

48. 337 U.S. 582 (1949).

49. Recall from chapter 2 that we need only consider a single Condorcet-producing rule to illustrate the problem that it would cause in an institution that is presumed obligated to produce collective decisions. *See supra* chapter 2, §II.A.

50. Because no justice takes the position, I have not included a potential fourth option, "not-*Crawford,* not-*Seattle.*"

51. Among jurisprudential theorists and judicial politics scholars, there exists a considerable debate concerning whether stare decisis operates to constrain the behavior of Supreme Court justices, especially in constitutional cases. For scholars arguing that stare decisis poses a minimal constraint in constitutional cases, see SAUL BRENNER & HAROLD SPAETH, STARE INDECISIS (1995). For scholars taking the opposite view, see LEE EPSTEIN & JACK KNIGHT, THE CHOICES JUSTICES MAKE (1998); Lee Epstein & Jack Knight, *The Norm of* Stare Decisis, 40 AM. J. POLI. SCI. 1018–35 (1996). For a recent symposium on this issue, see 40 AM. J. POLI. SCI. 971–1083 (1996). While it is not possible to review this literature in detail, it is worth commenting briefly on its relationship to the social choice model developed in the text. First, for purposes of that model, it is important to distinguish formal overruling from any other form of avoidance of precedent. As explained later in this chapter, distinguishing precedent often has the effect of generating alternative decisional paths. This phenomenon helps to explain some nonobvious doctrinal developments. *See infra* at 118–19. n.*, 181–87, 192–95. Second, while it is certainly correct that, given the difference in the costs of overturning

erroneous Supreme Court precedents in each context, the Court is far more inclined to overrule constitutional than statutory cases, the absolute number of overrulings nevertheless remains almost trivial. For a discussion of the percentage of overruled constitutional cases versus other overruled cases, see JEFFREY A. SEGAL & HAROLD J. SPAETH, THE SUPREME COURT AND THE ATTITUDINAL MODEL 51 (1993) (noting that from 1953 through 1990, the ratio of Supreme Court overrulings in constitutional cases to all others was 69 percent in the Warren Court, 68.2 percent in the Burger Court, and 68.4 percent in the Rehnquist Court). For a discussion of the absolute number of overruled Supreme Court cases, see EPSTEIN & KNIGHT, *supra* at 172–77. Professors Epstein and Knight observe:

No matter how one counts the alterations of precedent, the numbers border on the trivial: the Congressional Research Service reports that the Court has overturned prior decisions in only 196 of the cases decided through 1990; and Saul Brenner and Harold Spaeth, using a different rule, claim that the Vinson through Rehnquist Courts overruled about 2.5 cases per term.

See id. (citing Congressional Research Service, *The Constitution of the United States of American: Analysis and Interpretation* 2117–27 (1987); and *1990 Supplement,* 265–66; BRENNER & SPAETH, *supra*).

Finally, while one could rest upon these reported numbers alone to support the proposition that stare decisis does in fact operate as a significant constraint on judicial behavior even in constitutional cases within the Supreme Court, there is a more important methodological issue that separates the approach taken here from that employed by at least some judicial politics scholars, whether or not asserting that stare decisis operates as a meaningful constraint on judicial behavior. Judicial politics scholars attempt, in part, to assess the impact of precedent upon judicial behavior by comparing the number of favorable case citations in majority and dissenting opinions, leading to the conclusion that sufficient precedent exists to arrive at precisely opposite outcomes on the same question of law. *See, e.g.,* EPSTEIN & KNIGHT, *supra* at 173–74 (listing justice's citations to precedent in majority and dissenting opinions). While Professors Epstein and Knight express relatively strong support for the intuition that stare decisis is a meaningful constraint, this methodology nonetheless has the potential to understate the doctrine's constraining effect. The conceptual difficulty lies in the fact that precedent is generally cited with respect to the most contentious issues of law in the case, and is therefore focused upon a fairly narrow margin. Thus, for example, in an appeal from the denial of a due process claim by a convicted criminal, neither side is likely to challenge the power of federal courts to exercise judicial review; to do so against a contrary legal determination by a state court; to apply the Bill of Rights to the states; to do so in a manner that gives equal content to both federal and state applications; and to apply judicially created remedies to identified constitutional violations, just to name a few resolved—and respected—precedents. In each instance, the validity of the precedents that established these propositions is likely to simply be assumed. Stated differently, the relevant issue space within each case is restricted by a considerable backdrop of precedent, only some of which is likely to be close enough to the actual case, and potentially subject to judicial reconsideration, to warrant direct discussion.

52. For a formal definition of these Arrovian conditions, see *supra* chapter 2, § V.B.
53. *See supra* chapter 3, § II.B.

54. As in the illustrations of collective intransitivities within individual cases presented in chapter 3, the assumptions employed to generate a forward or backward cycle in *Crawford* and *Seattle* include each possible ranking over the remaining alternatives for the justices embracing each ideal point. *See supra* at 106 n. 35.

55. In *Seattle School Board,* the Seattle School Board brought suit in United States District Court to challenge the Washington initiative. *Seattle School Board,* 458 U.S. at 464. The district court held Initiative 350 unconstitutional, and a divided panel of the Ninth Circuit affirmed. *Id.* at 465–66. The state and various officers appealed to the Supreme Court, which noted probable jurisdiction. *Id.* at 467. In *Crawford,* the superior court found the constitutional amendment inapplicable to the revised plan that it had previously ordered, a ruling that was reversed on appeal. *Crawford,* 458 U.S. at 533. After the California Supreme Court denied hearing, the United States Supreme Court granted the petition for writ of certiorari filed on behalf of the minority schoolchildren. *Id.* at 534.

56. For a formal definition of "independence of irrelevant alternatives," see *supra* chapter 2, § V.B.

57. 438 U.S. 265 (1978).

58. 505 U.S. 833 (1992).

59. While I presented *Casey* in one dimension rather than two, *see supra* chapter 3, § IV.B, that was largely a function of the fact that the joint authors provided no indication independent of their outcome vote, which was nominally based upon stare decisis, as to how they would have voted on the question of whether the constitution protects a woman's right to abort in the absence of precedent.

60. 173 U.S. 537 (1896).

61. 347 U.S. 483 (1954).

62. These cases are discussed, *infra* § III.D.

63. *See, e.g.,* Coleman v. Thompson, 501 U.S. 722, 747 (1991) (observing that in Wainwright v. Sykes, 433 U.S. 72 (1977), the Supreme Court limited Fay v. Noia, 372 U.S. 391 (1963), to its facts).

64. *Casey,* 505 U.S. at 854.

65. While interest groups are presumed unable to raise the claims of others, under specified conditions, associations are permitted to raise the claims of their members. Thus, in Hunt v. Washington Apple Advertising Comm'n, 432 U.S. 333 (1977), the Court articulated the following three-part test for organizational standing:

> [An] association has standing to bring suit on behalf of its members when:
> (a) its members would otherwise have standing to sue in their own right;
> (b) the interests it seeks to protect are germane to the organization's purpose; and (c) neither the claim asserted nor the relief requested requires the participation of individual members in the lawsuit.

Id. at 343. Thus, the Washington Apple Advertising Commission was afforded standing to represent the interests of its member producers who were allegedly harmed by the North Carolina law under review, which prevented posting non-U.S.D.A. grading, thus precluding superior Washington grading to be posted on apple imports, because each part of the three-part test was satisfied.

66. *See supra* chapter 1, § III.A.

67. 430 U.S. 144 (1979).

68. 509 U.S. 630, 646–49 (1993).
69. 515 U.S. 900 (1995).
70. Justice Kennedy, writing for the majority stated:

> Nor can the argument that districting cases are excepted from standard equal protection analysis be resuscitated by *United Jewish Organizations of Williamsburgh, Inc. v. Carey*, 430 U.S. 144 (1977). . . . As we explained in *Shaw*, a majority of the Justices in *UJO* construed the complaint as stating a vote dilution claim, so their analysis does not apply to a claim that the State has separated voters on the basis of race. To the extent that any of the opinions in that "highly fractured decision," . . . can be interpreted as suggesting that a State's assignment of voters on the basis of race would be subject to anything but our strictest scrutiny, those views ought not to be deemed controlling.

Miller, 515 U.S. at 914–15.
71. *Id.* at 946 n. 11 (Ginsburg, J., dissenting). With respect to the argument that *Carey* was best understood as presenting a vote-dilution claim, rather than a claim of racial gerrymandering, Justice Ginsburg added:

> Nor is *UJO* best understood as a vote dilution case. Petitioners' claim in *UJO* was that the State had "violated the Fourteenth and Fifteenth Amendments by *deliberately revising its reapportionment plan along racial lines.*" *Id.* at 155 (opinion of White, J., joined by Brennan, Blackmun, and Stevens, JJ.) (emphasis added). Petitioners' themselves stated: " 'Our argument is . . . that the history of the area demonstrates that there could be—and in fact was—*no reason other than race* to divide the community at this time.' " *Id.,* at 154 n.14 (quoting Brief for Petitioners, . . .) (emphasis in Brief for Petitioners).

Miller, 515 U.S. at 946 n.11.
72. For a discussion of the two-tier framework, see *supra* chapter 1, § II.B.
73. Justice Thurgood Marshall did not participate in the *Casey* decision.
74. 430 U.S. at 165 (stating, "Whether or not the plan was authorized by or was in compliance with § 5 of the Voting Rights Act, New York was free to do what it did so long as it did not violate the Constitution, particularly the Fourteenth and Fifteenth Amendments; and we are convinced that neither amendment was infringed").
75. *See supra* note 51 and cites therein.
76. 163 U.S. 537 (1896).
77. RICHARD KLUGER, SIMPLE JUSTICE: THE HISTORY OF BROWN V. BOARD OF EDUCATION AND BLACK AMERICA'S STRUGGLE FOR EQUALITY 132 (1977) (quoting committee memorandum to Garland Fund Administrators).
78. As Kluger states: "To go after the problem as proposed in the fund's original memo by launching one suit in each of the seven most discriminatory states in an effort to force officials to provide equalized school facilities would be like trying to empty a swimming pool with an eye-dropper." *Id.*
79. *Id.* at 134 (quoting Margold).
80. *Id.* at 136–37.
81. 305 U.S. 337 (1938).
82. 332 U.S. 631 (1948). In *Sipuel,* the Court held that the State of Oklahoma must provide an equal legal education to a black woman denied admission to the only state law school due to her race. *Id.* at 632–33. The Court denied relief in Sipuel's

subsequent constitutional challenge to the adequacy of Oklahoma's hastily created black-only law school. *See* Fisher v. Hurst, 333 U.S. 147, 150–51 (1948); *see also* Dennis J. Hutchinson, *Unanimity and Desegregation: Decisionmaking in the Supreme Court, 1948–1958*, 68 Geo. L. J. 1, 6–9 (1979).

83. *Gaines,* 305 U.S. at 352; *Sipuel,* 332 U.S. at 632–33. The *Gaines* court rejected the State of Missouri's argument that it had met its equal protection obligation by offering Mr. Gaines scholarship assistance to attend an out-of-state law school that admitted black students. *Gaines,* 305 U.S. at 348–50. After the victory in *Gaines,* Missouri appropriated the necessary funds to create a black law school. While the NAACP thought the law school inferior in many respects and hoped to challenge its constitutionality in a successive suit, Gaines, the prospective law student, disappeared without a trace. *See* Lucile H. Bluford, *The Lloyd Gaines Story,* 32 J. Educ. Soc. 242, 245–46 (1959).

84. 333 U.S. 147 (1948).

85. 339 U.S. 629 (1950).

86. 339 U.S. 637 (1950).

87. 347 U.S. 483 (1954).

88. *See, e.g.,* Craig v. Boren, 429 U.S. 190 (1976) (Ginsburg on brief for ACLU as amicus curiae); Weinberger v. Wiesenfeld, 420 U.S. 636 (1975) (Ginsburg argued for appellee); Frontiero v. Richardson, 411 U.S. 677 (1973) (Ginsburg argued for ACLU as amicus curiae); Reed v. Reed, 404 U.S. 71 (1971) (Ginsburg on brief for appellant).

89. 118 S. Ct. 1428 (1998).

90. *See supra* chapter 1, § II.A.

91. 411 U.S. 677 (1973).

92. 429 U.S. 190 (1976).

93. In 1981, for example, the Court sustained a statutory rape statute, that prohibited sexual intercourse with a female, not the wife of the perpetrator, under the age of eighteen, against an equal protection challenge by a convicted male, who was himself a minor, *see* Michael M. v. Sonoma County Superior Court, 450 U.S. 464 (1981), and a mandatory draft registration law that only applied to men against a Fifth Amendment due process challenge, *see* Rostker v. Goldberg, 453 U.S. 57 (1981).

94. *See* Califano v. Goldfarb, 430 U.S. 199 (1977) (holding that dependency requirement for widowers, but not widows, under the Federal Old-Age, Survivors, and Disability Insurance Benefits program, violates equal protection); Wengler v. Druggists Mut. Ins. Co., 446 U.S. 142 (1980) (striking down similar scheme under Missouri law). In contrast, the Court unanimously sustained against an equal protection challenge a seemingly benign provision of the Social Security Act that allowed women, but not men, to exclude a number of low-earning years from their benefits computation to compensate for the historical difference in earnings between men and women. *See* Califano v. Webster, 430 U.S. 313 (1977).

95. As one civilian scholar has explained:

Although there is no formal rule of *stare decisis,* the practice is for judges to be influenced by prior decisions. . . . The judge may refer to precedent because he is impressed by the authority of the prior court, because he is persuaded by its reasoning, because he is too lazy to think the problem through himself, because he does not want to risk reversal on appeal, or for a variety of other reasons. These are the principal reasons for the use of authority in the common law tradition, and the absence of any formal rule of *stare decisis* is relatively unimportant.

John H. Merryman, The Civil Law Tradition: An Introduction to the Legal Systems of Western Europe and Latin America 144 (1969). I would add to the list that, whether or not knowingly, civilian jurisdictions might also employ stare decisis to avoid doctrinal instability resulting from cycling preferences.

96. *Accord* Lewis A. Kornhauser, *An Economic Perspective on* Stare Decisis, 65 Chi.-Kent. L. Rev. 63, 73 (1989) (describing stare decisis as "weak" obligation); Jonathan R. Macey, *The Internal and External Costs and Benefits of* Stare Decisis, 65 Chi.-Kent L. Rev. 93, 110 (1989) (describing stare decisis as imposing "optional" obligation); Erin O'Hara, *Social Constraint or Implicit Collusion? Toward a Game Theoretic Analysis of* Stare Decisis, 24 Seton Hall L. Rev. 736, 742 n. 26 (1993) (describing stare decisis as an "imperfect" obligation). While each of these characterizations is apt, I prefer to cast stare decisis as a "presumptive" obligation, which implies that a justice needs a reason beyond the mere desire to reach an alternative result in choosing not to adhere to an otherwise controlling, meaning indistinguishable, precedent. *See also supra* note 50 and cites therein.

97. *See supra* chapter 3, § III.

98. For an analysis demonstrating the breakdown of the *Marks* doctrine in cases with a multidimensional issue spectrum and asymmetrical preferences, see. *supra* chapter 3, § V.

99. 505 U.S. 444 (1992).

100. 469 U.S. 529 (1985) (overruling National League of Cities v. Usury, 426 U.S. 833 (1976)).

101. For the most recent example, see Printz v. United States, 521 U.S. 898 (1997) (holding that Brady Handgun Violence Protection Act, which temporarily required chief law enforcement officers of states to perform background checks on potential gun purchasers, violates the Tenth Amendment by commandeering state executive officers).

102. For another example, recall Justice Scalia's deference to precedent in explaining why he agreed that petitioner had standing in Miller v. Albright, 523 U.S. 420 (1998), even though as an initial matter he would have agreed with Justice O'Connor that standing should be denied. *See supra* chapter 1, § II.A.

103. *See supra* note 51 and cites therein.

104. For a discussion demonstrating that the New Deal Court conceived the modern standing doctrine to further this objective, see *infra* chapter 5, § II.

105. *Casey,* 505 U.S. at 861–64.

106. For a discussion of the narrowing of direct appellate jurisdiction in the Supreme Court after 1988, see John E. Nowak & Ronald D. Rotunda, Constitutional Law 27–28 (5th ed. 1995).

107. For a thoughtful analysis of the Rule of Four, see Richard L. Revesz & Pamela S. Karlan, *Nonmajority Rules and the Supreme Court,* 136 U. Pa. L. Rev. 1067, 1068–109 (1988); *see also* Robert L. Stern et al., Supreme Court Practice 162–222 (7th ed. 1993).

108. For an excellent analysis of en banc practices in the federal circuit courts, see Tracey E. George, *The Dynamics and Determinants of the Decision to Grant En Banc Review,* 74 Wash L. Rev. 213 (1999).

109. Circuit splits arise when different federal circuit courts of appeals provide contradictory holdings on underlying questions of federal law, including constitutional law.

110. The same analysis can be extended to explain the presumption against stare decisis among district court justices sitting in the same district. While district judges are single-member panels, and thus are not prone to formal path dependence, they may nonetheless be outliers on the courts on which they sit. Allowing the order in which cases are presented to individual judges to govern the evolution of law within a district as a whole would be potentially problematic for circuit courts, which would then have relatively less information about possible interpretations of the constitution, statutes, or other underlying legal materials, than in a regime where individual district judges are not bound by their colleagues' prior legal determinations. Again, by imposing stare decisis in vertical form, from the Supreme Court to the circuit courts, and from the circuit courts to the district courts, the higher court at each level in the pyramid retains the wherewithal to avoid fortuitous doctrine and to increase its information base for issuing corrections, in the form of full opinion affirmances and reversals.

111. *Cf.* Winter, *supra* note 7, at 1512 (positing that "[o]nce we recognize that legislation and adjudication are not dichotomous but are merely different points on a single normative spectrum, then we are free to assume responsibility").

112. This point was perhaps made best in Einer Elhauge, *Does Interest Theory Justify More Intrusive Judicial Review?* 101 Yale L.J. 31 (1991) (arguing that while interest group theory, or public choice, helps to expose the costs and benefits of certain lawmaking practices, the theory itself is uninformative in determining how to choose among revealed options).

113. 488 U.S. 361 (1989).

114. 18 U.S.C. § 3551 *et seq.* (1982 Supp. IV); 28 U.S.C. §§ 991–998 (1982 ed. Supp. IV).

115. *Mistretta,* 488 U.S. at 367 (noting exceptions where "the judge finds an aggravating or mitigating factor present that the Commission did not adequately consider when formulating guidelines"). The commission was required to submit the initial guidelines to Congress and to wait six months before they went into effect, *see* section 235 of Pub. L. No. 98–473, and to review periodically its established guidelines and to report any amendments or modifications to Congress subject to the same delay period before implementation. 28 U.S.C. § 994(p) (providing that such amendments shall take effect "no earlier than 180 days after being submitted and no later than the first day of November of the calendar year in which the amendment or modification is submitted"). *See also Mistretta,* 488 U.S. at 36 (describing the process for amendments to guidelines). The statutory delay requirements do not undermine the argument below that the commission's powers are essentially legislative in nature. Congress could always change the guidelines or the amendments and modifications to those guidelines through ordinary legislation. The sixth-month delay provision simply gives Congress an opportunity to do so before the guidelines and amendments or modifications go into effect.

116. 505 U.S. 833, 965 (1992). For a more detailed discussion and analysis of *Casey, see supra* chapter 1, § II.C; chapter 3, § IV.B.

117. *Id.* at 965 (Rehnquist, C.J., concurring in part and dissenting in part).

118. For a parallel comparison of underlying normative assumptions about the nature of legislative decision making, *see infra* chapter 6, § IV.A (discussing Clinton v. City of New York, 524 U.S. 417 (1998)).

119. For a recent analysis related to the one in the text, informed by comparative institutional transactions costs, rather than by social choice, see NEIL K. KOMESAR, IMPERFECT ALTERNATIVES: CHOOSING INSTITUTIONS IN LAW, ECONOMICS AND PUBLIC POLICY (1994).

120. See supra at 165 n.* (discussing etiology of the word case).

121. See, e.g., Bowen v. Owens, 476 U.S. 340, 348 (1986) ("Congress' adjustments of this complex system of [Social Security] entitlements necessarily create distinctions among categories of beneficiaries, a result that could be avoided only by making sweeping changes in the Act instead of incremental ones. A constitutional rule that would invalidate Congress' attempts to proceed cautiously in awarding increased benefits might deter Congress from making any increases at all"); Williamson v. Lee Optical, Inc., 348 U.S. 483, 489 (1955) ("The legislature may select one phase of one field and apply a remedy there, neglecting the others").

122. See, e.g., Katzenbach v. McClung, 379 U.S. 294, 303 (1964) (rejecting challenge to public accommodations provisions of the Civil Rights Act of 1964, premised upon "omission of a provision for a case-by-case determination—judicial or administrative—that racial discrimination in a particular restaurant affects commerce").

123. See also supra at 165 n.* (discussing etiology of the word case).

124. The only provisions not incorporated are the Second Amendment, the Third Amendment, the Fifth Amendment's requirement of grand jury indictment, and the Seventh Amendment. See GEOFFREY R. STONE ET AL., CONSTITUTIONAL LAW 811 (3d ed. 1996).

125. 347 U.S. 483 (1954).

126. See Keyes v. School Dist. No. 1, 413 U.S. 189, 219 (1973) (Powell, J., concurring in part and dissenting in part) ("In my view we should . . . formulate constitutional principles of national rather than merely regional application").

127. Subsequent to the completion of this book, the Supreme Court took certiorari and heard oral arguments in Dickerson v. United States, a case presenting the question whether Congress has the power to provide a substitute set of remedies for, and alternative set of prophylactic rules to safeguard against, coerced confessions. See 120 S. Ct. 578 (1999).

128. 461 U.S. 95 (1983).

129. 429 U.S. 1012 (1976).

130. I have used the term constitutional guarantees rather than constitutional rights deliberately; the issue is whether Mrs. Gilmore has the authority to bring a claim to prevent a violation of a constitutional guarantee, when the violation does not infringe one of her constitutional rights.

131. 429 U.S. at 1013 (Chief Justice Burger (joined by Powell)); id. at 1017 (Justice Stevens (joined by Rehnquist)).

132. 438 U.S. 59 (1978).

133. 438 U.S. 265 (1978).

134. See David Jackson, Supreme Court Lets California's Ban on Affirmative Action Stand; Supporters Expect Similar Measures to Pass Nationwide, THE DALLAS MORNING NEWS, Nov. 4, 1997, 1a (Home Final Edition) (noting, "The Supreme Court refused . . . to interfere with California's Proposition 209, allowing the state's ban on affirmative action programs to stand").

135. See Katzenbach v. Morgan, 384 U.S. 641, 646–47 (1966) (holding that Congress may expand substantive reach of the Fourteenth Amendment equal protection clause beyond that provided in Supreme Court decision interpreting that clause);

but see City of Boerne, Texas v. Flores, 521 U.S. 507 (1997) (rejecting *Katzenbach* analysis in striking down the Religious Freedom Restoration Act, through which Congress relied upon its enforcement authority under the Fourteenth Amendment to expand the scope of religious freedoms beyond that under prevailing Supreme Court case law against state infringement).

136. As Professor Fletcher has demonstrated, all standing determinations, although couched in procedural terms, can readily be transformed into substantive legal determinations. *See* Fletcher, *supra* note 38, at 234–39. Thus, for example, while the *Gilmore* Court declined to consider the merits of Mrs. Gilmore's underlying claims, it also effectively held as a matter of substantive law that at least as a presumptive matter, Mrs. Gilmore has no right to enforce her son's constitutional rights in federal court.

137. For articles taking this view, see Sunstein, *supra* note 23, at 166 n. 15 (observing that "one generalization—that the standing issue depends on the existence of a cause of action—is not [worthless]"); *see also* Cass Sunstein, *Standing and the Privatization of Public Law,* 88 COLUM. L. REV. 1432, 1474–75 (1988); Cindy Vreeland, *Public Interest Groups, Public Law Litigation, and Federal Rule 24(a),* 57 U. CHI. L. REV. 279, 286 n. 34 (1990) ("To the extent that Congress can create redressable injuries by creating new legal rights, constitutional standing and the existence of a cause of action are essentially the same"); Lee Albert, *Standing to Challenge Administrative Action: An Inadequate Surrogate for Claim for Relief,* 83 YALE L.J. 425, 426 (1974) ("A more illuminating way of looking at standing is to recognize that its determination is an adjudication of familiar components of a cause of action, resolved by asking whether a plaintiff has stated a claim for relief") (footnote omitted).

138. 471 U.S. 1, 11–12 (1985).

139. For a counterintuitive illustration of this principle, see Powers v. Ohio, 499 U.S. 400 (1991); see also *infra* chapter 6, § III.A.1 (discussing *Powers*).

140. For a discussion of interest group sponsorship of appeals by convicted criminals, see *supra* at 179 n.*.

141. *See, e.g., Powers,* 499 U.S. at 414; Secretary of State v. Joseph H. Munson Co., 467 U.S. 947, 956 (1984); Craig v. Boren, 429 U.S. 190, 194 (1976).

CHAPTER 5

1. *See* KARL R. POPPER, CONJECTURES AND REFUTATIONS: THE GROWTH OF SCIENTIFIC KNOWLEDGE 37 (5th ed. 1989) (" [T]he criterion of the scientific status of a theory is its falsifiability, or refutability, or testability"); *see also* THOMAS S. KUHN, THE STRUCTURE OF SCIENTIFIC REVOLUTIONS 66–91 (2d ed. 1970) (stating that inexplicable data create a crisis for a scientific theory and establish the need to devise new paradigms that account for that data). The argument in the text is not to suggest, of course, that a single contrary datum requires that scientists abandon existing theories. Instead, it means that further testing of the theory is indicated to determine whether the datum can be replicated and, if so, whether the theory can be modified to accommodate that datum. For that reason, most scientific theories develop incrementally. For a classic work on the nature of testing economic models, see MILTON FRIEDMAN, *The Methodology of Positive Economics, in* ESSAYS IN POSITIVE ECONOMICS 3 (1953) (positing that economic models must be evaluated based upon their empirical testability or robustness, rather than the realism of their underlying assumptions).

2. As Mancur Olson has explained: "The persuasiveness of a theory depends not only on how many facts are explained, but also on how diverse are the kinds of facts explained." MANCUR OLSON, THE RISE AND DECLINE OF NATIONS: ECONOMIC GROWTH, STAGFLATION, AND SOCIAL RIGIDITIES 13 (1982).

3. While some of the cases upon which the Court relied in developing modern standing doctrine were ancient by modern constitutional law standards, *see, e.g.,* Georgetown v. Alexandria Canal Co., 37 U.S. (12 Pet.) 91, 99 (1838) ("[T]he plaintiff cannot maintain a stand in a court of equity"), others were then quite recent. *See* Steven L. Winter, *The Metaphor of Standing and the Problem of Self-Governance,* 40 STAN.L. REV. 1371 (1988). One then-recent case, often cited as among the earliest standing cases, *see* Frothingham v. Mellon, 262 U.S. 447 (1923), was actually a case concerning the jurisdictional limits on federal court equitable powers. *See infra* note 68 and cites therein.

4. *See supra* at 164, table 4.3.

5. For a description of the ratchet effect, see RUDIGER DORNBUSCH & STANLEY FISCHER, MACRO-ECONOMICS 166–67 (2d ed. 1981) (describing ratchet effect and relationship to relative-income hypothesis, where consumers base their expenditures on peak annual incomes, even when faced with temporary annual declines).

6. As William E. Leuchtenburg states:

From the beginning of the Roosevelt era, Administration leaders had worried about Mr. Justice Roberts. Their anxiety had eased when Roberts had helped compose the majority in *Nebbia, Blaisdell,* and the gold clause cases. But when Roberts joined the Four Horsemen in striking down the Railroad Retirement Act, New Dealers recognized that the conservatives on the Court, for the first time since FDR took office, had gotten the upper hand. Furthermore, the language of Roberts's opinion led them to fear the worst—that this was no temporary defection but a signal that Roberts was permanently lost. In fact, in every important division on the Court for almost all of the next two years, Roberts was to align himself with the Conservative Four. The *Rail Pension* decision, then, loomed as far more important than the particular legislation at issue. May 6 was to be looked back on as the day of a historic shift of power on the highest bench.

WILLIAM E. LEUCHTENBURG, THE SUPREME COURT REBORN: THE CONSTITUTIONAL REVOLUTION IN THE AGE OF ROOSEVELT 42 (1995); *see also id.* at 168–74 (observing that between 1935 and 1937, Justice Roberts consistently joined the Four Horsemen).

7. 295 U.S. 555 (1935).

8. 295 U.S. 602 (1935).

9. 300 U.S. 379 (1937).

10. 298 U.S. 587 (1936).

11. 198 U.S. 45 (1905). In a series of recent articles, two scholars have called the conventional "switch in time" story, which finds 1937 to be a landmark year in Supreme Court doctrinal development, into question. Richard Friedman has argued that the change in Supreme Court doctrine was more incremental and began as early as 1930, with the appointments of Chief Justice Charles Hughes and Associate Justice Owen Roberts. *See* Richard D. Friedman, *Switching Time and Other Thought Experiments: The Hughes Court and Constitutional Transformation,* 142 U. PA. L. REV. 1891 (1994). And Barry Cushman, while agreeing that the doctrinal revolution attributed to the New Deal Court was more incremental than is generally understood, attributes the major change in commerce

clause jurisprudence to a later period, beginning in the early 1940s. *See* Barry Cushman, *Rethinking the New Deal Court,* 80 VA. L. REV. 201 (1994); Barry Cushman, *A Stream of Legal Consciousness: The Current of Commerce Doctrine from Swift to Jones and Laughlin,* 61 FORDHAM L. REV. 105 (1992). Resolving this debate is not necessary to the general point in the text, namely that the New Deal Court was generally not characterized by multidimensionality and asymmetry.

12. From 1937 through 1941, FDR appointed seven of the associate justices: Black in 1937; Reed in 1938; Frankfurter and Douglas in 1939; Murphy in 1940; and Byrnes and Jackson in 1941. *See* LEUCHTENBURG, *supra* note 6, at 220. He also promoted Stone, a consistent liberal dissenter, to replace Hughes as chief justice, in 1941. *See id.* Justice Byrnes, who resigned one year after his appointment, was replaced by Justice Rutledge, *see id.,* the only new associate with federal judicial experience prior to joining the Supreme Court. *See id.* at 212. He had served for two years on the United States Court of Appeals for the District of Columbia Circuit. *See* C. HERMAN PRITCHETT, THE ROOSEVELT COURT: A STUDY IN JUDICIAL POLITICS AND VALUES 1937–1947 13 (1963).

13. *See* LEUCHTENBERG, *supra* note 6, at 145; ROGER K. NEWMAN, HUGO BLACK: A BIOGRAPHY 214 (1994).

14. For a more detailed discussion of Black's jurisprudence, see *infra* § III.A.

15. *See* Earl M. Maltz, *The Prospects for a Revival of Conservative Activism in Constitutional Jurisprudence,* 24 GA. L. REV. 629, 638 (1990) (explaining that "[w]ithin five years [of FDR's re-election], the victory of the liberal forces was consolidated as Roosevelt appointed a number of justices who were both ideologically committed to the New Deal and vigorously opposed to the judicial activism of the *Lochner* era"); *see also* Robert E. Riggs, *When Every Vote Counts: 5–4 Decisions in the United States Supreme Court, 1900–90,* 21 HOFSTRA L. REV. 667, 682–84 (1993) (observing that when FDR elevated Justice Harlan Stone to chief justice in October 1941 (Stone was appointed associate justice by Calvin Coolidge), only Justice Stone and Associate Justice Owen Roberts had more than four years of experience on the Supreme Court).

16. Ironically, while *Humphrey's Executor,* 295 U.S. 602, which prevented FDR from removing an officer of the Federal Trade Commission who did not share FDR's political views, was viewed as a major setback to the New Deal, it ultimately helped pave the way for numerous New Deal programs by establishing the power to create independent federal agencies. *See* Paul R. Verkuil, *The Status of Independent Agencies After* Bowsher v. Synar, 1986 DUKE L.J. 779. Verkuil explains:

The independent agency has existed for one hundred years, since the formation of the Interstate Commerce Commission as the prototype. But its "independence" did not become a matter of constitutional concern until the 1930's, when the New Deal greatly expanded the number of agencies and commissions. Ironically, President Roosevelt, the great spawner of administrative government, was the victim as well as the beneficiary of the independence concept.

Id. at 780.

17. *See, e.g.,* Cargo of The Brig Aurora v. United States, 11 U.S. (7 Cranch) 382, 286 (1813); United States v. Grimaud, 220 U.S. 506, 517 (1911). For a more detailed history and analysis of the nondelegation doctrine, see Peter Aranson, Ernest Gellhorn, & Glen O. Robinson, *A Theory of Legislative Delegation,* 68 CORNELL L. REV. 1 (1982) (arguing for a revival of nondelegation doctrine based upon principles of public choice).

18. 276 U.S. 394 (1928).
19. *See* Panama Refining Co. v. Ryan, 293 U.S. 388 (1935) (striking down § 9(c) of the National Industrial Recovery Act, which allowed the president to prohibit the shipment of "hot oil," which was withdrawn from storage contrary to state law, in an effort to reduce the oil glut and to sustain prices); A.L.A. Schechter Poultry Corp. v. United States, 295 U.S. 495 (1935) (striking down provision of the act, that authorized trade associations to create fair codes of competition); Carter v. Carter Coal Co., 298 U.S. 238 (1936) (striking down the Bituminous Coal Conservation Act of 1935, which allowed predefined coal districts to set minimum prices and collective bargaining to set binding minimum wage and overtime restrictions).
20. *See, e.g.,* United States v. Rock Royal Coop., 307 U.S. 533 (1939) (sustaining fairly modest delegation of power); Yukas v. United States, 321 U.S. 414 (1944) (sustaining broad grant of regulatory power to the Office of Price Administration to fix commodity prices).
21. *See supra* at 167 n. 17 (quoting Theodore J. Lowi, *Two Roads to Serfdom: Liberalism, Conservatism and Administrative Power,* 36 AM. U. L. REV. 295, 298 (1987)); *see also* Richard J. Pierce, Jr., *Political Accountability and Delegated Power: A Response to Professor Lowi,* 36 AM. U. L. REV. 391, 391–93 (1987) (confirming Lowi's historical analysis but disagreeing on implications for the nondelegation doctrine).
22. *See* Aranson, et al., *supra* note 17, at 17 (The authors explain that "the Court . . . has never entirely abandoned the delegation doctrine. It continues to live a fugitive existence at the edge of constitutional jurisprudence"). The authors further explain that in addition to occasional references by individual justices, "[t]he Court sometimes refers to the doctrine . . . when interpreting broad statutes, using it in support of an otherwise tenuous effort to narrow statutory construction." *Id.* at 12.
23. 270 U.S. 144 (1992).
24. U.S. CONST. amend. X.
25. 22 U.S. (9 Wheat.) 1 (1824).
26. In contrast, state legislative powers are plenary, requiring no express delegation, but are also subject to the constraints of the federal and state constitutions. *See* James E. Costello, *The Limits of Popular Sovereignty: Using the Initiative Power to Control Legislative Procedure,* 74 CAL. L. REV. 491, 553 n. 329 (1986) (distinguishing state and federal legislative models).
27. 156 U.S. 1 (1895).
28. 247 U.S. 251 (1918).
29. 298 U.S. 238 (1936).
30. 317 U.S. 111 (1942).
31. 312. U.S. 100 (1941).
32. 317 U.S. 111.
33. 301 U.S. 1 (1937).
34. Thus, Hughes observed that the regulated works could "be likened to the heart of a self-contained, highly integrated body" that stretched limbs, arteries, and veins across multiple states. *See id.* at 27.
35. 312 U.S. at 124.
36. 317 U.S. at 127.
37. *See* Frothingham v. Mellon, 262 U.S. 447 (1923).
38. *See generally* Winter, *supra* note 3.
39. As Professor Steven Winter, who has documented the early evolution of standing, has shown, Justices Brandeis and Frankfurter drew upon early equity prin-

ciples to devise the standing doctrine in an effort to limit the class of plaintiffs who would be eligible to challenge the development of New Deal regulatory programs in federal court. *See* Winter, *supra* note 3, at 1420–22.

40. *See* Peter H. Irons, The New Deal Lawyers 13 (1982) (observing that the Hughes Court "shared with their lower-court brethren an equal commitment to the precepts of constitutional fundamentalism and a similar 19th-century perspective"); Joseph L. Rauh, Jr., *Lawyers and the Legislation of the Early New Deal*, 96 Harv. L. Rev. 947, 949 (1983) (book review) (observing that prior to the Roosevelt administration, "three successive Republican administrations had stacked the lower federal courts with judges hostile to federal action of almost any kind").

41. For an excellent, and more detailed, discussion of standing doctrine in this historical period, see William Fletcher, *The Structure of Standing*, 98 Yale L.J. 221, 226–27 (1988). Several of the examples in the text to follow are taken from this work.

42. *See, e.g.,* Act of Mar. 20, 1933, ch. 3, § 5, 48 Stat. 8, 9 (precluding veterans from challenging agency denials of benefits in federal court).

43. *See, e.g.,* Communications Act of 1934, § 402(b), 47 U.S.C. § 402(b)(6) (Supp. V 1993)) (conferring standing upon "any . . . person . . . aggrieved or whose interests are adversely affected by any order of the [Federal Communications] Commission"); *see also* Federal Communications Comm'n v. Sanders Bros. Radio Station, 309 U.S. 470, 476–77 (1940) (granting standing to complainant even though the claimed injury was not a factor that the commission was legally obligated to consider).

44. *See, e.g.,* Tennessee Elec. Power Co. v. Tennessee Valley Auth., 306 U.S. 118, 137–38 (1939) (denying standing to challenge TVA's regulatory conduct absent an allegation that the agency had invaded plaintiff's legal right, for example, one grounded in property, contract, or tort); Alabama Power Co. v. Ickes, 302 U.S. 464, 480 (1938) (denying standing to challenge federal loans and grants to competing municipal utilities, holding that plaintiff had no right to be immune from lawful municipal competition); *see also* Joint Anti-Fascist Refugee Comm. v. McGrath, 341 U.S. 123, 152 (1951) (directly linking standing inquiry to infringement of comparable common law right).

45. *See, e.g.,* Heart of Atlanta Motel v. United States, 379 U.S. 241, 261 (1964) (upholding the public accommodations provision of the 1964 Civil Rights Act against a challenge by the motel); Katzenbach v. McClung, 379 U.S. 294, 304–5 (1964) (upholding the same provision against challenge by a restaurant).

46. For a striking recent example, consider Swidler & Berlin v. United States, 574 U.S. 399 (1998). In that case, the Court rejected the efforts of independent prosecutor, Kenneth Starr, to obtain notes from a meeting, which former deputy White House counsel Vincent Foster had with his attorney shortly before he committed suicide, in connection with Starr's investigation into the dismissal of White House Travel Office employees. Starr had argued that the attorney-client privilege either did not attach to communications that took place prior to the client's death, or, alternatively, if the privilege did attach, it could be overcome in a case with a sufficiently significant public interest. Writing for a majority of six, Chief Justice Rehnquist rejected both arguments, thus honoring the privilege and refusing to order the disclosure of the attorney-client communications. Given the absence of either constitutional or federal statutory law on the subject, Rehnquist relied largely upon secondary treatises, many of which themselves were informed by state common law principles on the doctrine of attorney-client privilege.

47. See Melvin I. Urofsky, *Conflict Among the Brethren: Felix Frankfurter, William O. Douglas and the Clash of Personalities and Philosophies on the United States Supreme Court,* 1988 DUKE L.J. 71. The author explains:

> Following the constitutional crisis of 1937, the personnel of the United States Supreme Court changed rapidly as Franklin Roosevelt named new Justices whom he believed committed to the modern views of the New Deal. Roosevelt appointees constituted a majority of the Court by 1942, but instead of harmony, the Court entered one of the most divisive periods in its history. The economic issues which had dominated the Court's calendar for nearly a half-century gave way to new questions of civil liberties and the reach of the Bill of Rights, and these cast the jurisprudential debate between judicial restraint and judicial activism in a new light.

> *Id.* at 71.

48. 391 U.S. 145 (1968).
49. As Donald Lively has observed, while President Eisenhower labeled his appointment of Earl Warren as chief justice a mistake, he "could not really claim betrayal":

> Eisenhower's nomination of Warren can be regarded both as a payback for the latter's assistance in securing the Republican presidential nomination for Eisenhower in 1952 and a shrewd tactic designed to defuse political warfare between the more progressive Warren faction and the more conservative Nixon elements of the California Republican Party.

> Donald E. Lively, *The Supreme Court Appointment Process: In Search of Constitutional Roles and Responsibilities,* 59 S. CAL. L. REV. 551, 555 n.30 (1986) (citing BERNARD B. SCHWARTZ, SUPER CHIEF: EARL WARREN AND HIS SUPREME COURT—JUDICIAL BIOGRAPHY 21–22 (1983), and G. EDWARD WHITE, EARL WARREN: A PUBLIC LIFE 139–44 (1982)).

50. *See* RICHARD HODDER-WILLIAMS, THE POLITICS OF THE U.S. SUPREME COURT 30 (1980); Michael Comiskey, *Can a President Pack—or Draft—the Supreme Court? FDR and the Court in the Great Depression and World War II,* 57 ALB. L. REV. 1043, 1057 n. 93 (1994); Joseph L. Rauh, Jr., *An Unabashed Liberal Looks at a Half-Century of the Supreme Court,* 69 N.C. L. REV. 213, 230 (1990). For an interesting article questioning this conventional wisdom with respect to the appointment of Justice Brennan, see Stephen J. Wermeil, *The Nomination of Justice Brennan: Eisenhower's Mistake? A Look at the Historical Record,* 11 CONST. COMM. 515 (1994–95).
51. In his well-noted biography, Bernard Schwartz describes Earl Warren's transformation of the chief justice's role as follows:

> Frankfurter once compared a great Chief Justice's manner of presiding over the Court with Toscanini leading an orchestra. And Warren brought more authority, more *bravura,* to the Chief Justiceship than had been the case for years. The Justices who sat with him have all stressed that Warren may not have been an intellectual like Frankfurter, but then, as Justice Potter Stewart puts it, "he never pretended to be one." More important, says Stewart, he possessed "instinctive qualities of leadership." When Stewart was asked about claims that Justice Black was the intellectual leader on the Court, he replied,

"If Black was the intellectual leader, Warren was the *leader* leader." According to Stewart, Warren "didn't lead by his intellect and he didn't greatly appeal to others' intellects; that wasn't his style. But he was an instinctive leader whom you respected and for whom you had affection, and . . . as the presiding member of our conference, he was just ideal."

See SCHWARTZ, *supra* note 49, at 31.

52. *See, e.g.,* SCHWARTZ, *supra* note 49; WHITE, *supra* note 49.
53. 367 U.S. 643 (1961) (six to three).
54. 384 U.S. 436 (1966) (five to four).
55. 347 U.S. 483 (1954) (unanimous).
56. 358 U.S. 1 (1958) (unanimous on result).
57. 372 U.S. 335 (1963) (unanimous on result).
58. *See, e.g.,* Duncan v. Louisiana, 391 U.S. 145, 149 (1968) (holding sixth amendment right to jury trial to be a fundamental right applicable to states); Miranda v. Arizona, 384 U.S. 436, 467–73 (1966) (holding that police must provide specified warnings prior to interrogation, including the right to remain silent and to assistance of counsel, for those who cannot afford it); Malloy v. Hogan, 378 U.S. 1, 3 (1964) (applying the Fifth Amendment privilege against self-incrimination to the states); Gideon v. Wainwright, 372 U.S. 335, 344 (1963) (holding that indigent criminal defendants have a fundamental right to state-assisted counsel under the Sixth Amendment).
59. *See* Kirkpatrick v. Preisler, 394 U.S. 526, 536 (1969) (extending the equal population rule to congressional districts); Reynolds v. Sims, 377 U.S. 533, 568 (1964) (holding that equal protection requires that state legislative districts be equal in population); Baker v. Carr, 369 U.S. 186, 226–29 (1962) (holding that an equal protection challenge to a state's legislative redistricting is not a nonjusticiable political question).
60. *See* Heart of Atlanta Motel, Inc. v. United States, 379 U.S. 241, 261 (1964) (upholding application of the public accommodations provision of the Civil Rights Act of 1964 to a motel that claimed that it did not operate in interstate commerce); Katzenbach v. McClung, 379 U.S. 294, 304–5 (1964) (upholding application of the same provision to a restaurant that claimed that it did not operate in interstate commerce).
61. *See* The Civil Rights Cases, 109 U.S. 3, 13, 26 (1883) (invalidating the public accommodations provisions of the 1875 Civil Rights Act and articulating the state action doctrine).
62. 347 U.S. 483 (1954).
63. 410 U.S. 113 (1973).
64. 381 U.S. 479 (1965).
65. *Accord* Joan Mahoney, *A Sword as Well as a Shield: The Offensive Use of Collateral Estoppel in Civil Rights Litigation,* 69 IOWA L. REV. 469, 469 (1984) ("Many of the decisions of the Warren Court were predicated on the belief that federal constitutional issues ought to be tried, or at least finally resolved, in federal court. To that end, concepts of standing were broadened"); Arthur H. Abel, Note, *The Burger Court's Unified Approach to Standing and Its Impact on Congressional Plaintiffs,* 60 NOTRE DAME L. REV. 1187, 1189 (1985) (positing, based upon Baker v. Carr, 369 U.S. 186 (1962), that "[d]uring the Warren Court years, the standing requirement was designed simply to ensure that plaintiffs pursued their claims vigorously").
66. 392 U.S. 83 (1968).

67. 262 U.S. 447 (1923).
68. Steven Winter persuasively demonstrates that *Frothingham* is one of two pre–New Deal cases (the other is Fairchild v. Hughes, 258 U.S. 126 (1922)), in which the Supreme Court held that the claimants, taxpayers, challenging governmental spending policies, lacked the requisite form of injury to invoke the equitable powers of the federal courts. *See* Winter, *supra* note 3, at 1447. Winter further demonstrates that while Justice Brandeis sought to generalize these equitable limitations on the federal courts into a more generic standing principle in his effort to protect the federal judiciary from challenges to legislative policymaking, he did not succeed until well into the New Deal. Winter notes that the term *standing* was attached to these cases prior to the New Deal, but that standing did not become an Article III constraint (and even then only a prudential one) until the New Deal. *See id.* at 1447 and *id.* n. 435 (noting that "[n]either *Frothingham* nor *Fairchild* became cases of 'standing' until later," and that the later characterizations of these cases as standing cases "are little more than quotations of *Frothingham* with the characterization of 'standing' attached"). Winter further notes that it was not until the landmark case Coleman v. Miller, 307 U.S. 433, 460 (1939), which is better known as a political question case, that Justice Felix Frankfurter "linked the term 'standing' with [Article] III in his concurring opinion." Winter, *supra* at 1449. Winter adds that the *Coleman* majority rejected Frankfurter's analysis and conferred standing, but denied justiciability based upon the political question doctrine. *See id.*
69. 454 U.S. 464 (1982).
70. While the plaintiffs in both cases sued under the establishment clause, the *Valley Forge* Court distinguished *Flast* by resting, instead, upon the property clause, which the government had raised in its defense. *Id.* at 479–80.
71. 369 U.S. 186 (1962).
72. U.S. CONST. Art. IV, § 4.
73. 48 U.S. (7 How.) 1 (1849).
74. *See* Robert J. Pushaw, *Justiciability and Separation of Powers: A Neo-Federalist Approach,* 81 CORNELL L. REV. 393, 453–54 n. 289, 510 n. 575 (1996). Pushaw explains that, contrary to the presentation in Baker v. Carr, 369 U.S. 186 (1962), *Luther* did not establish that federal courts could not adjudicate guarantee clause challenges, but rather, it established that when a political branch of the United States has already recognized one of two claimed governments in a state as legitimate, the Court will not entertain a challenge by the other government under the guarantee clause. *See id.* at 453–54 n. 289. *See also* Akhil Reed Amar, *The Central Meaning of Republican Government: Popular Sovereignty, Majority Rule, and the Denominator Problem,* 65 U. COLO. L. REV. 749, 776 (1994).
75. *See* New York v. United States, 505 U.S. 144, 184–85 (1992) (explaining Court's erroneous construction of *Luther* in several twentieth-century cases, including Baker v. Carr).
76. *See, e.g.,* Planned Parenthood Ass'n v. Ashcroft, 462 U.S. 476 (1983) (upholding a parental notification provision for minors seeking an abortion); Planned Parenthood v. Danforth, 428 U.S. 52, 63–65 (1976) (upholding a state statute in which a preset number of weeks was rejected for determination of viability and noting that in Roe v. Wade, the Court had recognized that "viability was a matter of medical judgment, skill, and technical ability" and further noting that the Court wished to "preserve[] the flexibility of the term").

    Not surprisingly, the Rehnquist Court upheld substantially more restrictive abortion laws. See Planned Parenthood v. Casey, 505 U.S. 833 (1992) (upholding all but the spousal notifications provision of Pennsylvania's restrictive abortion statute and classifying abortion as a liberty interest, subject to a newly minted undue burden test, rather than as a fundamental right, subject to strict scrutiny); Webster v. Reproductive Health Serv., 492 U.S. 490 (1989) (plurality opinion) (upholding several restrictions on the right to abort and suggesting the abandonment of the trimester framework.)

77. *See* Board of Regents of the Univ. of Cal. v. Bakke, 438 U.S. 265, 315, 355 (1978) (holding that "race-conscious remedial action is permissible" but that the school's "special admissions program, focused *solely* on ethnic diversity, would hinder rather than further attainment of genuine diversity").

78. *See* United States v. Nixon, 418 U.S. 683, 707 (1974) (Burger, C.J.) (concluding that "the legitimate needs of the judicial process may outweigh Presidential privilege").

79. *See* Washington v. Davis, 426 U.S. 229, 246 (1976) (White, J.) (noting that "the disproportionate impact of [a particular literacy test does not] warrant the conclusion that it is a purposeful device to discriminate").

80. *See* Keyes v. School Dist. No. 1, 413 U.S. 189, 213 (1973) (Brennan, J.) (holding that a school system determined to maintain deliberate racial segregation in one portion of a system "has the affirmative duty to desegregate the entire system").

81. In his biography of Justice Powell, Professor John Calvin Jeffries, Jr., provides a similar account of the Burger Court, and further posits that Justice Powell, who served from 1972 to 1987, for most of the Burger Court and the first two years of the Rehnquist Court, was the fulcrum holding the balance between two often irreconcilable extremes. Justice Powell is therefore widely regarded as having had an unusually strong jurisprudential impact on the most divisive issues of the day, including busing, affirmative action, and the rights of criminal defendants. Professor Jeffries explains:

> The Supreme Court in Powell's time was neither consistently liberal nor dependably conservative, neither predictably activist nor reliably restrained. It was an era of judicial balance. The periods before and after were of a distinctly different character. In the liberal heyday of Chief Justice Earl Warren, the Justices commanded an end to segregation, greatly expanded the rights of criminal defendants, and zealously sought to reform many other aspects of American society and law. After Powell retired, the Supreme Court entered the conservative ascendancy associated with the Chief Justiceship of William Rehnquist.
>
> In between lay a period—lasting for the better part of a generation—in which neither liberals nor conservatives dominated the Supreme Court. These were years of ideological stalemate and political pragmatism, of conflict and compromise, of decisions that owed less to dogmas of the left or the right than to a flexible search for justice, order, and decency in a changing world. And this Court's most characteristic voice, the one that proved most often decisive, was that of its most reluctant member, Justice Lewis F. Powell, Jr., of Virginia.

JOHN C. JEFFRIES, JR., JUSTICE LEWIS F. POWELL, JR. 12 (1994).

82. *See, e.g.,* Cass R. Sunstein, *What's Standing After* Lujan? *Of Citizen Suits, "Injuries," and Article III,* 91 MICH. L. REV. 163, 167 (1992) (arguing that *Lujan* is a form of substantive due process from the right).

83. *See, e.g.,* Planned Parenthood of Southeastern Pennsylvania v. Casey, 505 U.S. 833, 954–55 (1992) (Rehnquist, C.J., concurring in the judgment in part and dissenting in part) (arguing against rigid adherence to stare decisis in constitutional cases, stating, "[e]rroneous decisions in . . . constitutional cases are uniquely durable, because correction through legislative action, save for constitutional amendment, is impossible"); *see also id.* at 993–1001 (Scalia, J., concurring in the judgment in part and dissenting in part) (providing a vitriolic attack on the joint opinion's argument that stare decisis requires continued adherence to protecting the right to abort).

84. For a recent example, see City of Boerne, Texas v. Flores, 521 U.S. 507 (1997), in which the Supreme Court struck down a provision the Religious Freedom Restoration Act ("RFRA"), which demanded an application of strict scrutiny to laws of general application that had an incidental effect in prohibiting religious practices. In 1990, the Supreme Court had instead held that such laws were subject to rational basis scrutiny. *See* Employment Div. v. Smith, 494 U.S. 872 (1990). In striking down RFRA, the Court rejected Justice Brennan's analysis in Katzenbach v. Morgan, 384 U.S. 641 (1966), which allowed Congress to expand the scope of equal protection, against a contrary Supreme Court precedent, through its enforcement power under section 5 of the Fourteenth Amendment. While three justices dissented in *City of Boerne,* none of them continued to adhere to the Brennan position, allowing Congress, through its enforcement authority under section 5, to expand the scope of substantive constitutional protections. For another recent example illustrating the more conservative characteristics of even the Supreme Court's nominal liberal wing, see Clinton v. Jones, 117 S. Ct. 1636 (1997), in which the Court unanimously declined to extend executive privilege to protect President Clinton from civil trial during the pendency of his administration.

85. From 1801 through 1955, the Supreme Court produced a total of 45 plurality opinions, while from 1955 to 1981, the Court produced 130 plurality decisions. *See* Note, *Plurality Decisions and Judicial Decisionmaking,* 94 HARV. L. REV. 1127, 1127 n.1 (1981). For some additional studies of Supreme Court plurality opinions, see Ken Kimura, Note, *A Legitimacy Model for the Interpretation of Plurality Decisions,* 77 CORNELL L. REV. 1593 (1992); John F. Davis & William L. Reynolds, *Juridical Cripples: Plurality Opinions in the Supreme Court,* 1974 DUKE L.J. 59; Comment, *Supreme Court No-Clear-Majority Decisions: A Study in* Stare Decisis, 24 U. CHI. L. REV. 99 (1956). While a complete statistical analysis of plurality opinions is beyond the scope of this book, it will be helpful to consider a breakdown of plurality decisions, by ten-year intervals, beginning in 1946, based upon the most current available data. The following summary is distilled from LEE EPSTEIN, JEFFREY A. SEGAL, HAROLD J. SPAETH, & THOMAS G. WALKER, THE SUPREME COURT COMPENDIUM: DATA, DECISIONS & DEVELOPMENTS 210–11 (2d ed. 1996): (table 3.5: Cases Decided by a Judgment of the Court, 1946–1994 Terms): 1946–55: 38; 1956–65: 29; 1966–75: 52; 1976–85: 59; 1986–94: 38.

A few general comments about these numbers might be helpful. I have argued that the period beginning in 1970 and continuing through the present is particularly significant because the Court in this period has been prone to multidimensionality and occasional asymmetry. It is worth noting that the ten-period from 1966 through 1975 can be subdivided into four- and six-year periods as follows: 1966–69: 10; 1970–75: 42. In addition, while the most recent nine-year period, 1986–94, marked a decline in the absolute number of plurality decisions relative to the prior ten-year period, beginning in late 1980s the total number of cases that the Supreme Court resolved by full opinion began to drop as follows: 1988: 156; 1989: 143; 1990: 121; 1991: 119; 1992: 111; 1993: 98; 1994: 90. This might reflect the increased influence of the conservative lower federal courts, following the Reagan and Bush administrations, in reducing the incidence of circuit conflicts. From 1973 through 1987, the Court resolved between a low of 142 (1974) and a high of 183 (1982) cases by full opinion each term, and an average of 158.8 cases per term. Finally, it is important to understand that plurality opinions are by no means a perfect proxy for multidimensionality and asymmetry. In most plurality opinions, a narrowest grounds opinion, or Condorcet winner, exists. As explained in chapter 3, relatively few plurality opinion cases can be expected to possess the characteristic features of multidimensionality and asymmetry from which it becomes possible to infer a collective intransitivity. Even so, as explained in chapter 4, over a long enough period of time, even cases with a unidimensional issue spectrum can become the fodder for path manipulation, and can thus contribute to effective doctrinal asymmetry.

86. For other descriptions of the present or recent political compositions of the Supreme Court, see Paul H. Edelman & Jim Chen, *The Most Dangerous Justice: The Supreme Court at the Bar of Mathematics,* 70 S. Cal. L. Rev. 63, 96 (1996) (positing that in the October 1994 and 1995 terms, Justices Kennedy and Ginsburg were the fulcrums on the Supreme Court); Lawrence C. Marshall, *Divesting the Courts: Breaking the Judicial Monopoly on Constitutional Interpretation,* 66 Chi.-Kent L. Rev. 481, 481 (1990) (explaining, "In 1990, it appears that the Court has a core conservative bloc of five (Rehnquist, O'Connor, Scalia, Kennedy & Souter), with one other (White) providing a rather consistent conservative vote"); David M. O'Brien, *On Supreme Court Commentaries and Developing Constitutional Law,* 81 Mich. L. Rev. 839, 845 n. 53 (1983) (describing Justice Potter Stewart as the Court's "second moderate conservative") (reviewing Jesse Choper et al., The Supreme Court: Trends and Developments, Volume 3: 1980–1981 (1982)); Robert E. Riggs, *When Every Vote Counts: 5–4 Decisions in the United States Supreme Court, 1900–90,* 21 Hofstra L. Rev. 667, 697 (1993) (describing Justice White, since 1981, as the Court's sole moderate, with a "continuing conservative tilt"); Linda P. Campbell, *Justice White: The Democrat Who Often Votes with Court Conservatives,* Chi. Trib., Mar. 21, 1993, at 18. *See also* Joan Biskupic, *When Court Is Split, Kennedy Rules,* Wash. Post, June 11, 1995, at A14 (noting that Justice Kennedy "holds the decisive vote").

87. 523 U.S. 420 (1998).
88. 505 U.S. 833 (1992).
89. 438 U.S. 265 (1978).
90. 410 U.S. 113 (1973).
91. 430 U.S. 188, 192 (1977).
92. 523 U.S. 420 (1998).
93. 450 U.S. 662 (1981).
94. 337 U.S. 582 (1949).
95. 458 U.S. 527 (1982).
96. 458 U.S. 457 (1982).
97. 430 U.S. 144 (1979).
98. 509 U.S. 630 (1993).
99. 115 S. Ct. 2475 (1995).
100. 478 U.S. 186 (1986).
101. The *Bowers* Court declined to reach the issue of whether homosexuals are a suspect class under the equal protection clause, an issue that it later ducked as well

in Romer v. Evans, 517 U.S. 620 (1996) (striking down Colorado constitutional amendment that prohibited any special status on the basis of gay, lesbian, or bisexual orientation, concluding that the law exhibited an unlawful animus to a particular class, and thus violates equal protection even under rational basis scrutiny).

102. *See supra* chapter 2, § III.E (citing Shepsle).

103. *See supra* chapter 2, § IV.B.

104. *See supra* chapter 4, § III.G.3 (explaining relationship between standing and certiorari).

105. *See* ROBERT STERN ET AL., SUPREME COURT PRACTICE 197–202 (7th ed. 1993) (discussing the importance of resolving circuit splits on questions of federal law as motivating grants of petitions for writ of certiorari).

106. *See infra* chapter 6, § III.A.1 (discussing Powers v. Ohio, 499 U.S. 400 (1991); Campbell v. Louisiana, 523 U.S. 392 (1998)).

107. Ch. 324, 60 Stat. 237 (1946) (current version at 5 U.S.C. §§ 551–559, 701–706 (1988)).

108. 397 U.S. 150 (1970). In the landmark 1970 *Data Processing* decision, the plaintiffs sought standing to sue in federal court based upon section 10(a) of the APA and upon two substantive statutes, section 4 of the Bank Service Corporation Act, 12 U.S.C. § 1864 (1988), and the National Bank Act, 12 U.S.C. § 24 (1988 & Supp. V 1993). In conferring standing, the Supreme Court interpreted the APA to require a federal court plaintiff to allege, first, that she suffered an "injury in fact" and, second, that "the interest sought to be protected by the complainant [be] arguably within the zone of interests to be protected or regulated by the statute or constitutional guarantee in question." *See Data Processing,* 397 U.S. at 151–52.

109. Ch. 324, § 10(a), 60 Stat. 237, 243 (1946) (codified as amended at 5 U.S.C. § 702 (1988)).

110. For a review of the early academic debate, dominated by Professor Kenneth Culp Davis, who claimed that the APA required an injury in fact, and Professor Louis Jaffe, who argued that the APA was not intended to alter prior standing law, see Fletcher, *supra* note 41, at 256–57.

111. *See id.* at 255 n. 151 ("It is fairly clear from the legislative history, as well as from the statutory text, that the APA was designed to preserve existing standing law").

112. Indeed, in the companion case, Barlow v. Collins, 397 U.S. 150 (1970), the petitioners conceded this point. *See* Fletcher, *supra* note 41, at 257 (citing petitioners' briefs). As stated above, *see supra* at 167 n. 21, and cites therein, the Court had previously suggested a connection between justiciability and Article III, but had not formalized the elements of standing, including most notably injury in fact, as a constitutional requirement growing out of Article III until this period.

113. The causation prong was first mentioned in Linda R.S. v. Richard D., 410 U.S. 614, 618 (1973) (holding that the plaintiff failed to establish injury in fact because enforcement of the statute would result in jailing the child's father without necessarily producing support payments), and was given constitutional status in Warth v. Seldin, 422 U.S. 490, 499 (1975) (observing that "[t]he Art. III judicial power exists only to redress or otherwise to protect against injury to the complaining party"). *See also supra* at 167 n. 21, and cites therein (citing cases providing earlier indications of connection between Article III and standing).

114. 479 U.S. 388 (1987).

115. For an article exposing some recent doctrinal confusion, and arguing that the zone of interest test should not apply when Congress confers standing broadly by

statute, see Robert A. Anthony, *Zone-Free Standing for Private Attorneys General*, 7 GEO. MASON. L. REV. 237 (1999).

116. For a more detailed analysis of this aspect the Court's much criticized *Data Processing* decision, see Maxwell L. Stearns, *Standing and Social Choice: Historical Evidence*, 144 U. PA. L. REV. 309, 400–404 (1995).

117. *See* Fletcher, *supra* note 41, at 255–59 ("The touchstone [of section 10(a)] is that anyone whom a 'relevant statute' considers to be adversely affected or aggrieved by agency action has standing to seek review of the action under that statute.").

118. *See, e.g.*, Trafficante v. Metropolitan Life Ins. Co., 409 U.S. 205, 212 (1972) (allowing "a generous construction" of the Fair Housing Act of 1968 and holding that any member of the housing unit who claimed injury from the owner's discriminatory actions had standing to sue under the statute); Flast v. Cohen, 392 U.S. 83, 105–6 (1968) (holding that a taxpayer had standing to challenge the financing of religious schools on establishment clause grounds). For a discussion of the recent decision, Friends of the Earth v. Laidlaw, 120 S. Ct. 693 (2000), which appears to restore some of the liberal statutory standing principles established in the cases listed in this note, in a manner that is in tension with *Lujan*, see *supra* at 169 n.31.

119. *See, e.g.*, Sunstein, *supra* note 82, at 177 (positing that "early English and American practices give no support to the view" that injury in fact is a requirement for Article III cases or controversies).

For an interesting recent decision, in which Justice Stevens discusses the novelty of modern doctrinal standing elements, with a particular focus on redressibility, *see* Steel Company v. Citizens for a Better Environment, 523 U.S. 83 (1998). For a majority, Justice Scalia rejected standing in a private enforcement action for the disclosure of information under the citizen suit provision in the Emergency Planning and Community Right-to-Know Act of 1986 that allowed suit to force disclosures "designed to inform the public about the presence of hazardous and toxic chemicals, and to provide for emergency response in the event of a health-threatening release." *See* 523 U.S. at 86. Among the defects Scalia identified with the claim was that under the statute, plaintiffs sought monetary damages for past wrongs that, with the exception of litigation costs (which Scalia determined could not alone provide the basis for redressibility), would be payable to the U.S. Treasury rather than to them.

In a separate concurrence, Stevens rejoined that at early common law, the objective of promoting deterrence was alone sufficient to allow private prosecutions. Stevens further noted that such deterrence can arise from fines paid, whether into public coffers or to private individuals, or from other potential criminal sanctions. Thus, Stevens explained:

History supports the proposition that punishment or deterrence can redress an injury. In past centuries in England, the American colonies, and in the United States, private persons regularly prosecuted criminal cases. The interest in punishing the defendant and deterring violations of law by the defendant and others was sufficient to support the "standing" of the private prosecutor even if the only remedy was the sentencing of the defendant to jail or to the gallows. Given this history, the Framers of Article III surely would have considered such proceedings to be "Cases" that would "redress" an injury even though the party bringing suit did not receive any monetary compensation.

Id. at 127–128 (Stevens, J., concurring in the judgment).

120. *See* Havens Realty v. Coleman, 455 U.S. 363, 373–74 (1982) (holding that a fair housing organization consisting of one white member and one African American member had standing under the FHA to challenge the dissemination of untruthful and discriminatory housing information, stating that the injury required by Article III may exist by virtue of " 'statutes creating legal rights, the invasion of which creates standing' " (quoting Linda R.S. v. Richard D., 410 U.S. 614, 617 n. 3 (1973)); *Trafficante,* 409 U.S. at 211–12 (upholding a Fair Housing Act provision granting standing to plaintiffs who claimed that the defendants unlawfully denied them truthful housing information because of their race, even though the plaintiffs were testers who were not interested in actually securing housing, but instead were raising the claim on behalf of others who failed to secure desired housing because of racial discrimination); *see also* Gladstone, Realtors v. Village of Bellwood, 441 U.S. 91, 109–15 (1979) (converting a third-party standing claim of residents not attempting to secure housing into a first-party standing claim to enjoy the "social and professional benefits of living in an integrated community"); Village of Arlington Heights v. Metropolitan Hous. Dev. Corp., 429 U.S. 252, 264 (1977) (conferring standing upon an African American in search of housing near his place of employment to challenge under the FHA the town's refusal to rezone for reasons related to race, where the developer's proposal created "substantial probability" that the project would be completed, even though development was contingent upon uncertain federal housing subsidies). For a thoughtful analysis of these and other FHA cases, see generally David A. Logan, *Standing to Sue: A Proposed Separation of Powers Analysis,* 1984 WIS. L. REV. 37, 64–81.
121. 504 U.S. 555 (1992).
122. 520 U.S. 154 (1997).

CHAPTER 6

1. 5 U.S.C. § 701 *et seq.*
2. 504 U.S. 555 (1992).
3. 429 U.S. 1012 (1976) (order of the Court terminating stay of execution).
4. *See, e.g.,* Powers v. Ohio, 499 U.S. 400, 412–14 (1991) (allowing a white criminal defendant to raise *Batson* challenge on the ground that the defendant was effectively raising the right of the potential African American juror not to be excluded); Campbell v. Louisiana, 523 U.S. 392 (1998) (allowing a white criminal defendant to raise *Batson/Powers* challenge to the exclusion of black person from the role of foreperson on the grand jury). For a critical analysis of *Powers,* see *infra* § III.A.1.
5. *See supra* at 10 n. 15 (describing the principal Fair Housing Act cases).
6. 504 U.S. 555.
7. Most recently, in Friends of the Earth v. Laidlaw, 120 S. Ct. 693 (2000), issued since this book was written, the Supreme Court began to retreat from its *Lujan* analysis of statutory standing. *See supra* at 169 n. 31.
8. It is worth noting that I have used the term *undistorted* rather than *unregulated* in the heading. My choice of terminology is intended to distinguish the standing cases in this category from the cases that marked the end of the *Lochner* era. In West Coast Hotel v. Parrish, 300 U.S. 379 (1937), the Court held in a case in which standing was not seriously disputed (as evidenced by the Court's failure to address the plaintiff's standing argument in its opinion, *see id.* at 386), that the Constitution no longer prevented prospective economic regulation that had been held off limits under *Lochner. West Coast Hotel* effectively held that there

is no right to transact in an unregulated market, at least as a matter of due process. In the standing cases, in contrast, plaintiffs are not claiming that economic regulation is per se unconstitutional. Instead, they are claiming that, if we assume that the regulation in question violates some independent constitutional guarantee, most commonly the equal protection clause, or a statute, then they have a right to have the regulation struck down if doing so would ultimately inure to their benefit. Thus, while *West Coast Hotel* held that the due process clause does not prevent market regulation, these standing cases effectively hold that plaintiffs do not have the right to the benefits associated with removing independently unconstitutional, or otherwise illegal, market distortions.

The heading also captures another important feature of these cases. Some illegal market distortions can be superimposed upon a regime that takes a set of legal regulations, instead of a state of laissez-faire, as its baseline. Thus, in Allen v. Wright, 468 U.S. 737 (1984), the plaintiffs alleged that the illegal market distortion resulted from the conferral of tax-exempt status in violation of the equal protection clause, and in Simon v. Eastern Kentucky Welfare Rights Org., 426 U.S. 26 (1976), the plaintiffs alleged that such a market distortion resulted from the conferral of tax-exempt status in violation of the Internal Revenue Code. Again, the claimed right is not to a market that is unregulated, but rather to a market, whether regulated or not, that is not distorted by illegal means.

9. *See infra* § III.C (discussing cases).
10. *See supra* chapter 4, § IV.
11. *See infra* § III.A.1 (discussing Powers v. Ohio, 499 U.S. 400 (1991), and Campbell v. Louisiana, 523 U.S. 392 (1998)).
12. Robert J. Pushaw, Jr., *Justiciability and Separation of Powers: A Neo-Federalist Approach,* 81 Cornell L. Rev. 393, 493 (1996).
13. 48 Stat. 955 (1934) (codified at 28 U.S.C. §§ 2201–2202 (1982)).
14. See Donald L. Doernberg & Michael B. Mushlin, *The Trojan Horse: How the Declaratory Judgment Act Created a Cause of Action and Expanded Federal Jurisdiction while the Supreme Court Wasn't Looking,* 36 UCLA L. Rev. 529, 561 (1989) ("The bill was introduced in every session of Congress from 1919 to 1932. . . . Finally, in 1934, the Act became law.").
15. *See* Aetna Life Ins. v. Haworth, 300 U.S. 227 (1937). While the Court had called the constitutionality of state declaratory judgment acts into question in Willing v. Chicago Auditorium Ass'n, 277 U.S. 274, 289 (1928), the Court ultimately sustained a state declaratory judgment act in Nashville, C. & St. Louis Ry. V. Wallace, 288 U.S. 249 (1933). *See also* Doernberg & Mushlin, *The Trojan Horse, supra* note 13, at 566–69.
16. 48 Stat. 955 (1934) (codified at 28 U.S.C. § 2201(a)).
17. *See* Pushaw, *supra* note 12, at 494.
18. 339 U.S. 667 (1950).
19. *See* Pushaw, *supra* note 12, at 493–96.
20. *See* Doernberg & Mushlin, *The Trojan Horse, supra* note 14, at 548.
21. See Doernberg & Mushlin, *The Trojan Horse, supra* note 14; Donald L. Doernberg & Michael B. Mushlin, *History Comes Calling: Dean Griswold Offers New Evidence Surrounding the Enactment of the Declaratory Judgment Act,* 37 UCLA L. Rev. 139 (1989).
22. *See* Doernberg & Mushlin, *The Trojan Horse, supra* note 14, at 548 (citations omitted).
23. *See, e.g.,* Raines v. Byrd, 521 U.S. 811 (1997) (holding challenge to Line-Item Veto Act unripe, despite statutory standing provision).

24. *See, e.g.,* National Endowment of the Arts v. Karen Finley, 574 U.S. 569 (1998); Secretary of State v. Joseph H. Munson, 467 U.S. 947, 956–57 (1984); Gooding v. Wilson, 405 U.S. 518 (1972); Broadrick v. Oklahoma, 413 U.S. 601 (1973).

25. *See* Michael Dorf, *Incidental Burdens on Fundamental Rights,* 109 HARV. L. REV. 1175, 1241 (1996); *see also* United States v. Salerno, 481 U.S. 739, 745 (1987).

26. *See, e.g.,* Papachristou v. City of Jacksonville, 405 U.S. 156, 162 (1972).

27. For a more general discussion of vagueness and overbreadth, see LAURENCE H. TRIBE, AMERICAN CONSTITUTIONAL LAW §§ 12–27 & 12–28 (2d ed. 1988).

28. The Supreme Court has described mootness as "the doctrine of standing set in a time frame: The requisite personal interest that must exist at the commencement of the litigation (standing) must continue throughout its existence (mootness)." United States v. Geraghty, 455 U.S. 388, 397 (1980) (*quoting* Henry P. Monaghan, *Constitutional Adjudication: The Who and When,* 82 YALE L.J. 1363, 1384 (1973)). In the recent decision, Friends of the Earth v. Laidlaw, 120 S. Ct. 693 (2000), Justice Ginsburg signaled a retreat from this characterization of mootness, stating that "[c]areful reflection on the long-recognized exceptions to mootness, however, reveals that the description of mootness as 'standing set in a time frame' is not comprehensive." *Id.* at 708. For a more detailed discussion of *Laidlaw,* see *supra* at 169 n. 31.

29. This analysis is largely consistent with the position advanced by Chief Justice Rehnquist in Honig v. Doe, 484 U.S. 305, 329–32 (1984) (Rehnquist, C.J., concurring), in which he acknowledged that for the thirty years prior to that decision, the Court had dismissed cases that became moot pending appeal to, or decision from, the Supreme Court, and that recent decisions had suggested that mootness was a requirement growing out of Article III. But Rehnquist then went on to argue that if the doctrine was truly a constitutional requirement, it would be impossible to reconcile the doctrine with the exceptions for cases raising claimed harms that are "capable of repetition, yet evading review," and for cases involving voluntary cessation of conduct that, if resumed, would produce recurrent injuries. For a more detailed discussion of the linkage of mootness to Article III, *see supra* chapter 4 n. 21.

30. For a recent related illustration, consider the combined efforts of various civil rights organizations to contribute to a rare postcertiorari settlement in Piscataway Township Bd. of Educ. v. Taxman, 522 U.S. 1010 (1997), a case that most civil rights leaders agreed presented the Supreme Court with a potentially attractive opportunity to limit, or even to end, affirmative action. *See* Paula Alexander Becker, *Affirmative Action and Reverse Discrimination: Does Taxman v. Board of Education of the Township of Piscataway Define the Limits of Lawful Voluntary Race-Conscious Affirmative Action,* 8 SETON HALL CONST. L. J. 13, 16 n. 14 (1997). For a student note evaluating the *Piscataway* settlement as an example of inverse path manipulation, see Lisa Estrada, *Buying the Status Quo on Affirmative Action: The Piscataway Settlement and its Lessons About Interest Group Path Manipulation,* 9 GEO. MASON U. CIV. RTS. L.J. 207 (1998/1999)

31. *See generally* Evan Tsen Lee, *Deconstitutionalizing Justiciability: The Example of Mootness,* 105 HARV. L. REV. 605 (1992). *See also supra* note 28 and cites therein.

32. *See, e.g.,* DeFunis v. Odegard, 416 U.S. 312, 316 (1974) (per curiam); North Carolina v. Rice, 404 U.S. 244, 246 (1971); *see also* Lee, *supra* note 30, at 610–12.

33. *See DeFunis,* 416 U.S. at 316; *Rice,* 404 U.S. at 246.

34. Roe v. Wade, 410 U.S. 113 (1973).

35. *See, e.g.,* Northeastern Fla. Chapter of Associated Gen. Contractors v. City of Jacksonville, 508 U.S. 656 (1993); City of Mesquite v. Aladdin's Castle, Inc., 455 U.S. 283 (1982); United States v. W.T. Grant Co., 345 U.S. 629 (1953).

36. 410 U.S. 113. While *Roe* is the most well known instance of this exception, as Chief Justice Rehnquist observed in his *Honig* concurrence, the exception was established in Southern Pacific Terminal Co. v. ICC, 219 U.S. 498 (1911). *See* Honig v. Doe, 484 U.S. 305, 329–32 (1988) (Rehnquist, C.J., concurring).

37. *See supra* note 34 and cites therein.

38. *See, e.g.,* Powers v. Ohio, 499 U.S. 400 (1991); Secretary of State v. Joseph H. Munson Co., 467 U.S. 947, 956 (1984); Craig v. Boren, 429 U.S. 190, 194 (1976); Craig R. Gottlieb, Comment, *How Standing Has Fallen: The Need to Separate Constitutional and Prudential Concerns,* 142 U. PA. L. REV. 1963, 1071 (1994) (arguing that the only constitutional basis for standing is the need to promote zealous advocacy); *cf.* Arthur H. Abel, Note, *The Burger Court's Unified Approach to Standing and Its Impact on Congressional Plaintiffs,* 60 NOTRE DAME L. REV. 1187, 1189 (1985) (observing that in the Warren Court, the standing doctrine was largely grounded in the desire to promote vigorous advocacy).

39. 429 U.S. 1012, 1013 (1976) (terminating a stay of execution on the grounds that Gary Gilmore "made a knowing and intelligent waiver of all federal rights he might have asserted after the Utah trial court's sentence was imposed").

40. 461 U.S. 95, 101 (1983).

41. *See generally* William Fletcher, *The Structure of Standing,* 98 YALE L.J. 221 (1988).

42. *See supra* chapter 4, § IV.A.

43. As stated in chapter 4, such groups can still sponsor litigation on behalf of the injured party, but doing so remains more costly in terms of the maneuverability of path manipulation than if the interest group were fully able to time cases on its own. *See supra* at 179 n.*. Moreover, the stringent requirements for associational standing raise the cost to associations of picking and choosing claims as a means of manipulating the order of precedent. See *supra* at 169 n.74 (discussing Hunt v. Washington Apple Advertising Comm'n, 432 U.S. 333 (1977)).

44. 523 U.S. 420, 445 (O'Connor, J., concurring in the judgment). *See supra* chapter 1, § II.A.

45. 42 U.S.C. § 3604 (1988).

46. *See* Trafficante v. Metropolitan Life Ins. Co., 409 U.S. 205, 208–12 (1972) (finding a congressional intention to define standing under the Fair Housing Act as broadly as is permitted by Article III). *See also* David A. Logan, *Standing to Sue: A Proposed Separations of Powers Analysis,* 1984 WIS. L. REV. 37, 65 (positing that "[b]ecause the *Trafficante* plaintiffs had alleged that they were themselves injured [by the inability to live in an integrated community], the injury in fact requirement was met even though the defendant's discriminatory practice was aimed at other persons who were not parties to the suit").

47. Gladstone, Realtors v. Village of Bellwood, 441 U.S. 91, 112 (1979) (relying upon *Trafficante* and a broad definition of standing under the Fair Housing Act to allow housing testers who live within the target area to evade summary judgment).

48. *See* Havens Realty Corp. v. Coleman, 455 U.S. 363 (1982).

49. *Id.* at 373 (relying upon *Gladstone, Realtors* to find injury in fact and thus standing to sue for a housing tester); *see also* Linda R.S. v. Richard D., 410 U.S. 614, 617 n. 3 (1972) (original source of quoted text).

50. *See supra* chapter 4, § IV.A.

51. 100 U.S. 303 (1880).

52. *See id.* at 305. In defining the defendant's claim, the Court stated:

> It is to be observed that the first of these questions is not whether a colored man, when an indictment has been preferred against him, has a right to a grand or a petit jury composed in whole or in part of persons of his own race or color, but it is whether, in the composition or selection of jurors by whom he is to be indicted or tried, all persons *of his race or color* may be excluded by law, solely because of their race or color, so that by no possibility can any colored man sit upon the jury.

> *Id.* (emphasis added). The italicized language reveals the limitations of the *Strauder* Court's gloss on the defendant's claim. As defined by the Court, the defendant claimed the right not to have persons of *his* race or color systematically excluded from jury service. Moreover, because a minority juror can be excluded in the trial of a white defendant, the Court implied that a prospective minority juror has no right to serve.

53. 396 U.S. 320 (1970).
54. *See id.* at 329–30. The *Carter* Court stated:

> Defendants in criminal proceedings do not have the only cognizable legal interest in nondiscriminatory jury selection. People excluded from juries because of their race are as much aggrieved as those indicted and tried by juries chosen under a system of racial exclusion.

> *Id.* at 329.
55. 476 U.S. 79 (1986).
56. *See Batson,* 476 U.S. at 86–87.
57. 499 U.S. 400 (1991).
58. 523 U.S. 392 (1998).
59. *See id.* at 1422–23.
60. *See id.* at 1426 (Thomas, J., concurring in part and dissenting in part).
61. *See supra* § I.
62. Thus, the *Powers* Court conferred third-party standing based upon a determination that Powers would litigate the issue zealously and that the Court, if it granted relief, would remedy whatever harm the race-based exclusion could be said to have caused Powers. The Court stated:

> This congruence of interests [between the defendant and the excluded jurors] makes it necessary and appropriate for the defendant to raise the rights of the juror. And, there can be no doubt that petitioner will be a motivated, effective advocate for the excluded venire persons' rights. Petitioner has much at stake in proving that his jury was improperly constituted due to an equal protection violation, for we have recognized that discrimination in the jury selection process may lead to the reversal of a conviction.

> *Id.* at 414. While it is undoubtedly true that the defendant would press the jurors' claims vigorously and that a favorable ruling would provide the defendant with the desired relief, the Court's analysis begs the question whether any relief afforded the defendant would flow from curing the violation of the defendant's rights or those of someone else. Had the Court construed its standing metaphors of zealousness and redressability as proxies for when to shift the burden of legislative inertia, rather than as justiciability criteria with independent content, it

would have recognized the anomaly that Powers had deployed all the trappings of a criminal appeal to stress the urgency of judicial creation of positive law in a context more appropriately suited to nonurgent civil litigation brought by someone else or not at all.

63. 405 U.S. 727 (1972).

64. 412 U.S. 669 (1973).

65. *Sierra Club,* 405 U.S. at 735 n. 8 (quoting paragraph 3 of the complaint).

66. *See Powers,* 499 U.S. at 414 (positing that "there can be no doubt that petitioner will be a motivated, effective advocate for the excluded persons' rights"); *see also* Secretary of State v. Joseph H. Munson Co., 467 U.S. 947, 956 (1984) (finding that "[w]here practical obstacles prevent a party from asserting rights on behalf of itself," a court should consider whether the litigant can be expected to present the issues "with the necessary adversarial zeal"); Craig v. Boren, 429 U.S. 190, 194 (1976) (noting that, because questions had been presented "vigorously" and "cogently," the denial of standing would "serve no functional purpose").

67. There can be little doubt that Mrs. Gilmore would actually have been more zealous than her son in pursuing his legal claims, given that Gary Gilmore elected not to pursue his legal remedies at all. Similarly, the Sierra Club would, without doubt, have litigated the legality of the proposed recreation facility as ambitiously as those who used the affected national park. On the other hand, no criminal defendant is ever thrown out of court—or summarily convicted—for not vigorously pursuing his claims. The state retains the burden of proof beyond a reasonable doubt even if the defendant puts on no defense at all. In short, zealousness, like the other standing elements or proxies, has no independent doctrinal significance to justiciability.

68. *Sierra Club,* 405 U.S. at 735 n. 8 (quoting the complaint).

69. 412 U.S. 669 (1973).

70. The Court described the "attenuated line of causation" as follows:

[A] general rate increase would allegedly cause increased use of nonrecyclable commodities as compared to recyclable goods, thus resulting in the need to use more natural resources to produce such goods, some of which resources might be taken from the Washington area, and resulting in more refuse that might be discarded in national parks in the Washington area.

Id. at 688.

71. *See* Fletcher, *supra* note 41, at 258–60 ("a perfectly plausible—and I believe the best—reading of NEPA is that anyone who can make a colorable claim . . . should have standing").

72. *See SCRAP,* 412 U.S. at 686 (quoting *Sierra Club,* 405 U.S. at 734).

73. While the Sierra Club apparently cited a number of substantive statutes in its complaint, the Supreme Court only noted these statutory arguments in a footnote and in the text stated, "The Sierra Club relies [for standing] upon § 10 of the Administrative Procedure Act (APA)." *See Sierra Club,* 405 U.S. at 730 n. 2. The Court stated:

As analyzed by the District Court, the complaint alleged violations of law falling into four categories. First, it claimed that the special-use permit for construction of the resort exceeded the maximum acreage limitation placed upon such permits by 16 U.S.C. § 497, and that issuance of a "revocable" use permit was beyond the authority of the Forest Service. Second, it challenged the proposed permit for the highway through Sequoia National Park on the grounds that the highway would not serve any of the purposes of the park, in alleged violation of 16 U.S.C. § 1, and that it would destroy timber and other natural resources protected by 16 U.S.C. §§ 41 and 43. Third, it claimed that the Forest Service and the Department of the Interior had violated their own regulations by failing to hold adequate public hearings on the proposed project. Finally, the complaint asserted that 16 U.S.C. § 45c requires specific congressional authorization of a permit for construction of a power transmission line within the limits of a national park.

Id. The Court's treatment of the Sierra Club's statutory claims suggests that they were sufficiently attenuated on standing that the Court did not need to resolve those standing claims on the merits. This position may well have been bolstered by the nature of the substantive statutory provisions on which the Sierra Club relied. With the exception of the Sierra Club's claim that the Forest Service and the Department of the Interior failed to hold public hearings in violation of their own regulations, none of the statutory claims, in contrast with those raised in *SCRAP*, appeared to suggest a right of public enforcement. Moreover, the public hearing provisions were not created by statute, but rather by administrative regulation.

74. *See SCRAP*, 412 U.S. at 686–87. The Court explained: "In *Sierra Club*, . . . we went on to stress the importance of demonstrating that the party seeking review be himself among the injured. . . . No such specific injury was alleged in *Sierra Club.*" *Id.* at 687.
75. *See* Fletcher, *supra* note 41, at 260–63 (arguing that the different outcomes in *SCRAP* and *Sierra Club* may have turned on whether Congress intended that the underlying statutes protect the plaintiffs' claimed rights).
76. *See supra* note 73.
77. 500 U.S. 72 (1991).
78. 498 U.S. 517 (1991).
79. 28 U.S.C. § 1442(a)(1) (as amended 1996).
80. The Court further rejected the NIH's argument that, regardless of the zone of interest of the federal removal statute, it would be futile to remand to state court given the lack of merit of the plaintiffs' underlying claim, noting that state and federal standing requirements might differ. 500 U.S. at 88–89.
81. 498 U.S. 517 (1991).
82. *Id.* at 520 (internal quotations omitted).
83. 454 U.S. 464 (1982).
84. 392 U.S. 83 (1968).
85. *See supra* at 233–234 (discussing relaxation of standing and justiciability generally in the Warren Court).
86. 418 U.S. 208 (1974).
87. 418 U.S. 166 (1974).
88. U.S. Const. art. I, § 6, cl. 2.
89. U.S. CONST. art. I, § 9, cl. 7.
90. 5 U.S.C. § 552 (1988).
91. *See supra* at 10 n. 16.
92. *See, e.g.*, National Recycling Coalition, Inc. v. Browner, 984 F.2d 1243, 1248 (D.C. Cir. 1993) (conferring standing under the Resource Conservation and Recovery Act of 1976 (RCRA), 42 U.S.C. § 6972 (1988), to challenge Environmental Protection Agency guidelines for government procurement of certain products); Sup-

porters to Oppose Pollution v. Heritage Group, 973 F.2d 1320, 1322 (7th Cir. 1992) (conferring standing under RCRA to oppose a landfill that had at least potential to cause them harm). For other federal environmental statutes with broad-based standing provisions, see Toxic Substances Control Act, 15 U.S.C. § 2619 (1988 & Supp. V 1993); Federal Water Pollution Control Act, 33 U.S.C. § 1365 (1988 & Supp. V 1993); Safe Drinking Water Act, 42 U.S.C. § 300j–8 (1988).

93. 410 U.S. 614, 617 n. 3 (1973).
94. 504 U.S. 555 (1992).
95. For a more detailed discussion, see *infra* § IV.
96. 468 U.S. 737 (1984).
97. 438 U.S. 265 (1978).
98. Justice Stevens's dissenting opinion in *Allen* is closest to the characterization of the plaintiffs' claim offered in the text:

> [The Court's] causation analysis is nothing more than a restatement of elementary economics: when something becomes more expensive, less of it will be purchased. . . . If racially discriminatory private schools lose the "cash grants" that flow from the operation of the statutes, the education they provide will become more expensive and hence less of their services will be purchased.

> *Id.* at 788.
99. 422 U.S. 490 (1975).
100. 426 U.S. 26 (1976).
101. Thus, the *Warth* Court, per Justice Powell, stated:

> We find the record devoid of the necessary allegations. . . . [N]one of these petitioners has a present interest in any Penfield property; none is himself subject to the ordinance's strictures; and none has ever been denied a variance or permit by respondent officials. . . . Instead, petitioners claim that respondents' enforcement of the ordinance against third parties—developers, builders, and the like—has had the consequence of precluding the construction of housing suitable to their needs at prices they might be able to afford. The fact that the harm to petitioners may have resulted indirectly does not in itself preclude standing. . . . But it may make it substantially more difficult to meet the minimum requirement of Art. III: to establish that, in fact, the asserted injury was the consequence of the defendants' actions, or that prospective relief will remove the harm.

> 422 U.S. at 504–5 (citation omitted).
102. *See Simon,* 426 U.S. at 28. While the *Simon* claimants relied upon a federal statute, rather than a constitutional provision, the analysis suggests that given the breadth of the tax code and the potential range of litigants that a contrary standing determination would have invited to challenge IRS policies in violation of the Code, the ruling in *Simon,* no less than in *Allen* and *Warth,* has the effect of reducing advertent litigant path manipulation.
103. While less obvious, until quite recently in any event, the Court had maintained that Congress also has the authority to expand the substantive reach of the Fourteenth Amendment equal protection clause to include claims that the Supreme Court has previously denied. *See* Katzenbach v. Morgan, 384 U.S. 641, 658 (1966) (upholding Congress's power to expand the reach of the equal protection

clause in a manner that the Court had expressly rejected in Lassiter v. Northampton County Bd. of Elections, 360 U.S. 45 (1959)). Applying this reasoning, even though the Court has been unwilling to treat wealth as a suspect classification for equal protection purposes, Congress presumably could expand the list of suspect classifications to include wealth status, thus creating a stronger basis with which to challenge Penfield's zoning ordinance. However, in recent years, the Supreme Court has suggested that Congress is substantially limited in its power to expand the reach of equal protection rights under the Fourteenth Amendment. *See, e.g.,* Adarand Constructors, Inc. v. Pena, 515 U.S. 200, 227 (1995) (imposing strict scrutiny and striking down federal affirmative action programs and overruling Metro Broadcasting, Inc. v. Federal Communications Comm'n, 497 U.S. 547 (1990), which had upheld an FCC affirmative action program based on intermediate scrutiny); *see also* Miller v. Johnson, 515 U.S. 900, 920 (1995) (applying strict scrutiny in evaluating a racially gerrymandered congressional district drawn to satisfy Department of Justice administrative preclearance under the Voting Rights Act of 1965, 42 U.S.C. §§ 1971–1972bb-2 (1988 & Supp. IV 1992)). Most importantly, the Court directly called the *Katzenbach* analysis into question in City of Boerne, Texas v. Flores, 521 U.S. 507 (1997). In *City of Boerne,* the Court struck down the Religious Freedom Restoration Act, through which Congress had attempted to elevate to strict scrutiny the test for applying laws of general application that have an incidental effect in restricting religious practices. In doing so, none of the justices, including those in dissent, continued to embrace the view expressed by Brennan in *Katzenbach,* that Congress could expand, in the name of enforcing, substantive constitutional protections.

104. 5 U.S. (1 Cranch) 137 (1803).
105. 232 U.S. 383 (1914).
106. 367 U.S. 643 (1961).
107. 384 U.S. 436 (1966).
108. See Dickerson v. United States, 120 S. Ct. 578 (1999) (grant of certiorari to United States Court of Appeals for the Fourth Circuit). As the Fourth Circuit explained, following *Miranda,* Congress enacted 18 U.S.C.A. § 3501 (1966), which liberalized the standard for determining the voluntariness of confessions and for determining the admissability of allegedly coerced confessions. See United States v. Dickerson, 166 F. 3d 667, 671 (4th Cir. 1999).
109. *See supra* chapter 3, § II. The fact that these rulings were decided by majority opinion does not undermine the argument in the text. The fact remains that, in contrast with legislatures, which have the power to remain inert, the Supreme Court, and lower federal courts, are collectively obligated to issue rulings, *whether or not* those courts possess Condorcet-winning preferences.
110. 438 U.S. 59 (1978).
111. 438 U.S. 265 (1978).
112. *See Duke Power,* 438 U.S. at 74–75 (citing the findings of the district court in Carolina Envtl. Study Group, Inc. v. United States Atomic Energy Comm'n, 431 F. Supp. 203, 219 (W.D.N.C. 1977)).
113. *See Bakke,* 438 U.S. at 280 n. 14. Recall that the California Supreme Court ordered Bakke's admission before the case reached the Supreme Court, analogizing the equal protection claim to one arising under Title VII and thus shifting the burden to the state to prove that, absent the minority admissions program, Mr. Bakke would not have been admitted. On petition for rehearing before the Supreme Court, the California Board of Regents conceded that they could not meet that burden. *See id.* at 280–81.

114. *See id.* For a recent example of a case in which the Court granted standing despite an attenuated causal chain, see Northeastern Fla. Gen. Contractors v. Jacksonville, 113 S. Ct. 2297, 2301 (1993) (conferring standing upon a contractor challenging a racial set-aside program using *Bakke*-style analysis in which injury is defined as the ability to compete rather than the ability to obtain a contract); *see also* Village of Arlington Heights v. Metropolitan Hous. Dev. Corp., 429 U.S. 252, 264 (1977) (conferring standing to challenge an alleged racially motivated denial of a variance even though the requested relief would not guarantee that the project would be built).

115. *See supra* § I.

116. 499 U.S. 400 (1991).

117. 118 S. Ct. 1419 (1998). *See also supra* § III.A (discussing *Powers* and *Campbell*).

118. This is not to suggest, however, that public enforcement actions generally lack clear antecedents in early federal court practice. For a more detailed discussion, *see supra* at 36 n. 112 and cites therein.

119. 504 U.S. 555 (1992).

120. 520 U.S. 154 (1997).

121. Prior to *Lujan,* the most serious effort to link standing to Article II was in an article written by then-professor Scalia. *See* Antonin Scalia, *The Doctrine of Standing as an Essential Element of the Separation of Powers,* 17 SUFFOLK U. L. REV. 881, 893–94 n. 58 (1983) (positing that "congressional approval and even encouragement [of relaxed standing] cannot validate judicial disregard of the boundary between the second and third branches"). Justice Scalia authored the *Lujan* and *Bennett* decisions.

122. *Lujan,* 504 U.S. at 571–72 (quoting 16 U.S.C. § 1540(g) (1988)).

123. *Id.* at 602 (Blackmun, J., dissenting).

124. *Id.* at 580 (Kennedy, J., concurring).

125. 5 U.S. (1 Cranch) 137 (1803).

126. *Lujan,* 504 U.S. at 576 (quoting *Marbury,* 5 U.S. (1 Cranch) at 170).

127. *Marbury,* 5 U.S. (1 Cranch) at 170.

128. *See id.* For two more recent cases demonstrating the Court's willingness to compel executive conduct as required by law, see Clinton v. Jones, 520 U.S. 681 (1997) (rejecting president's claim of immunity from civil suit growing out of alleged sexual harassment of a state employee, as governor of Arkansas, while sitting as president); United States v. Nixon, 418 U.S. 683, 702 (1974) (ordering President Nixon to release tapes that he withheld in response to a properly issued subpoena).

129. *See, e.g.,* Logan, *supra* note 45, at 42 (positing that "[i]n the statutory context, the Court should uniformly follow the approach it has used in a series of cases construing the Fair Housing Act, one which accords great deference to Congress' power to provide judicial redress to parties asserting even novel claims with attenuated causal relationships"); Richard J. Pierce, Jr., Comment: Lujan v. Defenders of Wildlife: *Standing as a Judicially Imposed Limit on Legislative Power,* 42 DUKE L.J. 1170, 1181 (1993) (observing that Justices Kennedy and Souter, in their concurrences in *Lujan,* "recognize that regulatory regimes often create judicially enforceable statutory rights that differ from traditional common law rights"); Cass Sunstein, *What's Standing after* Lujan? *Of Citizen Suits, "Injuries," and Article* III, 91 MICH. L. REV. 163, 177–78 (1992) (asserting that "[t]here is absolutely no affirmative evidence that Article III was intended to limit congressional power to create standing").

130. 5 U.S. (1 Cranch) at 177.
131. As noted previously, this is further supported by the intuition, derived from the etiology of the word *case,* that adjudicatory lawmaking is legitimated by the chance presentation of issues necessary to the resolution of cases for decision. *See supra* at 165 n.*, and cites therein.
132. 520 U.S. 154 (1997).
133. In addition to stating claims under the ESA, petitioners alleged that the challenged actions constituted arbitrary and capricious conduct and an abuse of discretion under the APA. *See Bennett,* 520 U.S. at 160.
134. The *Bennett* Court relied upon two earlier cases, Association of Data Processing Serv. Org., Inc. v. Camp, 397 U.S. 150 (1970), and Lujan v. National Wildlife Fed'n, 497 U.S. 871 (1990), for the proposition that "whether a plaintiff's interest is 'arguably . . . protected . . . by the statute' within the meaning of the zone-of-interests test is to be determined not by reference to the overall purpose of the Act in question (here, species preservation), but by reference to the particular provision of law upon which the plaintiff relies." *Bennett,* 520 U.S. at 175. But in fact, as the Ninth Circuit well documented, the overall weight of authority was contrary. *See* Bennett v. Plenert, 63 F.3d 915, 919–22 (9th Cir. 1995) (collecting authorities). Moreover, as the Supreme Court itself stated in Clark v. Securities Industry Ass'n, 479 U.S. 388 (1970), the companion case to *Camp,* the zone-of-interest test "denies a right of review if the plaintiff's interests are so marginally related to or inconsistent with the purposes implicit in the statute that it cannot be reasonably assumed that Congress intended to permit the suit." *Id.* at 399. Thus, the Ninth Circuit concluded, based upon *Clark,* that "the statutory purposes should be divined by considering the particular statutory provision that underlies the complaint within 'the overall purpose' of the act itself." *Plenert,* 63 F.3d. at 919. At a minimum, this understanding of the zone-of-interest test is more consistent with the pre-*Lujan* understanding that the purpose of standing is to determine whether Congress intended to allow the claimant to pursue his statutory cause of action in federal court.
135. *Plenert,* 63 F.3d at 918 n. 4 (citing *Lujan,* 504 U.S. at 570–80).
136. 409 U.S. 205.
137. *Bennett,* 520 U.S. at 175 (conceding that while plaintiffs' interests were economic, the "overall purpose of the [ESA]" is "species preservation").
138. *See id.* at 1162–63.
139. *Plenert,* 63 F.3d at 921–22.
140. *See supra* at 278.
141. *Lujan,* 504 U.S. at 572.
142. Thus, in *Lujan,* Justice Scalia distinguished cases in which the procedural injury, if remedied, will confer even de minimis monetary damages, in the form of a bounty. *Lujan,* 504 U.S. at 572–73. Based upon this insight, Professor Cass Sunstein has argued that *Lujan* might ultimately be inconsequential in that Congress could remedy whatever deficiencies were perceived in the standing provision by amending to include a cash bounty if plaintiffs succeed in their suit. *See* Sunstein, *supra* note 128, at 232.
143. For a discussion of the nondelegation doctrine, see *supra* chapter 5, § II.
144. 521 U.S. 811 (1997).
145. 524 U.S. 417 (1998).
146. *See, e.g.,* Michel v. Anderson, 14 F.3d 623, 625 (D.C. Cir. 1994); Barnes v. Kline, 759 F.2d 21, 28–29 (D.C. Cir. 1985); Moore v. U.S. House of Representatives,

733 F.2d 946, 950–52 (D.C. Cir. 1984); Kennedy v. Sampson, 511 F.2d 430, 435–36 (D.C. Cir. 1974). *See also Raines* 521 U.S. at 814 & 821 n. 4. The United States Supreme Court had never endorsed this practice. *See* id. at 814.

147. I have previously set out an analysis, based upon public choice theory, of the likely impact of the item veto on legislative bargaining within Congress, and between members of Congress and the president. *See* Maxwell L. Stearns, *The Public Choice Case Against the Item Veto,* 49 WASH. & LEE L. REV. 385 (1992). The article, which was written prior to the adoption of the Line-Item Veto Act, and which was directed at proposed constitutional amendments conferring item veto power upon the president, demonstrates that if we assume that members of Congress and the president behave rationally, the item veto will likely produce the opposite of its intended effect of curbing unwanted pork barrel legislation, while remaining largely neutral with respect to overall matters of legislative policy. If we assume, as seems probable, that the president has greater control in selecting which bills to support than in selecting with whom he must bargain in Congress to get those bills passed, then the president will likely find his hands tied with respect to the most egregious pork as the precondition to having his favored bills survive the various negative legislative checkpoints in Congress. At the same time, holding all else constant, those legislators seeking to claim credit with their constituents for securing special interest legislation will look more favorably to those bills, still in need of support, that the president supports, and for which they can secure a return commitment from the White House that if the bill is signed into law, the president will not separately veto the special interest item. The item veto is therefore likely to increase the president's power at the margin to determine which bills pass, while limiting the president's ability to excise the very pork against which the item veto is directed.

148. *See supra* § II (discussing ripeness doctrines and exceptions).

149. Pub. L. No. 104-30, 110 Stat. 1200, codified at 2 U.S.C.A. § 691 *et seq.* (Supp. 1997).

150. *Raines,* 521 U.S. at 814 (quoting 2 U.S.C. § 691(a) (Supp. 1997), with indentations omitted).

151. 2 U.S.C.A. § 691e(4)(A), (B), (C) (Supp. 1997); *see also Raines,* 521 U.S. at 814.

152. 2 U.S.C.A. § 691e(9)(a)(i), (ii) (Supp. 1997).

153. *See* U.S. CONST. art. I, § 7.

154. 2 U.S.C.A. § 692(a)(1) (Supp. 1997).

155. 2 U.S.C.A. § 692 (b), (c) (Supp. 1997).

156. Raines v. Byrd, 521 U.S. 811, 835 (1997) (Stevens, J., dissenting).

157. *See supra* note 133 and cites therein.

158. 307 U.S. 433 (1939).

159. *See supra* § II (discussing ripeness and exceptions).

160. In his separate dissent, Breyer went further and argued that the Court could not deny standing in *Raines* without overruling Coleman v. Miller, 307 U.S. 433 (1939). *See Raines,* 117 S. Ct. at 2329 (Breyer, J., dissenting). Because the Court had not overruled *Coleman,* Breyer would have decided the issue of standing based upon stare decisis, eschewing any inquiry into the merits of the underlying challenge. For a recent related decision conferring standing to challenge the use of statistical sampling for the 2000 decennial census under a federal statute upon a voter potentially disadvantaged in a congressional election and upon a group of voters potentially disadvantaged in state elections in counties that are apportioned according to federal census figures, see Department of Commerce v. United States House of Representatives, 525 U.S. 316, 119 S. Ct. 765 (1998).

The voters alleged that the use of statistical sampling violated the requirement in Article I, § 2, cl. 3, authorizing Congress to direct an "actual Enumeration." The Court declined to reach the substantive constitutional issue, resting its affirmance of the lower court decision to invalidate the statistical sampling procedure instead on amendments to the Census Act, 13 U.S.C.S. 1 *et seq* (as amended 13 U.S.C.S. 141(a) (1990)). The Court declined to address the more salient standing issue, namely whether Congress could confer standing upon the House of Representatives to challenge the use of statisical sampling to determine the size of each state's congressional delegation.

161. 524 U.S. 417 (1998).
162. Justice Kennedy also filed a separate concurring opinion.
163. *See supra* at 296–97 n.* (quoting U.S. CONST. Art. I, § 7).
164. 488 U.S. 361 (1989).
165. 505 U.S. 833 (1992).
166. *See supra* chapter 4, § IV.
167. Clinton v. City of New York, 524 U.S. at 434 (Breyer, J., dissenting).
168. *Id.* at 431 (Scalia, J., dissenting).
169. For a more detailed analysis along the lines presented in the text, see generally Stearns, Item Veto, *supra* note 146.

CHAPTER 7

1. 450 U.S. 662 (1981).
2. 458 U.S. 527 (1982).
3. 458 U.S. 457 (1982).
4. For a discussion of these articles, see *supra* chapter 2, § II; see also Maxwell L. Stearns, *The Misguided Renaissance of Social Choice,* 103 YALE L.J. 1219 (1994).
5. Indeed, I have since developed a course and course book on public choice, with a considerable emphasis on social choice. *See* MAXWELL L. STEARNS, PUBLIC CHOICE AND PUBLIC LAW: READINGS AND COMMENTARY (1997).
6. 118 S. Ct. 1428 (1998).
7. 505 U.S. 833 (1992).
8. 438 U.S. 265 (1978).
9. 468 U.S. 737 (1984).
10. 383 U.S. 413 (1966).
11. 430 U.S. 188 (1977).
12. 504 U.S. 555 (1992).
13. See Friends of the Earth v. Laidlaw, 120 S. Ct. 693 (2000). See also *supra* at 169 n. 31.

Bibliography

Articles

Abel, Arthur H. Note, "The Burger Court's Unified Approach to Standing . . . ," 60 *Notre Dame L. Rev.* (1985)

Albert, Lee. "Standing to Challenge Administrative Action," 83 *Yale L.J.* (1974)

Amar, Akhil Reed. "The Central Meaning of Republican Government," 65 *U. Colo. L. Rev.* (1994)

Anthony, Robert A. "Zone-Free Standing for Private Attorneys General," 7 *Geo. Mason L. Rev.* (1999)

Aranson, Peter H., Ernest Gellhorn, and Glen O. Robinson. "A Theory of Legislative Delegation," 68 *Cornell L. Rev.* (1982)

Ayres, Ian and Peter Crampton. "Deficit Reduction through Diversity," 48 *Stan. L. Rev.* (1996)

Bates, Robert H. "Comparative Politics and Rational Choice," *Am. Pol. Sci. Rev.* (1997)

Becker, Paula Alexander. "Affirmative Action and Reverse Discrimination," 8 *Seton Hall Const. L.J.* (1997)

Biskupic, John. "When Court is Split . . . ," 1995, June 11, *Wash. Post*

Blau, Julian. "The Existence of Social Welfare Functions," 25 *Econometrica* (1957)

Bluford, Lucile H. "The Lloyd Gaines Story," 32 *J. Educ. Soc.* (1959)

Braverman, William A. Note. "Janus Was Not a God of Justice," 68 *N.Y.U. L. Rev.* (1993)

Brennan, Geoffrey and Alan Hamlin. "Bicameralism and Majoritarian Equilibrium," 74 *Pub. Choice* (1992)

Caminker, Evan H. "Sincere and Strategic Voting Norms on Multimember Courts," 97 *Mich. L. Rev.* (1999)

Campbell, Linda P. "Justice White: . . . ," 1993, *Chi. Trib.*, March 21

Coase, R. H. "The Coase Theorem and the Empty Core," 24 *J. L. and Econ.* (1981) "The Nature of the Firm," 4 *J. L. and Econ.* (1988)

Comiskey, Michael. "Can a President Pack—or Draft—the Supreme Court?" 57 *Alb. L. Rev.* (1994)

Comment. "Supreme Court No-Clear-Majority Decisions," 24 *U. Chi. L. Rev.* (1956)

Costello, James E. "The Limits of Popular Sovereignty," 74 *Cal. L. Rev.* (1986)

Cushman, Barry. "A Stream of Legal Consciousness," 61 *Fordham L. Rev.* (1992) "Rethinking the New Deal Court," 80 *Va. L. Rev.* (1994)

Davis, John F. and William L. Reynolds. "Juridicial Cripples: Plurality Opinions in the Supreme Court," 59 *Duke L. Rev.* (1974)

DeBow, Michael E. and Dwight R. Lee. "Understanding (and Misunderstanding) Public Choice: A Response to Farber and Frickey," 66 *Tex. L. Rev.* (1988)

Demsetz, Harold. "Information and Efficiency: Another Viewpoint," 12 *J. L. & Econ.* (1969)

Doernberg, Donald L. and Michael B. Mushlin. "History Comes Calling: Dean Griswold Offers New Evidence . . . ," 37 *UCLA L. Rev.* (1989) "The Trojan Horse: How the Declaratory Judgment Act . . . ," 36 *UCLA L. Rev.* (1989)

Dorf, Michael. "Incidental Burdens on Fundamental Rights," 109 *Harv. L. Rev.* (1996)

Easterbrook, Frank. "Ways of Criticizing the Court," *Harv. L. Rev.* (1982)

Edelman, Paul H. and Jim Chen. "The Most Dangerous Justice: The Supreme Court at the Bar of Mathematics," 70 *S. Cal. L. Rev.* (1996)

Elhauge, Einer R. "Does Interest Group Theory Justify More Intrusive Judicial Review?" 101 *Yale LJ.* (1991)

Eskridge, William N. "Politics Without Romance: Implications of Public Choice Theory . . . ," 74 *Va. L. Rev.* (1988)

Estrada, Lisa. "Buying the Status Quo on Affirmative Action," 9 *Geo. Mason U. Civ. Rts. L. J.* (1998/1999)

Farber, Daniel A. and Philip B. Frickey. "Legislative Intent and Public Choice," 74 *Va. L. Rev.* (1988) "The Jurisprudence of Public Choice," 65 *Tex. L. Rev.* (1987)

Fletcher, William A. "The Structure of Standing," 98 *Yale L.J.* (1988)

Friedman, Richard D. "Switching Time and Other Thought Experiments," 142 *U. Pa. L. Rev.* (1994)

George, Tracey E. "Developing a Positive Theory of Decisionmaking in the U.S. Court of Appeals," 58 *Ohio St. L. Rev.* (1998) "The Dynamics and Determinants of the Decision to Grant En Banc Review," 74 *Wash. L. Rev.* (1999)

Ginsburg, Ruth Bader. "Remarks on Writing Separately," 65 *Wash. L. Rev.* (1990)

Gottlieb, Craig R. Comment. "How Standing Has Fallen," 142 *U. Pa. L. Rev.* (1994)

Halcombe, Randal G. "An Empirical Test of the Median Voter Model," 18 *Econ. Inquiry* (1980)

Hovenkamp, Herbert. "Arrow's Theorem: Ordinalism and Republican Government," 75 *Iowa L. Rev.* (1990)

Hutchinson, Dennis J. "Unanimity and Desegregation: Decisionmaking in the Supreme Court, 1948–58," 68 *Geo. L.J.* (1979)

Jackson, David. "Supreme Court Lets California's Ban on Affirmative Action Stand . . . ," 1997, November 4, *The Dallas Morning News*

Jenkins, John A. "The Partisan: A Talk with Justice Rehnquist," 1985, March 3, *New York Times*

Jensen, Erik M. and Jonathan L. Entin. "Commandeering, the Tenth Amendment, and the Federal Requisition Power," 15 *Const. Comm.* (1998)

Jones, Harry W. "Dyson Distinguished Lecture: Precedent and Policy in Constitutional Law," 4 *Pace L. Rev.* (1983)

Kennedy, Helen. "Ex-Wrestler Elected Minn. Governor," 1998, Nov. 4, *Daily News* (New York)

Kimura, Ken Noote. "A Legitimacy Model for the Interpretation of Plurality Decisions," 77 *Cornell L. Rev.* (1992)

Kornhauser, Lewis A. "An Economic Perspective on *Stare Decisis*," 65 *Chi.-Kent L. Rev.* (1989)

Kornhauser, Lewis A. and Lawrence G. Sager. "The One and the Many: Adjudication in Collegial Courts," 81 *Cal. L. Rev.* (1993) "Unpacking the Court," 96 *Yale L.J.* (1986)

Landes, William and Richard A. Posner. "Legal Precedent: A Theoretical and Empirical Analysis," 19 *J. L. and Econ.* (1976)

Lee, Evan Tsen. "Deconstitutionalizing Justiciability," 105 *Harv. L. Rev.* (1992)

Levine, Michael and Charles Plott. "Agenda Influence and Its Implications," 63 *U. Va. L. Rev.* (1977)

Levmore, Saul. "Parliamentary Law, Majority Decisionmaking, and the Voting Paradox," 74 *Va. L. Rev.* (1989) "Voting Paradoxes and Interest Groups," 28 *J. Leg. Stud.* (1999)

Lively, Donald E. "The Supreme Court Appointment Process," 59 *S. Cal. L. Rev.* (1986)

Logan, David A. "Standing to Sue: A Proposed Separation of Powers Analysis," 37 *Wis. L. Rev.* (1984)

Lowi, Theodore J. "Two Roads to Serfdom: Liberalism, Conservatism, and Administrative Power," 36 *Am. U. L. Rev.* (1987)

Macey, Jonathan R. "Promoting Public Regarding Legislation Through Statutory Interpretation," 86 *Colum. L. Rev.* (1986) "The Internal and External Costs and Benefits of *Stare Decisis,* 65 *Chi.-Kent L. Rev.* (1989)

McLean, Ian and Arnold B. Urken. "Did Jefferson or Madison Understand Condorcet's Theory of Social Choice?" 73 *Pub. Choice* (1992)

Mahoney, Joan. "A Sword as Well as a Shield," 69 *Iowa L. Rev.* (1989)

Maltz, Earl M. "The Prospects for Revival of Conservatism Activism in Constitutional Jurisprudence," 24 *Ga. L. Rev.* (1990)

Maltzman, Forrest and Paul J. Wahlbeck. "Strategic Policy Considerations and Voting Fluidity on the Burger Court,"90 *Am. Pol. Sci. Rev.* (1996)

Marshall, Lawrence C. "Divesting the Courts: Breaking the Judicial Monopoly . . . ," 66 *Chi.-Kent L. Rev.* (1990)

Mashaw, Jerry. "Prodelegation: Why Administrators Should Make Political Decisions," 1 *J. L. Econ., and Org.* (1985)

Mayton, William Ty. "The Possibilities of Collective Choice," *Duke L.J.* (1986)

Monaghan, Henry P. "Constitutional Adjudication," 82 *Yale L.J.* (1973)

Nichols, Gene R., Jr. "Justice Scalia, Standing, and Public Law Litigation," 42 *Duke L. J.* (1993)

Note. "Plurality Decisions and Judicial Decisionmaking," 94 *Harv. L. Rev.* (1981)

O'Brien, David M. "On Supreme Court Commentaries and Developing Constitutional Law," 81 *Mich. L. Rev.* (1983)

O'Hara, Erin. "Social Constraint or Implicit Collusion?: Toward a Game Theoretic Analysis of Stare Decisis," 24 *Seton Hall L. Rev.* (1993)

Pierce, Richard J., Jr. Comment. "*Lujan v. Defenders of Wildlife:* Standing as a Judicially Imposed Limit on Legislative Power," 42 *Duke L.J.* (1993) "Political Accountability and Delegated Power," 36 *Am. U. L. Rev.* (1987)

Pildes, Richard and Elizabeth Anderson. "Slinging Arrows at Democracy," 90 *Colum. L. Rev.* (1990)

Post, David and Steven Salop. "Issues and Outcomes, Guidance and Indeterminancy," 49 *Vand. L. Rev.* (1996) "Rowing Against the Tidewater: A Theory of Voting by Multijudge Panels," 80 *Geo. L. Rev.* (1992)

Pushaw, Robert J. "Justiciability and Separation of Powers," 81 *Cornell L. Rev.* (1996)

Rauh, Joseph L., Jr. "An Unabashed Liberal Looks at a Half-Century of the Supreme Court," 69 *N.C. L. Rev.* (1990) "Lawyers and the Legislation of the Early New Deal," 96 *Harv. L. Rev.* (1983)

Revesz, Richard L. and Pamela S. Karlan. "Nonmajority Rules and the Supreme Court," 136 *U. Pa. L. Rev.* (1988)

Riggs, Robert E. "When Every Vote Counts: 5–4 Decisions in the United States Supreme Court, 1900–90," 21 *Hofstra L. Rev.* (1993)

Riker, William H. "The Paradox of Voting and Congressional Rules for Voting on Amendments," 52 *Am. Pol. Sci. Rev.* (1958)

Rogers, John M. "'Issue Voting' by Multimember Courts," 49 *Vand. L. Rev.* (1996) "I Vote This Way Because I'm Wrong: the Supreme Court Justice as Epimenides," 79 *Ky. L.J.* (1991)

Romer, Thomas and Howard Rosenthal. "The Elusive Median Voter," 12 *J. Public Econ.* (1979)

Rowley, Charles K. "The Relevance of the Median Voter Theorem," 140 *J. Inst'l and Theoretical Econ.* (1984)

Scalia, Antonin. "The Doctrine of Standing as an Essential Element of the Separation of Powers," 17 *Suffolk U. L. Rev.* (1983)

Schwartz, Bernard. "Term Limits, Commerce, and the Rehnquist Court," 31 *Tulsa L.J.* (1996)

Schwartz, Edward P. "The Concurrent Dilemma," Department of Government (1999), Harvard University, working paper

Schwartz, John. "New Evolution Research Ruffles Some Feathers," 1996, Nov. 15, *The Wash. Post*

Sedler, Robert A. "Standing, Justiciability, and All That: A Behavioral Analysis," 25 *Vand. L. Rev.* (1972)

Sen, Amartya K. "Social Choice and Justice: A Review Article," 23 *J. Econ. Lit.* (1985) "Social Choice Theory: A Reexamination," 45 *Econometrica* (1977)

Shepsle, Kenneth. "Congress is a 'They,' Not an 'It,' " 12 *Int'l Rev. Law and Econ.* (1992)

Shepsle, Kenneth and Barry Weingast. "The Institutional Foundations of Committee Power," 81 *Am. Pol. Sci. Rev.* (1987) "Structure-Induced Equilibrium and Legislative Choice," 37 *Pub. Choice* (1981)

Skeel, David A. Jr. "The Unanimity Norm in Delaware Corporate Law," 83 *Va. L. Rev.* (1997)

Stearns, Maxwell L. "From Lujan to Laidlaw: A Preliminary Model of Environmental Standing," 11 *Duke Envtl. L. & Pol'y F.* (forthcoming 2000) "How Outcome Voting Promotes Principled Issue Identification," 49 *Vand. L. Rev.* (1996) "The Misguided Renaissance of Social Choice," 103 *Yale L.J.* (1994) "Mistretta Versus Marbury: The Foundations of Judicial Review," 74 *Tex. L. Rev.* (1996) "The Public Choice Case Against the Item Veto," 49 *Wash. & Lee L. Rev.* (1992) "Should Justices Ever Switch Votes?: *Miller v. Albright* in Social Choice Perspective," 7 *Sup. Ct. Econ. Rev.* (1999) "Standing and Social Choice: Historical Evidence," 144 *U. Pa. L. Rev.* (1995) "Standing Back from the Forest: Justiciability and Social Choice," 83 *Cal. L. Rev.* (1995) "The Case for Including *Marks v. United States* Within the Canon of Constitutional Law," 17 *Const. Comm.* (forthcoming 2000)

Stengle, Richard. "An Indelicate Balance," 1988, July 25, *Time*

Stout, Lynn. "Strict Scrutiny and Social Choice: An Economic Inquiry into Fundamental Rights and Suspect Classifications," 80 *Geo. L.J.* (1989)

Sunstein, Cass R. "Standing and the Privatization of Public Law," 88 *Colum. L. Rev.* (1998) "What's Standing After Lujan?" 91 *Mich. L. Rev.* (1992)

Thurmon, Mark Alan. "When the Court Divides: Reconsidering the Precedential Value of Supreme Court Plurality Decisions," 42 *Duke L.J.* (1992)

Tullock, Gordon. "Why So Much Stability?" 37 *Pub. Choice* (1981)
Tushnet, Mark V. "The New Law of Standing: A Plea for Abandonment," 62 *Cornell L. Rev.* (1997)

Urofsky, Melvin I. "Conflict Among the Brethren," 71 *Duke L. Rev.* (1988)

Vickrey, William. "Utility, Strategy, and Social Decisional Rules," 74 *Q. J. of Econ.* (1960)
Vreeland, Cindy. "Public Interest Groups, Public Law Litigation, and Federal Rule 24 (a)," 57 *U. Chi. L. Rev.* (1990)

Wermeil, Stephen J. "The Nomination of Justice Brennan," 11 *Const. Comm.* (1994–95)
Winter, Steven L. "The Metaphor of Standing and Problem of Self-Governance," 40 *Stan. L. Rev.* (1988)

Young, H. Peyton. "Condorcet's Theory of Voting," 82 *Am. Pol. Sci. Rev.*

Monographs

Ackerman, Bruce. *We, the People: Foundations* (1991) *We, the People: Transformations* (1999)
Arrow, Kenneth J. *Social Choice and Individual Values* (1951) *Social Choice and Individual Values* (2d ed., 1963)

Baker, Keith M. *Condorcet: From Natural Philosophy to Social Mathematics* (1975)
Becker, Gary S. *The Economics of Discrimination* (2d ed., 1971)
Bickel, Alexander M. *The Least Dangerous Branch: The Supreme Court at the Bar of Politics* (1962)
Black, Duncan. *The Theory of Committees and Elections* (1958)
Brenner, Saul and Harold Spaeth. *Stare Indecisis* (1995)
Buchanan, James and Gordon Tullock. *The Calculus of Consent* (1965)

Calamari, John D. and Joseph M. Perillo. *Contracts* (4th ed. 1987)
Choper, Jesse, et al. *The Supreme Court: Trends and Developments,* Volume 3:1980–81 (1982)

Dornbusch, Rudiger and Stanley Fischer. *Macroeconomics* (2d ed., 1981)

Ely, John Hart. *Democracy and Distrust* (1980)
Epstein, Lee and Jack Knight. *The Choices Justices Make* (1998)
Epstein, Lee, et al. *The Supreme Court Compendium: Data, Decisions, Developments* (2d ed., 1996)

Epstein, Richard A. *Bargaining with the State* (1993) *Forbidden Grounds: The Case Against Employment Discrimination Laws* (1992)

Farber, Daniel A. and Philip B. Frickey. *Law and Public Choice* (1991)
Federalist No. 10 (Madison)
Friedman, Milton. "The Methodology of Positive Economics" in *Essays in Positive Economics* (1953)

Green, Donald P. and Ian Shapiro. *Pathologies of Rational Choice Theory* (1994)

Hirshleifer, Jack. *Price Theory and Applications* (2d ed. 1980)
Hodder-Williams, Richard. *The Politics of the U.S. Supreme Court* (1980)

Irons, Peter H. *The New Deal Lawyers* (1982)

Jacob, Herbert, et al. *Courts, Law, & Politics in Comparative Perspective* (1996)
Jeffries, John C., Jr. *Justice Lewis F. Powell: A Biography* (1994)

Kluger, Richard. *Simple Justice: The History of* Brown v. Board of Education *and Black America's Struggle for Equality* (1977)
Komesar, Neil K. *Imperfect Alternatives: Choosing Institutions in Law, Economics, and Public Policy* (1994)
Kuhn, Thomas S. *The Structure of Scientific Revolutions* (2d ed., 1970)

Leuchtenberg, William E. *The Supreme Court Reborn: The Constitutional Revolution in the Age of Roosevelt* (1995)
Lieberman, Jethro K. *The Evolving Constitution* (1992)

McGovern, William M. *Trusts and Estates* (1988)
Merryman, John H. *The Civil Law Tradition: An Introduction to the Legal Systems of Western Europe and Latin America* (1969)
Mueller, Dennis. *Public Choice II* (1989)

Olson, Mancur. *The Rise and Decline of Nations: Economic Growth, Stagflation, and Social Rigidities* (1982)
Ordeshook, P. *Game Theory and Political Theory: An Introduction* (1986)
Orwell, George. *Animal Farm,* Harcourt, Brace, Jovanovich (1990)

Perry, H. W. *Deciding to Decide: Agenda Setting in the United States Supreme Court* (1991)
Popper, Karl R. *Conjectures and Refutations:The Growth of Scientific Knowledge* (5th ed., 1989)
Pritchett, C. Herman. *The Roosevelt Court: A Study in Judicial Politics and Values* (1963)

Riker, William H. *Liberalism Against Populism* (1982) *The Theory of Political Coalitions* (1962)

Schelling, Thomas C. *The Strategy of Conflict* (1960)
Schwartz, Bernard B. *Super Chief: Earl Warren and His Supreme Court* (1983) *The Ascent of Pragmatism: The Burger Court in Action* (1990)
Segal, Jeffrey A. and Harold Spaeth. *The Supreme Court and the Attitudinal Model* (1993)
Sen, Amartya K. *Welfare and Measurement* (1982)
Shakespeare, William. *The Tragedy of King Lear,* Riverside (1974)
Stearns, Maxwell L. *Public Choice and Public Law* (1997)
Stern, Robert, et al. *Supreme Court Practice* (7th ed., 1993)
Stone, Geoffrey R., et al. *Constitutional Law,* 3d ed. (1996)

Tideman, T. Nicolaus. *Collective Decisions and Voting,* unpublished manuscript (1999)
Tribe, Laurence H. *American Constitutional Law* (2d ed., 1988)

Indexes

Case Index

Subject Index